TRIAL TECHNIQUES

TRIAL TECHNIQUES

Sixth Edition

THOMAS A. MAUET
Director of Trial Advocacy
and Milton O. Riepe Professor of Law
University of Arizona

PUBLISHERS

1185 Avenue of the Americas, New York, NY 10036
www.aspenpublishers.com

Permissions
Aspen Publishers
1185 Avenue of the Americas
New York, NY 10036

Printed in the United States of America.

ISBN 0-7355-3240-0

2   3   4   5   6   7   8   9   0

Library of Congress Cataloging-in-Publication Data

Mauet, Thomas A.
    Trial techniques / Thomas A. Mauet. — 6th ed.
        p. cm.
      Includes index.
      ISBN 0-7355-3240-0
      1.   Trial practice—United States.   I.   Title.
    KF 8915 .M38   2002
    347.73'75—dc21   2002018624
                                                                              CIP

About Aspen Publishers

Aspen Publishers, headquartered in New York City, is a leading information provider for attorneys, business professionals, and law students. Written by preeminent authorities, our products consist of analytical and practical information covering both U.S. and international topics. We publish in the full range of formats, including updated manuals, books, periodicals, CDs, and online products.

Our proprietary content is complemented by 2,500 legal databases, containing over 11 million documents, available through our Loislaw division. Aspen Publishers also offers a wide range of topical legal and business databases linked to Loislaw's primary material. Our mission is to provide accurate, timely, and authoritative content in easily accessible formats, supported by unmatched customer care.

To order any Aspen Publishers title, go to *www.aspenpublishers.com* or call 1-800-638-8437.

To reinstate your manual update service, call 1-800-638-8437.

For more information on Loislaw products, go to *www.loislaw.com* or call 1-800-364-2512.

For Customer Care issues, e-mail *CustomerCare@aspenpublishers.com*; call 1-800-234-1660; or fax 1-800-901-9075.

Aspen Publishers
A Wolters Kluwer Company

SUMMARY OF CONTENTS

CONTENTS

III. JURY SELECTION

VI. EXHIBITS

VII. CROSS-EXAMINATION

IX. CLOSING ARGUMENTS

X.   OBJECTIONS

XI.   TRIAL PREPARATION AND STRATEGY

XII.   BENCH TRIALS

PREFACE

My experiences as a trial lawyer and trial advocacy teacher have made me realize that effective trial lawyers always seem to have two complementary abilities. First, they have developed an effective method for analyzing and preparing each case for trial. Second, they have the technical skills necessary to present their side of a case persuasively during trial. It is the combination of both qualities — preparation and execution — that produces effective trial advocacy.

This text approaches trial advocacy the same way. It presents a method of trial preparation and reviews the thought processes a trial lawyer uses before and during each phase of a trial. In addition, it discusses and gives examples of the basic technical courtroom skills that must be developed to present evidence and arguments persuasively to the jury. This is done in the firm belief that effective trial advocacy is both an art and a skill, and that while a few trial lawyers may be born, most are made. Artistry becomes possible only after basic skills have become mastered.

In trial work, as in many other fields, there is no one "right way" to proceed. There are just effective, time-tested methods that are as varied as lawyers are numerous. Consequently, while the text presents standard methods of examining witnesses, introducing exhibits, and making arguments, there are different approaches to all the tasks involved in trial work. Thus, the examples in the text are not the only way of effectively accomplishing the particular task involved. The text uses these examples because inexperienced trial lawyers need specific examples of effective techniques they can learn and use in court. Other effective ways of doing things are necessarily a product of experience, and only through experience will you learn what works best for you.

The emphasis of this text is on jury trials, since a lawyer who can persuasively try cases to a jury should also be competent during a bench trial. The examples are principally from personal injury and criminal cases, since they involve easily isolated examples of trial techniques, and they constitute the substantial majority of cases tried to juries. If the method and techniques applicable to uncomplicated, recurring situations presented here are mastered, more complex cases can be handled competently as well.

What's New in the Sixth Edition

I have made several additions and changes to this sixth edition. First, the most apparent change is that the text adds a new chapter on bench trials.

Chapter XII addresses a commonly asked question: how much of what we know about the psychology of persuasion in jury trials applies to bench trials? This chapter is based on "Bench Trials" published in *Litigation* (Summer 2002).

Second, the experts chapter has been revised to reflect the Supreme Court's decisions since *Daubert* and the amendments to Rules 701, 702, and 703 of the Federal Rules of Evidence effective in December 2000. In particular, Rule 703 may have a significant effect on the direct examinations of experts, and the chapter discusses how the new rule may change what lawyers are permitted to bring out during direct examinations.

Third, other chapters have been revised to reflect the other 2000 amendments to the Federal Rules of Evidence, Rules 103, 404(a), 803(6), and 902. These affect preserving error for appeal, presenting character trait evidence, and the foundation for business records. In particular, self-authentication, now permitted by Rule 803(6) as an alternative foundation for business records, will become a common way to admit business records at trial.

Finally, as with the previous editions, I have added numerous ideas throughout the text that I have picked up over the years, mostly because trial lawyers have been kind enough to pass them on to me. Particularly helpful have been Dominic J. Gianna, the most creative trial lawyer I know, and the Hon. Warren D. Wolfson, the best trial judge I know. They have been friends, partners, and colleagues for many years and represent the best of the bar and bench. Particularly supportive has been my wife, Gloria Torres Mauet, also a trial lawyer, who never seems to tire from listening to my latest ideas. I hope you will be pleased with the result.

Thomas A. Mauet

Tucson, Arizona
April 2002

TRIAL TECHNIQUES

I

THE TRIAL PROCESS

§1.1. Introduction

You have just been called into the office of a partner of the litigation firm that recently hired you. The partner tells you he has a case scheduled for trial soon that seems "just right" for you. Discovery has been completed. Pretrial motions have all been ruled on. Witnesses have been interviewed. Trial memoranda have been prepared. Settlement negotiations have just collapsed. The case now needs to be tried, and you're the person who will try it. With a smile, the partner hands you the file. Apprehensively, you walk out of his office, thinking: "My God. What do I do now?"

Jury trials are the principal method by which we resolve legal disputes parties cannot settle themselves through less formal methods. Although alternative dispute resolution methods such as arbitration, mediation, summary trials, private trials, and the like are becoming increasingly important, jury trials in the federal and state courts remain the most important dispute-resolving method in the United States.

In our jury trial system, the jury determines the facts, the judge determines the law, and the lawyers act as advocates for the litigants. Our adversary system is premised on the belief that pitting two adversaries against each other, with each interested in presenting her version of the truth, is the best way for the jury to determine the probable truth. The tools the litigants have, and must understand, are fourfold: substantive law, procedural law, evidence law, and persuasion "law." The first three, being principally legal, can be learned in a few years. The last, the psychology of persuasion, is what fascinates true trial lawyers, and they spend a lifetime learning about, and learning how to apply, psychology in the courtroom.

Integrating substantive law, procedural law, evidence law, and persuasion "law" and applying the result to our jury trial system is what this book is all about. Chapter I is an overview of the trial process. Chapter II discusses the psychology of persuasion. Chapters III through X cover all the specific stages of a jury trial, from jury selection through closing arguments and objections. Chapter XI provides a comprehensive approach to trial preparation and strategy. Chapter XII covers bench trials and discusses how the psychology of persuasion applicable to jury trials also applies, with modifications, to bench trials.

§1.2. *Local practices and procedures*

Jurisdictions differ in how they conduct trials. First, the applicable substantive law may differ. Second, the applicable civil and criminal procedural rules may differ. Although many jurisdictions follow the Federal Rules of Civil Procedure, many do not. Criminal procedural rules vary widely. Third, the applicable evidence law may differ. Although most jurisdictions have adopted the Federal Rules of Evidence, many states, particularly the more populous ones, have not. Fourth, court rules and local rules implementing procedural statutes can vary widely. Indeed, trial procedures and customs differ from county to county and judge to judge. Judges, particularly in federal court, may impose additional limitations on the parties, such as how many experts each side may call, how much time each side will have to present its case, and how much time can be used during opening statements and closing arguments.

Small wonder, then, that a trial lawyer's first job is to learn and understand all the "rules" that will be applied to the upcoming trial. Accordingly, the outline of the jury trial process in this chapter must be taken as an overview of that process. While common variations in practices and procedures will be pointed out, not all can be.

§1.3. *Trial date assignment*

Cases are set for trial in two basic ways: individual calendars and central assignment systems. With individual calendars, each trial judge is responsible for the overall handling of every case assigned to that judge's docket, including setting the trial date and trying the case. In civil cases, after discovery is completed and the parties state that the case is ready to be tried, the judge will set a trial date. That date will vary, but frequently the trial date in civil cases is at least three to six months after the case is ready to be tried. Criminal cases, because of speedy trial requirements, usually get trial dates within three to four months of arrest or arraignment.

Central assignment systems are found more frequently in large urban areas. Under that system, cases remain on one central calendar for trial assignment purposes. The oldest cases are at the top. New cases then creep their way from the bottom to the top of the list. Depending on the jurisdiction, this may take from perhaps one to more than five years. When the case reaches the top, it is sent to a judge for trial. Jurisdictions having a central assignment system usually publish the trial calendar in the daily legal newspaper, and it is the lawyers' responsibility to keep track of their cases as they move up the calendar.

§1.4.   Jury selection

Congratulations! It's the day of trial. You've done all the preparatory work (discussed in Chapter XI) and the case is actually going to trial. What happens now?

You and your opposing counsel arrive in the trial judge's courtroom at the designated date and time. Clients will usually be there. Sitting on the bench is the trial judge. Other courtroom personnel will include the court clerk, court reporter, and bailiff. Other lawyers and spectators may be present.

The clerk calls the case — your case — for trial. You, your client, and the other lawyer move up and sit at the lawyers' tables in the courtroom (frequently marked "Plaintiff" and "Defendant"; if not, find out ahead of time where the sides customarily sit). The judge asks whether both sides are ready for trial. You and the other lawyer both respond "ready, your Honor."

The judge next "orders a jury" and directs the bailiff or other court personnel to go to the jury room and bring a panel of 25 to 40 jurors back to the courtroom. In the meantime, the judge may again explore the possibility of settling the case, try to resolve any remaining procedural and evidentiary issues, and address any questions about how the jury will be selected. This may be done in the judge's chambers.

When the jurors are first brought into the courtroom, they usually sit in the back rows. The judge introduces herself, the lawyers, parties, and court personnel, mentions the case on trial, and explains how jury selection will be conducted. In a few jurisdictions, lawyers make short introductory statements about facts and issues of the case. The court clerk swears in the prospective jurors to answer questions asked by the judge and lawyers. Jury selection then begins.

How a jury is selected in a particular courtroom varies greatly, probably more than any other phase of a trial. Jury selection is controlled by statutes, court rules, and individual judicial practices. These control how jurors are initially called and qualified for jury service, how many jurors will decide the case, whether alternate jurors will be selected, the bases for cause challenges (statutory grounds to dismiss, or "strike," jurors), and the number of peremptory challenges (a party's right to strike a juror for almost any reason) each party will have and how they will be exercised. These also control what jury selection system will be used (the most common are the "strike system," used in most federal courts, and the panel system, used in many state courts), the permissible topics on which jurors can be questioned (will they include questions about law or be limited to questions about jurors' backgrounds and life experiences), and who will do the actual questioning (judge, lawyer, or both). Written questionnaires for jurors are frequently used in complex cases.

How long does the jury selection process take? While most cases take between one and three hours, in a complex or highly publicized case jury selection can take much longer. When the selection process is completed the jurors and any alternates are sworn in by the court clerk as trial jurors to decide the case.

§1.5.   *Preliminary instructions of law*

After jury selection and before opening statements, the judge usually gives the jury preliminary instructions on the law. This orients the jurors and lets them know what will happen during the trial. For instance, the judge will probably summarize their duties as jurors (to follow the law, determine the facts and credibility of witnesses, apply the facts to the law), instruct them on how to conduct themselves during recesses (do not discuss the case among yourselves or with others, do not visit the scene, do not research the case in any way), and describe how trials are conducted. In recent years more judges also summarize the pleadings and instruct the jury on the applicable substantive law. In a few jurisdictions, jurors are told that they may discuss the evidence during the trial when recesses occur, as long as all jurors are present in the jury room when the evidence is discussed. This usually takes only a few minutes.

By this time the lawyers probably will have asked the judge to order the exclusion of witnesses during the trial (sometimes called "separating witnesses" or "invoking the rule"). This prevents witnesses from sitting in the courtroom while other witnesses are testifying. The exclusion does not apply to parties, a party's representative, or someone whose presence is essential.

Some jurisdictions permit note-taking by jurors. Some jurisdictions encourage it by providing jurors with notepads and pencils. In lengthy trials, jurors are sometimes given notebooks containing photographs of each witness and paper for note taking. Other jurisdictions expressly bar note-taking.

§1.6.   *Opening statements*

Plaintiff and defendant now give their opening statements. The opening statements are the lawyers' opportunities to tell the jury what they expect the evidence will be during the trial. This helps the jury understand the evidence when it is actually presented. The opening statements should be factual, not argumentative, although jurisdictions and judges vary considerably in how much "argument" and discussion of law they allow in the openings. While many jurisdictions permit opening statements to be waived, this is rarely done.

Most opening statements are based on themes and storytelling, usually giving a chronological overview of "what happened" from either the plaintiff's or defendant's viewpoint. The statement should be engaging and memorable, presenting each side's case in the best possible light and drawing a picture that will make the jury want to find in that side's favor. Lawyers know the importance of a good opening statement. Research has shown that most jurors return verdicts that are consistent with their impressions made during the opening statements.

How much time do the opening statements take? Most last 10 to 30 minutes per side; longer statements run the risk of either boring the jurors or overloading them with details. The judge may put time limits on opening statements as well as on other phases of the trial.

Some jurisdictions require that plaintiff's opening statement make out a prima facie case because lawyers' statements are taken as admissions. If this is the case, plaintiff's lawyer (and defendant's lawyer, if affirmative defenses or counterclaims are also involved) must be sure that the opening statement is legally sufficient.

In some jurisdictions the defendant may reserve the opening statement until after the plaintiff has rested his case in chief. While this is infrequently done, the defendant may sometimes not want the plaintiff to know her specific trial strategy. (This may happen in criminal cases where the discovery rules are restrictive, the defendant plans to present an affirmative defense and doesn't want the plaintiff to know its details. This prevents the plaintiff from anticipating the defense during plaintiff's case in chief.)

Finally, a few judges have the lawyers make their opening statements to the entire jury panel, before jury selection is conducted. The idea is that jurors will be more likely to disclose attitudes they have that might affect their suitability to be jurors if they know more about the case being tried.

§1.7.   Plaintiff's case-in-chief

Plaintiff, having the burden of proof, presents evidence first. (This is always the case, unless defendant has admitted the plaintiff's facts, so that only affirmative defenses or counterclaims, on which the defendant has the burden of proof, remain to be proved.) This means that in the plaintiff's case-in-chief, plaintiff must present sufficient proof on each element of each legal claim alleged in the complaint or indictment, using four possible sources of proof: witnesses, exhibits, judicial notice, and stipulations.

When a witness is called to testify, he is first sworn to tell the truth by the court clerk. Once the witness is seated in the witness chair, questioning begins. Direct examination is that part of the questioning done by the plaintiff's lawyer (the side calling the witness). When the direct is completed (the lawyer usually says "nothing further on direct, your Honor," "pass the witness," or "your witness," depending on local custom), cross-examination by the defendant's lawyer begins. In most jurisdictions the scope of the cross-examination is limited to the subject matter of the direct. A few states, however, follow the "English rule" under which cross-examination can go into any relevant matter.

When the cross-examiner announces she is done, the direct examiner may conduct a redirect examination (limited to explaining or refuting matters brought out on cross). The cross-examiner may conduct a recross-examination (limited to matters brought out during the redirect). (In some jurisdictions the judge may ask the witness questions, and a few jurisdictions allow jurors, usually through written questions submitted to the judge for approval, to ask the witness questions.) The witness is then excused, and plaintiff calls another witness.

Exhibits are the other principal source of evidence. The four principal types of exhibits are real objects (guns, blood, drugs, machinery), demonstrative exhibits (diagrams, models, maps), writings (contracts, promissory notes, checks, letters), and records (private business and public records). Exhibits need "foundations" to be admitted; that is, the party seeking to introduce the exhibit in evidence must present evidence that the exhibit is actually what it purports to be and complies with the applicable rules of evidence. The foundation may come from witness testimony, certification, or other methods. The formalities required in establishing the appropriate foundation for a particular exhibit vary somewhat, depending on the jurisdiction. If admitted in evidence, the exhibits may be considered by jurors just like any other evidence presented during the trial.

Judicial notice is the third method of getting evidence to the jury. The judge can admit evidence through judicial notice when the fact is either well known in the jurisdiction where the trial is being held (the Empire State Building is in Manhattan) or the fact can be easily determined and verified from a reliable source (on June 1, 2000, the moon was full).

The fourth method of proof is in stipulations, an agreement between the parties that certain facts exist and are not in dispute. This makes the presentation of undisputed evidence more efficient. Stipulations are usually made in writing and are shown or read to the jury much like any written exhibit. The judge usually instructs the jury on what a stipulation is.

In what order does plaintiff present the various witnesses, exhibits, and other evidence in his case in chief? This is totally up to plaintiff; whatever is most persuasive (and logistically practical) is permitted. Plaintiff must have some idea how long the witnesses are likely to testify so that he will neither run out of witnesses during the day nor have witnesses wait hour after hour to testify. Most witnesses are on the stand between 15 and 90 minutes, although some, particularly parties and experts, may take substantially longer.

When plaintiff is finished presenting all his evidence, he "rests." This is done simply by standing up and announcing to the judge and jury, "Your Honor, plaintiff rests." The judge tells the jury that the plaintiff has finished presenting evidence; the judge then will probably take a recess to hear defendant's motions.

§1.8.   Motions after plaintiff rests

After plaintiff rests, and the jury has been excused and has left the courtroom, defendant usually moves for a directed verdict. While the motion may have different names in different jurisdictions (in criminal cases, for example, it is commonly called a "motion for a directed judgment of acquittal"; in federal civil cases it is called a "motion for judgment as a matter of law"), its purpose is identical. The defendant asks the judge to terminate the trial in whole or part, and enter judgment for the defense, because plaintiff has failed to "prove a prima facie case." While the motion is frequently made orally, the better and often required practice is to file a written motion with the court.

If plaintiff has failed to present any evidence to support any element of any claim brought in the complaint or indictment, the judge should grant the motion as to that unproved claim. The standard applicable to the motion is that the judge must view the evidence "in the light least favorable to the movant." Accordingly, if there is any credible evidence, either direct or circumstantial, supporting the claim, the motion should be denied. Hence, it is up to the defendant to point out why there has been a fatal absence of proof on any required element of plaintiff's claims, or that there is only one reasonable conclusion that can be drawn from the evidence that was admitted.

The judge may grant all, deny all, or grant part of the motion. For instance, the judge may grant the motion on one count of the complaint and deny the motion as to the other counts. In a criminal case the judge may grant the motion on the charged offense but deny it as to a lesser-included offense (grant the motion as to the murder charge but deny it as to the lesser manslaughter charge). The trial then continues.

§1.9. Defendant's case-in-chief

Defendant's case-in-chief has two possible components: evidence to refute plaintiff's proof, and evidence to prove any affirmative defenses and counterclaims (as well as cross-claims and third-party claims in multiple-party cases).

Defendant, if she elects to present evidence, proceeds in the same way that plaintiff did — by calling witnesses and introducing exhibits, judicially noticed facts, and stipulations. The procedures are identical.

When defendant is finished presenting all her evidence, she "rests" by standing up and announcing to the judge and jury, "Your Honor, defendant rests." The judge tells the jury that the defendant has finished presenting evidence; the judge then probably takes a recess to hear motions.

§1.10. Motions after defendant rests

After defendant rests, and the jury has been excused and has left the courtroom, the judge again hears motions. Plaintiff can move for a directed verdict on any of defendant's affirmative defenses and counterclaims. The judge must again view the evidence "in the light least favorable to the movant" in ruling on the motions. If there is a failure of proof on any required element of any affirmative defense or counterclaim, the judge should grant the motion as to that defense or counterclaim.

§1.11. Plaintiff's rebuttal and defendant's surrebuttal cases

After defendant rests, and after motions have been made and ruled on, plaintiff has an opportunity to introduce evidence that rebuts defendant's evidence. This rebuttal evidence usually proves a defense to defendant's counterclaims or contradicts other specific evidence presented by the defendant.

Defendant also has a last chance to rebut specific matters raised in the plaintiff's rebuttal case. This is called the defendant's surrebuttal case.

§1.12. Motions at the close of all evidence

When all the evidence is in, and both sides have rested, plaintiff or defendant may again move for a directed verdict at the close of all the evidence. Again, the standard remains the same: the judge must take the evidence "in the light least favorable to the movant."

In many jurisdictions a motion for a directed verdict at the close of all the evidence is required to preserve the right to move for judgment notwithstanding the verdict after trial.

§1.13. Instructions conference

At some point during the trial the judge will need to "settle instructions." This means that the judge must rule on which jury instructions will be submitted to the jury. The judge will probably have both plaintiff's and defendant's requested instructions before or at the beginning of trial (in civil cases the final pretrial memorandum submitted by the parties will usually contain each side's requested instructions and any objections to the other side's). Usually, however, the judge cannot reach final decisions on which instructions to submit to the jury until she has heard all the evidence. For that reason the instructions conference is usually held after both sides rest and before closing arguments.

During the instructions conference plaintiff and defendant argue why instructions should be given, denied, or modified. During the conference, which may be held in court (without the jury present) or in chambers, the court reporter should be present to record the objections and rulings. In most jurisdictions the lawyers must make specific objections on the record to requested instructions before a judge's giving that instruction to the jury, or refusing to give a requested instruction, can be raised as error on appeal.

§1.14. Closing arguments

Plaintiff and defendant now give their closing arguments. The closing arguments are the lawyers' opportunities to tell the jury what the evidence has been, how it ties into the jury instructions, and why the evidence and law compel a verdict in their favor.

Effective closing arguments integrate the facts and law and argue that the credible evidence, when applied to the law, requires a favorable verdict. Lawyers can argue inferences from the facts, refer to important testimony, use admitted exhibits, tell stories, employ analogies, and use a range of other techniques to persuade the jury.

How much time do closing arguments take? Most last 30 to 60 minutes per side. If too short, they fail to use the available time persuasively. If too long, they run the danger of boring or irritating the jury. The judge may put reasonable time limits on the closing arguments.

In most jurisdictions the party having the burden of proof, usually the plaintiff, has the right to argue first and last. That is, plaintiff has the right to argue first and, after defendant has argued, make a rebuttal argument. A few jurisdictions allow only one argument per side (and in some of these, the defendant argues first, plaintiff last).

In situations where the only issue for the jury to decide is whether an affirmative defense or counterclaim has been proved, and the defendant has the burden of proof on these issues, the defendant usually will have the right to argue first and last.

§1.15.   Jury instructions

The judge must instruct the jury on the law that applies to the case. Some judges instruct the jury before the lawyers make the closing arguments. Others instruct the jury after the closing arguments are completed. In most jurisdictions the judge will both read the instructions and give the jury a written set of the instructions to use during deliberations. A few jurisdictions follow the practice that instructions are only read to the jury.

The jury will also get verdict forms. There may be a number of verdict forms, since cases may have multiple parties, claims, counterclaims, and third-party claims. In some cases the jury may also get special verdict forms asking how the jury finds on various specific issues of fact and law.

Reading and explaining the instructions in most cases take perhaps 10 to 15 minutes, although in complex cases they can take much longer.

§1.16.   Jury deliberations and verdict

The jury is then sent to the jury room to begin deliberations. Before leaving the courtroom, however, alternate jurors, if any, are dismissed, and the court bailiff is sworn in to safeguard the jury's privacy during its deliberations.

The bailiff usually carries the admitted exhibits and the written jury instructions back to the jury room for use during the deliberations.

The only guidelines the jury receives on how it should organize and conduct itself are the standard instructions that the jurors should first select a foreperson to preside over their deliberations and that the foreperson and other jurors must sign the verdict forms that reflect their decisions. How the jury organizes itself and conducts the deliberations is largely up to the jury.

Jurors sometimes have questions during their deliberations. These are usually written down and brought by the bailiff to the judge, who then confers with the lawyers on how to respond. When a response is prepared, the jury is brought back into the courtroom and given the response. Deliberations then continue.

When the jury reaches a verdict (either a unanimous or majority verdict, depending on the jurisdiction) and signs the appropriate verdict forms, it signals to the judge (usually through a buzzer system) that it is ready to return the verdict. The lawyers, if they are not in the courthouse, are called, and everyone reappears in the courtroom. The jury is brought in, and the judge asks if the jury has reached a verdict. When the foreperson answers "yes," the foreperson is directed to give the verdict to the bailiff, who gives it to the judge (who checks to see that all verdict forms are accounted for and have been signed properly), who usually gives it to the court clerk to be read aloud.

After the verdict has been announced, the judge will ask whether any parties want to "poll the jury." If so (and it is common that the losing side requests it), the clerk will then ask each juror if the verdict read in court is that juror's verdict. If all say "yes," that ends the jury's service. If any jurors necessary for the verdict (some jurisdictions do not require unanimous verdicts in all cases) say "no," the jury continues deliberating.

How long does the jury deliberate? Most verdicts are probably reached in one to four hours, although every trial lawyer can tell a story about getting a 15-minute verdict or having a jury deliberate more than a day, perhaps several days, in a lengthy or complicated case.

What happens when the jury cannot agree on a verdict? The judge usually asks the jury whether further deliberations might be useful or whether the jury is hopelessly deadlocked. If the former, the judge often gives the jury an "Allen charge," which encourages the jurors to listen to each other's views and attempt to reach a verdict. If the latter, the judge declares a mistrial, excuses the jury, and schedules a retrial.

The court then usually sets a date for a hearing on any post-trial motions and, in a criminal case following a guilty verdict, sentencing.

§1.17.   Post-trial motions and appeal

After the verdict a party usually has a specific number of days in which to file written post-trial motions. The most common are a motion for judgment notwithstanding the verdict, which asks the judge to set aside the jury's verdict and enter judgment for the other side, and a motion for a new trial, which asks the judge to order a new trial because of claimed errors made during the first trial. These motions are frequently made alternatively. Also common in some jurisdictions are motions in civil cases for additur or remittitur, which ask the court to increase or decrease the dollar amount of the jury's verdict.

The judge will usually schedule a hearing on the motions and allow the parties to argue orally. The judge will then rule on the motions and usually will prepare a written order.

When post-trial motions have been decided, the judge enters judgment in accordance with the jury verdict and post-trial motions. Entering judgment is the jurisdictional fact that ends the case in the trial court. A party wishing to appeal the judgment must file a timely notice of appeal with the clerk of the trial court. In civil cases a party must usually post an appeal bond in the amount of the judgment. This act begins the appellate process.

§1.18.   Conclusion

There is nothing mysterious or complicated about trial procedure. The important thing to remember is that federal and state courts historically have developed different ways of conducting the various stages of a trial, and they continue to experiment with changes today. Consequently, every trial lawyer must know how his case will be tried in the court, and before the judge, where it is scheduled. If you don't know, you must find out. Ask the judge's law clerk, court clerk, and trial lawyers who have tried similar cases before that judge how cases are tried there. If all else fails, go to the courtroom and watch a case being tried.

II
THE PSYCHOLOGY OF PERSUASION

§2.1.   Introduction

Trials are a re-creation of reality — an event or transaction that happened in the past. In trials, there are usually three versions of reality: your side's reality, the other side's reality, and the jury's reality. Each party firmly believes that its version of reality is correct and tries to persuade the jury to accept its version. However, the only reality that ultimately matters is the jury's reality — what the jury believes actually happened — because that reality will control the jury's verdict.

Which side's version of reality will the jury accept as its own? This depends largely on which side is more persuasive in presenting its version during the course of the trial. If neither side is persuasive, the jury will construct a version of reality entirely on its own. To persuade juries, you need to understand juries — their backgrounds, beliefs, and attitudes, how they process information, how they think, and how they make decisions. Only when you understand the psychology of persuasion can you understand how to persuade a jury to adopt your version of reality as its own. This understanding will influence everything you do during a jury trial, from jury voir dire through closing arguments.

This chapter reviews what behavioral science and jury research have learned about juror backgrounds, beliefs and attitudes, how they process information, what influences them, how they make decisions, and discusses how trial lawyers can use this knowledge to shape how they try cases. Although for the most part this research is consistent with what effective trial lawyers have learned through experience, it has organized and explained jury behavior in a systematic way that significantly contributes to our understanding of how jurors think, how they decide, and how they can be persuaded.

§2.2.   Behavioral science and jury research

Until perhaps 50 years ago, a common view was that jurors objectively absorbed the evidence presented by both sides during a trial, withheld making premature judgments, dispassionately reviewed that evidence during deliberations, and ultimately reached a logical decision, based on the evidence and the applicable law. Behavioral science research, beginning in the 1940s, and jury research, beginning in the 1960s, have emphatically rejected that view. "They," the jurors, do not think and decide like "us," the lawyers.

A caveat is in order, however. Much of this jury research has been conducted in environments that have little to do with courtroom realities. For example, researchers frequently use written questionnaires answered by undergraduate students receiving extra credit to test the researchers' hypotheses. Researchers frequently show videotaped scenarios to volunteers, who then answer questionnaires. Whether such research yields results that can be applied with confidence to jury trials is somewhat doubtful. Fortunately, in recent years some of that research has become more realistic, by using trial lawyers to help create courtroom scenarios, and by using actual or representative jurors in real courtrooms to test the hypotheses. Such research results have more credibility in the world of trial lawyers. What does the credible behavioral science and jury research tell us?

1.   Affective reasoning

People have two significantly different approaches to decision making. Most people are primarily affective ("right brain") decision makers. Affective persons have several common characteristics. First, they are usually emotional and creative, and are more interested in people than problems. They see trials as human dramas, not legal disputes. Second, they use deductive reasoning, which is primarily emotional and impulsive, in which a few premises about how life works and relatively little factual information are used to reach decisions and attribute cause and blame quickly. Third, once they make decisions, they become committed to them, and they validate their decisions by selectively accepting, rejecting, or distorting later information to "fit" the already reached decisions. This allows them to justify their decisions and believe the decisions are logical and fair. People have an internal need to be consistent, which makes them committed to their original decisions despite the receipt of later conflicting information. Since information inconsistent with their decisions causes internal conflict and stress, they become resistant and soon hear and see only what they want to hear and see.

By contrast, cognitive ("left brain") decision makers are more interested in problems than people, enjoy accumulating information, defer making decisions until they have all the available information and, like trained scientists, use inductive reasoning to reach logical decisions. Cognitive decision makers are more likely to have higher education levels and math, hard science, or business backgrounds. After seeing a collision, affectives ask: "Was anyone hurt?" Cognitives ask: "Whose fault was it?" In short, affectives "feel"; cognitives "reason."

While most jurors are affective decision makers, most lawyers, trained in legal reasoning, are cognitive decision makers. The approach that is effective in persuading "them," the jurors, will not be the approach effective for "us," the lawyers. Lawyers must understand how jurors process information and make decisions before lawyers can communicate persuasively with them. This has significance at all stages of a jury trial.

2.   Beliefs and attitudes

Beliefs (what we know about something) are how we perceive life works — our value system. Attitudes (how we feel about something) are the expressions of our beliefs. Our attitudes are our convictions, biases, and prejudices about people and events, our sense of what's right and wrong, what's fair and unfair. We try to make sense of the world around us, and use stereotypes — our beliefs and attitudes — to organize our views of that world. Beliefs and attitudes are formed throughout our lives through parental training, formal education, television, news, and, most importantly, personal observations and experiences. Once developed, attitudes are usually held for life and change slowly, if at all, over time.

Attitudes subconsciously filter information about the world around us and help sort out conflicting information and fill in missing information. Attitudes are the rose-colored glasses through which we "see" information in our own unique way, accepting information that we like, and rejecting, minimizing, or distorting information that we dislike, thereby achieving personal consistency and comfort.

Most jurors do not passively sit and uncritically absorb evidence. They rarely have "open minds" that are receptive to new ideas. Instead, they "test" new information by how consistent it is with their preconceived ideas of how life works, and how it fits into the picture of the case they have constructed in their minds. Jurors rapidly construct stories of what probably happened in the case, then subconsciously use their attitudes to accept, reject, or distort evidence, or supply missing information, to create a complete, plausible story. This lets jurors reach decisions they believe are consistent with the evidence, and are therefore logical and fair. The more circumstantial the evidence of liability or guilt, and the more familiar jurors are with the subject matter of the trial, the more important jurors' beliefs and attitudes become.

Juror attitudes have great significance throughout a trial. These attitudes determine if the jurors will be receptive or resistant to the parties, evidence, and themes presented during the trial. Lawyers can only persuade if jurors are willing to accept, and jurors' attitudes, not logic or reason, control whether they will accept or reject particular information or messages during a trial. Therefore, lawyers need to understand the jurors' relevant attitudes, whether these attitudes are consistent with or in conflict with each other, and how intensely those attitudes are held. This must be explored before and during the jury selection process, since it is highly unlikely that any jurors will change their attitudes about any important matters during the course of a trial.

Although reliable juror demographic information (such as sex, race, age, marital status, family history, residence information, education, and job history) is easy to obtain, those demographics at best reflect likely general attitudes about life, and have limited use in predicting individual juror attitudes relevant to the issues in a particular trial. Single demographic characteristics, such as sex, race, and age are almost useless in predicting juror attitudes (unless, of course, the case itself involves issues of sex, race, or age).

By contrast, direct information of juror attitudes should be a better source. However, jurors are frequently inaccurate, whether intentionally or unintentionally, in describing their own attitudes about issues relevant to a particular trial. Self-disclosure of true attitudes during jury selection, particularly attitudes on sensitive issues, is notoriously unreliable, because the jurors' need to fit in and be accepted by others usually overrides the obligation to be truthful. As a result, jurors usually give socially acceptable answers to questions that probe attitudes on sensitive issues. Creating a relaxed, nonjudgmental environment for self-disclosure improves its reliability. Questioning jurors individually, out of the presence of the other jurors, improves the amount and accuracy of self-disclosure. Using written questionnaires, rather than questions in open court, also significantly improves the candor and completeness of self-disclosure.

Lawyers usually seek to learn juror attitudes indirectly, by asking about jurors' hobbies, interests, involvement with groups and organizations, and personal experiences in life, from which attitudes can be inferred. Personal experiences similar to the case being tried are particularly important, because jurors consider these experiences to be evidence and frequently spend as much time during deliberations discussing their collective experiences as they do discussing the formally introduced evidence.

Jury selection (assuming the law and court permit such latitude) usually pursues all these approaches — getting basic demographic information, as well as direct and indirect information on attitudes — so that lawyers can make informed decisions on which jurors to accept or reject in a particular case.

3.   Decision making

A jury verdict is a product of two forces: individual decision making, and group decision making. Individual juror decisions are influenced principally by affective reasoning and the jurors' beliefs and attitudes, discussed above. However, it is also important to understand that most jurors go through an emotional progression during the course of a trial, because that progression will influence how lawyers present themselves, their evidence, and their arguments. Lawyers who understand and respond to the jurors' emotional needs during the trial have a significant advantage.

At the beginning of a trial, particularly during the jury selection process, most jurors experience varying levels of anxiety. This is natural, since uncertainty creates anxiety. They are unsure of their role as jurors, unsure that they will be selected to sit as jurors, unsure of their capacity to understand what the case is all about, and unsure of their ability to reach the right verdict. For the rest of the trial those jurors are using subconscious strategies to cope with their unwanted anxiety.

As the trial begins, after they have been selected to sit as jurors, and after they have heard the opening statements, that uncertainty and anxiety, for most jurors, subsides. Their uncertainty lessens as they begin to understand courtroom procedure and their role in the trial process. They begin to come to terms with the case by constructing stories in their minds of what the case seems to be about. These stories may turn out to be accurate or inaccurate, but they are constructed just the same. The stories are the mental process by which jurors strive to make sense of the information they receive. This is not the same thing as reaching a final decision, but does have a great deal to do with how those jurors perceive the actual evidence when they receive it.

As the trial progresses, and they actually hear and see the evidence, jurors subconsciously accept, reject, or distort that evidence, depending on whether the evidence is consistent or inconsistent with the stories they have constructed in their minds. This is the filtering process, where jurors subconsciously use their attitudes and beliefs to screen the evidence as they hear and see it. For most jurors, the evidence, as filtered, serves to validate the stories they have already constructed in their minds, and serves to "prove" that their initial impressions were right. The anxiety most jurors experienced at the beginning of the trial has subsided, as these jurors become confident of what the right outcome of the case should be.

At the end of the presentation of evidence, most jurors, now confident of and committed to their decisions, look forward to sharing their views with others during deliberations. For these jurors, the closing arguments will have little influence, since they already know what the right decision should be (although hearing arguments supporting their decision may make them stronger advocates for that decision during deliberations). Closing argument will usually influence only those jurors who are still unsure of their decision, or who do not have confidence in their decision. Closing argument may also influence those jurors who realize that their decisions are not permitted under the verdict options given in the court's instructions on the applicable law, and must now reassess their decisions.

When the jurors retire to the jury room to deliberate, this is the time they may first realize that other jurors may not share their views and decisions, and group dynamics has a strong influence in determining whose decisions will prevail and speak for the jury as a whole.

Individual decisions are influenced by the dynamics of group decision making, since a jury is a group charged with reaching a decision — the verdict. Jury research has focused much of its attention on the dynamics of group decision making, the critical concern being the extent to which individual decisions can be overcome by group decisions.

Group dynamics do not involve an even exchange among the members of a group. Some members have more influence on the group than others. For these purposes members are usually defined as persuaders, participants, or nonparticipants.

Persuaders are persons who make assertive statements about the evidence, freely express their opinions, and actively build coalitions supporting their views. Persuaders are the opinion leaders who have the most influence and dominate the discussion in a group. They usually have higher education levels and have positions of authority or expertise in their work. They are articulate, talk readily, and are comfortable in group settings. Many will have prior jury service. Persuaders constitute approximately 25 percent of a group. In a typical jury deliberation, three jurors do more than 50 percent of the talking, and those are the persuaders.

Participants are persons who also engage in group discussions. However, they are followers, not leaders, and value social approval and acceptance by others. They defer to others' having stronger egos, more education and higher intelligence, more experience, and greater career success. Participants readily join coalitions, since the coalition validates their decisions, but they do not lead them. They will be actively involved in the deliberations, but are likely to state things in terms of their opinions, and do not actively try to have others accept their views. Participants constitute approximately 50 percent of a group. In a typical jury deliberation, about six jurors will be participants.

Nonparticipants are persons who rarely engage in group discussions. Jurors who are nonparticipants rarely become involved in deliberations other than to express agreement with a particular view or vote. Nonparticipants are usually followers who will go along with what the majority decides to do. (However, nonparticipants who are loners and are detached from and avoid involvement with others may exhibit independence and not be easily swayed by the majority's view.) Nonparticipants constitute approximately 25 percent of a group. In a typical jury deliberation, three jurors will be nonparticipants.

Categorization of potential jurors is, of course, particularly important at the jury selection stage of the trial, where the peremptory challenges should be used first to eliminate unfavorable persuaders. It is more important than trying to identify the potential jury foreperson, who, research has shown, is more likely to be a compromiser and consensus builder than an opinion leader or authoritarian personality.

4.   What influences the jury

What influences jurors to accept our version of reality as their own? Communication is based on perception. It is a process involving senders (witnesses and lawyers), messages (evidence and arguments), media (testimony and exhibits), and receivers (jurors). Learning, for the receivers, is also an active process involving receiving, processing, remembering, and retrieving messages. Learning and persuasion will only occur if the messages you intend to send to the jury are the same as the messages the jury actually receives and retains.

a.   Sender credibility

The senders — witnesses and lawyers — must be credible sources of information before they can influence the jury. Influence is largely a function of credibility, and credibility is largely a function of the sender's personal attributes. People develop opinions about others quickly, often within a few minutes. Three principal characteristics of credibility are trustworthiness, expertise, and dynamism.

First, trustworthiness refers to impartiality. Jurors obviously prefer witnesses who have no apparent bias, interest, or motive to slant testimony one way or another, or, if expert witnesses, are not hired guns willing to say anything for a fee. For lawyers, it means that the lawyers are candid in dealing with both good and bad facts, and do not try to pull the wool over the jurors' eyes.

Second, expertise refers to how knowledgeable the witnesses are about the facts and issues of the case. Knowledgeable and authoritative persons have more influence on others. With lay witnesses, it refers to how well the witnesses saw, heard, or knew about the relevant events and transactions, and how well they remember and recount the details surrounding them. With expert witnesses, it refers to the experts' education, training, and experience, and how thoroughly they did their tests and analysis. It also refers to the uniqueness of the experts' qualifications, since people put more weight on information seen to be scarce and therefore valuable. The less the jurors are able to understand the testimony, the more important trustworthiness and expertise of the witness becomes.

Third, dynamism refers to the witnesses' and lawyers' ability to communicate. Jurors prefer witnesses and lawyers who are likeable and attractive, both physically and personally. They are more influenced by people they like and who appear to be much like themselves. They prefer witnesses and lawyers who project energy, enthusiasm, and confidence when they testify or argue. All the components of effective delivery — verbal content (the actual spoken words), nonverbal delivery (paralinguistics, such as speech rate, volume, pauses, and voice inflection), and body language (kinesics, such as posture, body, arm, and hand movement, facial gestures, and eye contact) — must work in a coordinated way. Boredom is the enemy of effective communication, and dynamic delivery is the best antidote. Any lawyer or witness can be taught how to be a more effective communicator.

Finally, jurors think — erroneously — that they are good at detecting deception, and use stereotypes to make such assessments. They believe that mannerisms such as lack of eye contact, nervousness, hand over mouth, hesitancy in answering, and using words like "honestly" or "believe me" indicate uncertainty or deception. These are the kinds of mannerisms that witness training and preparation can minimize.

b.   Receiver capacities

The receivers — the jurors — come with diverse interests and abilities and represent a broad spectrum of today's adult population. Many, however, have limited attention spans, limited interest in learning, and limited channels through which they are willing to learn.

First, most people's attention spans are short. The average person can only maintain a high level of concentration for about 15 to 20 minutes. After that, attention levels drop significantly. That's why half-hour television programs are more common than one-hour programs — advertisers know that viewers are likely to change channels before the hour is over. In addition, listening to others talk occupies only a small portion of the brain's capacity, allowing the rest of the brain to fade in and out and think about other things. While some jurors will pay close attention throughout a trial, most jurors will have varying levels of attention, and periodically drift off and think about other things.

Second, most people have limited interest in learning, particularly when there is no perceived self-interest involved. Learning new things takes effort. Many jurors did not like formal learning, and once their schooling was done, resist situations that repeat their school-years experience. A trial, of course, represents in many ways the formality of classroom learning, which, for these jurors, dredges up unpleasant memories.

Third, most people have been trained, principally through television, how to expect new learning. They are part of the "sound bite" generation. They now want it fast, painless, interesting, and visual. They form perceptions quickly, based on little information. Observe any television news program. Notice how each news item is short, usually less than two minutes, leads off with a few seconds introduction from a "talking head," cuts quickly to visuals with a background voice, focuses on the human impact of the story, and wraps up before boredom sets in. If this is what makes people watch television news, it speaks volumes about how lawyers in today's environment should try cases to juries.

Fourth, what people see as "evidence" is different from what lawyers understand as evidence. When people become jurors, they see as evidence any information relevant to their decision, whether it is formally introduced evidence from witnesses and exhibits, their personal experiences in life they believe, rightly or wrongly, to be relevant to the case, and their attitudes about how life works. Everything that jurors see as evidence goes into their decision making. Jurors frequently spend as much time discussing their experiences in life — such as the automobile accidents they've been involved in, their experiences with doctors and hospitals, and their experiences with the police — which they feel are as relevant to their decision, as they do to the witness testimony and exhibits. It's all "evidence" to the jurors.

c. *Effective messages*

Effective communication must come from credible sources and must be attuned to the realities of today's listeners. The message itself, whether witness testimony, exhibits, or lawyer arguments, must also be effectively structured. Research has contributed much to understanding the components of effective communication.

First, memory is a severe limitation on what we can effectively communicate. It makes no sense to communicate if the listeners do not retain the essence of what has been communicated. The average person forgets most of any communication within a few hours, and after two or three days retains but a small part. Trial lawyers need to understand that memory is indeed fleeting, and must use strategies to improve jurors' retention of the key information presented during a trial.

Second, people use simplification strategies to deal with sensory overload. People are bombarded with information during a trial through testimony, exhibits, and arguments. They quickly become overloaded with information and subconsciously employ simplification strategies to cope with the avalanche of information, since sensory overload is a stressful situation that people try to avoid.

A key simplification strategy recognizes that people instinctively use psychological anchors, which are mnemonic devices to help them remember the gist of what they have learned. Much like we use yellow highlighters to mark key words and phrases on written material, jurors create psychological anchors to do mentally what highlighters do physically.

Psychological anchors are simply what trial lawyers call themes. A theme is a memorable word or short phrase — "this is a case about greed" — that summarizes and encapsulates lengthy descriptive and evaluative information. Research shows that it is human nature to condense voluminous information to an easily remembered word or phrase, so that hearing or seeing the word or phrase later will trigger some of the supporting detail. Anchoring information to a theme makes the information easier to retain and retrieve. If trial lawyers do not provide the themes during a trial, jurors will instinctively create themes themselves. An important part of trial preparation is selecting themes that are emotionally based, are catchy and memorable, summarize the liability and damages positions in the case, fit the undisputed and disputed evidence, and are consistent with the jurors' beliefs and attitudes. If this is done well, and used periodically during the trial, jurors will adopt your themes during their deliberations.

Third, this is the era of visual learning. People today are part of the television age or, more recently, computer age, and are used to receiving information visually. Trials, however, largely involve witness testimony. Research has shown that after two or three days listeners retain only about 10 percent of aural messages, but they retain about 20 percent of visual messages. Retention is improved several-fold if both aural and visual messages are used to present the same information. Trial lawyers have to focus on improving the level of retention from witness testimony and lawyer argument by using visual aids whenever possible to repeat and reinforce aural messages.

Fourth, research has shown that the impact of aural information — witness testimony and lawyer argument — can be significantly improved. Witnesses and lawyers can be trained to use "powerful language" to improve their persuasiveness and eliminate or minimize speaking styles that detract from credibility. Powerful language use the active voice, has good speech rate and volume, uses plain English and good diction, uses present tense, and makes descriptions vivid and visceral. It avoids using tentative language, such as hollow intensifiers ("very," "really"), unnecessary hedges ("I guess," "well"), and indications of uncertainty ("it seemed like"). Witnesses and lawyers can be taught to use sensory language to make what is verbal appear to be visual by creating unique images and symbols. They can be prepared to testify about details of events and transactions that enhance their credibility. They can be prepared to demonstrate what happened, rather than just tell what happened. They can be taught to create emotional messages, both positive and negative, and express confidence and certainty whenever possible.

Fifth, this is the era of the visual trial. Visual aids — photographs, diagrams, charts, models, enlarged documents, and computer simulations — that are large, clear, and vivid usually have much more immediate and lasting impact than the spoken word. They dramatically improve retention levels of the information. Whenever possible, show rather than just tell. Whenever the information is important, make it visual.

Finally, research has shown that several concepts can be used to increase memory and persuasion. Repetition is a powerful influence. Repeating a message — such as a theme in opening statements or closing arguments — three or four times substantially improves retention. More repetition can be effective, but its form must be modified so that jurors do not turn off to seemingly endless identical repetition, and the repetition does not become legally objectionable. Jurors may forget the details over time, but they will retain the impressions that have been repeated during the trial.

Cues are a powerful influence. A cue is simply a verbal or visual warning that something important is about to happen, so that listeners will pay particular attention. A cue can be direct — saying "this is important" — or indirect — using tone of voice, pregnant pauses, body language, rhetorical questions, and the like.

Rhetorical questions also have a strong influence because they stimulate active thinking. Self-generated ideas have greater strength and retention. When jurors respond to rhetorical questions and reach the desired conclusions themselves, their conclusions will have a stronger and more lasting impact.

Order effects are particularly important. Where a message is placed in relation to other information has much to do with how well the message is received and retained. Because most people make up their minds quickly and become bored and tune out quickly, it is particularly important to begin with information that has impact. People remember better what they hear first — this is the concept of primacy. On the other hand, people also remember better what they hear last — this is the concept of recency. It also is important to end with information that has impact. In short, the most important information should be at the beginning and end of any message.

Order effects can sometimes be used to enhance less credible sources. Because people tend to forget the source of information over time — the sleeper effect — information from a less impressive witness can be placed in the middle of the presentation.

Order effects are important within the component parts of a trial, such as opening statements, closing arguments, and direct examinations, as well as the trial as a whole. When trials are short, primacy is the more important concept. When trials last more than a few days, recency is probably more important.

There also are specific techniques that can effectively deal with the fact that trials involve two opposing sides that are constantly bombarding the jurors with conflicting information and messages. Forewarning and inoculation are particularly important techniques for the side presenting information or arguing first. Forewarning is giving the listeners advance warning that they are going to hear contrary information and appeals from the other side. Inoculation is anticipating the other side's argument and giving the listeners information and arguments that they can use to resist the other side's arguments. Research shows that when forewarning and inoculation are used, listeners become more resistant to later contrary information and arguments.

Two-sided argumentation is also important. Research shows that when one side has a strong case and the listeners are already favorably disposed, one-sided arguments — discussing only that side's strengths — are more persuasive, since they reinforce already held views. However, where both sides have reasonably equal cases and the listeners are not disposed one way or another, two-sided arguments — including the other side's arguments and a refutation of them — are more persuasive. Because most cases actually tried have strengths and weaknesses on both sides, two-sided argumentation will usually be the more effective technique.

§2.3. *What research means for trial lawyers*

What does this behavioral science and jury research tell us as trial lawyers about how to approach a jury trial? What are the keys we need to keep in mind throughout our trial preparation and the trial itself? Six concepts stand out.

1. Prepare from the jury's point of view

The only reality that counts in the courtroom is the jury's reality. The jury's perception of reality is *the* reality. Therefore, all courtroom communication must be juror centered — it must be planned and executed from the jury's point of view. If it's not persuasive to the jury, it's not worth doing, no matter how logical it may be to you. Always ask: What does the jury want to know? How does the jury want to learn it?

This means we must recognize that for many jurors, serving on a jury involves stress and anxiety. We must employ strategies that quickly and easily help jurors understand the trial process and what the case is all about. And it means we must understand that most jurors are affective decision makers, are emotional and people oriented, and make decisions quickly, based mostly on their preconceived views of how life works, then resist changing their minds. It means we must recognize that jurors filter evidence through their beliefs and attitudes and subconsciously decide whether to accept, reject, or distort it. It means we must make our witnesses, and ourselves, trustworthy, knowledgeable, and dynamic. It means we must make the trial vivid and visual. And it means we must be efficient, move the story forward, and make our points quickly before boredom sets in and jurors tune out.

Jurors, like everyone else, are a product of their environment. They have been trained, primarily through television and film, to expect drama, an emphasis on personalities, and sophisticated visual effects. They expect to get everything quickly, in simple, digestible sound bites. And they want it all to be interesting and enjoyable. Anything less and you've violated the "boring rule," and jurors will quickly change channels.

After a verdict, the losing lawyers often complains: "The jury just didn't understand the case." That is a lawyer problem, not a jury problem. The lawyer didn't understand that everything you do must be from the jury's point of view.

2. Develop a theory of the case

A theory of the case is a clear, simple story of "what really happened" from your point of view. It must be consistent with the undisputed evidence as well as your version of the disputed evidence and the applicable substantive law. It must not only show what happened, but also explain why the people in the story acted the way they did. It should be consistent with the jury's beliefs and attitudes about life and how the world works. It must be a persuasive story that will be the basis of your evidence and arguments throughout the trial. If you cannot state your theory of the case in a minute or two, it needs more work. If you do not construct a clear, simple story that puts all the evidence together into a coherent whole — your theory of the case — the jury will construct one without you.

The theory of the case obviously needs to be developed as the facts of the case become known, and well before trial. Consider, for example, an automobile collision case, where there is evidence that the plaintiff-driver may have been drinking before the collision with the defendant's car. Plaintiff must decide if her theory of the case is that (1) the accident was caused solely by the defendant's negligence and that no drinking occurred, (2) plaintiff had been drinking but her drinking played no part in causing the collision, or (3) plaintiff's drinking did play a part but the defendant's negligence was the primary cause of the collision. In a murder case, the defendant must decide if his theory of the case is (1) mistaken identity, (2) self-defense, or (3) accident. In a contract case, the plaintiff must decide if his theory of the case is (1) defendant failed to perform his obligations under the contract, resulting in consequential damages, or (2) defendant intentionally breached the contract in bad faith, resulting in punitive damages. Although alternative and inconsistent theories are proper and useful at the pleading stage, by the time of trial they must be distilled down to one simple, clear story.

Trials are in large part a contest to see which party's version of "what really happened" the jury will accept as more probably true. In civil cases, the opposing sides usually have directly competing versions of reality, and each side tries to present a persuasive version that the jury will adopt as its own. In criminal cases, this is also often true (particularly when the defense is presenting an affirmative defense), but frequently the contest is whether the jury will accept the prosecution's version, when the defense is defending on the existence of reasonable doubt and is not offering a competing version of reality.

3.   Select themes and labels

Themes and labels are the trial vocabulary that become the psychological anchors you want the jurors to accept and adopt as their own during the trial. Once you have developed your theory of the case, you have to condense it into themes and labels.

Themes are the anchors that summarize your case. They are the memorable words or phrases that encapsulate the essence of your case, your position on liability and damages, and project the images you want the jury to retain about the case. A case should not have more than three or four themes, which will be repeated throughout the trial, from jury selection to closing arguments. If selected properly, the jurors will adopt your themes as their own, and use your themes to argue for your side during deliberations.

A key part of trial preparation is selecting themes that are emotional, create memorable images, state your position on liability and damages, summarize what happened (conduct), who did it (people), and why they did it (motive), and are consistent with the jurors' beliefs and attitudes. The best themes come from time-honored sources that contain universal truths about life, such as the Bible, Aesop's Fables, or Americana sayings. Single words such as love, hate, fear, trust, honor, duty, responsibility, power, greed, and revenge are powerful explanations of human motives. Phrases such as "two seconds of carelessness," "a time bomb waiting to go off," and "desperate times call for desperate measures" create powerful images of events. Phrases such as "taking responsibility for your actions," "false friends," and "profits over safety" create strong moral images.

Themes should be selected with an eye toward the central issues in the case. Trials usually revolve around three kinds of issues. First, most trials involve elements issues. Have the parties proven, to the required degree of proof, each element of the claims and defenses? Second, many trials involve inferences issues. The parties do not disagree over the basic facts, but disagree over the inferences to be drawn from the facts. This is often the case when the issue is whether the facts circumstantially prove a mental state, such as intent or knowledge. Third, many trials involve credibility issues. When the testimony from witnesses clashes over important events, the jury must decide whose testimony to believe. Themes must be tailored to focus on the elements, inferences, and credibility issues the jurors will need to resolve to decide the case.

Labels are the tags you put on the people, events, and things involved in the case. Words convey images. Calling someone "the plaintiff" or "my client" conveys a different image than "Mrs. Johnson" or "Helen." Calling a tractor-trailer truck a "vehicle" conveys a different image than a "50,000 pound rig" or "eighteen-wheeler." Calling a death an event in which someone "died" is different from saying someone was "slaughtered." Calling an accident an "incident" or "event" is different from calling it a "collision" or "crash." In these examples, the plaintiff will want to use the emotional labels, the defendant will want to use the bland ones. You need to decide how you will label the parties, witnesses, events, and things to convey the emotional images you want the jury to see and accept, and use those labels consistently during the trial. They should be introduced in opening statements, carefully employed during witness examinations, and hammered home during closing arguments.

4.   Emphasize the people

Most jurors are people oriented. During trials, they want to hear about the people, not the legal problems. Jurors want to know who to silently root for, who wears the white hat. Jurors want to feel good about their decisions, and they can't unless they learn enough about the key people to get a feel for them and reach a verdict that is consistent with their feelings about those people. With key people, such as parties, jurors want three-dimensional information about them.

People do things for a reason. Jurors want to know not only what they did — the conduct — but also why they did it — the motivation. Jurors always want to know who the people are, what they did, why they did it, and what effect it had on their lives.

Notice how television news understands and uses this knowledge. Stories of an event invariably focus on the human element. Coverage of disasters, wars, and economic events all zoom in on a particular person and tell about the event through its effect on that person. This puts a human face on the news, which viewers like because they can relate to the story on a personal level. Good trial lawyers understand that trials involve the same elements.

5.   Use storytelling techniques

Storytelling is the way people have communicated with each other since the beginning of time. Long before written language, storytelling was the way information was passed on to others, and the way oral history was preserved. People instinctively use storytelling to communicate with others, and use the story framework to organize, understand, and remember information. Jurors do the same thing during trials. If lawyers do not organize the evidence into a clear, simple story, jurors will do so on their own. It's human nature.

Good stories organize, humanize, and dramatize. They have plot, characters, and emotion. They have a narrative structure. Notice how television and film use the story framework. Someone becomes involved in an event, a conflict arises, a crisis is reached, which culminates in a resolution. The story uses sensory language, vivid, visceral, and visual images, present tense, pace, and simplicity to give life to the story and dimensions to its characters. The story is told in a way that puts the members of the audience into the picture, engaging their hearts and minds, so that the audience cares about the people and what happens to them. The story's moral is consistent with the audience's beliefs and attitudes, so that the ending of the story is fair and justice is served. The story is highlighted with gripping visual aids. And the story is told efficiently and always moves forward, so that it never stalls or becomes boring.

Trials involve much more than merely introducing a set of facts; those facts must be organized and presented as part of a memorable story. Effective storytelling is the basis for much of what occurs during a trial, including the opening statement, direct examinations, and closing arguments. Small wonder, then, that good trial lawyers are invariably good storytellers.

6.   Focus on the key disputed facts and issues

In most trials almost all of the relevant facts are undisputed, so the few disputed facts are critical. Trial lawyers need to understand what is disputed and what is not, focus on the disputed facts, deal candidly with both the favorable and unfavorable evidence, and marshal and present that evidence so that the jury accepts your version of the disputed facts.

Focus on your best facts. How can you highlight the best facts, whether testimony or exhibits? How can you make them vivid, visceral, and visual? And how can you repeat your best facts in ways that maintain juror interest? Focus also on your worst facts. How can you minimize the impact of those facts? Can you anticipate them, using the techniques of forewarning, inoculation, and two-sided argumentation? And can you rebut the worst facts with evidence that has impact? If key facts and events are disputed because witnesses remember them differently, how can you make your witnesses and exhibits more persuasive than your opponent's on these key disputed matters?

Inexperienced lawyers usually spend too much time belaboring undisputed facts, thereby boring the jury, and too little time proving their version of disputed facts, thereby failing to persuade the jury. Experienced lawyers spend a great deal of time finding witnesses and exhibits that support their version of the disputed facts, and preparing them so that they are dynamic, confident, detailed, and vivid. They understand that wars are won or lost depending on which side wins or loses a key battle. The same is true for trials.

7.   Understand your role as an advocate

These first six concepts are not self-executing. They require an advocate. An advocate does more than represent a client, or protect a client's rights. An advocate exhibits unrelenting commitment to the client's cause, and actively seeks to influence jurors by reaching their hearts and minds. Your role as an advocate at trial begins on the way to the courthouse for the first day and ends only when the jury is polled after the verdict. Always assume that the jurors (as well as judge and opposing counsel) see and hear everything you, your client, and your trial team do and say. Always assume that you are "on camera," even when the trial is not in session.

An advocate is both a director and an actor. You are a director, because a trial is much like theater. While limited to the script (what the witnesses say and exhibits show), the director uses creativity in choreographing that script (how the witnesses say it and how the exhibits are presented). You are also an actor, because you are constantly on stage. In many cases you will be the most important "witness" as you communicate with the jurors throughout the trial.

An advocate is always credible. This requires that you act professionally and fairly with the judge and opposing counsel. You must be trustworthy, knowledgeable, and dynamic so that the jurors see you as the teacher, helper, and guide. And it means that you must be yourself, so that the jurors know you are genuine.

An advocate always conveys a sense of injustice. Jurors must recognize it and be compelled to correct it, so that they feel good in reaching their decision. Jurors subconsciously ask a critical question: Are you saying it because you've been paid to say it, or are you saying it because you believe it? You need to project passion and commitment to your cause, and expose the injustice to motivate the jurors to decide the case in your favor (without crossing the line into expressing personal opinions).

Finally, an advocate always seeks to control the atmosphere in the courtroom. An advocate grabs and holds the jurors' attention, sets the tone for the trial, and becomes the dominant influence as the trial progresses. Jurors should look to you for leadership and guidance, and look forward to when you do things. This means you need to plan how you, your client, and your trial team conduct themselves throughout the trial, not just in the courtroom, but also during recesses, during lunch breaks, and going to and from the courthouse. Plan how you interact with the judge, court personnel, opposing counsel, and your client whenever the jurors are present. And plan how to organize the visuals — your attire, counsel table, exhibits, notebooks, and files — down to the smallest detail. When you control the atmosphere in the courtroom, through your conduct and your visuals, you enhance your power to persuade.

In trials, good things happen when you make them happen. The true advocate understands this and acts on it.

§2.4.   *Conclusion*

These are the key concepts that trial lawyers must understand and use during trial preparation and at every stage of a jury trial. They will influence your jury voir dire and peremptory challenges, shape your opening statements and closing arguments, structure your direct- and cross-examinations, and design your trial exhibits. They will influence how you, the advocate, put them together into a persuasive whole. To repeat, the key concepts are:

- Prepare from the jury's point of view
- Develop a theory of the case
- Select themes and labels
- Emphasize the people
- Use storytelling techniques
- Focus on the key disputed facts and issues
- Understand your role as an advocate

Does this mean that, simply by using these concepts, any case can become a winner? Of course not. The facts of most cases determine their outcomes. In litigation, cases in which the facts strongly favor one side rarely go to trial. These usually settle. Cases in which both sides have strengths and weaknesses, so that the outcome is in doubt, are most likely to go to trial. And in these cases, effective trial lawyers — advocates — do make a difference.

III

JURY SELECTION

§3.1. Introduction

Within the field of trial work, perhaps no area is the subject of more theory and speculation than jury selection. Every trial lawyer develops his own approach. Every trial lawyer has a favorite story that can disprove any other lawyer's approach. Some believe that jury selection is so unpredictable that any group of jurors will, in a given case, reach the same general conclusions. Others believe that a case is largely won or lost by the time the jury has been selected. Nevertheless, anyone aspiring to be a complete trial lawyer must become familiar with the methods by which juries are selected and the various approaches on which their selection can be based.

This chapter discusses the initial decision to request a jury trial, various methods by which jurors are examined, empaneled, and challenged, basic approaches and theories employed for the selection process, and the ways prospective jurors should be questioned.

§3.2. Do you want a jury?

In most jurisdictions, both parties to a lawsuit, whether civil or criminal, usually have a right to a jury trial. Where the right exists, it can be waived, either by failing to make a timely jury demand or by waiving it later. Parties in both civil and criminal cases must therefore make a threshold decision: Should you, if you have the right, demand a jury trial or try your case to the court? This decision is based on two considerations.

1. Who is the judge?

Some jurisdictions, usually in larger cities, use central assignment systems for their trial calendar. Consequently, you will not know who your judge is until your case is assigned to a trial judge, which frequently happens just before the case goes to trial. In many jurisdictions, however, your case will be assigned to a specific judge either when the case is first filed or at least well in advance of the trial date. Regardless of the assignment method used, you can and should make every effort to determine your judge's track record at the earliest possible time. Is he plaintiff- or defense-oriented in personal injury cases? What kind of judgments has he entered in similar civil cases? Do his trial rulings have any particular bent? In criminal cases, is he prosecution- or defense-minded? Does he have known attitudes in certain types of cases? What sentencing disparity does he have between bench and jury trials? Ask lawyers familiar with the judge and other knowledgeable sources what your reasonable expectations should be in your upcoming trial.

2.   Does your case have jury appeal?

Plaintiff's lawyers in personal injury cases usually demand jury trials on the theory that most of their cases have emotional appeal; thus, a jury in such a case is more likely to find liability and award substantial damages, while a judge who has heard it all before will have a more detached view of the evidence and take a harder look at the issues of liability and pain and suffering damages.

Defense lawyers in criminal cases usually will demand a jury trial if the client is presentable, the prosecution's case appears strong, the facts do not shock the jury, and the case has no substantial legal defenses to be raised. But if the prosecution's case appears weak or if a substantial defense, either legal or factual, can be developed, defense lawyers will sometimes prefer a bench trial, particularly when a heinous crime or aggravating facts would be shocking to the jury.

Commercial litigation cases frequently involve complex issues of law and fact revolving around substantial quantities of documentary proof. The cases themselves often involve multiple parties, usually corporations or other artificial entities. In these types of cases the parties, especially the party that believes it has the stronger case, may prefer a bench trial since the facts can be both confusing and boring to a jury.

The decision whether to use the right to a jury trial can be intelligently made only if done on a case-by-case basis, considering the facts, witnesses, parties, lawyers, and judge involved and considering the characteristics of the jury pool. For example, large-city jury pools are usually seen as favoring plaintiffs, particularly in personal injury cases. While generalizations are useful guides, they should not override evaluation of an individual case.

The final decision whether to try the case to a jury or waive a jury and try the case to the court must also be discussed with the client, who must be advised of the competing considerations in the case. This is particularly so in criminal cases, where the defendant's constitutional right to a jury trial can be waived only if the defendant makes a knowing and intelligent waiver of that right.

§3.3.   *Jury examination and selection methods*

If you have decided on a jury trial, you must seek answers to several preliminary questions before the jury selection process begins:

1. How many jurors and alternates will be selected?
2. What jury questioning system will be used?
3. What kinds of questions will be permitted?
4. What jury selection system will be used?
5. How many challenges does each side have, and how will they be exercised?

Jurisdictions vary more in jury selection than in any other phase of trial. Therefore, in preparing a case for trial every trial lawyer must review the applicable statutes, practice rules, local customs, and individual judge's practices.

1. How many jurors and alternates will be selected?

The number of jurors (and alternates, if applicable) who will decide a particular case is principally controlled by statutes and practice rules.

The number of jurors who will decide a case varies significantly among the jurisdictions. In federal courts, for example, criminal cases have 12 jurors, civil have 6. In state courts, juries commonly consist of 6, 8, or 12 jurors. In criminal cases, the number of jurors sometimes depends on the type of charge or possible sentence. For example, capital cases may require more jurors than noncapital cases.

The number of alternate jurors is also controlled by statute or rule, although they frequently are discretionary. The judge usually will decide to add alternate jurors if the trial will take more than two or three days, since this increases the likelihood that a regular juror may be unable to complete the trial. If, for instance, a trial will take no more than one week, most judges will seat one or two alternates; if the trial will take two or three weeks, many judges will seat three or four alternates. This should avoid a mistrial owing to an insufficient number of jurors remaining at the end of a trial to decide a case.

The point to remember is to review the applicable statutes and rules before trial to make sure what will happen in your particular case. A good practice is to have a photocopy of the applicable statutes and rules in your trial notebook before jury selection begins.

2. What jury questioning system will be used?

There are several systems by which courts question the prospective jurors, commonly called the "venire." The examination itself is usually called the "voir dire" examination. These systems vary significantly, depending on the jurisdiction, type of case, and the judge. The only safe procedure is to research the applicable statutes and rules and ask the judge, his court personnel, or knowledgeable trial lawyers how your judge intends to conduct voir dire in your particular case.

There are several systems used today to question prospective jurors.

a. Lawyer examination

Traditionally the lawyers conduct the entire voir dire examination. The judge, following her introductory remarks to the jury, merely turns the jury pool over to the lawyers and limits her participation to ruling on objections made during the examinations.

b. Judge examination

In recent years the trend, particularly in federal courts, has been for the judge to conduct the entire voir dire examination. The lawyers' role is restricted to submitting requested questions to the judge and exercising challenges. Although most trial lawyers object to this trend, claiming that their right to examine jurors personally is an inherent right as well as necessary to intelligently exercise challenges, many judges favor it since it is more efficient and keeps the lawyers from "trying their case" during the voir dire examinations.

If your judge will conduct the entire examination herself, determine what questions she will ask in your type of case. If there are certain questions you feel should be asked to enable you to exercise challenges intelligently, present your proposed voir dire questions in writing to the judge, obtain a ruling on whether they will be asked, and make sure that your proposed questions and the judge's rulings on them are on the record.

c. Hybrid system

The third method is a hybrid of the first two. The judge asks all preliminary questions of law and determines whether any prospective jurors have fixed attitudes or experiences in life that have slanted their outlook of the case. This is designed to identify jurors who may be challenged for cause. The lawyers are then permitted to ask additional questions so that they can intelligently exercise their peremptory challenges.

d. Questionnaires

In recent years juror questionnaires have become common, particularly in lengthy or heavily publicized cases where juror attitudes on the issues are particularly important. There is substantial research showing that written juror responses to written questions are significantly more accurate and truthful than oral responses made to questions asked in the courtroom. This is particularly so where the responses involve juror attitudes about sensitive social issues and personal experiences, and where the case is a high profile case with substantial media coverage.

Each side usually submits proposed questions to the judge before trial. The judge rules on which questions will be permitted, how the questions will be phrased, and the order of the questions. Each prospective juror answers the questionnaire in writing. The questionnaire is typically drafted like an interrogatory with spaces for the jurors to write down answers. The completed questionnaires are then given to the judge and lawyers to review.

The questionnaires are convenient for both the prospective jurors and the lawyers. While many judges dislike jury questionnaires on the grounds that they are unnecessary and take an excessive amount of time to administer, a short questionnaire, perhaps two or three pages long and containing only several questions touching on key matters, can be an effective and efficient way to explore juror attitudes on sensitive matters. Bases for challenges for cause, and other reasons to excuse a juror, frequently are apparent from the questionnaire answers.

Questionnaires are often used in conjunction with one of the other methods discussed above.

e.   Individual and group questioning

In some jurisdictions all jurors are questioned individually. The questions are usually asked in the courtroom with the other jurors present, although the jurors are sometimes questioned privately, one at a time, in the judge's chambers. In others the jurors are questioned on general information and attitudes as a group. The jurors are then questioned individually on specific topics and on responses they made to the group questions. For example, the judge may ask the entire venire if any have ever been involved in a car accident. After three jurors raise their hands, those three jurors can be asked specific follow-up questions on the accidents they were involved in. This shifting from group to individual questions is more efficient and avoids some of the repetitive questioning. Lawyers, if they are permitted to question the venire, may use the same approach.

3.   What kinds of questions will be permitted?

a.   Open approach

Jurisdictions and individual judges also vary widely on the permissible scope of questions the prospective jurors may be asked. Some, following the more traditional approach, permit far-ranging questions designed not only to cover jurors' backgrounds and experiences but also to sound out the jurors' receptivity or hostility to applicable law and to test jurors' reactions to the likely evidence they will hear and see later in the trial.

b.   Restrictive approach

Many jurisdictions and judges today restrict the scope of questions, and statutes or court rules permit the lawyers to inquire only into jurors' backgrounds and experiences. They will not permit questions about law or questions that test jurors' attitudes on legal and factual issues related to the case. Judges following this approach, an increasingly common one, basically define an allowable question according to whether it is designed principally to learn *about* the juror or to convey information *to* the juror. The former type of question is permitted, the latter is not. This approach is more efficient and keeps the lawyers from "trying the case" during the jury selection process.

If your judge restricts the scope of questions, make sure you submit to the judge, in advance, questions of law you want the judge to ask the prospective jurors. In highly publicized cases or those in which the trial issues are particularly volatile, you will probably want the judge to question the prospective jurors more extensively on their knowledge of the case and their attitudes about the issues and experiences in life relating to the trial. Written questionnaires are particularly useful in these kinds of cases. Since the questions the jurors will be asked are within the judge's discretion, it is important to bring your requests to the judge in a written motion well before trial.

4. What jury selection system will be used?

The jury selection system to be used in your case is controlled by statutes, rules, local practices, and the judge's preference. As always, the only safe procedure is to research the applicable statutes and rules and ask the judge, his court personnel, or knowledgeable trial lawyers what selection system, and what procedures, your judge intends to use in your particular case.

There are many variations in jury selection systems, but almost all are based on two principal systems used today.

a. Strike system

Under this system every juror in the entire pool of prospective jurors, called the venire (typically between 15 and 40 jurors, depending on the case) is brought to the courtroom and is seated, usually in the spectator section. The jurors are then questioned. The questioning is done collectively, individually, or as a hybrid of the two, depending on the practice in that jurisdiction and before that judge. In many jurisdictions the order of the prospective jurors is chosen at random by the clerk, although some jurisdictions have statutes and rules regulating the order in which prospective jurors are questioned.

When all the questioning of the prospective jurors is completed, and the judge has ruled on whether any jurors should be excused for cause, the lawyers for the parties simply designate the jurors against whom they wish to exercise their available peremptory challenges. There are two ways this is done. In some jurisdictions each party gets a list of all the prospective jurors (usually from the court clerk at the end of the jury selection process) in the order in which they were questioned. The lawyer for each party then marks on her list the jurors she wants excused, usually by drawing a line through the juror's name and initialing it. The clerk then gets the list from both sides and calls the first 12 names (assuming a 12-person jury) that neither side has excused. In other jurisdictions, the lawyers work off one list, usually taking turns, first plaintiff, then defendant, using their available peremptory challenges.

If the case requires alternate jurors, the clerk simply calls the next two names (assuming that the judge has decided to have two alternates in the case).

The strike system has several advantages and one disadvantage. Its disadvantage is that it requires questioning every juror in the venire. Its advantages, however, probably account for its growing popularity: first, it avoids most of the gamesmanship of the traditional selection system; second, it keeps jurors from knowing which side excused them; third, lawyers know the background of the entire venire before using any peremptory challenges; and fourth, alternate jurors don't know who they are, since only at the end of the trial, just before deliberations begin, are any excess jurors excused, and they are excused either at random or because they were the last jurors accepted from the list.

b. Panel system

The traditional jury selection system, still common today, simply fills the jury box with the necessary number of jurors. Only the prospective jurors in the box are questioned by one of the methods described above. If lawyers also ask questions, the plaintiff's lawyer usually goes first, and then exercises the peremptory challenges he wishes to use at that time. The challenged jurors are excused and they are replaced by new jurors from the venire, sitting in the spectator section of the courtroom. The new jurors are then questioned and plaintiff's lawyer again can use peremptory challenges. This process goes on until plaintiff's lawyer accepts the panel and "tenders the panel" to the defense.

The defense lawyer then goes through the same steps, questioning the jurors and exercising his peremptory challenges, replacing the challenged jurors with new jurors from the venire, and continues this process until he also accepts the panel and tenders it back to the plaintiff. The plaintiff then can question the new jurors he had not previously questioned and exercise peremptory challenges against those jurors. This process goes back and forth until both sides accept the same panel of jurors. Alternate jurors, if necessary, are picked the same way.

The panel system has one advantage and several disadvantages. Its advantage is that only jurors in the jury box need to be questioned. But the system permits more gamesmanship during the selection process; it forces the lawyers to exercise peremptory challenges without knowing the backgrounds of the remaining jurors, since they have not yet been questioned; and it identifies the jurors who are alternates, making it less likely that they will give the trial the same degree of attention as the other jurors.

Keep in mind that the two basic selection methods described above are not the only ones used. There are numerous variations of these systems. The safest course is always to learn in advance exactly how the jury will be selected for your case and before your judge.

5. How many challenges does each side have, and how will they be exercised?

a. Cause challenges

There are two kinds of challenges (sometimes called "strikes"): challenges for cause and peremptory challenges. The grounds to excuse a juror for cause are usually enumerated by statute or rules. Common grounds include that the juror does not meet the statutory qualifications for jury service or that the juror cannot be fair and impartial in this particular case, usually because of a close relationship to one of the parties or because the juror has a fixed opinion of how the case should come out. No limit is placed on the number of cause challenges.

b. Peremptory challenges

Peremptory challenges are those given by statute or rules to each party to use as each party sees fit. Each party has a predetermined and limited number of peremptory challenges. There are several things you must always remember about those challenges.

First, the free rein that lawyers traditionally enjoyed to use peremptory challenges for any, or no, reason has been limited by several Supreme Court decisions in the past few years. The leading cases at present are *Batson v. Kentucky*, 476 U.S. 79 (1986), *Powers v. Ohio*, 499 U.S. 400 (1991), *Edmonson v. Leesville Concrete Co.*, 500 U.S. 614 (1991), *Georgia v. McCollum*, 505 U.S. 42 (1992), *J.E.B. v. Alabama*, 511 U.S. 127 (1994), and *Purkett v. Elem*, 514 U.S. 765 (1995). In *Batson* the Court held that in criminal cases a prosecutor cannot exercise peremptory challenges to eliminate members of the defendant's race from the jury solely on account of their race. In *Powers* the holding in *Batson* was extended to white defendants challenging the prosecution's exclusion of black jurors. In *Edmonson* the Court extended the holding in *Batson* to civil juries. In *McCollum* the Court applied *Batson* to the defense's exercise of peremptory challenges in criminal cases. *J.E.B.* applied the *Batson* holding to peremptory challenges based on gender. Finally, *Purkett* clarified the three-step *Batson* procedure for analyzing and ruling on objections to peremptory challenges. Once the opponent of a peremptory challenge makes out a prima facie case of racial discrimination, the party exercising the peremptory challenge must come forward with a race-neutral explanation for the challenge, which need not be persuasive or even plausible. If a race-neutral explanation is made, the opponent then must prove purposeful racial discrimination, which is decided by the trial judge. While the Supreme Court to date has applied *Batson* to race and gender, it has not yet extended it to other constitutionally recognized categories such as religion and ethnicity, although some lower courts have done so.

Second, never run out of challenges. Under the strike system this is not a serious problem since all the jurors will be questioned before exercising challenges. Under the panel system, however, this is vital since you will be exercising challenges without knowing the backgrounds of the remaining unquestioned jurors. Hence, you must always keep the remaining jurors in mind when exercising challenges. Watch those jurors as they sit in the back of the courtroom. How those jurors look and act will have a substantial effect on how frequently you use challenges. Always try to save at least one peremptory challenge. The cases are legion in which one lawyer used all his challenges before the complete jury was picked only to discover that the last juror seated was disastrous for him. Save your last challenge for such an emergency. However, keep in mind that many jurisdictions require you to exhaust your peremptory challenges to preserve error in the court's denial of any challenges for cause.

Third, if the panel system is being used you must determine if you will be allowed to "reinvade the jury." The right to reinvade refers to your right to use peremptory challenges on jurors you previously accepted during the selection process. In some jurisdictions the practice is that once you accept a juror you cannot later challenge her. In others the practice is that you can challenge jurors you initially accepted and tendered to the other side when the panel is later tendered back to you. Find out in advance what procedure you will be required to follow.

c. How many peremptory challenges does each side have?

The number of peremptory challenges varies according to the jurisdiction, the kind of case on trial, and the number of parties. In most jurisdictions the number of challenges is contained in statutes and rules. The numbers vary widely, and you must always read the applicable statutes and rules to find out. For example, the number may be as low as three challenges per side in a civil case or as high as ten per side in a criminal case.

The kind of case also may affect the number of peremptory challenges. Civil cases usually have fewer challenges than criminal cases. In multiple-party situations, statutes and rules frequently provide for additional challenges. Some add a certain number of challenges for each additional party. Others may add challenges for each additional party but sometimes provide that all plaintiffs will always have the same total number of challenges as all the defendants. In multiple-party situations some courts allow all plaintiffs or all defendants, if they agree, to "pool" their challenges and use them collectively.

Some jurisdictions give the trial judge discretion to allow additional challenges. If alternates are to be picked, most jurisdictions provide for additional peremptory challenges. Practices vary widely, so the recurring advice again applies: Read the applicable law to be sure.

d. How will challenges be exercised in court?

In jurisdictions using the strike system, the usual procedure is that the court clerk prepares a list of the jurors who have been questioned. That list will usually contain only enough jurors to add up to the number of jurors required in the case and the number of challenges each side has. For example, if the case will be tried by 12 jurors and have 2 alternates, and each side is entitled to 6 challenges, the list needs to have 26 jurors on it (after any challenges for cause have been ruled on).

The parties then get the list. In some jurisdictions both sides use one list, and plaintiff and defendant alternate taking turns using their challenges. In other jurisdictions both parties get a copy of the list and use their challenges. Under the latter system the parties do not know the jurors the other side has struck (and sometimes both sides strike the same juror). The list or lists are then given to the court clerk, who calls the jurors that neither side has challenged. In the event the parties either do not use all their challenges or duplicate some challenges, the clerk usually calls the jurors from the top of the list. These jurors then are sworn in as trial jurors and take their seats in the jury box.

In jurisdictions using the panel system, practices vary greatly. In some jurisdictions judges ask the lawyers to come to the bench and hold a side-bar conference at appropriate times to learn which jurors will be challenged. The judge will then excuse the challenged jurors. (The same approach is used for cause challenges. The judge asks whether either side is requesting that any jurors be excused for cause, hears any arguments, and rules.)

In other jurisdictions the lawyers are required to exercise challenges, both peremptory and for cause, in open court, where all the jurors can hear what is being said. If this is the practice, a bit of psychology is crucial. Most jurors hate to be excused. Waiting in the jury room to be called for another case is tedious. Therefore, if you are required to exercise challenges in open court, be polite to the juror being excused.

Example:

> *Plaintiff counsel:* Your Honor, at this time we ask that Mr. Smith be excused.
>
> *or*
>
> Your Honor, plaintiff thanks but excuses Mr. Smith.
>
> *Court:* Mr. Smith, you are excused. Please return to the main jury room.

If you are required to exercise challenges for cause in open court, make sure you have demonstrated why you are asking, and why you are entitled to, a challenge for cause.

Example:

Plaintiff is suing a truck driver for injuries arising out of a highway collision.

> *Plaintiff counsel:* Mr. Smith, what kind of work do you do?
> *Juror:* I'm a truck driver.
> *Plaintiff counsel:* How many years?
> *Juror:* Eighteen years.
> *Plaintiff counsel:* Over those years, were you ever involved in a collision with another car?
> *Juror:* Yes, three times.
> *Plaintiff counsel:* Did you ever get involved in a lawsuit from these collisions?
> *Juror:* Well, I got sued on one of them.
> *Plaintiff counsel:* Mr. Smith, because you have the same job as the defendant here, and you've also been a defendant in a lawsuit, do you think you might start off in this case a bit on the defendant's side?

Juror: Well, I always figure that a professional driver is probably not going to be the person that caused the accident.

Plaintiff counsel: Your Honor, under the circumstances we ask that Mr. Smith be excused from this case, for cause.

Judge: Yes. Mr. Smith, you are excused. Thank you for your candor.

If the judge refuses to excuse the juror for cause, you must of course use one of your peremptory challenges to get this obviously unfavorable and now probably hostile juror off the jury. You have made your reasons clear to the other jurors, and they should not hold it against you.

§3.4.   *Psychology of prospective jurors*

1.   What are prospective jurors feeling and thinking?

Put yourself in the shoes of a prospective juror. You recently received your notice to appear for jury duty. This morning you arrived at the courthouse, waited in the jury room most of the morning, read a pamphlet or watched a videotape about jury service, and were finally called, with about 30 other persons, and brought to a courtroom. You just entered the courtroom and sat down in the spectator rows. You can see the judge on the bench, and various other persons in the front of the courtroom. And then you wait some more. What is that juror thinking and feeling?

Most jurors have little or no experience in the courtroom. They are in the midst of strangers. They are apprehensive and intimidated. They are worried that their ignorance about the jury trial system will show. They are concerned about their life's secrets being exposed.

What do you do about it? As a lawyer, turn it around. Change from being a stranger to being the jurors' friend. If they feel intimidated, reassure them. If they are among strangers, make them feel comfortable. If they are worried about their ignorance, help them become informed. If they are concerned that secrets in their past will be exposed, reassure them. In short, the jury selection process is an opportunity for a trial lawyer to become the jurors' friend and guide by helping them understand the trial system, by reassuring that they do belong here, and by letting them know that their participation is important to you and your party.

How do you do it? Remember that empathy is important, and that you need to give before you can get. Remember that public speaking in front of strangers is one of the most commonly held fears. If permitted, tell the jury that you understand what it's like to be questioned about their lives in front of strangers in the courtroom, and that you are sensitive to their needs. If allowed, tell the jurors something about your life, so that you will not be seen as prying when you ask them questions about their lives. The lawyers (and judges) who get honest answers from the jurors are the ones who create a comfortable environment for disclosure and initiate the disclosure process by revealing parts of themselves before asking jurors to do the same.

2.   What are you trying to accomplish during jury selection?

As an advocate for a party, your purpose during the jury selection process is clear: You want to select a jury that will be open-minded, receptive to your proof, favorably disposed to you and your party, and ultimately will return a favorable verdict. Your opponent, of course, while also looking for a jury with an open mind, is also looking for a jury that will react favorably to her, her client, and her case. What constitutes a good jury depends on which side of the case you represent and determines how you will use your peremptory challenges. When two evenly matched adversaries participate in the jury selection process, injecting their concepts of a good jury into that process, they will probably select a jury that will fairly consider the evidence and return a fair verdict.

With these points in mind, what are your specific purposes during the voir dire examination of prospective jurors? There are three:

a.   Present yourself and your party in a favorable light before the jury. You must show the jury that you are confident, committed, and prepared. You must humanize your party. You must create a psychologically positive and receptive courtroom atmosphere.
b.   Learn about the jurors' beliefs and attitudes so that you can exercise your peremptory challenges intelligently.
c.   Familiarize the jurors with applicable legal and factual concepts, if permitted by the judge.

Notice that of these three aims only the second is directly related to voir dire itself. The others are related more to the broader concern of trial advocacy, which begins when the jurors first enter the courtroom and continues until they return a verdict. You, your client, and the facts are all on trial and affect its final outcome. While you are picking the jurors, the jurors are picking the lawyer that they like and trust. The perceptive trial lawyer is the one who understands this and conducts himself accordingly throughout the trial.

3.   Approaches to questioning prospective jurors

Go back about one hundred years. The United States was a land of immigrants. The first waves of immigrants, during the eighteenth century and the 1840s and 1850s, were largely English, German, and Scandinavian. The second wave, between 1890 and 1914, brought millions of new immigrants to this country, and they were increasingly from Eastern and Southern Europe and Asia. Concentrated in the cities, these immigrants truly made the United States an ethnic melting pot.

With millions of first-generation immigrants, the standard jury selection approach was based on perceived characteristics of the various ethnic groups. Lawyers usually assumed that certain ethnic groups had deeply rooted beliefs derived from family and other social peer groups and that these beliefs would be carried into the jury room. For example, plaintiff's personal injury lawyers usually favored Irish, Italian, Greek, and Eastern European jurors under the belief that such jurors were more likely to respond to a sympathetic story and an emotional appeal. Defendants in such cases usually preferred English, German, and Scandinavian jurors under the belief that such jurors were more responsive to law-and-order arguments and were against windfall damages. In criminal cases the same logic prevailed, except that prosecutors preferred Nordics, defense lawyers preferred Mediterraneans.

Modern jury selection methods have moved beyond these early attempts to generalize likely attitudes of jurors, in part because the United States is no longer principally a country of first-generation immigrants, in part because over the past generation social science research has done much to increase our understanding of how people develop beliefs and attitudes, how they process information, and how they make decisions. Consequently, the principal approaches to jury selection today are the following.

a.   Beliefs and attitudes

Social science research during the past 25 years has shown that most people are affective, not cognitive, thinkers. That is, most people are emotional, symbol oriented, selective perceivers of information who base their decisions largely on previously held attitudes about people and events. Most people are also deductive, not inductive, reasoners. That is, they are impulsive, use few basic premises to reach decisions, and then accept, reject, or distort other information to fit their already determined conclusions. People use their preexisting beliefs and attitudes about people and events to filter conflicting information, accepting consistent information and rejecting, distorting, or minimizing inconsistent information. People reach decisions quickly and resist changing their minds. Finally, people are unable to absorb most of the information they receive, since sensory overload occurs quickly; thus, they base their decisions on relatively little information that their attitudes have subconsciously filtered.

Social science research has also demonstrated that many people are less than candid when asked directly about their beliefs and attitudes, particularly in front of strangers in a group setting. The desire to fit in and be accepted by others is strong, and people frequently tell others what they think the others want to hear. Hence, likely beliefs and attitudes are more accurately learned through indirection. Rather than asking prospective jurors directly about their attitudes, it is probably more effective to learn the backgrounds and life experiences of the jurors and use them to draw inferences about the jurors' likely beliefs and attitudes. There are several basic background characteristics that are seen as the best, although admittedly imperfect, predictors of likely attitudes:

1. age
2. education
3. employment history

4.   residence history
5.   marital and family history
6.   hobbies and interests
7.   reading, television, and computers
8.   participation in organizations
9.   experiences in life related to case on trial

Under this approach, questioning jurors is principally a matter of getting background information from which you infer likely beliefs and attitudes relevant to the case being tried. While every case needs to be individually analyzed to determine the kind of jurors you want and don't want, certain generalizations are probably true. Plaintiff's lawyers in personal injury cases and defense lawyers in criminal cases typically prefer jurors whose backgrounds suggest greater receptivity to emotional appeals, such as single and young persons or young married couples, artists, actors, writers, and other creative individuals, and persons at both extremes of the social and income scales. Prosecutors in criminal cases and defense lawyers in personal injury cases typically prefer middle-aged or retired jurors with average incomes and stable marriages and families, who work at blue-collar or white-collar jobs, are businesspeople or government employees, or hold other jobs that demonstrate traditional work ethics and values and a deference to authority.

This beliefs-and-attitudes approach is probably the most popular approach to jury selection today. This is probably so because the amount of social science research available on jury selection supports the validity of that approach and because in those jurisdictions where the judge does the entire questioning of prospective jurors this is the only approach that is readily applicable. A word of caution is in order, however. The beliefs-and-attitudes approach is attractive to lawyers in part because it is easy to ask prospective jurors about their backgrounds, interests, and experience in life. The shortcoming is that jurors may not disclose this information accurately, or the information, if accurately disclosed, may not accurately predict the jurors' relevant attitudes. Background information, particularly a single demographic category such as age or sex, frequently is a poor if not useless predictor of jurors' attitudes. Experiences in life, on the other hand, have a higher predictive value, but the value depends principally on how accurately and completely a juror discloses this information. In short, it is the totality of a juror's background, interests, and experiences in life, particularly the latter, that become reasonably useful predictors of that juror's likely attitudes on the key trial issues.

In cases where the damages are large or pretrial publicity is extensive, lawyers frequently hire jury research firms to assist in selecting a jury. The firms usually survey the community from which the jurors will be drawn, determine what the community's attitudes are on issues relevant to the trial, and draw up a demographic profile of favorable and unfavorable jurors. While the cost of using jury research firms is prohibitive in many cases, it does demonstrate how the beliefs-and-attitudes approach to jury selection has become the most utilized approach today.

b. Likability

We tend to like, and therefore find credible, people with whom we have a shared set of values and beliefs. Conversely, we tend to distrust, and therefore find less credible, people with whom we have little in common. Social science research supports the idea that likability has much to do with credibility; thus, jurors will naturally, though subconsciously, give greater weight to the testimony of witnesses whose backgrounds are similar to theirs.

Some lawyers therefore focus on the parties and the key witnesses in the case, analyze their characteristics and backgrounds, and try to select jurors that have similar backgrounds to their party and key witnesses. This approach, of course, applies only when the parties and the witnesses for each party have substantially different backgrounds. For example, in a personal injury case where the plaintiff and her main witnesses are blue-collar workers and the defendant is a business executive, plaintiff probably will prefer jurors who are workers, not people high on the socioeconomic scale.

c. Body language

This approach has become increasingly popular, due in part to a growing awareness — supported by psychological and communications research — that voir dire examinations can sometimes be extremely inaccurate in determining jurors' true attitudes. Since most jurors want to be chosen, they will often hide their true feelings and attempt to answer questions about themselves the way they think the questioner wants them answered. This may be subconscious, or it may be intentional. In addition, trial lawyers are increasingly realizing that the jurors' attitudes toward, and reactions to, the lawyers are important aspects of trial work and can have a significant impact on the outcome of a case.

Consequently, this approach focuses on a juror's appearance, behavior, and nonverbal responses since these may give a more accurate picture of the juror's attitudes than the verbal answers. It considers the juror's attire. Is she dressed appropriately for her age, work, and class? Are his clothes compensating for a perceived inadequacy? Does her immaculate attire suggest a juror who is meticulous and analytically oriented? Do his clothes suggest what he would like to be, but isn't?

The body language approach also considers physical responses in conjunction with verbal answers. Hands over mouth, licking lips, sighing, swallowing, blushing, and appearing restless all suggest that the juror may be sensitive or nervous about the subject being discussed. The approach also considers the juror's attitude toward the lawyer. Leaning back, turning sideways, crossing arms and legs, and looking at everyone but the questioning lawyer all suggest a negative attitude toward or rejection of that lawyer.

Finally, the body language approach considers the nonverbal responses in conjunction with the verbal responses. Are the juror's nonverbal signals consistent with his answers? Do his responses have unusual or abnormal pauses? Does she hesitate and look elsewhere before answering? Does his pattern of responses change when certain topics are discussed? Does she hedge her answers? Do these add up to distortion or deception?

If, as most trial lawyers believe, a juror's subjective response to you as a lawyer is important, learning to read a juror's body language is an important part of the selection process. A word of caution is in order here as well. Nonverbal cues can be misleading, and determining if a gesture is simply a mannerism or has significance is, at best, an inexact science. This fact explains why jury consultants are increasingly being used during the actual jury selection process to help trial lawyers interpret the jurors' verbal and nonverbal responses.

d.   *Persuaders, participants, and nonparticipants*

This approach — again supported by psychological and communications research — divides prospective jurors into three categories: persuaders, participants, and nonparticipants.

Persuaders, also called leaders, are those jurors whose backgrounds and personalities suggest that they are take-charge types who will attempt to control the jury's deliberations. Research shows that a typical 12-person jury will have three leaders who explicitly state their views and actively try to persuade others to accept their views. Those three leaders will usually talk more than the rest of the jurors put together.

Participants, also called followers, take part in the jury deliberations by stating their thoughts and by agreeing or disagreeing with the views of the leaders. However, followers do not actively try to persuade others to accept their views and are more willing to compromise to reach a verdict. About 50 percent of a typical jury will be followers.

Nonparticipants take little or no part in the jury deliberations other than voting on the verdicts. Nonparticipants sometimes are not receptive to other jurors' arguments, whether logical or emotional, since their minds are already made up. Nonparticipants can become holdout jurors, which is important in cases that require a unanimous verdict. Nonparticipants constitute about 25 percent of a typical jury.

The significance of this approach is based on the limited number of peremptory challenges, particularly in civil cases, which generally allow fewer challenges than in criminal cases. For example, in federal civil cases each side has only three challenges. This means that challenges must be used sparingly in situations where they will make a difference. Using this approach, two things should be kept in mind.

First, use your challenges to strike jurors who are persuaders and appear to have attitudes unfavorable to your side. These are the jurors who will influence the other jurors during the deliberations, and you must use your challenges to eliminate the strongest leaders having the strongest unfavorable attitudes. This is particularly true for plaintiffs, who need unanimous or near-unanimous verdicts, and therefore often prefer jurors who are participants and compromisers because they are likely to eventually go along with the views of the majority. Defendants, on the other hand, frequently prefer strong jurors, since jurors who are take-charge types and used to having their way are more capable of assuming independent views and resisting the opinion of the majority.

Second, use your challenges to strike jurors who are nonparticipants and appear to have attitudes unfavorable to your side. Nonparticipants are dangerous because they are independent and will do whatever they want to do, uninfluenced by the arguments of the other jurors (and, perhaps, the evidence and applicable law as well). This is particularly important for prosecutors in criminal cases, who usually need unanimous verdicts, but is significant for civil cases as well. It only takes one such juror to create a hung jury in a criminal case, or to force a compromise in a civil case if that juror's vote is necessary to reach a verdict.

As with any approach involving human nature, the validity of these approaches is difficult to prove conclusively, although in recent years social science research has studied the factors that help predict how a particular type of juror will probably react to different cases. In large cases, both civil and criminal, trial lawyers frequently use clinical psychologists to determine who their best and worst jurors are likely to be in their case. The best that a new trial lawyer can do is to become familiar with these principal approaches, use common sense and experience in determining what his best and worst jurors are for each case, and develop intelligent questions to uncover as much useful information about the jurors as possible.

4.   Juror profile chart

Using the jury selection methods discussed above, your next step is to organize a jury profile chart. Well before trial, you must learn how prospective jurors are likely to feel about your case, and identify the background characteristics of your best and worst jurors. In large cases, trial lawyers frequently use jury consultants to make these determinations. This information should be placed on a profile chart and kept in the jury section of your trial notebook.

In civil cases, where the jury decides both liability and damages, you may want to further break down your juror profile chart. For example, if the case is strong on liability, but weak on damages, will that influence your juror profile? Businesspeople are usually seen as defendant's jurors in personal injury cases, but if liability is strong, and your damages case depends primarily on lost future income, perhaps a businessperson, who will understand future income projections and is used to dealing with substantial amounts of money, may be a good juror.

You should also prepare a jury questions checklist. A checklist is simply the special topics you plan to question jurors about during the voir dire examination. This checklist will be the basis for a motion to request questions in jurisdictions where the judge does the entire voir dire examination of the prospective jurors.

Example:

You represent plaintiff pedestrian, a 23-year-old cocktail waitress, who was struck by a truck in an intersection. Both liability and damages are in dispute.

JUROR PROFILE

Good jurors	Bad jurors
Young	Professional drivers
Students	Owners/mgr. of businesses
Service occupations	Nondrinkers
Socially active	Stay-at-home types
Outdoors, athletic	Sedentary lifestyles
High school education	College education

Topics to ask about:

1. Social habits — restaurants, taverns
2. Attitudes toward social drinking
3. Any professional driving — cabs, trucks
4. Accident and injury history
5. Similar lawsuit history — self, family, friends

§3.5. *How to question jurors*

Questioning jurors effectively involves two basic skills: knowing what topics to discuss with the jurors, and developing a questioning style that is honest and nonjudgmental. This gets the jurors to reveal their essential background history so that you can intelligently decide whether to accept or challenge each juror in the venire.

1. Topics checklist

The following areas should be considered in deciding what questions to ask prospective jurors. The general questions about the law and case on trial are, in most jurisdictions, asked by the judge to all the prospective jurors as a group, to determine if there is any basis to excuse a juror for cause. For example, if any juror says that she disagrees with what the law is and could not follow the judge's instructions, or knows one of the parties to the lawsuit and already is leaning one way because of that fact, the judge will usually excuse the juror for cause.

  a. *Law (usually asked by judge)*
     • Follow the law, even if you disagree with it.
     • This is not the place to change the law.
     • Set aside sympathy or bias in reaching a verdict.
     • Anything about the case that starts you off favoring one side.
     • Wait until all the evidence is in before making up your mind.
     (civil cases)
     • Plaintiff has burden of proof, by greater weight of evidence.
     • Substantive law involved in case.
     • Award damages if the evidence supports it.

(criminal cases)
- Defendant presumed innocent.
- Prosecution has the burden of proof, beyond a reasonable doubt.
- Defendant doesn't have to prove anything or testify.
- Substantive law involved in case.

b. *Case on trial (usually asked by judge)*
- Know the judge.
- Know the lawyers.
- Know any of the parties.
- Ever work for any of the parties.
- Know any of the witnesses.
- Heard about the case.
- Any feelings about being a juror in this kind of case.
- Any knowledge about the parties or case that might influence you in deciding this case.

c. *Jurors (usually asked by judge)*
- Any medical problems — back, hearing, and so on — prevent juror from hearing case.
- In longer cases, will length of case cause serious difficulties for juror.

Questions about juror backgrounds are designed to allow the lawyers to exercise their peremptory challenges intelligently. Keep in mind that you want to learn about the jurors' backgrounds and experiences in life so that you can learn their likely beliefs and attitudes that will probably control how they will decide the case.

The following checklist covers the general background topics you will cover in most cases. Some may not be important in certain cases, and other topics, not on the list, may be important in others. Nevertheless, this checklist should help you tailor your questions for any specific case. Keep in mind that some of this information may already be available from juror cards or questionnaire answers.

1. *Age*
    Age should be obvious just by looking at the juror. If exact age is important, you can usually get it indirectly from other facts, such as the age of any children or how long the juror has been retired. Many jurors, especially older ones, do not like being asked to reveal their exact age.

2. *Education*
    - last school attended
    - degrees, institutions (if college background)
    - military service
    - legal, medical, etc., training

3. *Employment history*
    - present job — job title and what it involves
    - previous jobs
    - supervisory and managerial experience

4. *Residence history*
   - present address
   - previous addresses
   - own or rent (if important)
5. *Marital and family history*
   - present marital status
   - spouse, children, parents
   - occupations of family members
   - schools of children
6. *Hobbies and interests*
   - what juror likes to do in spare time
7. *Reading and television*
   - newspapers, magazines frequently read
   - types of books enjoy reading
   - favorite radio and television programs
   - computer use
8. *Organizations*
   - clubs and organizations juror active in
9. *Experiences in life*
   - prior jury duty
   - involvement in lawsuits
   - involvement in crime
   - work for insurance company
   - involvement in similar situations as case on trial

2.   Questioning techniques

Once you have developed a checklist of the topics you want to discuss with the jurors (and are permitted in your jurisdiction), what you do depends on whether the lawyers, the judge, or both are allowed to question jurors.

If the judge is going to ask all the questions, or those questions dealing with legal issues, prepare a written list of questions you would like the judge to ask and submit them before the trial starts. Get a ruling on which questions will be allowed and make sure that your requests and the judge's rulings are on the record.

If the lawyers are allowed to ask questions, you must convert your topics checklist into questions that will be effective in communicating with the jurors.

a.   Getting information from jurors

Most of your questions will be designed to get enough information about each prospective juror so that you can intelligently decide which jurors to challenge. Here your questioning technique, and the atmosphere you create during the questioning, is all-important.

Social scientists know the importance of reciprocity and empathy when questioning people to get information. Reciprocity means that before you can get, you need to give. Self-disclosure by the questioner substantially improves self-disclosure by the person being questioned. If the judge will allow it, tell the jurors a little about yourself before asking them to reveal things about themselves. Empathy means that you need to create a friendly, nonjudgmental atmosphere before candid self-disclosure will occur. Asking your questions in a relaxed, conversational way will stimulate the jurors to open up about themselves and lessen the fear that they are being judged.

i. Short, open-ended questions. Questions that are short, nonleading, open-ended, and get the jurors to talk, and that are asked in a warm and friendly way, work best. These questions draw more substantial responses from jurors. Remember that when jurors talk, you are getting not only the verbal response but also the more important inflections that interpret the response.

Example:

Q. Mr. Johnson, where do you work?
A. The Ajax Widget Works.
Q. What does your company do?
A. We make a full line of consumer products.
Q. What kind of products?
A. Well, we make radios, TVs, furniture, kitchen appliances, things like that.
Q. How did you get your job at Ajax?
A. They came to me and offered me the job of head of sales. I was working at a competitor at the time.
Q. What is it you like most about your job?
A. They leave me alone. I get to do my job without interference from above. That seems to work well for all of us.

These questions gently force the juror to talk about himself without invading the juror's sense of privacy.

ii. "What, when" questions. The "what" and "when" questions draw out the basic biographical information.

Example:

Q. What do you do for the XYZ Company?
A. I'm an expediter. I make sure that all the things we need on the production line are there when we need them.
Q. When did you start that job?
A. Two years ago.

These questions get the basic backgrounds and are a good beginning. The key is to then move on to get information about a juror that would not appear on a resume.

iii. "How, why" questions. The "how" and "why" questions get the explanations and attitudes behind the basic facts.

Example:

> Q.   How did you feel about your experiences as a juror in that case?
> A.   It was good. We got to know each other as people, not just as ju-
>   rors. We argued a lot, but at the end we all agreed on what to do
>   and we parted as friends.

Example:

> Q.   Why did you leave the ABC Company after just three months?
> A.   They worked everyone to death. Typical business. They squeezed
>   every bit of work out of you and thought they were doing you a
>   favor by paying you.

Example:

> Q.   How do you feel about motorcycles?
> A.   They're all right, I guess.
> Q.   Does anyone in your family ride one?
> A.   No.
> Q.   If your son wanted to buy a motorcycle, would you let him?
> A.   I don't think so.
> Q.   Why not?
> A.   They're too dangerous. They don't protect you if you're in an ac-
>   cident.

These questions go beyond basic background and elicit attitude information. Here it is important to note not only what is being said but how
the juror is saying it.

iv.   No notes.   Jury questioning is not a job interview. It is your opportunity to communicate with the jurors as equals. Accordingly, get away from
counsel table (unless you are required to remain there), stand up in front
of the jurors, maintain eye contact, and talk with them. Get rid of your
notes. Have someone else take notes to record important facts if you alone
are trying the case. If you stand, without notes, and concentrate on developing a rapport with the juror you are questioning, with the attitude that
this is a friendly conversation with someone you just met and are interested
in, the juror will probably respond by opening up and talking candidly.

v.   Active listening and follow-up questions.   Effective juror questioning
requires active listening. Concentrate on the answers, showing the jurors
that you are genuinely interested in what they are saying. Repeat their answers to show that you are listening and understand what they are saying.
Use follow-up questions to develop important information.

Example:

> Q.   How do you feel about persons who drink alcoholic beverages?
> A.   Well, I guess it's okay.
> Q.   Why do you say that?
> A.   Well, it's legal if you're over 21.
> Q.   Do you drink socially yourself?

A. No.
Q. Why not?
A. I've seen too many people ruin their lives with alcohol.
Q. Anyone close to your family?
A. My brother ruined his life with alcohol.
Q. Do you disapprove of just hard liquor, or beer and wine as well?
A. I don't approve of any of it.

Example:

Q. Mrs. Johnson, this case involves an accident using an all-terrain vehicle, which is like a big tricycle with a motor. Have you or any members of your family ever owned an ATV?
A. My younger brother had one for a while.
Q. When was that?
A. Back when he was in high school.
Q. How long did he keep it?
A. About two years.
Q. Why did he get rid of it?
A. He had a couple of close calls going through the woods and decided he'd better sell it before something bad happened.
Q. How did you feel about that?
A. I was relieved. I tried to talk him out of getting it in the first place.

In these situations a few follow-up questions uncovered the true depth of the juror's feelings, revealing an attitude substantially stronger than the first, seemingly innocuous, response.

vi. Never embarrass a juror. There is one cardinal rule you cannot forget when questioning jurors: Never embarrass a juror. Make sure you never force a juror to reveal anything embarrassing about her job, family, home, education, or background.

Tell the jurors at the beginning to let you know immediately if you happen to ask questions on any subject that any juror prefers not to talk about, or at least not in front of other jurors. You have to let jurors know you are sensitive to their privacy rights. While it may sometimes be necessary to ask questions about sensitive subjects, don't press a juror if he appears reluctant to talk. Ask the juror if he would rather talk about something in the privacy of the judge's chambers or at least at side bar. Most judges will permit this if it seems appropriate and the topic is important to the case.

Example:

Q. Mrs. Smith, have any members of your family ever been victims of a crime?
A. Yes.
Q. Could you tell us about that?
A. Well, it's rather personal.
Q. Mrs. Smith, would you prefer that we talk about this in the judge's chambers?

> *A.* I'd sure prefer that.
> *Q.* Your Honor, could we discuss this with Mrs. Smith in your chambers for just a minute?
> *Court:* Certainly. (Judge, lawyers, and court reporter go to the judge's chambers.)
> *Q.* Mrs. Smith, do you feel you can share with us here what happened?
> *A.* Well, my sister was raped several years ago. We've tried to keep this private for her sake.
> *Q.* Mrs. Smith, we appreciate your letting us know this. Could that experience affect you in deciding this case?
> *A.* I don't think so.

b.   *Conveying concepts to jurors*

Most jurisdictions today do not allow the lawyers to go into matters of law while questioning the jurors. In some jurisdictions, however, the rules are much broader, and lawyers are not restricted to questioning the jurors about their backgrounds and experiences in life. In those jurisdictions the jurors may be questioned by the lawyers about legal concepts involved in the case. This, of course, allows the lawyers to test out concepts before the jurors to gauge their reactions.

Example (defendant in civil case):

> *Q.* Mr. Johnson, just because the plaintiff was injured in an accident doesn't automatically mean she's entitled to get money damages, does it?
> *A.* That's right.
> *Q.* Plaintiff also has to prove to you that we were at fault and caused the accident, before she's entitled to get any money, isn't that right?
> *A.* Yes.
> *Q.* You understand that's what the law says, don't you?
> *A.* Yes.
> *Q.* Mr. Johnson, it's natural to feel sorry for the plaintiff for what happened to her, isn't it?
> *A.* Sure.
> *Q.* But it wouldn't be fair to give her money simply because we might feel sorry for her, would it?
> *A.* I guess not.
> *Q.* If the plaintiff proves she was injured, but fails to prove we were at fault and caused the collision, what would your verdict be?
> *A.* I guess we'd have to find in favor of the defendant.

Example (defendant in criminal case):

> *Q.* Mrs. Jones, the prosecution has the burden of proving guilt beyond a reasonable doubt. You understand that, don't you?

> A. Yes.
>
> Q. Does that rule bother you?
>
> A. Well, I guess that's the law.
>
> Q. You wouldn't find Mr. Smith guilty just because you think he *might* have robbed the store, would you?
>
> A. No.
>
> Q. That wouldn't be fair, would it?
>
> A. I guess not.
>
> Q. Mrs. Jones, can you promise us that you'll hold the prosecution to its burden of proof — *beyond* a reasonable doubt?
>
> A. Yes.
>
> Q. And if the prosecution fails to prove guilt beyond a reasonable doubt, what would your verdict be?
>
> A. I guess I'd have to find him not guilty.

These questions, most of which were leading and suggested the desired answer, rarely get unexpected responses. But some lawyers, particularly those representing defendants, feel they serve an important purpose by introducing the jurors to the important legal concepts in the case that the jurors will have sworn to follow. In addition, by discussing the law you demonstrate to the jurors that you are not afraid of the applicable law in this case. If jurors show hesitation about the law, tactful, more neutrally phrased follow-up questions can gently probe further.

The trend in most jurisdictions, however, is to avoid these indoctrinating kinds of questions. Judges increasingly bar the lawyers from asking these and other kinds of questions designed primarily to test juror reactions to the law or evidence. Jury research also shows that many jurors react negatively toward lawyers who try to sell the merits of their case during jury selection or try to get verdict commitments before the jurors have heard the evidence.

c.   Introductory and concluding comments

In jurisdictions where the lawyers do all the questioning, most allow the lawyers to make a short, nonargumentative statement summarizing the case.

Example:

> Q. Members of the jury, I'm Alex Jones and I represent Ellen Smith, the plaintiff. Ellen, stand up for a moment. (Plaintiff stands up and sits down.) Ms. Smith was severely injured when the defendant's truck crashed into the side of her car. She was out of work for several months and has not, and never will, completely recover. What we're going to do this morning is talk with all of you so that we have 12 of you who will hear the evidence and decide this case fairly.

The lawyer then begins to question the prospective jurors.

At the end of the questioning, some lawyers ask general concluding questions designed to cover anything they may have failed to ask about specifically. These are always a good idea, because jury research has shown that voir dire examinations frequently fail to uncover important background information that is significant in learning the juror's attitudes on important issues.

Example:

    Q. Mr. Phelps, I guess we could talk all morning, but we can't take that much time, so I'm just going to ask you this: Is there anything about you, and the experiences in life that you've had, that you think we ought to know about?

    A. I can't think of anything.

This kind of open-ended question can sometimes trigger disclosure of important additional information.

Example:

    Q. Ms. Johnson, is there anything about you and your family we should know about that we haven't talked about yet?

    A. Well, my former husband was involved in a serious car crash a few years ago.

    Q. Were you still married at the time?

    A. Yes.

    Q. Can you tell us what happened?

    A. Sure. He was coming home at night when another driver, who was drunk, ran a stop sign and crashed into his car.

    Q. Was your former husband hurt?

    A. He was seriously hurt. He had a concussion, some broken ribs, and lots of bruises and cuts in his face. He was in the hospital for a week, and missed four months of work.

    Q. Did you ever sue the other driver?

    A. We thought about it, but our lawyer told us it wasn't worth it. The other guy was uninsured, and didn't have any money.

    Q. How did you feel about that?

    A. We were robbed. The other guy walked away from it and never ended up paying a dime.

    d. *Group questions*

In some jurisdictions jurors are questioned individually, but in many both individual and group questions are permitted. Questions to the jurors as a group are an effective way to get into basic topics. Follow-up questions can then be directed to individual jurors.

Example:

> *Q.* Do any of you have family or close friends in law enforcement — city police, county sheriff, prison guard? (Two jurors raise their hands.)
>
> *Q.* Mr. Andrews, let's start with you. Who do you know in law enforcement?
>
> *A.* My nephew is a deputy sheriff.
>
> *Q.* Does his work ever involve being at traffic collisions?
>
> *A.* I suppose so.
>
> *Q.* Does he ever discuss those cases with you?
>
> *A.* Well, he sometimes mentions them when we get together for family functions, but I wouldn't say that he really talks about them.
>
> *Q.* I take it that you won't have any problems in deciding this case only on what you hear in the courtroom?
>
> *A.* No.
>
> *Q.* Mrs. Fields, what about you? Who do you know in law enforcement?
>
> *A.* I have a neighbor who is a retired police officer.
>
> *Q.* Does that neighbor ever talk about his experiences?
>
> *A.* No. I didn't even know he had been a cop until this year.

Group questions, followed by individual questions, are an effective way of getting into relevant experiences in life, such as involvement with law enforcement personnel, lawyers, traffic accidents, and other experiences that may be important to a particular case.

3. Example of voir dire

Example:

You represent the plaintiff in an automobile collision case. Plaintiff is a 23-year-old cocktail waitress whose car collided with defendant's truck. You have already made a juror profile chart. This is the first juror. In this jurisdiction you are allowed to ask questions only about the juror's background and experiences in life. The judge has already asked questions about the law and questions designed to identify any jurors who can be challenged for cause.

> *Q.* Mrs. Blivitz, good morning. Why don't we start off by finding out a little about yourself and your family. First, your juror card says you work at the Ajax Widget Company?
>
> *A.* That's right.
>
> *Q.* What do you do at Ajax?
>
> *A.* I'm a secretary.
>
> *Q.* Tell us about your job.
>
> *A.* Well, I've been there for 12 years. I've worked for the same boss most of that time. Mr. Bellows is now the head of sales.
>
> *Q.* Your husband, Mrs. Blivitz, tell us about him.
>
> *A.* Ed and I have been married for 20 years. He's a computer programmer at Xerox.

Q.   How long has he been there?

A.   About 8 years.

Q.   Has he always worked as a computer programmer?

A.   Yes, but he worked for several companies before settling down at Xerox.

Q.   Tell us about your children.

A.   There's Chad, age 17, and Barbara, who's 15. They both go to school at the local high school.

Q.   How are they doing?

A.   Fine. Barbara's the real student. Chad is involved with sports right now, but he's doing okay in class.

Q.   How about your and your husband's schooling?

A.   I graduated from high school and was attending the community college until we got married. Ed graduated from the state university with a degree in physics.

Q.   Mrs. Blivitz, where do you live?

A.   Over on Cherry Lane almost next to the elementary school.

Q.   How long have you been there?

A.   The whole time we've been married — 20 years.

Q.   Mrs. Blivitz, do you have any hobbies or interests that you spend time on?

A.   Well, with teen-agers in the house, it's pretty busy, but I do like to stay active. We do a lot of camping, my husband and I still try to play tennis regularly, and keep up with the gardening.

Q.   How about reading and television? Do you have things you like to read or watch on TV?

A.   I mostly read and watch the news. I like *60 Minutes,* the *NewsHour* on PBS. If there's a good movie on TV, we'll usually watch it.

Q.   Do you subscribe to any magazines?

A.   Just *Time, National Geographic,* and *Redbook.* My husband gets a few computer magazines, but you'd have to ask him about those.

Q.   Do you and your husband belong to any organizations — clubs, things like that — that you can share with us?

A.   Ed's very active in the local Rotary Club. Of course we participate in our school's PTA, but that's about it.

Q.   Mrs. Blivitz, have you ever been a juror before?

A.   Once, a few years ago.

Q.   Did you actually serve and decide a case?

A.   Yes.

Q.   Tell us about the case.

A.   It was a contract dispute between two businesses.

Q.   Anything about that experience that might affect how you feel about serving in this case?

A.   No. I liked being a juror, and Ajax Widget Company gives us time off with pay when we serve, for up to one week.

Q.   Our case involves a collision between Mary Jones's car and the defendant's truck. Have you ever been involved in a collision?

A.   Yes.

Q.   Could you tell us about it?

A. Sure. One time I was in a fender bender in a parking lot. We just exchanged names and things like that, and took care of it ourselves. The other time was when I got rear-ended at a traffic light. It was the other guy's fault.

Q. What happened to you in that rear-ender?

A. The car was pretty seriously damaged. I got a whiplash injury to my neck.

Q. Tell us about your neck.

A. Well, it was pretty sore. I saw my doctor, and he gave me some medication to relax the muscles and reduce the pain. I took a few days off from work, then went back.

Q. When did all this happen?

A. About three years ago.

Q. How's your neck now?

A. It's okay. I haven't had any problems with it.

Q. Were you satisfied with the medical care you received at the time?

A. Yes. I just went to my family doctor, who took care of me until my neck got better.

Q. Mrs. Blivitz, did you hire a lawyer or bring a lawsuit over that case?

A. No.

Q. Why not?

A. It was obviously the other driver's fault. His insurance paid for all my expenses and time off from work, so there wasn't any need to get a lawyer.

Q. Was there anything about that experience that might make you think either side should win here?

A. No, that was pretty different from what this case sounds like.

Q. Mrs. Blivitz, is there anything you've experienced in your life that we haven't asked about you think we should know about?

A. No, nothing that comes to mind.

Q. Thank you, Mrs. Blivitz.

Talking with the jurors in a conversational, nonjudgmental way, projecting your interest in the juror as a person, using open-ended questions, mixing the "what" and "when" questions with the "how" and "why" questions all help to create an atmosphere that promotes candor and honesty, and results in jurors voluntarily disclosing the information you need to intelligently select jurors for this case.

§3.6. *Summary checklist*

The earlier sections of this chapter have discussed the various procedures courts use to select jurors. Before you participate in that process, make sure you can answer the following:

1. How many jurors and alternates will be selected?
2. What jury questioning system will be used?
3. What kinds of questions will be permitted?

4. What jury selection system will be used?
5. How may challenges will I have, and how will I exercise them?
6. What are the best and worst jurors for my profile chart?
7. What topics do I need to cover when questioning jurors?
8. Have I submitted written voir dire questions to the court (if the judge will do the questioning)?
9. Have I prepared my questioning style to create honest, candid communication with the jurors?

IV
OPENING STATEMENTS

§4.1.   Introduction

The opening statement will be your first opportunity to tell the jury what the case on trial is all about. As such, it is a critical part of the trial that must be carefully planned, developed, and delivered, yet is frequently the most overlooked part of the jury trial process.

Trial lawyers agree that opening statements often make the difference in the outcome of a case. Studies have shown that jury verdicts are, in the substantial majority of cases, consistent with the initial impressions made by the jury during the opening statements. As in life generally, the psychological phenomenon of primacy applies, and initial impressions become lasting impressions. Accordingly, make sure your case gets off on the right footing. This can be achieved only when you forcefully deliver a logical opening statement that clearly establishes your themes and demonstrates the facts that entitle your party to a favorable verdict.

This chapter will discuss the elements and structure of effective opening statements and will present illustrative opening statements in representative civil and criminal cases.

§4.2.   Opening statements from the jury's perspective

Jury selection has been completed, and the selected jurors have just been sworn in to try the case. The following ritual usually happens next:

Judge: Are both sides ready?
Plaintiff's lawyer: Ready, your Honor.
Defendant's lawyer: We're ready, your Honor.
Judge: Members of the jury, we're now going to hear the opening statements from the lawyers. The opening statements should give you an overview of what the lawyers expect to show through the witnesses and other evidence they will introduce during the trial. This should help you understand the actual evidence when you receive it. Plaintiff, please proceed.

What are the jurors thinking and feeling at this point? First, they are anxious and worried about courtroom procedure and their role as jurors. Second, they are curious and wondering what the case is all about. Third, they want to know whom, other than the judge, they can trust and rely on for help. Fourth, they are more open-minded and receptive to information than at any other stage of the trial. Experienced lawyers understand what the jurors are thinking and feeling and use this knowledge to organize and deliver effective opening statements.

What does all this say about opening statements? From the jury's perspective, effective opening statements must incorporate the key concepts of jury persuasion discussed in Chapter II.

1.   Explain your theory of the case

The opening statement is your first opportunity to tell the jury your theory of the case. A theory of the case is your side's version of "what really happened." It should incorporate all the uncontested facts as well as your side's version of the disputed facts. It must be logical, fit the legal requirements of the claims or defenses, be simple to understand, and be consistent with the jurors' common sense and their perception of how real life works.

For example, in a contract case the plaintiff must decide if her theory of the case is that defendant simply failed to perform under the contract, resulting in consequential damages, or that the defendant intentionally breached the contract for personal gain, resulting in bad faith and punitive damages. Inconsistent and alternative pleadings are proper at the pretrial stage, but not by the time you go to trial. At trial you need to select the best theory of the case and go with it.

A jury trial is essentially a competition to see which party's theory of the case the jury will select as more probably true. Seize the opportunity! Give the jury a coherent overview that puts all the evidence together in an interesting and compelling way. Jurors know that trials involve disputes that they are called on to resolve, so they want to know what your side of the dispute is. If you fail to do so, the jury will not understand where you stand on the facts and issues. Worse yet, the other side during closing arguments may argue that you never had a theory of the case at all, but were merely waiting to hear all the evidence before committing yourself to one.

2.   Themes, labels, and the first minute

Themes are the psychological anchors that jurors instinctively create to distill and summarize what the case is about. That's because information during a trial becomes complicated and overwhelming. Themes become the essential tool jurors use to reduce a large amount of information and summarize their attitudes about that information in easily remembered words and phrases. If jurors instinctively create themes on which to anchor their thoughts and attitudes, doesn't it make sense for trial lawyers to use themes in their opening statements to summarize their side's theory of the case in a way that jurors will adopt as their own?

Every case can, and should, be distilled into not more than three or four themes that summarize your positions in an engaging, easily remembered way. Sometimes a theme can be a single word, at other times a short phrase. Some cases can be organized around a single theme, but many can use different themes for different considerations, such as liability and damages issues, or the motivations of a party or key witness. Today almost all judges permit lawyers to use themes in opening statements (unless excessively argumentative), because the themes help jurors understand the parties' different positions and help jurors focus on what the disputes in the case are.

Good themes are based on the universal truths about people and events we learn during our lives. Good sources of themes are the great works of literature, religious classics such as the Bible, and popular sayings that are part of our everyday speech.

Examples:

> *"This is a case about taking chances."*
> *"Mary Jones had a dream and a plan."*
> *"This is a case about a company that refuses to do business the American way."*
> *"Everything that happened here happened because of greed."*
> *"Revenge. That's what this case is all about."*
> *"This is a case about taking responsibility for your own conduct"*
> *"This is also a case about pain. Mr. Johnson's only companion today is constant pain."*
> *"This is a case about police brutality."*

In addition to selecting themes, you need to select labels. Labels are simply the trial vocabulary you select to refer to the parties, events, and other important things during the trial. Labels are important because they convey attitudes and messages. There is a difference between calling your party "the plaintiff" and "Bobby Smith," between calling a vehicle a "car" and a "big black Jaguar sports car," and between calling a crash an "accident" and a "collision."

Decide how you will label your party, the opposing party, the events, transactions, vehicles, weapons, and other things important to the case. Chose the labels that personalize your party and depersonalizes the opposing party, that projects the images you want of the other things, then use them consistently during the opening statement, and the rest of the trial.

Example (automobile-negligence case):

Plaintiff's labels:	*Defendant's labels:*
Ms. Smith (plaintiff)	*Frank Johnson (defendant)*
that defendant	*the plaintiff*
defendant's two-ton truck	*our delivery van*
crash/collision	*accident/incident*
shattered arm	*the injury*

When do you bring out your themes and theory of the case? Right away! First impressions become lasting impressions. The jurors, in a matter of minutes, will make impressions about you, your client, and your case. Hence, the first minute or two of the opening statement should unfold your theory of the case, state your themes, and convey them in a positive, interesting, human way. Convey the seriousness of the case and why the other side is responsible.

Example (personal injury):

This is a case of drunk driving. On May 8, 2000, that defendant, while drunk, ran his Cadillac through a red light, crashed into the front driver's side of Jane Smith's car, and crushed her behind the steering wheel of her car. Jane Smith has never been able to walk again. We're here today asking that you give Jane Smith, and her family, justice.

Your opening statement, from the beginning on, must be delivered in a forceful, energetic way that lets the jurors know that you are eager to get the trial under way, enthusiastic about your case, and confident that the jurors will do the right thing at the end. While lawyers deliver their opening statements in a variety of personal styles, the good ones all project one thing: We expect to win this case.

3. Storytelling and people

Effective opening statements, like so much of trial work, are usually based on good storytelling. After all, a trial is essentially a contest to see which side's version of a disputed event or transaction the jury will ultimately accept as true.

Several ingredients collectively create good storytelling. First, focus on the people, not the problem. Most jurors view the world through emotional eyes. They are interested in the people and what makes them do the things they do. This means that you must focus on, and personalize, your party and key witnesses. It also means that you must emphasize the events they were part of, not the legal issues involved.

Personalizing your party is particularly important because jurors want to help people they like. If your client is likeable and sympathetic, the jurors will identify with her, and they will be more likely to return a favorable verdict. That's simply human nature.

Example (sexual assault prosecution):

This case is the story about Mary Martin, who was born and raised in our city. She had just completed college and was starting her first job as a buyer at the Smith Department Store. She had her own apartment for the first time. Life was exciting and new. It was around 2:00 A.M. when the nightmare started. Mary was sleeping, alone in her apartment. Suddenly she was startled by a noise. At first she thought it was outside. But when she heard it a second time she knew what it was:

the creak of the wooden floor in her living room. That's when Mary knew that a stranger was in her home.

Second, your storytelling must be vivid and re-create for the jury the events that happened to your party. Where appropriate, your storytelling should be emotional and dramatic, since you want to draw the jurors into your story and create empathy for your party. Dramatic, emotional storytelling is memorable and holds the jury's attention. It "puts the jury into the picture" and lets the jurors relive the event from your perspective.

Example (personal injury):

It's April 25, 2000, at around 4:00 P.M. John Smith was walking along Spring Street, just around the corner from his home. Suddenly, a car came from behind, ran right through a stop sign, made no attempt to stop, slow down, or swerve, and crashed into John from behind. John didn't knew what hit him. The impact crushed his ribs, broke his back in two places, and threw him into a ditch. Those were the last steps John Smith ever took. He will never walk again.

Example (personal injury):

At 5:30 P.M. Mr. Cannon was driving home from work. Everything was normal. He was in a line of cars driving south on Main Street. He could see the intersection with Elm Street a short distance ahead. Just before Mr. Cannon got to Elm Street, however, that defendant drove out of an ally, without looking, without stopping, right in front of Mr. Cannon's car! Mr. Cannon reacted as fast as he could and slammed on his brakes, but it was too late.

Example (products liability):

Folks, let's walk through the defendant's plant and watch as they manufactured the brake system that failed to work properly. Their process starts at the front of the assembly line . . .

Third, storytelling must be organized in a simple, logical way. Most of the time the best way to organize is chronologically, since jurors are used to hearing stories that move from beginning to end. A chronology is easy to follow and understand.

Example (assault prosecution):

There had been bad blood between the defendant and Bobby Short before. Just the week before, in fact, the two had been in the tavern and had gotten into an argument. The defendant tried to push Bobby around, but Bobby refused to get involved. Instead, Bobby simply left the tavern and went home.

One week later, April 10, the same thing happened. The defendant and Bobby Short were again at the tavern. Again the defendant got into an argument with Bobby, and again tried to pick a fight. Again Bobby refused and tried to leave. This time, however, he was not so lucky, because the defendant blocked the doorway and refused to let Bobby leave.

If, however, the case allows for a different approach, consider it. For instance, you might organize your storytelling by describing the last event first, then loop back and describe earlier events that led up to the last event. The important point to remember is that your organization must be simple, clear, and easy to follow.

Example (medical malpractice):

Visit with Martha Johnson today and see what her life is like. She's always in bed. She can't move. She can't feed herself. She can't talk. All she can move is her eyes. And all she has left is terrible, constant pain. But she wasn't always like this. Two years ago Martha Johnson was an active young woman in the prime of her life. What happened to her? And who did this to her?

It all began two years ago, when Martha made an appointment with the defendant, Dr. Williams . . .

Sometimes you can juxtapose the chronology of the two parties to create a vivid contrast that will capture the jury's attention.

Example (personal injury):

At 4:30 P.M. Mrs. Wood was finishing up some paperwork at her office. She didn't know that, at the same time, the defendant was ordering his second double martini at the Racehorse Tavern. At 5:00 P.M. Mrs. Wood left her office and was walking to the parking lot to drive home to her family. She didn't know that, at the same time, the defendant had just finished his third double martini, had stumbled out of the tavern, and was trying to remember where his car was.

Fourth, the opening statement can alert the jurors to coming attractions. Giving the jurors a preview of important testimony heightens their anticipation and keeps their attention during the trial. This is particularly important for the defendant, who presents evidence only after the plaintiff has rested.

Example:

Listen when Dr. Johnson tells you what happens to a rib cage when it is struck by a two-ton truck, and you will know why Mary Smith will never again be able to work and support her family.

Example:

When the plaintiff testifies, listen when I cross-examine him about what he told the police officer a short time after the crash. You'll then understand why it is so important to know what he said then, not what he's going to say here.

4.   Request a verdict

Jurors want to know what you want. Let them know what a favorable verdict is from your point of view. Too many inexperienced lawyers tell the jury "what happened" without ever ending the opening statement with a specific request for a verdict.

Example:

> *Members of the jury, at the end of the case we will ask you to return the only verdict that this evidence supports, a verdict of guilty of murder. Thank you.*

Example:

> *When you have heard all the evidence, you will understand that Mr. Johnson did nothing wrong, and that this accident was caused entirely by the plaintiff's own carelessness. Because of that, we will ask you to find against the plaintiff and in favor of the defendant, William Johnson.*

Plaintiffs in civil cases are usually concerned about both liability and damages. In commercial cases, such as breach of contract, the allowable damages frequently can be accurately calculated and plaintiffs often tell the jury that they will ask for a specific amount in damages. However, plaintiffs in personal injury cases usually ask for a verdict on liability, but do not ask for a specific amount in damages. This is largely because damages in personal injury cases are based on intangibles such as pain and suffering, are impossible to calculate, and are largely within the jury's judgment. For that reason, plaintiff's lawyers prefer to focus on the liability aspects of the case in opening statements, and usually ask for damages for the permissible elements, without asking for a precise dollar amount. This gives them flexibility to adjust the dollar amount they will ask for in closing arguments, depending on how well the trial went.

Example:

> *Based on that evidence, we ask you to return a verdict finding that this tragedy was the defendant's fault, and 100 percent his fault, and we will also ask you to compensate Mary Johnson — fully and completely — for what she has lost, for what she has suffered, and for what her life will be like for the rest of her life.*

§4.3. Strategic and evidentiary considerations

Several strategic and evidentiary considerations also play a significant role in structuring and delivering your opening statement.

1.   Be efficient

Jurors have limited attention spans. They have limited capacities to retain information. Hence, your opening statement must be efficient. Efficiency in opening statements — as in the other stages of a trial — means two things. First, research shows that the longest time period that most persons can maintain a high level of concentration is 15 to 20 minutes. Even during that time, minds regularly wander away and return. Second, research also shows that memory decays rapidly. Within a short time most persons have forgotten most of what they heard. Within a few hours they have forgotten the great majority of what they heard. Research also shows that repetition is a key ingredient in improving memory and that repetition of information three or four times significantly aids memory.

For the lawyer the message should be clear. Most opening statements should take perhaps 10 to 30 minutes. Using more time is counterproductive: Jurors will be overwhelmed, confused by details, and will respond by refusing to listen. Instead, it is usually more effective to select memorable themes, touch on fewer details, focus on your most important facts and phrases, and repeat them three or four times. This is particularly important with your themes, the anchoring devices for your opening statement.

2.   Do not argue or state personal opinions

Arguments are reserved for closing arguments. They are improper in opening statements. An easy way to keep the distinction in mind is to remember that opening statements state facts. Closing arguments, in addition to stating facts, can also argue characterizations, conclusions, inferences, credibility of witnesses, common sense, common experiences in life, and other matters beyond the evidence itself. Ask yourself: Do I have witnesses or other evidence that will prove the facts I am telling the jury about in my opening statement? If so, it is proper to include those facts in your opening statement.

Stating the rule against arguments is easy. Determining where the line is, or when you have crossed it, is not easy, since judges differ widely in their interpretation of what constitutes impermissible argument. Some give considerable leeway; others give the prohibition a strict interpretation. In addition, practices vary between jurisdictions. The only solution is to learn what your particular judge's attitude is and adjust to it. Do this before trial, and then plan your opening statement to eliminate anything potentially objectionable, so that your opening will flow smoothly, without interruption. This is not the place to draw objections from the other side.

Example:

Proper:	*Improper:*
He was going 50 mph in a 30-mph zone.	*He was racing his car, scattering everything in his path.*
He drove off the road on a clear, dry day on a straight section of the road.	*He was a loose cannon, charging down the road.*
She will say that she took a handgun away from a 250-lb. football player.	*Common sense tells you that she couldn't have done what she claims she did.*

There is another reason why lawyers should not argue during opening statements: At this stage of the trial, it does not persuade. Good facts, which create memorable mental pictures, have more impact. Rather than describing someone as "drunk," it is better to describe someone as "crawling on all fours." Rather than describing someone's driving as "reckless," it is better to describe it as "driving his 6,000 pound delivery truck 35 mph through a crowded elementary school crosswalk, where the posted speed limit is 10 mph." Good facts, expressed through strong nouns and verbs, are much stronger than characterizations and conclusions.

It is also improper to state directly your personal opinions about the facts or the credibility of witnesses. Phrases like " I believe," " I think," "I know," or even " we believe" state personal opinions and are usually objectionable, not only in opening statements but at any stage of the trial. Moreover, they are not persuasive ways to present things to the jury. These phrases should be eliminated from your trial vocabulary before they become a bad habit.

3.   Do not overstate the evidence

The only thing a trial lawyer has to sell to the jury is his credibility. Hence, nothing is more damaging than to overstate facts in your opening statement. The jury will remember it, resent your misrepresentation, and no longer trust you. Your opponent during closing arguments will in all likelihood point out each misrepresentation that you failed to deliver on.

Accordingly, if you do err, do so on the side of caution. When in doubt, understatement is the better part of wisdom. The jury will be pleasantly surprised to learn that your case is even better than it had expected.

4.   Consider using exhibits and visual aids

Exhibits in opening statements are a mixed blessing. On the one hand, they can be an effective tool to make key facts clear for the jury. Exhibits that are graphic and vivid can grab the jury's attention and create an impression that words alone cannot equal. Where such exhibits exist, using them in opening statements is effective, since first impressions often become lasting impressions. On the other hand, exhibits can also distract the jurors' attention from you, and once seen will no longer be new evidence when reused during the trial. Hence, using exhibits during opening statements should be done only after weighing the benefits and costs involved.

If a chart, diagram, or other exhibit is essential for the jurors' understanding of the case, then it must be used. This is commonly true in commercial cases, where the parties, facts, and events can be complex. In those cases a chart showing the parties and their principal witnesses, a chronological chart of a series of related events, or a flow chart showing the sequence of important activity can be effective during opening statements.

If the exhibit you wish to use in your opening statement has already been admitted in evidence through a pretrial order or by stipulation of the parties, there should be no problem with using it in your opening statement. It is always a good idea, however, to inform the judge and opposing lawyer of your plans so that any objections or logistics can be ironed out in advance.

If the exhibit is not in evidence, tell the judge that you plan to use it during your opening statement and that you will establish a proper foundation for the exhibit during the trial. If you want to use a visual aid, such as a chart showing the relationships of the parties and their key employees, the visual aid is merely a supplement to your opening statement and will not be admitted in evidence (since it is not "evidence"). Nevertheless, today almost all judges permit using visual aids during the opening statements, since they help the jury understand what the case is about. Again, inform the judge and opposing counsel of your plans beforehand so that any objections can be resolved.

5.   Anticipate weaknesses

Often a difficult decision in opening statements is whether, and if so how, to volunteer weaknesses. This involves determining your weaknesses and predicting whether your opponent intends to use them at trial. There is obviously no point in volunteering a weakness that would never be raised at trial. Where, however, that weakness is apparent and known to the opponent, you should volunteer it. If you don't, your opponent will, with twice the impact. How do you volunteer the weaknesses? The key is to mention the weakness without emphasis and to present it in its least damaging light, when it will blend easily into the story.

Example:

Your client is the plaintiff in a personal injury action. He was involved in a collision with another automobile at an intersection. The defense is contributory negligence, based in part on the fact that your client had been drinking.

On April 25, 2000, John Smith went to work as usual. At 4:00 P.M., when his shift got out, he and several of his fellow employees went to Frank's Tavern, as they often did, and he had a couple of beers and talked with the other men there. After about one hour, John left to drive home for dinner with his family. It was on the way home that he was struck by the defendant's car.

Some lawyers believe that volunteering their own weaknesses only puts undue emphasis on those weaknesses. They feel that it is better to let the opponent bring them out. This approach fails to recognize, however, that over the course of the trial the only thing that a lawyer has to sell is his credibility. Once the jurors feel that a lawyer is not being honest and candid with them, that credibility is lost. Credibility is best maintained by always being candid, which includes honestly disclosing weaknesses in opening statements and discussing them frankly in closing arguments. Social science research has demonstrated that "drawing the sting" by volunteering the weakness is the more effective approach, principally because it enhances the lawyer's credibility. This is best done by making the weaknesses part of your story, giving the jury the message that these "weaknesses" do not affect the overall merit of your case.

6.   Waiving or reserving opening statements

Experienced trial lawyers look forward to opening statements since this is their first real opportunity to communicate directly with the jurors and tell them about the case. In some jurisdictions the party with the burden of proof, normally the plaintiff, must make an opening statement that demonstrates a prima facie case. In others, there is no legal requirement that either party make an opening statement. Moreover, some jurisdictions permit the defendant to reserve an opening statement until he begins the defense's case in chief.

It is difficult to imagine a situation where a party, either plaintiff or defendant, would find it advantageous to waive making an opening statement. Remember that trials are conducted to see which viewpoint of a disputed set of facts the jury will accept as true. Making an effective opening statement gives you a head start over your opponent. Take advantage of the opportunity.

The defendant, however, has a more realistic decision to make: if permissible, should he make an opening statement immediately after the plaintiff or should he reserve it for the defense case in chief? Most defendants open immediately after the plaintiff. Reserving the opening statement means that plaintiff's version of the facts will go unchallenged. Coupled with a strong case in chief, the plaintiff may well have convinced the jury before you get a chance to tell your side of the case. Some defense lawyers prefer to reserve opening statements because they will have the benefit of hearing the plaintiff's evidence before deciding exactly what to say. However, reserving the defendant's opening statement necessarily creates the impression that you did not have a defense, so you waited to see what the plaintiff's case looked like before devising one.

Nonetheless, the defendant should at least consider reserving his opening statement where he has a strong case and there are significant strategic advantages in that approach. This situation exists most commonly in criminal cases where a strong affirmative defense exists and, because of limited discovery, the prosecution does not know what the defense evidence will be. Reserving the opening statement in such a situation will prevent the prosecution from altering its case in chief to blunt the anticipated defense. The defendant might also reserve his opening statement when he has more than one defense to raise, and cannot make up his mind which one to raise until he has heard the prosecution's case in chief. For example, in a murder case where the prosecution's evidence is weak on identification, the defense could be based on that issue. If the identification evidence is strong, the defense of self-defense could be asserted.

7.   Lawyer's position and delivery

During opening statements, unless required to use a fixed lectern, you should position yourself in the courtroom to maximize your presence before the jury. Although this is partly a matter of personal style, the most advantageous position is usually directly in front of the jury, a few feet away, where you can comfortably maintain eye contact with each of the jurors. Standing at either end of the jury box gives the impression of favoring some jurors and ignoring others. Standing too far away reduces your presence, while too close makes jurors uncomfortable by invading their personal zone.

Example:

   In this schematic diagram of a courtroom, the lawyer should usually stand near the position "X."

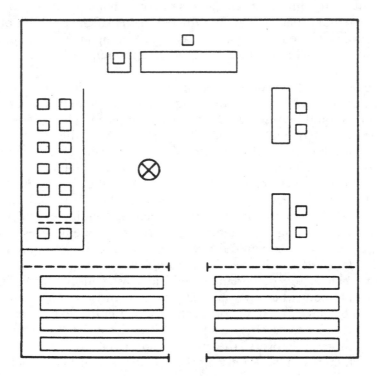

   How do you deliver an effective opening statement? How you say it is just as important as what you say. What you say is discussed in the next section. How you say it involves both verbal and nonverbal considerations, but the overall impression must lead to one conclusion: You have a good case, and you expect to win! Jurors are always subconsciously thinking: Which side is glad to be here? Which side expects to win?

An opening statement is not a speech. Think of it as a conversation with a group of people about a subject you feel strongly about, and this is your opportunity to show them why they should join you in your thinking.

Verbal considerations are important. Research shows that speakers who use the active voice and plain English, employ an energetic pace and volume, modulate their speech rate, pitch, volume, and pauses to maintain interest, and avoid hollow intensifiers and signs of hesitancy are seen as more authoritative and persuasive.

Nonverbal considerations are also important. Think of gestures and body movement as the ways you reinforce and punctuate what you say. Movement draws the listener's eye, and people hear better when they watch the speaker. Upper body movement is reinforcing, since it draws attention to the speaker's face. Hand and arm gestures, shoulder and head movement, and facial gestures are the kind of movement that punctuate your speech and reinforces it. Eye contact with individual jurors, for a few seconds at a time, is important, because each juror needs to feel that you are including him or her in your discussion.

On the other hand, lower body movement is usually distracting. Hands hanging down, hands in pockets, hands holding or playing with pens draw the listener's eye away from the speaker's face. Constant and aimless wandering back and forth merely advertises the speaker's nervousness. Instead, use lower body movement positively. When talking, stand in front of the jury, facing them directly, and use only upper body movement. Use lower body movement to signal breaks, such as the end of a topic and the beginning of a new one. For example, if you have finished describing how a collision happened, pause for a few seconds, move a few feet to a new position, then again face the jury and begin the next segment of your opening statement. Remember that upper and lower body movement should always reinforce your speech, not distract from it.

A trial lawyer should know his case well enough and have prepared his opening so that extensive notes are unnecessary. If possible, avoid notes altogether. If impossible, reduce your opening statement outline to a single sheet, which contains in large print only the key topics and ideas you need to cover, and refer to the outline only if it becomes necessary. This permits you to exude confidence, use your hands and arms for effective gestures, and maintain continuous eye contact with each of the jurors. Lawyers who can give an opening statement without notes have a decided advantage over their opponents.

§4.4.   *Content of effective opening statements*

The following checklist should be useful in organizing your opening statements. While no checklist should be religiously adhered to under all circumstances, following an outline will force you to prepare, organize, and deliver an opening statement that will present your evidence in a logical and clear progression that the jury can follow and remember.

1. introduction
2. parties
3. scene
4. instrumentality
5. date, time, weather, and lighting
6. issue
7. what happened
8. basis of liability/nonliability or guilt/nonguilt
9. anticipating and refuting other side
10. damages (civil cases only)
11. conclusion

While this type of checklist should be useful, it is by no means the only way an opening statement can be organized. Like most aspects of trial work, nothing is etched in stone. It can and should be modified to meet the unique facts of each case, your personality and style as well as that of your opponent. Only time and experience will determine what approaches work best for you.

Although the checklist is advisory, the requirement of preparation and organization is not. Like any other phase of the trial, the opening must be carefully organized, planned, and delivered. Giving an opening statement "off the top" usually leads to disaster.

1. Introduction

The beginning of your opening statement is your first opportunity to speak directly with the jury. It is your first chance to impress them with the merits of your case and your abilities as an advocate. First impressions are usually lasting impressions. Within the first minute or so you should be able to achieve three purposes:

a. present your themes
b. present your theory of the case
c. demonstrate your enthusiasm, confidence, and integrity through your delivery and demeanor

Example (plaintiff — civil):

May it please the Court, counsel, members of the jury. This is a case about carelessness and how it ruined another person's life. That's because on April 25, 2000, John Smith had his leg crushed when, at the intersection of North and Clark Streets in this city, he was walking across North Street with the walk light, and the defendant, running the red light, crashed into Mr. Smith's leg. The force of the crash crushed his leg, shattered it in several places, and Mr. Smith's leg, and his life, have never been the same.

Example (defendant — civil):

> *This is a case about taking responsibility for your own conduct. On April 25, 2000, the plaintiff, who was in a hurry, took a chance, and, without looking, stepped off the curb before the light had changed. The plaintiff now wants to blame someone else for his own carelessness.*

Example (plaintiff — criminal):

> *Members of the jury, this is a case of first degree murder. That defendant took a fully loaded .38 caliber revolver, pointed it at the victim, Jimmy Smith, who was not armed in any way, and from a distance of less than three feet shot Jimmy in the head. He did it intentionally, and he did it for revenge.*

Example (plaintiff — criminal):

> *This case is simple. Bobby Williams wasn't there. He wasn't there when Jimmy Smith was shot. He wasn't anywhere near there. He was miles away, at home with his family. This is a case of mistaken identity.*

Is a theme improper in an opening statement because it constitutes argument? While some courts still adhere to the traditional test — only if a witness will testify to it can you say it in opening statements — most courts today allow reasonable latitude and recognize that themes and other devices that grab attention, while technically perhaps "argument," should be allowed because they help the jurors understand the positions of the opposing parties. Themes, if direct inferences from the evidence to be introduced at trial, are usually allowed. Since the propriety of an opening statement is, like so many things, within the discretion of the trial judge, obviously you need to know your judge.

If your trial judge is a traditionalist, you will need to modify or even drop your themes from your opening statement. Adding the time-honored phrases, "We expect the evidence to show," and "We will prove to you," incanted at the beginning and repeated once or twice during the opening statement, will usually satisfy the judge.

2. Parties

You should introduce the essential people, both parties and critical witnesses, to the extent appropriate. As plaintiff, your description of the plaintiff in a personal injury case should include his activities at work, home, and play. Tell a story about your client. Build him up and make him a human being the jury can relate to and sympathize with. In addition, remember that the credibility of your important witnesses is determined not only by what they say and how they say it, but by who the witnesses are. As defendant, discuss the important parties and witnesses the plaintiff either did not mention or glossed over.

As always, make sure that whatever you do bring out about any parties or witnesses will be supported by testimony at trial. Since a witness' background will usually only be brought out through that witness' testimony, discussing the background in the opening statement may commit you to calling the witness at trial. For this reason, defense lawyers in criminal cases will rarely discuss the defendant's or other defense witnesses' backgrounds in their opening statements, unless they are certain these persons will testify. In this way they remain flexible in deciding to present a defense at all.

Example (plaintiff):

Folks, meet John Smith. [John, please stand up.] John is an accountant. He had worked steadily as an accountant at the XYZ Company for 15 years, supporting himself and his three children. He has lived in our community all his life. [John, please take your seat.]

Before April 25, 2000, John Smith was a completely healthy man. He was physically active. He did all the work around the house, including building an addition a few years ago. He enjoyed playing tennis, hiking and camping with the family, and other athletic activities. Never did he have any problems with his back or legs.

Example (defendant):

To understand this case you need to understand Bob Jones. Bob's a professional driver. He drives all kinds of trucks for ABC Construction. He's done that for more than eight years now. Bob was so professional in his work that two years ago he was promoted to head driver, a responsibility that involves hiring, firing, training, and scheduling all the other drivers.

In cases that involve artificial entities, such as corporations, or multiple parties, consider using a chart showing who the plaintiffs and defendants are, and the names of officers and employees for those parties that are important or will appear as witnesses during the trial. The jury will appreciate your making the added effort to help them understand the case.

3. Scene

In most personal injury and criminal cases, the scene of an occurrence is usually important. In these cases you should describe the scene so that the jury can visualize it. Remember that the key to describing scenes is to develop verbal pictures such that if you close your eyes and listen to the description you should actually be able to form a mental picture of the scene described. Here clarity is critical. If the jury cannot visualize what you are describing, the rest of your opening will make little sense.

Juries, like lay people, often have difficulty in understanding compass directions. Instead, it is usually more effective to ask the jury to assume that they are facing a given direction, then "walk" the jury through the scene involved. Give one fact at a time, slowly enough to be absorbed and make a mental picture of it. It's generally best to give the jury the minimum amount of detail necessary to accurately picture the scene. Too much detail at this time runs the danger of confusing the jury.

Example (plaintiff):

This collision occurred at the intersection of Clark Street and Division Street. Picture a car traveling south on Clark Street toward the intersection of Division Street. Clark Street is a two-lane street. There are parking lanes on both sides, which are always filled. Both sides of Clark Street near the intersection have commercial buildings approximately three stories high. Division Street is a four-lane street which intersects at right angles with Clark Street. It has no parking lanes and is also lined with commercial buildings. Consequently, as you drive down Clark Street you can't see the traffic coming down Division Street until you are in the intersection itself.

Defendant, speaking after the plaintiff, should describe those details of the scene plaintiff left out, or with which you disagree.

Examples (defendant):

Counsel has described part of the scene to you but he failed to mention that . . .
It is important to keep in mind that . . .

A diagram, enlarged photograph, or other exhibit can be an effective aid in your opening statement, but several considerations must be kept in mind in deciding whether to use them. First, find out if the judge will allow you to use the exhibit during your opening statement. If you represent to the court that you can establish a foundation for the exhibit, or your opponent has no objection to its admission, the judge will ordinarily permit use of the exhibit during your opening statement. Second, keep in mind that the exhibit can be both an attraction and a distraction. It is attractive because the exhibit is vivid and, in an appropriate case, can help the jury understand the case. On the other hand, the exhibit is distracting, because jurors will find it much more interesting than listening to you talk. The best way of dealing with this problem is to use the exhibit only when necessary, then move it out of sight when done. Third, using the exhibit during opening statements will mean that the exhibit is no longer new when it is formally introduced in evidence later. Where the exhibit will help spice up a tedious but necessary examination, consider saving it to use for the first time during that examination.

4. Instrumentality

In many cases, particularly personal injury and products liability, the instrumentality is an important part of the case. These would commonly involve vehicles, machinery, equipment and other products. In such cases the instrumentality should be described fully. Use the same picturization technique used to describe scenes.

Example:

> *This bus was 40 feet long and had front and rear exits on its right side. Each exit had three steps. There were handrails on both sides of the exits. There were large caution signs on all the glass doors as well as on the steps.*

Example:

> *The scaffolding used on this construction site consisted of a platform 20 feet long and 2 feet wide, which was suspended from the roof by two steel cables. An electric winch was attached to each cable.*

Example:

> *These life insurance policies had a face value of $50,000. They also had a double indemnity clause, a clause that said that in the event of an accidental death, the insurance company would pay twice as much.*

This is another place to consider using a diagram, photograph, or an actual object to make your points vividly.

Example:

> *This [holding up the lighter] is the same cigarette lighter that caused the fire here. Notice that the stem, which acts like a match, pulls out of the top [demonstrating]. The metal stand on the bottom unscrews [demonstrating], and here's where you put the two batteries that make the lighter operate.*

5.   Date, time, weather, and lighting

In cases where the date and precise time of an event are important, or the weather and lighting conditions are significant, describe these in detail.

Example:

> *This collision occurred on April 25, 2000, just before 3:00 P.M. It had been a sunny day. Although showers were expected, the streets were still clear and dry.*

Example:

> *This robbery occurred at 11:30 P.M. on April 25, 2000. Although it was nighttime, this intersection was well lighted. There was a streetlight directly over the spot where Mr. Smith was robbed. There were other streetlights farther down the street in each direction, on both sides of the street. There was additional lighting from the storefronts that lined the street on both sides.*

6.   Issue

As defendant, your picture of what happened should be preceded by a denial of the plaintiff's version of the disputed facts of the case that the jury has just heard. How you make your denial is critical. It must be done directly and with conviction. You must force the jury to get away from plaintiff's version of the facts and keep an open mind about your evidence.

Plaintiff, of course, can also state what the issues in the case will be. However, it is usually preferable for him to proceed directly into the "how it happened" phase, since plaintiff will not usually want to tell the jury that the defense disagrees with his version immediately before he tells it.

Example (defendant):

Counsel for the plaintiff has told you that he expects to prove that this accident was caused by Mr. Johnson's negligence. But that's not what the evidence will show here!

What really happened on that day? We will prove that we were driving safely, and that if anyone caused this accident, it was the plaintiff himself who was negligent and at fault.

7.   What happened

You have now established the necessary foundations for your picture of the occurrence involved. You have set the stage: The parties, scene, instrumentality, weather, lighting, date, and time have all been described. A complete background has been created. The jury has a mental picture against which you can describe the action. You are now able to make an uninterrupted description of the actual event involved, with the kind of force and pace that will recreate the event and make it come alive. Action can only come alive if you present it in an uninterrupted way.

Remember that you are competing with your opponent to create the more plausible picture of how the event actually occurred. If you can make the jury visualize the event *your* way, you are well on the road to a favorable verdict. To do this successfully, your description must be a logical progression, simply yet forcefully stated; it must be paced so that the jury can follow easily; and it must be given from the perspective most advantageous to you.

As defendant, your primary problem is to persuade the jury to see the event *your* way, the way your evidence shows it really happened. You should directly deny that the event occurred in the way plaintiff has claimed, if you have evidence that will contradict the other side's version. If you have such evidence, you can in good faith deny their version and tell the jury what your side's proof is. However, what do you do if you have no contradictory evidence? Ethical considerations may keep you from directly denying your opponent's version or stating it's not true. You can, however, state that your opponent's evidence will be unpersuasive, will fail to convince, or will not meet his burden of proof. There is nothing improper in challenging your opponent's ability to prove what he is required to prove.

Example (plaintiff — civil):

Ladies and gentlemen, what happened the day this tragedy occurred? John Smith was driving south on Clark Street. He was driving at about 25 mph and was looking out for other cars and pedestrians. He could see the intersection of Elm Avenue ahead. The light was green for the Clark Street traffic. There were no cars in the intersection. Mr. Smith slowed down as he approached the intersection and could see no traffic or pedestrians. When he was halfway through in the intersection, without warning another car came from his left, ran the red light, and rammed Mr. Smith's car in the left rear.

Example (defendant — civil):

What really happened at the intersection? Frank Jones was driving westbound on Elm Avenue. As he approached the intersection of Clark and Elm, the light was red. Mr. Jones let his foot off the accelerator and began to slow down. Just before he reached the intersection, the light turned green. Mr. Jones accelerated and entered the intersection. Suddenly, another car shot through the intersection late, directly in front of Mr. Jones' car. Mr. Jones, although he had the green light, slammed on his brakes, but it was too late. The front of his car struck the other car on the rear driver's side.

Example (plaintiff — criminal):

Suddenly, at 9:05 A.M., three men with guns and masks burst through the front door of the bank. One man, armed with a shotgun, stood by the front door. The other two men ran to the tellers' area. One leaped over the counter and herded the tellers into a corner. The man standing before the counter announced, "This is a stickup. Don't do anything stupid."

Example (defendant — criminal):

At 11:30 P.M., while somebody else was robbing the unfortunate victim, Frank Jones was three blocks away, walking home from a movie. Suddenly, a police car with lights flashing came around the corner and pulled up next to Frank. Both officers, with guns drawn, ordered Frank to stand against a wall; Frank kept asking, "What's this all about?" One of the officers said, "You are under arrest for robbery." That, ladies and gentlemen, was the first time Frank Jones ever knew that a robbery had occurred.

8.   Basis of liability/nonliability or guilt/nonguilt

As plaintiff, this should be a high point in your opening statement. You want to make a summary of the facts and conclude that your client is entitled to win. This should be done in a suitably indignant and forceful manner. State the basis of liability immediately after your narration of your version of the facts.

As defendant, it is sometimes safer not to directly challenge the plaintiff's ability to prove certain facts. Assume that plaintiff will introduce some evidence to support his version. The safer approach is to suggest that plaintiff's picture of the disputed events will not be persuasive or convincing, then emphasize your *own* picture and conclusion.

Keep in mind that an opening statement cannot be argumentative, and that judges differ on what constitutes improper argument.

Example (plaintiff — civil):

Members of the jury, this evidence will show that the defendant did not keep a proper lookout for other cars, did not look out for pedestrians, did not slow down, and did not stop at the red light.

Example (defendant — civil):

The evidence will show that Mr. Jones was at all times driving carefully, and obeyed all the traffic signals on the streets. This accident was caused because the plaintiff ran the red light and drove his car into that intersection.

Example (plaintiff — criminal):

The evidence, in short, will prove that on April 25, 2000, this defendant, while armed with a loaded revolver, took $60 in U.S. currency and personal papers from the victim, Robert Smith.

Example (defendant — criminal):

We will show, then, that Bobby Smith, far from robbing anyone on April 25, 2000, was, at the time this robbery occurred, working as usual at his job as a dockworker at ABC Trucking Co.

Example (defendant in criminal case not intending to present a defense):

This evidence, which the state is required to present, will lead to only one conclusion. It will show that the state failed to prove, beyond a reasonable doubt, that Bobby was the robber. If it convinces you of anything, it is that the police arrested the wrong man.

Of course, there are situations where you may want to challenge the other side's facts with a direct denial. Where you do, however, make sure that you can prevail on the disputed facts. Nothing will damage your credibility faster than to directly claim that the other side's version is incorrect, then fail to prove it. Save such denials for safe situations.

9.   Anticipating and refuting other side

Lawyers sometimes wish to blunt the other side's anticipated evidence. This is particularly true for plaintiffs, since during opening statements plaintiffs go first and have no right of rebuttal. Can you refer, in your opening statement, to what you anticipate the other side's evidence will be? This is a difficult issue, and depends on whether it is the plaintiff's or defendant's opening statement.

For defendants the answer is easy. Defendants in both civil and criminal cases can ordinarily discuss the plaintiff's expected evidence, since the plaintiff's opening statement comes first and plaintiff will already have discussed its evidence. The defense can always talk about evidence the plaintiff has already talked about.

For plaintiffs the answer is more subtle, for both legal and advocacy reasons. Plaintiffs in civil cases cannot directly state what the anticipated defense evidence will be, because the defense may decide not to present any evidence during the trial. (This sometimes happens even though the defense, in the final pretrial statement, has listed witnesses and exhibits it plans to use at trial.) However, the plaintiff can present *its* evidence in a way that will implicitly reject the anticipated defense. The key is to defuse the defense, without appearing defensive.

Example (plaintiff — civil):

Notice how Ms. Torres was driving her car. She was going 20 mph in a 25-mph zone. She had her car lights on. She was maintaining a safe distance from the car ahead of her. She was watching the other traffic nearby. She was also looking at the traffic light at the upcoming intersection with Elm Street.

This rebuts the anticipated defense of contributory or comparative negligence.

The prosecution in a criminal case also cannot refer to evidence it anticipates the defense will present during the trial. This is because the defense in a criminal case has a constitutional right not to present any evidence. If the prosecutor refers directly to any expected defense evidence (e.g., "The defendant is going to say that . . ." or "The defense will try to prove that . . ."), this is clearly improper and may well result in an immediate mistrial. The most that the prosecution can do is refer to its *own* evidence, and then state the facts that will rebut the anticipated defense, without improperly commenting on defense evidence.

Example (plaintiff — criminal):

This evidence will show that at no time was the victim, Mr. Smith, armed in any way, nor did he do anything to provoke the defendant's assault.

This rebuts the anticipated defense of self-defense, without mentioning any defense evidence.

10.   Damages (civil cases only)

As plaintiff, you should describe what happened to the plaintiff, particularly where the injuries are extensive. In some injury cases, liability will not be seriously contested, so the only remaining issue is the extent of damages. Your organization of damages should therefore include symptoms, diagnosis, immediate treatment, prognosis, and conclusion. Most plaintiffs' lawyers do not tell the jury the dollar amount plaintiff will request, allowing flexibility in modifying the request based on how well the evidence was received. Most plaintiffs' lawyers also do not tell the jury the percentages of fault each party should bear, in comparative fault jurisdictions, again retaining flexibility. (During closing arguments, of course, plaintiffs usually suggest dollar amounts of damages and percentages of comparative fault.)

As defendant, you should express your regret that the plaintiff was injured, but firmly state that it was the plaintiff's fault, or certainly not your client's, particularly if you are defending solely on the issue of liability.

Example (plaintiff):

   a. Symptoms.
       What happened to Mr. Smith? The truck crashed into his hip and Mr. Smith collapsed on the pavement. He felt a sharp, stabbing pain in his hip. (Demonstrate on your own body where these injuries were.)
   b. Diagnosis.
       Several persons came to Mr. Smith's help and they tried to make him comfortable. Finally, an ambulance came, attendants put Mr. Smith on a stretcher, placed him in an ambulance, and drove him to the Mercy Hospital emergency room. Shortly afterwards, Dr. Franklin arrived, examined him and ordered X rays and other tests. The examination, X rays, and lab tests all showed that Mr. Smith had sustained multiple fractures of his left leg and hip.
   c. Immediate treatment.
       Mr. Smith's leg was placed in traction. He was given shots to relieve the radiating pain in his leg. After one week, his leg and pelvis were placed in a cast. The cast extended from his waist to his ankle.
   d. Further treatment.
       Several weeks later it became apparent that the leg and hip were not healing properly. Dr. Franklin performed another operation to correct this problem.
   e. Prognosis.
       What is Mr. Smith's condition today? He was examined as recently as last week. The examination revealed that his left leg was almost one inch shorter than the right. His left thigh and calf were substantially smaller and weaker. Arthritis had developed in the hip joint.
   f. Conclusion.
       Mr. Smith was in the hospital for four weeks. He incurred substantial hospital and medical bills. He was out of work for eight months. Even today he is no longer able to work a full day, play with his children, or do ordinary household chores. To this date, he has a continuous shooting pain that radiates from his left hip to his foot.

Example (defendant — where the defense is primarily on liability):

It is, of course, unfortunate that the plaintiff was injured. In this case, however, plaintiff's injuries were simply not our fault. The evidence will show that he was in a hurry, crossed the street without a walk light, and, without looking, stepped directly in front of a car that had no chance to stop. Because of this, the plaintiff must be responsible for the results of his own negligence.

11. Conclusion

Both plaintiff and defendant should conclude the opening statement by simply and directly telling the jury that the facts of the case will support his side, and ask for a verdict. Tell the jury what you want it to do. As plaintiff in a personal injury case, you should make a request for damages a part of your conclusion. Most lawyers generally advise against mentioning the specific monetary amount of damages you are seeking. Simply state that you are going to ask for adequate, lawful compensation and a verdict in the plaintiff's favor. After the jury has seen the plaintiff and understands how seriously he was injured, a large specific damages request will appear reasonable and realistic. On the other hand, other lawyers think it is better to begin conditioning the jury on damages by requesting a certain sum.

Example (plaintiff — civil):

Members of the jury, at the end of the trial, we will ask you to award lawful compensation to Mr. Smith for the losses and injuries he has sustained as a result of this collision. We will ask compensation for his medical expenses, compensation for his past and future loss of earnings, and compensation for his continuing pain and suffering, mental anguish, and inability to enjoy a healthy, normal life. In short, we will ask you to make it right.

Example (defendant — civil):

Based on that evidence, we will ask you to return the verdict that says "We, the jury, find in favor of defendant Jones and against plaintiff Smith."

Example (plaintiff — criminal):

After you have heard the evidence, we are confident that you will find the defendant guilty of each count in this indictment: armed robbery and murder.

Example (defendant — criminal):

At the conclusion of this case, you will have grave doubts that Frank Jones was anywhere near the robbery when it occurred. If anything, you will be convinced that someone else did it. Consequently, Frank Jones is simply not guilty of anything.

§4.5.   *Examples of opening statements*

1.   Criminal case (murder): *People v. Sylvester Strong*

(The defendant, Sylvester Strong, has been charged with murdering Shelley Williams on April 25, 2000. The prosecution claims that the shooting was in retaliation for a prior incident. The defense claims the shooting was justifiable self-defense.)

Opening statement — prosecution

May it please the court, counsel, members of the jury: this is a case of murder. You are here because on April 25, 2000, that defendant, Sylvester Strong, took a handgun and intentionally shot and killed an unarmed man, Shelley Williams.

There are several persons whose names will be mentioned frequently throughout the trial. First, there is the victim, Shelley Williams, who was 23 years old when he was shot to death. His mother, Rosie Garrett, and brother, Clarence Williams, both lifelong residents of Chicago, were both present when the shooting occurred. Of course there is the defendant, Sylvester Strong, who, as we will learn, shot and killed the victim with a handgun. He obtained that gun from George Howard, his brother-in-law. These are some of the names you will constantly hear about during the course of the trial.

This shooting happened on April 25, 2000, at approximately 3:30 P.M. It was a clear and bright day.

The shooting itself happened in the 2300 block of Bloomingdale Avenue in Chicago. Bloomingdale is a two-lane residential street that runs east and west. The south side of this block of Bloomingdale Street has an elevated railroad track, so the entire block on that side consists of a concrete wall about 10 feet high. The other side of the street, the north side, has a typical sidewalk and a mixture of residential buildings and small businesses. Most of what happened that afternoon occurred on the sidewalk near the middle of the 2300 block of Bloomingdale Avenue.

What, then, happened on Bloomingdale around 3:30 during the afternoon of April 25? The

(Introduction)

(Parties)

In this case the names and backgrounds of the principal witnesses are not significant, so they are mentioned in a cursory way. Another possibility is to skip this part entirely.

(Date, time, weather, and lighting)

These issues are not in dispute.

(Scene)

The location of the crime is, as is the case in most criminal cases, an important point. Consequently, it should be described in sufficient detail to give the jury a solid mental impression of the scene, so that the action will make sense to them. In short, set the stage before describing the action. This would be a good place to use a photograph or diagram in the opening statement.

(What happened)

evidence we will bring to you during this trial will show the following:

Earlier that afternoon Rosie Garrett and Shelley Williams had decided to drive to the home of Rosie's sister. They drove in two cars. Rosie had about seven people in her car, while Shelley had his brother and two friends in his. On the way back they decided to drive over to another sister who lived on the 2300 block of Bloomingdale. Shelley drove first, followed by Rosie. They drove down Winnebago until they reached the corner of Bloomingdale.

After turning the corner, the first car, driven by Shelley Williams, stopped a short distance down Bloomingdale when he saw the defendant, Sylvester Strong, riding a bicycle down the street. He stopped his bicycle a few feet from the car. Shelley got out of his car, walked up to the defendant and exchanged some words with him. This quickly escalated into an argument. The argument was based upon an argument the defendant had gotten into with Shelley's mother the previous day.

While this argument was going on, Rosie Garrett, Shelley's mother, arrived at the corner in her car and parked the car a short distance from Shelley's. She saw her son and the defendant having words. Her son motioned to her, so she got out of her car and walked to where Shelley and the defendant were standing. Shelley asked her, pointing to the defendant: "Is this the one who cursed you out?" She said: "Yes, it is." Shelley demanded an apology.

At this time George Howard, the defendant's brother-in-law, came to the corner and asked Shelley's brother, Clarence, and one of his friends what was going on. Both said they didn't know what the argument was all about. George Howard then took a gun out of his pocket and fired the gun twice into the air. Nobody was hurt. The defendant walked up to his brother-in-law and said: "You're not trying to hit him, give me the gun." He then took the gun from his brother-in-law.

It is sometimes advantageous to tell the jury up front that "you believe" the evidence will show certain things. Do this once, then go into the narrative of the events. This allows you to tell what happened without constantly repeating that phrase "we believe the evidence will show that . . ." (which a few courts still require).

Note how the action is described in an active, immediate way, which gives the jury a "feel" of how it really happened.

The defendant immediately aimed that gun at Shelley Williams and shot him once through the arm. When Shelley turned to get away, the defendant fired a second shot in his back. Shelley then fell to the ground, face down. The defendant then walked up to him and fired a third shot into his back.

Immediately after firing the third shot, the defendant ran down the sidewalk and attempted to escape. The victim's brother, Clarence, having just seen the defendant shoot his brother, jumped into his brother's car, drove it a short distance down Bloomingdale and cut off the defendant as he tried to run away. The defendant ran into the car and was knocked down to the ground. Clarence got out of the car and kicked the defendant in the head, trying to keep him on the ground and hold him for the police.

The defendant repeatedly tried to get up and Clarence kept trying to subdue him. A relative of the defendant brought a baseball bat from her house and came to the scene, but Rosie took the baseball bat from her. Rosie then took that baseball bat and hit the defendant over his head to keep him down until the police came.

When the police arrived at the scene, they found the defendant being held right by the car. He had been beaten up, but was being held for the police. They also recovered the gun, which had been taken to Rosie's house for safekeeping. An ambulance was called, but by the time he could be taken to a nearby hospital, the victim, Shelley Williams, was dead. A later autopsy showed the fatal bullet to be one that entered the victim's back, piercing his lungs and heart.

That, ladies and gentlemen of the jury, is what we expect the evidence to show. It will prove that on April 25, 2000, the defendant, Sylvester Strong, committed the crime of murder when he intentionally took a handgun and fired three shots into an unarmed victim, Shelley Williams. The third shot, the fatal shot, entered the victim's back as he lay helpless on the sidewalk, face down. The evidence will show that

The heart of the case can be acted out. Here the prosecutor can act out how the defendant held the gun and fired it.

A weakness in the prosecution case is that the defendant was, in fact, severely beaten by the victim's friends and family following the shooting. This problem is usually best handled by volunteering the unfavorable evidence now, so that its impact will be blunted before the defense can discuss the weakness the way it wants to.

(Basis of guilt)

This summary should be stated emphatically.

Since the defense need not present evidence, the prosecutor cannot comment on the anticipated defense directly.

the defendant was in no way justified in shooting Shelley Williams.

Based on this evidence, we will ask that you find the defendant, Sylvester Strong, guilty of the crime of murder as charged in this indictment.

(Conclusion)

Opening statement — defense

May it please the Court, counsel, ladies and gentlemen of the jury, good morning. We are here only because on April 25, 2000, Sylvester Strong had to use a gun to keep Shelley Williams from killing him. This is a case of self-defense, nothing more.

(Introduction)

In a criminal case, the prosecution, having the burden of proof, presents evidence first. Only after the prosecutors have presented their case will Sylvester Strong have an opportunity to present his case. We ask that each of you waits until you have heard from all the witnesses, ours as well as theirs, before deciding what really happened. However, before I talk to you about what we believe the evidence will show, I want to make one fact perfectly clear to each of you. We do not contest the fact that Sylvester Strong did in fact shoot and kill the deceased, Shelley Williams, on April 25, 2000, on Bloomingdale Avenue in Chicago. We agree that this happened. That fact, however, is not the issue in the case.

(Issue)

Framing the issue in a way most advantageous to your position is extremely important.

The *only* issue in this case is whether Sylvester Strong was defending himself when the shooting happened. In other words, ladies and gentlemen, was Sylvester Strong justified in defending himself under the facts and circumstances that unfolded during the afternoon of April 25? Please remember that we, as the defense, don't have to prove anything. It's the *prosecution* that has to prove, beyond a reasonable doubt, that Sylvester Strong was *not* justified in defending himself. The evidence will show that Sylvester Strong was in fact justified in doing what he did and thus is not guilty of any crime. In short, this is simply a case of self-defense.

After stating the issue, you must then emphatically answer it, then move directly into a review of the facts that support your position on that issue.

What really happened before and during the incident? On April 24, the day before, there was an argument involving the family of Shelley Williams with Sylvester Strong. On April 25, the very next day, Sylvester Strong was riding a bicycle on Bloomingdale when he was confronted on the street by Shelley Williams, his family, and other friends of the Williams family.

The evidence will show that Sylvester Strong was first struck in the face by Shelley Williams. Immediately thereafter Williams and his family attacked Sylvester with baseball bats and two-by-fours. Sylvester was unarmed and tried to protect himself from the people who were attacking him, but to no avail. He was repeatedly struck on his head and body. In desperation, he grabbed a gun from George Howard, who had arrived at the scene. With blood streaming down his face, he repeatedly fired the weapon, striking Shelley Williams.

The only reason he fired that gun was to get that crowd off of him, a crowd that was attacking him with two-by-fours and baseball bats, deadly weapons.

When this group of individuals who had been assaulting Sylvester realized that the gun was empty, they continued their assault with baseball bats and two-by-fours. Sylvester's head and face were a mass of blood.

Knowing that his life was in danger, he attempted to flee by running across the street, but was chased and caught by the mob, knocked to the ground, and again beaten until he lost consciousness. The only reason his life was spared was that the police arrived moments later.

In short, ladies and gentlemen, we expect the evidence to show that under these circumstances Sylvester did nothing more than what any other reasonable person would have done under those circumstances. He simply defended himself from an armed mob. Therefore, he is simply not guilty of murder or any other crime.

(What happened)

Note that the narrative of this action is done this time from the defendant's perspective.

There's nothing wrong with giving the defendant a sympathetic portrayal.

(Basis of nonguilt)

As with the plaintiff, this is the high point of the opening, and must be stated with emotion and conviction.

I ask you, ladies and gentlemen, at this time to withhold your judgment until you have heard all the evidence from all of the witnesses, and I am confident that upon hearing all of the evidence you are going to render a verdict in this case that will be fair. We believe that the prosecution will not be able to prove, beyond a reasonable doubt, that Sylvester was *not* justified in defending himself. We expect that after you deliberate and carefully weigh all the evidence in this case you will return the only possible verdict, a verdict of not guilty. I thank you.

(Conclusion)

The jury must be reminded that the prosecution has the burden on the issue of reasonable self-defense, since it's entirely likely that some of the jurors will assume that the defense should have to prove any defense it chooses to raise.

2.   **Civil case (products liability):** *Hi-Temp, Inc. v. Lindberg Furnace Company*

Hi-Temp, a company that treats metal products in furnaces, purchased an industrial vacuum furnace in September 1999 from the defendant manufacturer. On December 31, 2000, the furnace exploded. Hi-Temp had the furnace repaired. Hi-Temp claims that a design defect in the furnace, particularly in a valve, was the cause of the explosion. Lindberg maintains that the furnace was safely designed and manufactured.

Opening statement — plaintiff

Good afternoon, ladies and gentlemen.

(Introduction)

Hi-Temp is a company in business in Northlake, Illinois. Hi-Temp treats various metal products using high-temperature vacuum furnaces. The defendant, Lindberg Furnace Company, designs, manufactures, and sells such furnaces. In 1999 Hi-Temp entered into negotiations with the defendant for the purpose of purchasing a vacuum furnace.

(Parties)

Vacuum furnaces come in all shapes and sizes, but they all have the same basic components. The central part is a lined vacuum chamber. A large hatch allows materials to be placed in the chamber. The furnace works through a series of pumps, valves and heating elements. After the materials are placed inside, all the air is removed from the furnace, using the pumps and valves.

(Instrumentality)

Since this case centers on a mechanical device, it should be described with appropriate detail.

The heating elements then go on and heat whatever is in the furnace to the required temperature. This process tempers the metals, making them stronger and harder.

This would be a good place to use a diagram or photograph in the opening statement.

When Hi-Temp negotiated with Lindberg for the vacuum furnace, they told Lindberg the necessary requirements for the furnace. They told Lindberg the kind of heat that would be needed. They told Lindberg the pressures that would be needed. They told Lindberg all the specifications and requirements that the furnace would have to meet.

Lindberg adjusted their design and manufactured a vacuum furnace for Hi-Temp at a cost of $103,000. This purchase was made with the understanding that the furnace would do what it had been manufactured to do, that is, to heat the materials that Hi-Temp needed.

The furnace went into operation some time in September 1999. The whole time the furnace was in operation, the maintenance, care and concern shown by Hi-Temp for this furnace was meticulous. If there were any maintenance problems, repair problems, or anything of that sort, they were immediately dealt with. Often Lindberg itself was called in to consult on how to fix a problem.

(Anticipating defenses)

The expected defense is that the explosion was somehow caused by faulty maintenance, operation, or misuse. This statement helps rebut the expected defense.

On December 31, 2000, the furnace was in operation. During the afternoon this furnace was heating turbine blades and other aircraft parts. The heat was cycled to a temperature of 2,000 degrees and then cooled, and then heated again to a temperature of 1,800 degrees and then cooled. This went on in a series of stages. Everything was routine.

(Scene)

That evening the furnace was loaded with more turbine parts and was set in operation again. All the instruments were set properly. The loading was done properly. Everything was done the way we had been told to do it, and the way it had always been done.

The anticipated defense is again rebutted forcefully.

Around 8:30 that evening there was an explosion that tore off the sides of the furnace and damaged other parts. Immediately after the explosion an investigation was started to try to determine the cause of the explosion. Based upon all the evidence here, you will conclude that

(What happened)

there was a defect in the design of the vacuum furnace which was directly responsible for the explosion.

This furnace was designed in such a way that it would pump down from atmospheric pressure to a vacuum. The pressurized portion of the furnace was separated from the vacuum portion by a valve attached to the main vacuum pump, called a foreline valve. The furnace was manufactured and designed in such a way that this foreline valve could open between the atmospheric portion and the vacuum portion without first shutting down the furnace and without being coordinated with other valves on the unit. If the foreline valve somehow opened, atmospheric pressure would rush right into the vacuum portion, under incredible speed and pressure, creating shock waves in the furnace.

In this case the plaintiff's major problem is explaining causation — how the alleged design defect actually caused the explosion that occurred. Hence, this part of the opening is very carefully stated, so that there is no direct claim that the plaintiff, through its experts, will precisely be able to explain why the explosion occurred.

That, ladies and gentlemen, is what happened on December 31, 2000. After the foreline valve improperly opened, atmospheric pressure rushed into the vacuum portion, creating gigantic shock waves, which knocked off the sides of the furnace and did other damage.

(Basis of liability)

Plaintiff's theory of the case is simply stated — if the valve had a safety lock, there would have been no explosion.

You will learn that this explosion was directly caused by Lindberg's design and manufacture of this foreline valve, and that the explosion could have been prevented if Lindberg had simply built a foreline valve that had a locking safety device on it.

After the explosion, Hi-Temp had the vacuum furnace rebuilt. This took several weeks, during which time they could not process any of their customers' orders. The loss to Hi-Temp for the repairs, as well as for the business interruption, was $55,000.

(Damages)

The real issue in this case is liability, so damages are only mentioned briefly.

At the end of all the evidence, we will be asking you to return a verdict in favor of Hi-Temp and against Lindberg for the sum of $55,000.

(Conclusion)

Opening statement — defendant

May it please the Court, counsel, members of the jury: I represent the Lindberg Furnace Company.

(Introduction)

Lindberg's business is devoted to designing and building what are called vacuum furnaces for purchasers throughout the world. We have been in this business since 1947, and build furnaces based on the individual customer's requirements.

(Parties)

We will show that the design of the furnace Hi-Temp bought was a standard one with proven performance and safety over 20 years. We have built thousands of these furnaces over the past 20 years, without problems. The design is safe, and we make and test them carefully. Whatever caused the furnace to explode, it had nothing to do with its design or manufacture. If anything caused the explosion, it must have been Hi-Temp's maintenance, operation, or use of the furnace.

(Basis of nonliability)

Furthermore, we will show that the furnace could have been repaired in about two weeks at a cost far less than $55,000, and that it could have been put back into service after that time.

(Damages)

While the defense is on liability, it is usually desirable to at least touch on damages.

Simply put, the plaintiff will not be able to prove, by a preponderance of the evidence, that we did anything wrong here in designing and manufacturing this furnace that produced this so-called explosion. Accordingly, at the close of all the evidence we will ask that you return a verdict against the plaintiff and in favor of the Lindberg Furnace Company.

(Conclusion)

This unusually short opening has the advantage of sounding extremely confident. It forcefully states that the plaintiff will be unable to prove either a design defect or causation. In openings, brevity can sometimes be an effective technique.

V
DIRECT EXAMINATION

§5.1.   Introduction

Experienced trial lawyers recognize that most trials are won on the strengths of their case in chief, not on the weaknesses of their opponent's case. Consequently, effective direct examinations that clearly, forcefully, and efficiently present the facts of the case will usually have a decisive effect on the outcome of the trial.

The direct examination should be the jury's opportunity to relive reality from your side's perspective. The witness should show, not tell, the jury what happened so that the event is re-created for the jury's benefit. All this must be done while keeping in mind the elements of your claims or defenses, your theory of the case, your themes and labels, and the need to tell people stories that engage the hearts and minds of each juror. This is difficult and requires planning and witness preparation. If done well, each of the jurors will understand, accept, and remember the witness' testimony.

Consequently, direct examinations should let the witness be the center of attention. The lawyer should conduct the examination so that he does not detract from his witness. After all, a witness will be believed and remembered because of the manner and content of his testimony, not because the questions asked were so brilliant. Witness credibility is determined by who the witness is (background), what he says (content), and how he says it (demeanor). If the jurors remember one of your witnesses as being particularly convincing, but are not sure who conducted the direct examination, you have done your job well.

This chapter will discuss the components of effective examinations and review the kinds of direct examinations of nonexpert witnesses that are repeatedly encountered in civil and criminal trials. Expert witnesses are discussed in Chapter VIII.

§5.2. *Elements*

A good direct examiner is like the director of a film crew. Although limited by the script, the director can inject his own approach and perspective into the production. He has many variables to work with in portraying an event. He can choose the locations of his cameras, the angles of the shots, and the types of lenses. He can use panoramic shots, closeups, stop action frames, and slow motion. When the shooting is complete, he has the luxury of editing. The final product, while still a film of a recognizable event, is a unique product of the director.

A good trial lawyer approaches witness testimony the same way. He does much more than simply "get the story out." He decides how he wants to portray a certain event or scene, then makes the technical decisions necessary to achieve the desired result. Unimportant matters are avoided or glossed over. Important ones are stressed, details are zoomed in on, and action is slowed down. Critical matters can be shown in stop-action sequences.

The important point is that trial lawyers view trials, and particularly direct examinations, as a creative art, one which allows you to tell a story to the jury in a way that is most advantageous to your party. The tools for this creative approach are analyzed in this section.

Effective direct examinations exhibit recurring characteristics that should be remembered each time you plan any direct examination. These include the following.

1. Keep it simple

Inexperienced trial lawyers often make two interrelated mistakes. On the one hand, they elicit too much unimportant testimony. On the other, they spend too little time on the critical part of what the witness has to offer. The former results in the jury being bored or, even worse, becoming confused about what is important. It also permits opposing counsel to develop additional points for cross-examination. The latter, by rushing through the critical facts, fails to fully develop them so that the jury understands and appreciates them.

Remember that the jury is laboring under two handicaps: It has never heard the testimony before, and it is receiving the information aurally. Any person's ability to absorb and retain aural information is limited. Attention spans drop significantly after 15 to 20 minutes, so any examination should be short and focused. Therefore, don't make the jurors' difficulties greater by injecting into the direct examination unnecessary information and details. Determine in advance what the critical part of the witness' testimony is, get to it quickly, develop it sufficiently, then stop. In short, keep your direct examinations simple. In direct examinations, as in your case in chief, brevity is the better part of wisdom.

2.   Organize logically

Once you have determined what the key elements of the direct examination will be, you must organize those points in a logical order. Usually, but not always, this will result in a chronological presentation of the testimony. Experience has shown that jurors, like other people, are best able to comprehend a series of events or other information if they are presented in the same chronological order as they really occurred. Jurors are used to hearing stories presented chronologically, so they will be more likely to grasp and retain evidence at trial if a story is presented in this way.

With occurrence witnesses in personal injury and criminal cases, a logical and most frequently used sequence is:

1.   personal background
2.   scene description
3.   action description
4.   exhibits to highlight and repeat
5.   damages description (if applicable)

Example:

The witness, the plaintiff in an automobile collision case, should usually present testimony in the following order:

a.   background
b.   description of collision location
c.   what occurred just before the collision
d.   how the collision actually occurred
e.   what happened immediately after the collision
f.   emergency room and initial treatment
g.   continued medical treatment
h.   present physical limitations and handicaps
i.   exhibits that highlight the main points

Although a straight chronological narrative is the usual way of organizing direct examinations, particularly of occurrence witnesses, it is not invariably the only way testimony can be presented.

Presenting the most dramatic or important testimony early in the direct examination, when the jury is most alert and its retentive power is greatest, can sometimes be the better approach. Thereafter, earlier events or substantiation of conclusions can be brought out.

As in most areas of trial work, there are no easy rules available. The trial lawyer must exercise his best judgment and decide, with each witness, the order that will most effectively present his testimony.

3.   Use introductory and transition questions

Since jurors know nothing about the witness when he first gets on the stand, introductory questions are useful because they let the jurors know what to expect.

Example:

> Q. Officer Rich, you were the first police officer at the Johnson house?
> A. Yes.
> Q. You arrested the defendant?
> A. Yes.
> Q. And you ran the lineup?
> A. Yes.
> Q. I'm going to ask you questions first about arriving at the Johnson house. When did you get there?

With these orienting questions, jurors know what to expect, and not to expect. Since the questions are preliminary, the fact that they are leading does not matter.

Transition questions are also useful devices; they operate like sign posts during direct examination. When the witness will testify on several topics, transition questions let the jurors know when the questioning on one topic is finished and the testimony on the next topic is to begin. They operate like chapter headings in a book, making the direct examination much easier to follow, and serving to periodically renew the jury's interest in the testimony.

Example:

> Q. Ms. Smith, I'm going to ask you first about your professional background.
> Q. Let's turn now to the day you bought the machinery from the ABC Manufacturing Company.
> Q. Ms. Smith, I'm going to ask you questions now about what happened during the afternoon of June 15.
> Q. I want to take you back in time, to June 15, 2000, at about 3:00 P.M.

4. Introduce witness and develop background

Whenever a witness takes the stand, three questions will go through the jurors' minds. "Who is she?" "Why is she here?" "Why should I believe her?" Hence, your first order of business on direct examination is to let the jury know why the witness is here, and why the witness should be believed.

The first two purposes, showing who the witness is and why she is here, can be quickly disclosed.

Example:

> Q. Ms. Smith, please introduce yourself to the jury.
> A. I'm Jennifer R. Smith.
> Q. Ms. Smith, you were standing near the collision when it happened?
> A. Yes.

This simple question orients the jury to the general nature of the testimony.

The third purpose, showing why the witness should be believed, can also be efficiently done. The jurors want to know a little bit about the witness so that they have an initial basis for assessing credibility. Jurors feel comfortable with people that are like themselves. Show them that the witness is a normal person; if she moved into the jurors' neighborhood they'd be happy about it. Hence, you should quickly develop some general background with a few short questions.

Example:

> Q.   Mrs. Jackson, where do you live?
> A.   At 3742 Tulip Street.
> Q.   For how long?
> A.   About 15 years.
> Q.   Does anyone live there with you?
> A.   Yes, my husband and two teen-aged boys.
> Q.   Do you work outside the home?
> A.   Yes, I'm an accountant for the order department at Jewel Foods.
> Q.   How long have you worked there?
> A.   Almost 8 years.

With a few simple questions you have shown that the witness is married, has children, is a long-time resident of the community, and holds a responsible job; all facts that show the witness is a mature, responsible person, much like the members of the jury.

Jurors also like to get a "feel" for the witness. Hence, consider having the witness talk about something, such as her job or family, that gets her to express herself. While perhaps not highly relevant to witness credibility, most courts will allow such additional background development if it is efficiently done and the witness is a party or key witness.

Example:

> Q.   Ms. Williams, what does your job as an expediter at Ajax Manufacturing involve?
> A.   Our manufacturing process involves an assembly line. My job is to make sure that all the raw materials needed for manufacturing a product are where they're supposed to be on the assembly line and when they're supposed to be there.
> Q.   What happens when the raw materials aren't there?
> A.   You've got about 100 people on the assembly line standing around doing nothing, because the whole line is shut down.

Example:

> Q.   Mr. Johnson, what made you decide to move here after all those years in New York City?

    A. I'd always dreamed of starting my own business. About five years ago, I had an opportunity to start an advertising company here, and I jumped at the chance. Best move I ever made in my life, and I've never looked back.

Simple background questions should be asked of all witnesses, because credibility is always an issue. Whether the background should be developed further depends on who the witness is and how important the witness testimony is. The plaintiff in a personal injury case, the defendant in a criminal case, and experts such as police officers should have appropriate additional background facts developed. Key witnesses need to be three-dimensional, so that the jurors can get a real sense of who they are. These types of witnesses are discussed in detail later in this chapter.

The third purpose, showing why the witness should be believed, also involves nonverbal communication. That communication begins the moment the witness first enters the courtroom and continues until the witness leaves the courtroom. Frequently these nonverbal cues are controlling and will dominate over the actual testimony. Jurors quickly have gut reactions about people, then look for facts to justify and support their reactions.

If jurors assess credibility with their eyes as much as their ears, what can you do about it? Physical attractiveness is an important component of trustworthiness. While we can't change the physical characteristics of witnesses, we can influence their attire and nonverbal conduct in the courtroom. First, decide what the witness should wear in court. Don't simply tell the witness to "dress appropriately," since he may have no idea what this means. Determine precisely what the attire will be, down to the accessories. For men, this usually means a suit or at least a conservative blazer jacket. For women, it usually means a conservative dress or skirt and jacket. Another possibility is for witnesses such as police officers, security guards, and store personnel to wear their work uniforms, particularly if their testimony is related to their work, since uniforms usually enhance credibility. Jewelry, aside from watches and rings, should be kept to a minimum. The clothes should make the witness feel comfortable and give the jury the sense that the witness is taking his appearance in court seriously.

Second, rehearse how the witness will enter the courtroom, how he will walk to the witness stand, where and how he will take the oath, how he will sit in the witness chair, and how he should maintain eye contact. Keep in mind that when you say "Your Honor, we call Mr. Johnson as our next witness," and the bailiff or someone else goes outside the courtroom to bring the witness in, all jurors' eyes are fixed on the courtroom doors. Those jurors will be watching and assessing the witness as he enters, walks to the witness stand, is sworn, and settles in. These steps may take a full minute, during which time the jurors are actively engaged in "sizing up" the witness before he ever says a word. This is frequently the critical moment where credibility is determined. The image each of your witnesses should project is someone who is prepared to testify, is confident in the courtroom, takes the oath seriously, and is comfortable in the witness role.

5. Set the scene

The chapter on opening statements stressed the importance of organizing openings so that the description of parties, the scene, and other significant information precedes the description of the occurrence. The jury should have a description of the scene before hearing about the action. The stage should be set before the action begins.

The same approach should normally be used in direct examinations, particularly of occurrence witnesses. All necessary preliminary descriptions and information should be elicited before reaching the action. Why? Action testimony is most effectively and dramatically presented if presented in an uninterrupted manner. Once into the action part of the direct examination, you should never have to interrupt to provide additional background. This is disruptive, and reduces the impact of the action testimony.

It is often better *not* to use exhibits such as photographs or diagrams during the action testimony. The exhibits also interrupt the action. The more dramatic the witness' testimony, the more you don't want exhibits to distract from emotional storytelling. Keep the spotlight on the witness. Save the exhibits for use after the witness has described what happened. The exhibits will then highlight the important points.

Direct examinations, particularly where occurrence testimony is involved, should create sensory images. The witness' responses should paint a picture that the jury can actually visualize. This should be your goal, even if you have photographs, diagrams, and charts to supplement the testimony. The direct examination should provide enough information so the jury will understand what happened and relive it through the witness. However, avoid unnecessary detail. Too much technical information clutters up the direct examination, detracts from your central points, and bores the jury. Exact distances, times, and other details are things the cross-examiner will usually stress in his search for inconsistencies. When you elicit such detail during the direct, you succeed only in giving the cross-examiner additional facts to use during the cross.

Jurors are accustomed to getting information in the 5- to 15-second "sound bites" they see on the evening news. Go from the general to the specific, much like a zoom lens will begin with a panoramic view, then zoom in on the details important to the story. This makes it easy for the jurors to translate the oral testimony into a mental image of the scene.

Example:

> *Q.* Mr. Benson, where did the crash happen?
> *A.* Right at the corner of Elm and Maple.
> *Q.* You know that intersection?
> *A.* Sure. I go through that intersection every day on the way to work.
> *Q.* What kind of neighborhood is the intersection in?
> *A.* It's mainly a neighborhood retail area. Both Elm and Maple have small retail stores, mostly single story buildings. Behind Elm and Main it's basically residential.

> *Q.* Tell us about Elm Street.
> *A.* Elm runs north and south. It has one lane of traffic in each direction, and parking on both sides of the street.
> *Q.* What about Maple Street?
> *A.* It runs east and west. It's pretty much like Elm — one traffic lane in each direction, with parking on both sides.
> *Q.* What time did the crash happen?
> *A.* A few minutes after 6:00 P.M.
> *Q.* What was the traffic like then?
> *A.* It was near the end of rush hour. The traffic was steady, but it wasn't backed up.
> *Q.* Tell us about the weather that evening.
> *A.* It was clear and dry.
> *Q.* Tell us about the lighting.
> *A.* It was getting dark, but the corner had street lights on, and there was more light coming from the stores. You could see without any trouble.
> *Q.* Where were you when you saw the crash?
> *A.* I was standing on the southwest corner, waiting to cross Elm Street.

Here you have painted a general description of the location of the accident and of the lighting conditions that existed at the time. More detailed elaboration is unnecessary. Let the cross-examiner ask exactly how wide Maple Street was, exactly how far the witness was from the location of the accident, and how far each streetlight was from the accident.

These details will not substantially add to your direct examination. Prepare your witness for those detail questions, of course, but committing your witness to those details on direct adds nothing except grist for the cross-examiner's mill.

On the other hand, in some situations you will want the witness to describe details. If the witness' testimony will be disputed by another witness, jurors will look for reasons to accept one witness' memory over another's. Here details can enhance credibility. Jurors usually believe that if one witness has a superior memory of surrounding details, that witness will remember the disputed event or transaction better than the other witness.

Example:

Plaintiff's version of a conversation with the defendant, in which the details of a contract were worked out, will differ from the defendant's version.

> *Q.* Ms. Fisk, when did you meet with the defendant to work out the details of your agreement?
> *A.* We met in his office at 410 Main Street, at 2:30 in the afternoon.
> *Q.* Was anyone else present?
> *A.* No, although his secretary walked in a few minutes after we started talking about the details of the deal. She brought in a single sheet of paper, gave it to him, then left without saying anything.

Q. Where did you sit?

A. We sat in a sitting area next to his desk. I sat on a small green couch, and he rolled his desk chair so that it was facing me, on the other side of a small coffee table.

Q. Were the blueprints there?

A. Sure, they were rolled up and tied with a string, lying on the coffee table.

In this situation, having the plaintiff describe surrounding details of the meeting will subconsciously enhance her credibility, because she remembers the details so clearly. This can be used effectively during closing arguments, when you will argue that the plaintiff's memory of the meeting is better, and therefore more believable, than the defendant's. If plaintiff remembers the details of the scene so well, it stands to reason that she also remembers the details of the conversation.

Many scene descriptions use compass directions — north, south, east, and west — to orient the jurors to the location. This usually works well when the scene involves streets or open areas. Another common way to describe scenes is from the point of view of the witness, using the witness' orientation. This works well for smaller areas such as buildings and rooms, where compass directions are unimportant. This approach gets the jurors to "see" the scene from a particular perspective.

Example:

The scene is a small neighborhood bar where the defendant shot the victim following an argument. The witness is a patron who had just entered the bar as the argument began.

Q. Describe O'Toole's Tavern.

A. It's a small neighborhood bar in an old two-story brick building on Main Street.

Q. What does the front look like?

A. It's got a door in the middle, with big glass picture windows on either side of the door.

Q. When you walk through the door, what do you see?

A. When you walk in, you're in the front room. The bar counter is along the left wall. The counter has maybe seven or eight bar stools for customers. Along the right wall there are three small booths. If you go straight back past the counter and booths, there's a back room with a pool table and more booths. In the left rear, past the bar, that's where the kitchen is.

Q. What's the lighting like inside O'Toole's Tavern?

A. It's typical bar lighting. There are lights over the bar, lights over each of the booths, and lights from several beer signs around the room. You can see what's going on without any difficulty.

Notice that the scene description includes the lighting, which is important to the reliability of the eyewitness testimony.

6.   Recreate the action

Effective direct examinations of occurrence witnesses recreate the action so that the jurors become involved and experience the event through the witness. Doing this effectively is difficult and takes time to organize. There are four basic considerations involved in recreating the action: point of view, pace, sensory language, and present tense. Each needs to be considered whenever you are preparing the direct examination of an occurrence witness.

a.   Point of view

The first task is to organize the direct exam so that the jury "sees" the action from an advantageous point of view. This usually will be through the eyes of the witness.

Example:

Plaintiff in a collision case usually will want the jury to see the collision from the plaintiff's point of view. Put the jurors in the car with the plaintiff, so they see the collision through the plaintiff's eyes.

Q.   Mr. Berg, let's see what you see as you're going southbound on Main Street. As you look out your windshield, what do you see in your lane of traffic in front of you?
A.   I see a string of cars in front of me, going about 20 mph.
Q.   What do you see in your rear-view mirror?
A.   The same thing. There's a string of cars behind me.
Q.   What do you see in the northbound lane?
A.   There's no oncoming traffic. I can see that there's a car in the northbound lane, stopped in the intersection at Elm, trying to make a left turn, and there are cars behind it.

This kind of testimony puts the jury in the back seat of the car, seeing what the plaintiff sees, and is an effective way to get the jurors to picture the action from your point of view.

b.   Pace

Jurors also want to get a "feel" of what happened, and this is influenced by pace. Pace involves controlling the speed of the examination. This is particularly important where occurrence testimony is concerned. Pace, fortunately, can be easily controlled by the examiner, simply by eliciting the witness' testimony in small segments at the most advantageous rate.

Remember that the jury, unlike you and the witness, has never heard the testimony before. Its ability to receive, digest, and comprehend is limited. The critical part of most automobile collisions, for instance, will take place in a few seconds. In such a situation pace can be controlled to *slow down* the action. You may want to present the occurrence frame-by-frame, much like a slow-motion or stop-action movie. Only by slowing down the action will the jury be able to picture how the collision actually happened.

Example:

Plaintiff in some collision cases will want to slow down the action to demonstrate that he was exercising due care under the circumstances.

Q. As you approached the intersection of Elm and Maple, did you see any traffic?
A. No, not at that time.
Q. What was your speed at that time?
A. About 30 mph.
Q. As you got near the intersection, what did you do?
A. I slowed down and looked left and right.
Q. Where was your car when you first saw the other car?
A. I was entering the intersection.
Q. How fast were you driving then?
A. About 25 mph.
Q. Where was the other car then?
A. It was coming from my left, going towards the intersection.
Q. How fast was he going?
A. I couldn't tell.
Q. What did you do next?
A. I kept going through the intersection.
Q. Did you see the other car again?
A. Yes.
Q. When?
A. When I was in the middle of the intersection.
Q. How fast were you going then?
A. About 25 mph.
Q. At that time, could you estimate the other car's speed?
A. Yes.
Q. What was it?
A. Around 30 to 35 mph.
Q. Where was the car?
A. It was coming right at me, in the intersection.
Q. How far from your car was his?
A. Around 15 feet.
Q. What did you do?
A. I stepped on my brakes and turned my wheel.
Q. What happened next?
A. His car rammed mine, right on my door.
Q. What part of the intersection was the collision in?
A. Almost exactly in the middle of it.
Q. What part of his car struck what part of yours?
A. His left front bumper struck the left rear side of my car.
Q. Where did the cars end up?

    A.   My car stopped near the southeast corner of the intersection. His car was still stuck to the rear left side of my car, perpendicular to it.

In the above example, you have slowed down the action by having the witness describe four separate segments of the occurrence: (a) approaching the intersection, (b) just before the collision, (c) the collision itself, and (d) where the cars stopped. By having the witness describe each sequence, you have created a slow-motion word picture of what actually took very few seconds. The jury is able to follow the testimony, understand it, and form a picture of the collision. In addition, you have created an impression that the driver was totally alert as he drove to the intersection and could not possibly have caused the collision.

    In some situations you will want to convey the impression that an event happened very quickly, unexpectedly, without time to deliberate or react. In those situations you will want the pace *speeded up.*

Example (defendant, in the above example):

    Q.   Mr. Jones, as you entered the intersection of Elm and Maple, did you see any other traffic?
    A.   No.
    Q.   How fast were you going?
    A.   Around 30 mph.
    Q.   What's the next thing you did?
    A.   I kept going straight ahead through the intersection.
    Q.   What happened next?
    A.   Well, I was about in the middle of the intersection when suddenly another car flashed in front of me, coming from my right. Before I even had a chance to hit my brakes, our cars hit.

By delivering the critical testimony quickly, you create a sense of how unexpectedly and quickly the accident occurred. The impression the jury gets from this examination, the one you want to convey, is that the accident was inevitable.

    In every witness' testimony, therefore, you must decide if you want to expand, shorten, or leave alone the pace of your witness' description of the occurrence in the way you want the jury to view it, and frame your direct examination questions accordingly.

    c. Sensory language

    Effective witness testimony uses simple, sensory, language. Language needs to be simple, so all the jurors will understand it. Language needs to be sensory, so that it becomes vivid and memorable for the jurors. Experienced trial lawyers understand that developing an effective "trial vocabulary" with your witnesses is an essential part of effective direct examinations.

    First, keeping direct examinations simple involves choosing simple words and phrases for your questions and training witnesses to use simple words and phrases in answering your questions. Psychological studies have repeatedly demonstrated that how a question is phrased has a significant impact on how it is answered. Word choice, that is, affects the answer. Asking a witness "how fast" a car was traveling, rather than "how slowly," will invariably get a greater speed from the witness. Terms such as "smash" and "collided" convey different impressions than "struck" or "hit." In each case, therefore, you must decide in advance what words and phrases you want to employ to create advantageous impressions, then use them consistently during your examinations of witnesses and the other phases of the trial.

Eliminate "police talk" and other jargon from your vocabulary, as well as your witnesses'. Consider the following:

Example:

When did you exit from your vehicle?	vs.	*When did you get out of your car?*
Did you have an occasion to converse with him?	vs.	*Did you ever talk to him?*
How long have you been so employed?	vs.	*How many years have you been a bricklayer?*
Subsequent to your arrest, what, if anything, happened?	vs.	*What happened after they arrested you?*

The phrasing in the right column is obviously preferable. It is a clear, simple, and understandable way of asking a question. Communications research has shown that jurors find simple but grammatically correct English more persuasive than "police talk" and other stilted or unnecessarily complex speech, both from lawyers and witnesses.

Second, train your witnesses to use sensory language. Vivid words have impact, and are remembered better. However, most witnesses do not instinctively use sensory language, and an important part of developing an effective direct examination is helping a witness find his own sensory vocabulary. For instance, when asked "what happened to you after the crash?" most witnesses will state "I was hurt" or "I hurt my arm." When you are preparing the witness for testifying, ask him sensory questions: "When you hurt your arm, how did you know it was hurt?" "What did your arm look like?" "What did your arm feel like?" "What were you thinking at the time?" When you ask sensory questions, the witness will naturally respond with sensory answers, which will give the jurors a better, more vivid picture of what really happened.

Example:

Q. Ms. Wilson, just before the impact, what were you doing?
A. I just remember screaming as I saw the other car go through the red light.

Q. And then?

A. There was a huge crash. I was thrown into the steering wheel. I could hear the crunch of the metal and the tinkling of the glass.

Q. What happened to you?

A. The force of the crash threw me forward, and my arm got caught up in the steering wheel, and it snapped.

Q. What did you hear?

A. I heard the bone break. It was kind of a snapping sound.

Q. What did you see?

A. My arm was bent at a crazy angle at the elbow. It was bent back, the way it's not supposed to bend.

Q. What did you feel?

A. I felt an immediate hot shooting pain, something like being touched by a fireplace poker, running up my arm, and it kept getting worse.

Q. What did you do?

A. I remember starting to cry, and then I passed out.

And so on. Sensory language is vivid, and helps the jury visualize what happened. Every witness has a natural vocabulary that can make testimony come alive. Your job as a trial lawyer is to find and use it.

d. *Present tense*

Using the present tense, in both the lawyer's questions and the witness' answers, is an effective technique to recreate a dramatic event. It gives the jurors an opportunity to relive the event, through the witness' eyes, and become emotionally involved in the story.

Example:

Q. Mr. Berg, let's turn now to the collision itself. When you look at the light at Main and Elm, what color is it?

A. It's green, and then it turns yellow when I'm 50 feet away.

Q. What do you do?

A. I take my foot off the gas and keep rolling toward the intersection.

Q. What happens as you get near the crosswalk?

A. Suddenly the car facing me on Main makes a quick left turn, right in front of me.

Q. What do you do?

A. I slam on the brakes, but it's too late.

And so on. Recreating an event, so that the jury becomes emotionally involved, and relives the event through the witness' senses and feelings, is a difficult task, and usually involves all four techniques: point of view, pace, sensory language, and present tense. When done well, it can create magical moments in the courtroom.

7. Use nonleading questions

Basic to the rules surrounding direct examinations is the general prohibition against leading witnesses. Inexperienced lawyers usually lead too much on direct. Although it is a rule of evidence with, of course, certain exceptions, it is also a rule of persuasion. By suggesting the answer in your question, you diminish the impact of having the witness volunteer the facts himself. Jurors will wonder if the witness would have given that answer if the lawyer had not practically put it in the witness' mouth. If the witness gives only "yes" and "no" answers, the jury has no adequate way of assessing his credibility. A cardinal rule on direct examination is that the lawyer should never do anything that will detract from his witness or diminish the impact of his witness' testimony. Leading, suggestive questions do exactly that.

Example:

What kinds of streets are at the intersection?	vs.	*The streets at the intersection are both two lanes, aren't they?*
Please describe what the man looked like.	vs.	*Was the man six feet tall and about 25 years old?*
What happened after he announced a robbery?	vs.	*Did the man take the wallet from your purse after announcing a robbery?*

The examples in the left column are obviously the nonleading ones. These don't put words in the witness' mouth, and are much more effective before the jury.

On the other hand, preliminary matters that are not in dispute can often be brought out more smoothly and effectively by leading. This will get you to the important testimony more quickly, before the jury gets bored, and is usually permitted under FRE 611.

Example:

> Q. Ms. Wilson, you were on the corner of Main and Elm Streets when the collision happened, right?
> A. Yes.
> Q. Let's talk about what you saw.

Example:

> Q. Mr. Johnson, you were present on June 30, 2000, when the contract was signed?
> A. That's right.
> Q. Let's begin with who was present when the contract was signed.

Effective direct examinations are best achieved by using open-ended questions that elicit descriptive responses. This serves two functions. First, such questions let the witness tell the story and reveal the important evidence himself. Second, they minimize the presence of the lawyer. Remember that during direct examinations the witness should be the center of attention. Your questions should merely guide the witness from one area to another as he testifies, and break up the testimony into digestible capsules.

Once you have directed the witness to a certain area, your questions can become short, open-ended, and nonleading, so that the witness does the talking and becomes the center of attention. These questions simply break up the testimony into short, digestible pieces that the jurors can quickly absorb.

Example:

    Q. What happened (next)?
    Q. What did you see (next)?
    Q. What did you hear (next)?
    Q. What did you (he, she, they) do (next)?

On the other hand, these kinds of questions have a downside: They can become monotonous, and they give up control. To avoid monotony, periodically mix the short, open-ended questions with more focused questions. Ask explanatory and follow-up questions where appropriate.

Example:

    Q. What did the defendant do?
    A. He stuck a gun in my face and said: "give me the money."
    Q. What did you do then?
    A. I handed over my wallet!
    Q. Mr. Becker, what exactly did the defendant take from you?
    A. He took about $80 in cash, my credit cards, my driver's license, and all the other identification cards I keep in my wallet.

When the witness gives a particularly good or important answer, consider using the answer as part of the next question. Remember, however, that this is effective only when sparingly used.

Example:

    Q. What were the exact words he used?
    A. He said: "Give it up, sucker."
    Q. After the defendant said: "give it up, sucker," what did you do?

Short, open-ended questions necessarily give up control over the witness. That's why training witnesses to give 5- to 15-second sound bites, regardless of the question, is so important for direct examinations. This gives the jurors information in easily digestible bites.

Some witnesses, however, ramble on and simply like to talk, and long narrative answers are both objectionable and unpersuasive. For them, more focused questions will be necessary. For example, instead of asking "What happened next?" ask "What's the first thing you did?" or "What's the first thing you saw?" Instead of asking "What did you do?" ask "What was your first reaction?" These kinds of focused questions ask the witness to give a smaller bit of information, and are useful to control the rambling witness.

Effective direct examinations mix introductory and transition questions, focused nonleading questions, and open-ended questions to effectively guide the witness and control the pace, detail, and images of the examination.

8.   Have the witness explain

Many times a witness will say something that makes no sense, is unclear, or uses a technical term or phrase. Since your overall purpose is to give the jury a clear understanding of the events involved, any confusion should be clarified immediately. Put yourself in the jury's shoes. If the jury looks confused or wants an explanation, you must get it for them. This, however, must be done without embarrassing or demeaning the jury. When seeking additional details or explanations, use narrowly phrased questions that go directly to the problem area.

Examples:

> Q.   I'm sorry, Mr. Doc, I didn't follow you there. Where were you
>   standing when you actually saw the collision?
> Q.   When you saw him later, what time was that?
> Q.   Mr. Johnson, you used the term "ER." What does "ER" stand for?

The jury will appreciate your immediately having something important clarified or explained, without having suggested that they didn't understand it the first time.

9.   Volunteer weaknesses

Conventional wisdom has it that you should volunteer weaknesses during the direct examination. In this way, it is believed, you will "draw the sting" out of the weakness by voluntarily disclosing it before the cross-examiner can effectively use it. Volunteer before you are exposed. This protects both the witness' and lawyer's credibility.

While this conventional wisdom is useful as a general proposition, its intelligent application to any given witness is often difficult. How damaging is the weakness? Does your opponent know about it? Will this weakness become apparent during the course of the direct examination? Can you gracefully volunteer the weakness? Does your opponent have trial skills that can effectively expose the weakness during the cross-examination? These are the kinds of considerations that must be evaluated and weighed before deciding whether to volunteer the weakness during the direct examination. Remember, however, that direct examinations should be positive and forceful. Volunteering weaknesses necessarily works against this goal. Consequently, unless the weakness is significant, and other considerations point to volunteering it, the weakness might better remain undisclosed.

When you do decide to volunteer a weakness, it is usually best to bury it in the middle of the direct examination and make it part of the story. Remember that jurors, like people in general, remember best what they hear first and last. (These are the general principles of "primacy" and "recency.") Accordingly, it is usually best to start the examination on a positive note, disclose the unfavorable information afterwards, and end on another positive point. For example, suppose the plaintiff in a personal injury case had been drinking before the crash happened. The direct examination could introduce the plaintiff's background, describe the scene, bring out that the plaintiff had drunk two beers after work, establish that his driving was in no way impaired, and then describe how the collision happened.

The weakness will have less impact when volunteered after the witness has made an initial good impression. Studies have shown that people are reluctant to change their initial impressions when confronted by unfavorable facts.

10.   Use exhibits to highlight and summarize facts

Exhibits should be used during the direct examination to highlight the central facts of your case and explain important details to the jury. The preferable time to use exhibits is after the witness has substantially completed his oral testimony. This is particularly true of parties and key eyewitnesses in personal injury and criminal cases, who have dramatic stories to tell. In this way the exhibit will not interrupt or detract from the oral testimony. Using exhibits after the action testimony is usually an effective way to repeat and emphasize the important facts brought out by the witness. For example, suppose that a key eyewitness is the plaintiff's first witness in a personal injury case. The direct examination could bring out the witness's background, describe the scene, and then describe what happened. After this testimony is brought out, introduce the diagrams and photographs that corroborate and highlight the testimony. The effective use of exhibits at trial is discussed in §6.4.

11.   Listen to the answers

While attentiveness is usually thought of as applying to cross-examinations, it has equal application to direct examinations. Although your position during direct examinations should be behind the jury if possible, jurors will from time to time look at you, as well as everyone else in the courtroom. Accordingly, appear interested in the witness' answers. Maintain eye contact with him. Nod your head to let him know that you understand his answers and that everything is going well. You can hardly expect the jury to hang on the witness' words if you look and sound bored. Appearing interested has other consequences. It carries over to and infects the witness. It eliminates any suggestion that the direct has been scripted in advance. Finally, it helps you avoid making mistakes and makes you alert to the unexpected answers that inevitably appear.

12.   Lawyer's position

In many jurisdictions, lawyers are permitted to walk around the courtroom and place themselves in the most strategic locations during examinations. In others, particularly in federal courts, the lawyers are required to conduct their examinations from a lectern or counsel table. Where court rules permit, however, you should use the available arena to the fullest possible extent. This means, during direct examinations, that the witness' contact with the jury is maximized while yours is minimized. This is best achieved by conducting your examination near the far end of the jury box.

Example:

In the following schematic diagram of a courtroom, you can effectively conduct the direct examinations near the position marked "X."

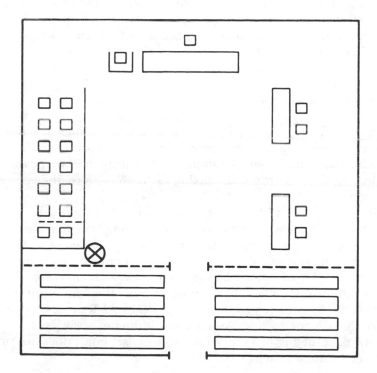

Doing this has several immediate benefits:

a.   It removes you from the jury's line of sight to the witness, thereby eliminating a visual distraction.
b.   It allows you to use written notes for the examination without the jury being actively aware of it.
c.   It forces the witness to speak up, since he will subconsciously talk loudly enough for you to hear him, thereby ensuring that every juror will easily hear his testimony.
d.   It forces the witness to look at the jurors, thereby maintaining critical eye contact with them.
e.   Perhaps most importantly, it allows you to watch the jurors as they listen to the witness, giving you instant feedback. Are they listening? Bored? Confused? Restless? Watch the jurors and be ready to shift gears in response to the nonverbal messages the jurors are sending.

Consider letting the jurors know, with your first witness, why you are standing where you are.

Example:

Q.   Ms. Franklin, I'm going to ask you questions from back here. Please keep your voice up so we can all hear you easily.

Some believe, however, that jurors find it important to watch, as well as hear, the interaction between lawyer and witness. If this is a concern, you might begin the examination by standing closer to the witness, in a place visible to the jury, then slowly move back to the end of the jury box as the jurors understand that the witness is the main attraction on whom they should focus their attention.

13.   Prepare the witness

Preparing a witness to testify involves at least three things: the nonverbal communication, the actual testimony, and potential problems. Some non-verbal communication considerations — trial attire, and demeanor when first entering the courtroom and taking the oath — were discussed earlier (see §5.2).

When you meet with a witness to prepare that witness for testifying during trial, tell the witness why you are meeting. Let the witness know that it is entirely proper for lawyers to meet with witnesses to determine what their testimony will be, and to prepare them for testifying. Let the witness know that the other lawyers may cross-examine him about this meeting, unless it is with a client, in which case the communications are protected by the attorney-client privilege. (Model Rule 3.4(b) prohibits improperly influencing a witness, such as inducing a witness to color his testimony or testifying in a way known to be false, but it does not prohibit preparing a witness to testify.)

During the meeting, review the facts the witness can testify about, and having the witness review all his earlier statements and testimony. Review the organization of the planned direct and why you are organizing it this way. Practice the planned direct with the witness, simulating the courtroom environment. Review potential problems, such as refreshing recollection, the procedure for handling exhibits and their foundations, and impeachment with prior inconsistent statements. Decide explicitly how the witness should dress for court. Review the nonverbal communication that occurs when the witness walks into the courtroom, takes the oath, and sits down in the witness seat. Review the importance of eye contact with the jurors, and maintaining a positive, friendly demeanor at all times. When you have done this, repeat and practice some more.

Lawyers usually give witnesses standard advice on testifying. Some do it in person, others put it in writing, and still others use commercially available videotapes. That advice should always include the following:

- Take your time in answering questions.
- Make sure you understand the question; if you don't, say so.
- Use plain English.
- Keep your answers simple; don't volunteer facts.
- Don't guess; if you don't know or don't remember, say so.
- Be polite and patient at all times.
- Above all, always tell the complete truth.

Inexperienced lawyers frequently encounter two recurring problems. First, they prepare the witness for testifying, yet are surprised and disappointed when the planned examination fails in the courtroom. Often this happens because the lawyer has not sufficiently practiced the direct examination with the witness. You need to ask the actual questions you will ask in the courtroom, and see how the witness actually answers them. You need to do this until the witness feels comfortable with your questions and you feel comfortable with the way the witness answers them. If the witness is important, consider taking her to the courtroom where the trial will be held, and practice the direct examination in that or another empty courtroom. Doing this will help reduce the stress that all witnesses experience when they testify.

Second, the witness sometimes sounds flat and rehearsed. This can be caused by too much preparation, although that is rarely the cause. A more common reason is that inexperienced lawyers often write out their questions and the witness' expected answers, and use that as a script for the direct examination. This rarely works well. There are ways of organizing your direct examination notes into topic checklists that will keep this from happening. These are discussed in Chapter XI.

Another reason is that the lawyer asking the questions sounds flat, causing the witness to sound the same. Remember that direct examination is a conversation between lawyer and witness in which the jurors are silent participants, and that real conversations sound fresh and have a certain energy level. In addition, the witness looks for subtle signs of approval, some indication that the testimony is going well. The lawyer needs to give the witness nonverbal feedback, using facial gestures and head nods, to indicate that all is well. The lawyer also needs to use some movement, such as hand gestures. Witnesses tend to imitate the questioner. If the lawyer is forceful and confident, and uses reinforcing movement and gestures, the witness will probably do the same, making the witness appear more forceful and confident as well.

§5.3.   *Occurrence witnesses*

The most common type of witness in trials is the occurrence witness. Also call a fact witness or percipient witness, an occurrence witness is simply any witness with first-hand knowledge who saw, heard, or did anything relevant to the case. Most trials involve either personal injury or criminal cases in which one event, usually an accident or a crime, forms the core of the case. Since these cases involve events, the eyewitnesses will be critical witnesses at trial. How persuasively these witnesses testify will in large measure determine the outcome of the trial. Accordingly, the ability to forcefully and clearly present an occurrence witness at trial is an essential skill every trial lawyer must possess.

Presenting occurrence witnesses effectively requires two skills: the testimony must be organized, and it must be dramatized, humanized, and visualized.

First, organize. The direct examination must be simply and logically organized. A common and effective organization is:

1.   introduce witness and background
2.   set the scene
3.   recreate the action
4.   introduce exhibits to highlight the testimony

There must be enough witness background so the jury can answer the three basic questions it always asks: Who is this witness? Why is he here? Why should I believe him? Witnesses who have educated themselves, hold responsible jobs, are stable residents of the community, and are successfully raising a family will usually be seen as credible witnesses. While courts differ in how much witness background they will allow (on the issue of witness credibility), most courts permit more extensive background for plaintiffs in personal injury cases and defendants in criminal cases.

The scene ordinarily should be described next, because the jury needs to be able to visualize the place where the action happened. Using the witness to describe the scene orally first does two things: it keeps the jury's attention focused on the witness, and it enhances the witness's credibility. (If the witness is good at describing the scene, it stands to reason that he will also be good in describing what happened.) The jury will be able to visualize the scene more easily if the testimony goes from the general to the specific. For example, if the testimony involves an accident at an intersection, have the witness describe the general neighborhood first, then the streets, then the traffic controls, much like a camera that starts with a wide angle shot, then zooms in on the specific details that are important.

The action description should come next. Once the scene has been described, the action — what happened — can then be brought out in an uninterrupted way. The testimony should be organized so that the witness recreates with sensory language what happened, so that the jury can relive the event through that witness.

Finally, exhibits can be introduced to highlight and summarize the key facts. Remember that some jurors are more responsive to emotional evidence, and oral testimony that is dramatic will have more impact on them. Other jurors are more responsive to logical evidence, and exhibits such as diagrams, charts, and photographs that explain things will have more impact for them. Presenting the evidence first orally, then using exhibits afterwards, reaches both kinds of jurors and allows you to highlight and summarize the key points without running afoul of the rule against repetitive testimony.

The second skill needed to effectively present occurrence witnesses is the ability to dramatize, humanize, and visualize. Jurors expect the testimony to be interesting, hopefully even dramatic. Jurors are interested in the people, not the problem, so the testimony should focus on the key people, not the technical details. And jurors like the testimony to be visual, which helps them relate to the case and the people involved, and to relive the event and experience it vicariously. In short, get the jurors involved.

How do you do this? Remember that jurors are a product of their environment. This is the age of television, and jurors expect a certain energy level from witnesses and lawyers and drama in the presentation of the case. They want to be shown, not told, what happened, both through vivid testimony and attractive supporting exhibits. They want to know about the people involved, and what motivated them to do what they did. They want to experience not only what the witnesses saw, heard, and did, but also the atmosphere and intensity of feelings that existed during the event. And they want to get it all effortlessly and efficiently.

Therefore, train your witnesses to give "visual sound bites" — answers that use sensory language, create memorable images in 5 to 15 seconds, focus on the people, and move the story forward. A direct examination that achieves these objectives, that clearly recreates the event for the jury to experience, may be the most difficult yet most rewarding achievement a trial lawyer can attain.

Types of occurrence witnesses are numerous, and it would achieve little to attempt to illustrate all representative types. Instead, this section will present the direct examinations of a few common types of occurrence witnesses in question-and-answer form, with an accompanying explanation showing why the questions were asked and framed as they were. When the reasoning underlying these direct examinations is understood, that knowledge can be applied equally well to any type of occurrence witness.

1. Example — direct examinations in a civil case

In the following civil case, plaintiff James Smith has filed suit against defendant Frank Jones, alleging that he was injured when Jones negligently drove into him as he was walking across the street at the intersection at Elm and Maple Streets on December 13, 2000. Jones has denied liability, claiming that he had the right of way and that Smith walked against the light. Hence, at trial the central issues are whether the defendant was negligent and whether the plaintiff was contributorily negligent.

Following are the direct examinations of the plaintiff and an eyewitness to the collision, two common types of witnesses in personal injury cases.

Example (victim in an automobile collision case):

Plaintiff James Smith — direct examination

Q. Mr. Smith, please tell us your full name.

A. I'm James P. Smith.

Q. Where do you live?

A. At 1650 N. Maple.

Q. How long have you lived there?

A. For 7 years.

Q. Where are you from originally?

A. I've lived in Chicago all my life, 36 years.

Q. Tell us about your family.

A. There's my wife, Judy, and our two daughters, Betsy and Becky.

Q. How old are your daughters?

A. Well, Betsy's 5 and Becky is 3.

Q. Is your wife employed outside your home?

A. Not right now, but she used to be a school teacher before the kids came.

Q. What kind of work do you do?

A. I'm also a school teacher.

Q. What school do you teach at?

A. At Central School, on Harrison Street.

Q. How long have you been at Central?

A. Eight years.

Q. What grades do you teach?

A. I've always taught eighth- and ninth-grade math.

Q. Do you have any other jobs?

A. During the school year I've coached the junior high boys' basketball team. During the summer I'm a counselor at Camp Thatcher, a co-ed day camp for children.

Q. How long have you been doing these jobs?

A. Ever since I started teaching.

Q. Mr. Smith, where did you receive your basic schooling?

A. I attended Chicago public schools.

Q. After that, where did you go to college?

(Background)

This is a traditional beginning. These are the usual background questions. They enhance his credibility as a witness by showing him to be a normal man, and allow him to relax and get used to testifying in the courtroom environment. There is no need for an introductory statement, since the jury already knows he is the plaintiff.

Notice that the witness gives short, factual answers to the background questions. Answers that are too flowery and obviously self-serving can backfire before a jury.

A. First I attended the University of Illinois and received a bachelor's degree in 1981. I then continued my studies in mathematics at Northwestern and received a master's degree in 1982.

Q. Mr. Smith, let's turn now to where the collision happened. Are you familiar with the intersection of Elm and Maple Streets?

A transition question.

A. Yes, I am.

Q. How many times have you been there?

(Scene)

A. I've been there thousands of times. It's just down the street from my house.

The description of the intersection is important in this case, so it should be described clearly, even if you have photographs and charts to supplement the intersection testimony. The witness' ability to describe the intersection accurately will enhance his credibility.

Q. What's the neighborhood around Elm and Maple like?

A. It's a residential area, with single family homes.

Q. Which directions do Elm and Maple go?

A. Elm is an east-west street. Maple runs north and south.

Q. How many lanes do they have?

A. Elm has four traffic lanes as well as parking lanes on both sides of the street. Maple has two lanes of traffic and parking on both sides.

The description will often include:
a. direction of streets
b. size of streets
c. lane markers
d. traffic lights
e. pedestrian lights and crosswalks
f. stop lines

Q. Does the intersection have any traffic controls?

A. Yes, it has traffic lights.

Q. Where are those located?

A. There are lights on poles on each corner. These include traffic signals and pedestrian lights.

Q. Does the intersection have other markings or controls?

A. Yes, sir.

Q. How are they marked?

A. The traffic lanes are marked with white dotted lines. There are four pedestrian crosswalks marked with solid white lines, and white stop lines in front of the crosswalks.

Q. Let's talk now about the collision on December 13, 2000. What time were you hit?

Another transition question.

A. It was at approximately 12:30 P.M.

Q. What was the weather like at that time?

The description should also include:

A. It was clear and dry.

a. weather

Q. What were the traffic conditions like?

b. road surface conditions

A. It was fairly busy. There were lots of cars as well as pedestrians.

c. traffic conditions

Q. What were you doing at that time?

A. I was walking on the sidewalk, northbound, on the east side of Maple, going toward Elm.

Q. Did you reach Elm?

A. Yes, I did.

Q. As you reached Elm, for which streets were the lights green?

A. They were green for Elm Street traffic.

Q. What did you do?

A. I stopped and waited for the lights to change.

Q. Were there any other pedestrians waiting for lights?

A. Not at my corner. I think there were people waiting on the others.

Q. Were there any cars waiting for the light?

A. There were cars on Maple Street.

Q. What happened next?

A. I stood at the corner, looking north at the traffic lights on the northeast corner. The light for Maple turned green and the walk-light for pedestrian traffic across Elm turned to "walk."

Q. What did you do?

A. I stepped off the curb and started walking on the crosswalk across Elm.

Q. What happened next?

A. I took three or four steps off the curb and was walking in the cross-walk when I was smacked from behind by a car. I remember the car crashing into my left leg, and being thrown into the street. I remember hearing brakes screeching after I was hit.

Q. Mr. Smith, what is the first thing you noticed about yourself?

A. All I can remember is a stinging, burning kind of pain coming from my left knee. I remember I couldn't move my leg. My shoulder was throbbing where I had landed on it and there were shooting pains going up my arm.

Q. Where were you at this time?

A. I was more or less facedown in the street.

Q. What happened next?

A. Several people ran to me and told me not to move.

Q. Then what happened?

A. I stayed on the street for I don't know how long, and finally an ambulance came. They put a stretcher next to me and they slowly

---

The background description is now completed. It is time to begin the action part of the testimony.

(Action)

The action can now begin without the interruption of further description. This makes the action flow with sufficient pace.

Show due care and caution, and absence of contributory negligence.
Notice how short the questions have become. They don't detract from the witness, particularly during the critical part of the testimony.
Notice also that the pace of the testimony has quickened. Good pace makes the testimony come alive. This is the worst place to bore the jury with testimony that drags on. Developing the victim's condition immediately after the collision is important to the issue of damages.

(Exhibits)

If you are going to use exhibits — diagrams

eased me on the stretcher. They then put me in the ambulance and took me to the Memorial Hospital emergency room.

Q. On the way to the hospital, how did you feel?

A. Not very well. I kept having these shooting, stinging pains going up and down my left leg and began feeling very dizzy and nauseated.

Q. What happened when you reached the Memorial Hospital emergency room?

A. The ambulance attendants took me out of the ambulance and wheeled me into one of the emergency rooms.

Q. What happened there?

A. Some nurses cut off my trouser leg, others were attaching a tube to my arm and drawing blood. They moved a portable X-ray unit to my table and started taking X rays. A doctor came over and talked to me, and gave me a shot of anesthesia and that's the last thing I remember.

Q. Mr. Smith, what is the next thing you can remember happening?

A. Next thing I remember is waking up in a hospital room.

Q. What is the first thing you noticed about yourself?

A. Well, I remember feeling very groggy and heavy. I had this dull throbbing, pulsating kind of pain in my left leg. I looked down at my leg and saw that they had applied a cast from my left toe that reached up to my crotch.

Q. How long did you remain at Memorial Hospital?

A. About five days.

Q. What did you do during those five days?

A. Nothing, really. I just lay on my back, and they had my left leg up on a pile of pillows to reduce the swelling.

Q. During those five days, how did you feel?

A. Well, I started getting very stiff and sore because I was always lying on my back. I had trouble sleeping in that position. I could not get up for anything. I had to use a bedpan for bowel movements. The pain in my leg changed to a dull throbbing ache.

and photos — this is a good place with this witness, the plaintiff in a personal injury case. Another choice is at the end of the examination.

(Damages)

The testimony should review the medical treatment and recovery, since pain and suffering will be a substantial part of any verdict in this case.

    a. immediate treatment in hospital

    b. postoperative period in hospital

Notice that the pace has slowed down, since the immediate trauma of the collision and emergency-room treatment has passed.

Q. Mr. Smith, let's talk now about your condition after you left the hospital. First, how did you get home?

Another transition question.

A. The attendants wheeled me outside in a wheelchair with my foot elevated. They helped me get into my car, on the back seat, and helped me put my leg on the seat. My wife drove me home. When I got home I was carried into the house, and put to bed, and again put my left leg as high as I could.

c. initial recovery period at home

Q. How long did you remain in bed at home?

A. About two more weeks.

Q. After that two-week period were you able to do anything else?

A. I started to get up for a few minutes at a time, using metal crutches. Usually I went to the bathroom or got up to stretch for a few minutes.

Q. Did you notice anything about your leg during those times?

A. Yes. Every time I would get up and use the crutches the throbbing in my leg would get a lot worse. The leg would start swelling and feel very warm.

Q. What did you do when that happened?

A. I would have to lie down and raise my leg again.

Q. After going home, did you see the doctor again?

A. Well, I saw Dr. Bartells at the hospital about six weeks later. He removed the cast and put on another one.

d. continued medical treatment

Q. What kind of cast was this one?

A. It was like the first one. It was from my ankle up to my crotch.

Q. How long did you have that second cast on?

A. About eight more weeks.

Q. During that period of time, what was the condition of your leg?

A. The pain and throbbing were getting better, except if I kept my leg down for any period of time. Then I would have to put the leg up again.

Q. When was the next time you saw Dr. Bartells?

A. About eight weeks later I went back to his office. Dr. Bartells removed the second cast and took more X rays. He then wrapped my knee and calf with an elastic bandage.

Q.   What did you notice about your leg after the cast was removed?

A.   The first thing I noticed was how skinny it was. My left thigh was maybe half the size of the right one. In addition, I could only move my knee maybe three or four inches in either direction.

Q.   What happened when you tried to bend your knee?

A.   It just wouldn't bend much and hurt when I tried to bend it.

Q.   Could you walk without crutches?

A.   No, I didn't start putting weight on the leg for another month.

Q.   Let's talk about the therapy for your leg. What did that involve?

A.   I had to apply heat from hot water bottles and wet towels to the knee, then bend the knee back and forth to increase the range of motion. I had to do that several times a day.

Q.   How did you feel during this therapy?

A.   It was mainly very painful. You had to stretch the ligaments in the knee to get the motion back.

Q.   How long did you do this treatment?

A.   I did it continuously for about three months. After that I did it a couple of times a day for maybe three more months.

Q.   Did you ever get full motion back in your knee?

A.   Not completely. I could straighten my leg all the way, but I could never bend it the other way as far as it used to go.

Q.   Mr. Smith, let's talk for a moment about the effect all this had on your teaching job. When was the first time you returned to work?

A.   I went back to work after spring vacation, which would have been the middle of April.

Q.   From the day of the accident until you returned to work, were you able to do any kind of work at all?

A.   No.

Q.   After returning to work, were you able to do all the things you used to?

A.   No, by that time I was walking without

A transition again.

c. continued therapy

It is important to show that plaintiff, at considerable pain and effort, tried to rehabilitate the leg to its former condition.

Also important is any permanent disability from the injury. (You might have the plaintiff demonstrate the degree of movement and appearance of the leg to the jury, although some lawyers feel this can backfire.)

This testimony is necessary to establish the lost wages element of damages.

crutches, but still limping a great deal. I couldn't coach basketball or do anything like sports.

Q. After returning to work, did you have further therapy on your leg?

A. Yes, sir. I still continued the heat treatment, the bending exercises, every day. I also did weight exercises to build up the muscles in that leg.

Q. Finally, Mr. Smith, let's talk about how you feel and what you can do now. What is the condition of your leg today?

A. Well, the leg is still smaller than the other one. The pain is gone as long as I take it easy on the leg.

Q. Is there anything you cannot do today that you could do before the collision?

A. Yes, sir. I can't play basketball or go hiking like I used to.

Q. What happens when you attempt these activities?

A. My knee swells up. It starts aching and throbbing.

Q. Have you ever played or coached basketball since the collision?

A. No, sir. I tried it once or twice, but it just doesn't work. It just hurts too much.

Q. Mr. Smith, before this collision occurred, what was your health like?

A. I was in perfect health; I didn't have any problems.

Q. Before all this happened to you, how did you like to spend your spare time?

A. Mainly outdoors activities—playing with my daughters, basketball, and hiking.

Q. Do you do those things now?

A. Basketball and hiking are out. The knee just doesn't take the strain. It swells up and starts throbbing whenever I try it. I can still play some with the girls, but I have to be careful in what I do.

Q. Has this affected your relationship with your family?

A. Judy, my wife, has been wonderful. She's been very supportive. It's been tough with the girls. They're too young to understand why daddy can't do some of the things with them he used to do.

Q. How do you feel about that?

This is another place where you could introduce and use exhibits.

Continuing present pain is also important on the issue of damages.

Permanent limitation of activities should be demonstrated.

Notice that the witness is testifying in a very factual way, avoiding the danger that too emotional a presentation will cause a jury reaction.

Prior good health should be shown.

These last questions and answers sum up the changed circumstances of the plaintiff's life and relate it to his family. After such a high point, stop.

A.   It's mainly frustrating. You want to do all the things you used to be able to do, especially with your kids. I'm still learning to adjust to the way things are.

Q.   Thank you, Mr. Smith. Your Honor, we have no further questions on direct.

Note that the plaintiff was *not* used to prove the dollar amounts of damages. Use other witnesses and exhibits to do this whenever possible.

Example (eyewitness to an automobile collision case):

The following witness, an eyewitness to the same collision, will be called after the plaintiff has testified. Because of this, certain areas the plaintiff already covered need not be duplicated. Instead, the witness will be used to corroborate certain critical facts and sequences that establish that the defendant was negligent and the plaintiff was not.

Witness John Doe — direct examination

Q.   Mr. Doe, please introduce yourself.

A.   I'm John J. Doe.

Q.   Mr. Doe, you're the person who saw the collision at Main and Elm on December 13, 2000?

A.   Yes.

Q.   Where do you live?

A.   I live at 1550 N. Maple.

Q.   How long have you lived there?

A.   About 1½ years.

Q.   Whom do you live there with?

A.   I'm single. I live by myself.

Q.   What kind of work do you do?

A.   I'm the custodian of the 1500 N. Aster Street condominium.

Q.   How long have you been working for that building?

A.   About 2 years.

Q.   Have you always been employed in the building maintenance field?

A.   Yes, sir, for about 20 years.

Q.   Mr. Doe, are you familiar with the intersection of Elm and Maple Streets?

A.   I sure am.

Q.   How often do you go there?

A.   I go by there two times a day, on my way to work and coming back.

Q.   Let's talk about what you saw at the intersection of Maple and Elm Streets on December 13, 2000, around 12:30 P.M. Where at that intersection were you?

(Background)

A more modern start. An introductory statement lets the jury know immediately the witness' role in the case.

Notice that, since this is an occurrence witness, not the plaintiff, only those aspects of his background that bear directly on his credibility as a witness are brought out.

(Scene)

Notice that the witness is only asked to establish his familiarity with the intersection. He should not describe it again. This has already been done by the plaintiff. Moreover, he might contradict the plaintiff's description in some respects.

A. I was on the northeast corner of the intersection waiting on the light.

Q. When you say waiting "on the light," exactly what do you mean?

When the witness says something that is not clear, have him explain the term.

A. I was standing on the corner, waiting for the green walk light so I could walk south across Elm Street.

Q. When you first got to that corner, what color were the lights?

A. The lights were green for the Elm traffic. The crosswalk light for crossing Elm was on "don't walk."

Since the walk-lights are an important issue, this witness should corroborate the plaintiff's version of the facts (that he had the green walk-light when he stepped off the curb).

Q. When that crosswalk light changed to "walk," where were you?

A. I was still on the northeast corner facing south.

Q. After the walk light changed, what did you do?

A. I started to step off the sidewalk into the street.

(Action)

Q. At that time did anything happen?

A. It sure did.

Q. What was that?

A. As I was stepping into the street, another man was also stepping into the street from the other corner, walking directly toward me.

At this point the pace should pick up to help recreate the occurrence.

Q. Which corner was the man on?

Q. What happened next?

A. Suddenly, a car going north on Maple made a righthand turn from Maple going eastbound on Elm.

Q. What happened next?

A. As the car was completing the turn, it struck the man right in the side.

Q. What part of the car struck what part of the man?

A. The right front bumper of the car struck the man's left leg.

Q. Where was the man when he was hit?

A. He was in the crosswalk around one-third of the way across the street.

Q. What happened after that?

A. The car screeched to a halt and the man was knocked down on the ground.

Notice that no unnecessary detail is elicited here. The witness testifies to the important facts efficiently. Exact times and distances are avoided. (These are the kinds of details the cross-examiner will probe. Why make it easier for him by committing the witness to the details in advance?)

Q. After you saw all this happen, what is the first thing you did?

A. I ran over to where the man was lying on the street and told him not to move and not to try to get up.

Q. What did you notice about the man?

A.   His face was all contorted and he was sort of squirming on the ground. He kept trying to grab his left knee.

Q.   What happened next?

A.   I and some other people tried to make him comfortable and keep him quiet until an ambulance could come.

Q.   Did an ambulance come?

A.   Yes, five or ten minutes later.

Q.   What happened then?

A.   The ambulance people put the man on a stretcher, very slowly, put him in the ambulance, and drove off.

Q.   What is the next thing you did?

A.   By that time some policemen were there directing traffic and talking to people, so I talked to one of them and told them what I had seen when all this happened

Q.   Mr. Doe, are you sure you saw where the man was when he was struck by that car?

A.   I'm sure. He was right in the crosswalk, walking with the walk light.

Q.   Thank you. I have no further questions.

> The evidence of the victim's pain and suffering should be brought out.

> Notice that this witness' direct examination is short. He contributes a few corroborative details on important points, then stops.

> Try to end on a high note, that reinforces a key point.

> **(Exhibits)**
>
> If exhibits will be used with this witness, this would be a good place to introduce and mark a diagram of htc intersection. The exhibit will highlight and repeat the key liability facts of the plaintiff's case.

2.   Example — direct examinations in a criminal case

In the following criminal case, John Smith is charged with raping Sharon Jones in the bedroom of her apartment on April 10, 2000. The defendant, while denying he committed the rape, does not contest that a rape occurred. Hence, the central issue in the case is the identification of the offender.

Following are the direct examinations of the victim and the first police officer who arrived at the scene of the crime, probably the two most common witness types in criminal cases.

Example (victim in a rape case):

Victim Sharon Jones — direct examination

Q.   Ms. Jones, please tell us your full name.

A.   Sharon Jones.

Q.   How old are you?

> **(Background)**
> The victim's age is a necessary element in a rape case under some state statutes.

A. I am 23.

Q. Are you single or married?

A. I'm single. I've never been married.

Q. Do you live here?

A. Yes, I live on the north side.

Q. How long have you lived there?

A. About 5 years.

Q. Where are you from originally?

A. I was raised in Rockford and lived there until I finished high school.

Q. Did you attend any schools after high school?

A. Yes, I went to college at the University of Illinois.

Q. Did you receive a degree?

A. I received a bachelor of arts degree with a specialty in education.

Q. What did you do after graduating from college?

A. For the past year I've been working as a seventh-grade teacher in the public school system.

Q. Which school do you teach at?

A. I teach at Hawthorne School on the south side.

Q. Ms. Jones, on April 10, 2000, where were you living?

A. I was living at 2501 North Halsted Street.

Q. Did you live there with anyone?

A. No, I lived there by myself.

Q. What kind of building is that?

A. It is a two-flat building. I lived in the second-floor apartment.

Q. Describe the entrances to your second-floor apartment.

A. There is a front door that serves both apartments. There is an inside stairwell which leads up to my apartment. There is also a rear porch with a stairwell leading to the second floor. The rear entrance from the porch goes to my kitchen.

Q. Do the doors at the top of the stairs and in the kitchen have locks?

A. Yes, they do.

Q. Were those doors locked when you last entered your house the evening before?

A. Yes, they were.

Q. Describe the rooms in your second-floor apartment.

Up to this point the questions have elicited the victim's background. By this time she should feel more at ease.

(Scene)

The scene of the crime is important. Hence, the witness is asked to describe it in some detail. This must be done in a logical, progressive fashion.

Note that a diagram or photograph is *not* used here. This keeps the spotlight on the victim, the critical witness in the case.

A.   The apartment has four rooms. When you go up the front steps, you enter into the living room. Behind the living room toward the rear of the apartment, a kitchen is in one corner and my bedroom is in the other corner. The bathroom is between the living room and the kitchen.

The description has progressed from the building, to the apartment, and finally to the bedroom, where the rape actually took place.

Q.   Describe your bedroom as it looked on April 10.

A.   As you stand in the doorway there is the far wall which has two windows. Against the right-hand wall there is my bed. Against the left-hand wall there are two dressers. On top of a dresser is a lamp.

Q.   What are the approximate sizes of the windows?

Since the primary trial issue is identification, the lighting conditions must be described and explained in detail.

A.   Each of the two windows is about two feet wide and four feet tall.

Q.   Did those windows have curtains?

A.   Yes, they did.

Q.   Were the curtains open or closed that morning?

A.   The curtains were open.

Q.   What was the weather like that morning?

A.   It was a bright, sunny day.

Q.   What were the lighting conditions like in the bedroom that morning?

A.   It had good lighting. I had no trouble seeing things in the room.

Q.   Ms. Jones, where were you during the morning hours of April 10, 2000?

A.   I was dozing in bed.

Q.   How long had you been in bed?

A.   Since about 2:00 A.M. that morning.

Q.   What kind of clothing were you wearing?

A.   I was wearing a nightgown.

Q.   Had you awakened at any time that morning?

The description of the setting is now complete. The action portion of her testimony can now safely begin.

A.   Yes, I did.

Q.   When was that?

A.   I woke up around 10:00, drank a glass of water and went back to bed.

Q.   Did you fall back to sleep?

A.   Well, I was dozing on and off.

Q.   Ms. Jones, at approximately 12:30 P.M., did anything happen?

(Action)

A.   Yes.

Q.   What was that?

A.   I heard a noise that startled me. I looked

up and saw a man standing in the doorway to my bedroom.

Q. What was that man doing?

A. He just stood there.

Q. What did that man look like?

A. Well, he was white, 25 to 30 years old, around 6 feet tall, and weighed 180 to 200 lbs.

Q. Did you notice anything about his face?

A. I noticed that he had dark hair and a mustache.

Q. What kind of clothing was he wearing?

A. I remember he had on a dark blue V-neck sweater and dark-colored, casual-type slacks. I didn't notice his shoes.

Q. Ms. Jones, the man you saw standing in your doorway on April 10, 2000, at approximately 12:30 P.M., do you see him in court today?

A. Yes, I do.

Q. Would you please point to him and describe what he is wearing in court today?

A. He is the man right over there (pointing). He is wearing a blue suit with a light blue paisley shirt.

Q. Your Honor, may the record reflect that the witness has pointed to and identified the defendant, John Smith?

Court: The record will so reflect.

Q. When you saw the defendant standing in your doorway, what did you do?

A. I screamed.

Q. What happened next?

A. He walked from the doorway, leaped on my bed, and grabbed my throat.

Q. What happened next?

A. We were struggling on the bed. He kept on grabbing my throat, and I was screaming and trying to get his hands off me.

Q. Which direction was he facing?

A. He was looking down at me.

Q. Which direction were you facing?

A. I was looking up at him.

Q. How far was your face from his face?

A. No more than two feet apart.

Q. During this time did the defendant say anything?

A. He kept saying he would kill me if I didn't do what he said.

Since the issue is identification, the victim's description of the offender, particularly when it is very accurate, should be brought out in detail.

Here the witness is asked to identify the offender as the defendant as early in the testimony as is possible. Thereafter, you can refer to him as the "defendant," which depersonalizes him and gets the jury to look at him each time he is mentioned.

The testimony, now being in the action part, should have pace. It should move to recreate the horror of the event. The questions are short, and merely help break up the narrative into digestible segments.

The face-to-face confrontation is important to the identification.

Q. What happened next?

A. He pulled the blankets off the bed and pulled my nightgown up.

Q. What happened after that?

A. While he was holding me by the throat he kept telling me to shut up and he was undoing his belt and trousers with his other hand.

Q. While he was doing that, what were you doing?

A. I was just trying to breathe and push him off.

Since penetration is a required element in a rape case, this fact must clearly be established.

Q. What happened next?

A. He started to have intercourse with me.

Q. Exactly what did he do?

A. Well, you know, he forced his penis in my vagina.

Q. How long did that go on?

A. Maybe a couple of minutes, I'm not sure.

Q. What happened after that?

A. He just lay there for a few minutes, then got up, pulled up his trousers and ran out of the bedroom.

Q. From the time you first saw the defendant in the doorway to the time he ran out of the bedroom, how much time had passed?

A. Maybe ten minutes.

Q. What happened after the defendant left?

A. I lay there for a couple of minutes, trying to get my breath back. Then I called the police. Then I just cried.

Q. Did any police arrive?

A. Yes.

Q. Who were they?

A. Two policemen in uniforms came up to the apartment. I don't remember their names.

Q. Did you talk with them?

A. I did, but I don't remember what I told them.

At this point the pace can begin to slow down again.

Q. How long were the policemen in your apartment?

A. Maybe ten minutes.

Q. What happened next?

A. They took me downstairs to their squad car and drove me to Memorial Hospital, to the emergency room.

Q. What happened there?

A. Some nurses and doctors examined me. They examined my neck and they gave me a pelvic exam. They also gave me some medication.

Q. How long were you in the emergency room at Memorial Hospital?

A. About one hour.

Q. What happened after that?

A. The same two policemen drove me to my friend's home.

Q. How long did you remain there?

A. I stayed there for several days.

Q. Did you ever go back to your apartment?

A. No, I never went back there.

This question again reminds the jury how terrifying the event was for the witness.

Q. Other than seeing the defendant in your bedroom on April 10, 2000, had you ever seen him before?

A. No.

Q. Is there any question in your mind today as to the man who attacked you on April 10, 2000?

A. No.

Q. Who was it?

A. The defendant, the man right over there.

Q. Your Honor, we have no further questions.

This is a good way to stop. Have the witness re-identify the defendant as the last question of the direct examination.

Example (police officer at scene of rape):

Just like the eyewitness in the automobile collision case, the police officer is being called to corroborate certain important facts — that a rape did in fact occur, and that the lighting conditions were sufficient for the victim to observe the offender and subsequently identify him.

Witness Officer McCarthy — direct examination

Q. Please introduce yourself to the jury.

A. I'm Jane J. McCarthy. I'm a police officer with the City Police Department.

(Background)

With this kind of witness you want to show the professional, not personal, background.

Q. For how many years?

A. Five.

Q. Where are you presently assigned?

A. Third District.

Q. How long have you been in that district?

A. All five years.

Q. What have your assignments been over those five years?

A. I've been a patrol officer doing regular patrol duty.

Since the witness has described herself as a patrol officer, no further description is really necessary.

Q. Officer McCarthy, were you working as a police officer on April 10, 2000?

A. Yes, I was.

Q. What shift were you working that day?

A. I was on the day, the 8 to 4 shift.

Q. Were you working with anyone?

A. Yes, sir, my partner, Officer Byrne.

Q. What was your assignment that day?

A. We were on routine patrol duty in our squad car.

Q. What area were you patrolling?

A. Our beat was between North and Fullerton Avenues along the lakefront.

Q. At approximately 12:45 P.M., did anything happen?

A. Yes.

Q. What happened?

A. We received a message over our police radio.

The actual content of the message will often be hearsay.

Q. After receiving the message, what did you do?

A. We went to 2501 N. Halsted St., to the second-floor apartment.

(Action)

Q. How did you enter the apartment?

A. We walked up the front stairs and walked into the front room.

Note that the action testimony here comes *before* the scene description. Scene description is unnecessary here, since the victim has already testified.

Q. Was anyone in the apartment?

A. Yes. We met a young woman, a Sharon Jones, in the front room.

Q. When you first saw her, what did Sharon Jones look like?

A. She was dressed in a nightgown. Her hair was messed up. She was crying and shaking.

This is the first important fact elicited on direct. This circumstantially corroborates the fact that the victim had just experienced something traumatic.

Q. Did you talk to her?

A. Yes.

Q. Other than yourself, your partner, and Ms. Jones, was anyone else in the apartment?

A. No.

Q. What's the first thing she said to you?

A. As we walked in, she said: "I've just been raped. The man that did it ran out a couple of minutes ago."

The prompt outcry of a rape victim is usually admissible as an exception to the hearsay rule.

Q. What happened next?

A. She sat down and started to cry.

Q. What is the next thing you did?

A. I sat down next to her and tried to comfort her. My partner got her a pair of shoes and overcoat. She put on the shoes and overcoat.

Q. What happened next?
A. I went over to the bedroom.
Q. What did the bedroom look like?
A. Well, the sheets on the bed were all crumpled. There was a blanket half on the floor, and a pillow on the floor next to the bed.
Q. What was the lighting in the bedroom like?
A. It was pretty light in there. The bedroom has two windows, and it was early afternoon.
Q. What happened next?
A. We put Ms. Jones in the squad car and drove her to the Memorial Hospital.
Q. What happened at the hospital?
A. We walked her into the emergency room and took her to one of the examining rooms. Some nurses and a doctor came to the room. We stayed outside in the waiting area.
Q. About how long was Ms. Jones in the examining room?
A. Perhaps an hour.
Q. After that hour, what happened?
A. We went into the examining room and talked with Ms. Jones for awhile.
Q. What was her condition at this time?
A. She had calmed down quite a bit. She had no difficulty talking to us about what had happened.
Q. How long did you talk to her?
A. About 15 minutes.
Q. What happened next?
A. We drove her in our squad car to a friend's house that Ms. Jones wanted to go to.
Q. What did you do next?
A. We went back to the station and prepared a written report summarizing what we had done in this case.

(Scene)

The condition of the bedroom and the lighting conditions are important facts which must be corroborated, since they support the victim's testimony that she was violently attacked.

Notice how quickly this direct examination went. The witness corroborated the victim on a few important facts — that she was raped, that it occurred in the bedroom, and that the lighting conditions there were good — then stopped. Nothing unnecessary was asked.

3. Example — direct examinations with a different organization

Not all occurrence witness testimony needs to follow the most common progression — background, scene, action, and exhibits — described above. If there is a good reason to organize the examination differently, in a way that makes the testimony more vivid, yet remain clear and understandable, consider it.

Example (defendant in a criminal case):

The following witness is the defendant in a criminal case, who has been charged with aggravated assault. The defense is self-defense. The defendant is the last witness in the defense's case-in-chief.

Q. Mr. Jones, let's get right to it. Did you stab Hector Smith on June 1, 2000?

A. Yes sir, I did.

Q. Why?

A. He said I was going to be dead meat, and I believed him. When he came at me, I stabbed him before he could kill me.

> This start immediately and dramatically establishes self-defense.

Q. Before we talk more about what happened that night, let's first learn a little about you. Where did you grow up?

A. Right here in Los Angeles. I've lived here all my life.

> Now the direct loops back to the witness's background.

Q. Tell us about your family.

A. Well, there's my mom and dad, and four kids. My dad worked at the auto plant until he died two years ago. My mom works as a checker at a food store. My younger sister, Janet, and I still live at the house. My older brothers are grown up.

> Although the witness' family history may not have much relevance on credibility, most judges will permit it for a key witness such as the defendant in a criminal case.

Q. Tell us about your schooling.

A. I went to Central High School, and I graduated last year.

Q. And after high school?

A. I go part time to Glendale Vocational. I'm learning to be an auto mechanic. I work part time at a Safeway Food Store as a bagger.

Q. Are you married?

A. No, but my girlfriend, Maria, and I are talking about it.

Q. Bobby, let's turn to the party during the evening of June 1, 2000. Were you invited?

> A transition.

A. Yes. It was at the house of Jim Burns, a friend of mine from school. Jim invited me over and some of our other friends. It was to celebrate the end of the spring semester.

Q. Did Maria go with you?

> This is important to bring out.

A. No, she works the evening shift at Safeway. I was going to pick her up when she got off at midnight.

Q. When did you get to Jim Burns' house?

A. About 7:00 P.M.

Q. What was going on when you got there?

A. There were about 25 people there. Some were in the back yard around a barbecue grill. Others were in the living room, talking and listening to music. It was a pretty typical party.

Q. Was there liquor?

A. Sure. You were expected to bring something, beer or soda, and something to eat.

Q. Did you know the people there?

A. Some of them, maybe half, were from school. The others I assumed were friends of Jim.

Q. Between 7:00 P.M., when you got there, and 9:00 P.M., when this incident happened, what were you doing?

A. I was talking to people I knew, ate a burger and potato salad, and drank some beer.

Q. How much beer?   Another important

A. I'd had two Miller Lites.   fact to bring out.

Q. Between 7:00 and 9:00, was anything unusual going on?

A. No, it was just a nice party.

Q. Bobby, let's talk about what happened at   A transition.
    9:00. First, where were you then?

A. I was in the kitchen.

Q. What were you doing there?

A. I'd gone there a few minutes earlier to get a beer from the cooler. There was a girl there and I started talking to her.

Q. Who was she?

A. I didn't know. I'd never seen her before I went in the kitchen.

Q. Anyone else in the kitchen with you?

A. Not really. A couple of people went to the cooler to get beer or soda, but nobody stayed.

Q. Did you talk to the girl?

A. Sure. It was just get acquainted talk — who you are, what do you do — like that.

Q. Was she there with anyone?

A. Not that I knew of. She didn't say she was with anyone.

Q. So what happened around 9:00 P.M.?

A. We're just talking, like I said, when this big guy comes in the kitchen. He looked at me, then the girl, then he said to me: "What's going on here?" She said: "It's okay" or "He's okay," something like that.

Q. What did you do?

A. Nothing. I just stood there.

Q. And then?

A. He walked over and stood in front of me.

Q. What did you notice about him?

A. He looked and smelled drunk. He was glassy eyed, kind of weaving back and forth. He smelled like booze, some kind of hard liquor.

Notice the sensory language. Imagery is important here.

Q. What did you do?

A. I tried to walk around him to get out of the kitchen.

Q. What happened?

A. He stepped in front of me, blocking my way.

Q. And then?

A. He said: "Nobody messes with my girl. You're dead meat."

Q. What did you do?

A. I started to back away from him, and the girl ran out the door.

Q. And then?

A. He said: "You're dead meat" again, and started coming towards me.

Q. What did he look like?

A. He had this wild, glassy-eyed look.

Q. What was going through your mind?

A. I thought "This guy is crazy. He's going to kill me. If he gets his hands on me, it's all over."

The defendant's state of mind is relevant to self-defense, and must be clearly established.

Q. Why did you think he was going to kill you?

A. He was a big guy, around 6' 2" and maybe 210 pounds, a lot bigger than I am.

Another important point.

Q. How big are you?

A. 5' 8", 155 pounds.

Q. So what did you do?

A. As he walked over to me I grabbed a knife off the kitchen table, held it in front of me, and yelled: "Stay away from me."

Q. What did he do?

A. He laughed at me, kept coming, and tried to grab the knife out of my hand.

This is crucial to the question of whether the defendant's actions were reasonable.

Q. And then?

A. He lunged at me, and I swung the knife at him. I cut him in the chest, and he just stared at me, and then slumped on the floor. I ran into the living room and yelled at someone to call an ambulance.

Q. What happened after that?

A. People ran into the kitchen, and I just sat

in a chair in the living room trying to calm down. After a while the ambulance people came and they took the big guy out of the kitchen. A while later one of my friends drove me home.

Q. Bobby, why did you swing that knife at Hector Smith on June 1, 2000?

A. I was trying to save my life. He said I was dead meat, tried to grab the knife, and I thought he was going to stab me with it.

Q. How did you feel when it was all over?

A. Very scared, but very glad to be alive.

More "state of mind" testimony, and a strong way to end the direct examination.

Example (surviving spouse in a wrongful death case):

The following witness is the husband of a woman who was killed when she was struck by a car while crossing the street. The husband was not an eyewitness to the collision.

Q. Mr. Potts, please introduce yourself to the jury.

A. My name is John Potts.

Q. Mr. Potts, where were you when you received the telephone call?

A. I was at work.

Q. What did the caller tell you?

A. It was a police officer. She said that Anne had been in an accident and had been taken to St. Mary's Hospital.

Q. What did you do?

A. I ran out of the office and drove over to the hospital.

Q. What did you do when you got there?

A. I went to the emergency room to find her.

Q. Did you?

A. Yes, she was in one of the surgery rooms.

Q. Tell us what you saw.

A. She was unconscious. She was all covered with blood. There were all sorts of tubes going into her. There were nurses and doctors all over the place. One of them told me I'd have to stay outside the room.

Q. What did you do?

A. I sat in a chair outside, and waited and prayed.

In this case, immediately beginning with the phone call is a dramatic, vivid way to start the testimony. The jurors know who the witness is anyway, and there is no good reason to develop his background first. The testimony can then bring out what Mr. Potts did, and what was going through his mind, until his wife Anne died, and the funeral that followed.

The direct examination can then loop back to develop the history of Mr. and Mrs. Potts.

Q. John, let's turn back now to happier times. Where did you first meet Anne?

A.   It was at a company picnic. I was in the computer department. She was in public relations, but I'd never met her. I don't think I'd ever seen her before. She was standing by the food tables, and asked me if I wanted something to drink.

The testimony can then develop how the relationship between John and Anne developed, when they married, and what their future plans were. When all that has been brought out, consider ending the examination on another dramatic, vivid note.

Q.   John, the place the company picnic was held where you first met Anne. Where was that?
A.   That was at the picnic grounds in MacArthur Park.
Q.   Since Anne passed away, have you ever been back?
A.   No.
Q.   Why not?
A.   I just can't do it. It would only remind me of the life I once had.

§5.4.   *Conversations and statements*

Conversations are frequently introduced as evidence in trials. However, since these conversations are out-of-court statements, they are usually hearsay and are inadmissible unless they are being offered for a non-hearsay purpose or are an exception to the hearsay rule. Accordingly, whenever you intend to introduce a conversation or statement in evidence, review the evidentiary basis for its admission. First, is the statement being offered for the truth of the matters asserted in the statement? If not, there is no hearsay problem. If so, the statement is hearsay. Second, if it is hearsay, is there any exception to the hearsay rule that applies? If so, the statement is admissible. You should always review FRE 801, 803, and 804 to determine if any exception is applicable.

The most common exception is admissions by party opponents, governed by FRE 801(d)(2). Whenever one party makes a statement and an opposing party wishes to introduce it, the statement is ordinarily admissible. If the statement made by a party opponent is part of a conversation, the conversation between the party opponent and another person is admissible, since the entire conversation is necessary to put the party opponent's statements in context.

Statements by agents and employees of party opponents are also admissible. These statements are admissible against the principal, the party opponent, if there is independent evidence that the agency relationship existed, that the agent's statements were made during the course of the agency relationship, and that the statements were about matters within the scope of the agent's employment. The same basic rules also apply to statements made by co-conspirators in criminal cases.

There are, of course, many hearsay exceptions to out-of-court statements. Common ones include excited utterances, statements against interest, statements of then-existing mental or physical conditions, and statements made for the purpose of diagnosis and treatment. As always, you must think expansively whenever you are trying to introduce out-of-court statements. Where necessary, research the problem and have supporting authority available when you introduce the statement in evidence.

Conversations also need proper foundations to be admissible. The basic requirement is authentication, that is, the witness must reasonably identify the participants to the conversation. (See FRE 901(b)(5).) The foundation should be established for every conversation, even if the opposing side may not object to its absence. First, opposing counsel can always decide to object, thereby breaking up the flow of your direct examination. Second, the foundation enhances your witness' credibility by demonstrating his ability to remember details.

Elements:

The following foundation elements must be established to admit in evidence a conversation between two or more persons:

1. when the conversation occurred
2. where the conversation occurred
3. who was present during the conversation
4. who said what to whom

It is not necessary that the witness actually have participated in the conversation. He may properly testify to a conversation he witnessed between two or more other persons as long as the conversation is otherwise admissible under hearsay rules.

Example (admission by party-opponent):

Q. Did you personally talk with Frank Jones?
A. Yes, I did.
Q. When did that conversation with the defendant take place?
A. I talked to him on April 25, 2000.
Q. What time of day was that?
A. That was about 3:00 in the afternoon.
Q. Where did that conversation take place?
A. We talked in his office.
Q. What's the address of his office?
A. It's at 150 North Clark Street, Suite 100.
Q. Who was present during that conversation?
A. There was just myself and Mr. Jones.
Q. What did you and Mr. Jones say at that time?
A. I said: "Mr. Jones, you still owe me $2,500 for the roofing job on your house." He said: "I know I do. I just don't have the money to pay you right now."

Example (excited utterance):

Q. What happened right after you heard the shot?

A.   Well, people came running to the scene.

Q.   Did you know any of them?

A.   Other than my wife, no.

Q.   What happened next?

A.   Well, there was a middle-aged man standing just a few feet from me, and he suddenly screamed: "Look out! He's got a gun!"

§5.5.   *Telephone conversations*

Telephone conversations, also commonly admitted in trials, are introduced in much the same way as face-to-face conversations, but have an additional element. The witness must be able to identify the speaker on the other end of the line. (See FRE 901(b)(5), (6).) There are four basic factual situations under which the foundation for the identity of the other speaker can be established.

1.   Witness knows other person

Elements:

The following elements must be established for a telephone conversation between two persons, where the witness knows and recognizes the other person's voice.

1.   when the conversation occurred
2.   where the conversation occurred (where witness was)
3.   witness recognized the other voice
4.   how witness knows the other voice
5.   whose the other voice was
6.   what other persons participated
7.   who said what to whom

It is not necessary to show who placed the call. Where this is known, of course you should show it, since it adds to the credibility of the witness and the reliability of the voice identification, but that knowledge is not a necessary element of the foundation. As in face-to-face conversations, it is also not necessary that the witness have personally participated in the conversation, just that he heard it.

Example:

Q.   At approximately 4:00 P.M. on April 25, 2000, where were you?

A.   I was in my house.

Q.   Did anything happen at that time?

A.   Yes.

Q.   What happened?

A.   The telephone rang.

Q. What did you do?
A. I picked up the phone and said "hello."
Q. Where were you when the telephone rang?
A. I was in the kitchen right next to the phone.
Q. What happened next?
A. A voice answered.
Q. Did you recognize that voice on the other end of the line?
A. Yes, I did.
Q. How did you recognize that voice?
A. I have talked to the same person numerous times over the past several years, in person and over the telephone.
Q. Whose voice was it?
A. It was Frank Jones'.
Q. Did anyone else take part in that telephone conversation?
A. No.
Q. Tell us what you said and what he said during that conversation.
A. He said: "Hi, this is Frank Jones." I said: "Hi." He said: "You still owe me $2,500 for the roofing job on your house." I said: "No, I don't. Your job was defective. I won't pay it."

Note that it is not necessary to show that the voice on the other end can be recognized because of previous telephone conversations. Face-to-face conversations are a sufficient basis for the identification. Of course, where the previous conversations were on the telephone, this enhances the reliability of the identification.

It would be improper to bring out that the caller identified himself before establishing the foundation. The concept behind the foundation requirement is voice recognition, which should eliminate imposters posing as someone else. The identification of the caller can properly be brought out in the conversation itself. (See FRE 901(b)(6)(A).)

2.   Witness does not know other person, but later learns identity through subsequent conversations

Elements:

The following elements must be established for a telephone conversation between two persons, where the witness learns the identity of the other person through later face-to-face conversations.

1. when the conversation occurred
2. where the conversation occurred (where witness was)
3. witness did not recognize the other voice at the time
4. at later dates, witness talked to the other voice personally
5. witness now recognizes other voice during the call
6. who other voice was
7. what other persons participated
8. who said what to whom

Example:

> Q. On April 25, 2000, at approximately 4:00 P.M., where were you?
> A. I was in the kitchen of my house.
> Q. What happened at that time?
> A. The phone rang.
> Q. What did you do?
> A. I picked up the phone and said "hello."
> Q. Did you recognize the voice on the other end?
> A. Not at that time.
> Q. Mr. Smith, on April 30, at approximately 4:00 P.M., where were you?
> A. I was in Frank Jones' office at 150 North Clark St., Suite 100.
> Q. Did you have a conversation with him?
> A. Yes, I did.
> Q. Since that day, have you had any other conversations with Frank Jones?
> A. Yes.
> Q. About how many?
> A. Maybe 10 or 12.
> Q. Mr. Smith, turning back to the telephone call you received on April 25, 2000, are you now able to recognize whose voice was on the other end?
> A. Yes, I am.
> Q. Whose voice do you now recognize it to be?
> A. Frank Jones'.
> Q. Were any other persons present during that conversation?
> A. No.
> Q. What did you say and he say at that time?
> A. He said: "You still owe me $2,500 for the roofing job on your house." I said: "No, I don't. The job is defective."

3.   Witness does not know the person, but later learns identity through some transaction

Elements:

The following elements must be established for a telephone conversation between two persons, where the witness learns the identity of the other person through either a prior or subsequent transaction (other than a conversation).

1. when the conversation occurred
2. where the conversation occurred
3. witness did not recognize the other voice at that time
4. witness was engaged in a prior or subsequent transaction that identified the voice for him (in some jurisdictions the subsequent act that identifies the voice must have occurred prior to the beginning of litigation)

5. witness now knows the other voice
6. what other persons participated
7. who said what to whom

Example:

Q. On April 25, 2000, at approximately 4:00 P.M., where were you?
A. I was in the kitchen of my house.
Q. Did anything happen at that time?
A. Yes, the phone rang.
Q. What did you do?
A. I picked up the phone and said "hello."
Q. Did you recognize the other voice at that time?
A. No.
(Show Plaintiff's Exhibit #1 to opposing counsel.)
Q. Mr. Smith, I show you Plaintiff's Exhibit #1. Do you recognize it?
A. Yes, I do.
Q. When did you receive this letter?
A. I got it around April 30, 2000.
Q. Is that letter in the same condition now as it was on the date you received it?
A. Yes, it is.
Q. Do you recognize the signature at the bottom of the letter?
A. Yes. I've seen it several times before.
Q. Whose signature appears at the bottom?
A. Frank Jones.
(Offer the exhibit in evidence. After it has been admitted, proceed as follows:)
Q. Please read the first line of that letter to the jury.
A. "Dear Mr. Smith, I am writing to confirm the substance of the telephone call I made to you the afternoon of April 25, 2000."
Q. Do you now know who the voice on the telephone was on April 25, 2000, at approximately 4:00 P.M.?
A. Yes, I do.
Q. Whose voice was it?
A. It was Frank Jones'.
Q. Did anyone else take part in the telephone conversation?
A. No.
Q. What was said during the conversation?
A. He said: "Mr. Smith, I am calling you about your roofing problem. We can resurface your roof for $2,500." I said: "That looks pretty good to me."

What have you established? There was only one person speaking on the telephone. Hence, only that person, in addition to yourself, could reasonably know the nature of the conversation. When the subsequent letter arrives, you know from its contents who the previous caller was. The letter identifies the caller and is admissible as an admission of the party-opponent. While not as reliable as voice recognition, it is sufficient to qualify the conversation for admission.

4. Witness does not know the person, but has dialed a listed business telephone number and spoken with the person there

Many jurisdictions hold that dialing a business number listed in a telephone directory is prima facie proof that you have called the listed party or his agent. (See FRE 901(b)(6)(B).)

Elements:

1. when the conversation occurred
2. where the conversation occurred
3. witness obtained business number from the current telephone directory
4. witness dialed the number listed in the directory
5. voice on the other end acknowledged it was the business entity
6. what other persons participated
7. who said what to whom

Example:

Q.   On April 25, 2000, at 4:00 P.M., where were you?
A.   I was in the kitchen of my house.
Q.   What did you do at that time?
A.   I got out the telephone directory and looked up the number of the ABC Company.
Q.   Was the ABC Company listed in the directory?
A.   Yes, it was.
Q.   What did you do next?
A.   I dialed the number for the ABC Company listed in the directory.
Q.   After you dialed that number, what happened?
A.   Someone picked up the phone at the other end and a voice said, "ABC Company; can I help you?"
Q.   Did anyone else take part in the conversation?
A.   No.
Q.   What was the conversation you had at that time?
A.   I said: "I want to order some roofing tar paper." The other person said: "That's no problem at all. What kind of tar paper do you need?"

§5.6.   *Refreshing a witness' recollection*

Witnesses often find testifying in court a frightening experience. They are in strange surroundings and must follow unfamiliar rules. They are expected to testify from memory. Hence, it is not surprising that many times a witness will simply forget an important part of his anticipated testimony. When that happens, the lawyer must refresh the witness' recollection, that is, jog the witness' memory. Although anything can be used to refresh recollection, this is most commonly done through writings such as statements, documents, reports, and depositions and through exhibits such as photographs.

A certain litany must be followed to establish the foundation for refreshing recollection. Explain the litany to your witness before he testifies. Explain that there is nothing wrong with failing to remember and reading a document to refresh recollection while on the witness stand. Explain that the cue words, "Do you recall, or remember, anything else," indicate that the witness forgot something important and that you are about to begin the refreshing recollection litany.

Elements:

The following elements must be demonstrated to establish a foundation for refreshing the recollection of a witness who is on the witness stand:

1. Witness knows the facts, but has a memory lapse on the stand.
2. Witness knows his report (or other document or exhibit) will jog his memory.
3. Witness is given and reads the pertinent part of his report.
4. Witness states his memory has now been refreshed.
5. Witness now testifies to what he knows, without further aid of the report.

Example:

A police officer recovered a coat, shoes, and gun from the defendant's house. These facts are all contained in his police report.

Q.   Did you remove anything from the defendant's house?
A.   Yes, I did.
Q.   What items did you remove?
A.   Let's see. . . . I got a coat from a closet and his shoes from a hallway.
Q.   *Do you recall removing anything else?* (The cue words.)
A.   No, that's all I can remember.
Q.   Officer, would anything refresh your recollection?
A.   Yes.
Q.   What is that?
A.   I'm sure my report would.
Q.   Ms. Roberts, please mark this two-page report State Exhibit #1. (Ms. Roberts, the court clerk, marks report.)
Q.   I am now showing State Exhibit #1 to opposing counsel. (Shows report to defendant's lawyer.)
Q.   Officer, I am handing you what has been marked State Exhibit #1. Do you recognize it?

A.   Yes, that's my report.

Q.   Please read it to yourself. (Witness reads report.)

Q.   Do you now remember the items you removed from the defendant's house?

A.   Yes, I do.

Q.   May I have the report back, please. (Officer returns report.) Please tell us what those items were.

A.   Yes, sir. In addition to the coat and shoes, I recovered a revolver from a bedroom.

Inexperienced lawyers commonly make three mistakes when attempting to refresh recollection. First, they fail to have the document marked as an exhibit and show it to opposing counsel. The document should be marked for identification purposes even though you will not offer it in evidence. Second, they fail to retrieve the document after the witness has read it. This will often cause the opposing lawyer to object that the witness does not really have a present recollection but is merely reading from the report. Eliminate this problem by getting the report back before asking the final questions. Third, lawyers fail to use the *do you recall* or *do you remember* language. Instead, they will ask: "Did you remove any other items?" and the witness will answer: "No." When they then attempt to refresh the witness' recollection, the opposing lawyer may object on the ground that the witness has answered the question, and there is no need to refresh recollection.

Finally, remember that under FRE 612 anything used to refresh recollection, both while or before testifying, must be made available to opposing counsel for use during cross-examination. If what you used to refresh recollection has not previously been made available to the other side, this could affect your decision to use it at all, since the documents may contain other facts that can be effectively used during cross-examination. In most instances, of course, a witness' prior statements will be in the other side's possession through pretrial discovery. Even more important, FRE 612 permits the opposing side to introduce into evidence the relevant portions of the document used to refresh recollection.

When a witness has made a previous record of an event, and the record does *not* refresh his recollection, it may be admissible as past recollection recorded. The foundation requirements for this are discussed in §5.3(15).

§5.7.   *Opinions of lay witnesses*

While in general only experts can give opinions in areas beyond the knowledge and experience of ordinary laymen, certain exceptions exist. Several kinds of facts, while perhaps technically opinions, are facts that repeatedly occur in the experiences of lay witnesses. For that reason, lay witnesses are permitted to give opinions, if based on the perception of the witness and helpful to a clear determination of a fact in issue. (See FRE 701 and 602.) Common facts on which such opinions are allowed include age, speed, sobriety, and handwriting.

Example:

The witness is testifying that he saw the driver of a car involved in an accident and that the driver appeared to be under the influence of alcohol. First establish the witness' background and his presence at the accident; then:

Q. Mr. Doe, were you able to watch the driver after he got out of the car?
A. Yes.
Q. How long were you able to watch him?
A. About two minutes.
Q. What was he doing during that time?
A. He was kind of walking and talking to various people.
Q. Did you notice anything about his walk?
A. Yes, he was walking in a hesitant, stumbling sort of way. He almost tripped once or twice.
Q. What did he look like during this time?
A. Well, his face was red and sweaty, and his eyes looked kind of glazed.
Q. Were you able to hear him talk?
A. Yes.
Q. Did you notice anything about his speech?
A. His speech was very slurred and halting.
Q. Mr. Doe, have you ever seen persons when they were under the influence of alcohol?
A. Of course.
Q. How many times during your adult life have you seen persons under the influence of alcohol?
A. Probably a few hundred times.
Q. Mr. Doe, were you able to tell what condition the driver of that car was in?
A. Yes, sir, I could.
Q. What was it?
A. He was under the influence. I'd say he was drunk.

§5.8. The records witness

In today's trial environment, records are an increasingly common sight. Although always present in commercial cases, records are often a significant part of personal injury and even criminal cases. Consequently, being able to present records witnesses, introduce records into evidence, and use them effectively is becoming an increasingly indispensable trial skill in every type of trial. This is so even though business records are frequently admitted by pretrial order, stipulation, or without opposition.

Business records, of course, are hearsay. Since the 1930s, however, when the first business records legislation appeared, all jurisdictions have enacted statutes that, when certain requirements are met, permit business records to be admitted in evidence. All these statutes, including the present federal rule in FRE 803(6), have the same underlying rationale: reliability. When a business has created documents on a recurring basis, has relied on their accuracy to conduct the affairs of the business, and has developed systems to store and retrieve those records, that rationale has been met.

The records witness has two principal functions at trial. First, he must be able to establish the foundation requirements to get the exhibit admitted in evidence, and do it in a way that maximizes the weight the jury will give to the exhibit. Second, he must be prepared to read and explain the contents of the records to the jury; the evidence is in the records, and an effective witness will explain and interpret the records and show why they are reliable and important.

There is a tendency to present such witnesses in summary fashion: quickly establish the witness as custodian of the pertinent documents, recite the foundation litany, and get the records into evidence. However, you should resist the temptation to treat such witnesses casually. Remember that the evidentiary impact of documents is affected primarily by how systematically the information on the documents is compiled, how accurately the records are prepared, and how carefully they are stored. Accordingly, what the witness has to say about the records, over and above merely laying the foundation for their admissibility, can be significant. Do not miss an opportunity to enhance the quality of this part of your proof.

How do you do this? Several separate considerations are involved:

1. Thoroughly qualify your witness. Show that he has substantial knowledge of the records involved, works with them on a daily basis, and knows the storage and retrieval methods the business uses.

2. Show how the records are made, who makes them, and the primary source of the information contained on them. The witness should be able to trace all the transactions contained in the records, from their initial creation by the first person who conducted the transactions to their inclusion in some permanent record.

3. Show how the records are distributed, stored, and subsequently retrieved for use. Essential to the credibility of records is a showing that the records, once created, are stored in such a way as to minimize the risk of loss, destruction, or alteration.

4. Show what use the records have for the business creating them. Where you can show that the business constantly uses the records, and that accurate and complete records are essential to the successful operation of that business, you will substantially enhance the impact those records will make at trial.

The following example illustrates the kind of development a records witness can provide in a direct examination. This should obviously not be done in every instance. When, however, the records are the primary evidence of a transaction, not merely corroborative evidence, and must stand on their own, you should always consider this kind of development for your qualifying witness.

Example:

The office manager has been called as a witness to qualify certain shipping documents of a trucking company.

Q. Ms. Doe, what is your occupation?

A. I am the branch manager of the Chicago office of the XYZ Trucking Company.

Q. How long have you been the branch manager of the Chicago office?

A. Approximately 5 years.

Q. Before becoming branch manager, what kind of work did you do?

A. I originally started as a supervisor in the loading dock area. I then moved to the Billing Department. I then became manager of the Billing Department before moving to my present job.

Q. How many years in all have you worked for XYZ Company?

A. Almost 12 years.

Q. Has that entire time been spent in the Chicago office?

A. Yes, it has.

Q. Ms. Doe, what kind of business does XYZ Trucking Company do?

A. We're what they call an over-the-road carrier; that is, we carry goods in tractor-trailers between major cities throughout the United States and Canada.

Q. How many offices does XYZ Trucking have?

A. We have 11 regional and 46 local offices.

Q. How many persons do you employ at the Chicago office?

A. Right now we have 14 full-time and 6 part-time employees. The number varies depending on the season.

Q. What kind of work does the regional office in Chicago do?

A. We receive orders for goods, pick them up, and deliver them to the designated locations. We also receive shipments from other cities and either store them for pickup by the consignee or deliver the goods directly to him. It all depends on the nature of the shipping contracts. As a large carrier we can work out almost any kind of shipping arrangement.

Q. What kind of records does your office regularly generate during the course of its business?

A. Our standard records that we make for each shipment are bills of lading, shipping orders, shipping invoices, and billings.

Q. Ms. Doe, did you recently receive a subpoena directing your company to produce certain records for this trial?

A. Yes, we did.

Q. Did you bring those records with you today?

A. Yes, I did.

Q. Ms. Roberts, please mark this document Plaintiff's Exhibit #1. (Clerk does so.) May the record reflect that I am showing Plaintiff's Exhibit #1 to defense counsel. (Shows exhibit to defense counsel.)

Q. Ms. Doe, I am now showing you what has just been marked Plaintiff's Exhibit #1. Do you recognize it?

A. Yes, I do. That is the record I brought here pursuant to the subpoena.

Q. What kind of record is it?

A. This record is what we call a shipping invoice.

Q. What use does your company make of that kind of record?

A. That is the basic record which contains all the information about one shipped order. We use that form so that we have a complete record of that shipment on one document. We also use it for billing purposes. It's a key record in our business.

Q. What kind of information is on a shipping invoice?

A. It contains the date the shipment was picked up, where it was picked up, what the shipment consisted of, the weight of that shipment, delivery instructions, and billing instructions.

Q. Who receives and enters the information that appears on the statement?

A. Two people normally fill out the form. First, an office clerk who receives a shipping order, whether in person or on the telephone, fills out the entire form except the weight. The shipping invoice is then given to the driver. When the driver picks up the shipment, he weighs it on our scales and then writes in the weight on the form. Both the office clerk and driver must initial the form.

Q. When do they fill out the form?

A. Right when they're doing the work on the order.

Q. What then happens to the form?

A. The form itself has four copies. The driver gives the first two copies to our office after weighing the shipment. He takes the other two forms with him. When the shipment is delivered, he gives a copy to the party receiving the shipment. On the other copy he gets the signature of the receiving party, and returns that copy to our billing department.

Q. What does your office do with the copies?

A. We send one copy to the party placing the order. We send the other one, the original, to the billing department. When the signed copy is received from the driver, we send out our bill.

Q. What ultimately happens to the two bills, the original and signed copy?

A. The original goes into our permanent records files which we maintain in a separate room. The Billing Department sends the signed copy along with a bill to the party to be billed.

Q. How long does your company keep the forms?

A. At least five years. After that they're put on microfilm.

Q. This exhibit, Plaintiff's Exhibit #1, was it made under the procedures you have just described?

A. Yes.

The foundation for admission is now complete, without using the stilted language of FRE 803(6). The exhibit can now be offered in evidence. If, however, the judge still wants to hear the foundation litany of FRE 803(6), this can easily be done.

> Q. Ms. Doe, I am again directing your attention to the XYZ Company record marked Plaintiff's Exhibit #1: Was that record made by a person with knowledge of (or made from information transmitted by a person with knowledge of) the acts and events appearing on it?
> A. Yes.
> Q. Was it made at or near the time of the acts and events appearing on it?
> A. Yes.
> Q. Is it the regular practice of the XYZ Company to make such a record?
> A. Yes.
> Q. Was that record kept in the ordinary course of a regularly conducted business activity?
> A. Yes.

Once the exhibit is in evidence, the witness can show, read, and explain the exhibit to the jury. Remember that a good records witness does more than merely get the exhibit in evidence. She can also, and should, explain things on the exhibit.

Example:

> Q. Ms. Doe, please look at the shipping invoice, Plaintiff's Exhibit #1, now in evidence. In the top left-hand corner of the form is a box with the words "shipping date." What is a shipping date?
> A. That's the date the goods actually leave our warehouse.
> Q. Down at the bottom right of the form is another box with the words "due date." What's a due date?
> A. That's the date when payment in full for the shipment is due. After that we start charging interest for late payment.

The witness can also translate the information on the exhibit into an understandable story. This makes records come alive for the jury, which can follow along with the records as the story is told.

Example:

> Q. Ms. Doe, I've placed the two records, the stock purchase form, which is Plaintiff's Exhibit #1, and the confirmation form, which is Plaintiff's Exhibit #2, on the easels so that the jurors can see them. What do these two records tell us?
> A. These two records tell us that Mr. Joseph ordered the purchase of 100 shares of IBM common stock on June 1, 2000. Our Ms. Williams took the telephone order from Mr. Joseph and handled the transaction. The stock was purchased that same afternoon,

and Mr. Joseph was sent a confirmation that the purchase was completed on June 2, 2000, and that he would be billed for the purchase.

§5.9.   *Character witnesses*

1.   Law

Character witnesses occupy a unique niche in trials. Infrequently used and, when called, usually appearing in criminal cases, such witnesses are nevertheless potential witnesses in any trial. The law of character evidence must be clearly understood before an intelligent decision to present such evidence at trial can be made. Substantial differences may exist between federal and state courts regarding the admissibility, presentation, and examination of such evidence. You should always review FRE 404 and 405 beforehand, because the procedural rules are technical.

Character evidence is of two distinct types: evidence of specific character traits, admissible as direct or circumstantial evidence; and evidence of truthfulness, admissible only to affect the credibility of witnesses who have testified. Each is properly admissible in limited situations after certain foundation requirements have been met.

a.   Evidence of specific character traits can be either direct or circumstantial. Where a character trait is an "essential element" of a claim or defense, it is direct evidence and can be introduced in both civil and criminal cases. This use of specific character traits evidence is rarely used. For example, in a libel action where the defendant called the plaintiff a drug addict, and the defense is truth, it raises as an essential element of the defense whether the plaintiff is in fact an addict. In an employment discrimination action, where the defendant claims the plaintiff was fired for being a thief and a drunk, the defense raises as an essential element whether the plaintiff is in fact a thief or drunk. When a specific character trait is an essential element of a claim or defense, it can be shown by reputation, opinion, or specific instances of conduct.

Evidence of specific character traits of the defendant and victim is also admissible as circumstantial evidence, but in criminal cases only. This is allowed because a person's reputation for a specific character trait shows that on the pertinent date that person probably acted consistently with that character trait. For example, showing that a defendant has a good reputation for honesty makes it less likely that he committed a theft. In an assault case where the defense is self-defense, showing that the defendant has a good reputation for peacefulness, or that the victim has a bad reputation for peacefulness, is circumstantial proof supporting the defense.

The procedure for using specific character trait evidence as circumstantial evidence is important. Only the defendant in a criminal case may initiate character trait evidence. He does this by calling a witness who testifies, in either reputation or opinion form, to the pertinent character trait of the defendant or victim. Once the defendant has initiated this proof, the prosecution can rebut with the same type of proof. (There are two exceptions to this general rule. First, if the case is a homicide charge involving the defense of self-defense, and the defendant has introduced evidence that the victim was the initial aggressor, the prosecution can rebut with evidence of the victim's good character for peacefulness. For example, if the defendant testifies that the victim attacked him first, the prosecution can rebut by showing that the victim has the character of being a peaceful person. Second, because FRE 404(a) (1) was amended in 2000, if the defendant has introduced evidence of a pertinent character trait of the *victim,* the prosecution may now rebut with evidence of the *defendant's* character trait for the same character. For example, if the defendant introduces evidence that the victim is a violent person, the prosecution can now rebut with evidence that the defendant is a violent person.)

b.   Evidence of truthfulness is governed by different rules. (See FRE 608(a).) Evidence of *bad* character for truthfulness, in reputation or personal opinion form, may be introduced by the opposing party, after a witness has testified, to attack the credibility of that witness. The evidence is admitted solely to diminish the credibility and weight of the witness' testimony. This rule applies to any witness, including any party, who has testified at trial. A party always has the right to attack any witness called by the opposing party with such evidence. Once a witness' truthfulness has been attacked, the proponent of the witness thereafter can offer contrary reputation or opinion evidence.

The procedural differences between evidence of truthfulness and specific character traits must be kept clear. Where character trait evidence as circumstantial proof of conduct is involved, the defendant in a criminal case has the exclusive right to decide whether to raise the relevant trait as an issue. The defendant does this by presenting evidence of that trait, in reputation or personal opinion form. Only after he has done so can the prosecution present rebutting evidence, and the prosecution can rebut only what the defense has elected to raise.

Where a witness' truthfulness is involved, different rules apply. Here both sides have the right to attack any witness who has testified for the opposing party by presenting evidence, in the form of reputation or personal opinion testimony, of that witness' bad character for truthfulness. Moreover, only after the witness has been attacked by such evidence can the party initially calling that witness present contrary evidence.

2.   Foundation

Several foundation requirements must be met before character trait evidence is properly admissible at trial. Although certain differences exist, the foundations for character trait evidence and truthfulness evidence are essentially similar.

First, the evidence must come from a qualified witness. Where reputation evidence is involved, the witness must be able to testify that he has heard the reputation discussed by other persons in the community. Where personal opinion is involved, the witness must be able to testify that he has had periodic contacts with the person about whom he is testifying. In both situations there must be an adequate basis shown for either the reputation or personal opinion.

Second, reputation evidence must be based on a relevant community or neighborhood. Any identifiable community in which the person spends a considerable period of time — residence, work, school, organizations — can be an appropriate community for supporting such evidence.

Third, the evidence must be based on a proper time period. Where the issue is a specific character trait, the relevant time period is the date the act charged was committed or a reasonable prior period. When the issue is truthfulness, the relevant time is the date the person to whom the reputation, or opinion, applies testified at trial or a reasonable prior period.

3.   Tactics

Several factual considerations should be weighed before deciding to present character evidence at trial. A list, by no means exhaustive, includes the following:

a.   How effective will the character evidence be in the type of case on trial? (It is probably more effective in primarily circumstantial cases.)

b.   Is the character evidence consistent with other evidence at trial?

c.   Will the reputation witnesses be able to testify about the reputation in all relevant communities? (Incomplete reputation evidence is always suspect.)

d.   Will the defendant testify? (Jurors may resent a defendant who does not testify, yet calls character witnesses that attack the other side's witnesses.)

e.   Are the character witnesses vulnerable on cross?

f.   Is the person to whom the reputation applies vulnerable on cross?

Once the decision to present character evidence has been made, appropriate witnesses must be selected. For this purpose the following should be considered:

a.   Objective, nonfamily witnesses with diverse backgrounds and no financial relationship to the person in question are preferable.

b.   Witnesses should be selected who can collectively testify to the person's reputation in every relevant community—residence, work, or other qualified areas.

c.   Witnesses should never be called unless they are intimately familiar with the person's reputation or with the person.

d.   Witnesses should be selected that a jury feels comfortable with, who have backgrounds similar to the jurors.

If, after the above considerations have been weighed, the decision to present such evidence is made, then a direct examination can be conducted along the following lines:

Example (reputation for peacefulness):

Q. Please introduce yourself to the jury.
A. My name is Robert Smith.
Q. Where do you live?
A. I live at 123 Rose Lane, Oak Park, Illinois.
Q. Who lives there with you?
A. My wife, Mary, and three children, Tom, Ted, and Betsy.
Q. How long have you lived there?
A. Fourteen years.
Q. What kind of work do you do?
A. I'm a typographer.
Q. How long have you been a typographer?
A. Fifteen years.
Q. What are your duties as a typographer?
A. I set the type for printing and design the ad layouts.
Q. What company do you work for?
A. The Donnelly Press.
Q. What kind of business is the Donnelly Press engaged in?
A. It publishes all kinds of advertising catalogs and pamphlets.
Q. How long have you worked for the Donnelly Press?
A. Six years.
Q. What is your present title?
A. I'm the assistant manager of the typography section.
Q. Do you know John Doe?
A. Yes, I do.
Q. How long have you known him?
A. Fourteen years.
Q. Are you related to him in any way?
A. No.
Q. Do you have any business dealings with him?
A. No.
Q. During the 14 years you have known him, how often would you come into contact with him?
A. Two or three times a week, on the average.
Q. Do you know where he lives?
A. Yes.
Q. What is his address?
A. 136 Tulip Lane, Oak Park.
Q. How long has he lived at that address?
A. About 10 years.
Q. Where is that address in relation to your home?
A. It's on the next block west of my block.
Q. During the years you have known John Doe, have you known other people in the community in which he lives who also know him?

A.   Yes.
Q.   Who are these people?
A.   Other people who live in the neighborhood.
Q.   Have you ever been present when those people discussed John Doe?
A.   Yes, I have.
Q.   How many persons have you heard discuss John Doe?
A.   Probably a couple dozen.
Q.   How many times have you heard them discuss John Doe?
A.   Probably at least a hundred times over the past 14 years.
Q.   Have you heard the reputation of John Doe for peacefulness in the community in which he lives, as it was around April 1, 2000?
A.   Yes, I have.
Q.   What is that reputation?
A.   It's excellent. He's known as a peaceful guy.

If the witness can also give a personal opinion, that can be quickly obtained.

Example (personal opinion):

Q.   Mr. Smith, other than having heard about John Doe's reputation, do you have a personal opinion whether Mr. Doe is a peaceful person?
A.   Yes.
Q.   What is your opinion?
A.   I think he's an extremely peaceful, quiet, gentle kind of guy.

§5.10.   Adverse witnesses

This chapter has evaluated the direct examinations of witnesses that are presumably favorable to the direct examiner. In those situations the witness will cooperate in the development and presentation of his testimony, since his interest is in maximizing the impact of that testimony.

A diametrically different situation exists with adverse witnesses. An adverse witness is any witness who, because of his position as a party or because he has special relationships to a party, will be presumed to give testimony detrimental to the other parties. As the name implies, such a witness favors your opponent. He will use every available opportunity to hurt you. Accordingly, it is usually preferable not to call a witness who is adverse unless necessary to establish an element of a claim or defense. About the only time you might choose to call an adverse witness, although not necessary to prove a claim or defense, is when you are certain that the adverse witness will make a poor impression on the jury.

When you do call a witness that is adverse, you have a witness outside of your control. Because of this, you are permitted to examine the witness as if on cross-examination, so you can control the witness by leading him.

Determine in advance whether the court will permit you to call someone as an adverse witness. Party opponents are adverse witnesses, as well
as officers, directors, and managing agents of parties. These can usually be
presumed to be identified with an adverse party. However, many times a
witness' status is unclear. FRE 611(c) speaks of "a witness identified with
an adverse party," which enlarges the traditional scope of the definition of
an adverse witness. In multiparty litigation, a witness may be adverse to
some, but not all, parties. Make sure you determine in advance that you
will be allowed to treat the witness as if on cross-examination.

When you do call an adverse witness to the stand, make sure you let
the court know what you are doing.

Example:

*Your Honor, at this time we call the defendant, Frank Smith, as an adverse
witness.*

As noted earlier, don't call an adverse witness unless necessary to
prove a claim or defense. If the witness is critical, and must be called, it is
safer to call him in the middle of your case where he will be sandwiched
between favorable witnesses. Make his testimony as brief as possible by
leading directly to the necessary facts, draw them out, and stop. The
longer such a witness is on the stand, the greater the opportunity he has
to hurt your case. When dealing with adverse witnesses, brevity is the safest
approach. Some plaintiff's lawyers, however, sometimes like to start their
case by calling the defendant as an adverse witness. This approach can be
effective when you reliably know that the defendant will make a bad impression on the jury (his deposition showed this), or has horrible facts that
he must admit (his deposition and records have locked him in on these
facts), or has not been adequately prepared to testify as an adverse witness
(the busy executive syndrome).

§5.11. Hostile witnesses

A hostile witness is one who surprises you and unexpectedly turns against
you during his testimony at trial. When a witness becomes hostile, the
same rules as those on adverse witnesses apply: You may examine that witness as if on cross-examination, since leading questions are "necessary to
develop the witness's testimony." (See FRE 611(c).)

The hostile-witness rule stems from the traditional rule that a party
calling a witness vouched for his credibility. Since he was presumably favorable to your side, you were in essence stuck with his testimony, for better or worse. Only if the witness unexpectedly failed to give the testimony
you anticipated could you have the witness declared hostile. The Federal
Rules of Evidence have swept away this questionable presumption, so that
a party does not vouch for the credibility of the witnesses it calls. (See FRE
607.) The Rules, therefore, accept the reality that parties are generally
stuck with the witnesses that are available, and that these are called at trial

from necessity, hardly by choice or design. When such a witness is hostile, he can be asked leading questions (FRE 611(c)).

In those jurisdictions adhering to the traditional rule, having a witness declared hostile, so that you can lead him, requires a showing of surprise. The usual procedure is as follows: When the witness surprises you at trial by giving totally unexpected answers adverse to your side, ask enough additional questions so that your surprise is made apparent to the court. Ask for a side-bar conference or a short recess. Once you are out of the presence of the jury and witness, explain to the judge that you have been surprised and that you had anticipated substantially different testimony. In many jurisdictions you must show surprise *at trial.* In those jurisdictions, where you learn in advance of the trial (usually at the final trial preparation stage) that the witness intends to change his testimony, you cannot make an adequate showing of surprise. You must also demonstrate that you anticipated the witness' testimony to be materially different. Tell the court what your pretrial interviews showed. Where you have interview notes, or the witness made previous written statements, make these available to the judge. You might also conduct a voir dire examination of the witness, still out of the jury's presence, about any prior inconsistent statement. If the witness admits making it, you have demonstrated hostility.

In the presence of the jury, have the witness again admit making the prior inconsistent statement, then proceed with a cross-examination of the witness. Lead, elicit the wanted information, and stop. As with adverse witnesses, the safer approach is to conduct as short an examination as can be done under the circumstances.

§5.12.   *Using deposition transcripts and videotapes*

Most trials involve "live" witnesses. Sometimes, however, witnesses are unavailable by the time the trial begins. Where this is the case, you can introduce a transcript of the witness' former testimony if the requirements of FRE 804(b)(1) are met. Basically, the witness must be "unavailable" under FRE 804(a), and the party against whom the former testimony is now being introduced must have been present and had an opportunity to question the witness, and the same or similar motive for questioning the witness, at the earlier proceeding. The most commonly introduced former testimony is deposition transcripts.

Another way transcripts are commonly introduced at trial is as admissions of the party-opponent, or admissions of an agent of a party-opponent, under FRE 801(d)(2).

When you plan to use an unavailable witness' deposition transcript at trial, you must determine two things: what parts of the transcript will be submitted to the jury, and how you will be permitted to present the transcript in court.

First, advise the court and your opponent which parts of the transcript you intend to read. Opposing counsel should then designate which additional parts he wants read. All evidentiary objections should be made and ruled on in advance. By raising and obtaining rulings on these matters in advance, you will be able to read the admissible transcript sections to the jury uninterrupted by objections. These matters are often taken care of at the pretrial memorandum and pretrial conference stage in civil cases.

Second, advise the court in advance how you intend to read the transcript. The most effective method is to have someone play the role of the witness and actually take the witness stand. You play the role of the questioner. Since both you and the witness will have a copy of the transcript (marked to show what parts will be read), you can now reenact the testimony for the jury. Using this approach is the best way to make a cold record come alive, with a reading that can closely approximate what the actual testimony was like. This works particularly well if the person playing the role of the witness is of the same age and sex as the witness.

If the deposition was videotaped, the same procedures apply. You and the opposing counsel designate the parts to be presented, and the court rules on all evidentiary objections. A videotape editor must then edit the tape to include only the admissible sections. All this should be done well in advance of trial.

When the deposition is of a party in the case, the deposition can be used in two different ways. First, the deposition can be used to impeach the party if he testifies at trial inconsistently with the transcript. Second, the deposition, being an admission of a party-opponent, can be introduced as substantive evidence in the other party's case in chief.

If you decide to use the opposing party's deposition in your case in chief, proceed the same way as with unavailable witnesses. Determine what parts you want read to the jury, have any evidentiary objections ruled on in advance, and have someone else play the role of the party when the transcript is read to the jury. The only difference is that, while all or most of the transcript of an unavailable witness is usually read to the jury, only those parts of the transcript of a party that contain the admissions are normally read. Consequently, reading admissions of a party to the jury is usually accomplished quickly. Another approach is to show the appropriate sections of the transcript to the jury, either by using a large screen projector or television monitor, or by putting key questions and answers on a large foam-core poster board.

Which method is more effective: reading a deposition in court or using a videotaped deposition? This depends on the quality of the videotape and the purpose behind introducing the testimony during trial.

Most deposition videotapes have poor visual and sound quality, at least in comparison to what jurors expect from watching television, and the witness rarely looks and sounds as convincing in the videotape as the witness would look and sound testifying live in the courtroom. This is because deposition videotapes rarely use commercial grade equipment and lighting, the setting has not been adequately planned and prepared, and deponents are rarely trained how to look and act before a camera. For this reason, consider using videotapes of adverse witnesses, especially those who appear nervous, hesitant, or argumentative, since the videotape will show these negative characteristics effectively.

Depositions of favorable witnesses are usually more effectively presented in court by reading the deposition. Keep in mind two things, however. First, keep the reading as short as possible by using only the key segments of the deposition. Second, find a person who can role-play the deponent effectively. In other words, match the characteristics of the deponent to the jurors' expectations of the kind of person the deponent is. For example, if the deponent is a school teacher, use someone who looks and sounds like a school teacher, and train that person to read the deposition answers persuasively.

§5.13. *Judicial notice and stipulations*

1. Judicial notice

Judicial notice is governed by FRE 201. Its purpose is to increase trial efficiency and admit indisputable evidence where formal proof of these facts would be both difficult and time consuming.

Judicial notice can be taken in two areas. First, the court can take judicial notice of facts that are generally known in that particular geographic area. In San Francisco, for example, it is generally known that the Golden Gate Bridge is between San Francisco and Marin County. Second, the court can judicially notice facts that can be accurately and easily verified from a reliable source. Common examples are Department of Labor actuarial tables showing life expectancy, and almanac facts, such as when a full moon or high tide occurred, or what day of the week a certain date was.

The party wishing to have the court judicially notice a fact must ask the judge to take judicial notice, and the opposing party must have an opportunity to state objections. If the court takes judicial notice of the fact, the jury is informed of the fact through an instruction. In civil cases the jury must conclusively take a fact judicially noticed as being true, but this is not so in criminal cases. Because of due process concerns, juries in criminal cases are instructed that they may, but are not required to, accept a judicially noticed fact as being true.

Example:

In a civil case, the court would tell the jury: *In this case, you must accept as a fact that . . . .*

In a criminal case, the court would instruct: *In this case, you may, but are not required to, accept as a fact that . . . .*

In practice, judicial notice is not commonly used. If a fact is so obvious that it can be judicially noticed, the standard way of getting the fact before the jury is through a stipulation.

2. Stipulations

A stipulation is simply an agreement between the parties that certain facts are true and are not in dispute. If the stipulation involves an absent witness, the agreement usually states that if the witness were called at trial, he would testify to certain things. Regardless what the stipulation is about, it must be brought to the attention of the jurors. The usual, and best, procedure is to prepare the stipulation in writing, have the lawyers sign it, and present it to the court in advance. The stipulation is then usually marked as an exhibit and read to the jury at an appropriate time. (See §6.3(19).)

§5.14. *Redirect examination*

When the cross-examination of a witness has been completed, the direct examiner may conduct a redirect examination of that witness. The proper purpose of the redirect examination is to rebut, explain, or further develop matters raised during the cross-examination; it is not the place to repeat or rehash the direct examination. This means that the scope of the redirect will be limited to what the cross-examiner chooses to raise during his examination. Judges vary widely, however, on the latitude they permit during the redirect examination. Some will strictly forbid going beyond the scope of the cross-examination. Others will give the redirect examiner a free rein. This is within the court's discretion under FRE 611(a).

Should you redirect? Every redirect examination necessarily implies that something was either forgotten, or needs fixing. Therefore, decide first if anything needs to be addressed, or if it can be ignored. If it's not broken, don't fix it. If you can't fix it, don't try. Most of the time you can anticipate what the cross-examiner will do, and deal with it during the direct examination.

What can you do on redirect examination? Three basic things. First, you can rehabilitate a witness who has been impeached with a prior inconsistent statement by asking the witness to explain why the inconsistency happened. The explanation will sometimes eliminate or lessen the impact of the inconsistency. Second, you can ask the witness to correct cross-examination testimony that was wrong or misleading. Where the witness has said something that is factually wrong on cross-examination, or where the cross-examiner's questions have left an impression that is misleading, you can have the witness correct it on redirect. Third, you can use the redirect examination to develop the new matters brought out on cross. These are all permitted responses to the cross-examination. In addition, the redirect should return to the mood of the direct examination, so that the jurors turn away from the atmosphere created by the cross.

What should you avoid on redirect examination? Don't redirect merely because you have the opportunity. Avoid discussing minor matters that the jury will soon forget. Redirect should focus on key points that make a difference. Therefore, when you redirect, go immediately to a key point, make it forcefully and efficiently, and go to the next point. End on a high note, then immediately stop. If you don't have an important point that you can make forcefully, don't redirect at all.

Some lawyers frequently withhold an important point from the direct examination with the idea that this point will have more impact if it is disclosed for the first time on redirect examination. This is dangerous. "Sandbagging" may be great when it works, but is a disaster when it fails. Holding back a choice piece of information from the direct examination in the hope that the cross-examiner will ask about it and choke on it is a dangerous tactic. The cross-examiner, either through design or luck, may decide not to cross-examine at all, or probe areas totally divorced from the withheld topic, thereby preventing you from eliciting the testimony at all. (If this happens, you can always try asking the court for permission to reopen the direct examination or recall the witness later. This is discretionary with the court. Even if permitted, however, the testimony will not appear as convincing, since the jury will view it as an afterthought.) The safer approach is always to bring out all the important testimony during the direct examination.

Another common tendency is for the direct and cross-examiners to constantly ask "just one more question," under the theory that it is always advantageous to have the last word. Keep in mind that constantly seesawing back and forth, so that the redirect is followed by the re-recross, and so on, inevitably develops no further information and is viewed by the jury as boring and nit-picking. If you have nothing substantial to develop, don't redirect or recross solely to rehash already existing testimony. Tell the court you have no further questions of the witness. The jury will appreciate both your professionalism and brevity.

The most common redirect examinations involve situations where the cross-examination has called into question the witness' conduct, or where the cross-examination has brought out only parts of a conversation or occurrence, or the witness has been impeached with a prior inconsistent statement. In each situation the redirect examination can develop additional facts that tell the complete story or explain why the inconsistency occurred.

Example:

The cross-examination of a rape victim has stressed the fact that the victim waited two hours after the rape before she called the police. The implication is that a rape really never occurred. On redirect the following question is proper:

Q. Why didn't you call the police for two hours?
A. I was upset and afraid. He said he'd come back and kill me if I called the police.

Example:

The cross-examination of an eyewitness to a shooting brought out that the witness said nothing about seeing the shooting when interviewed by the police. The implication is that the trial testimony has been fabricated. On redirect the following question is proper:

> Q. Bobby, why did you tell the police that you saw and heard nothing, when you tell us today that you saw and heard the entire thing?
> A. I didn't want to get involved. I know all the people involved.

Of course, these are also the kinds of things the direct examiner should anticipate and bring out during the direct. That is entirely proper, since FRE 607 permits a witness to be impeached during the direct, after which the explanation for the inconsistency can be brought out.

Example:

The cross-examination has elicited part of a conversation, that part that helps the cross-examiner. On redirect the following question is proper:

> Q. Other than "I'm sorry this whole thing happened," did you say anything else to Mr. Smith at that time?
> A. Yes, I also said: "However, if you don't pay me the money you owe, I'll have to hire a lawyer to collect it."

When a witness has been impeached by a prior inconsistent statement, it is proper on redirect to "rehabilitate" the witness. This is done by having the witness explain how or why the inconsistency occurred. If there is a sensible, logical explanation for the inconsistency, the impact of the inconsistency will be significantly lessened.

Example:

On direct examination a police officer has testified that the defendant he arrested stated "I shot John Doe and he deserved it." The cross-examiner impeached the police officer by showing that the defendant's statement does not appear on the officer's initial case report (impeachment by omission). On redirect the following questions are proper:

> Q. Did you make out any other case reports?
> A. Yes, I made two supplementary reports.
> Q. Did you put the defendant's statement in those reports?
> A. Yes, in both of them.
> Q. Is there a reason the statement wasn't put in your initial report?
> A. Yes. The initial report covered only the events up to the defendant's arrest at his house. He made the statement at the station, and what happened there is covered by the supplementary reports.

Under limited circumstances a witness impeached by a prior inconsistent statement can be rehabilitated with a prior consistent statement. This is proper only when the cross-examination suggests a recent fabrication or improper influence or motive, and the prior consistent statement was made before the time a reason to change the testimony arose. Under FRE 801(d)(1)(B) the prior consistent statement is then admissible, since under these circumstances it rebuts the implication of recent fabrication or improper influence or motive.

Example:

A defense witness in a personal injury case is cross-examined as follows:

> Q. You know the truck that was involved in the collision with the plaintiff's car was a truck owned by United Parcel Service, the defendant in this case?
> A. Yes.
> Q. Three months after the accident, you got a job with UPS, right?
> A. Yes.
> Q. And now you claim that the UPS truck was driving properly at the time of the accident?
> A. That's right.

This cross-examination has suggested that the witness's testimony is a product of the witness being hired by the defendant after the accident. Since the cross-examination has suggested an improper influence, the redirect examiner can rebut it with a prior consistent statement, made before the time of the claimed improper influence.

> Q. (On redirect) Did you talk to a policeman at the scene of the accident?
> A. Yes, I did.
> Q. What did you tell the policeman at that time?
> A. I told him that the UPS truck was driving properly at the time of the accident.

This redirect examination rebuts the cross-examination's suggestion that the witness is testifying favorably to the defendant because she was hired by the defendant after the accident, since the witness said the same thing to a police officer right after the accident, before being hired by the defendant.

VI

EXHIBITS

§6.1. Introduction

Ours is the age of visual media. Television has become the dominant information-transmitting source in our society. Printed and aural communications have taken a back seat to the visual media. A whole generation of Americans has been raised and educated primarily by seeing. Children learn by watching TV, not by reading. Critics complain that the art of clear speaking and clear writing is becoming lost.

Whether this change is desirable can be debated, but not its existence. Visual communications have grown by leaps and bounds. Advertising on TV, magazines, and billboards is often predominantly nonverbal, influencing its viewers by subconscious appeals.

Social science research supports the shift from the aural and written to the visual. Studies show that learning and retention are significantly better if information is communicated visually. Studies also show that repeating basic facts and ideas approximately three or four times substantially improve retention. Finally, studies confirm that if information is presented through multiple "channels" — aural, written, and visual — understanding and memory are again substantially improved. In short, visual exhibits are important not only in presenting new information in an attractive, memorable way but also in highlighting and summarizing information already presented through another medium. "Show and tell" works.

These changes have hardly gone unnoticed in the courtroom. Led by imaginative personal injury lawyers, other lawyers began to realize that, in the courtroom as well, a picture was indeed worth a thousand words. If a picture was so useful, so too could be a map, chart, diagram, model, movie, experiment, or in-court demonstration. Trial lawyers began using aerial photographs. Automobiles and machinery were reassembled in court. "A day in the life" movies portrayed personal injury plaintiffs. Elaborate models of buildings and accident sites appeared. In-court demonstrations became common. Computer-generated graphics and three-dimensional simulations were admissible. In short, exhibits assumed a new importance.

What can be an exhibit? In its broadest sense an exhibit can be anything, other than testimony, that can be perceived by the senses and be presented in the courtroom as evidence. Any trial lawyer who has ever been involved in a case that used exhibits creatively knows the impact they have on the jury.

The exhibits become the center of attention. They make an immediate and lasting impression on the jury. It sees the exhibits as not only more interesting, but also more reliable. Accordingly, any aspiring trial lawyer must learn more than how to establish the foundation for common as well as more dramatic exhibits. He must also learn when to use exhibits and other visual aids, and how to present them effectively at trial.

This chapter will discuss the proper procedures for having exhibits admitted in evidence, the foundation requirements of exhibits commonly encountered during trials, and how and when to use exhibits and other visual aids effectively during all the stages of a trial.

§6.2. *How to get exhibits in evidence*

Most jurisdictions follow the rule that exhibits can only be offered in evidence by the party currently presenting evidence. This means that only the plaintiff can introduce exhibits in evidence in the plaintiff's case-in-chief, and only the defendant in the defendant's case-in-chief. It also means that while the cross-examiner may use other exhibits during cross-examinations of the opponent's witnesses, the cross-examiner can only offer those exhibits in evidence when it is the cross-examiner's turn to present evidence. Some jurisdictions, however, permit a cross-examiner to introduce exhibits in evidence during cross-examinations of an opponent's witnesses, provided that a proper foundation has been established. These procedures are governed by FRE 611(a) and are in the trial judge's discretion.

Exhibits can be admitted in evidence only when a sequence of procedural steps has been followed. These steps are part of a litany that should be smoothly and efficiently demonstrated for each exhibit, using a qualified witness.

Your preliminary consideration is witness selection. Many times you will have more than one witness who is competent to qualify an exhibit for admission in evidence. When this is so, you will ordinarily select the witness who has the most knowledge of the exhibit and its required foundation and makes the best impression on the jury. Call the witness early in your case in chief, since it is usually advantageous to get your exhibits before the jury as soon as possible. (If you have witnesses who may become confused by the exhibits, consider calling them *before* the exhibits are introduced.) Keep in mind that some exhibits may need more than one witness to establish a proper foundation. In such cases, do not offer the exhibit in evidence until the last necessary witness has testified.

The following steps for getting exhibits into evidence constitute the most complete procedure. Most courts have relaxed some of the requirements. For instance, many courts permit or require marking exhibits before trial. Many do not require asking permission to approach the witness. Nevertheless, you must be familiar with the most formal procedural requirements, then determine in advance of trial which ones have been re-laxed or eliminated by your particular court. Be sure to make a good record of what you are doing in the courtroom by stating what you are doing as you do it.

Step 1.   Have the exhibit marked

Every exhibit must be marked so it can be differentiated from all others. Exhibits are most commonly given sequential numbers or letters (e.g., 1, 2, 3). Where certain exhibits are part of a series, they can be marked 1A, 1B, 1C, or 1-1, 1-2, 1-3. Sets of exhibits that should remain together should be marked as group exhibits. Use any numbering system that logically marks the exhibits in your type of case. Exhibits are usually marked to show which party offered them (e.g., Plaintiff, Defendant, Government, Defendant Smith), although the practice in some jurisdictions is not to designate which side offered the exhibit. In that case, a common practice is to allocate certain numbers to the plaintiff, others to the defendant (e.g., plaintiff has #1–99, defendant has #100–199).

In most jurisdictions exhibits are simply marked "Plaintiff's Exhibit #1," "Defendant's Exhibit #1," and so on. A few jurisdictions mark exhibits "for identification," as in "People's Exhibit #5 for identification." If the ex-hibits are not marked before trial, the court clerk or the court reporter, depending on local practice, usually marks them. In most jurisdictions ex-hibit labels are put on the exhibits, either on the front or the back of the exhibit. The exhibit labels, which are often color-coded, usually show which side offered the exhibit, the exhibit number, and when it was first introduced.

Example:

> *Counsel:*   (To court clerk) Please mark this Plaintiff's Exhibit #1. (Hand the exhibit to the clerk, who will attach a label to the exhibit, mark it "Plaintiff's Exhibit #1," and return it to you.)

If your jurisdiction permits or requires premarking exhibits, make sure your labels clearly designate which party's exhibits they are. If the ex-hibit has previously been used during the trial, it will already be marked, so this step is unnecessary.

Step 2.   Show the exhibit to opposing counsel

Fairness requires that the opposing lawyer see the exhibit so that she knows what kind of exhibit it is and what the proper foundation for that exhibit is, and so that she can make a timely objection if the foundation is not properly established or another evidentiary problem exists. Most ju-risdictions require that the exhibit be shown to the opposing lawyer before the foundation is established, and the common practice is to state what you are doing so that the trial record is clear.

Example:

> Counsel: For the record, I am now showing Mr. Smith Plaintiff's Exhibit #1. (Hand the exhibit to counsel, who should have a reasonable opportunity to inspect or read the exhibit, and get the exhibit back.)

In a few jurisdictions the practice is to show the exhibit to the opposing counsel only when the exhibit is offered in evidence. This is not the preferred approach, however, since it does not give the opposing counsel a timely opportunity to examine the exhibit to determine what the proper foundation for that exhibit is, or to make an early objection.

Step 3.   Ask the court's permission to approach the witness

Example:

> Counsel: Your Honor, may I approach the witness?
> Court: You may.

This formal requirement has been eliminated in many jurisdictions. In addition, the court bailiff in some jurisdictions hands exhibits to the witnesses.

Step 4.   Show the exhibit to the witness

Example:

> Counsel: Mr. Johnson, I am handing you Plaintiff's Exhibit #1. (Walk to the witness and hand the exhibit to him or place it in front of him.)

You should hand the exhibit to the witness so that the jury cannot see what the exhibit contains, since the jury should not see the exhibit unless it has been admitted in evidence. If the opposing lawyer has indicated that he has no objection to the exhibit, there is no problem. However, if you expect the opposing lawyer to object, this is important. Photographs, documents, and records can easily be handed to the witness without the jury seeing their contents. Physical objects and large diagrams, however, sometimes cannot be handled in the courtroom without the jury's seeing them. As the opponent, if you have a serious objection to the exhibit, ask the judge to require that the foundation for such an exhibit be first made out of the jury's presence and that you be permitted to cross-examine the witness. If the judge sustains your objection, the jury never sees the exhibit and cannot be improperly influenced by it. This is a useful procedure when potentially inflammatory or misleading exhibits are involved.

Step 5.   Lay the foundation for the exhibit

You are now ready to establish the required foundation for the particular kind of exhibit you have. Section 6.3 of this chapter will cover the foundations necessary for different types of exhibits commonly introduced in trials.

Step 6.   Offer the exhibit in evidence

Once you have established the proper foundation for the exhibit, offer it in evidence. The opposing lawyer may make an objection, briefly stating the evidentiary basis for it. Show the exhibit to the judge when you offer it in evidence, if the judge needs to see the exhibit to rule on any objections.

Example:

> *Counsel:*   Your Honor, we offer Plaintiff's Exhibit #1 in evidence.
> *Court:*   Any objections, counsel?
> *Opposing counsel:*   Yes, your Honor. It's hearsay.
> *Court:*   The objection is overruled. Plaintiff's Exhibit #1 is admitted.

If the objecting lawyer wants to make a more lengthy argument on the objection, or the judge wants to hear further argument, this should be done at a "side bar," out of the jury's hearing. This means that the lawyers will come to the front or side of the judge's bench and make their arguments in quiet voices so that the jurors cannot hear the legal arguments being made. The judge will then rule. On particularly important issues the judge may excuse the jury from the courtroom, or take the lawyers into the judge's chambers, to hear the arguments. Regardless of the procedure, the important thing to remember is that legal arguments should not be heard by the jury, and it is improper for a lawyer to make an evidentiary objection in front of the jury in a way that is calculated to influence the jury.

If you have a serious objection, or you think you can destroy the foundation for the exhibit, as the opposing counsel you can ask the judge for permission to cross-examine the witness on the exhibit's foundation. This is sometimes done out of the jury's presence.

Example:

> *Opposing counsel:*   Your Honor, may I voir dire the witness on the exhibit?
> *Court:*   You may.

Whether a proper foundation can be established can only be determined at trial, since a witness is usually necessary to establish a proper foundation. However, other objections such as privilege or hearsay can often be ruled on in advance. Where this is the case, you should make a motion in limine before trial to raise the objection and get a ruling. In civil cases rulings on objections are sometimes made at the final pretrial conference, where the judge usually rules on the various objections raised in the joint pretrial memorandum.

Step 7.   Have the exhibit marked in evidence

When the exhibit is admitted in evidence, a record must be made. In most jurisdictions the court clerk marks the exhibit "admitted" and notes the date and time the exhibit was admitted. This is usually marked on the exhibit label. In these jurisdictions you simply hand the exhibit to the clerk, who makes the appropriate notation. In other jurisdictions, which still label exhibits "for identification," the clerk or court reporter shows that the exhibit is now in evidence by crossing out the "for identification" notation on the exhibit label. Whatever the procedure, make sure you follow it so that the record clearly shows that the exhibit is now in evidence.

Step 8.   Have the witness use or mark the exhibit, if appropriate

Once the exhibit has been admitted in evidence, you should always consider how the exhibit can be used or marked to increase its usefulness. Tangible objects can be held to show how they were used. Diagrams and photographs can be marked to show locations and distances. Documents and records can have their significant sections underlined or highlighted. The various techniques for marking and using exhibits effectively are discussed in §6.4.

Keep in mind that some courts still do not allow documents and records to be marked, on the theory that underlining or circling important terms or sections alters exhibits. However, most courts take the view that the witness's markings on exhibits are just illustrations of the witness's testimony that do not change the admissibility status of the exhibits.

Some courts require reoffering the exhibit in evidence, after a witness has marked it, particularly when demonstrative exhibits are involved, otherwise the witness markings are not considered to be in evidence. And some courts bar any witness markings on an exhibit after the exhibit has been admitted in evidence. The moral is obvious: Know your local practices.

Step 9.   Obtain permission to show or read the exhibit to the jury

Example:

> *Counsel:*   Your Honor, may we show Plaintiff's Exhibit #1 in evidence to the jury at this time?
> *Court:*   You may.

This is a matter of the judge's discretion. The judge will usually allow the exhibit to be shown or read to the jury if it can be done efficiently. If the exhibit is a document several pages long, the judge may tell you to continue with your examination, as the jury will get a chance to see the exhibit during a break or other more convenient time.

Step 10. "Publish" the exhibit

"Publishing" an exhibit is simply the act of showing or reading an exhibit to the jury. How and when an exhibit should be published with maximum effectiveness will be discussed in detail in the next section. In general, however, how you publish the exhibit depends for the most part on what kind of exhibit it is. Many exhibits, such as photographs and tangible objects, are usually shown to the jury.

Example:

> *Counsel:* Your Honor, may we show Plaintiff's Exhibit #1 to the jury?
> *Court:* You may.
> (Then hand the exhibit to the first juror, who will look at it and pass it on to the next juror until all jurors have seen it. Then get the exhibit back after all the jurors have seen it, and give it to the court clerk.)

Other exhibits, principally documents and records, can be published either by showing or reading them to the jury. Where the documents are simple, such as with checks or promissory notes, the exhibit can easily be shown or read to the jury. If read, either the counsel or the witness can read it.

Example (counsel):

> (Counsel stands before the jury.)
> *Counsel:* Ladies and gentlemen, Plaintiff's Exhibit #1 reads as follows:
> (Then read the exhibit to the jury.)

Example (witness):

> Q. Mr. Smith, please read Plaintiff's Exhibit #1 to the jury.
> A. (Witness then reads the exhibit.)

Many records, however, are lengthy or complicated, and showing or reading them to the jury may be ineffective. The better technique is to ask the witness to read the important parts of the record to the jury. The jury can then look at the entire exhibit during a recess.

Example:

> Q. Mr. Smith, does that invoice, Plaintiff's Exhibit #1, show on what date the shipment was made?

A. Yes, it was made on December 12, 2000.
Q. Does it reflect the gross weight of the shipment?
A. Yes, it was 1,936 lbs.
Q. Does the invoice have a place where the addressee acknowledges receipt of the shipment?
A. Yes.
Q. What is contained in that place on the invoice?
A. The place is captioned "Received the above shipment." It bears the signature R. Schwartz and the date of December 14, 2000.

At the conclusion of your case in chief, it is always a sound procedure, before resting, to reoffer your exhibits in evidence or check with the judge that you have correctly recorded the admission of the exhibits. The judge will then usually run down his list of exhibits and report what his ruling was on each one. This creates a clear record and avoids possible confusion later in the trial or on appeal.

These steps are the most formal requirements for admitting exhibits in evidence. Most jurisdictions have eliminated some of the formalities. For instance, having the court reporter or clerk mark exhibits, marking them "for identification," or asking for permission to approach the witness are frequently no longer required. You should use the most efficient procedure allowed in your court.

The following example illustrates the exhibits procedure usually followed in federal courts.

Example:

(Exhibits have been marked before trial.)
Q. Your Honor, may the record reflect that I am showing Plaintiff's Exhibit #1 to counsel? (Hand exhibit to opposing counsel, and get it back.)
Court: It will.
Q. (Hand exhibit to witness.) Mrs. White, I'm showing you Plaintiff's Exhibit #1. Do you recognize the scene in that photograph?
A. Yes.
Q. What scene does it show?
A. It shows the corner of Elm and Maple Streets where the accident happened.
Q. Does the photo fairly and accurately show how that intersection looked at the time of the collision?
A. Yes, it does.
Q. Your Honor, we offer Plaintiff's Exhibit #1 in evidence.
Court: Any objections, counsel?
Counsel: No, your Honor.
Court: It's admitted.
Q. Mrs. White, does the photograph show where the two cars collided?

A. Yes.

Q. Using this red felt pen, please put an "X" where the cars collided.

(Witness marks photograph.)

Q. Does the photograph show where you were standing when the cars collided?

A. Yes.

Q. Using this blue felt pen, please put a "W" in a circle where you were standing.

(Witness marks photograph.)

Q. Your Honor, may we show Plaintiff's Exhibit #1 to the jury?

Court: You may.

(Hand photograph to first juror.)

How do you handle exhibits that are already admitted by pretrial order or by stipulation of the parties? Keep in mind that although the exhibit is in evidence and therefore can be shown or read to the jury, the jury has not seen it before and does not know why it is reliable. Hence, it is best to use a witness to provide a quick introduction, although a formal foundation is unnecessary.

Example:

(Get the exhibit from the court clerk.)

Q. Ms. Johnson, I'm showing you Plaintiff's Exhibit #6, which has already been admitted in evidence. Do you know what this exhibit is?

A. Sure, it's one of my company's standard invoices which we make each time we sell something to a customer.

Q. Let's talk about the information on the invoice. First, does it show who the customer is?

A. Yes, a Robert Parker.

The same approach can be used when an exhibit is used again at trial, after it has already been admitted in evidence through an earlier witness. It is best to have the witness quickly identify the exhibit and acknowledge its accuracy, although you do not need or want to go through the formal foundation litany.

Example:

Q. Mr. Williams, I'm showing you a diagram, already admitted in evidence as Defendant's Exhibit #4. Do you recognize the intersection on the exhibit?

A. Sure, that's the corner of Main and Elm Streets.

Q. Please draw a "W" in a circle showing where you were standing when the two cars collided.

(Witness marks the diagram.)

§6.3. *Foundations for exhibits*

Every foundation must meet three basic requirements before the exhibit can be admitted in evidence. These are:

1. The qualifying witness must be competent.
2. The exhibit must be relevant and reliable.
3. The exhibit must be authenticated.

The first two requirements rarely cause problems. The witness will ordinarily have first-hand knowledge because he previously saw the exhibit, or knows the facts underlying the exhibits. Relevance can usually be established through the testimony of the witness or by having the judge examine the exhibit. Reliability, which is involved whenever documentary exhibits are offered, can be established by showing that the exhibit is either nonhearsay or falls within a hearsay exception.

Authentication is the principal issue raised at trial. Authentication, governed primarily by FRE 901 and 902, involves establishing that the exhibit is in fact what it purports to be. In a contract action, for example, a contract that is shown to be signed by the defendant has been authenticated and is relevant; if this contract was not in fact signed by the defendant, it cannot be authenticated and is irrelevant. In trial lawyer's language, you must "lay a foundation" for the exhibit. When you lay a proper foundation for a particular kind of exhibit, you have established both its relevance and its reliability. This section sets out the necessary foundations for the kinds of exhibits frequently introduced at trial.

Keep in mind that you are establishing a foundation for both the judge and jury. The judge, concerned only with admissibility, is interested in seeing if you have made a prima facie showing under FRE 901(a) that the exhibit is what it purports to be. The jury, concerned only with credibility and weight, is interested in how persuasive your witness and foundation testimony is. Hence, your foundation must be technically adequate, to satisfy the judge, and factually persuasive, to convince the jury.

Always ask yourself: what else should I ask, beyond what is legally required for admissibility, to convince the jury that the exhibit is authentic and reliable? When the exhibit is important, it takes only one or two additional questions to convince the jury.

Example:

Q. Officer Wilson, I'm showing you what has been marked as State's Exhibit #4. Do you recognize it?
A. Yes, I do.
Q. What do you recognize it to be?
A. That's the gun I took from the defendant's jacket pocket at the time I arrested him.
Q. Is that gun, State's Exhibit #4, in the same condition now as it was when you took it from the defendant?
A. Yes.

This is a legally sufficient foundation for admissibility. However, if the gun is a key piece of evidence, ask additional questions to convince the jury.

Q.   Officer Wilson, how do you know that's the same gun?
A.   When I took the gun from the defendant, I scratched the date and my badge number on the handle. You can see the date — 6/1/00 — and my badge number — 5627 — on the wooden handle. In addition, I described the gun and recorded the serial number in my police report, and it matches this gun.

Although there are numerous kinds of exhibits, most of them fit into one of four categories, and the basic foundation requirements are the same for all exhibits within a category. These categories are as follows:

1.   *Real evidence.* Since "real evidence" is the actual tangible object involved, the exhibit is admissible if it is actually what it purports to be. Common examples are weapons, clothing, drugs, blood, and other objects. Hence, the proponent must show that the exhibit is the actual one, and not a substitute, and that it is in basically the same condition now as it was on the relevant date.

2.   *Demonstrative evidence.* "Demonstrative evidence" is not the actual object itself, but is evidence that represents or illustrates the real thing which is admissible as substantive evidence. Common examples are photographs, diagrams, maps, models, and computer graphics. Hence, demonstrative evidence is admissible if it fairly and accurately represents the real thing and helps the trier of fact understand the real thing.

3.   *Writings.* Writings are documents that have legal significance. As such, the documents are nonhearsay. Common examples are written contracts, letters that form contracts, promissory notes, checks, and wills. These writings are admissible if they were in fact executed by the person they appear to have been signed by. Hence, the signatures must be identified as being genuine before these writings are admissible.

4.   *Records.* Business records are hearsay, and are admissible as hearsay exceptions only if the foundation requirements of FRE 803(6) are met. Business records include not only common records like invoices, shipping documents, and bills, but can also include things like telephone memos and diaries. A custodian or other qualified witness must testify that the record involved was made under the requirements of that rule, since this shows that the record was accurately made and maintained by the business. Public records are admissible if the requirements of FRE 803(8) and 902 are met.

The following exhibit types described in this section expand on these four basic categories and demonstrate the foundation requirements necessary for admission. Keep in mind that each required step of the admissions procedure, from marking the exhibit to reading or showing the exhibit to the jury, must be followed each time an exhibit is introduced into evidence.

The admissions procedure and foundation should be done smoothly and efficiently. Leading questions are proper when doing this since there is no nonleading way the foundation information can reasonably be obtained from the qualifying witness. Hence, leading questions that use the words of the foundation requirements are proper, and this is the standard way of establishing the necessary foundation.

The foundations that follow are legally adequate from the judge's point of view. Beyond the legally required foundation, however, you should always ask what additional questions you can ask that will convince the jury, which is free to accept or reject the admitted exhibit, that the exhibit is what it purports to be and is reliable.

1.   Tangible objects

Elements:

  a. Exhibit is relevant.
  b. Exhibit can be identified visually, or through other senses.
  c. Witness recognizes the exhibit.
  d. Witness knows what the exhibit looked like on the relevant date.
  e. Exhibit is in the same condition or substantially the same condition now as when the witness saw it on the relevant date.

The above elements pertain to any tangible object that can be positively identified by the senses, usually because the witness previously saw it. Common examples are weapons, clothing, and other objects that can be identified visually, either because the article is inherently unique in appearance, or because a serial number, markings or identifying symbols make it unique. In these situations a chain of custody is not required.

Example:

A police officer has testified that he found a handgun at the defendant's house.

  Q. Please describe the weapon you saw on the dresser in the bedroom.
  A. It was a .38 caliber blue steel Colt revolver, five-shot, with a brown wood handle and a two-inch barrel.
Step 1. Have exhibit marked.
Step 2. Show exhibit to opposing counsel.
Step 3. Ask permission to approach witness.
Step 4. Show exhibit to witness.
Step 5. Establish foundation:
  Q. Officer Doe, I show you Plaintiff's Exhibit #1 and ask you to examine it. (Witness does so.) Have you seen it before?
  A. Yes, I have.
  Q. When was the first time you saw this exhibit?
  A. When I saw it on the dresser in the bedroom on December 13, 2000.

Q. How are you able to recognize this as being the same revolver?

A. Well, I remember what kind of gun it was and what it looked like. I can remember the notches that were cut in the wooden handle (pointing). I also recorded the serial number appearing on the barrel in my report. In addition, I scratched the date and my initials on the trigger guard, and they're still there: "12/13/00, T.A.D."

Q. Is Plaintiff's Exhibit #1 in the same or substantially the same condition today as when you first saw it on December 13, 2000?

A. Yes, sir, it is.

Q. Is there anything different about this exhibit today compared to when you first saw it?

A. Other than where I scratched the date and my initials, no, sir.

Step   6.   Offer exhibit in evidence.

Step   7.   Have exhibit marked in evidence.

Step   8.   Have witness use exhibit.

Step   9.   Ask permission to show exhibit to jury.

Step 10.   Show exhibit to jury.

If the physical object is so large that it cannot be brought into the courtroom, or if aids such as photographs and diagrams do not adequately show a scene, the jury can be taken to the object or scene. This is called a "view." The procedure is sometimes regulated by statute, but otherwise deciding whether to permit a view and how it should be conducted is usually within the discretion of the trial judge.

2.   Tangible objects — chain of custody

Where an object cannot be uniquely identified through the senses, a chain of custody must be established to demonstrate that it is the same object that was previously found. Although most common in cases involving narcotics such as pills or powdered drugs, a "chain" may be necessary in many other circumstances. A bullet, wire, rubber tubing, paint chips, and dirt samples may have no identifying markings and are too small to be marked. Liquids such as blood or brake fluid cannot be marked. In all these cases a chain of custody must be established to prove that the object is the same one, and has not been switched, altered, or tampered with, before it can properly be received in evidence.

Elements:

There are two basic methods to show a chain of custody:

a. Show that the exhibit has been in one or more persons' continuous, exclusive, and secure possession at all times.

b. Show that the exhibit was in a uniquely marked, sealed, tamperproof container at all times.

Example (method a):

A police officer has testified that he removed a broken hydraulic brake-fluid tube from a car immediately after an accident.

Q. Officer Doe, what did that tubing look like?
A. It was a black rubber tube, eight inches long, one inch in diameter. It was covered with a black fluid and had a large crack running lengthwise.
Q. What did you do with the tubing after you removed it from the car?
A. I put it in a small cardboard box, labeled the box, and placed it in my evidence locker.
Q. Was the tubing in your possession from the time you removed it from the car to the time you put it in your evidence locker?
A. Yes, sir.
Q. Did anyone else handle it?
A. No, sir.
Q. Did you do anything to or with the tubing during this time?
A. No, sir.
Q. What does your evidence locker consist of?
A. There's a room in the station we reserve to store evidence. Every officer has his own steel locker with a lock on it. It's about the size of a file drawer.
Q. Who has access to your evidence locker?
A. Only me. I've got the only key to the lock.
Q. After placing the tubing in your locker, what's the next thing you did?
A. I locked the door to it.
Q. Between December 13, 2000, and today, did you ever remove the box or tubing from your locker?
A. No.
Q. Did you ever allow anyone else to open and enter your locker?
A. No.
Q. Did you ever give your locker key to anyone else?
A. No.
Q. Did you do anything with the tubing today?
A. This morning I went to my locker, unlocked it, took out the box with the tubing, and took it with me to court.
Q. Has the tubing been in your possession since you removed it from your locker this morning?
A. Yes, it has.
Q. Did you do anything to or with the tubing today?
A. No, sir.
Q. May I have the tubing, please? (Obtain tubing from witness.)

Step 1. Have exhibit marked.
Step 2. Show exhibit to opposing counsel.
Step 3. Ask permission to approach witness.
Step 4. Show exhibit to witness.

Step 5. Establish foundation:

> Q. Officer Doe, I show you what has just been marked Plaintiff's Exhibit #1. Is this the tubing you removed from your evidence locker and brought to court today?
>
> A. Yes, it is.
>
> Q. Is it in substantially the same condition now as when you first saw it on December 13, 2000?
>
> A. Yes.

Step 6. Offer exhibit in evidence.

Step 7. Have exhibit marked in evidence.

Step 8. Have witness use exhibit.

Step 9. Ask permission to show exhibit to jury.

Step 10. Show exhibit to jury.

Notice that the witness was *not* asked if this tubing was the same tubing that he obtained on December 13, 2000. The answer to that question necessarily follows from the testimony.

Example (method b):

A quantity of powdered heroin in a plastic bag was seized by a police officer, given to a laboratory custodian, and then to a chemist.

Police officer testifies.

> Q. Officer Doe, after taking the bag containing the brown powdery substance from the defendant on December 13, 2000, what did you do with it?
>
> A. I kept it in my possession and took it with me to headquarters. I then placed the bag containing the powder in one of our plastic evidence bags, labeled it, and sealed it.
>
> Q. How did you label the evidence bag?
>
> A. The bag has a special texture on the inside of the opening where you can write. I put the date, subject's name, address, and time of seizure, my name, badge number, and the case number.
>
> Q. How did you seal the evidence bag?
>
> A. We have a special machine which seals the opening by heating it so the two sides melt into each other. It's sort of like laminating plastic. The sealed strip is about one-and-a-half inches wide, and it also seals in the identifying marks I made.
>
> Q. What did you do with the bag after labeling and sealing it?
>
> A. I carried it to the chemistry section of our crime laboratory.
>
> Q. What did you do with it there?
>
> A. I gave the bag to the record custodian, who gave me a receipt.
>
> Q. At the time you gave the evidence bag to the custodian, what was its condition?
>
> A. It was still in a sealed condition.

Step 1. Have exhibit marked.

Step 2. Show exhibit to opposing counsel.

Step 3. Ask permission to approach witness.
Step 4. Show exhibit to witness.
Step 5. Establish foundation.

Q. Officer Doe, I show you what has been marked Plaintiff's Exhibit #1. (Witness examines it.) Do you recognize it?
A. Yes, I do.
Q. What do you recognize it to be?
A. That's the evidence bag in which I placed the plastic bag containing the powder I seized from the defendant on December 13, 2000.
Q. How can you recognize it to be the same particular bag?
A. I can see the label I placed on it by the heat seal.
Q. Is that heat seal in the same condition today as when you placed it on the bag on December 13, 2000?
A. Yes, sir.
Q. Is there anything different in the condition of the evidence bag today from the time when you delivered it to the crime lab on December 13, 2000?
A. Yes, sir. There's another heat seal on the opposite side of the bag from the one I made.
Q. Did you make that second seal?
A. No, sir.
Q. From December 13, 2000, until today, did you ever see that evidence bag?
A. No.

Chemist testifies.

Q. Ms. Rae, I show you what has been previously marked Plaintiff's Exhibit #1. (Witness examines it.) Have you ever seen it before?
A. Yes, I have.
Q. When was the first time you saw it?
A. On December 16, 2000.
Q. Where did you first see it?
A. I saw it in the evidence room of the chemistry section when our custodian removed it and gave it to me.
Q. When you first received Plaintiff's Exhibit #1, what condition was it in?
A. It was in a sealed condition.
Q. Where was it sealed?
A. It had only one seal — on the side by the label.
Q. What was the condition of the bag itself?
A. It was in the normal condition. It had no signs of tampering or alteration.
Q. What did you do with the exhibit?
A. I cut open the side opposite from the seal, removed the contents, and weighed it. I removed a small portion of the contents on which I performed certain chemical tests. The remainder I put back in the same bag.
Q. What did you do after putting the contents back in the bag?

A.   I put my label in the bag and heat-sealed the edge I had opened.

Q.   What did you do with the bag?

A.   I returned it to our evidence locker.

Q.   When did you next see Plaintiff's Exhibit #1?

A.   This morning the custodian removed it from the evidence locker, and I brought it to the courtroom.

Q.   When you received the bag this morning, what was its condition?

A.   It was sealed.

Q.   Was there anything different about the bag this morning from the way it was when you returned it to the evidence locker on December 16, 2000?

A.   No, the bag was still sealed, looked the same, and had no signs of tampering.

Step   6.   Offer exhibit in evidence.

Step   7.   Have exhibit marked in evidence.

Step   8.   Have witness use exhibit.

Step   9.   Ask permission to show exhibit to jury.

Step 10.   Show exhibit to jury.

Note that you have traced the bag from the moment the officer obtained it from the defendant to the time the chemist received it, tested it, and brought it to court. The evidence custodian is *not* a necessary witness because the evidence bag was still sealed when the chemist received it, nor is it necessary to show that no one else handled the bag. The important point is that no one, other than the chemist, had access to the bag's contents. This is conclusively demonstrated by showing that the bag remained sealed and had no signs of tampering from the time the police officer delivered it to the crime laboratory to the time the chemist received it. Hence, you have proved that the evidence is what it purports to be. Of course, if your opponent seriously challenges your chain of custody, the evidence custodian should be available as a witness.

3.   Photographs, motion pictures, and videotapes

Elements:

    a.   Photograph is relevant.

    b.   Witness is familiar with the scene portrayed in the photograph.

    c.   Witness is familiar with the scene at the relevant date (and time, if important).

    d.   Photograph "fairly and accurately" shows the scene as it appeared on the relevant date.

Example:

Q.   Mr. Doe, have you ever been at the intersection of North and Clark Streets?

A.   Yes.

Q.   How many times have you been there?

A. About 50 times.

Q. Are you familiar with the intersection as it looked on December 13, 2000?

A. Yes, I am.

Step 1. Have exhibit marked.

Step 2. Show exhibit to opposing counsel.

Step 3. Ask permission to approach witness.

Step 4. Show exhibit to witness.

Step 5. Establish foundation:

Q. I show you what has been marked Plaintiff's Exhibit #1 and ask you to examine it. (Witness does so.) Do you recognize the scene in that photograph?

A. Yes.

Q. What scene is shown in the photograph?

A. It shows the intersection of North and Clark Streets.

Q. Mr. Doe, does Plaintiff's Exhibit #1 fairly and accurately show that intersection as it appeared on December 13, 2000?

A. Yes, sir, it does.

Step 6. Offer exhibit in evidence.

Step 7. Have exhibit marked in evidence.

Step 8. Have witness mark exhibit.

Step 9. Ask permission to show exhibit to jury.

Step 10. Show exhibit to jury.

In recent years motion pictures and videotapes have been used with increasing frequency at trial, particularly in personal injury cases. Plaintiff's lawyers use movies to illustrate graphically how the plaintiff's injuries have affected his lifestyle. These day-in-the-life movies show the plaintiff's activities during a typical day much more effectively and dramatically than is possible through oral testimony. Defense lawyers, on the other hand, have used movies of the plaintiff to demonstrate that the plaintiff's injuries and subsequent limitations have been exaggerated or even fabricated.

Where motion pictures and videotapes are introduced, the foundation elements are essentially identical to that for still photographs. However, the mechanical procedures in establishing those foundation elements parallel that for sound and video recordings. (See subsection 8 below.)

There are three evidentiary issues that commonly arise when photographs are offered in evidence. First, since camera lenses and the angles from which the pictures are taken can distort and mislead, make sure that the photographs fairly show the scene and do not mislead, distort, or confuse. Otherwise, object on the basis of FRE 403. Second, photographs can distort the lighting that existed at the relevant time. For instance, if the event happened at night, a photograph taken with a flash will necessarily distort the lighting. Again, object on the basis of FRE 403. In this situation courts commonly admit the photograph for a limited purpose (showing the scene), and give a cautionary instruction that the jury is to use the photograph for that purpose only and not for the lighting that existed at the relevant time. Third, photographs can be gruesome and inflammatory. This arises commonly in homicide cases when the prosecution offers morgue photographs of the deceased. Again, the objection should be based on FRE 403. If there is no issue over the cause of death (as will be the case when the issue is identification), such photographs are frequently excluded. If the condition of the deceased is actually relevant to a trial issue (as will usually be the case when the issue is self-defense), the photographs are usually admitted.

If photographs or similar exhibits do not give the jurors an adequate picture of the scene, the court may permit a "view." This is done by taking the jury to the location involved, so that the jury can personally view the scene. Such a trip is discretionary with the judge and, because of the logistics, time, and cost concerns, is seldom done.

4.   Diagrams, models, and maps

Elements:

  a.   Diagram, model, or map is relevant.
  b.   Witness is familiar with the scene represented by the diagram, model, or map.
  c.   Witness is familiar with the scene at the relevant date (and time, if important).
  d.   Diagram, model, or map is reasonably accurate or to scale.
  e.   Diagram, model, or map is useful in helping the witness explain his testimony to the jury. (This is not required in many jurisdictions.)

Keep in mind that jurisdictions can differ in their treatment of these exhibits, depending on the accuracy of the exhibit itself. When an exhibit is "to scale," all jurisdictions will admit the exhibit in evidence.

When the exhibit is "reasonably accurate," courts differ in their approach. Most still admit the exhibit in evidence since its probative value is still substantial. A few still take the view that the exhibit is merely an "illustrative" aid to help the witness explain his testimony to the jury, so the exhibit is not admitted in evidence. Hence, it does not go to the jury duing deliberations. Make sure you learn in advance what your judge's approach to diagrams and other demonstrative evidence is.

Example (exhibit not to scale):

  Q.   Mr. Doe, are you familiar with the intersection of North and Clark Streets?
  A.   Yes, it's a block from my house.
  Q.   Are you familiar with that intersection as it looked on December 13, 2000?
  A.   Yes.
Step   1.   Have exhibit marked.
Step   2.   Show exhibit to opposing counsel.

Step 3.   Ask permission to approach witness.
Step 4.   Show exhibit to witness.
Step 5.   Establish foundation:

    Q. I show you Plaintiff's Exhibit #1. Does that diagram fairly and ac-curately show the intersection of North and Clark Streets as it ex-isted on December 13, 2000?

    A. Yes, sir. I'd say it does.

    Q. Would that diagram help you explain what happened?

    A. I think so.

Step 6.   Offer exhibit in evidence.
Step 7.   Have exhibit marked in evidence.
Step 8.   Have witness mark exhibit.
Step 9.   Ask permission to show exhibit to jury.
Step 10.   Show exhibit to jury.

If the exhibit has been prepared to scale, the person preparing it could testify as follows:

Example (exhibit to scale):

    Q. Mr. Doe, were you at the intersection of North and Clark Streets on approximately December 30, 2000?

    A. I was.

    Q. At whose direction did you go there?

    A. You asked me to.

    Q. When you got to the intersection, what did you do?

    A. I measured every important distance such as street widths, side-walk widths, crosswalks, traffic controls, and so forth.

    Q. After completing these measurements, what did you do next?

    A. I went to my office and prepared a diagram of the intersection.

Step 1.   Have exhibit marked.
Step 2.   Show exhibit to opposing counsel.
Step 3.   Ask permission to approach witness.
Step 4.   Show exhibit to witness.
Step 5.   Establish foundation:

    Q. Mr. Doe, I show you what has been marked Plaintiff's Exhibit #1. Do you recognize it?

    A. Yes, that's the diagram I prepared.

    Q. Does that diagram accurately portray the intersection of North and Clark Streets as it existed on December 30, 2000?

    A. Yes, it does.

    Q. Is the diagram to scale?

    A. Yes, it is.

    Q. What scale is it?

    A. I prepared the diagram using a scale of one inch equaling five feet.

Step 6.   Offer exhibit in evidence.
Step 7.   Have exhibit marked in evidence.
Step 8.   Have witness mark exhibit.

Step 9.   Ask permission to show exhibit to jury.
Step 10.   Show exhibit to jury.

Note that since the witness obviously prepared the "to scale" diagram some time after the occurrence, it may be necessary to have another witness testify that the intersection looked the same on the date of the occurrence as it looked on the date the diagram was prepared.

The requirement that the diagram helps explain the witness testimony is derived from older notions of relevance. Since the diagram was not the "real thing," but only "illustrative," it was viewed as only a supplement to the witness' oral testimony and was properly in court only if the witness used it to explain his testimony. In most jurisdictions this concept has been discarded, and demonstrative exhibits are treated for relevancy purposes like any other evidence. Hence, you can usually dispense with the "does the diagram help you explain what happened" type of question, since this is not a logical requirement for the exhibit's admission.

5.   Drawings by witnesses

Drawings by witnesses in court are usually things to be avoided. It is difficult to create an adequate record, particularly where the witness uses a blackboard. Moreover, witness drawings are often inaccurate and misleading. The better practice is to prepare a diagram and have the witness prepared to qualify it. If you must have an in-court drawing, use artist's paper so that the drawing can be preserved as part of the record.

Elements:

    a.   Drawing is relevant.
    b.   Witness is familiar with the scene at the relevant date.
    c.   Drawing is reasonably accurate and is not misleading.
    d.   Drawing is useful in helping the witness explain what he saw. (This is not required in many jurisdictions.)

Example:

    Q.   Mr. Doe, are you familiar with the intersection of North and Clark Streets as it looked on December 13, 2000?
    A.   Yes, I am.
    Q.   Mr. Doe, would making a drawing of the intersection of North and Clark Streets help you explain what happened?
    A.   Yes, I think so.
    Q.   Your Honor, may the witness step down from the witness stand and approach the exhibit stand?
    Court: He may.
    Q.   Using the black felt pen, please make a drawing of that intersection on the artist's paper, which is marked Plaintiff's Exhibit #1. (Witness does so.) What does this line represent? (pointing)

A. That's the curb line between the sidewalk and street. (Have the witness identify the major parts of the drawing, and label as is necessary. Then:)

Step 6. Offer exhibit in evidence (if the Court will admit in evidence a drawing that is not to scale).

Step 7. Have exhibit marked in evidence.

Step 8. Have witness mark exhibit.

Step 9. Ask permission to show exhibit to jury.

Step 10. Show exhibit to jury.

6. Demonstrations by witnesses

Witnesses are generally allowed to display body parts to the jury, demonstrate physical acts, or reenact an event. This is usually done by having the witness step down, stand before the jury box, and display the body part (such as a foot), or demonstrate a physical act (such as bending a knee), or act out an event.

Keep in mind, however, that some personal injury lawyers disapprove of having their clients display injuries to the jury. They feel that this runs a grave risk of offending the jury, and that the injuries can better be demonstrated by using photographs. In addition, the opponent can object that the demonstration's inflammatory effect outweighs its probative value.

Making an accurate record of the demonstration is also difficult. If you must use a witness demonstration, be sure that you narrate for the record exactly what the witness does, and ask the judge to confirm the basic accuracy of your narration.

Elements:

a. Demonstration is relevant.

b. Probative value of the demonstration exceeds any prejudicial effect.

Example:

Q. Your Honor, may the witness step down from the stand and approach the jury box?

Court: He may.

Q. Mr. Doe, would you please step down and stand before the jury? (Witness does so.)
The scars on your face that you have previously described, would you please point them out to the jury?

A. The scar over my left eye is right here (witness points, while facing jury). The scar on my left cheek is right here (pointing).

Q. Your Honor, may the record show that Mr. Doe has pointed to a white scar approximately two inches long, running horizontally about one inch over his left eye, and a reddish scar approximately four inches long, a half inch wide, which runs vertically starting about one inch below his left eye?

Court: That looks pretty accurate to me. Any objection to that description, counsel?

Counsel: No, your Honor.

Q.   Thank you, Mr. Doe. Please return to the witness stand. (Witness does so.)

Example:

Q.   Your Honor, may the witness step down and stand by the jury box?

Court: Of course.

Q.   Mr. Doe, would you please step down and stand before the jury? (Witness does so.) Before the collision, how far could you bend forward?

A.   I could bend all the way over and touch my toes.

Q.   Since the collision, how far have you been able to bend your back?

A.   Just a little bit, not nearly as far as before.

Q.   Mr. Doe, please demonstrate to the jury the extent to which you can now bend your back. (Witness does so.) Your Honor, may the record show that the witness has bent over and touched his legs so that his fingertips reach his thighs about six inches above the knees?

Court: The record will so show. Any objection, counsel?

Counsel: No, your Honor.

Q.   Is that the furthest you are able to bend over at the present time?

A.   Yes, sir.

Q.   How long has that condition existed?

A.   It's been that way for over a year now.

Q.   Thank you. Please return to the witness stand.

7.   X-ray films

X-ray films can usually be admitted in evidence using either of the two following approaches. First, the X ray and accompanying label can be qualified as a business record, since doctors and hospitals routinely take, label, and maintain X rays under established procedures and rely on them for diagnosing and treating patients. Second, the X ray is like a photograph and a qualified witness, usually the treating physician, can identify the X ray as being of the particular patient. Today the prevalent approach is to qualify the X rays as part of the business records of the hospital, clinic, or medical office.

Elements (business records):

a.   X ray is relevant.

b.   Witness is the "custodian or other qualified witness."

c.   X ray is a "record" of the hospital.

d.   The X-ray label was "made by a person with knowledge" of the facts, or was "made from information transmitted by a person with knowledge" of the facts.

e.   X ray was "made at or near the time" of the "conditions" appearing on it.
f.   X ray was made as part of "the regular practice" of the hospital.
g.   X ray was "kept in the course of a regularly conducted business activity."

Example:

(See the examples in subsection 13 dealing with business records.)

Elements (photographs):

a.   X ray is relevant.
b.   Witness is familiar with the patient's physical condition at the relevant date.
c.   X ray "fairly and accurately" shows the condition of the patient's body as it was at the relevant date.

Example:

The treating physician is testifying. He has already described his initial examination of the patient.

Q.   Dr. Doe, did you order any X rays of John Smith during the course of your examination and treatment on December 13, 2000?
A.   I did.
Q.   What parts of the body did you order X rays of?
A.   I ordered two X rays of the left knee, a lateral view and an anterior-posterior view.

Step 1.   Have exhibit marked.
Step 2.   Show exhibit to opposing counsel.
Step 3.   Ask permission to approach witness.
Step 4.   Show exhibit to witness.
Step 5.   Establish foundation:

Q.   Dr. Doe, I show you Plaintiff's Exhibit #1. Do you recognize it?
A.   Yes.
Q.   What do you recognize it to be?
A.   This is an X-ray film of John Smith's left knee I had taken on December 13, 2000.
Q.   How are you able to recognize this particular X-ray film as being of John Smith?
A.   Well, the corner label is exposed on the film when the X rays are taken. The label always has the patient's name, date, and hospital on it. This X ray's label in the corner shows it to be of John Smith and taken on December 13, 2000. In addition, I remember seeing this particular plate, the anterior-posterior view, with these fracture lines on December 13, 2000, and can identify the plate

on that basis. Finally, my examination of the patient disclosed a probable fracture of Mr. Smith's left femur just above the knee, which corresponded to the fracture disclosed on the films.

Q.   Does Plaintiff's Exhibit #1 fairly and accurately portray the bones and other internal structures of John Smith's left knee as they were on December 13, 2000?

A.   Yes, it does.

Step   6.   Offer exhibit in evidence.
Step   7.   Have exhibit marked in evidence.
Step   8.   Have witness use exhibit.
Step   9.   Ask permission to show exhibit to jury.
Step 10.   Show exhibit to jury.

8.   Sound and video recordings

Sound and video recordings present complex authentication problems. A witness must be able to testify that the recording is an accurate reproduction of the events involved. Therefore, the equipment used to record the original event, as well as the equipment used to show it in court, must be in good working condition. In addition, a qualified witness must be able to identify the scenes, persons, or voices on the tape. Finally, the tape recording itself must be securely stored, to prevent the possibility of erasing, editing, or other tampering.

Elements:

a.   Recording is relevant.

b.   Recording machine was tested before being used and was in normal operating condition.

c.   Recording machine that was used can accurately record and reproduce sounds/images.

d.   Operator was experienced and qualified to operate the recording machine that was used.

e.   Witness heard/saw what was being recorded.

f.   After the recording was made, the operator replayed the tape and the tape had accurately recorded the sounds/images.

g.   Tape was then labeled and sealed, placed in a secure storage vault to guard against tampering, and later removed for trial, still in a sealed condition.

h.   Recording machine in court is in normal operating condition and can accurately reproduce the sounds/images on the tape.

i.   Witness recognizes and can identify the voices on the tape/locations and persons seen on the tape.

Note that more than one witness may be necessary to completely qualify a recording. For instance, in a sound recording of a telephone conversation, you may need three witnesses, each of whom can testify to one of the following required elements: (1) qualify the machines and recording, (2) demonstrate the custody of the tape, and (3) identify the voices on the tape.

Example:

The following example involves a police officer who made a sound recording of a telephone conversation.

Q.   Officer Doe, what kind of sound-recording machine did you use to record this telephone conversation?
A.   A Uhr tape recorder, using a half-inch magnetic tape.
Q.   Are you familiar with the operation of that machine?
A.   Yes, sir.
Q.   How many times have you used it?
A.   I've used this particular type of machine probably 200 to 300 times.
Q.   Did you do anything with the machine before recording the call?
A.   Yes, I tested it.
Q.   How did you test it?
A.   I attached the microphone of the tape recorder to the telephone, dialed the number of our department, and talked shortly to our receptionist. I recorded the call and then played it back on the machine.
Q.   What was the result of your test?
A.   The machine was working properly. It was accurately recording and playing back.
Q.   What happened next?
A.   I turned the machine on again. Mr. Smith picked up the receiver, dialed a number, and engaged in a conversation for about two minutes. He then put down the receiver and I turned off the machine.
Q.   Did you do anything during the conversation?
A.   Yes, I was listening to the conversation on an extension phone.
Q.   Did you recognize the voice on the other end?
A.   Yes.
Q.   Had you ever heard it before?
A.   Oh yes, lots of times.
Q.   Whose voice did you recognize it to be?
A.   Mr. Jones'.
Q.   After the conversation, what is the next thing you did?
A.   Immediately after the conversation, I rewound the tape and played it.
Q.   Did the tape completely and accurately record the conversation you had just heard?
A.   Yes, it did.
Q.   What did you do with that tape?
A.   I labeled it, put it in an evidence bag, sealed the bag, and placed the bag in my evidence vault.
Q.   Did you ever see the tape again?

    A.   Yes, this morning.

    Q.   Where did you see it at that time?

    A.   I took it out of my evidence vault.

Step 1.   Have exhibit marked.

Step 2.   Show exhibit to opposing counsel.

Step 3.   Ask permission to approach witness.

Step 4.   Show exhibit to witness.

Step 5.   Establish foundation:

    Q.   Officer Doe, I show you what has been marked Plaintiff's Exhibit #1. Do you recognize it?

    A.   Yes.

    Q.   What do you recognize it to be?

    A.   That's the tape I previously made on December 13, 2000.

    Q.   What is the condition of the bag at this time?

    A.   It's still in a sealed condition.

    Q.   Is this bag with the tape in it in the same condition now as when you sealed it on December 13, 2000?

    A.   Yes, sir, it is.

    Q.   Your Honor, at this time we offer Plaintiff's Exhibit #1 in evidence.

Court: It will be admitted.

    Q.   Officer Doe, do you recognize the machine on the table in front of you?

    A.   Yes, sir,

    Q.   What is it?

    A.   That's a Uhr cassette tape recorder. In fact, that's the same kind of machine I used to record the telephone conversation.

    Q.   Is this machine in proper working order?

    A.   Yes. I tested it just before bringing it to the courtroom.

    Q.   Your Honor, may the witness unseal Plaintiff's Exhibit #1 and play it on the machine for the jury?

Court: He may.

(Witness sets up machine, unseals the tape, puts it on the machine.)

    Q.   Officer Doe, before playing the tape, would you describe which voice is Mr. Smith's and which is Mr. Jones'?

    A.   Smith has a very low, deep voice. Jones has a high-pitched voice with a slight accent.

    Q.   Please play the tape for the court and the jury. (Witness plays tape.)

Where the voices cannot be easily described, it may be preferable to play the first few seconds of the tape, stop the machine, then ask the witness to identify the voices which were just heard.

Example:

    Q.   Officer Doe, please stop the tape. (Witness does so.) Whose voice said "Hello"?

    A.   That was Mr. Jones.

    Q.   Whose voice said "Frank, it's me"?

A. That's Mr. Smith.
Q. Please continue playing the tape.

Where sound recordings are involved, it is usually advantageous to offer in evidence a transcript of the recording. A copy of the transcript can then be given to each juror to read as the recording is played. Following along on the transcript while the tape is being played makes the tape much easier to understand. Whether the transcript can be used in addition to the recording, or whether it goes to the jury during deliberations, rests in the sound discretion of the trial judge. Where allowed, the witness who prepared the transcript must testify that it is a true and accurate verbatim transcript of the recording involved.

Finally, remember that establishing the foundation for a recording and presenting it in court is a complicated procedure. For this reason, many courts will require you to demonstrate the complete foundation out of the jury's presence before permitting you to present it before the jury.

9.   Computer-generated graphics and animations

Computer-generated graphics have become realistic alternatives to two-dimensional diagrams and three-dimensional models. If a computer has a computer-assisted design program, graphics of things like machines, buildings, and body organs can be enlarged, moved, and rotated on the television monitor. Animations of events like an automobile collision can recreate the event with stunning clarity. These graphics and animations, when used with a testifying expert, become powerful, persuasive tools. Anyone who has seen a computer-generated animation of an industrial explosion or airplane crash knows how vividly it can illustrate an event for the jury.

Computer-generated graphics are used the same way as other demonstrative evidence, such as diagrams and models, and the foundation is identical. A qualified witness must testify that he is familiar with the scene or object, that the graphic fairly and accurately represents the scene or object, and (in some jurisdictions) that the graphic helps the witness explain his testimony to the jury. When this is done, the graphic will be admitted in evidence.

Computer-generated animations are principally used to recreate an event in a way that reflects the expert's conclusion of how the event occurred, based on the available objective data and the mathematical model on which the computer program is based.

Elements (computer animation of airplane crash):

a.   Exhibit is relevant.
b.   The data used by the expert and put into the computer program are accurate (e.g., the data came from the flight recorder of the aircraft that crashed).
c.   The integrity of the data was maintained (e.g., the chain of custody of the flight recorder was maintained).

d. Data were accurately transferred into a properly functioning computer.

e. The computer software program used to create the animation is based on valid and accepted scientific methodology.

f. The computer animation accurately reflects how the event happened.

g. The computer animation will help the jury understand or determine a fact in issue.

Note that more than one witness may be needed to qualify the computer animation as an exhibit. For example, one witness may establish the chain of custody on a flight recorder, another may testify that the data from the flight recorder was accurately put into the computer, and a third may establish the validity of the computer program used to create the animation.

Today most courts admit properly qualified computer animations in evidence as substantive evidence. Some courts, however, still categorize computer animations as either demonstrative evidence or substantive evidence, depending on the foundation that is established. If the animation is being offered only to "illustrate" an expert's opinion, the only foundation necessary is the expert's testimony that the animation fairly and accurately illustrates her opinion and is helpful for the expert to explain her opinion to the jury. If so, the animation is only "demonstrative evidence," meaning that the jury sees it only in conjunction with the expert's testimony. It is not admitted as an exhibit, the lawyers cannot use it during closing arguments, and the jury does not see it during its deliberations. On the other hand, if the animation is being offered as an actual recreation of a specific event (sometimes called a "simulation"), the foundation necessary is the technical foundation detailed above. Validating the computer program used to create the animation must meet the applicable standard for expert opinion testimony, usually either the *Daubert* or the *Frye* test. These tests are discussed in §8.1. If the foundation is successfully established, the animation is admitted as an exhibit, the lawyers can use it during closing arguments, and the jury may (subject to the court's discretion) see it during its deliberations. The law in this area is jurisdiction specific and continuously evolving, so research will be necessary whenever you plan to introduce computer-generated animations at trial.

Since the foundations for animations are technical, courts usually require that opposing parties have an adequate opportunity to examine them beforehand, including the computer software program and the data that was fed into the program, and will usually hold pretrial hearings to determine the admissibility of the animations.

10.   Signed instruments

Signed instruments such as wills, contracts, and promissory notes are writings that have independent legal significance, and are nonhearsay. Whenever a signed instrument is introduced at trial, such as in a contract action, the authentication requirement must be met by proving that the party actually signed the instrument involved. If this is shown, the instrument is admissible against the party that signed it. This requirement protects against fraudulent claims based on forged instruments.

There are a variety of ways to prove that the signature on the instrument was made by the person whose signature it purports to be. These include:

1. Call a witness who saw the party place his signature on the document.
2. Call a witness who is familiar with the party's signature and can identify it.
3. Call the signing party as an adverse witness to admit the signature as being his.
4. Call a handwriting expert who can testify that, based on handwriting comparisons, the signature was made by the party.

Keep in mind that a writing that has independent legal significance is nonhearsay. Therefore, trying to establish the writing as a business record under FRE 803(6) does nothing. Whenever the instrument is being introduced against a signator, you must prove that the signature on the instrument was in fact made by the signator.

Elements:

a. Document is relevant.
b. Document bears a signature (or is handwritten).
c. Signature (or handwriting) is that of the party or his agent.
d. Document is in the same condition now as when it was executed.

Example:

The witness saw the promissory note signed by a party.

Step 1. Have exhibit marked.
Step 2. Show exhibit to opposing counsel.
Step 3. Ask permission to approach witness.
Step 4. Show exhibit to witness.
Step 5. Establish foundation:
   Q. Mr. Doe, I show you what has been marked Plaintiff's Exhibit #1. Have you seen it before?
   A. Yes.
   Q. When was the first time you saw it?
   A. I saw it on December 13, 2000.
   Q. Where were you at that time?
   A. In my office.
   Q. Did you see who prepared Plaintiff's Exhibit #1?
   A. Yes, I prepared that note myself.
   Q. After preparing it, what did you do with it?
   A. I gave it to Mr. Jones, who was sitting in my office.

Q. What did Mr. Jones do with it?
A. He signed it at the bottom.
Q. Did you actually see him sign it?
A. Yes.
Q. After Mr. Jones signed Plaintiff's Exhibit #1, what did you do with it?
A. I took the signed note and put it in my files.
Q. Is Plaintiff's Exhibit #1 in the same condition now as when Mr. Jones signed it?
A. Yes, sir, nothing's been done to it since he signed it.
Step 6.   Offer exhibit in evidence.
Step 7.   Have exhibit marked in evidence.
Step 8.   Have witness mark exhibit.
Step 9.   Ask permission to show/read exhibit to jury.
Step 10.   Show/read exhibit to jury.

Example:

The witness sent a contract to a party, who returned the contract signed. The witness can identify the party's signature.

Step 1.   Have the exhibit marked.
Step 2.   Show the exhibit to opposing counsel.
Step 5.   Ask the Court's permission to approach the witness.
Step 4.   Show the exhibit to the witness.
Step 5.   Establish foundation:
Q. Mr. Doe, I show you Plaintiff's Exhibit #1. Have you seen it before?
A. Yes.
Q. When was the first time you saw it?
A. On December 13, 2000, when I prepared it.
Q. What did you do with it?
A. I mailed it to Mr. Jones.
Q. Did you see it again?
A. Yes.
Q. When was that?
A. About one week later I received it in the mail.
Q. Was anything different about Plaintiff's Exhibit #1 at that time?
A. Yes, it had been signed at the bottom.
Q. Did you recognize the signature?
A. Yes.
Q. Had you ever seen that signature before?
A. Oh yes, many times.
Q. Under what circumstances had you seen it?
A. I've seen it on correspondence and contracts. Several times I've actually seen Mr. Jones sign his name.
Q. Mr. Doe, showing you Plaintiff's Exhibit #1, do you recognize the signature that appears at the bottom of page 2?
A. Yes, that's Mr. Jones' signature.

> *Q.* Is this document in the same condition now as when you received it on approximately December 22, 2000?
>
> *A.* Yes, sir.

Step 6.   Offer exhibit in evidence.

Step 7.   Have exhibit marked in evidence.

Step 8.   Have witness mark exhibit.

Step 9.   Ask permission to show/read exhibit to jury.

Step 10.   Show/read exhibit to jury.

Note that a qualified witness can identify the signature on the document, even if that witness had nothing to do with the preparation or execution of the document itself.

11.   Checks

Checks are negotiable instruments and therefore have independent legal significance. Since checks are nonhearsay, they must be authenticated the same way as all instruments. A witness must be able to identify the signature of the drawer before the check is admissible as proof that the drawer made the payment. A witness must be able to identify the endorsement signature of the payee to prove receipt by the payee.

Checks are commonly used at trial as proof of payment from drawer to payee. There are several ways the signatures of the drawer and payee can be authenticated, so that the check can be admitted to prove payment.

a.   Call the drawer of the check to testify that he personally made and gave the check to the payee or his agent.

b.   Call the payee or his agent as an adverse witness to prove his receipt, endorsement, and cashing of the check.

c.   Call a handwriting expert to testify that the endorsement on the back of the check is in the payee's handwriting.

d.   Call a representative of the payee's bank to qualify a microfilm of the canceled check as a business record and show that the check was deposited to the payee's account.

Of these methods, the most common approach involves calling the drawer of the check as the only or primary witness.

Elements (drawer of check):

a.   Check is relevant.

b.   Witness made payment by check.

c.   Witness prepared the check and signed it.

d.   Witness gave the check to the payee.

e.   Witness received canceled check from his bank some time later.

f.   Canceled check had payee's endorsement on the back.

g.   Witness recognizes handwriting of endorsement as payee's.

h. Canceled check is in the same condition now except for the endorsement and markings on the back of the check.

Example (drawer of the check is testifying):

Q. Mr. Doe, did you pay the bill sent to you by the XYZ Hardware Company?

A. Yes.

Q. How did you pay the bill?

A. By check.

Q. What bank was that check drawn on?

A. That was on my account at the First National Bank.

Step 1. Have exhibit marked.

Step 2. Show exhibit to opposing counsel.

Step 3. Ask permission to approach witness.

Step 4. Show exhibit to witness.

Step 5. Establish foundation:

Q. Mr. Doe, I show you Plaintiff's Exhibit #1. Do you recognize it?

A. Yes, I do.

Q. What kind of document is it?

A. It's a check.

Q. Do you recognize the drawer's signature on the front?

A. Yes, it is my signature.

Q. Do you recognize the handwriting on the face of the check?

A. Yes, it's all in my handwriting. I prepared that check.

Q. What did you do with Plaintiff's Exhibit #1 after you prepared it?

A. I gave it to Mr. Roe at the hardware store.

Q. Are you familiar with Mr. Roe's signature?

A. Oh yes, I've seen him write his name many times.

Q. Mr. Doe, please look at the back of the check. Do you recognize the signature appearing there?

A. Yes, I do.

Q. Whose signature do you recognize it to be?

A. That's Mr. Roe's signature.

Q. After giving that check to Mr. Roe, did you ever see it again?

A. Yes.

Q. When did you see it next?

A. The following month I got the check from my bank, as part of that month's batch of canceled checks.

Q. Was there anything different about the check when you got it from your bank?

A. Yes.

Q. What was that?

A. The back of the check had Mr. Roe's signature on it and various bank stamps.

Q. Other than those added items, did the check appear in the same condition as when you gave it to Mr. Roe?

A. Yes.

Step 6. Offer exhibit in evidence.

Step 7.   Have exhibit marked in evidence.
Step 8.   Have witness mark exhibit.
Step 9.   Ask permission to show exhibit to jury.
Step 10.   Show exhibit to jury.
(Make sure you offer *both* sides of the check in evidence.)

Note that in the above example one witness was able to testify to both preparing and presenting the check as well as to the identity of the endorser. Many times, of course, two or more witnesses would be necessary to complete the required proof.

In criminal cases, checks are sometimes introduced at trial, most commonly in fraud and forgery cases. In such cases, the identity of the handwriting on the face of the check as well as the endorsement may be in issue. Since the defendant cannot be called as a witness by the prosecution, proof of these facts can be through:

   a. a witness who recognizes the handwriting on the check as the defendant's
   b. a witness who saw the defendant write out the check or endorse it
   c. a handwriting expert who can testify that the handwriting is the defendant's

Note that while the operative portions of the check have independent legal significance and are nonhearsay, this is not the case with other parts of the check. The "memo" portion of a check, which is frequently filled out to show the purpose for writing the check, is probably hearsay. The bank stamps on the back of a check, which show the clearing process, are probably hearsay as well.

12.   Letters

Letters can present complicated evidentiary issues. First, letters can be hearsay or nonhearsay, depending on their contents and use. Where an exchange of two letters forms a contract, the letters, being words of offer and acceptance, have independent legal significance and are nonhearsay. A letter containing defamatory words, a letter offered to show the writer's state of mind, and a letter offered to show notice or knowledge are also nonhearsay. However, facts asserted in a letter will usually be hearsay, and some exception, most commonly party admissions, must be applicable to make the letter admissible. Second, letters must be authenticated. A witness must be able to identify the signature on the letter as being in fact that of the person it purports to be. This authentication requirement is designed to prevent the possibility of forgery. Third, letters may not be relevant unless it can be shown that the intended addressee actually received the original. This is required where the letters form a contract, or a letter constitutes notice to the addressee. Fourth, where the original has been sent out and is unavailable, and there is a genuine dispute over authenticity, the original documents rule, FRE 1001-1004, requires production of the original or that its absence be explained before a copy is admissible. All these issues — hearsay, authentication, proof of receipt, best evidence, and copies — can arise whenever a letter is offered in evidence at trial.

The following examples illustrate what are probably the two most common authentication, receipt, and copy problem areas; both involve letters sent between parties.

a. Letter sent to your party by another party

Elements:

    a. Letter is relevant.
    b. Witness received the letter.
    c. Witness recognizes the signature as the other party's.
    d. Letter is in the same condition today as when first received.

Note that the receipt of the letter and the identity of the signature can be established by separate witnesses. If the witness who can testify to receiving the letter cannot identify the signature, the signature must be proved by a witness who can identify the handwriting, or by expert handwriting comparisons.

Example:

The witness can testify that he received a letter and can identify the signature on it.

Step 1. Have exhibit marked.
Step 2. Show exhibit to opposing counsel.
Step 3. Ask permission to approach witness.
Step 4. Show exhibit to witness.
Step 5. Establish foundation:

    Q. Mr. Doe, I show you Plaintiff's Exhibit #1. Do you recognize it?
    A. Yes.
    Q. Have you seen it before?
    A. Yes, I received this on approximately December 13, 2000.
    Q. Do you recognize the signature at the bottom?
    A. Yes, I do.
    Q. Have you seen that signature before?
    A. Yes, sir, lots of times.
    Q. Under what circumstances?
    A. (Witness explains how he has acquired personal knowledge.)
    Q. Whose signature is it?
    A. It is Frank Jones' signature.
    Q. Is this letter in the same condition today as when you received it on approximately December 13, 2000?
    A. Yes, sir. It looks the same.
Step 6. Offer exhibit in evidence.

Step 7.   Have exhibit marked in evidence.
Step 8.   Have witness mark exhibit.
Step 9.   Ask permission to show/read exhibit to jury.
Step 10.   Show/read exhibit to jury.

    b.   Letter sent by your party to another party

The more difficult situation involves the mailing of a letter to another party. This presents two problems. First, there is usually no direct way to prove receipt by the addressee, absent an admission. Second, unless the original of the letter has been produced by the addressee, it will be necessary to introduce a copy of that letter at trial. The essential element is proof of proper mailing, to raise the inference of receipt. A copy of the original can then be introduced.

Elements:

    a.   Letter is relevant.
    b.   Witness dictated the letter, addressed to a party.
    c.   Witness saw the typed original and copy (carbon or photocopy) of the letter.
    d.   Witness signed the original letter.
    e.   Original letter was placed in a properly addressed and post-marked envelope, bearing a proper return address.
    f.   Envelope was deposited in a U.S. mail depository.
    g.   Carbon or photocopy of original is a true and accurate copy of original.
    h.   Original letter and envelope were never returned to sender.

Example:

The witness is the secretary who typed and mailed the original letter.

Step 1.   Have exhibit marked.
Step 2.   Show exhibit to opposing counsel.
Step 3.   Ask permission to approach witness.
Step 4.   Show exhibit to witness.
Step 5.   Establish foundation:
    Q.   Ms. White, I show you what has been marked as Plaintiff's Exhibit #1. Have you ever seen it?
    A.   Yes, I have.
    Q.   What kind of document is it?
    A.   It is a carbon copy of a letter.
    Q.   Did you have anything to do with the preparation of this copy?
    A.   Yes, I did.
    Q.   What was that?
    A.   I took the dictation for this letter from Mr. Smith and typed an original and a carbon copy of the letter.
    Q.   When did you prepare the original and copy?

A. The same date that is on the letter, December 13, 2000.

Q. What did you do after you prepared the original and copy?

A. I gave the original to Mr. Smith. He signed it and gave it back to me.

Q. What did you do next?

A. I prepared an envelope that had the same address as appeared on the letter. I then put the signed original in the envelope, sealed the envelope, and put a first-class stamp on it.

Q. What happened next?

A. At the end of the day I mailed the letter by putting it in the mailbox in front of our building.

Q. Did that envelope contain a return address?

A. Yes, it did.

Q. What was that address?

A. Our office stationery, including the envelopes, has our complete office address on it.

Q. Who is in charge of incoming mail in your office?

A. I am.

Q. Did you ever receive back the letter and envelope you sent Mr. Smith?

A. No, that letter never came back to us.

Q. After mailing the original, what did you do with the copy?

A. I put it in our files.

Q. The copy of that letter, Ms. White, is that the same document that has been marked Plaintiff's Exhibit #1?

A. Yes, sir. That is the copy.

Q. Is Plaintiff's Exhibit #1 a true and accurate copy of the letter you sent to Mr. Jones on December 13, 2000?

A. Yes, sir, it's identical.

Q. How are you able to recognize this copy as a copy of the letter you prepared and sent that day?

A. Because both Mr. Smith's initials and mine appear in the lower lefthand corner of the copy. This shows that I typed this particular letter for Mr. Smith on that date.

Q. Is this copy in the same condition now as when you mailed the original to Mr. Jones on December 13, 2000?

A. Yes, it is.

Step 6.   Offer exhibit in evidence.

Step 7.   Have exhibit marked in evidence.

Step 8.   Have witness mark exhibit.

Step 9.   Ask permission to show/read exhibit to jury.

Step 10.   Show/read exhibit to jury.

Preparation is rarely a problem because the secretary will routinely place initials on every letter typed. In many cases, however, the secretary cannot independently remember having mailed the particular letter to the addressee. In those instances, it is necessary to show the usual established business practice of the office in mailing letters, proper under FRE 406, to prove circumstantially that the letter in question was, in fact, mailed to the addressee.

Example:

Q. Ms. White, do you remember what you did with the original of this letter after you prepared it?

A. I cannot tell you what I did with this particular letter. It's just been too long ago.

Q. Do you have a standard established office procedure in preparing and handling letters?

A. Yes, we do.

Q. Was that procedure followed in December 2000?

A. Oh yes, we've been doing it the same way for years now.

Q. Please describe that procedure for us.

A. Well, after I type the original and make one copy I give it to the proper person for signing. I never mail a letter unless it has been signed by the person indicated. I then put the original in an envelope that has the same address as appears on the letter. The envelope bears the return address of our office. I then seal the envelope and put it in our office mailbox.

Q. What happens next?

A. Around 5:00 P.M. I take all the letters that have been prepared that day, stamp them with the proper postage on our stamp machine, and tie all the letters together. When I leave the office, I take that mail package and put it in the mailbox located in front of the building.

Q. Did you go through that procedure on December 13, 2000?

A. Yes, sir. I do that every day I work, and I worked that day.

13.   Business records

Business records are the most common type of documentary evidence introduced in trials. Introducing such records in evidence can be accomplished simply by following the foundations set out in FRE 803(6).

The federal business records rule has substantially relaxed certain requirements previously required under older statutes. The witness no longer need be the records custodian, but also can be any "other qualified witness." A business now includes any "business, institution, association, profession, occupation, and calling of any kind, whether or not conducted for profit." A record can be any "memorandum, report, record or data compilation, in any form, of acts, events, conditions, opinions or diagnoses." The record must be "made by . . . a person with knowledge" or "made . . . from information transmitted by a person with knowledge." The witness in court should be able to identify the type of person working for the business who had firsthand knowledge of the facts and initially received, recorded, or transmitted the information that ultimately appeared on the record.

Under FRE 803(6), business records can now be introduced in evidence through either of two ways: certification that complies with FRE 902 or through a properly qualified foundation witness.

The certification method, permitted since FRE 803(6) was amended in 2000, allows "certification that complies with Rule 902(11), Rule 902(12), or a statute permitting certification."

Elements (certification of domestic records):

    a.   Record is relevant and reliable.

    b.   "Written declaration of its custodian or other qualified person . . . certifying that the record" (A) was made at or near the time of the occurrence of the matters set forth by, or from information transmitted by, a person with knowledge of those matters; (B) was kept in the course of the regularly conducted activity; and (C) was made by the regularly conducted activity as a regular practice.

    c.   All adverse parties have notice of the intention to introduce the record under FRE 902(11) and have a sufficient opportunity to inspect the record to have a fair opportunity to challenge admissibility.

This new certification method, which permits certification much like that permitted for public records, is likely to become a popular method for getting routine business records admitted in evidence, since it eliminates the need to call a foundation witness at trial. FRE 902(12), governing the admissibility of certified foreign records in civil cases, has similar requirements. At trial, the certified business record need only be marked as an exhibit and offered in evidence. Once admitted, it can be shown or read to the jury.

The other foundation method is to use a properly qualified foundation witness. This, of course, is the traditional method.

Elements (foundation witness):

    a.   Record is relevant and reliable.

    b.   Witness is the "custodian or other qualified witness."

    c.   Record is a "memorandum, report, record or data compilation in any form."

    d.   Record was "made by a person with knowledge" of the facts or was "made from information transmitted by a person with knowledge" of the facts.

    e.   Record was "made at or near the time" of the "acts, events, conditions, opinions, or diagnoses" appearing on it.

    f.   Record was made as part of "the regular practice of that business activity."

    g.   Record was "kept in the course of a regularly conducted business activity."

The following example shows how easily the required technical elements of FRE 803(6) can be met with a qualified witness.

Example:

> Q. Mr. Doe, please state your occupation.
> A. I'm the records keeper of the XYZ Corporation.
> Q. What does your job involve?
> A. I collect, keep, and maintain all the company records according to our filing system.

Step 1. Have exhibit marked.
Step 2. Show exhibit to opposing counsel.
Step 3. Ask permission to approach witness.
Step 4. Show exhibit to witness.
Step 5. Establish foundation:

> Q. Mr. Doe, I am showing you what has been marked Plaintiff's Exhibit #1. Do you recognize it?
> A. Yes, it's one of our records.
> Q. Was that record made by a person with knowledge of, or made from information transmitted by a person with knowledge of, the acts and events appearing on it?
> A. Yes.
> Q. Was the record made at or near the time of the acts and events appearing on it?
> A. Yes.
> Q. Is it the regular practice of the XYZ Corporation to make such a record?
> A. Yes.
> Q. Was that record kept in the course of a regularly conducted business activity?
> A. Yes.

Step 6. Offer exhibit in evidence.
Step 7. Have exhibit marked in evidence.
Step 8. Have witness mark/explain exhibit.
Step 9. Ask permission to show/read exhibit to jury.
Step 10. Show/read exhibit to jury.

The above example illustrates how quickly the minimum foundation requirements can be established. As a vehicle of persuasion, of course, it may not be adequate. Where the record is an important part of your case, the credibility of the witness and the record should be enhanced by developing both fully. Developing the witness' background has been previously shown. (See §5.7 and the accompanying example.) The following example demonstrates how the exhibit itself can be enhanced, and how the requirements of FRE 803(6) can be met without using the technical language of the rule, so that the foundation is persuasive to the jury.

Example:

Step 1. Have exhibit marked.
Step 2. Show exhibit to opposing counsel.
Step 3. Ask permission to approach witness.
Step 4. Show exhibit to witness.

Step 5. Establish foundation:
  Q. Mr. Doe, I am showing you Plaintiff's Exhibit #1. Do you recognize it?
  A. Yes, I do.
  Q. What kind of record is it?
  A. This is a monthly statement for a checking account.
  Q. What use does the bank make of the monthly statement?
  A. It's the basic record on which we record all transactions involving that account. We also send it to our customers to advise them of the current status of their accounts.
  Q. What kind of information is recorded on a monthly statement?
  A. It contains all the checks, deposits, charges, and other debits and credits for that account, as well as a daily balance for the particular month involved.
  Q. Who receives and enters the transactions that appear on the statement?
  A. That's done by a clerk in our accounting department. The clerk receives all checks and deposits and enters them on the appropriate account ledger.
  Q. When are the transactions entered on the ledger?
  A. All transactions, like checks, deposits, and other charges, are posted on the account ledger within 24 hours of their receipt by the bank.
  Q. When are these transactions entered on the monthly statements?
  A. At the end of every month all transactions entered on the account ledger are printed on the monthly statement form.
  Q. What's the difference between the account ledger and the monthly statement?
  A. They both contain the same information, but the ledger is a continuous record. The statement simply takes this month's ledger transactions and prints them on an almost identical form. The statement is really just a reprint of the last part of the ledger.
  Q. What happens to the statement after it is printed?
  A. One copy is mailed to the customer. The other copies are kept in the bank's auditing department.
  Q. How long does the bank keep copies of the monthly statement?
  A. We're required to keep them at least seven years.
  Q. This procedure you have just described — is it used for the monthly statements for all the bank's checking accounts?
  A. Yes.
  Q. Mr. Doe, let's turn back to Plaintiff's Exhibit #1. Was that monthly statement made under the same bank procedures you have just described for us?
  A. Yes.
Step 6. Offer exhibit in evidence.
Step 7. Have exhibit marked in evidence.
Step 8. Have witness mark/explain exhibit.
Step 9. Ask permission to show/read exhibit to jury.
Step 10. Show/read exhibit to jury.

Note how the example established the required elements of FRE 803(6) without using the rule's technical language. The record was explained in language any layperson can understand. Keep in mind, however, that judges may be used to hearing the technical foundation litany of FRE 803(6). Therefore, to satisfy such judges, simply add the litany from the earlier example for business records.

Finally, as the party opposing the admission of the record, always keep in mind that many objections to its admission can be made. In addition to a lack of foundation, you can object on grounds of relevance or "lack of trustworthiness" of the record. You can object to parts of the record if it contains double hearsay or violates some other evidentiary rule, such as mentioning insurance, settlement offers, or privileged communications. For these reasons, you must carefully review the contents of the records for additional bases for objections to their admission in evidence.

"Double hearsay" or "hearsay within hearsay" is a common evidentiary objection to business records that lawyers frequently overlook, and is governed by FRE 805. Remember that qualifying a business record under FRE 803(6) merely eliminates the first level of hearsay. The business records foundation eliminates the need to call the actual maker of the record as a witness at trial. It does not eliminate double hearsay problems, which arise whenever the record contains information that came from persons who are not employees of the business (and therefore have no "business duty" to report and record information accurately). For example, whenever an accident report contains the statements of the drivers of the cars involved, and of bystanders, these statements are double hearsay and are not admissible unless a separate hearsay exception applies (here, admissions of a party opponent, or excited utterances, may apply) to make those statements admissible. If no separate hearsay exception applies, the double hearsay portions of the business record must be physically deleted before the record can be admitted in evidence and shown to the jury.

The absence of a business record can be admissible evidence. Under FRE 803(7), if an event or transaction had occurred, and the business would create a record of the event or transaction had it actually occurred, proving that the event or transaction never occurred can be done by showing that there is no business record for the claimed event or transaction.

Proving the absence of a record is done by calling a custodian or other qualified witness to testify about how the business creates records to record events and transactions. The witness can then testify that he searched the business records but could find no record for the claimed event or transaction.

Note that if one party wants to introduce an *opposing* party's business record, the record also may qualify as an admission by a party-opponent under FRE 801(d)(2). In that case you will need a witness to testify that the record was made by the party-opponent, or by a person authorized by the party, or by the party's agent or servant and is about a matter within the scope of employment and made during the time of the employment. However, you should not need to establish a formal business records foundation. (During pretrial discovery, particularly in requests to admit and interrogatories, parties frequently ask the opposing parties to produce or identify their business records, which may establish a foundation for this purpose.) This can be a useful alternative to the business records rule, particularly where the business contends that the record does not meet all the technical requirements of FRE 803(6).

Example:

Plaintiff is attempting to introduce the defendant's shipping record, which shows that a shipment of goods was made to plaintiff. The witness is a manager in the defendant's business, called as an adverse witness in plaintiff's case in chief.

> Q. Ms. Fairchild, I'm showing you Plaintiff's Exhibit #1. That's one of your company's records, right?
>
> A. It's one of our shipping records.
>
> Q. Look at the bottom of the form. The form was prepared by a Robin Johnson, right?
>
> A. Yes.
>
> Q. Robin Johnson is one of your shipping supervisors?
>
> A. Yes.
>
> Q. Mr. Johnson was employed by your company on the date this record was prepared, right?
>
> A. Yes.
>
> Q. And his job at the time involved preparing such shipping records?
>
> A. Yes.
>
> *Plaintiff's counsel:* Your honor, we offer Plaintiff's Exhibit #1 in evidence.
>
> *Judge:* Any objections?
>
> *Defendant's counsel:* We object, your Honor. Plaintiff has not established a business records foundation under FRE 803(6).
>
> *Plaintiff's counsel:* We agree, your Honor. But we have established that this is a statement made by an employee of the defendant, and that it qualifies as a party admission under FRE 801(d)(2)(D). It's properly admissible under that rule.
>
> *Judge:* Plaintiff's Exhibit #1 will be received in evidence as a party admission.

14. Computer records

The use of computers by business organizations is rapidly eliminating traditional methods of record-keeping. Even where traditional account books and ledger systems are still employed, such data are often periodically transferred to computer banks and the original records are destroyed. Where computers are used to store business records, the retrieval of such information is done through a computer printout. Hence, such computer printouts are common evidence in trials.

Since FRE 803(6) includes "data compilations," computer printouts can be qualified for admission like any other business record. It is not necessary to prove that the computer printout was made at or near the time of the transaction involved, since frequently this will not have been the case. However, so long as the data was initially recorded on some record, at or near the time the event or transaction occurred, either as input into the computer's data bank or on a traditional paper record, the reliability requirement of the business records rule has been substantially met. When the computer printout was actually printed, or when the data were transferred from a paper record to the computer's data bank, should not matter, at least as far as admissibility of the printout is concerned.

A recurring issue is whether the computer printout offered in evidence is the complete record. Since computers are capable of printing out data in any form, and selectively, there is always a question whether the printout offered in evidence is the complete record of a transaction or selectively shows only certain facts. The rule of completeness, FRE 106, requires that when a writing is offered in evidence, all parts of that writing that in fairness should be considered at the same time must also be offered in evidence. This rule prevents offering parts of writings taken out of context. In the computer printout area, this is of major concern, since the printout itself does not show whether it is only part of the record of a particular transaction. These problems are often worked out at the discovery stage when business records are first produced and the completeness problem first arises.

Another approach is to treat computer printouts that show only selected information as a summary, which is admissible only if the requirements of FRE 1006 are met. That rule requires that the records on which the summaries are based be available for examination and copying by the opposing party. It also requires notifying the opposing party of an intent to introduce summaries at trial. This ensures that opposing parties can check the accuracy of the summary chart. (See subsection 18 below.)

A final approach is to authenticate computer-generated evidence under FRE 901(b)(9), which requires a showing that a process or system was used to produce a result, and that the process or system in fact produces an accurate result. This is a useful rule to establish a foundation for computer records that are automatically created by a particular computer system, such as automated telephone call records.

15. Recorded recollection

Under FRE 803(5), a memorandum or record is admissible as a recorded recollection if the record was made when the facts were fresh in the witness' mind, the record was accurate when made, and the witness now has insufficient recollection "to testify fully and accurately." This exception to the hearsay rule should be considered whenever the witness has a partial memory failure and the memorandum does not qualify as a business record.

If properly qualified, the record may be read to the jury. The idea is that reading the pertinent parts of the record is a proper substitute for the witness's forgotten memory. However, the record itself is not admitted in evidence as an exhibit unless offered by an adverse party.

Elements:

    a.   Exhibit is relevant and reliable.
    b.   Witness has no full or accurate present recollection of the facts.
    c.   Witness had firsthand knowledge of facts when they occurred.
    d.   Witness made record of the facts when the facts were fresh in the witness' memory.
    e.   Record was accurate and complete when made.
    f.   Record is in the same condition now as when made.

Example:

Witness has testified that he recorded the serial numbers of every automobile on a dealership lot on a certain date.

    Q. Mr. Doe, how many cars did you see on the lot that day?
    A. About 300.
    Q. Did each car have a serial number?
    A. Yes.
    Q. Can you tell the jury what the serial numbers on the cars were?
    A. No, sir, I can't possibly remember them.
    Q. Did you make any record of those serial numbers?
    A. Yes, sir, I made a list.
    Q. When did you make that list?
    A. I made it at the time I was on the dealership lot.
    Q. Was the list you made accurate and complete?
    A. Yes, sir.
    Q. Mr. Doe, would that list refresh your recollection as to what those serial numbers were?
    A. No, I couldn't possibly remember them, even if I reviewed the list.

Step 1.   Have exhibit marked.
Step 2.   Show exhibit to opposing counsel.
Step 3.   Ask permission to approach witness.
Step 4.   Show exhibit to witness.
Step 5.   Establish foundation:
    Q. I show you what has been marked Plaintiff's Exhibit #1. Do you recognize it?
    A. Yes.
    Q. What is it?
    A. That's the list I made of the serial numbers on the cars I saw at the car dealership.
    Q. Is the record in the same condition now as when you made it?
    A. Yes, nothing on it has been changed.

Step 6.   Offer contents of exhibit in evidence.
Step 7.   Have contents of exhibit marked in evidence.
Step 8.   [Not applicable.]
Step 9.   Ask permission to read exhibit to jury.
Step 10.   Read exhibit to jury.

16.   Copies

Under the Federal Rules of Evidence copies of writings are usually just as admissible as the originals. FRE 1001-1004, the original documents rule, provides that copies, now called "duplicates," are just as admissible as an original, unless there is a genuine dispute over authenticity, as would be the case where an important document is alleged to be a forgery or altered. Only in this situation must an original be produced. If an original cannot be produced, its absence must be satisfactorily explained before a copy is then admissible. Duplicates include carbon copies, photocopies, or any accurate reproduction of an original.

The federal rule generally permits copies to be introduced in any trial. Keep in mind, however, that some states that have not adopted the federal rules may still require originals, unless their unavailability is explained, in which case copies and other secondary evidence such as oral testimony may be admissible.

Where the absence of the original must be explained before the copy is admissible, the following foundation should be established.

Elements:

   a.   Copy is relevant.
   b.   Executed original once existed.
   c.   Copy of the original was made.
   d.   Copy was a true and accurate copy.
   e.   Original was unintentionally lost, is unavailable, etc.
   f.   A thorough search for the original in every possible location failed to produce it.

Example:

Step 1.   Have exhibit marked.
Step 2.   Show exhibit to opposing counsel.
Step 3.   Ask permission to approach witness.
Step 4.   Show exhibit to witness.
Step 5.   Establish foundation:
   Q.   Ms. White, I show you what has been marked as Plaintiff's Exhibit #1. Do you recognize it?
   A.   Yes, I do.
   Q.   What kind of document is it?
   A.   It is a photocopy of an agreement.
   Q.   Was there an original to the copy?

A. Yes, there was.

Q. What did you have to do with the creation of the original and the copy of the agreement?

A. I typed the original and made two photocopies of it.

Q. What did you do with the original?

A. After it was signed I put the original in the appropriate file in the file cabinets.

Q. What did you do with the copies?

A. One I put in our files with the original. The other I mailed to Mr. Jones.

Q. Ms. White, did you receive a subpoena calling for the production of that agreement?

A. Yes, I did.

Q. Pursuant to the subpoena did you locate the original?

A. No, I couldn't.

Q. Where should the original have been?

A. It should have been in our files with the copy, but when I went to get it, only the copy was there.

Q. Did you conduct a search of your office to find the original?

A. Yes, I did.

Q. What did that search consist of?

A. I notified everybody in the office to look for it. I personally went through every file in every cabinet in the office and every desk in our clerical area to look for it.

Q. How long did you search for the original?

A. I spent about 12 hours looking for it.

Q. Did you or anyone else find the original?

A. No, we finally had to give up. I just don't know where it could have gone.

Step 6.   Offer exhibit in evidence.

Step 7.   Have exhibit marked in evidence.

Step 8.   Have witness mark exhibit.

Step 9.   Ask permission to show/read exhibit to jury.

Step 10.   Show/read exhibit to jury.

Note that under 28 U.S.C. §1732, copies of business records are admissible, regardless of whether the originals are in existence and available.

17.   Certified records

Under FRE 902, certified copies of public records are self-authenticating. A record is certified when there is a statement attached to it stating that the record is in fact a record from that public agency. It usually bears the seal of the agency and has a blue or red ribbon attached. Hence, no witness is necessary to qualify the exhibit for admission. It need only be offered, then published to the jury. The only evidentiary objection possible is relevance.

Example:

> *Counsel:* Your Honor, we offer in evidence Plaintiff's Exhibit #1. It is a certified copy of a State of Illinois Department of Motor Vehicles vehicle registration. (Show the exhibit to the opposing counsel.)
>
> *Court:* Any objection, counsel?
>
> *Opposing counsel:* No objection, your Honor.
>
> *Court:* It's admitted.

Ask for permission to read or show it to the jury.

18.   Summaries

In an age when trials are becoming increasingly complex, it is hardly surprising that summary charts of technical evidence and other data are becoming increasingly common. Such charts can effectively compile financial records and other statistical data, clearly depict a chronological sequence of events, or graphically illustrate any number and type of transactions and relationships. When properly qualified as exhibits and admitted in evidence, such charts can be persuasive weapons.

There are two types of summary charts that are admissible at trial: summary charts of evidence produced at trial and summaries of voluminous records. The usual procedure in establishing the necessary foundation for a summary chart of evidence is to have it prepared by a witness who will actually sit in court while the evidence is being presented. Each fact appearing on the chart must then be related to the exhibit or witness that established the particular fact. This is usually done on the chart itself. At the appropriate time this witness can be called to demonstrate the evidentiary sources of the facts as well as any resulting mathematical computations he performed. When so qualified, the chart is admissible if it will aid the jury in understanding the evidence.

Example:

The following summary chart shows the cash loss to a bank following a robbery. A summary witness will be necessary to explain the audit procedures employed on the chart. (GE# refers to the government exhibits in evidence that prove each entry.)

Second Federal Savings & Loan Association
Cash Loss Audit on 5/2/00

	Teller #1	*Teller #2*	*Teller #3*
Cash on hand 4/30/00	$12,101.86 (GE# 20E)	$6,388.96 (GE# 20C)	$25,162.00 (GE# 20A)
Cash deposits 5/2/00	100.00 (GE# 21D)	340.00 (GE# 21D)	0

Cash withdrawals 5/2/00	427.50 (GE# 22A, 23)	0	0
Net change	$11,774.36 (GE# 20F)	$6,728.96 (GE# 20D)	$25,162.00 (GE # 20B)
Cash on hand	11,774.36 (GE# 20F)	6,728.96 (GE# 20D)	9,162.00 (GE# 20B)
Difference	0	0	$16,000.00 loss

Summaries of voluminous records are governed by FRE 1006. Under FRE 1006, summaries of writings, recordings, or photographs that cannot be conveniently produced in court can be admitted without first producing in court and getting into evidence the writings, recordings, or photographs. The underlying sources for the summaries can be examined and copied by the parties prior to trial, and the court can still require their production at trial if appropriate. Remember that FRE 1006 requires giving other parties notice of your intent to introduce summaries at trial.

Many courts will treat records generated from computer data bases as summaries under FRE 1006, if the exhibit in court is a compilation of data selectively extracted from the original data bases and not a print-out of the data in the same form as it was originally put into the data bases. In other words, such records are not business records under FRE 803(6), since the exhibit in court is not in the same form as the original data entered into the data bases. They are now summaries of voluminous records, and the requirements of FRE 1006 must be met.

FRE 1006 can be used to summarize the deposition of an unavailable witness. If the deposition is lengthy, and reading it in its original form would be a needless consumption of time (see FRE 611(a)(2)), the court may allow a summary of the witness' answers to be introduced instead of the deposition transcript.

Summary charts of evidence and summaries of voluminous records should be distinguished from charts, diagrams, or drawings that lawyers may make on poster boards or sketch pads during closing arguments. When made by the lawyers during closing arguments, the charts and drawings are not evidence and do not go to the jury during deliberations. They are merely visual aids that the lawyers may use to supplement their closing arguments.

19.   Stipulations

Stipulations can be both oral and written, although they are usually in a written form. Where written, they should be marked as an exhibit for purposes of the record and offered in evidence. The stipulation is usually read to the jury by the attorney who requested the stipulation.

Example:

> *Counsel:* Your Honor, may we read a stipulation, which has been marked Plaintiff's Exhibit #1, to the jury at this time?
> *Court:* Have you agreed to this stipulation?

    Opposing counsel: We have, your Honor.

    Court: Members of the jury, a stipulation is simply an agreement between the parties that certain facts are true and are not in dispute. Counsel, read the stipulation.

    Counsel: Ladies and gentlemen of the jury, this stipulation, or agreement, between the parties, states as follows: (Read the entire stipulation.) At the bottom is my signature as attorney for Mr. Smith, the plaintiff, and the signature of Mr. Doe as attorney for Mr. Jones, the defendant. (Give the executed original to the court clerk for safekeeping with the other exhibits.)

Stipulations are customarily drafted in either fact or witness form. A stipulation in fact form usually states that "the parties agree that the following facts are true," and recites the agreed facts. A stipulation in witness form usually states that "the parties agree that if Jane Smith were called as a witness she would testify to the following," and recites what the witness would say. When you use the witness form, make sure you include appropriate backgrounds for both lay and expert witnesses because the jury needs a basis for determining the witness' credibility.

20.   Pleadings and discovery

Pleadings and discovery answers, when they contain admissions, may be shown or read to the jury. The most common examples are the answers to the complaint, interrogatory answers, and responses to requests to admit facts. Since the papers were previously filed with the court, they have already been authenticated as coming from a particular party. Consequently, they need only be "published" to the jury. Since introducing such court papers is not a common procedure, perhaps it is best to ask for a side-bar conference to determine how to publish the exhibit. Before it is published, the judge will usually explain what the exhibit is and how it was made. The lawyer then reads the appropriate parts to the jury.

Example:

    Counsel: Your Honor, at this time we offer in evidence the contract attached to our complaint as Exhibit A. The existence and execution of this contract have been admitted in the defendant's answer.

    Court: It may be admitted.

The contract can then be shown to the jury like any other exhibit.

Example:

The defendant will introduce one of the plaintiff's interrogatory answers.

Counsel: Your Honor, before reading the pertinent part of the exhibit to the jury, we ask that the jury be instructed as to the significance of interrogatories and interrogatory answers.

Court: Very well. Members of the jury, before trial the parties customarily send each other what are called "interrogatories," which are simply written questions about the case. Their purpose is to permit the parties to learn more about the case and find out what facts are not disputed. The party answering the interrogatories must answer in writing, under oath, and sign the answer. Please proceed, counsel.

Counsel: Ladies and gentlemen, Defendant's Interrogatory #3 reads as follows: "State whether the plaintiff's vehicle involved in the accident had been inspected at an official motor vehicle inspection station within 12 months of the accident, and if so, where and when was it inspected?" The plaintiff's answer to Interrogatory #3 reads as follows: "The vehicle was not inspected within 12 months of the accident."

Before attempting to introduce a pleading or discovery answer at trial, research the applicable law. In general, verified pleadings ("judicial admissions") and unverified pleadings ("evidentiary admissions") are both admissible. However, parties often amend pleadings and other discovery responses prior to trial. Under certain circumstances, the original pleading or response, particularly if unverified, may not be introduced as an admission.

§6.4. Planning, preparing, and using visual aids and exhibits

1. Develop a visual strategy

This is the age of visual learning, so trials must become more visual as well. Since visual aids and exhibits are often dramatic, and seeing is usually more persuasive than hearing, always consider using them. While visual aids and exhibits can be both overused and misused, you should always explore creative ways to use them in any case. The best way is to develop a visual strategy, well before trial, that implements your trial strategy. After all, you develop a strategy for witness testimony; why not go through the same process for the visual part of the trial? How do you do this? You need to decide *what* to use, *when* to use it, and *how* to present it.

First, decide *what* visual aids and exhibits to use during the trial. Think broadly. Too many lawyers think only of exhibits that will be offered and formally admitted in evidence during the direct examination of witnesses in their case in chief. But visual aids can be used during all stages of the trial — opening statements, closing arguments, and cross examination — not just during direct examinations. For example, the opening statement might use a chart showing the key employees of the corporate parties, and a chronology of events. The closing argument might use a checklist of key points and a summary of the key damages instruction. The direct examination of an expert might include a diagram outlining the steps in a chemical reaction or a flow chart illustrating a manufacturing process. These visual aids are not exhibits in the sense of exhibits that will be formally admitted in evidence, yet they may be critical to presenting the case persuasively. Courts routinely permit the use of such visual aids, which are merely a visual representation of what the lawyer or witness is saying. As long as they are factually accurate and based on admissible evidence, their use will be proper.

What visual aids will send the messages you want to send? Do they create a compelling atmosphere or image? Is there one visual aid that can hit a home run, be the focus of your case, and visualize a key theme or fact? How many can you use effectively during the trial? How can you sequence visual aids and exhibits throughout the trial to maintain juror interest, yet repeat your key facts and messages? Determine if the exhibit will be admissible in evidence (and will usually go to the jury room during deliberations), or if it will be a visual aid used during the opening statement, closing argument, or expert testimony (and will usually not be admitted as an exhibit, hence will not go to the jury during deliberations). Begin by taking an inventory of the exhibits you have, then expand from that and develop a coordinated approach to using visual aids and exhibits throughout the trial, weighing the pros and cons of using each one during a particular stage of the trial. An experienced jury consultant or graphic arts expert can be valuable in creatively thinking of ways to make a trial more visual.

Second, decide *when* to use each visual aid or exhibit during the trial. Will it be a visual aid used during your opening statement? Will it be an exhibit formally offered in evidence during your case in chief? Will it be a teaching tool used to illustrate the testimony of your expert? Will it be an exhibit used during the cross-examination of your opponent's witnesses? Will it be a visual aid that summarizes liability or damages evidence during closing arguments? Can the visual aid or exhibit be used effectively more than once during the trial? How can you keep moving forward during the trial by giving the jurors new visual information? These questions also need to be asked well before trial, when you are developing your trial strategy, the content of your opening statement, closing argument, and the direct and cross-examinations of witnesses.

Third, decide *how* to present the visual aids and exhibits during the trial. Will they be documents, records, transcripts, videotaped testimony, objects, photographs, charts, diagrams, or models? How can they be presented most effectively to the jury? Should they be read by a witness, shown to the jury, or both? Should jurors be given individual exhibit books containing all the exhibits? Should exhibits be enlarged and mounted on poster boards? Should an overhead projector be used? Will modern technology — CD-ROMs, laptop computers, TV monitors, and the like — be useful or necessary? Will such technology be available in the jury room so that jurors can review the exhibits during their deliberations? Again, using a jury consultant or graphic arts expert can be valuable in exploring the possibilities. How to present the visual aids and exhibits should be the last question when developing a strategy. Remember that technology is a tool; it is not a strategy. Technology is simply the tool that implements a visual strategy that in turn supports your trial strategy.

For example, consider a corporation that has brought a breach of contract case against another corporation, claiming that the defendant breached a specific clause in the contract. What visual aids and exhibits will be the key components of plaintiff's visual strategy? During opening statements plaintiff might use (1) a chart showing who the plaintiff and defendant are, and the key employees of each who had major roles in the case; (2) a chronology of key events from the time contract negotiations began to when the breach and losses occurred; (3) a poster board showing the key language in the contract. During its case in chief plaintiff might use (1) a poster board containing a page of the contract, with the key language highlighted; (2) a computer projection of an important admission by defendant's key employee; (3) a summary chart prepared by an accountant showing plaintiff's losses computation. During cross-examination of defendant's witnesses, plaintiff might use (1) a poster board containing an excerpt of defendant's key employee's important admission; (2) a poster board of a letter by another of defendant's employees containing another important admission. Finally, during closing arguments plaintiff might use (1) poster boards of key jury instructions on liability and damages; (2) a chart containing a checklist of the reasons why defendant is liable, tied to key exhibits and instructions; (3) a chart of plaintiff's losses, tied to key exhibits and instructions. The important point to remember is that plaintiff's visual strategy keeps the jury interested, provides it with new visuals as the trial progresses, and focuses on the key themes, issues, and facts.

Finally, you need to learn additional things before settling on the visual strategy for a particular trial. Learn the physical characteristics of the courtroom in which the trial will be held. Courtrooms vary greatly in the size, shape, and location of the judge's bench, jury box, lawyer's tables, court personnel, and available floor and wall space. Some courtrooms have windows providing natural light, others have only artificial lighting, and the extent to which that lighting can be controlled varies greatly. Courtrooms differ in the amount and location of electrical outlets and what technical hardware is already in place. These variables significantly influence what visual aids and exhibits will be effective in that courtroom.

Learn the judge's attitudes and procedures about visual aids and exhibits, because they can differ. Judges routinely permit using exhibits during opening statements and closing arguments, if the exhibits will be, or have been, admitted in evidence. Most judges give lawyers considerable latitude in using visual aids during opening statements and closing arguments, as well as during witness testimony. Some traditionally minded judges, however, may impose limits on what visual aids can be used during these stages of the trial. In addition, opposing lawyers may make objections. If these are concerns, let the judge and opposing lawyers know what visual aids you plan to use in your opening statement and closing argument. Do this just before you give it (unless the judge's pretrial or other order requires earlier disclosure of visual aids as well as exhibits), so that any issues about their use can be resolved, and your opening statement and closing argument can be presented smoothly. Finally, learn your own, and your witness', comfort level with technology. If the lawyer using the visual aid, and the presentation medium, is not comfortable with it, it will affect the lawyer's performance. If the witness is not comfortable with it, the witness' performance will suffer as well.

When you have developed an overall visual strategy, you are then ready to consider preparing and presenting courtroom visual aids and exhibits.

2.   Prepare courtroom visual aids and exhibits

Graphic arts experts have several basic rules for preparing any visual aid or exhibit. First, it must have a clear message, one that jurors immediately comprehend. Second, it should usually be simple, since jurors can absorb only a limited amount of information from a single exhibit. It must be free of distractions, so that the jurors focus on the message. Third, it must be attractive: It must be big, colorful, and visually appealing. Graphics artists sometimes refer to the "billboard test": Is your exhibit designed so that it grabs the attention of motorists, and conveys the intended message within a few seconds? (Fig. 1)

On the other hand, in some trials one party is in favor of clarity, the other in favor of confusion. If your position is that the case is complex and confusing, visual aids and exhibits can also make that point, by collecting complex and confusing information and portraying it visually. (Fig. 2)

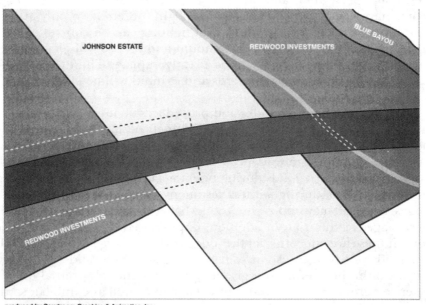

produced by Courtroom Graphics & Animation, Inc.

Fig. 1

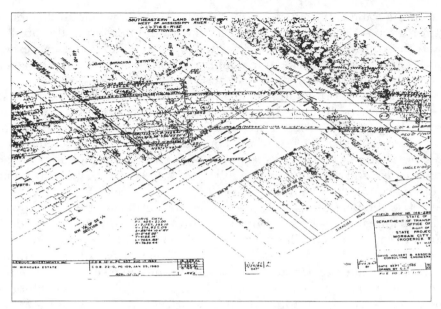

Fig. 2

Keep in mind that your key visual aids and exhibits should highlight and summarize your proof of liability and damages in such a visually compelling way that the jurors will instinctively use *your* exhibits, not your opponent's, as reference points during their deliberations. For example, in an automobile collision case, you want the jury to use *your* intersection diagram as the focal point for its deliberations on liability, and *your* damages chart as the focal point for its deliberations on damages. If your exhibits are more attractive and informative, the jurors will use them instead of your opponent's when deciding the case.

How do you make your visual aids and exhibits more appealing? And how do you choreograph their presentation in court to maximize their impact? The answers depend in part on the kind of visual aid or exhibit involved.

a. Objects

Think back to the last time you saw a press conference on the evening news during which the police announced a major drug seizure. The police chief, backed up by several uniformed police officers, was standing at a lectern in a press room. On a nearby table were stacks of drugs, all within view of the TV cameras. While the chief announced the details of the seizure, the cameras focused on and slowly scanned the drugs.

Good trial lawyers use the same kind of choreography in the courtroom. They know that objects — drugs, weapons, appliances, machinery — have a dramatic impact. To heighten that impact, they usually keep the object out of sight, then introduce it into the courtroom with a dramatic flair. For example, prosecutors in large drug cases usually bring the drugs into the courtroom in shopping carts during the direct examination of a key witness and display them before the jury. They know that this heightens juror interest. Plaintiffs in product liability cases often bring the product into the courtroom, such as a defective tire that exploded at expressway speed and caused an accident that injured the occupants. Seeing the actual object has a powerful psychological impact on the jury. (Fig. 3)

Plaintiffs' attorneys in personal injury cases, where the plaintiff is severely injured or disfigured, often keep the plaintiff out of the courtroom until the plaintiff is brought in to testify, keep the examination short, and then keep the plaintiff out of the courtroom afterward. They know that seeing a severely injured or disfigured plaintiff has a tremendous impact on the jury, and removing the plaintiff afterward keeps the jurors from becoming comfortable with that injury.

Use the same strategy in presenting objects during the trial. If your case involves a gun, keep it out of the jurors' view (this should be done anyway, since the gun will not yet be admitted in evidence), then reveal it during the direct examination when you will maximize its impact. If your exhibits include the actual forceps used during a delivery, keep the forceps out of the jury's view (even if the forceps already have been admitted in evidence), then introduce them in your case in chief where they will have the most impact. Unveiling objects can be moments of high drama, and drama always has a place in the courtroom.

b. Photographs and videotapes

If the real thing can't be brought into the courtroom, the next best thing is to use photographs and videotapes to show the real thing.

Fig. 3

Photographs and videotapes, properly taken and presented in the court-room, have an enormous impact.

How do you create effective courtroom photographs? First, make them large. The originals should be taken so that they can be enlarged to 8″ × 10″ or poster board size without significant loss of clarity. Avoid taking pictures with film smaller than 35mm, since such film is difficult to enlarge for courtroom use without the pictures becoming fuzzy or grainy. Double reflex cameras, which use $2\frac{1}{4}$″ × $2\frac{1}{4}$″ film, will produce much better enlargements. Second, use color whenver possible. Color is much more attractive to jurors than black and white, and color is particularly important when the object or scene has low contrast. Third, film is inexpensive. Use professional-quality film suitable for making poster-sized enlargements. Take enough photographs so that you can select the best ones for use in the courtroom. If you are an experienced photographer and have the proper equipment, you can take photographs yourself. (Make sure, however, that someone else can testify at trial to provide a proper foundation for the admission of the photographs.) If not, hire a commercial photographer.

If you have photographs enlarged to 8″ × 10″, mount them on foam-core poster board. This makes them much easier to handle in the court-room and more noticeable during deliberations, when you want your photographs to stand out. If a photograph is critically important, have it enlarged to 30″ × 40″ or larger and mounted on poster board. Have the photos printed with a dull matte finish to minimize glare and reflection. Commercial photography and photocopy stores can do this easily.

How do you compose effective photographs? Here jury psychology controls. You need to take photographs that will give the jury the pictures it needs to see and "feel" what's involved. Use both panoramic views and close-ups. If a close-up, make sure that the photograph is taken close enough so that the key scene and objects fill the photograph, yet does not distort the perspective. Courtroom photographs commonly are taken too far from the key points. Remember that jurors want to become emotionally involved in the case, and effective photographs are a critical component in getting the jury to see the case from your point of view.

For example, consider an intersection collision case. You could use overhead photographs that give a neutral bird's-eye view of the intersection. However, photographs taken from your party's (or key witness') perspective may be more effective. Photographs taken at the eye level of your party, at the same time of day as the collision, can show how the intersection looked from various distances. Sequential photographs can replicate your party's view as she approached the intersection. Showing what your party saw can make the jurors visualize the collision from your point of view, and that's important. (Figs. 4a – 4c)

Consider a burglary case. The first photograph can be of the house burglarized. Successive photographs can show the window where entry was made, a close-up can show the pry marks on the window frame and broken glass, and other photographs can show the interior of the house. The sequence of photographs will show how the burglar gained entry to the building and what he did once inside.

Fig. 4a

Fig. 4b

Videotapes can be dramatically effective exhibits. For example, a "day in the life" videotape of a permanently disabled plaintiff can make the physical reality of the plaintiff's daily routine come alive much more effectively than oral testimony or photographs. A videotape tour of a manufacturing plant can recreate the "feel" inside the plant more effectively than other evidence.

Where a videotape will be an effective vehicle for presenting evidence, you will need to employ an experienced videographer so that the

Fig. 4c

end product is of professional quality and fairly portrays what it contains. Make sure that the videographer is available for trial to provide a proper foundation for admission of the videotape. In addition, make sure the videographer retains and preserves all edited portions of the tape (the "out-takes"), since these are usually discoverable and are important in determining if the final videotape fairly and accurately portrays what it purports to portray.

c.   Diagrams, models, and charts

Diagrams have great usefulness in the courtroom. While they are not as detailed as photographs in showing real things, diagrams have other virtues: They can filter out extraneous details, and they can be marked to highlight what is important to your case. For instance, an intersection diagram can be drawn to contain only the important details. It can use car figures to show the positions of the vehicles before and at the time of the collision, and can be marked to show distances, times and speeds, as well as the location of eyewitnesses. A floor plan of a crime scene can show the layout of a house and can be marked to show what happened and where the witnesses were. (Fig. 5)

Models, since they are three-dimensional, can show spatial relationships more effectively than two-dimensional diagrams. A working model, built to scale, can recreate an object or structure, sometimes more effectively than a computer animation. (Fig. 6)

Charts are a particularly effective way to display information, and the relationships of key facts to each other and over time. Each of the four

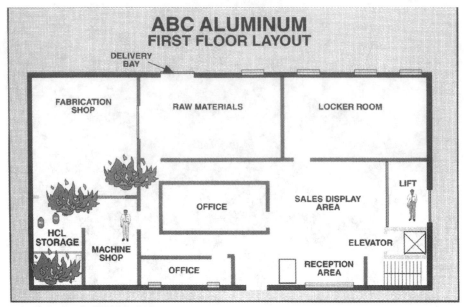

produced by Courtroom Graphics & Animation, Inc.

Fig. 5

Fig. 6

basic chart types — line, bar, pie, and table — has specific strengths. A line chart (sometimes called a fever chart) plots points on a grid having two axes; its principal use is to show changes in quantities over a period of time. A bar chart uses a series of columns placed vertically or horizontally on a grid; its principal use is to allow size comparisons of different data, particularly statistical information. A pie chart slices up a circle into various pie segments; its principal use is to show the components of the whole so that the relative sizes of the components can be visualized. A table orders specific data on a grid; its principal use is to allow exact comparisons of statistical data when a bar chart is not precise enough.

Line, bar, pie, and table charts are particularly useful when a case involves detailed data, such as sales records, production records, or financial figures, that must be analyzed over time or compared to each other. Therefore, charts are most frequently used in commercial cases. (Fig. 7)

Flow charts are also useful in organizing information in sequential or other logical order, and are commonly used to show a series of related steps or events. For example, a flow chart can show steps in a manufacturing process or stages of a chemical reaction. (Fig. 8) A chronology or time chart can show when various related events occurred. (Fig. 9)

Flow charts and chronologies are frequently used during opening statements and closing arguments, since they organize complex information in easily understood ways. Flow charts are also frequently used to illustrate an expert's testimony, for the same reason. When used for these purposes, they are visual aids, not exhibits, usually are not formally admitted in evidence, and usually do not go to the jury room during deliberations.

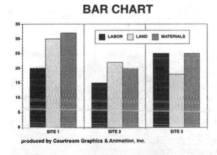

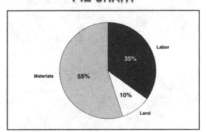

Fig. 7

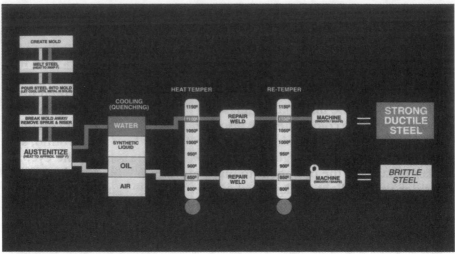

produced by Courtroom Graphics & Animation, Inc.

Fig. 8

Trial lawyers have a great deal of latitude in preparing such diagrams and charts, and the principal concern is what will be effective before the jury. Several graphics arts "guidelines" should be kept in mind. First, make sure the exhibit is large enough. Common foam-core poster board sizes are 30″ × 40″, 36″ × 48″, and 40″ × 60″. These have a rigid center, and are easy to keep on an easel. Although larger sizes are often available at art supply stores, they are awkward to bring to and use in the courtroom. Don't use a white board, since this provides too strong a contrast with black lines and letters. (It makes the letters "bleed," or appear to swim when stared at for any extended time.) An off-white board with a light gray, tan, or blue tone (10-15 percent tone) is more effective. The board

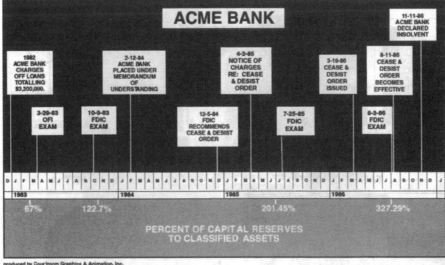

produced by Courtroom Graphics & Animation, Inc.

Fig. 9

should have a dull matte or textured finish to minimize glare and reflection.

Second, in addition to black, use not more than three or four high-contrast colors, such as red, blue, yellow, and green, keying the colors to the same points on all related exhibits so that they become visual cues. For example, the plaintiff's car can be blue, the defendant's red, on all the diagrams in the case. Color can also suggest ideas. For example, green suggests money, red suggests danger, and blue suggests calm. However, keep in mind that a significant number of persons (mostly males) have some level of visual color deficiencies. The most confusing colors are bland reds and greens. An effective approach is to make the basic diagram in black on an off-white background, then use bold colors for the important things you want the jury to focus on. (Fig. 10)

Reversing the color scheme is also frequently done, and has certain advantages. For example, having light lettering on a dark background, such as gold lettering on a burgundy background, is pleasing to the eye and makes it hard for the opponent to mark on your exhibit. (Fig. 11) For that reason, consider using a light background where you want your witness to mark the diagram; consider using a dark background where the diagram will be complete and you want to prevent other parties from marking it.

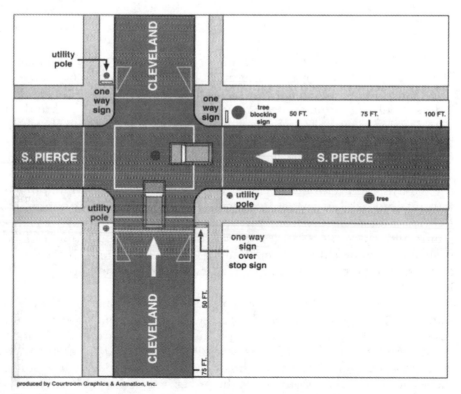

produced by Courtroom Graphics & Animation, Inc.

Fig. 10

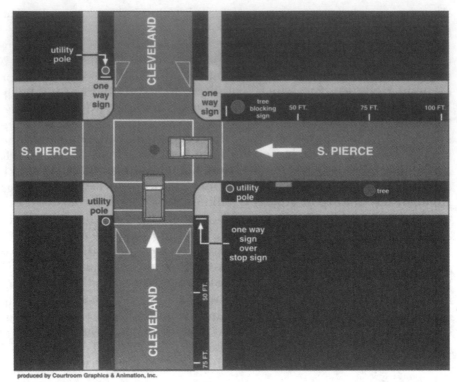

produced by Courtroom Graphics & Animation, Inc.

Fig. 11

Third, how lines and lettering are made are critical to a diagram and chart's effectiveness. Obviously they must be large enough to be seen easily by everyone. Since a juror may be more than 20 feet from the exhibit, letters should be simple in design and at least one inch high. A standard lettering that meets these requirements is 120-point Helvetica type, which is a sans serif type available in art supply stores in both stick-on and rub-on lettering. This or similar lettering is routinely part of computer graphics software programs.

Fourth, be careful not to clutter the diagram or chart with too much information. Exhibits are more effective if kept simple and to the point. Lawyers are among the worst offenders here, and commonly treat diagrams and charts as a contest to see how much information can be squeezed into one exhibit. Keep in mind the "billboard test": If the jurors don't get the point of the exhibit in a few seconds, it contains too much information.

Finally, give thought to how you organize informational charts such as summaries, chronologies, and damages charts. These must be carefully composed so that they attract attention, and can be easily read and understood. Graphics arts designers have several guidelines that are useful when creating a chart on a large poster board. First, use a border of at least two inches of white space. (Don't frame the poster board, since this only draws attention to the border.) Second, use standard one-inch high Helvetica or similar type consistently on the exhibit. Be careful in using all capital letters, since these are sometimes more difficult to read for persons with marginal reading skills. Use a capital letter to start a line, otherwise use lower case letters. For a diagram or chart heading, use the same type style used in the body, except with thicker or larger lettering. The heading should be bold weight, the rest of the diagram medium weight. (This will give the heading the appearance of being in bold type.) Third, spacing between letters and lines is important to the exhibit's overall visual effect. As a general rule, the spacing between letters should be about equal to the thickness of the letters. The spacing between lines should be at least equal to the height of the capital letters. The spacing between the heading and next line should be a double space. Finally, the left margin should be justified, the right margin ragged. If each line has a separate item of information, numbering or using a "bullet" (a large dot) on the left margin is useful.

Using these guidelines, a chart on a 30″ × 40″ or 36″ × 48″ poster board can contain a heading and about eight lines of text. Each line can contain about 10 characters (letters, punctuation, and spaces). (Fig. 12) If you have more information than can be contained in this format, use a second chart, not a larger single chart.

Knowing these format guidelines will help you prepare a rough sketch, and will be useful whether you or a graphic artist prepares the actual courtroom exhibit. Such an exhibit will be clean, organized, visually attractive, and send a clear, understandable message to the jury. Even more important, the jury will want to use your exhibit, not your opponent's, as a reference during its deliberations on liability and damages.

MEASURE OF DAMAGES

NATURE, EXTENT, DURATION OF INJURY	$ _____
PAST PAIN AND SUFFERING	$ _____
FUTURE PAIN AND SUFFERING	$ _____
PAST MEDICAL EXPENSES	$ _____
FUTURE MEDICAL EXPENSES	$ _____
LOST INCOME TO PRESENT DATE	$ _____
FUTURE LOST EARNINGS CAPACITY	$ _____

produced by Courtroom Graphics & Animation, Inc.

Fig. 12

d. Records and documents

From the jury's point of view, records and documents are usually boring. Unfortunately, in many cases, particularly commercial cases, the key evidence is in business records, correspondence, and other documents. Accordingly, the principal task for the trial lawyer is how to make paper exhibits interesting to the jury, and this task is not easy.

First, accept the fact that many jurors will not pay much attention to a pile of records that have introduced in evidence. Some jurors won't read them at all. It's simply a case of boredom combined with information overload.

Second, simplify. Almost all cases involving documentary proof have a handful of key documents that will make or break the case. One way to make your key exhibits stand out is to reduce them to the absolute minimum. This guarantees that the jury will focus on those exhibits, since their attention will not be distracted by less important ones. Another way is to make the significant part of a long record or document a separate exhibit. For example, even though you may need to introduce the entire contract in a contract case, put the key paragraph of the contract on a separate exhibit. Again, this guarantees that the jury will focus on the key words.

Third, use the exhibit in conjunction with a live witness. Many jurors only pay attention to paperwork if you make it easy for them. Whenever possible, have a well-qualified witness ready to explain what the exhibit is (even if the exhibit is already admitted in evidence), what its key provisions are, and why those provisions are so important. The witness should also translate into plain English any key terms and phrases that are not self-evident. Using the exhibits with a live witness works particularly well when the exhibits deal with a transaction or series of events. The exhibits can be mounted on large poster boards and placed sequentially before the jury, and the witness can then tell a story of what happened, using the exhibits to walk the jury through the transaction or events.

Fourth, make the exhibits visually attractive. There are several approaches. As always, bigger is better. Have the key documents enlarged to $30'' \times 40''$ or larger and mounted on poster board. Highlight the key provisions with color or other attention-getting marking. (Fig. 13) A key advantage of such poster boards is that they will go into the jury room during deliberations, where they will continue to grab the jury's attention.

Another approach is to make transparencies of the documents, then use an overhead projector in the courtroom and have a witness highlight, circle, underline, and explain key provisions and terms. The shortcoming of transparencies is that their visual quality does not match that of other exhibits, and they are difficult for the jury to use during deliberations.

Yet another approach is to load the documents into a computer, so that they can be projected from the computer on a large TV monitor or screen. (Fig. 14) These exhibits can be bar-coded and retrieved simply by moving an electronic pen over a bar code. The exhibits can then be marked, highlighted, and enlarged by either the lawyer or witness. Jurors are usually interested in these new technologies and will probably pay more attention to the exhibits. The only shortcoming is that the jury may

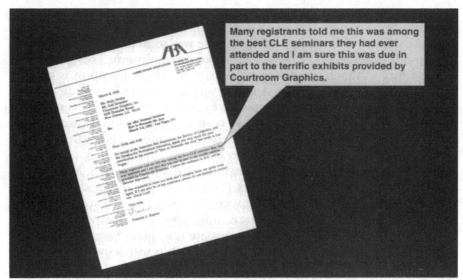

Fig. 13

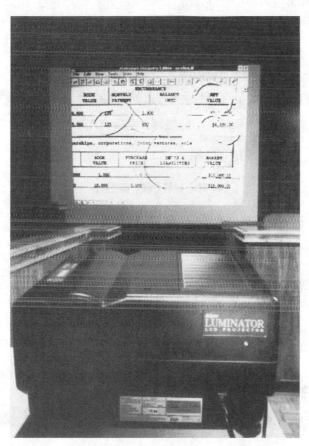

Fig. 14

not be able to see the exhibits again during deliberations, unless the jury room also has the necessary technology.

e. Summaries

The term *summary* actually includes two different types of exhibits. First, under FRE 1006, if records are so voluminous that it is impractical to bring them to the courtroom, summaries of those records are admissible if the other parties are on notice of your intent to introduce them in evidence, and the other parties have an opportunity to check the accuracy of the summaries by comparing them to the original records.

Keep in mind that many courts hold that if business records are stored in a computer data base and later printed out, such printouts are business records under FRE 803(6) only if they are in the same form as the original input entered into the computer. If the data base is searched and only selected data is printed out, those printouts will probably be considered summaries, not business records, and FRE 1006, not FRE 803(6), controls their admission.

Rule 1006 also presents an opportunity to create effective courtroom exhibits. For example, if a case involves a chemical or manufacturing process, a chart can be prepared showing the chronological steps in the process. (Fig. 15) Such a summary is much more effective than introduc-

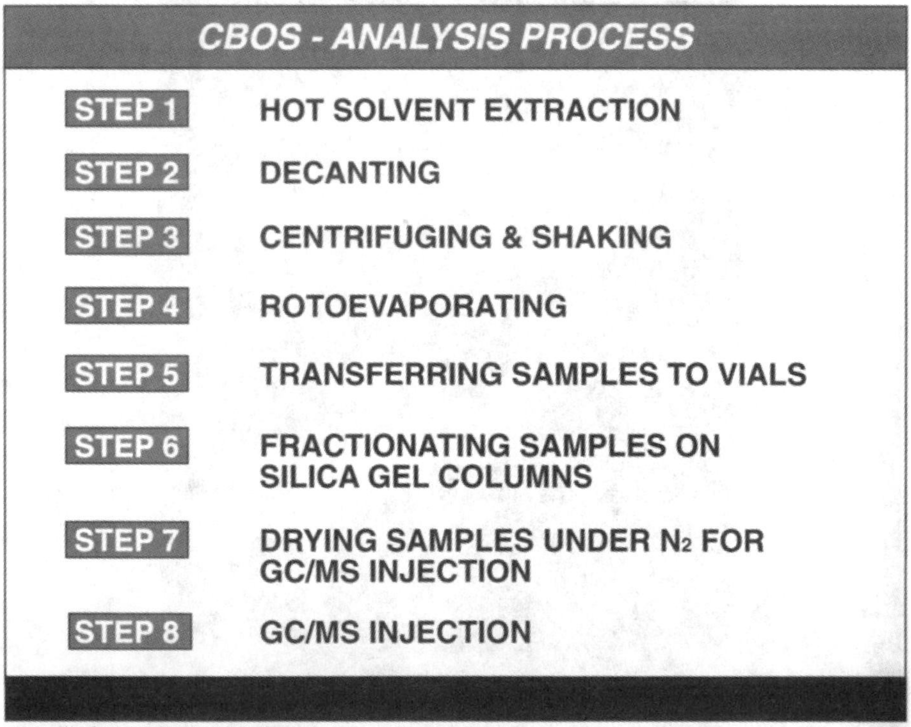

CBOS - ANALYSIS PROCESS

STEP 1	HOT SOLVENT EXTRACTION
STEP 2	DECANTING
STEP 3	CENTRIFUGING & SHAKING
STEP 4	ROTOEVAPORATING
STEP 5	TRANSFERRING SAMPLES TO VIALS
STEP 6	FRACTIONATING SAMPLES ON SILICA GEL COLUMNS
STEP 7	DRYING SAMPLES UNDER N_2 FOR GC/MS INJECTION
STEP 8	GC/MS INJECTION

produced by Courtroom Graphics & Animation, Inc.

Fig. 15

ing and then dealing with numerous pages of records or manuals that explain the process in unnecessary detail. (Make sure you have a qualified witness who can establish the appropriate foundation.)

A second kind of summary involves a summary of admitted evidence prepared by a testifying expert. For example, in criminal tax fraud prosecutions and in civil actions for an accounting where damages calculations are important, the parties frequently call accountants as summary witnesses to testify to losses calculations, based on the admitted evidence. These accountants usually prepare summary charts showing how they made the losses calculations. (Fig. 16) If these summaries are accurately based on admitted evidence, they are routinely admitted in evidence.

Lawyers sometimes loosely (and inaccurately) use the term summaries to refer to visual aids that they make for or during opening statements, closing arguments, and, where permitted, cross-examination. For example, a lawyer may create a chart showing the relationships of the parties in a multiparty case, and showing the witnesses from each party that are expected to testify at trial, and use it during her opening statement. (Fig. 17)

More commonly, lawyers make charts for, or during, closing arguments. The most common use of such charts is by plaintiffs in personal injury cases to summarize the damages amounts they are asking for on each element of permitted damages. An effective method is to have the chart completed in advance, then either have the dollar amounts covered with magnetic overlays, which are removed as each item of damages is discussed, or write in the dollar amounts as each item is discussed. (Fig. 18)

These kinds of visual aids are not summaries. In fact, they are not evidence at all, since they have not been introduced in evidence, and the

SECOND FEDERAL SAVINGS & LOAN ASSOCIATION
CASH LOSS AUDIT
MAY 2, 1984

DATE	TRANSACTION	TELLER #1	TELLER #2	TELLER #3
4-30-84	CASH ON HAND	(Exh. #10) $12,101.86	(Exh. #11) $6,388.96	(Exh. #12) $25,162.00
5-2-84	CASH DEPOSITS	(Exh. #13) 100.00	(Exh. #14) 340.00	0
5-2-84	CASH WITHDRAWALS	(Exh. #15) 427.50	0	0
	NET CHANGE	(Exh. #16) $11,774.36	(Exh. #17) $6,728.96	(Exh. #18) $25,162.00
	CASH ON HAND	(Exh. #19) 11,774.36	(Exh. #20) 6,728.96	(Exh. #21) 9,162.00
	DIFFERENCE	0	0	Loss $16,000.000

produced by Courtroom Graphics & Animation, Inc.

Fig. 16

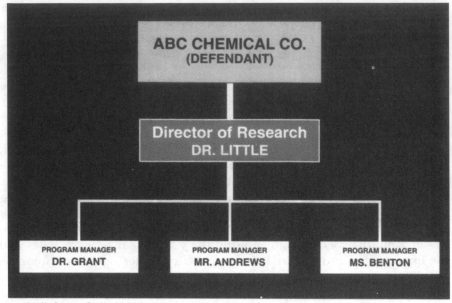

Fig. 17

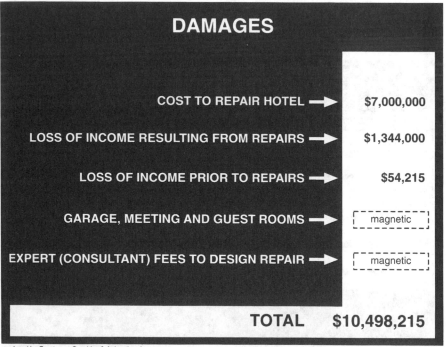

Fig. 18

jury will not have them in the jury room when they deliberate. Nonetheless, almost all courts allow the use of such visual aids during opening statements and closing arguments because they help the lawyers communicate the essence of their positions more effectively to the jury. The exhibits are merely visual representations of the lawyer's argument.

f. Computer graphics, animations, and data storage

In recent years computer technology has opened up a whole new world of possibilities for visual aids and exhibits. An industry has sprung up to service the demand for sophisticated courtroom graphics and animations. The technology has created two distinctly different courtroom uses.

First, optical scanners now enable lawyers to scan documents, photographs, transcripts, and court papers and store them on CD-ROMs. Each disk can contain thousands of pages of images. This means that all visual aids, exhibits, and transcripts, keyed to bar-codes, can be contained on CD-ROMs. With a swipe of an electronic pen over the appropriate bar-code, any page can be brought to a TV monitor or screen almost instantaneously. Once on the monitor or screen, the images can be enlarged, highlighted, underlined, or marked in a variety of ways. The images can be moved and enlarged. They can be printed out. CD-ROM technology has become common, perhaps even the norm, in complex cases that invariably involve numerous records and documents. A lawyer need only put bar codes in the appropriate places in her trial notebook, making it easy to pull up the correct exhibit when needed.

Second, computers with appropriate software programs can create sophisticated graphics and animations. Computer generated graphics are inexpensive and can be easily converted to slides, transparencies for overhead projectors, large courtroom exhibits, or can be projected directly on a television monitor or screen. Computer animations, prepared by experts using special software programs, can re-create complex events and graphically and convincingly illustrate the expert's opinion. Watching just one such computer animation (e.g., re-creating the last minute in an airline cockpit before a crash, with an animation that shows the pilot's view through the front windshield of the cockpit, shows the aircraft's key instrument readings, and plays the pilot's actual voice) will convince anyone of the new technology's power in the courtroom. The cost of this computer technology, while expensive, is dropping rapidly, and there is no question that it is the wave of the future. (Fig. 19)

3. When to use exhibits

Exhibits are visual and grab attention. That is precisely why you want to use them as much as possible. On the other hand, their very attractiveness can be a problem. Exhibits draw attention away from oral testimony. They win the battle for the jury's attention. That is why exhibits should complement testimony, rather than compete with it. How you should use exhibits in a case depends on the witness, the nature of the witness'

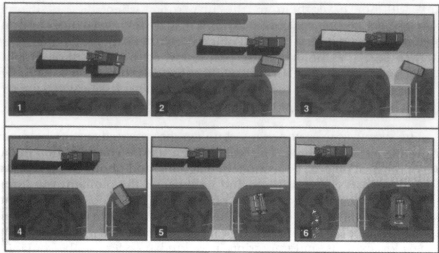

produced by Courtroom Graphics & Animation, Inc.

Fig. 19

testimony, the kind of exhibit, and how the trial judge permits exhibits to be presented to the jury.

Earlier chapters discussed why, during direct examinations, descriptive testimony ("the scene") ordinarily should precede and not interrupt occurrence testimony ("what happened"), since occurrence testimony is most effectively presented in a well-paced, uninterrupted way. The same approach should be taken whenever possible where exhibits are involved. Do not let the exhibits interrupt the pace and flow of the occurrence testimony, particularly if that testimony is graphic and dramatic.

Exhibits can be "published" to the jury in several ways: (1) they can be handed to the jury (objects such as weapons, drugs, consumer products, and machine parts); (2) they can be shown to the jury (photographs, maps, charts, and diagrams); and (3) they can be read to or by the jury (letters, documents, and other records). Once these exhibits are produced in the courtroom, jurors usually want to handle and examine them. They will be frustrated by lawyers who introduce exhibits in evidence and then fail to give them the exhibits. This will not be a serious consideration in the case of large objects, models, diagrams, and photo enlargements, which the jurors can readily see and probably understand the moment you bring them into the courtroom. However, small objects, photographs, and documents present different problems. These the jurors cannot understand unless they actually touch, see, or read them. Give them that opportunity as soon as permissible.

Trial judges can vary significantly in their approach to exhibits. Most will give counsel a free rein in deciding how and when the exhibits will be published. Others seem to view exhibits, particularly documents, as disruptive influences that slow a trial down, and may not allow the jury to read them in the courtroom, particularly if the exhibit is lengthy. Learn what your judge's attitude is on publishing your types of exhibits. If he will not let you show or read some exhibits immediately after their admission in evidence, or in the way you would like, plan accordingly. Whenever possible, reduce lengthy records to their key sections and mount them on large poster boards, or project them on television monitors or screens, so that the jury can immediately read them. If this is not possible, always let the jury know the reason why they cannot see the exhibits now.

Example:

> *Counsel:* Your Honor, may we show Plaintiff's Exhibit #1 to the jury at this time?
>
> *Court:* We'll do that at the end of the direct examination. Please continue with your examination.

Despite these differences in judicial attitudes, there are three basic ways to use exhibits during witness examinations.

a. During the direct examination

Where witnesses are occurrence witnesses and the exhibits are objects, the exhibits can be introduced when they are first mentioned during the direct examination. This method works well for exhibits such as weapons, drugs, and other objects. The foundations for these exhibits can be quickly established (particularly if they will not be contested) without significantly interrupting the flow of the direct examination. From their very nature, they need not be immediately shown to the jury, since the jury saw each exhibit while its foundation was being established. For example, a police officer can testify about arresting and searching the defendant, finding a gun, establish the foundation for the gun, and then continue with his testimony of what happened.

In some situations an exhibit must be introduced during the direct examination. Where the exhibit must be explained, or later testimony depends for its relevance on the admission of the exhibit, that exhibit must be introduced first. This often occurs where documents and records are involved, since the qualifying witness may have to explain technical terms in the documents and records and testify further about transactions appearing on them. For example, a witness in a commercial transaction case will need to explain how the exhibits show how a particular transaction was done. In such cases the records tell the story, and the records witness acts as an interpreter. Here the key exhibits that tell the story — the contract, shipping records, and the like — should be enlarged and placed in proper sequence before the jury, and the witness, can then describe what happened, using the exhibits as the focal points.

b. At the end of the direct examination

Another method is to wait until the direct examination is essentially completed before introducing and qualifying any exhibits. This has several advantages. First, it avoids interrupting the pace and flow of eyewitness testimony, which is important when the testimony is graphic and emotionally compelling. It keeps the exhibits out of sight, where they will not compete with, and draw attention away from, the witness. Second, it allows you to publish the exhibits to the jury immediately after their foundations are established, and allows the witness to explain the exhibits if necessary. Finally, using exhibits at the end of the direct examination allows you to highlight key parts of the direct, since the exhibits will often operate as visual summaries of events just described. The jury is seldom bored, because the exhibits themselves are usually interesting, and the looping back makes visual the direct examination's key points.

Using exhibits at the end of the direct examination works particularly well with key occurrence witnesses, especially those that are called early in that party's case in chief. Frequently such a witness will be the plaintiff in a personal injury case, the victim or defendant in a criminal case, or an important eyewitness. With these witnesses the critical part of the testimony, the action description, should flow and have pace. Once the event has been described, and the jury has experienced the event through the witness, the examination can loop back, and the witness can qualify for admission in evidence the physical evidence, photographs, and diagrams. The witness can then mark the photographs and diagrams to show the locations of parties and events he previously described. When the witness is through with the exhibits, they can immediately be given to the jury.

c. Handling multiple exhibits

Where only a few exhibits need to be shown to the witness and qualified for admission in evidence, each exhibit is usually handed to the witness individually, and the foundation for its admission is established before moving on to the next exhibit.

Sometimes, however, this procedure is unsatisfactory. Establishing the foundation for numerous exhibits individually is both needlessly time-consuming and boring. (This is why the parties often stipulate to the admission of most of each other's exhibits before trial.) Particularly where large numbers of documents and records are involved, the witness can identify the documents and records individually, then qualify them for admission as a group. This should be considered whenever a substantial number of exhibits have identical foundation requirements.

Example:

Where a custodian of the records has been called to qualify 20 bills of lading, show all 20 to the witness at one time. (The bills of lading can be individually marked, or can be marked as a group exhibit.) After she has looked at each bill of lading and has stated that they are all records of her company, ask the FRE 803(6) foundation requirements once for the whole group.

In commercial cases involving numerous documents and records, lawyers frequently put their exhibits into individual ring binders for the judge, lawyers, and each juror. This makes it easier for everyone to follow the testimony of the witnesses as they discuss the events and transactions, since those witnesses will invariably need to refer to the exhibits. The admissibility of the exhibits in these cases will usually be decided at the final pretrial conference or shortly before trial. Make sure the exhibits are numbered and put in the most logical order in the ring binders.

4. How to use exhibits

Having decided when to introduce your exhibits, you must next decide how they can be most effectively presented. This involves the mechanics of bringing the exhibit to the witness, and presenting the exhibit to the jury. Make sure you know how the judge wants you to proceed, so that your procedure will smoothly publish the exhibits during your case in chief. There are four common situations.

a. Have the witness hold the exhibit

The easiest method is to walk to the witness, hand him the exhibit, and return to your normal position near the far end of the jury box to ask the foundation questions. This has the benefit of making the witness speak up and maintain eye contact with the jury. Once the proper foundation has been established and the exhibit has been admitted in evidence, you can retrieve the exhibit from the witness and, if permitted, show it to the jury. This method is effective with objects such as weapons and drugs.

b. Have the witness mark or read from the exhibit

The second method can be used where the witness will have to mark or read parts of the exhibit. In these situations the lawyer may need to remain by the witness stand. Two rules should be followed. First, never block the jury's view of the witness, and never turn your back to the jury during the examination. You can avoid this by standing at either of the places indicated on the diagram on the next page.

Either of these positions gives the jury an unobstructed view of the witness. You will still be able to speak and look toward the jury when asking questions, yet be immediately next to the witness and the exhibit.

Second, make sure the record reflects what the witness is doing with or to an exhibit. When the witness points to or, preferably, marks the exhibit, make sure the record accurately reflects what has occurred.

Example:

The witness has established the foundation for a photograph of a lineup, and the photo has just been admitted in evidence.

> *Q.* Does Plaintiff's Exhibit #2 show the person you identified at the lineup?
> *A.* It does.

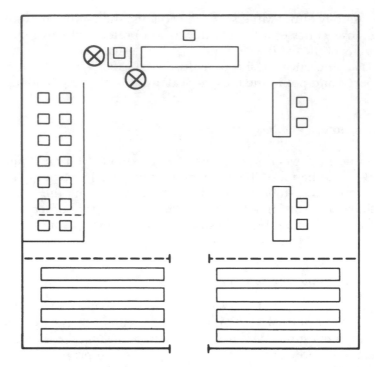

> Q. Using this red pen, please draw a circle around the head of the
> person you identified, and place your initials next to the circle.
> (Witness does so.) Your Honor, may the record show that Mr.
> Doe has placed a red circle around the head of the third person
> from the left, and has placed the initials "TD" next to the circle?
> *Court:* The record will so reflect.

Example:

The witness has testified to seeing a pedestrian struck at an intersection. A diagram of the intersection has been admitted in evidence.

> Q. Does Plaintiff's Exhibit #2 show where Mr. Smith was standing
> when he was struck by the car?
> A. Yes, it does.
> Q. Using this blue pen, please place the word "Smith" in a circle at
> that location. (Witness does so.) Your Honor, for the record, the
> witness has placed the word "Smith" in a circle in the crosswalk,
> near the lower right corner of the exhibit.

The marked exhibit can then be shown to the jurors.

    c. Use enlargements of photographs, documents, and illustrations

The third method is to use enlargements of photographs, documents, maps, plats, diagrams, or charts in the courtroom. The most common approach is to enlarge the exhibit and mount it on a 30″ × 40″, 36″ × 48″, or 40″ × 60″ poster board. Such an exhibit holds the jury's attention, and allows the witness to step down from the witness stand and illustrate his testimony using the exhibit.

An exhibit should first be admitted in evidence before it can be shown to the jury, although not all judges require this. If it is apparent that you can establish a foundation, the judge may allow you to place the exhibit before the jury on a stand while the foundation for its admission is being established. (As the opponent, if you intend to oppose the admission of the exhibit, ask that the other side be required preliminarily to establish the foundation for the exhibit out of the jury's presence.) Place the stand and exhibit in the most advantageous position. When possible, this is directly before the jury, about ten feet away. This treats all jurors equally, and places the exhibit at a distance where jurors wearing bifocal glasses can see it easily. Of course, the judge and lawyers may not be able to see the exhibit from the bench or counsel table. If this happens, the usual solution is for the judge and the other lawyers to position themselves so they can see. If the judge will not allow this, you must, of course, place the exhibit where he directs, most commonly next to or behind the witness stand.

Establish the foundation for the exhibit while the witness is still on the stand. Offer the exhibit in evidence. After it has been admitted, ask the judge for permission to have the witness leave the stand and go to the exhibit. When you receive permission, tell the witness what you want him to do, where to stand, and in what direction to face.

Example:

> *Counsel:* Your Honor, may the witness leave the stand and continue his testimony by the exhibit?
>
> *Court:* Of course.
>
> *Counsel:* Mr. Johnson, please step down and stand next to the right side of the exhibit, facing the jury.

The witness should then step down and stand at one side of the exhibit. (Please refer to the diagram on the next page). As always, the key is not to block the jury's view. Remind him to speak up, in the jury's direction. To force the witness to speak up and look at the jury when talking, you should ask questions from your usual position near the end of the jury box. Don't stand by the diagram. Have the witness mark the exhibit to highlight his testimony whenever possible.

Example:

The witness is standing next to a large diagram of an intersection. The diagram has been admitted in evidence.

> *Q.* Mr. Doe, is the grocery store that you left just before you saw the collision shown in this diagram, Plaintiff's Exhibit #2?
>
> *A.* Yes, it is.

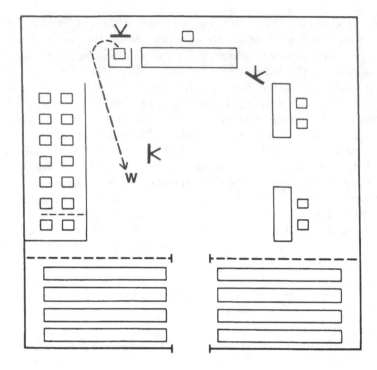

> *Q.* Please write the word "store" with this blue marker where the grocery store is. (Witness does so.) Does this diagram show where you stood at the time of the collision?
> *A.* It does.
> *Q.* Please place your last name in a circle at that spot with this red marker. (Witness does so.)

This approach has two advantages. First, it tells the witness precisely how to mark the diagram. Don't ask the witness to "indicate" or "mark" on the diagram, since you want to select symbols that are clear and highlight your key facts. Second, telling the witness how to mark the diagram usually eliminates the need to "make a record" of what the witness is doing. Hence, you should not need to add "your Honor, for the record the witness is . . . ," since it is obvious from your question what the witness has placed on the diagram.

How the witness marks exhibits has a substantial impact on the exhibit's effectiveness. Use your imagination, focusing on your key facts and issues. Documents and records can be underlined or circled with colored felt-tip markers to highlight the critical parts. Appropriately selected colors and symbols logically connect information on a diagram to the evidence. For example, if the cars involved in a collision were blue and green, use the same colors to show their locations on the diagram. Appropriately selected symbols can enhance the exhibit's usefulness. Use boxes or car figures to represent cars. Stick figures can represent persons, particularly where their body positions are important. Other important features, such as lights, can be marked in yellow. There are usually better ways to show objects and locations than the standard "X" markings.

Diagrams, maps, and photographs can also be marked to show distances, speeds, and times. For example, if the distance from a witness to the scene of an event is important, and good for your side, have the witness draw a line between the two points and mark the distance on it. The same approach can be used to show speeds and times. For example, if a car went a given distance in a certain amount of time, and the time is important, have the witness draw a line between the two points and label the time involved. If a car was speeding, put the speed on the diagram next to the car figure. If a traffic light was yellow for three seconds, put this information, if important, on the diagram.

Diagrams can be used to show sequences much like a stop-action movie. In automobile collision cases, for instance, it is often effective to use colored boxes to represent the cars involved. Boxes with an adhesive on the back, so they can simply be pressed on the diagram (and not later be moved around), work well. The boxes can then be put on the diagram to represent three time sequences: where the cars were when the witness first saw them, at the point of impact, and where they finally came to rest. Numbers can be put in each box to show the first, second, and third positions. Dotted lines can show the path of the cars, and distances can be marked on them. While doing this effectively requires rehearsing the sequences with the witness, it can be a persuasive trial technique. If the diagram will look too cluttered, consider using a separate clear-plastic overlay, or a separate diagram, for each of the time sequences. The possibilities are limited only by the limits of your imagination. Using an experienced graphics expert is extremely useful in designing and preparing such courtroom exhibits.

Finally, keep in mind that using a witness to mark a diagram involves risk. Some lawyers fear that a witness will make a mistake, and therefore prefer to have a completely marked diagram prepared before trial. The witness' role at trial is then limited to qualifying the completed diagram for admission in evidence. This approach has the advantages of safety and a professional-looking exhibit. However, because the jurors know that the lawyer had the diagram prepared in advance, its credibility suffers. By contrast, when the witness marks the exhibit in front of the jury, the jurors know that the information comes from the witness, not the lawyer, and this enhances both the credibility of the witness and the exhibit. Most witnesses can do a persuasive job of marking diagrams and charts if you let them know what you want them to do and practice it so that it can be done smoothly during trial.

d. Using exhibits during the cross-examination

Your opponent has a right to cross-examine the witness using any exhibit that was used during the direct examination. The question arises whether the cross-examiner also can have the witness mark additional things on the exhibit. If the cross-examiner is marking the exhibit only to clutter it up to destroy its impact, or to confuse the jury, an objection based on relevance and FRE 403 should be sustained. If the cross-examiner wants other relevant things marked to complete the diagram or that in fairness should be marked, an objection should be overruled. These issues are governed by FRE 611(a), which gives the judge power to control the mode of presenting evidence.

To preserve the integrity of the exhibits that you have introduced during the direct examination, have a plastic overlay attached to the exhibit and ask the judge to require that any cross-examiner's markings be made on the plastic overlay. Another approach is to have an identical diagram available and ask that this diagram be used during cross-examination. While this is discretionary, many judges feel that the cross- examiner has no right to mark up your exhibits with additional details when the real purpose is to destroy the clarity and persuasiveness of the exhibits.

The question also arises whether the cross-examiner has a right to introduce his exhibits during cross-examination. For example, may the defense, during cross-examination of a plaintiff's witness, use and introduce in evidence a defense exhibit? Judges will allow *using* new exhibits during cross-examination, provided they are within the scope of the direct or are relevant to the witness' credibility. For example, using the witness' prior written statements or deposition testimony during cross-examination to impeach the witness is proper and commonly done. Judges usually permit *showing* the exhibit to the jury while it properly is being used during cross-examination. For example, when a witness is being impeached with a prior inconsistent statement, judges will usually permit the impeaching statement to be enlarged and shown to the jury, either by placing the statement on a large poster board or projecting it on a screen.

Most judges, however, hold that such exhibit use is limited to otherwise proper cross-examination, and the exhibit itself cannot be formally admitted in evidence (assuming it is admissible) until it is the cross-examiner's turn to introduce evidence. This is because most judges feel that each party has the right to control what witnesses and exhibits are presented in its case in chief, limited only by exhibits that properly may be used during cross-examination. These issues again are controlled by FRE 611(a).

e. *Exhibits and jury deliberations*

The expectation is that exhibits will go to the jury during the jury deliberations, but their treatment depends on the kind of exhibit or visual aid involved. Exhibits that have been formally admitted in evidence during the trial ordinarily will go to the jury. There are two possible exceptions. First, dangerous exhibits, such as weapons, drugs, and chemicals, may be kept from the jury, in the discretion of the judge. Second, demonstrative exhibits ordinarily go to the jury. However, some judges still take the position that since they are only "illustrative," they do not go to the jury.

Visual aids that the lawyers have made and used during opening statements or closing arguments, or during the direct or cross-examinations of witnesses, ordinarily will not go to the jury. The most common of these are visual aids made for closing arguments, such as damages charts or checklists of major points. These are merely visual aids used to supplement the closing argument, and are not evidence. Therefore, they do not go to the jury during deliberations.

VII

CROSS-EXAMINATION

§7.1. Introduction

Cross-examination. The term itself commands respect and even generates fear among seasoned trial lawyers. Certainly, as far as the novice is concerned, no other area of trial work generates as much uncertainty and mystery. How many times, at the conclusion of a direct examination, has the thought flashed through every cross-examiner's mind: "My God! What do I do now?"

That countless writers have called cross-examination an art or intuitive skill hardly helps. Copying a model cross-examination from a "how to" text rarely helps, because every witness, in the context of a particular trial, is unique and must be treated as such. That 20 to 25 jury trials are usually necessary to acquire the experience essential for a moderate degree of polish in cross-examinations (as well as other aspects of trials) is hardly comforting. The novice trial lawyer needs help and he needs it now.

Because of this, the purposes of this chapter are threefold. First, it presents an analytical approach to threshold decisions and organization. Second, it presents a conceptual approach to the realistically attainable purposes of cross-examination. Third, it discusses and illustrates the technical skills needed to conduct successful cross-examinations and impeachment.

§7.2. Should you cross-examine?

The decision to cross-examine cannot be intelligently made unless you have prepared the cross-examination in advance and have a realistic understanding of what you can expect to achieve during the cross-examination of any given witness. The key, as always, is thorough preparation before trial. You know what your opponent's theory of the case will probably be. Through discovery you know what the witness will probably testify to at trial. You know your theory of the case, themes, and labels, and you know what the key disputed facts and issues are. Therefore, you can decide on your purposes in a cross-examination, then plan it and organize it in advance.

Since modern discovery in civil and, to an increasing extent, criminal trials is usually complete discovery, the element of surprise has been greatly reduced. Correspondingly, the need for thorough preparation to achieve an effective cross-examination has been greatly increased. The days of "let's see what he says on direct" are over, and a "wait-and-see" attitude will usually guarantee failure.

Although you have prepared your cross-examination in advance, this does not invariably mean that you will undertake it at trial. No one is required to cross-examine every witness who testifies at trial. Whenever you get up to cross-examine, the jury assumes that the witness has hurt you. When this is not the case, simply telling the judge, "Your Honor, we have no questions for this witness," or "No cross, your Honor," sends confident messages to the jury. Ask yourself the following questions whenever a witness has finished his direct testimony, before automatically rising to begin your cross-examination.

1.   Has the witness hurt your case?

Not every witness will have a devastating impact at trial. Some witnesses may only establish a required technical element of a claim or defense, or provide the foundation for exhibits not in dispute. Others will simply be corroborative witnesses, and you have already established your points with earlier ones. Where the witness has not damaged your position, cross-examining him is not essential.

2.   Is the witness important?

Keep in mind that jurors have certain preconceived notions about trials, which include the notion that every witness can and will be cross-examined by the opposing counsel. You must acknowledge and accommodate the jury's expectations. Where the witness has a significant role in the trial, this ordinarily means that you should undertake some type of cross-examination. Failure to do so may generate negative impressions for the jury and invite negative comments from opposing counsel during closing arguments.

3.   Was the witness' testimony credible?

Sometimes a witness will not "come off right" and his testimony is not believable. Other times a witness will be substantially contradicted by other witnesses. In those situations the damage has been done before you can do anything, so leaving well enough alone may be the soundest approach.

4.   Did the witness give less than expected on direct?

Has the witness (or his lawyer) omitted an important part of his testimony? If so, conducting a cross-examination may give the witness (or his lawyer) time to realize the mistake and attempt to repair it on redirect. Don't give the opposition a second chance.

   Do you think the witness has intentionally withheld a damaging part of his testimony on direct, hoping you will pursue it on cross? In other words, is the witness (or his lawyer) "sandbagging"? Remember that damaging testimony is twice as damaging if elicited during the cross-examination. Where you think the opposition is sandbagging on an important point, consider foregoing cross-examination, in whole or in part.

5.   What are your realistic expectations on cross?

Do you have any real ammunition to use during cross-examination? If the witness is credible and your ammunition is weak, consider avoiding cross-examination altogether or conducting a cursory cross on a peripheral point. Remember that during cross-examinations, where a witness has made a reasonable impression on direct, the jury will side with the witness. The jury sees the lawyer as sharp, crafty, and battle-tested, the witness as inexperienced, frightened, and in need of protection. While these attitudes may not always accurately reflect the true situation, they result in the same conclusion by the jury: In the cross-examination game, ties go to the witness. Accordingly, unless you can realistically expect to score points during your cross-examination, avoid it or conduct a cursory inquiry.

6.   What risks do you need to take?

Trial lawyers always dream of taking to trial an invincible case, one where witness upon witness simply overwhelms the opposition. This rarely happens, because perfect cases, if they exist at all, are usually settled. Consequently, trials invariably involve calculated risks. The number and extent of the risks depend on how good your case is. If your case is solid and you can reasonably expect to win, keep your risks to a minimum. If, however, your case is a probable loser that cannot be settled, you can cast caution to the winds and conduct a risky cross that searches for the break that might turn the case around. If, as is likely, that never occurs, your case will hardly be worse off than before. Accordingly, "safe" cross-examinations should always be utilized in those cases where the facts are close or favor your side. However, where your facts are bad and, barring luck, you can confidently expect to lose, conducting "risky" cross-examinations is something you can consider.

§7.3.   *Purposes and order of cross-examinations*

There are two basic purposes of cross-examinations:

a. *Eliciting favorable testimony (the first purpose).* This involves getting the witness to admit those facts that support your case in chief and are consistent with your theory of the case, themes, and labels.

b. *Conducting a destructive cross (the second purpose).* This involves asking the kinds of questions that will discredit the witness or his testimony so that the jury will minimize or even disregard them.

Understanding these two basic, broad purposes, and their order of use, is essential to conducting effective cross-examinations. While you may utilize only one of the approaches with some witnesses, you should always consider eliciting favorable testimony from the witness before you attempt a destructive cross-examination.

Why this order? At the end of the direct examination, most witnesses will have testified in a plausible fashion and their credibility will be high. This is the time to extract favorable admissions and information from the witness, since the witness' credibility will enhance the impact of the admissions. Such admissions will have less impact, and be less likely to occur, if you have previously attacked the witness.

Should you always undertake a destructive cross-examination? Not necessarily. Remember that a destructive cross is one that attempts to discredit a witness or his testimony so that the jury will minimize or even disregard what the witness has stated. If you have been successful in obtaining significant admissions, you may well decide to omit any discrediting cross at all. Remember that trials make it difficult to have your cake and eat it too. Jurors will be understandably skeptical if you argue that a witness' favorable testimony should be believed, while that part of the testimony you attacked should be disbelieved. Accordingly, where the witness' admissions have been helpful, thereafter conducting a destructive cross-examination will only undermine the admissions. Discretion is often the better part of valor in such situations.

§7.4.   *Elements of cross-examinations*

1.   Structure

Successful cross-examinations follow a preconceived structure that gives the examination a logical and persuasive order. That structure is based principally on the following considerations.

a.   *Have your cross-examination establish as few basic points as possible*

Your cross should preferably have no more than three or four points that support your theory of the case, themes, and labels. Why no more? Always remember the jury's finite capacity to retain information. The jury receives facts aurally, and it often receives them only once. Attempting too much on cross-examination creates two problems: the impact of your strongest points will be diluted, and the less significant points will be forgotten entirely by the time the jury deliberates on its verdict. Therefore, stick with the strongest ammunition and avoid the peripheral material. Always ask yourself: What will I say about this witness during closing arguments? Is this point one I will discuss during closing arguments? If the point is not important enough to make during closing arguments, it is probably not worth raising during the cross-examination either.

b.   Make your strongest points at the beginning and end of your cross-examination

Open with a flourish and end with a bang. Why? Again, the nature of the jury dictates this approach. Jurors remember best what they hear first and last. These are the principles of "primacy" and "recency." Their first and last impressions made during the cross-examination will be the lasting ones. Try to use your themes and labels at the beginning and end of the cross examination.

c.   Vary the order of your topics

Successful cross-examinations are sometimes based on *indirection* — the ability to establish points without the witness perceiving your purpose or becoming aware of the point until it has been established. Varying the order of your topics from the direct examination will make it less likely that the witness will anticipate the purpose of a given line of questions. After all, the direct examination was organized to be clear and persuasive. Why automatically adopt that organization for your cross-examination? On the other hand, constantly jumping from point to point is ineffective, since usually the jury and you become more confused than the witness.

d.   Don't repeat the direct examination!

This may be the most commonly violated maxim of good cross-examinations. Many are the lawyers whose standard approach is to have the witness "tell it again," in the groundless hope that the witness' testimony will somehow fall apart during the second telling. This approach almost invariably fails. It has merit only in the rare situations where the witness' testimony appears memorized, or where major parts of the direct examination support your theory of the case.

2.   Rules for cross-examinations

Your chances of conducting successful cross-examinations improve when you follow certain rules that have withstood the test of time. While these, like any other rules, can be ignored or violated in appropriate situations, following them is usually the safest approach. These rules include the following.

a. Start and end crisply

The first minute sends messages! When you start your cross-examination, the jury expects you to do something noteworthy. If you don't, the jury will quickly conclude that your cross-examination will add nothing to what they already learned from the witness. Accordingly, don't start your cross with useless introductory comments like "I just have a few questions I need to ask you" or "Mr. Johnson, I'd like to go over part of your earlier testimony." This does nothing for the jury other than to tell them you have nothing important to say. Start immediately with something that grabs the jury's attention. A first question like "Mr. Johnson, you're a convicted felon, aren't you?" tells the jury that you're going to be interesting and informative. The same psychology applies to your last point: Make it an important point, make it interesting, and make it crisp.

b. Know the probable answer to your questions before you ask the questions

Play it safe. Many witnesses will seize every opportunity to hurt you. Cross-examination is not a discovery deposition. This is not a time to fish for interesting information or to satisfy your curiosity. Its sole purpose is to elicit favorable facts or minimize the impact of the direct testimony. Accordingly, your cross-examination should tread on safe ground. Ask questions that you know the witness should answer a certain way, or, because he might not give exactly the expected answer, questions that you know you can handle his response to.

c. Listen to the witness' answers

This may appear to state the obvious, but the fact remains that lawyers often forget to do just that. Witnesses constantly surprise you. Unless you are watching and listening, you will miss nuances and gradations in the witness' testimony. Reluctance and hesitation in answering will be overlooked. Don't bury your face in your notes, worrying about the next questions while the witness is answering the last one. Organize your notes into cross-examination topics, then formulate your actual questions spontaneously. This way you can watch the witness as he listens and answers, gauge the witness' reaction to your question and the tone of his answer, and intelligently formulate follow-up questions. (See §11.14 on organizing the cross-examination.)

d. Don't argue with the witness

Cross-examination can be frustrating. The answers will often not be to your liking. The temptation, therefore, to argue with the witness is always present. Resist the temptation. Arguing is legally improper. It is also unprofessional. In terms of maintaining your credibility with the jury, it is a disaster. Lawyers who succumb to this weakness are usually those who conduct cross-examinations like fishing expeditions. Repeatedly getting bad answers, they begin to argue with the witness. The possibility of this happening can be substantially reduced simply by carefully organizing and structuring your cross-examinations in advance.

e.   Don't ask the witness to explain

Open-ended questions are inappropriate on cross-examinations. Hostile witnesses are always looking for an opening to slip in a damaging answer. Questions that ask "what," "how," or "why" or elicit explanations of any kind invite disaster. These kinds of questions are best avoided altogether on cross-examination. They're the kind of questions the redirect examination should ask.

f.   Don't ask the one-question-too-many

The traditional approach to cross-examinations was to make all your points during the cross-examination itself. The modern approach has an entirely different emphasis and level of subtlety. You ask only enough questions on cross-examination to establish the points you intend to make during your closing argument. This means that you will avoid asking the last question that explicitly drives home your point. Instead, your cross will merely suggest the point. During the closing argument you will rhetorically pose that last question and answer it the way you want it answered, when the witness is not around to give you a bad answer.

Example:

You want to establish that the witness did not see the collision until *after* the initial impact and therefore really doesn't know how the accident happened.

Q.   You weren't expecting a collision at the intersection, were you?
A.   No.
Q.   You'd gone through that corner many times without any collisions occurring, hadn't you?
A.   Yes.
Q.   The weather was good?
A.   Yes.
Q.   The traffic was normal?
A.   Yes.
Q.   As you approached the corner you were talking with your passenger, isn't that right?
A.   Yes.
Q.   The first unusual thing you heard was the sound of the crash, wasn't it?
A.   Yes.
Q.   And that's when you noticed that a crash had just occurred, isn't that true?
A.   Yes.

At this point, stop! You've made your point. Don't ask the last obvious question: "So you didn't really see the cars *before* the crash occurred, did you?" The witness will always give you a bad answer. Instead, save it for your closing argument:

Example:

> *Remember what Mr. Doe said on cross-examination? He testified that the first unusual sound he heard was the crash, and then he noticed that a crash between the two cars had just happened. Did he see the crash itself? Of course not. Did he see where the cars were before the crash? Of course not.*

The problem is always recognizing what that last question you shouldn't ask is, before you inadvertently ask it. Perhaps the best safeguard against doing this is to ask yourself: What's the final point about this witness that I'll want to make during closing arguments? When you decide on the point, make sure you don't ask it as a question during the cross-examination.

g.   Stop when finished

Cross-examination continuously tempts you to keep going on. There is always one more question you could ask. There is always one more point that you might be able to establish. Resist this natural temptation to fish for additional points. It's dangerous. Moreover, the jury has a limited attention span and can maintain a high level of concentration for only 15 to 20 minutes. Stick with your game plan and get to your last big point before the jury gets restless or bored. Make your point, stop, and sit down.

3.   Questioning style

Cross-examination requires a different attitude and verbal approach by the lawyer from those on direct examination. Effective direct examinations normally require you to assume a secondary role, remain in the background, and ask open-ended questions that let the witness dominate the jury's attention. Cross-examination, in terms of the lawyer's position and manner of questioning, is the mirror opposite of direct examinations. Accordingly, you should follow certain rules when conducting cross-examinations.

a.   Make your questions leading

This is an oft-violated rule. Questions like "What's the next thing you did?" and "Describe what the intersection looked like" have little place on cross, particularly where important testimony is involved. A leading question is one that suggests the answer and is the basic form you should use for cross-examinations. Inexperienced trial lawyers usually make two interrelated mistakes: they lead too much on direct and too little on cross. The best way to cure such mistakes is to consciously avoid them before they become an irreversible habit.

Example (proper leading forms):

> Q. Mr. Doe, on December 13, 2000, you owned a car, didn't you?
>
> Q. You left that intersection before the police arrived, isn't that correct?
>
> Q. You had two drinks in the hour before the collision, right?

These are all obviously leading questions. Another approach is to make the question leading, not through your language, but through your intonation and attitude, which make it obvious to the witness what answers you are expecting. The advantage of this approach is that the questions are simpler, making it effective when you want to establish a series of related points.

Example:

> Q. Ms. Jones, the robbery happened around 9:00 P.M.?
>
> A. Yes.
>
> Q. It was dark?
>
> A. It was nighttime.
>
> Q. The sun was down?
>
> A. Yes.
>
> Q. Stores were closed?
>
> A. Yes.
>
> Q. Not many cars driving around?
>
> A. Not many.
>
> Q. You said there were lights from the street lights?
>
> A. Yes.
>
> Q. And they were at the street corners?
>
> A. Yes.
>
> Q. But there weren't any street lights in the middle of the block?
>
> A. No.
>
> Q. And that's where the robbery happened, didn't it?
>
> A. Yes.

The only time you can safely ignore the rule is when the answer is not important — you know that the witness must give a certain answer because he has been previously committed to that answer by prior statements — or because any other answer will defy common sense or other evidence. You can then safely ask a nonleading question, because you can effectively impeach any unexpected answer.

Asking nonleading questions can break up the monotony of constantly leading questions. However, whenever you get near important, contested matters, the leading form is the only safe questioning method.

b.   Make a statement of fact and have the witness agree to it

During cross-examination you are the person who should make the principal assertions and statements of facts. The witness should simply be asked to agree with each of your statements. In a sense, you testify, the witness ratifies. By phrasing your questions narrowly, asking only one specific fact in each question, you should be able to get "yes," "no," or short answers to each question. Keep in mind that whenever the witness is given the chance to give a long, self-serving answer, he will.

> c. *Use short, clear questions, bit by bit*

Cross-examination is in part the art of slowly making mountains out of molehills. Don't make your big points in one question. Lead up to each point with a series of short, precise questions that establish each point bit by bit.

Example:

The cross-examiner wants to establish that the witness did not actually see the pedestrian get hit by a car. Don't ask: "You didn't really see the pedestrian get hit by the car, did you?" This is the classic "one-question-too-many." It's the point you will argue later in closings. The witness will always give you an unfavorable answer, and it's much better to lead up to that point by several short questions.

> Q. You're familiar with the intersection of North and Clark?
> A. Yes.
> Q. In fact, you've driven through that intersection over the past five years, haven't you?
> A. Yes.
> Q. You usually go through the intersection on your way to and from work?
> A. Yes.
> Q. So over the past five years, you've driven through the intersection over a thousand times?
> A. Probably.
> Q. You never saw a pedestrian hit by a car there before, did you?
> A. No.
> Q. On December 13, 2000, the weather was clear and dry?
> A. Yes.
> Q. The traffic was pretty much the way it always is at that time of day, wasn't it?
> A. Yes, I'd say so.
> Q. Nothing was going on that made you pay more than your usual attention to the road?
> A. No.
> Q. In fact, just before the accident you were thinking about what you were going to do at work that morning, weren't you?
> A. I might have been.
> Q. So the first unusual thing that you noticed that morning was the sound of the crash, wasn't it?

A.   Yes.
Q.   And that's when you saw that someone had been hit by a car, wasn't it?
A.   Yes.

Notice that by a series of interrelated, progressive questions you have demonstrated that the witness was not expecting a crash and really did not notice anything until after hearing the sound of the crash. You have made your point by indirection. Notice that what would be a last question, "So you didn't really see the pedestrian before the crash, did you?" was not asked. The witness will invariably say "yes," or something even more damaging. As noted above, that is the question you want to save and answer in your closing argument.

d.   Keep control over the witness

Control comes in large part by asking precisely phrased leading questions that never give the witness an opening to hurt you. But it has another facet. Control means forcing the witness to obey evidentiary rules, particularly those involving nonresponsive answers. When the witness continuously gives such answers, a common approach is to move to strike the answer and, if warranted, ask the court to admonish the witness.

Example:

Q.   You recognized the driver of the car, didn't you?
A.   Yes.
Q.   It was Frank Jones, wasn't it?
A.   Yes. He was weaving and looked drunk.
Q.   Objection, your Honor, we ask that the answer after "yes" be struck as nonresponsive, and the jury be instructed to disregard it.
Court: The answer will be stricken. The jury will disregard it.

Of course the jury cannot disregard it, since you cannot "unring a bell." However, it does serve a valuable purpose by letting the jury know that the witness' conduct is improper, adversely affecting the witness's credibility. If the witness repeatedly gives nonresponsive answers, consider asking the court to admonish him.

Example:

Q.   Your Honor, could the witness be admonished to answer the question and only the question?
Court: Yes. Mr. Smith, you will only answer the questions asked. This is not the place for speeches.

If after such an admonition the witness continues to volunteer answers, the jury will realize how biased and partial the witness is and judge his testimony accordingly.

The disadvantage of moving to strike and disregard is the message it sends the jury about you, the cross-examiner. The subliminal message the jury gets is that you are incapable of handling a problem witness and need to run to the judge for help. For that reason, many lawyers choose not to move to strike and disregard unresponsive and other improper answers unless doing so is necessary to preserve an important point as error on appeal.

A more effective approach to controlling problem witnesses is to let the witness know that you will not be deterred by an unresponsive answer and will insist on a proper one. If the witness then gives a proper answer, you have made your point. If the witness refuses to give a proper answer, you have demonstrated to the jury that the witness is being evasive or unfair, and you have again scored points by discrediting the witness. You can do this simply by repeating the same question, or rephrasing it slightly. If the other side objects that your question is repetitive, your response will be that the witness has yet to answer it properly.

Example:

Q. Mr. Jones, between 8:00 and 9:00 P.M., you drank five bottles of beer in the tavern, didn't you?
A. Well, we were all drinking.
Q. Mr. Jones, my question is, you drank five bottles of beer during that hour, didn't you?
A. I guess so.

Another method of control is to let the witness know that you have total command of the facts and will immediately know if the witness is telling you anything less than the total truth.

Example:

Q. Mr. Jones, there were three other persons sitting at your table in the tavern, weren't there?
A. Yes.
Q. They were Jimmy Smith, James Oliver, and Wilbur Franklin, correct?
A. Yes.
Q. Wilbur was sitting across from you?
A. Yes.
Q. And he's tall, thin, and has a deep voice, isn't that right?
A. Yes.
Q. And it was during that time in the tavern that you told Wilbur and the others, "I ditched the stolen car in the parking lot," isn't that right?
A. I guess so.

By demonstrating to the witness, before asking the important question, that you know the facts — because you probably talked to the other persons present in the tavern — you have a much lesser risk that the witness will give you an inaccurate or altogether false answer under the mistaken impression that you don't really know the true facts.

e.   Project a confident, take-charge attitude

On cross-examination, you should be the center of attention. Consistent with proper procedure and good taste, act the role. Ask questions in a voice and manner that projects confidence, both to the jury and the witness. Let the jury know your attitude about the facts. On direct examination, how a witness answers is as important as the answer itself. On cross-examination, how you ask a question is as important as the question itself. Projecting humor, incredulity, and sarcasm are all a proper part of cross-examination. Use them in appropriate situations. Above all, make sure the witness understands and feels your attitude about the facts of the case and your expectations in your questioning. Projecting that attitude usually has a significant impact in obtaining the answers you want.

Projecting confidence, however, is different from being unnecessarily hard on the witness. Cross-examination does not require examining crossly. The jury will react negatively if you sound and act tough on the witness without a good reason for your attitude.

f.   Be a good actor

Every cross-examiner, no matter how experienced, careful, and talented, will get bad answers to questions. When this happens, a good poker face is invaluable. Juries, when they hear what appears to be a devastating answer, will look around the courtroom and gauge the reaction of the judge, lawyers, and spectators. When the witness does drop a bomb, don't react to it. Simply go on as if nothing really happened. If you refuse to make anything of the answer, you have minimized its impact, and the jury may well conclude that the answer was not as damaging as it first appeared to be.

g.   Use a natural style

While trying cases requires you to conform your conduct as a lawyer to certain rules, there is a great deal of latitude that permits the personalities of the lawyers to come out. As in other phases of trial work, there are many styles with which you can conduct cross-examinations. However, there is only one solid rule you should follow: Use the style that is natural to you, that you feel comfortable with. Juries will immediately spot any lawyer who is attempting to copy someone else's style. The style that is natural for you will invariably be the one that is the most effective as well.

4.   Lawyer's position

Yours should be the dominant physical presence during the cross-examination, since you want to capture the jury's attention. Staying in the jury's line of sight will force them to watch you and concentrate on your questions. Where local rules do not restrict you to a council table or a lectern, standing directly before the jury, as you would during opening statements and closing arguments, is the most dominant position.

Use your voice and appropriate gestures to maintain the jury's attention. Moving around the courtroom periodically can also be useful. If you look and sound confident, you have a substantially better chance of making the cross-examination effective.

Standing directly before the jury has a second advantage. It allows you to maintain constant eye contact with the witness. In many cases maintaining eye contact gives the witness the impression that you are totally in command and know when the witness is wavering and hedging in his answers. It also forces the witness to either look at you or avoid your gaze by looking down. This keeps the witness from looking at the jury when he answers your questions.

Example:

In the following schematic diagram of a courtroom, you would usually stand near the area marked "X."

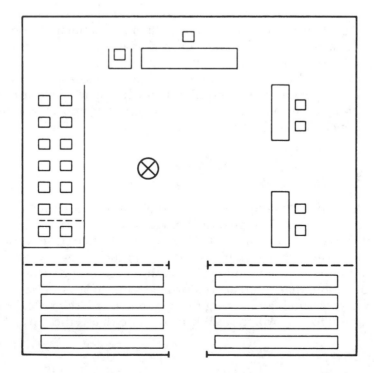

§7.5.   *Eliciting favorable testimony*

The cross-examiner's primary purpose, as mentioned earlier, is to elicit facts from the witness that will support your case in chief and be consistent with your theory of the case, themes, and labels. This should be done first, because the witness at the beginning of the cross-examination will be minimally adverse. If you are pleasant and courteous to the witness, your chances of obtaining favorable testimony will be maximized. The witness will relax and be much more likely to cooperate with you in achieving your purposes.

What constitutes favorable testimony? Here a little imagination and ingenuity is useful. You must keep your theory of the case in mind, because the purpose of this phase of the cross-examination is to obtain facts which support your theory or contradict theirs. Consider the following possibilities.

1.   Did part of the direct examination help?

Only rarely is an entire direct examination damaging. Usually the witness will testify to a number of facts that are either neutral or are helpful to your position. In those circumstances, it is useful to have the witness repeat the favorable facts, because the jury is much more likely to retain the information when you draw it out during the cross-examination.

Example:

In a criminal case where the issue is identification, the victim has testified he was robbed at midnight in an alley and has identified the defendant as the robber. The cross-examination can emphasize that it was nighttime and the crime occurred in poor lighting.

2.   Can the witness corroborate your case?

Often it is advantageous to determine if the witness can corroborate aspects of your case, even if those aspects were not directly covered during the direct examination. Review the central parts of your case and determine if the witness can testify to any facts that support it. Such admissions are always more impressive when obtained through the other side's witnesses.

Example:

A common cross-examination technique is to use the other side's witnesses to establish the foundations for exhibits you want to introduce during the trial. If the witness has the necessary first-hand knowledge to establish the required foundation, this is an effective technique, and later you can argue during closing arguments that the exhibits must be credible because the other side's witnesses established their foundations. Two issues sometimes arise, however. First, if establishing the foundations for the exhibits goes into new matter, an objection may be made that the cross-examination is beyond the scope of the direct. Scope issues are governed by FRE 611(b), and the judge has discretion to permit additional inquiry into new matters. Second, some judges permit an exhibit to be introduced in evidence during cross-examination immediately after a proper foundation has been established. Other judges permit the exhibits to be formally admitted only when it is the cross-examiner's next opportunity to present evidence (his case in chief or rebuttal case). These issues are governed by FRE 611(a), and are again discretionary with the judge.

Example:

In a contract case, plaintiff has testified that the parties entered into an oral contract. The cross-examination can point out that the plaintiff received a letter from the defendant, after the date of the claimed oral contract, which stated that certain terms still needed to be negotiated. The plaintiff can be shown the letter, marked as a defense exhibit, can be asked to identify the signature as being the defendant's, and can be asked to admit receiving the letter. (In most jurisdictions the letter cannot be admitted in evidence or shown to the jury until the defendant's case-in-chief.)

Another effective procedure is to use the other side's witnesses to corroborate specific facts that your witnesses have, or will, testify about. During closing arguments you can point out that these facts must be true, because even the other side's witnesses agreed with your's.

3.   What must the witness admit?

Review what the witness' prior statements are, as well as statements of your opponent's other witnesses. Where these prior statements contain favorable information, it is safe to ask the witness about the information. If the witness contradicts his own prior statement, he can be effectively impeached. If he contradicts another of your opponent's witnesses, you have established a contradiction in your opponent's case. The same procedure can be used with exhibits you know your opponent intends to introduce or has introduced at trial.

4.   What should the witness admit?

While this category is obviously less safe than the previous one, nevertheless it should always be considered. What the witness should admit can be gauged by common sense, logic, probabilities, and by what your other witnesses will say. If the witness does not admit what you believe he should, the testimony will probably not be accepted by the jury either.

Example:

In a personal injury case, you can probably get the driver of a car involved in a collision to admit that he was not anticipating an accident and wasn't driving any differently than he normally does. If the witness disagrees and claims that he was particularly careful that day, the jury probably will not believe him.

Example:

In a criminal case, the victim was robbed at gunpoint. You can probably get the victim to admit that he was frightened, afraid he was going to be shot, and was staring at the gun pointed at him. If he does not, the witness will have contradicted common sense and logic, and the jury will probably disbelieve that part of his testimony.

§7.6. *Discrediting unfavorable testimony*

Discrediting cross-examinations, regardless of the witness involved, have one fundamental purpose: to demonstrate or suggest that the witness is less credible or the testimony is less probably true than appeared at the end of the direct examination. This is sometimes called "increasing the improbabilities." Whether your approach is to obtain unlikely explanations, retractions, contradictions, inconsistencies, or implausibilities, the effect is the same.

The emphasis in a discrediting cross-examination is *not* on "destroying the witness." This almost never occurs in actual trials. Rarely will you cross-examine a perjurer and be able to demonstrate that he has totally fabricated his testimony. While some witnesses lie, more are confused or forgetful. Most witnesses, much like any other person telling a story, inject their own attitudes, perspectives, and selective recall into their testimony. It is this coloring, usually unintentional and often subconscious, that can realistically be developed and exposed.

There are two basic methods by which cross-examination can increase the improbabilities: discredit the testimony, and discredit the conduct.

1. Discredit or limit the testimony

The most common type of cross-examination, particularly in cases involving occurrence testimony, is one that challenges the reliability of the testimony or limits the importance of the testimony. Experience tells us that, although most witnesses are honest, attempt to be objective, and try to present an accurate narrative of an event, often just the opposite results. The witness himself is usually not aware of this. Witnesses often see only parts of an event, and "fill in" the gaps of their observations by what they think are the logical facts. After a while they honestly believe that they actually observed the filled-in facts, since their memory has blurred the distinction between actual observation and the filled-in facts. Consequently, the cross-examination cannot be a direct assault on the witness' integrity, because the jury will resent and reject this tactic.

The sounder approach is to accept the witness' honesty, but have your cross-examination suggest that certain factors adversely affect his testimony and undermine its impact. The basic methods are to discredit the witness' perception, memory, and ability to communicate.

a. Perception

A common challenge to occurrence testimony centers on the witness' ability and opportunity to observe the event involved. Usually this will involve showing that an event occurred quickly and unexpectedly, that the witness was frightened or surprised, and that the lighting was poor. When this is done effectively, the jury will realize that the circumstances under which the witness made the observations were not conducive to accuracy.

Example:

A witness has testified to driving down a street and observing a collision between two other cars. The cross-examination will show that the collision occurred quickly and unexpectedly, and that the witness was too far away to accurately observe what really happened.

Q. Ms. Jones, Maple Avenue is a north-south street and Elm Street runs east-west, correct?
A. Yes.
Q. The accident you say you observed was at that intersection?
A. Yes.
Q. When the accident happened, you were driving toward the intersection on Elm Street, correct?
A. Yes.
Q. You were about one-half block from the corner when it happened, isn't that so?
A. Yes.
Q. It's fair to say that you weren't expecting an accident that day, isn't it?
A. Yes.
Q. So you were driving the way you usually would just before the accident, weren't you?
A. Yes.
Q. You had a passenger in the car?
A. Yes.
Q. You were talking with him while driving?
A. Yes.
Q. Ms. Jones, each block in this city is one-eighth of a mile long, isn't it?
A. I think so.
Q. So each block is about 600 feet long, isn't it?
A. That sounds about right.
Q. This means that you were about 300 feet from the corner when the accident happened, weren't you?

A. I guess so.

Q. Three hundred feet is the length of a football field, isn't it?

A. Yes.

Q. Both Maple and Elm have buildings on both sides of the street, don't they?

A. Yes.

Q. As you were driving toward the corner, you couldn't see traffic on Maple other than at the intersection, could you?

A. No.

Q. That's because the buildings were blocking your view?

A. Yes.

Q. So you couldn't see the two cars involved in the accident until they were actually in the intersection, could you?

A. No.

Q. Ms. Jones, there was other traffic on Elm Street as well as Maple that morning, wasn't there?

A. Yes.

Q. You were watching that other traffic as you were driving?

A. Yes.

Q. Elm Street has a good amount of traffic during the rush hour, doesn't it?

A. Yes.

Q. There were probably cars going in both directions on Elm Street, weren't there?

A. Probably.

Q. Some of those cars were in your lane, while others were in the opposite lane, weren't they?

A. That's possible.

Q. And some of the cars were in front of you, while others were behind you, weren't they?

A. That's possible, but I'm not sure.

Through this cross-examination you have demonstrated that the witness was a good distance from the accident, could not see the cars involved until they were in the intersection, and probably had traffic blocking her view at the critical moments. In short, her observations are not as reliable as they first appeared to be.

Example:

A robbery victim has testified that he was robbed at knifepoint in an alley, and has identified the defendant as the robber. The cross-examination will show that the robbery happened suddenly and unexpectedly, that the robber was lighted from behind, and that the victim was focusing on the knife, not the robber's face.

Q. Mr. Archer, all this happened around 11:00 at night?

A. Yes.

Q. It was dark?

A. Yes.

Q. The robber pushed you from behind into the alley?
A. Yes.
Q. You never saw the robber until after you were in the alley, right?
A. That's right.
Q. And there weren't any street lights in the alley, were there?
A. No.
Q. The robber was facing into the alley?
A. That's right.
Q. And you were facing toward the street?
A. Yes.
Q. Then you noticed he had a knife in his hand?
A. Yes.
Q. Describe the knife.
A. It had a shiny blade, about six inches long, and a wooden handle.
Q. Mr. Archer, you must have been concerned that he might use the knife against you?
A. Yes.
Q. You kept your eye on the knife?
A. I suppose so.
Q. He then said "give me your wallet" and you gave it to him?
A. Yes.
Q. He then ran down the alley, away from the street?
A. Yes.
Q. From the time he said "give me your wallet" to the time he ran past you down the alley, that took about ten seconds?
A. I'm not sure of the exact time.
Q. And during that time, he always had the knife where you could see it?
A. Yes.

Notice that this cross-examination makes its major point by indirection. By showing that the victim kept looking at the knife (during the few seconds it took to complete the robbery), it demonstrates that the victim was understandably not concentrating on the robber's face (which was not lighted anyway), which is the key to a credible identification.

Example:

The Drug Enforcement Agency (DEA) conducted a surveillance of a "stash house" in which drugs were later found. A DEA agent has testified about various persons who were seen entering and leaving the house, including the defendant. The cross-examination will not contest that the defendant was there, but will point out that the agent could not see into the house, and could not hear what was going on in the house when the defendant was there. Hence, an innocent interpretation for the defendant's presence is clearly possible.

Q. Agent Zapata, you did your surveillance from a car?
A. Yes.

Q.   That car was about 100 feet from the house?
A.   About that.
Q.   You could see the people coming and going?
A.   Sure, particularly with my binoculars.
Q.   You couldn't see inside the house, could you?
A.   Not unless a window or door was open.
Q.   Even your binoculars can't look through walls, can they?
A.   No.
Q.   You couldn't see what was going on inside the house, could you?
A.   Not unless the door was open.
Q.   And you couldn't hear what was going on inside the house, could you?
A.   No.
Q.   You saw Frank go to and leave the house three times in three days, right?
A.   Yes.
Q.   Each time he went there Frank was inside at least one hour, right?
A.   Yes.
Q.   Once Frank was inside, you couldn't see what he was doing?
A.   That's right.
Q.   And you couldn't hear what was being said.
A.   That's right.
Q.   You couldn't see if he was visiting a friend, could you?
A.   No.
Q.   And you couldn't hear if he was chatting with a friend, could you?
A.   No.

Notice that this cross-examination accomplishes two things. First, it shows that the witness couldn't see or hear anything going on inside the house. Second, it raises the defense's theory of the case: The defendant was simply visiting a friend, not engaging in any drug activities.

b.   *Memory*

The witness' ability to remember details of an event, and his efforts to record or otherwise preserve these details, are often important considerations. Even where the witness had an excellent opportunity to make accurate observations of an event, the time between an event and the witness' testimony in court may be substantial. When this happens, cross-examinations often point out that the witness has forgotten details, has made no effort to record them, or cannot really separate this event from other similar ones.

Example:

A police officer has testified that he arrested the defendant in a hotel room and took a statement from him. The cross-examination will show that the officer did not put the statement in his report and, because of the intervening time and the number of arrests he has made during that time, cannot possibly remember what the defendant said.

> Q. Officer Jones, this arrest you made took place over a year ago?
> A. Yes.
> Q. One of a police officer's duties is to make arrests, isn't it?
> A. Yes.
> Q. How many arrests would you estimate you make each week?
> A. Oh, perhaps two or three, on the average.
> Q. This means that in the year since this arrest, you've arrested as many as 150 persons?
> A. It's possible. I can't really say how many.
> Q. It's impossible to remember all the details of every one of those arrests, isn't it?
> A. I suppose so.
> Q. Because of this, you prepare police reports?
> A. Yes.
> Q. The reports are made to refresh your memory about the details of every arrest?
> A. Yes.
> Q. You write the report to include everything you think could be important, don't you?
> A. I try to.
> Q. The report you made in this case, previously marked Defendant's Exhibit #1, included those things you thought were important, didn't they?
> A. Yes.
> Q. But your report doesn't say anything about a statement other than the notation, "Defendant made statement," does it?
> A. No.
> Q. Your report says nothing about what the defendant actually said, does it?
> A. No.

Example:

Plaintiff's secretary has testified that she mailed to the defendant a letter that accepted a previous offer the defendant made to the plaintiff. The defendant has denied receiving plaintiff's letter. The cross-examination will demonstrate that, because the secretary types and processes so many letters, she cannot possibly remember how this particular letter was handled.

> Q. Ms. Jones, you've been Mr. Doe's secretary for some five years now?
> A. Yes.
> Q. The events to which you just testified took place almost three years ago?

A.   Yes.

Q.   How many letters, on the average, do you type during a working day?

A.   It varies, of course, but it's probably around 5 a day.

Q.   So you would type approximately 25 letters a week, right?

A.   Approximately.

Q.   That would make about 100 each month?

A.   Approximately.

Q.   And over 1,000 each year?

A.   I guess so.

Q.   This means that you've probably typed over 5,000 letters for Mr. Doe since you started working for him, correct?

A.   Probably.

Q.   Ms. Jones, now and then Mr. Doe will make changes on a letter you've given him to sign, won't he?

A.   Yes.

Q.   In those instances you'll type a new draft of the letter?

A.   Yes.

Q.   How often does that happen?

A.   Oh, perhaps once or twice a week.

Q.   Now and then Mr. Doe will decide not to send a letter you've typed at all, won't he?

A.   Yes.

Q.   How often does that happen?

A.   Oh, maybe a couple of times a month.

Q.   Every now and then Mr. Doe will keep a letter on his desk that you've typed, won't he?

A.   Yes.

Q.   Every now and then you've probably had to remind him to send a letter out, haven't you?

A.   Yes.

Q.   Ms. Jones, as you sit here now, you can't remember which letters over the past five years you've retyped, can you?

A.   No.

Q.   Or which letters Mr. Doe decided not to mail?

A.   No.

Q.   Or which letters you had to remind him to put in the mail?

A.   No.

Q   It's simply a case of too many years and too many letters, isn't it?

A.   Yes.

c.   *Communication*

Another method of discrediting testimony is to examine the witness' ability to communicate. What good does it do for a witness to have observed an event, remember what happened, yet be unable to describe the event logically and accurately to the jury? The observations are only as good as is the witness' ability to tell what actually happened. A common cross-examination technique is to test the witness' ability to describe details and directions and to estimate distances and time, to demonstrate that the witness cannot accurately re-create a picture of what actually happened for the jury.

Example:

A witness has testified to the details of a collision and the times and distances involved. The cross-examination will demonstrate that the descriptions, times, and distances are inaccurate and unreliable.

> Q.   Mr. Jones, you were sitting on the porch of your house when the accident happened?
> A.   Yes.
> Q.   From your porch you could see both cars involved in the accident, right?
> A.   Yes.
> Q.   The impact between the two cars happened right in front of your house?
> A.   Yes.
> Q.   The defendant was pulling out of his driveway across the street from you, right?
> A.   Yes.
> Q.   How long is that driveway?
> A.   Well, it's a long driveway, so it's maybe 100 feet.
> Q.   How long did you estimate it took for the car to go the length of the driveway?
> A.   Maybe four seconds or so.
> Q.   The plaintiff's car on the street going toward you was moving at about 40 mph, is that your estimation?
> A.   Yes.
> Q.   How far away from you was the plaintiff's car when you first saw it?
> A.   Oh, maybe 500 feet away.
> Q.   And how long did it take the plaintiff's car to travel 500 feet?
> A.   Oh, maybe 20 seconds or so.
> Q.   Mr. Jones, could you estimate the distance from the witness stand to the doors at the back of the courtroom?
> A.   Well, that's about 25 feet.
> Q.   Your Honor, may the record reflect the distance is actually 38 feet?
> *Court:*   It may — we've measured that before.

You now have, partly by indirection, generated ammunition that you can use in closing arguments to demonstrate that this witness is an unreliable source of information, because he is not capable of accurately estimating distances. The second part of the cross-examination demonstrated this. When you can get a witness to make significantly inaccurate estimates of distances and time, it undermines the credibility of his entire observations. However, this approach should be used only in circumstances when you have a realistic possibility of success. It works best with children or persons who do not deal with technical information on a daily basis.

The first part of the cross-examination can also be used fruitfully in closing arguments. Every lawyer handling automobile cases soon learns that 15 mph = 22 ft./sec. The witness said the defendant's car traveled 100 feet in 4 seconds, or over 15 mph. As plaintiff, you can argue that this was an excessive rate of speed for a driveway. The witness also stated that the plaintiff's car traveled 500 feet in 20 seconds, or less than 20 mph. As plaintiff, you can easily argue that this was a safe speed to be traveling on a residential street. This type of cross-examination, pinning the witness down to specific estimates of distances, time, and speed, is a common technique in accident cases and often reveals internal inconsistencies.

2.   Discredit the conduct

A witness will sometimes testify in a seemingly reasonable manner, yet have acted inconsistently with the testimony. In these instances, the cross-examination should emphasize the inconsistency between the testimony and the conduct. This is based on the established principle that actions speak louder than words.

Example:

The defendant in an automobile collision case has testified that he was not negligent in the operation of his car. The cross-examination will develop that he left the scene of the collision without calling the police, never told his wife about it, and never reported it to either the police or anyone else.

> Q.   Mr. Jones, this collision happened about 7:30 at night?
> A.   Yes.
> Q.   There are gas stations at that corner, aren't there?
> A.   Yes.
> Q.   They were open when the collision occurred?
> A.   Yes.
> Q.   You only remained at the scene of the collision for approximately 15 minutes, didn't you?
> A.   Yes.
> Q.   You were not injured during the collision, were you?
> A.   No.
> Q.   At no time following the collision while you were at the corner did you call the police, correct?
> A.   No.
> Q.   You never attempted to flag down any police cars?
> A.   No.
> Q.   When you drove away from that corner, you didn't drive to the police station, did you?
> A.   No.
> Q.   You drove straight home?

A. Yes.

Q. When you got home your wife and family were home?

A. Yes.

Q. You didn't tell your wife or children that you had just been involved in a collision, did you?

A. No.

Q. At no time that evening did you call the police to report that fact, did you?

A. No.

Q. In fact, you never reported this collision to the police at any time, did you?

A. No.

Q. And you never reported this collision to anyone else, did you?

A. No.

Example:

The defendant in a criminal case is charged with sexually assaulting Ms. Smith. On direct examination he denied the charge. His defense is consent. The cross-examination will show his consciousness of guilt by his actions following the incident.

Q. Mr. Jones, on December 13, 2000, you were working at the XYZ Company, weren't you?

A. Yes.

Q. That date was a Tuesday?

A. Yes.

Q. You were living at 1420 Maple Street?

A. Yes.

Q. You were with Ms. Smith during the evening of December 13 until about 11:00 P.M., weren't you?

A. Yes.

Q. You then left?

A. Yes.

Q. You didn't go back to your apartment that night, did you?

A. No.

Q. You didn't go to work the next day, did you?

A. No.

Q. You weren't sick though, were you?

A. No.

Q. You didn't go home either, did you?

A. No.

Q. You didn't tell anyone at work where you were, did you?

A. No.

Q. You didn't tell any friends or family where you were, did you?

A. No.

Q. In fact, you were staying at a friend's house?

A. Yes.

Q. That's where you stayed for the next three days?

A. Yes.

Q. During those three days, you never went to work?
A. No.
Q. You never returned home?
A. No.
Q. And the only person who saw you at your friend's house was your friend, isn't that so?
A. Yes.

§7.7.   *Impeachment*

Impeachment is the most dramatic trial technique in the lawyer's arsenal. Selectively used and effectively employed, it can have a devastating effect at trial. Jurors appreciate effective impeachment. They enjoy seeing a witness get "caught" changing his story. Impeachment, however, should be selectively used because, like any dramatic weapon, its impact is diluted with overuse. Impeachment must be effectively employed because it must be dramatically executed using a persuasive technique. Consequently, learning when and how to use impeachment is an essential skill for any trial lawyer.

Impeachment is a cross-examination technique that discredits the witness or his testimony. Its purpose is simple: show the jury that this witness, or this part of his testimony, cannot be believed. Many lawyers mistakenly attempt the same thing through the refreshing recollection technique. Remember that refreshing recollection is a direct examination technique that steers a favorable but forgetful witness back on the beaten path. It is an accrediting technique and should usually not be used during cross-examination.

Impeachment is governed by a series of technical rules from the Federal Rules of Evidence, case law, and custom. Under FRE 607 any party can impeach any witness. This permits a party to "volunteer" impeaching facts on direct examination, an approach usually called "drawing the sting."

There are seven basic impeachment techniques:

a. bias, interest, and motive
b. prior convictions
c. prior bad acts
d. prior inconsistent statements
e. contradictory facts
f. bad character for truthfulness
g. treatises

Each of these will be discussed later in detail. Treatises will be discussed in Chapter VIII.

1.   Impeachment requirements

Impeachment procedures are governed by statutes, case law, local custom, and rules of persuasion. These rules for the most part apply regardless of the particular impeachment technique used. While the Federal Rules of

Evidence are largely silent on impeachment procedure, the common law developed certain procedural requirements to ensure that impeachment would be both fair and efficiently done, and most courts continue to follow them.

a. Must have good faith

Central to impeachment is the requirement of good faith. You must have a good faith basis for believing that the impeaching fact you are disclosing is in fact true. Unless you have such a good faith belief, you cannot inquire into it. The judge may require you to disclose to him your good faith basis for going into a particular matter. In addition, case law ordinarily requires that you prove up an important impeaching matter if the witness denies its existence. If you cannot prove up something that you may be required to, you cannot ask about it. This requirement protects a witness from being attacked with unsupportable impeachment. The good faith requirement is also an ethical rule. (See Model Rule 3.4.)

b. Must raise on cross-examination

If you intend to raise an impeaching matter, most jurisdictions require you to do so during cross-examination of the witness you are impeaching. (Of course, the direct examiner can impeach her own witness under FRE 607, but most impeachment occurs during cross-examination.) The reasons are fairness and judicial economy. Fairness requires that a witness be asked about an impeaching fact, so that he can admit, deny, or explain it. Judicial economy requires that an impeaching fact be brought out on cross because if the witness admits the impeachment, there is no need to prove it up with extrinsic evidence. In addition, an impeached witness can explain away, or reduce the effect of, impeachment on redirect examination, an efficient way of dealing with this situation.

c. Must prove up if required

Whether you must prove up an impeaching matter depends on two questions. First, did the witness admit the impeachment? If the witness unequivocally admits the impeachment, there is nothing left to do. If the witness denies or equivocates, however, you may be required to prove up the impeaching matter. Equivocations such as "I'm not sure," "I don't remember," or "I might have" are treated like denials.

Second, whether the impeaching matter is "collateral" or "noncollateral" determines whether you will be required to prove up a denial or equivocation. The reason is again based on judicial economy. Only noncollateral matters that are denied must be proved up with extrinsic evidence. If a collateral matter is denied, you must "take the witness' answer" and cannot prove up a denial. Whether a matter is noncollateral or collateral is really a practical question addressed to the judge's discretion. Is the matter that was denied by the witness important enough, given the issues of the case and significance of the witness, that we should use court time to prove up the denied matter with extrinsic evidence? If the answer is "yes," it is noncollateral. For instance, if an important eyewitness says he was 20 feet away when he saw an accident, and denies saying previously that he was 200 feet away, this fact is obviously important, or noncollateral. On the other hand, if the witness says that he was 20 feet away, and denies saying previously that he was 30 feet away, this inconsistency is relatively unimportant, or collateral. Some categories of impeachment are viewed as always noncollateral, others are always collateral, while some may fall in either category.

d. When to prove up

If a witness denies or equivocates on a noncollateral matter, you must "prove up the denial" or "complete the impeachment" with "extrinsic evidence" when you next have the opportunity to call witnessess or introduce exhibits. For example, if a plaintiff witness denies a noncollateral matter during cross-examination, defendant's lawyer must wait until the plaintiff rests and it is the defense's turn to call witnesses in the defense's case in chief. Only then can the defense call the prove-up witness. If a defense witness denies a noncollateral matter during cross-examination, plaintiff's attorney must wait until the defense rests and it is plaintiff's turn to call rebuttal witnesses. Only then can plaintiff call a prove-up witness. How this is done is discussed later in this section.

Once the basic procedure regulating impeachment is understood, the persuasive impeachment techniques can be learned. The techniques depend in large part on the particular impeachment method being used.

2. Bias, interest, and motive

This category includes bias, interest, and motive. While there is no federal rule on this category, bias, interest, and motive are always considered non-collateral. If the witness does anything other than admit the matter, you must prove it up with extrinsic evidence.

Regardless of the particular area, the approach is the same. Your cross-examination must, bit by bit, carefully suggest the impeaching facts, then stop. An overly zealous cross-examination runs the considerable danger of offending the jury. Accordingly, subtlety is essential. The jury will respect your good taste and reach the proper conclusion on its own.

a. Bias and prejudice

Bias and prejudice are particular tendencies or inclinations that a person has that prevent him from being impartial. A person is biased in favor of, or prejudiced against, some person or position. This usually involves exposing a family, personal, or employment relationship that renders the witness incapable of being impartial and objective.

Example:

The defense in a criminal case is alibi. The defendant's mother has testified that the defendant was at home when the crime was committed. The cross-examination will develop the mother's obvious bias for her son.

Q. Mrs. Jones, your son was living with you on the date this robbery was committed, wasn't he?
A. Yes.
Q. In fact, he's still living with you now?
A. Yes.
Q. So you see him just about every day?
A. Yes.
Q. You talk to him?
A. Yes.
Q. He talks to you when he has problems?
A. Yes.
Q. Mrs. Jones, you've probably talked with your son about this case many times, haven't you?
A. Yes.
Q. Would it be fair to say you talk about it with him almost every day?
A. Probably.
Q. You weren't subpoenaed to come to court today, were you?
A. No.
Q. Your son and his lawyer asked you to come?
A. Yes.

Notice that the cross-examination was fairly gentle. In such a situation the jury can easily sympathize with the poor woman whose son obviously put her up to testifying for him. In this kind of cross-examination, being gentle and brief is being safe. For this reason, lawyers frequently choose not to raise obvious bias on cross-examination, preferring instead to discuss it during the closing arguments. This is an effective alternative if the facts establishing bias are already in evidence.

b. Interest

Interest refers to the witness' possible benefit in, or detriment from, the outcome of a particular case. Most commonly, though not always, the witness' interest is financial. Since human greed is one of the most common motivations, demonstrating it can a powerful adverse effect on the witness' credibility.

Example:

In a will contest suit, the heirs at law who were excluded by the will have challenged the testator's mental capacity to execute the will. The witness is an heir who would receive part of the estate under intestacy should the will be barred.

Q. Mr. Jones, you are one of the late William Jones' children, aren't you?

A. Yes.

Q. You're one of three surviving children?

A. Yes.

Q. You knew your father had substantial property and other assets, didn't you?

A. Yes.

Q. When you learned that his estate was valued at over $300,000, that didn't surprise you, did it?

A. No.

Q. But when you learned that he had willed his entire estate to three different charities, that did surprise you, didn't it?

A. Yes.

Q. You knew that this meant that the three charities would get all your father's money, right?

A. Yes.

Q. Shortly after you learned the contents of your father's will, you consulted a lawyer?

A. Yes.

Q. You learned that if the will were invalid, the state laws of intestacy would apply, correct?

A. Yes.

Q. Those laws would provide that you, as one of three surviving children, would get one-third of his estate?

A. Yes.

Q. So, you knew that if the will were declared invalid, you would get about $100,000 from the estate, isn't that true?

A. Yes.

Q. But you also knew that if the will were upheld, you wouldn't get one dime, isn't that also true?

A. Yes.

   c.   Motive

Motive is the urge that prompts a person to think and act in a certain way. Common examples are greed, love, hate, and revenge. Each, in the right circumstances, can be a compelling emotion. Where such a motive can be effectively suggested, it is a powerful weapon because, like bias and interest, it taints the credibility of the witness, regardless of how plausible his testimony might appear to be.

Example:

Defendant is charged in a criminal case with forging endorsements on stolen checks and then cashing them. The cross-examination is designed to show his financial plight and obvious need for money as the motive for committing the crime.

Q. Mr. Jones, over the past two years you've invested in the stock market?

A. Yes.

Q. You bought over $100,000 worth of commodities stock?

A. Yes.

Q. Commodities are high-risk investments, aren't they?

A. Yes.

Q. It would then be fair to say you were speculating in the commodities market, wouldn't it?

A. I suppose so.

Q. You bought the stock on a 10 percent margin?

A. Yes.

Q. This meant you had to put up only 10 percent, or $10,000, of your own money to buy all the stock, isn't that true?

A. Yes.

Q. However, because of this, if the market value dropped by 10 percent, you'd lose your entire investment unless you put up more money, isn't that also true?

A. Yes.

Q. That's what's known as a margin call?

A. Yes.

Q. On December 13, 2000, you got a margin call from your brokerage firm, didn't you?

A. Yes.

Q. And it was the day after the margin call that you deposited these checks in your savings account, wasn't it?

A. Yes.

Q. The same day you used that money to meet the margin call, didn't you?

A. Yes.

3. Prior convictions

Prior convictions are governed by FRE 609, a highly technical rule that has two basic provisions. First, any felony conviction, and any conviction involving dishonesty or false statements, can be used to impeach the credibility of any witness who has testified. However, the conviction, or release from confinement, must have been within ten years of the present date. Second, a balancing test is applied in two situations: where the witness is a defendant in a criminal case and the prior conviction is a felony, and where the conviction is more than ten years old. In these situations the court must determine whether the probative value of the conviction outweighs its prejudicial effect. If so, the conviction can be used to impeach.

Prior convictions must be raised on cross (unless the witness has already "volunteered" it on direct examination, a situation that frequently occurs). This can be quickly done.

Example:

> Q. Mr. Smith, you've been convicted of a crime, haven't you?
> A. Yes.
> Q. You were convicted of a felony?
> A. Yes.
> Q. In fact, you were convicted of armed robbery five years ago, isn't that right?
> A. Yes.

If a witness denies or equivocates about the prior conviction, you must be prepared to prove it up with extrinsic evidence, since prior convictions are always considered noncollateral.

It is always a good idea to raise the question of using prior convictions to impeach before trial to get a ruling on precisely what convictions can be used to impeach. In recent years courts have frequently used the balancing test required when the witness is a criminal defendant to permit the fact of the conviction to be raised, but bar any reference to the actual crime. For instance, the court might rule that the defendant can be shown to have a "felony conviction," but not that the conviction was for armed robbery, in order to reduce the prejudicial effect of the conviction. This is sometimes done when the prior conviction is for the same or similar crime as the one for which the defendant is currently on trial, since there is a danger that the jury may use the prior conviction to conclude that "once a robber, always a robber," which is an improper use of the prior conviction.

When cross-examining a witness, the rule in most jurisdictions is that any fact appearing on the judgment order, or record of conviction, can be raised. This usually includes the jurisdiction, presiding judge, date of conviction, the crimes the witness was found guilty of, and the sentence imposed. If the witness has volunteered only part of this information on direct, the cross-examiner may still develop the remainder.

Example:

> Q. Mr. Doe, you told us that in 2000 you were convicted of income tax evasion, right?
> A. Yes.
> Q. In fact, you were convicted on June 30, 2000, on three counts of that charge, weren't you?
> A. Yes.
> Q. That was before Judge Smith in the U.S. District Court for the Northern District of Indiana, wasn't it?
> A. Yes, it was.
> Q. Judge Smith sentenced you to six months' imprisonment and five years' probation on all three counts, didn't he?
> A. Yes, he did.

Impeachment with a prior conviction is a technical area, and the rules governing it may vary substantially in those jurisdictions not following FRE 609. Consequently, you must do two things whenever you plan to use prior convictions at trial. First, make sure you know the applicable law. Second, raise prior conviction matters before trial, since improperly impeaching with a prior conviction can easily result in a mistrial.

4. Prior bad acts

Prior bad acts are admissible under FRE 608(b) if the acts are "probative of truthfulness." This is a change from the common law, and today some jurisdictions that have not adopted the Federal Rules of Evidence do not permit this type of impeachment. Hence, research is required in these jurisdictions to determine the admissibility of prior bad acts. Bad acts that are probative of truthfulness commonly include submitting false loan applications or inaccurate employment applications or other intentional factual misrepresentations.

   Prior bad acts are viewed as collateral. The cross-examiner must "take the witness' answer," and the bad act cannot be proved up extrinsically. This being the case, the cross-examiner should pursue the cross-examination to get the witness to admit the bad act, or show that a denial is not believable.

Example:

> Q. Mrs. Johnson, you filled out an employment application at Sears last year?
> A. Yes.
> Q. You submitted it on March 31 of last year, correct?
> A. Around then.
> Q. And you signed it?
> A. I think so.
> Q. Mrs. Johnson, on the line asking for the extent of your education, didn't you write down "received a B.A. degree in economics from U.C.L.A. in 1981"?
> A. Yes.
> Q. In fact, Mrs. Johnson, you haven't received a B.A. degree from U.C.L.A., have you?
> A. No.

As a matter of technique, you should ask about the bad act by revealing enough detail that lets the witness and jury know that you have done your homework on this subject. The witness is then more likely to admit it, or the jury is unlikely to believe a denial.

5. Prior inconsistent statements

Raising prior inconsistent statements is the most frequently used impeachment method at trial. More than any other impeachment method, however, impeaching with prior inconsistent statements requires a precise technique to be effective before the jury.

FRE 613 expressly requires that the witness have an opportunity to admit, deny, or explain making the inconsistent statement. Hence, most courts require that you raise it during the cross-examination of the witness. Prior inconsistent statements can be either collateral or noncollateral. If it is noncollateral, and the witness does not admit making it, you must prove it up later with extrinsic evidence.

What is the evidentiary status of a prior inconsistent statement used to impeach during trial? This depends on the witness, the kind of prior inconsistent statement involved, and the jurisdiction's evidence law. A prior inconsistent statement can always be used to impeach, and a hearsay objection will never be proper, when the statement is used for the limited purpose of impeachment. If the statement was made by a party, however, it will also always qualify as an admission under FRE 801(d)(2), and can be used both to impeach and as substantive evidence. If the statement was made by a nonparty, it can always be used to impeach, but under FRE 801(d)(1)(A) it is admissible as substantive evidence only if the statement was made under oath at a trial, hearing, proceeding, or deposition. (A few state jurisdictions, however, permit the introduction of any written prior inconsistent statement in evidence merely because it was used to impeach the witness during trial, on the theory that the jury should be able to see, as well as hear, the impeaching statement.)

a. Techniques

The impeachment technique must be both structured and simple. The basic structure involves three steps — commit, credit, and confront. First, commit the witness to the fact he asserted on direct, the one you plan to impeach. Use the witness' actual answer on direct when you commit him, since he is most likely to agree with the actual answer, rather than a paraphrasing.

Second, credit, that is, build up the importance of the impeaching statement. Direct the witness to the date, time, place, and circumstances of the prior inconsistent statement, whether oral or written. Under FRE 613(a), you no longer need to show an impeaching writing to the witness before using it, although you must show it to the opposing counsel on request. However, it is usually more effective to show the witness his prior written statement and make him admit having made or signed it. Building up the impeaching statement also involves showing that the statement was made when the witness' memory was fresher, and under circumstances showing that the statement was seriously made.

Third, confront the witness with the prior inconsistent statement by reading the appropriate parts to the witness and asking him to admit having made it. Use the actual words of the impeaching statement. If you are using a lengthy statement such as a deposition, tell opposing counsel the page you are reading from. You can also have the witness read the impeaching statement, but this usually is not as effective, since the witness will not be as forceful in reading the impeaching section.

Finally, project your attitude! Your attitude during the impeachment signals to the jury what its attitude should be. Is your attitude that the witness was lying, confused, or forgetful? If lying, broadcast it by using a suitably hard demeanor. If confused or forgetful, broadcast it by using a more sympathetic tone. Your attitude during the impeachment also should be consistent with your attitude during closing arguments when you discuss the witness' inconsistency.

Example:

> Q. Mr. Jones, you say you were about 50 feet from the accident when it happened?
> A. Yes.
> Q. There's no doubt in your mind about that?
> A. No.
> Q. Weren't you actually *over 100 feet* away?
> A. No.
> Q. Mr. Jones, you talked to a police officer right at the scene a few minutes after the accident, didn't you?
> A. Yes.
> Q. Since you talked to him right after the accident, everything was still fresh in your mind?
> A. Yes.
> Q. You knew the police officer was investigating the accident?
> A. Yes.
> Q. And you knew it was important to tell the facts as accurately as possible?
> A. Yes.
> Q Mr. Jones, you told that police officer, right after the accident, that you were *over 100 feet away* when the accident happened, didn't you?
> A. Yes.

Here the basic technique — commit, credit, and confront — was executed cleanly and simply. A simple fact — 50 feet — was singled out for impeachment, then contrasted cleanly with the contradictory earlier oral statement — 100 feet. Effective impeachment is like holdiing up two flash cards before the jury, one white, one black, so everyone can see and understand the contrast.

Since the answer was "yes," the witness has admitted the prior inconsistent statement and nothing else needs to be done. If the answer were "no" or an equivocation like "I don't know" or "I'm not sure," you will have to "prove up" the statement if the statement is important, or noncollateral. Proving up, or completing, the impeachment is discussed later in this section.

Simplicity is essential for the jury to understand the contrast, but is often difficult to achieve. Three problems frequently arise. First, you cannot effectively impeach long statements, paragraphs, or even lengthy sentences. These have to be reduced to a critical fact or essential few words that can be effectively contrasted with a prior statement. Second, you cannot effectively impeach several facts at one time. To make the inconsistencies clear and understandable, each fact you intend to impeach should be brought up separately and contradicted separately. This keeps things clear, and clarity is essential. Using phrases like "you say today" and "today you claim" as you recommit the witness to a fact that he said on direct examination signals to the jury not to believe it, and that you will soon show why.

Example:

> Q. Mr. Jones, did I hear you right — you say today you were about 50 feet away when you saw the accident?
> A. That's right.

Build up the impeaching statement, in this case an oral statement to a police officer shortly after the accident, then:

> Q. You told Officer Adams that you were *over 100 feet* away, didn't you?
> A. Yes.
> Q. Mr. Jones, you say today that you'd been at that corner for 30 minutes?
> A. Yes.
> Q. But you told Officer Adams that you'd gotten there *only moments earlier,* isn't that right?
> A. Yes.
> Q. Mr. Jones, you claim today that you had a clear view of the accident?
> A. Yes.
> Q. However, you told Officer Adams, a few minutes after the accident, that you were looking away and only saw the crash *after* it happened, isn't that right?
> A. Yes.

This basic technique, impeaching one simple fact at a time, is applicable to every type of prior inconsistent statement.

In many jurisdictions you are permitted to use a chalkboard or butcher's paper during your cross-examinations. If permitted, this is a persuasive technique for making prior inconsistent statements visual and obvious to the jurors. Create two columns, labeled "Today" and "At scene" or similar labels for different times the witness has made statements. As you commit the witness to the direct testimony, and bring out the impeaching inconsistency, put the key words on the chalkboard or paper.

Example:

In the preceding example, while doing the same impeachment, you would create the following chart:

Today	At scene
1. "50 feet away"	1. "over 100 feet away"
2. "at corner 30 minutes"	2. "got there only moments before"
3. "clear view of accident"	3. "saw crash after it happened"

So long as the chart fairly and accurately states what the witness says, it is proper. Note that in those jurisdictions permitting this technique, the chart is not substantive evidence. Therefore, it is not admitted as an exhibit and the jury does not see it during its deliberations.

Third, you cannot effectively impeach unless you commit the witness to facts that clearly contradict the impeaching statement. If the contradiction is not obvious, you must first convert the fact asserted on direct examination to a fact that is clearly contradicted by the impeaching statement.

Example:

The witness on direct stated that "the northbound car ran the red light." In an oral statement to an investigator he said that "the plaintiff ran the red light."

Q. Mr. Smith, you say that the northbound car ran the red light, right?
A. Yes.
Q. The northbound car was driven by Jones?
A. Yes.
Q. Jones is the defendant here?
A. Yes.
Q. So you're saying that the *defendant* ran the red light, correct?
A. That's right.
   (After building up the impeaching statement:)
Q. Mr. Smith, didn't you tell that investigator that the *plaintiff* ran the red light?
A. Yes.

Finally, the basic three steps approach — commit, credit, and confront — can be varied to make the contrast sharper. It is sometimes more effective to build up the impeaching statement *first,* then recommit and contrast. This works better with inexperienced lay witnesses. Experienced witnesses, such as police officers, will quickly realize that you are setting up an impeachment routine.

Example:

Q. Mr. Jones, you talked to a police officer at the scene a few minutes after the crash happened, didn't you?
A. Yes.
Q. Everything was fresh in your mind then?
A. Sure.

Q. You knew it was important to tell the investigating officer every-
thing you knew, as accurately as possible, right?
A. Yes.
Q. Mr. Jones, you say today that you were about *50 feet* from the ac-
cident when it happened, correct?
A. Yes.
Q. But you told that police officer, right after the accident, that you
were *over 100 feet away* when the accident happened, didn't you?
A. Yes.

These impeachment examples have all assumed that your purpose is
to attack the witness' credibility by forcefully exposing the changed testimony. If your approach is that the witness is mistaken or forgetful and may
freely change his testimony, it may be more effective not to recommit the
witness to his direct examination. Instead, simply bring out the prior statement and have the witness agree that it is true and accurate. In this way
the witness adopts his earlier testimony.

b.   *Prior testimony*

Prior testimony includes any testimony given under oath, such as depositions, former trials, evidentiary hearings such as preliminary hearings
and grand jury proceedings, and hearings before governmental bodies
such as inquests. Because prior testimony is under oath — subject to perjury penalties — made at a formal proceeding, its impeachment value is
high, and it is particularly important to build up the prior testimony.

Example:

Witness testifies in a personal injury case that he saw the cars involved
before the collision. At his deposition he testified that he saw the cars only
after hearing the crash.

Q. Mr. Jones, you saw the two cars before they actually collided, is
that what you're telling us?
A. Yes, I did.
Q. There's no question in your mind that you saw them before the
collision?
A. No, sir.
Q. Mr. Jones, you gave what's called a deposition in this case last
year, didn't you?
A. I think so.
Q. Well, you remember you were in my offices on March 15, 2000,
don't you?
A. Yes, it was about then.
Q. You knew you would be asked questions about the collision?
A. Yes.
Q. And at that deposition, Mr. Franklin, the other lawyer, the court
reporter, you, and I were all present, isn't that right?

A. Yes.

Q. Both Mr. Franklin and I asked you questions about the collision?

A. Yes.

Q. Before you answered those questions you raised your right hand and were sworn by the court reporter to tell the truth, weren't you?

A. Yes.

Q. That's the same oath you took today?

A. Yes.

Q. You did tell the truth, didn't you?

A. Of course.

Q. After you finished testifying you had a chance to read your testimony to make sure it was accurate?

A. Yes.

Q. All of those questions and the answers you gave were in a typed booklet, called "Deposition of William Jones," right?

A. Yes.

Q. After reading it to make sure it was correct, you signed it at the end, didn't you?

A. Yes.

Q. You testified at that deposition just four months after the collision, right?

A. Yes.

Q. So how the collision happened was still pretty fresh in your mind, wasn't it?

A. I guess so.

Q. Mr. Jones, I'm going to read from a page of your deposition — page 18, line 6, counsel. Please follow along to make sure I read the questions and your answers right. (Reading transcript while showing to witness):

  Q. What's the first thing that drew your attention to the collision?

  A. Well, I guess when I heard a loud crash.

  Q. What did you do then?

  A. I looked over and saw that two cars had just collided.

  Q. Was that the first time you actually saw the cars?

  A. Yes.

Q. Did I read it right?

A. That's what it says.

Q. You were also asked this question and gave this answer, didn't you? — page 33, line 12, counsel.
(Reading transcript):

  Q. Did you see the cars before the collision?

  A. No, I didn't really notice them then.

Q. Did I read it right?

A. Yes.

When impeaching from a transcript, read the questions and answers verbatim. It is improper to summarize or paraphrase the testimony. When impeaching with any kind of writing or recorded statement, make sure that it is materially and fairly impeaching. Avoid using statements that only marginally impeach. Not only is it questionably admissible, it is ineffective as a technique. Avoid asking "do you remember" questions, since they allow a witness to avoid the substance of the question. Avoid asking the witness "did you say that?" since the witness may equivocate; simply ask him "did I read it right?" or "is that what it says?" Most of all, avoid impeaching with statements taken out of context. Under FRE 106, your opponent can require you to read the entire relevant portion of the statement.

c. Written statements

Written statements include statements in either narrative or question-and-answer form, and are written by the witness or signed by him. Although written statements are usually statements given to investigators or police officers, they can include any other writings such as letters and records.

Example:

Witness testifies in a criminal case that the person who robbed him was about 24 years old and 5 feet 11 inches tall. In a signed written statement to a police detective, he stated the robber was about 18 years old and 5 feet 7 inches tall.

Q. Mr. Doe, you now say that the man who robbed you was about 24 years old and about 5 feet 11 inches tall?
A. Yes.
Q. You were face to face with him for perhaps two minutes, weren't you?
A. Yes.
Q. There was plenty of light?
A. Yes.
Q. So you had an opportunity to see his face and gauge his height, didn't you?
A. Yes.
Q. How tall are you, Mr. Doe?
A. I'm 5 feet 8 inches.
Q. So the robber was about three inches taller than you?
A. Yes.
Q. And he was about 24 years old?
A. Yes, about that.
Q. Your estimate of his age at 24 and his height at 5 feet 11 inches was based on your two-minute face-to-face confrontation, is that correct?
A. Yes.
Q. Mr. Doe, you made a written statement the same day of the robbery, didn't you?
A. Yes.
Q. That was made to Detective Smith?
A. Yes.

> *Q.* At the police station?
> *A.* Yes.
> *Q.* After he typed your statement he gave it to you?
> *A.* Yes.
> *Q.* He asked you to read it and make any corrections necessary?
> *A.* Yes.
> *Q.* You did that?
> *A.* Yes.
> *Q.* You wanted to be sure that your statement was accurate, didn't you?
> *A.* Yes.
> *Q.* After making sure it was accurate, you signed the statement?
> *A.* Yes.
> *Q.* (Have the statement marked as an exhibit, show it to opposing counsel, then to the witness.) Mr. Doe, I'm showing you a two-page document marked Defendant's Exhibit #1. That's your signature at the bottom, isn't it?
> *A.* Yes.
> *Q.* This is the signed statement you made for Detective Smith, isn't it?
> *A.* Yes.
> *Q.* I'm going to read from your written statement — page one, counsel — "The man looked about 18 years old. He was approximately 5 feet 7 inches tall"? That's what your statement says, right?
> *A.* Yes.

Make sure your reading of the written statement is verbatim, not a summarization. As noted above, FRE 613 now gives you the option of not showing the prior inconsistent statement to the witness before impeaching him with it. However, most lawyers prefer to use the traditional method demonstrated in the example, on the theory that it is a more persuasive technique. If you don't show the witness the statement, it looks unfair to the jury, and the witness may not admit making the impeaching statement unless you show it to him first.

d. Oral statements

Oral statements most commonly are made to police officers or private investigators. However, any statement made by the witness to any person can be used to impeach if it is inconsistent with the in-court testimony on an important fact.

Example:

Same fact situation as above, except that the statement to the police detective is oral. The detective summarized the oral statement in his report. Use the same approach as above to lock the witness into his direct examination testimony that the robber was 24 years old and 5 feet 11 inches tall. Then proceed in the following manner.

Q.   Mr. Doe, you talked to Detective Smith a couple of hours after the robbery, didn't you?

A.   I think so.

Q.   That was in an interview room at the police station?

A.   That's right.

Q.   Detective Smith's partner was also in the room?

A.   Yes.

Q.   Detective Smith asked you all about the robbery, didn't he?

A.   Yes.

Q.   And you told him everything you could remember?

A.   Yes.

Q.   You told him everything as accurately as you could?

A.   Yes.

Q.   You wanted to make sure that the right person was arrested, didn't you?

A.   Yes.

Q.   Detective Smith and his partner were taking notes during your conversation, weren't they?

A.   I think so.

Q.   Mr. Doe, didn't you tell Detective Smith, in the presence of his partner, that the robber was 24 years old?

A.   Yes.

Q.   Didn't you also tell him that the robber was approximately 5 feet 7 inches tall?

A.   Yes, I think that's what I said.

When impeaching with an oral statement that was noted in someone else's report, you cannot impeach the witness with the report itself, because the witness did not write the report. Hence, in the above example it would be improper to ask: "Didn't you say in Officer Smith's report that . . ." The report is Officer Smith's, not the witness', and it is unfair to cross the witness using someone else's report. This is a frequent mistake when impeaching with oral statements.

e.   Pleadings and discovery

Any court document that is signed by the witness, such as answers to interrogatories, or an affidavit in support of a motion, may be used to impeach. It can happen, however, that a party or witness forgets what was stated in a court document and testifies inconsistently. In those situations, the document can be used to impeach.

Example:

Defendant in a contract action has stated on direct examination that he cannot remember receiving an acceptance letter from the plaintiff. In his answer to interrogatories he admitted receiving the letter.

Q.   Mr. Eastwood, you say that you can't remember if you received a letter from the plaintiff accepting your offer, is that your testimony?

A. That's right.

Q. This letter, Plaintiff's Exhibit #1, dated July 5, 2000 — you received that letter, didn't you?

A. I'm not sure.

Q. Mr. Eastwood, after you were sued you and your lawyer received a copy of what are called interrogatories, didn't you?

A. Yes.

Q. Those are written questions that you were required to answer?

A. Yes.

Q. Under oath?

A. Yes.

Q. In writing?

A. Yes.

Q. You answered those questions in writing, under oath, didn't you?

A. Yes.

Q. And sent me a copy of your answers?

A. I suppose my lawyer did.

Q. Mr. Eastwood, I'm handing you the interrogatories, marked Plaintiff's Exhibit #2, and your written answers, marked Plaintiff's Exhibit #3. Those are the interrogatories and your written answers, right?

A. Yes.

Q. And your answers are signed by you?

A. Yes.

Q. Under oath?

A. Yes.

Q. Interrogatory #5 says: (Reading) "On or about July 8, 2000, did you receive a letter, attached as Exhibit #1, from the plaintiff accepting her offer?" Did I read it right?

A. Yes.

Q. Answer #5 of your signed and sworn answers says: (Reading) Defendant admits he received the letter attached as Exhibit #1 to Plaintiff's Interrogatories. Did I read your answer right?

A. That's what it says.

f. Omissions

Impeachment by omission is a common trial technique whenever a witness testifies who previously prepared a written report of his activities. While impeaching by omission can be powerful, don't use it on inappropriate witnesses. Save it for witnesses who have been trained how to make and fill out reports and records and have control over what goes into them. Police officers and other investigators commonly fall into this category. Whenever such a witness testifies to any important fact that he failed to include in his report, he can be impeached by the omission of this fact from his report. The technique is the same as for impeachment with a prior written statement, only that the prior statement is nonexistent. The purpose is obvious: If what he is saying now was so significant, why didn't he put it in his report?

The buildup is critical. You must establish that the witness knows how to prepare good reports, because he knows when information is important enough that it would always be included. Once this has been driven home, force the witness to admit that the omitted fact is an important one that should always be included in a report. With this established, the conclusion is obvious: The claimed fact never actually occurred.

Example:

A police officer has testified that immediately after arresting the defendant, the defendant said, "I don't know what got into me. It just happened." That statement is not in his written report.

Q. Officer Doe, right after you arrested Bobby you claim he said, "I don't know what got into me. It just happened." Is that what you're telling us?
A. Yes, sir.
Q. You're sure that's what he said?
A. Yes.
Q. Officer Doe, you prepared a written report of this incident, didn't you?
A. Yes.
Q. You received training on how to prepare such written reports at the police academy, didn't you?
A. Yes.
Q. You were taught to prepare complete and accurate reports?
A. Yes.
Q. You were also taught to include everything about the incident that was important?
A. Yes.
Q. That's because you, your commanding officer, and the county attorney all rely on that report to evaluate the case, don't they?
A. Yes.
Q. One of the most important things to write down is what any person arrested says about the incident, right?
A. Yes.
Q. In fact, you're taught to write down the actual words someone you arrest uses, aren't you?
A. Yes.
Q. (Have the officer's report marked as an exhibit, show it to opposing counsel, then to the witness.) I show you what has been marked Defendant's Exhibit #1. That's your written report?
A. Yes.
Q. Your narrative of the incident covers the entire back side of the form, and is in single-spaced type?
A. Yes.
Q. After typing it you read it over?
A. Yes.
Q. You wanted to make sure it was complete and accurate, didn't you?

A. Yes.

Q. And that it included everything that was important, right?

A. Yes.

Q. After making sure it was complete and accurate, you signed that report, correct?

A. Yes.

Q. The purpose of the report is to have an accurate record of what you saw, heard, and did, correct?

A. Yes.

Q. You also use such a report to refresh your memory before testifying about the incident, isn't that also correct?

A. Yes.

Q. That's important, because everyone's memory fades with time, doesn't it?

A. Yes.

Q. In fact, you read this report today before testifying here, didn't you?

A. Yes.

Q. Officer Doe, nowhere in this report that you prepared did you state Bobby said, "I don't know what got into me. It just happened." Isn't that so?

A. That's not in the report.

Q. In fact, your report says absolutely nothing about any statement, does it?

A. No.

While this is an effective approach, there are more persuasive techniques to expose an important omission. One way is to have the witness look over his report and attempt to find the absent information. Another is to give the witness a pen and ask him to circle the absent information. The witness' obvious inability to do this effectively exposes the omission.

Example:

Q. Officer Doe, show me where in your report you state Bobby said, "It's all my fault. I just lost my head."

A. (Looks at report) It's not there.

Q. Show me where your report contains anything at all about anything Bobby said.

A. There's nothing in my report.

Example:

Q. Officer Doe, please take this red felt pen and circle on your report where it states Bobby said, "It's all my fault. I just lost my head." (Give pen to witness)

Q. Officer, you haven't circled anything with the pen. Is there a problem?

A. It's not in my report.

6. Contradictory facts

A cross-examiner may wish to show that certain facts are different from what the witness claims. This is usually called impeachment by contradiction. How the fact is asserted on cross-examination determines whether you are under an obligation to prove up the asserted fact if the witness denies it.

Example:

> Q. Did you drink any alcoholic beverages that day before the accident?
> A. No.
> Q. Didn't you have three double martinis at O'Malley's Pub one hour before the accident?
> A. No.

The first question, because of its form, does not directly assert a fact, and the denial ends the matter. In the second question, however, its form directly suggests that the drinking in fact occurred, and if the witness denies it, you may be required to prove it up. As always, you cannot ask such an impeaching question unless you have a good faith basis to believe that the facts you are suggesting as true are in fact true.

If the witness denies the contradictory facts suggested by the cross-examination, whether you are required to prove it up with extrinsic evidence depends on whether the contradictory facts are collateral or noncollateral. This is the same distinction used for prior inconsistent statements. If it is noncollateral, you must prove it up. If it is collateral, you cannot prove it up.

Example:

> The witness in an automobile negligence action testifies he was wearing a green tie and was ten feet from the accident when it happened. On cross the witness is asked: "weren't you wearing a red tie?" and "weren't you really 100 feet from the accident?" and he denies both facts.

In this example the cross-examiner has directly suggested that both contradictory facts are true. However, only the denial of the 100 feet distance is important, and the cross-examiner must prove it up. The denial that his tie was red is collateral and cannot be proved up.

7. Bad character for truthfulness

Whenever any witness testifies at trial, his credibility is in issue. Hence, the witness' character for truthfulness is relevant to his credibility and under certain circumstances may be introduced at trial.

The procedural requirements must be kept clear. Under FRE 608(a) and most state rules, a witness must have his character for truthfulness attacked before it can be supported. This is because witnesses are presumed to be truthful and must be discredited before they can be accredited.

Hence, the opponent must first call a witness to testify that the earlier witness' character for truthfulness is bad. This is proper, under FRE 608(a), through either reputation or personal opinion. Once attacked, the proponent of the earlier witness can present supporting reputation or personal opinion evidence. Remember that the reputation or opinion witness must be properly qualified by showing the basis for the reputation or opinion, before he can testify what it is.

Example:

Plaintiff calls Smith as a witness. After plaintiff rests, defendant calls Johnson to testify that Smith has a bad reputation for truthfulness. After defendant rests, plaintiff in rebuttal calls Edwards to testify that Smith has a good reputation for truthfulness.

Keep in mind that calling a reputation witness has a built-in risk. The reputation witness can be asked on cross-examination if he knows, or has heard, anything that is inconsistent with the claimed reputation. This may open the door to specific acts of misconduct that might not otherwise come out at trial.

Example:

The defendant in a criminal case testifies. The prosecution later calls Jones, who says that the defendant has a bad reputation for truthfulness. The defense counters this evidence by calling Johnson, who says the defendant has a good reputation for truthfulness. On cross-examination of Johnson the prosecutor may ask, "Did you hear that the defendant was arrested for credit card fraud last year?" This is a proper test of Johnson's knowledge, even though it raises the defendant's arrest, which would otherwise be inadmissible in the trial. Of course, the cross-examiner must have a good faith basis to believe that the defendant was in fact arrested for credit card fraud last year, otherwise he cannot ask the question.

8.   Completing the impeachment

Whether you will be required to "prove up" an impeaching fact with extrinsic evidence depends on two things. First, did the witness unequivocally admit the impeachment? If so, nothing more needs to be done. If the witness either denied or hedged with responses, such as "I don't remember," "I may have," or "I'm not sure," you may be required to prove up. Second, was the impeachment noncollateral? For trial efficiency reasons, proving up is permitted and required only for noncollateral matters, those matters that are important enough, in the overall context of the trial, to use court time to prove up. Some impeachment methods are always considered noncollateral: bias, interest, motive, and prior convictions. Another method is always considered collateral: prior bad acts. Still others can be either collateral or noncollateral: prior inconsistent statements and contradictory facts. (This dichotomy does not apply to bad character for truthfulness or to treatises.)

In short, you must have both noncollateral impeachment and something short of an unequivocal admission by the witness before you are permitted and required to prove up the impeachment with extrinsic evidence. How you do this persuasively depends on the particular type of impeachment involved.

You prove up impeachment the next time it is your turn to call witnesses. For example, if you have impeached a plaintiff's witness during the plaintiff's case in chief, you can prove up the impeachment only after the plaintiff has rested and it is the defense's turn to call witnesses. You should then call a witness who can testify to the impeaching fact sometime during the defendant's case-in-chief.

Hearsay is never a proper evidentiary objection to prove up testimony when you are proving that a witness made a prior consistent statement, because the testimony is being offered only to prove that the witness made the statement, not that it is true. (However, remember that FRE 801(d)(1)(A) makes a prior inconsistent statement made under oath non-hearsay, meaning that it is admissible for its truth.)

a.   Bias, interest, and motive

Where a witness on cross-examination has not admitted a fact showing bias, interest, or motive, you must prove up that fact, since bias, interest, and motive are always noncollateral. You must call a witness or present an exhibit that demonstrates that the fact showing bias, interest, or motive actually is true. For instance, if a witness has denied being financially indebted to a party, call a witness who has personal knowledge of the indebtedness, or present documentary proof of it.

b.   Prior convictions

To prove up a prior conviction, simply obtain a certified copy of the witness' record of conviction. The certified copy is self-authenticating and is admissible without further foundation. Simply offer the certified copy as an exhibit at your next opportunity to present evidence, and ask the court for permission to read or show the record to the jury.

Where the name of the witness is the same as the name on the record, this usually creates a presumption that the witness is the same person as named on the record. Where the names are different (and changing names is not uncommon) or the witness denies he is the person named on the record, you must be prepared to prove the witness is the same person as named in the record. Usually the underlying prison record, which includes fingerprints, photographs, and signatures, will be adequate to demonstrate that the convict is the same person as the witness in court.

c.   Prior inconsistent statements

These are the most common impeachment sources that may require proving up, particularly oral inconsistent statements, which are the type most frequently denied during cross-examination.

When proving up, call the prove-up witness, establish his familiarity with the inconsistent statement, lead the witness to the actual inconsistency, and establish that it was in fact made. A common error is to have the prove up witness testify to the entire statement, not just the inconsistent part of it.

i. Prior testimony.   To prove up statements made under oath during a deposition or other judicial proceeding, you must call as a witness the court reporter who made the verbatim stenographic notes of the testimony. Establish that the court reporter is a certified shorthand reporter, that he was present at the proceeding, had sworn the witness to tell the truth, and prepared verbatim stenographic notes of all questions and answers. Have the reporter identify as an exhibit his stenographic notes (not his transcript — that is not the original record of the testimony). Establish that the exhibit includes the testimony of the witness involved. Finally, have the witness read from the notes the exact questions and answers that prove up the impeachment. (Have the reporter go through his notes in advance and mark the part that contains the impeaching questions and answers).

In practice this is frequently handled by a stipulation between the parties that states that if the court reporter were called as a witness, he would testify that the transcript is accurate and verbatim. You would then read the appropriate transcript section to the jury.

ii. Written or signed statements.   To prove up statements that are written or signed, simply call any witnesses who can identify the writing or signature or who saw the person write or sign the statement. Have the witness establish his presence at the writing or signing of the statement (if he was in fact present), show the statement to the witness (have it marked as an exhibit), and have the witness either identify the handwriting or signature as that of the person or describe having seen the person write or sign the statement. Finally, have the witness read from the written statement the part that proves up the impeachment.

Make sure your witness reads fairly, so that the impeaching words are not taken out of context. When impeaching with a writing, FRE 106 permits the adverse party to require that you read or introduce any other parts of the writing or statement which in fairness should be included. The purpose of the rule is to prevent impeachment by using statements taken out of context. Requiring that all relevant parts of the statement be introduced prevents this unfairness.

iii. Oral statements.   To prove up oral statements, simply call any witness who was present when the person made the prior inconsistent statement. Establish the usual foundation questions for oral conversations, then bring out the specific inconsistent statements. Since this type of statement is the one most likely to be denied on cross-examination, take the time to develop the background of the prove-up witness and the circumstances under which the statement was made, because this will build up the credibility of the impeachment.

Example:

Jones on cross-examination has denied telling a police officer at the scene of an automobile accident that he only saw the cars involved after hearing them collide. To prove that Jones made that statement, you must later call the police officer as a prove-up witness. Establish the police officer's background, how he came to the accident scene, and what he did after he arrived. Then proceed as in the following manner.

> *Q.* Officer Martin, while you were at the scene of the accident, did you talk to any witnesses?
> *A.* Yes.
> *Q.* Was one of them a Roger Jones?
> *A.* Yes.
> *Q.* Did you tell Mr. Jones why you needed to talk to him?
> *A.* Yes, I told him I needed to find out exactly what everyone saw so I could prepare a report about the accident.
> *Q.* Did you ask Mr. Jones what he had seen and heard?
> *A.* Yes.
> *Q.* What was the first thing he said he noticed?
> *A.* He said he was walking down the street, heard a crash, looked up, and saw that two cars had collided in the intersection.
> *Q.* Did Mr. Jones ever tell you he had seen those two cars *before* the crash?
> *A.* No. He specifically told me he first saw them after hearing the crash.

A common mistake is to attempt to introduce as an exhibit the police officer's report that contains the witness' statement. This is improper, since the witness did not prepare or sign the report.

iv. Discovery and affidavits.   It is highly uncommon for a witness to deny signing discovery or an affidavit that contains an inconsistent statement. Showing the document to the witness and drawing his attention to his signature on it will invariably draw out the admission. If this does not happen you must prove that the signature on the document was the witness', then ask the court for permission to read the appropriate parts to the jury.

Since an attorney is an agent of the party, pleadings signed and filed by the attorney will be binding on the party as admissions. However, since the party did not sign the pleading, it probably cannot be used to impeach unless you can establish that the party read the pleading and approved it before it was filed.

v. Omissions.   It is also unlikely that a witness, after being shown his previous statement, will deny that what he testified to in court is not in the statement. If anything, the witness will claim that what he said is implicitly stated in the statement.

To prove that a prior written statement does not contain facts or statements that the person testified about at trial, you must put in evidence the entire statement to show that the facts and statements are omitted from the written statement. Use the same method as used to prove up a prior inconsistent written statement. Since the witness will in all likelihood admit having made the prior written statement, the statement need only be shown to the jury to demonstrate the omission.

d.   Contradictory facts

Contradictory facts, like prior inconsistent statements, can be collateral or noncollateral. If it is noncollateral, and the witness did not admit it, you must prove up the fact with extrinsic evidence.

Example:

On direct examination a plaintiff witness says she was 20 feet from an intersection when she saw the accident. On cross-examination she denies arriving at the intersection after the collision. Since this denied fact is noncollateral, the defendant during the defense case in chief must call a witness who will testify that the plaintiff's witness came to the scene after the collision had already happened.

e.   Failure to prove up

What happens if the cross-examiner fails to prove up an impeaching fact that he is obligated to prove up? There are two basic approaches to the problem.

First, make a motion to strike the cross-examiner's question and the answer, and ask the judge to instruct the jury to disregard them. Obviously the jury cannot "unremember" the unproved fact, particularly if the judge just reminded them of it. However, it does alert the jury to the fact that the cross-examiner failed to prove the fact he suggested was true during his cross-examination and, since the witness denied it, it must be considered untrue. Ask the judge to tell this to the jury expressly, rather than casually admonishing the jury to "disregard it." Making the motion is of course necessary to preserve error on appeal. If the violation is serious enough, move for a mistrial.

Second, consider *not* making the motion for tactical reasons. If the cross-examiner's failure to prove up is not important, then failing to preserve error for appeal is also unimportant; consider not making the motion to strike so you can comment on it during closing arguments. If the cross-examiner had no affirmative evidence to present, and only attacked your witnesses, commenting on the opponent's tactics and showing that his insinuations were never proved can be an effective approach during closing arguments.

9.   Impeaching out-of-court declarants

Statements of an out-of-court declarant are frequently admissible since they often qualify for admission as hearsay exceptions. The most common example is a deposition transcript qualified as former testimony. The opponent may wish to attack the credibility of the out-of-court declarant using one of the permitted impeachment methods.

This situation is governed by FRE 806. Since the declarant is not in court, it is impossible to ask him the impeaching questions normally required on cross-examination. However, the opponent can introduce extrinsic evidence to impeach the out-of-court declarant whenever the impeachment is noncollateral.

Example:

In an automobile negligence action, plaintiff introduces the deposition of Jones, who has recently died. Since Jones is unavailable, his deposition transcript qualifies as former testimony under FRE 804(b)(1). In the defense case the defendant can introduce the fact that Jones was convicted of perjury five years ago, since this prior conviction is admissible to attack Jones' credibility under FRE 609. This would be done by introducing a certified copy of Jones' record of conviction.

FRE 806 is an important rule, because the jury frequently receives statements and testimony from out-of-court declarants. It is often used to attack the credibility of expert witnesses, who do not appear in person at the trial, but testify through the introduction of their deposition transcript as former testimony.

§7.8. *Special problems*

Cross-examiners commonly must deal with certain recurring tactics that witnesses employ to frustrate or defeat the purposes of the cross-examination. These include the following.

1. Evasive witnesses

Often a witness who had no difficulty testifying on direct examination will become evasive the moment you begin your cross-examination. The evasion can take several forms. The witness' tone and demeanor change. He constantly repeats your question or asks that you repeat the question. He is slow in answering. He constantly answers, "I don't know," "I don't remember," "I can't recall," "I'm not sure," "I might," "I could," or avoids answering directly.

The key to cross-examining such a witness is to keep in mind that all this evasive activity is making a horrible impression on the jury, an impression that can spill over on the other parts of your opponent's case. Accordingly, you should not attempt to squeeze better answers out of him. Instead, continue in the same vein. Extract as many "I can't remember" responses as possible. Ask the witness if he has difficulty hearing or understanding your questions. Ask the witness "That didn't answer my question, did it? Try to get evasive responses to some of the same questions that the witness had no difficulty answering during the direct examination. The jury will quickly recognize what the witness is doing and treat his testimony appropriately.

2. Argumentative witnesses

The explaining or arguing witness presents the opposite cross-examination problems from those of the evasive witness. This witness wants to expound on everything. He wants to answer your question with one of his own. He wants to argue over everything. The key to such a witness is control. Where the witness argues with you or answers your question with a question, make your questions particularly short and clear, and the only possible answer obvious. Repeat the question and insist on a responsive answer. If the witness continues in the same vein, the jury will again quickly comprehend what is going on.

Avoid doing what many lawyers commonly do. When the witness starts a nonresponsive answer, or attempts to argue or elaborate, resist the temptation to cut the witness off.

Example:

Q. You were standing on the corner at that time, right?
A. I was right on the corner when the big Buick came charging . . .
Q. Thank you, Mr. Williams, you've answered the question. My next question is . . .

Why should this be avoided? Research shows that jurors intensely dislike lawyers who constantly cut witnesses off, because it gives the appearance that the lawyer is trying to keep something from the jury, which is fatal to the lawyer's credibility. The better technique is not to cut the witness off, then demonstrate to the jury that the witness is not playing by the rules.

Example:

Q. You were standing on the corner at that time, right?
A. I was right on the corner when the big Buick came charging through the red light and crashed into the Toyota.
Q. Mr. Williams, my question was, where were you standing?
A. Right on the corner.

Example:

Q. You were standing on the corner at that time, right?
A. I was right on the corner. That's when the big Buick came charging through the intersection.
Q. Mr. Williams, we'll get to the Buick in a minute. Right now my question is, you were standing on the corner?
A. Yes.

If the witness continues to give answers that go beyond what you are asking for, the jury will understand what the witness is doing and assess his credibility appropriately.

Also avoid asking the judge to strike the unresponsive answer and direct the witness to answer only the question asked (unless this is essential to preserve error on appeal). Research has shown that jurors do not heed the admonition. If anything, it strengthens the jurors' memory of the improper answer, and demonstrates to the jury that you are incapable of controlling the witness. Instead, patiently repeat the question until you get a responsive answer. If the witness continues to make speeches, the judge will usually eventually admonish the witness without your asking, which creates an entirely different impression.

Another approach is to make a "contract" with the witness.

Example:

> Q. Mr. Franklin, before I begin my cross-examination, I'd like to agree with you on how to go about it. I'm going to ask you questions as clearly as I can. If it's not clear, let me know, all right?
> A. Okay.
> Q. If my questions are clear, you'll answer them simply and clearly, all right?
> A. Yes.
> Q. Can we agree on this?
> A. Yes.
> Q. That's fair, isn't it?
> A. Yes.

It's hard for a witness not to agree to such an arrangement. Then, if the witness is evasive or argues with you, the jury will view the witness as violating a fair arrangement he himself agreed on.

3.   Memorized or identical stories

While not a common phenomenon, sometimes a witness on direct examination will give clues that his testimony, at least in critical parts, is memorized, or is so similar in certain respects to another witness' testimony that it suggests they got together and planned identical stories. The clues may be words and phrases that are not natural for the witness. They may be that the witness has testified to details that normally would not be remembered, or has omitted facts that would ordinarily be recalled. A clue may be in the deliberateness of the testimony or some other unusual delivery. Whatever the clue, the approach is the same. These witnesses can be asked to violate one of the cardinal rules of cross-examination: Never repeat the direct examination. Witnesses who have memorized parts of their testimony, particularly children who have been coached, will usually repeat the testimony essentially verbatim, using the same words, phrases, and details as before. These witnesses will often claim to remember details you would not expect them to, or fail to remember facts that they normally would remember. They will sometimes use a vocabulary that is not natural for them. The jury will usually pick up on the striking similarity between the two narrations, or the peculiar recall of the witnesses, or an odd word choice. Once this has been demonstrated, you should inquire whom the witness talked to before testifying, to uncover the origins of the memorization.

4.   "Apparent" cross-examinations

While cross-examinations are not required, under most circumstances the jury will expect some type of cross. This is particularly so when the witness is a significant one for your opponent. In such a case some sort of cross-examination is called for, and you should always consider using any of the standard techniques discussed in this chapter.

Sometimes, however, you will have neither a realistic expectation of eliciting favorable admissions nor any real ammunition for conducting an effective, discrediting cross-examination. In short, you have nothing that has a chance of succeeding, yet the jury will expect some kind of cross-examination. In these situations your best approach may be to conduct an "apparent" cross-examination. Consider examining the witness on the following collateral points:

a.   Who asked him to be a witness?
b.   Was he subpoenaed?
c.   Who has he talked to about the case?
d.   Discussed testimony with lawyer?
e.   Attend any meetings with other witnesses present?
f.   Read other materials to prepare his testimony?
g.   Make any notes on the incident?
h.   Read depositions and prior statements?
i.   Know any of the parties or witnesses?
j.   Compensation as a witness?

None of these topics directly attempts to attack the testimony. However, pursuing the appropriate ones can plant a seed of doubt in the jury's mind so that it will at least think about the testimony rather than blindly accept it.

Another technique that can sometimes be effectively used when you have no ammunition for cross-examination, is to use the cross-examination to get *your* version of the facts before the jury, even though the witness will deny it. At least it tells the jury that there is a second side to the lawsuit they will hear. This technique can work well for the defendant, since he presents his evidence second, and suggests to the jury that it should keep an open mind and hear all the evidence before deciding who is right. Keep in mind, however, that using this technique will probably obligate you to actually produce evidence of your version during your case in chief.

5.   Opposing counsel

Although regrettable, it is nonetheless a fact of life that some lawyers will step beyond the bounds of proper evidentiary objections and make objections solely to help or coach a witness who is being cross-examined.

While it is always proper to make any objection whenever a good faith basis for the objection exists, it is improper to make an objection solely to warn or coach the witness so that he gives a safer or better answer. There are three basic problems.

First, lawyers will constantly interject "if he knows" objections after a proper question has been posed. Invariably the witness will then answer the question: "I don't know." This kind of interjection is improper and is an obvious attempt to coach the witness in answering the question. You should object forcefully if your opponent constantly resorts to such tactics and, if necessary, ask the court to direct your opponent to desist. Regardless of what the court does, the jury will quickly realize what the lawyer is doing.

Another tactic is the "clarification" request. When the witness has given an answer on cross that the lawyer does not like, he will interrupt your examination and say, "Your Honor, could the witness tell what he means by the term ''transfer'? I'm not sure that was clear to the jury," or some similar interjection. The effect, of course, is to interrupt the flow of your cross-examination and, at the same time, cue the witness that the last answer was not very good. When this happens, you should again object to the lawyer's conduct and point out that these "clarifications" can properly be made during the redirect examination.

Probably the most common problem the cross-examiner faces is the lawyer who constantly makes speeches in conjunction with the objections. (E.g., "Objection, your Honor. I don't see how the witness can possibly answer the question in light of the other evidence which has clearly shown that . . .") Objections, of course, should state only the legal basis for the objection. Any argument should be out of the jury's hearing. The lawyer who constantly objects is trying to disrupt your examination and make periodic summations to the jury. Pointing this out to the judge promptly and forcefully will usually cure the problem.

§7.9.   *Special witnesses*

This chapter has emphasized developing a methodology that will systematically allow you to identify and achieve realistically attainable objectives during cross-examinations. If the methodology is learned and followed, you should be able to cross-examine any witness in a competent way — not just occurrence witnesses.

Certain special types of witnesses, however, do appear with some frequency at trials, and it is useful to analyze the additional methods of cross-examinations that can be effective with them.

1.   The records witness

The records witness has two principal functions at trial: to qualify records and other documentary evidence for admission in evidence and, where necessary, interpret and explain the records for the jury. Since the records witness is neither an occurrence nor an expert witness and will only rarely have made prior statements of any kind, many of the usual cross-examination techniques will be ineffective. Although records witnesses are frequently not cross-examined at all, you should always consider the alternative approaches that are possible with such a witness.

With a records witness your first cross-examination approach is to attempt to keep the records from being admitted in evidence. The usual bases for attacking the records are the grounds of relevance, foundation, or multiple hearsay. However, if you have been unsuccessful in keeping the records from being admitted in evidence, or you have decided as a matter of trial strategy not to object to their admission, you should then consider the following additional approaches.

a. Look for favorable material in the records and have the witness point it out.

b. Look for inconsistencies, errors, and incompleteness in the records and have the witness point them out.

c. Point out that the witness is merely the custodian of the records, has no firsthand knowledge of the underlying facts, and has made no attempt to verify the accuracy of those facts. An alternative approach is to get the witness to repeatedly assert the records' accuracy despite having no firsthand knowledge that the facts are accurate.

d. Stress that no one is infallible, that mistakes can be and sometimes are made, and that the witness has no way of knowing if they occurred here. Point out that the business generating the records has no independent verification system or internal audit controls that would discover and correct any mistakes.

Note that your first purpose is, as always, to use the witness to point out evidence in the records favorable to your side. If none exists, your secondary purpose must be to minimize the significance and impact of the records themselves. Remember, however, that records witnesses are often clerical personnel who, although able to provide the necessary foundation for the records admission, are not experts on complicated company procedure. Accordingly, do not attack the witness for something he is not. Save your challenges for the records themselves.

2.   The character witness

Under FRE 404, 405, and 608, a witness can testify to a pertinent character trait of another person, in reputation or personal opinion form. Such a witness can be cross-examined much like any other witness. He may be asked with whom, where, and when he actually discussed the reputation. He may be questioned about the nature and extent of his relationship with the person about whom he is testifying. He may be examined regarding any bias, prejudice, or interest in the outcome of the case.

In addition, under FRE 405(a) and 608(b) other matters can be probed. The cross-examiner may expose relevant specific instances of conduct, inconsistent with the type of reputation evidence involved. This is allowed, not as proof of prior misconduct, but as a legitimate inquiry into the knowledge and credibility of the witness. Accordingly, the cross-examiner may ask about reports of prior acts, arrests, and convictions of the person relevant to and inconsistent with the claimed reputation, if such reports arose in the time period relevant to the type of reputation evidence involved. However, the witness may not be used to establish the truth of such reports, nor may the cross-examiner by the manner of his questioning directly suggest that the reports are true. The traditional proper form for cross-examination of a reputation witness is: "Have you heard . . ." "Do you know" was improperly suggestive. This has been the approach adhered to in most jurisdictions, including the federal courts. However, since FRE 405 and 608 allow character trait evidence based on personal opinion, the "do you know" form is now proper when cross-examining such a witness.

The cross-examiner, faced with a reputation witness, should consider the following approaches:

First, as in any trial where the witness has been unconvincing or his testimony ineffectively presented, no cross-examination at all might well be the safest approach. However, consider asking a single question emphasizing that the witness was not present during the event involved may be appropriate.

Example:

> Q. You weren't in Joe's Tavern on April 1, 2000, between 8:00 P.M. and 10:00 P.M., were you?
>
> A. No.

Some courts, perhaps more technically oriented, might sustain an objection that this question is beyond the scope of the direct. Other courts might overrule an objection, reasoning that pointing out that the witness has no knowledge beyond what he has stated on direct does not elicit any new information that is beyond the scope of the direct. As a practical matter, since the cross-examiner can always recall the witness later to make the point, there appears little point in sustaining a scope objection.

When the witness has personal or business ties to the person in question, a cross examination designed to emphasize his apparent bias and interest may be effective.

A common approach on cross-examination of a reputation witness is to show that the witness has only limited knowledge on which he bases his testimony. This is usually done by demonstrating that the witness has talked to few people, on infrequent occasions, and that his conclusion is no more than his own opinion. This works best on a witness who has been inadequately prepared.

Example:

> Q. Whom have you talked to about John Doe?
>
> A. I've talked to Fred Smith, a neighbor.
>
> Q. When was that?

    A.   I can't really remember the times.

    Q.   Whom else have you talked to?

    A.   Jack Jones.

    Q.   Where was that?

    A.   I can't recall.

    Q.   Other than Fred Smith and Jack Jones, whom else can you remember specifically talking to about John Doe?

    A.   I can't remember the names right now.

    Q.   Where did you talk about John Doe with these other people whose names you can't remember?

    A.   I can't remember.

Finally, the witness may be cross-examined in most jurisdictions on specific rumors and reports about the person in question inconsistent with the reputation expressed, provided a good faith basis for asking the questions exists.

Example (witness has testified that Doe's reputation for peacefulness is good):

    Q.   Have you heard that John Doe was arrested for battery and disorderly conduct on April 1, 2000?

    A.   No.

    Q.   Have you heard that John Doe was involved in a fight in the Blarney Tavern on January 30, 2000?

    A.   No, I didn't hear about that.

§7.10. *Summary checklist*

The preceding sections have discussed the various approaches and techniques of cross-examinations and the sequence under which they should be employed. Before you conduct any cross-examinations, always ask yourself the following questions, which are organized in the way you should approach each cross-examination of any witness that has testified for the other side:

1. *Must I cross-examine this witness?*
    a. Has the witness hurt my case?
    b. Is the witness important?
    c. What are my reasonable expectations?
    d. What risks do I need to take?
2. *What favorable testimony can I elicit?*
    a. What parts of the direct helped me?
    b. What parts of my case can he corroborate?
    c. What must the witness admit?
    d. What should the witness admit?
3. *What discrediting cross-examination can I conduct?*
    a. Can I discredit the testimony? (perception, memory, communication)
    b. Can I discredit the witness' conduct?

4.   *What impeachment can I use?*
   a.   Can I show bias, interest, and motive?
   b.   Can I use prior convictions?
   c.   Can I use prior bad acts?
   d.   Can I use prior inconsistent statements?
   e.   Can I show contradictory facts?
   f.   Can I show bad character for truthfulness?
   g.   Can I use treatises?
   h.   How will I prove up the impeachment if necessary?

VIII

EXPERTS

§8.1. Introduction

Experts play a role in modern litigation with unparalleled frequency. Personal injury cases use physicians and economists; products liability cases use design and safety experts; construction cases use structural engineers and architects; criminal cases use fingerprint and DNA experts. The list could go on and on. In the great majority of cases, trial lawyers are using experts to explain how and why things happened the way they did, or didn't happen the way they were supposed to. Because of this, the ability to present expert testimony persuasively, and to cross-examine the opponent's experts effectively, are essential skills every trial lawyer must have.

Expert testimony must meet two tests. First, it must satisfy the judge by complying with evidence law. Second, it must satisfy the jury by complying with persuasion "law." This chapter examines the law of experts, the jury's expectations about experts, and discusses and illustrates various effective direct and cross-examination techniques.

§8.2. The law of experts

Expert testimony must pass certain evidentiary tests before it is properly admissible. These tests are best understood as a series of sequential questions. These questions also provide an analytical approach for the opponent seeking ways to object to expert testimony.

1. Is the subject matter appropriate for expert testimony?

FRE 702 provides that expert testimony is proper if it will "assist the trier of fact to understand the evidence or to determine a fact in issue." In short, does the expert testimony help the jury understand the facts and resolve the issues? This "helpful" standard depends, of course, on the legal and factual issues in the case. For example, a doctor in a personal injury case can testify that the plaintiff's injuries are permanent, since this testimony helps the jury to determine the seriousness of the injuries and appropriate compensation.

2.   Is the expert qualified?

FRE 702 provides that an expert is anyone "qualified as an expert by knowledge, skill, experience, training, or education." An expert must have greater knowledge than a lay person to make his testimony "useful" to the jury. For example, a young doctor who just graduated from medical school can be a qualified expert, even though many doctors have superior qualifications. Once the expert is shown to have some expertise, the issue then is one of credibility, which is for the jury to decide.

3.   Is the expert's testimony reliable?

For many years the standard for admissibility of expert testimony based on scientific tests and methods in federal courts and most state courts was the "Frye test," based on *Frye v. United States,* 293 F. 1013 (D.C. Cir. 1923). *Frye* held that before expert testimony based on scientific tests or principles is admissible, those tests or principles "must be sufficiently established to have gained general acceptance in the particular field in which it belongs." Under *Frye,* the relevant scientific community principally determines admissibility, not the judge.

In 1993 the Supreme Court decided *Daubert v. Merrell Dow Pharmaceuticals,* 509 U.S. 579 (1993). *Daubert,* applicable to federal courts, held that the Federal Rules of Evidence, and FRE 702 in particular, replaced the Frye test. The key inquiry now is whether the offered expert testimony is relevant and reliable. The trial judge must determine initially if the expert will "testify to scientific knowledge that will assist the trier of fact to understand or determine a fact in issue," which requires the trial judge to assess "whether the reasoning or methodology underlying the testimony is scientifically valid and whether that reasoning or methodology properly can be applied to the facts in issue." Factors bearing on this inquiry include (1) whether the theory or technique can and has been tested, (2) whether it has been subjected to peer review and publication, (3) the known or potential rate of error, and (4) whether the theory or technique has been generally accepted by the scientific community. Under *Daubert,* the judge, not the scientific community, controls admissibility. Since the judge is the gatekeeper, "Daubert hearings" are required to make this assessment whenever a party seeks to introduce expert testimony based on scientific tests and methods.

Some state courts continue to follow *Frye,* and life goes on much as before. The expert himself can testify that the scientific tests and methods on which his testimony is based have gained "general acceptance" in the relevant scientific community and, if he does so, his testimony can be presented to the jury.

In federal court, of course, things are different, because *Daubert* (and *Kumho Tire,* infra) must be followed. While *Daubert* was first seen as a victory for plaintiffs attempting to introduce expert testimony based on new scientific tests and methods, its history has proven otherwise. For plaintiffs seeking to prove causation in toxic tort and similar complex tort cases, *Daubert* has been a disaster. Based on its holding, judges in the federal district courts have rejected expert testimony numerous times, and almost all of the rejected testimony has been offered by plaintiffs.

Four years later, the Supreme Court decided *General Electric v. Joiner,* 522 U.S. 136 (1997). The Court held that the proper standard on appeal to trial court rulings excluding expert testimony was the "abuse of discretion" standard, which is the standard applied to evidentiary rulings in general. However, the Court in *Joiner* went further, and analyzed whether the trial court had in fact abused its discretion in excluding expert testimony on cancer causation based on four scientific studies in mice and humans. The Court concluded that the trial court had not abused its discretion in rejecting the plaintiff's expert testimony. The Court held that the mice study was too remote to the facts of the case, that the other three human disease studies did not have statistically significant results, and that the studies, even if taken in combination, were inadequate to support the experts' conclusions. Hence, the trial judge's rulings excluding the proposed expert testimony were upheld.

Joiner has been criticized for violating the very point the Court had taken pains to make in *Daubert:* The trial judge's inquiry is "solely on the principles and methodology, not on the conclusions they generate." In *Joiner* the Court blurred the line between methodology and conclusions, and permitted the trial judge to conclude that "there is simply too great an analytical gap between the data and the opinion offered." *Joiner* appears to be a tremendous grant of power to district court judges, since the judge can look for analytical gaps in both the scientific methods and conclusions, knowing that appellate reversal under the abuse of discretion standard is highly unlikely.

Finally, *Kumho Tire Co. v. Carmichael,* 526 U.S. 137 (1999), addressed an important question not resolved by either *Daubert* or *Joiner.* Does *Daubert* apply only to expert testimony based on "hard" science, such as chemistry and physics, or does it apply also to other expert testimony, not based on scientific tests and methods, that is grounded principally in training, observation, and experience? In short, does the *Daubert* analysis apply to all expert testimony in federal district courts?

In *Kumho Tire* the Court held that the trial judge's "gatekeeping" function applies to all expert witnesses, not just those experts providing "scientific" testimony. This is because the then-existing FRE 702, governing the admissibility of such testimony, does not distinguish between scientific knowledge and technical or other specialized knowledge. The controlling question remains the same: Is the expert's testimony relevant and reliable so that the jury will be allowed to hear it? If the expert's testimony is based on scientific tests and methods, the full *Daubert* analysis will apply. If the expert's testimony is not based on scientific tests and methods, the judge must still determine if the testimony is reliable and, in making this determination, may consider one or more of the *Daubert* factors.

This inquiry into the reliability of such an expert's testimony is necessarily a flexible one, which must be tied to the particular facts involved.

In *Kumho Tire* the issue was the admissibility of plaintiff's expert's testimony in a products liability case brought against a tire manufacturer in federal district court. The trial judge excluded the testimony of the expert, a tire failure analyst, and granted summary judgment for defendants. The expert's opinion (that the tire failure was caused by a defect, not tire abuse) was based on the expert's visual and tactile inspection of the tire, as well as his theory that the absence of certain physical symptoms of tire abuse showed that the tire failed from a defect. The trial judge concluded that there were insufficient indications of reliability of the expert's methodology in determining the cause of the failure of the particular tire involved. The Supreme Court held that the trial judge's ruling was proper, particularly under *Joiner*'s abuse-of-discretion standard. To date, few states have followed the *Kumho Tire* holding in determining the admissibility of testimony from trained and experienced experts.

In 2000, FRE 701 and 702 were amended. FRE 701 was amended to provide that expert witnesses cannot avoid the trial court's "gatekeeping" scrutiny required by FRE 702 by testifying as lay witnesses under FRE 701. FRE 702 was amended to make it clear that an expert may testify if "(1) the testimony is based upon sufficient facts or data, (2) the testimony is the product of reliable principles and methods, and (3) the witness has applied the principles and methods reliably to the facts of the case." This wording incorporates the holdings of *Daubert* and *Kumho Tire*.

4.   Were tests properly done in this case?

In most cases, of course, the scientific methodology underlying the tests is well established, and the principal trial issue is whether the tests were correctly conducted following proper procedures and using reliable equipment. For example, in a paternity case, even though the scientific basis of blood tests to establish paternity is well established, the proponent must still prove that the blood tests were properly conducted, using reliable equipment. In a drunk driving case, even though the scientific basis for the Breathalyser test is well known and accepted by courts, the proponent must still prove that the test was conducted properly, and that the Breathalyser unit was a reliable one that had been tested and calibrated to make sure that it was functioning accurately. This is usually shown through the testimony of the technician or police officer conducting the test.

5.   Are the sources the expert relied on proper?

FRE 703 provides that if the facts or data upon which the expert bases an opinion are "of a type reasonably relied upon by experts in the particular field . . . the facts or data need not be admissible in evidence." This means that the expert can base his testimony on facts and data not in evidence, so long as the facts and data are the type such experts reasonably use in their field. For example, a physician can base his opinions on lab reports and X rays, even though those sources have not been admitted in evidence.

6. When should the sources be disclosed?

FRE 705 provides that an expert can testify "without first testifying to the underlying facts or data, unless the court requires otherwise." However, the cross-examiner can require the expert to "disclose the underlying facts or data" on which the expert's testimony is based.

On direct examination, the expert can testify to his opinions without first stating the bases for the opinions. This permits the direct examination to be structured and ordered in whatever way will be most persuasive to the jury. Tactics principally control the order in which the expert testifies on direct examination. For example, a doctor may give his opinion followed by the reasons, or give the basis for the opinion before stating the opinion.

7. Are the sources themselves admissible?

FRE 703 permits the expert to testify without first having the facts and data that testimony is based on admitted in evidence. As noted above, a physician can base his opinions on lab reports and X rays, even though those sources have not been admitted as exhibits.

If the expert relied on certain facts and data, are those sources admissible in evidence because the expert relied upon them and they are of a type commonly relied upon by such experts, or must the sources have an independent evidentiary foundation before they can be admitted in evidence?

Before the 2000 amendment to FRE 703, courts were divided on the admissibility of the sources underlying the expert's opinions. If the sources had an independent basis for admission — for example, the underlying sources were business records that had been formally admitted in evidence — there was no problem. If the sources had no independent basis for admission — for example, an expert's interviews of eyewitnesses, which are hearsay — courts were divided on whether the sources were admissible. Some courts held that an expert could refer to the sources that formed the basis of the expert's opinions, but the sources themselves were inadmissible. Most courts, however, held that the sources were admissible merely because the expert had used them as the bases for the expert's opinions. This gave rise to the complaint that lawyers were using FRE 703 to expose the jury to "back door hearsay" that the jury otherwise would never hear.

The 2000 amendment to FRE 703 makes it clear that the bases for the expert's opinions are presumptively inadmissible, unless the trial judge rules otherwise. FRE 703 now provides that: "Facts or data that are otherwise inadmissible shall not be disclosed to the jury by the proponent of the opinion or inference unless the court determines that their probative value in assisting the jury to evaluate the expert's opinion substantially outweighs their prejudicial effect." This rule, of course, creates uncertainty for direct examiners, who no longer will be able automatically to admit the bases underlying the expert's opinions. This issue must be addressed before trial.

8.   Are the forms of the expert's testimony proper?

FRE 702 permits the expert to testify "in the form of an opinion or otherwise." For example, the expert can testify to an "opinion" or, as is required in some jurisdictions, an "opinion to a reasonable degree of scientific certainty." The expert can testify, if appropriate, to a "conclusion." The expert can still testify to a hypothetical question. This flexibility allows the expert to testify with an appropriate level of certainty, in a way that most effectively develops his testimony for the jury. For example, the expert can properly state that "in my opinion, the plaintiff's scars are permanent." The expert can also state that "the plaintiff's scars are permanent. They will never go away."

   On the other hand, the expert's testimony cannot be conjecture or speculation. For example, it should not be proper for an expert to testify that "it is conceivable that . . ." Such testimony is not relevant because it is not useful to the jury to hear opinions that are just guesswork or possibilities.

9.   Can the expert testify to ultimate issues?

FRE 704 provides that expert testimony "otherwise admissible is not objectionable because it embraces an ultimate issue to be decided by the trier of fact" (except for mental states in criminal cases). However, FRE 702 also requires that expert testimony "assist the trier of fact to understand the evidence or to determine a fact in issue." Putting the two rules together creates the proper rule: An expert may testify to "ultimate issues" if the testimony is "helpful" to the jury.

   For instance, a psychiatrist in a civil commitment proceeding testifies that the patient is a paranoid schizophrenic with organic brain damage. The expert should also be allowed to testify that the patient is a danger to herself and to the community (the "ultimate legal issue"). That testimony is helpful to the jury, since it is not equipped to use the expert's clinical evaluation to resolve the legal issue. By contrast, an accident reconstruction expert in a personal injury case testifies that from her analysis of the physical evidence, she concluded that the defendant's car was on the plaintiff's side of the road when it collided with the plaintiff's car. The expert should not be allowed to testify that the accident was the defendant's fault or that the defendant was negligent, since this testimony is not helpful to the jury. The jury can use the expert's factual conclusions to resolve the ultimate issues just as well as the expert.

§8.3.   *Experts from the jury's perspective*

Step into the jury box for a moment. An expert has been called as a witness, has made her way to the witness chair, and has just been sworn. What are the jurors thinking about that expert? What are their expectations? What are their concerns? How can we use the jury's expectations and concerns to create expert testimony that meets their needs?

1.   The jury's concerns about experts

To a jury, experts present an intimidating prospect. After all, an expert by definition is there to tell the jury about some sophisticated, technical subject the jury knows little or nothing about. What, then, are the jury's concerns?

First, the jury expects the testimony to be complicated and confusing. ("Oh my God! This antitrust expert is going to talk about market dominance. I probably won't be able to understand a word of it.") How do you deal with this expectation? Turn it around. If the jury expects it to be complicated, make it simple by avoiding details and focusing on the process. Use a logical, clear organization, and train the expert to use nontechnical language. Make sure the jury gets answers to three basic questions: What did you do? How did you do it? What does it mean?

Second, the jury expects the testimony to be boring. ("They're calling an accountant. I fall asleep every time I talk to my tax accountant.") How do you deal with this expectation? Turn it around. If the jury expects it to be boring, make it interesting by making the testimony fast paced and interspersing it with attractive visual aids.

Third, the jury wonders if the expert is really an expert. ("That doctor looks pretty young. How much can he really know?") How do you deal with the jury's doubt? Turn it around. If the jury wonders about the witness's expertise, show that the witness has packed an impressive amount of training and experience into those years.

Fourth, the jury wonders if the expert is biased. ("I'll bet that chemist testifies for the drug industry all the time. He's probably making a fortune.") How do you correct the jury's attitude? Turn it around. Show the jury that the expert is fair minded, reached his conclusions based on good data and objective analysis, and is being reasonably compensated for his time.

Fifth, the jury expects the expert to be condescending. ("He acts like a big know-it-all. He's talking down to us.") How do you deal with this? As before, turn it around. Show the jury that behind the expertise is a normal human being who's here to help, not to preach.

In short, effective expert testimony recognizes the jury's concerns about experts, focuses on those concerns, and turns the jury's concerns around by doing just the opposite of what it expects. A good expert witness can be understandable, interesting, authoritative, fair, and likeable. All you have to do is make him so.

2.   Expert as a teacher

An expert is simply a witness who explains things to the jury. The expert's job is to take something that appears complicated and boring to a jury and make it simple and interesting. Along the way the expert must show she has the expertise, has analyzed the issues fairly, and comes across as a like-able person. When this is done, the jury will understand and accept the expert's testimony.

How do you do this? Think back to high school. Who were your fa-vorite teachers? They were the ones who made the subject interesting, easy to understand, and fun to learn. They really understood the subject. They were likeable people who treated you with respect. The good teacher could get you to understand and like something you never imagined you would ever understand or like, make you feel glad you were in the class, and she could do it all in one class period! Transfer those images to the expert in the courtroom. Make the expert that teacher all the jurors re-member fondly.

3.   How jurors decide between competing experts

If one party calls experts at trial, so usually will the other. The jury will, in most cases, hear from opposing experts who will disagree about the im-portant issues in the case. Jurors do not remain neutral long. They will pick one expert's testimony and accept it over the testimony of an oppos-ing expert. How do they do that? What is it that makes the jury accept the testimony of one expert over another?

Persuasive experts always have several qualities. First, they have ex-pertise. ("That doctor certainly knew what he was talking about. He's been dealing with that condition for years.") Expertise is a combination of for-mal education and training in the particular discipline with practical ex-perience in applying that training and education to solving real problems. Jurors put more stock in actual experience, since most of them became competent in what they do for a living not by getting a degree, but by get-ting hands on experience until they developed expertise.

Second, experts are trustworthy. ("That professor sounded like a straight shooter. He didn't sound like he was trying to sell one point of view.") Jurors find witnesses more credible if they tell the truth based on the best information available to them, untainted by biases and agendas.

Third, they are likeable. ("That Dr. White seemed like such a nice young man.") Just as with any other witnesses, jurors find experts more persuasive if they have likeable personalities. Likeable witnesses have com-mon bonds with jurors, such as coming from the same locality, being phys-ically attractive, having dynamic personalities that make them interesting to listen to, and having strong communication skills.

In short, remember how the jury evaluates experts, put experts in the teacher mode, and focus on the attributes that make experts persuasive in the courtroom.

§8.4. *Direct examination*

Knowing the jury's concerns about experts, what a persuasive expert is, and how the jury decides between competing experts, how can we use that information to select, prepare, and present experts at trial?

1. Selection and preparation of experts

a. *Selection*

The first step is to select an appropriate expert. Often, of course, you have no choice. For example, the doctor who treated the patient in the emergency room is probably a necessary witness in a personal injury case. However, many times you will need to "find" an expert for trial. What should you look for?

The expert must be a qualified expert, but that alone is not enough. The expert must, above all, be a good communicator who can teach the jury about the issues from your point of view. Where do you find such an expert? Probably the best source for effective courtroom experts is other trial lawyers you know who have tried cases similar to yours and have used the same kinds of experts you need. The advantage of asking other trial lawyers is that they know the experts who are persuasive communicators in court. Talk to the other lawyers that have actually used the expert in a trial, since expertise in litigation and jury trials is particularly important here. Was the expert responsive to the lawyer's needs? Were the expert's charges reasonable? How did the expert handle being cross-examined during the deposition? Most important, what kind of impression did the expert make at trial on the jury?

Other sources should include the faculty at local universities, since juries usually respond well to local experts. Consider also specialized organizations such as Technical Advisory Service for Attorneys (TASA), Association of Trial Lawyers of America (ATLA), and Defense Research Institute (DRI), which have lists of experts by area. Probably at the bottom of the list should be experts who advertise in legal journals; experts who actively solicit consulting work are often vulnerable to attack at trial. Be particularly wary of the "jack of all trades" who professes expertise in many diverse areas.

b. *Preparation*

Once you have selected an expert, the expert has reviewed the case, has given you her report, and has been deposed, preparation of the expert has just begun. Preparing the expert for trial involves working with the expert, deciding what the expert will cover on direct examination and what exhibits she will work with, practicing the direct examination in a realistic setting, and preparing for cross-examination. Insist that the expert give you adequate time to accomplish these effectively.

First, you need to decide what the expert will testify about and, just as important, what he will not talk about. Remember that the expert often wants to tell the jury everything he knows about the subject. This is usually fatal to a case. The jury should be told only what it needs to know to understand the subject and accept this expert's opinions. What the jury needs to know is a small fraction of what the expert actually knows. The expert needs to focus on the process, not the details. Hence, your first task is to pare down, with the expert's help and understanding, the information the expert will testify about on direct examination.

Part of this process will involve agreeing on a "trial vocabulary." Juries dislike witnesses who use stilted, technical language, and prefer those who can communicate in plain English. You and the expert need to agree how to translate technical terms into understandable language, without insulting the jury's intelligence. The better approach is to avoid technical terms entirely. If the expert does use them, make sure the expert immediately explains what the term means in clear, simple English.

Second, you need to decide what exhibits the expert will work with during his testimony. Remember that visual aids such as large diagrams, three-dimensional models, and more sophisticated exhibits such as computer animations have an immense impact on the jury, both as persuasive devices and as aids to memory. With the expert's help, you need to decide what exhibits will most effectively illustrate the points the expert will make during his testimony.

Third, you need to practice the direct examination with the expert. Review the considerations that apply to any witness. (See §5.2.) Emphasize not just the content of the testimony but also the communication concerns, the paralinguistic (speech patterns) and kinesic (gestures and body movement) overtones that control how the jury perceives the expert. Practice getting the expert out of the witness chair and standing before the jury (if permitted in your jurisdiction), assuming the teacher mode, and working with visual aids. Practice in a realistic setting using the actual questions and answers you plan on using in court. Use videotape to show the expert where his testimony is effective and where it can be improved.

Fourth, prepare the expert for cross-examination. Review the considerations that apply to any witness. (See §§7.2 and 7.3.) Independently verify the expert's academic and other credentials. Make sure the expert has reviewed his own publications and speeches. Make sure he knows the basic treatises on the subject and what they say. Make sure he has reviewed his deposition transcript in this case, as well as his deposition transcripts in other similar cases. These will be potential impeachment sources on cross. Review the opposing expert's report, since it will probably suggest the points the cross-examiner will raise. Have someone practice both a gentle and hard cross-examination with the expert.

Getting experts to spend the amount of time necessary to become well prepared to testify is difficult. Some experts are "too busy" and are rarely available for pretrial preparation. Some believe that the preparation for their deposition is adequate to prepare them for trial. Some experts believe they already know all there is to know about testifying. Whatever the reason, be careful about experts who will not give you the time you need to prepare yourself, and them, for trial. Like any witness, practice is important. If an expert will not commit himself to spend adequate time to prepare for trial at the beginning of the engagement, you may need to find another expert.

2.   Order of direct examination

The Federal Rules of Evidence allow flexibility in structuring the direct examination. Since an expert under FRE 705 can give opinions without first stating the bases for the opinions, and the qualification requirements are so easy to meet, different orders are possible. A common organization for experts is:

    a.   introduction
    b.   education, training, and experience
    c.   opinions
    d.   reasons for the opinions

Different approaches are possible. For example, the expert could give his opinions shortly after being introduced and qualified. Another possibility is for the expert to state the bases for the opinions and save the actual opinions for the end. Another is to use specific qualifications details to support the opinions. The rules are flexible enough that the primary concern is not satisfying the evidence rules, but presenting the expert's testimony in whatever order will best make that testimony persuasive and memorable to the jury.

3.   Introducing the expert

The expert has just been sworn in and is now sitting in the witness chair. All eyes are on her. What do you do next? How do you get started?

    Remember that a jury always asks three basic questions whenever an expert witness appears: who is she, what did she do, and can I trust her? These concerns need to addressed, and resolved, in the first minute.

a.   *Who is the expert?*

First, who is the witness? The conventional way follows.

Example:

    Q.   Dr. Jones, tell us your full name.
    A.   Marian Jones.
    Q.   What do you do?
    A.   I'm a medical doctor.
    Q.   Do you specialize in a particular field?
    A.   Yes, I specialize in orthopedics.
    Q.   What's orthopedics?

And so on. This conventional approach has shortcomings, however. It doesn't focus on the witness and doesn't give the witness much chance to express herself as a person. Consider something with a little more energy that lets the expert's personal side come out.

Example:

> Q. Dr. Jones, please introduce yourself to the jury.
> A. I'm Marian Jones. I'm a doctor here in town, and I specialize in orthopedics. My office is at Main and Elm, right across from Mercy Hospital.

Personalize the expert. Have her disclose something about herself that shows that she is a human being the jury can relate to, not just someone who can narrate a series of credentials.

Example:

> Q. Why did you decide to specialize in orthopedics?
> Q. What made you decide to become a veterinarian?
> Q. What's so interesting about studying the pancreas?

b.   What did the expert do?

Second, what did the expert do? The conventional way follows.

Example:

> Q. Dr. Jones, do you know the plaintiff, Mary Smith?
> A. Yes, I do.
> Q. How did you come to meet her?
> A. She became a patient of mine in June of 1999.
> Q. Under what circumstances?
> A. I was the attending orthopedic surgeon at Mercy Hospital when Ms. Smith was brought in.

And so on. Again, however, this conventional approach has shortcomings. As before, consider something with a little more energy.

Example:

> Q. Dr. Jones, you're the orthopedic specialist who treated Mary Smith at Mercy Hospital following the crash on June 1, 1999?
> A. Yes.
> Q. You did the surgery on her leg?
> A. Yes.
> Q. And you did the follow up medical treatment?
> A. Yes.

> Q. Dr. Jones, are you prepared to tell us today about Mary Jones' leg and what the future holds for her?
> A. Yes, I am.

This approach is better. It tells the jury immediately what role this doctor has in the case, and the jury knows what to expect. The questions may be leading, but leading questions are proper for introductory and background information and matters not in dispute. You can take this approach with any witness.

Example:

> Q. Professor Wilson, please introduce yourself.
> A. I'm Sharon Wilson. I'm an engineering professor at the state university.
> Q. Professor Wilson, did I ask you to examine the brake system that this lawsuit is all about?
> A. Yes, you asked me to examine it and prepare a written report of my findings.
> Q. You did that?
> A. Yes, I finished the report about three months ago.
> Q. Professor Wilson, are you prepared today to tell us what your findings about that brake system are, and the reasons for them?
> A. Yes, I am.

There may be times when you want to let the jury know early what the expert did not do. This avoids the possibility that the jury will be disappointed by the limited role the expert has in the case.

Example:

> Q. Dr. White, you didn't treat Mr. Gable at the Mercy Hospital emergency room yourself, did you?
> A. No, he was attended by Dr. Johnson.
> Q. You first saw him following his discharge from the hospital?
> A. That's right. I saw him as an outpatient a few days after his discharge.
> Q. You supervised his recovery and therapy?
> A. Yes.
> Q. Are you prepared to tell us today what the future holds for Jim Gable?
> A. Yes.

c. Can I trust the expert?

Third, can the witness be trusted? This depends primarily on how capable a communicator he is. However, when you introduce the expert may be the appropriate time to mention fees. Normally, when both sides have experts who are being reasonably compensated for their work and court appearance, there is little to be gained by either side bringing out the details. If you feel your expert may be cross-examined on this topic, however, consider volunteering the appropriate information now.

Example:

> Q. Professor Williams, have you been compensated for your work in this case?
> A. Yes.
> Q. That includes time spent in court?
> A. Yes.
> Q. Tell us how you are being compensated.
> A. Well, my usual fee for any consulting work, regardless of who asks for my help, is $200 per hour. That fee is paid by whoever retained me, regardless of what my opinion turns out to be.
> Q. What has your fee been up to now?
> A. I spent 15 hours working on this case and preparing my written report, so my fee for that work was $3,000.
> Q. Are you being compensated for being here today?
> A. Yes, at my usual hourly rate.

If you feel the other side may take the "hired gun" approach on cross-examination, consider refuting it now.

Example:

> Q. Professor Williams, how often do you do consulting work in lawsuits?
> A. Maybe three or four times a year.
> Q. In what kinds of cases?
> A. I'm usually asked to analyze consumer products designs for their safety aspects.
> Q. Who usually retains you?
> A. It all depends. Sometimes it's the plaintiff, sometimes the defendant. It seems to vary from year to year.
> Q. Do you make your living doing consulting work?
> A. No. My main job is to teach and do research in electrical engineering at the university. I do a little consulting from time to time if the issues look interesting.

Let the jury know that the expert has been previously qualified and testified as an expert in court.

Example:

> Q. Dr. Adams, have you been accepted as an expert in orthopedic surgery by the courts of this country?

A. Yes.

Q. How many times?

A. I believe it's been 14 times.

When these introductory points have been established, you can then move to the next topic. This is best done with a transition question. This orients the jury and lets it know what to expect next.

Example:

Q. Dr. Adams, let's turn now to your medical training and experience.

Or, you can spell out the blueprint for the rest of the examination.

Example:

Q. Dr. Adams, I'm going to ask you next about your medical training and experience. After that we'll talk about your treatment of Mr. Henderson, and end up with your opinions about what his back will be like in the future, and the reasons for your opinions.

You are now ready to move on to the next part of the direct examination.

4.   Background

Before the jury will accept the expert's testimony, it has to accept the expert. How does the jury assess expertise? It looks at two components: formal education and training, and actual working experience. Lawyers tend to over-emphasize formal education, probably because lawyers themselves have substantial formal education and are impressed by others with similar backgrounds. However, keep in mind that few jurors will have the same level of education as an expert. Most jurors developed competence in their jobs simply by doing it until they got good at it. Hands on experience means more to them. In short, you need to bring out both the paper credentials and the actual working experience to convince the jury that the witness is a well-qualified expert.

a.   *Education and training*

In presenting the expert's formal education and training, remember that you are trying to accomplish two seemingly contradictory objectives. On the one hand, you want the expert to be impressive, which requires developing his considerable accomplishments. On the other hand, you want the expert to be likeable, which requires that he appear modest and unassuming. How do you accomplish this?

There are two approaches. First, keep it short and use leading questions to volunteer the expert's most impressive credentials. When you bring up the credentials, and the expert merely agrees with you, it keeps the expert from sounding pompous. The leading questions are proper because these are preliminary matters not in dispute. (However, keep in mind that under FRE 611 the court "shall exercise reasonable control over the mode" of interrogating witnesses. Some traditionally minded judges may sustain objections to using leading questions for foundational testimony.)

Example:

> Q. Dr. Johnson, let's talk about your education and training. You graduated from Stanford University?
> A. Yes.
> Q. That was followed by the Harvard Medical School?
> A. Yes.
> Q. What year did you graduate?
> A. 1975.
> Q. You did your residency at Massachusetts General Hospital?
> A. Yes.
> Q. What was your residency in?
> A. Orthopedics.
> Q. Describe the residency program at the hospital.
> A. It's a four-year program. You basically treat patients with orthopedic conditions under the supervision of experienced orthopedics specialists. The idea is to learn by getting hands on experience treating thousands of patients with all kinds of bone and joint conditions, ranging from broken bones from accidents to joint arthritis in elderly patients.
> Q. You completed the program?
> A. Yes.
> Q. Dr. Johnson, you're board-certified in orthopedics, right?
> A. Yes.
> Q. Is that the highest certification recognized by your field?
> A. Yes.
> Q. How does an expert like yourself become board-certified in orthopedics?
> A. Certification is controlled by the regulating body in each area of medical specialization, in my case by the American Board of Orthopedics. To become board-certified you need to complete the four-year residency program, and pass a two-day written and oral examination.
> Q. You successfully completed each of those requirements?
> A. Yes.
> Q. Dr. Johnson, I believe you also teach orthopedics to medical students, right?

And so on. Raise the impressive credentials in the questions, and have the doctor modestly agree with them. The follow-up questions can then ask the doctor to explain the credentials. This works much better than simply asking the doctor to describe his background ("Doctor, could you tell us a little bit about your education and training?"), which requires the expert to give a long-winded answer about himself. That rarely works well.

The usual credentials you will want to bring out include:

1. undergraduate and graduate education and degrees
2. licenses and certifications
3. teaching and publications
4. positions held in important professional associations
5. public offices held
6. previous experience as an expert witness
7. any other accomplishments that have a direct bearing on the witness's expertise

Second, supplement the qualifying examination with the expert's résumé or curriculum vitae. The résumé will further detail the expert's background and should be admissible as an exhibit, either as a business record under FRE 803(6) or as reliable hearsay under FRE 807. This is particularly useful for detailing credentials like publications, which look impressive on paper but sound boring in the courtroom. Be careful, however. Most experts create résumés with an eye toward impressing their professional colleagues, not lay people. Make sure your expert's résumé is comprehensible and persuasive to a jury. In addition, keep in mind that some courts consider the résumé as cumulative, and will let you ask about the expert's qualifications, or introduce the résumé, but not both. In this situation you will probably prefer to establish the key credentials orally, then introduce a shortened résumé containing the background facts not covered orally, such as publications and memberships in professional organizations.

Finally, tie the expert's background and experience to what was done in this case. For example, a treating orthopedist, who will testify that the plaintiff's condition is permanent, might be asked: "Dr. Stein, is there anything in your training and experience that you found particularly useful in evaluating the degenerative arthritis in Mrs. Smith's hip?" This allows the doctor to discuss any special training, research, and publications that helped him in his assessment of the plaintiff in a way that gives it more significance for the jury.

b. Experience

The expert's actual experience should come next. Remember that most jurors will relate more to this part of the expert's qualifications, since most jurors became good at what they do simply by doing it repeatedly. Jurors find big numbers persuasive. After all, if an expert has done something hundreds or thousands of times, shouldn't she have gotten good at it? Go from the general to the specific, the specific being the precise matter involved in the trial, and bring out the numbers if they are impressive.

Example:

> Q. Dr. Johnson, let's talk now about your actual experience as an or-thopedics specialist over the past 15 years. Have you ever treated patients with joint injuries?
>
> A. Of course.
>
> Q. How many times?
>
> A. Probably thousands. I see some kind of joint problem every day in my office.
>
> Q. Have you ever treated patients for joint dislocations?
>
> A. Yes.
>
> Q. Is that common?
>
> A. Sure. I see a joint dislocation patient two or three times a week.
>
> Q. Dr. Johnson, this case involves a posterior dislocation of the right elbow. Have you ever treated patients for that specific condition before?
>
> A. Oh yes. That's a common dislocation, particularly with children who fall down, instinctively stick out their arm, and end up with a posterior dislocation of the elbow.
>
> Q. Over the past 15 years, how many posterior elbow dislocations have you treated?
>
> A. I'd estimate I've treated about 200 to 300.

Experience should also include the expert's previous publications, if they have obvious relevance to the issues on which the expert is testifying. (If not, irrelevant publications just provide ammunition to the cross-examiner.)

Example:

> Q. Dr. Winfield, have you contributed to the literature in your field?
>
> A. Yes. I've written one text and 12 articles on orthopedics.
>
> Q. Doctor, this case is about traumatic arthritis in the knee joint. Do any of your publications deal with that condition?
>
> A. Yes. My orthopedics text discusses arthritis in the joints in a general way, and three of my articles are about traumatic arthritis. One of them is about traumatic arthritis in the knee joint.

Experience should also include the expert's previous experience as an expert witness, particularly the number of times he has been qualified in court in the same or similar area.

Example:

> Q. Dr. Waters, have you previously been accepted as an expert in the area of product safety design in the courts of this country?
>
> A. Yes.
>
> Q. How many times?
>
> A. I believe it's been 15 times.

How much time should you take developing the expert's credentials? While this is a judgment question, most experts can and should be qualified in a few minutes, if you focus on the important background facts and develop them efficiently. If you take much more time, you run the risk that the jury will become bored and tune out before the expert ever talks about her opinions and reasons for those opinions. However, if your expert appears youthful or inexperienced, you may need to spend more time on credentials.

c.   Tendering the witness as an expert

In some jurisdictions the practice is to "tender the witness as an expert" after the qualifications have been established. If the other side wishes to challenge the fact that the expert is qualified, the other side can ask to "voir dire the witness" on his qualifications, although this is infrequently done.

Example:

Q.   Your Honor, we tender Dr. Johnson as an expert in the field of orthopedics.
Court: Counsel, any objection?
Opposing attorney: Your Honor, we'll ask our questions during the cross-examination.
Court: Very well. Please continue.

In some jurisdictions the court will formally state before the jury that "The court accepts Dr. Johnson as an expert in the field of orthopedics." The direct examination then continues.

d.   Stipulations to qualifications

Decide how to handle offered stipulations about expert qualifications. The opposing party may offer to stipulate, either before trial or in the courtroom, that your expert is qualified, so that establishing his expertise becomes legally unnecessary. Unless your expert has minimal qualifications (if this exists, the opposing party won't make the offer), resist the offer. If it happens in the courtroom in front of the jury, turn down the offer with a brief explanation. (Keep in mind, however, that some judges disapprove of making offers to stipulate in the presence of the jury.)

Example:

Q.   Professor Stein, let's talk next about your education and training.
Opposing attorney: Your Honor, we agree that Professor Stein is a qualified witness. To save time, we're willing to stipulate to that.

> *Q.* Your Honor, Professor Stein's extensive qualifications are critical
> to the jury's decision on whose opinions it will accept. It will take
> me just a few minutes to bring out his education, training, and
> experience.
> *Court:* Very well. Continue.

Some judges may pressure you to accept the stipulation. While the judge
does not, under the law of most jurisdictions, have the legal power to
force parties to stipulate to facts, the judge still has substantial influence
as a practical matter. However, you don't want to cave in just to accommodate the judge when the effect will be that the jury does not get to
hear your expert's superior background. If pressured, you might suggest
a different and more favorable stipulation ("Your Honor, if counsel is willing to stipulate that Dr. Jones is the most qualified orthopedist in the area
of traumatic arthritis, we're willing to accept it."). The other side will invariably refuse it, and you can then continue with your examination.
Another approach is to offer to stipulate, with the understanding that
your adversary will also be precluded from going into his expert's qualifications as well.

5.   Opinions

a.   *"Opinion or otherwise"*

Now it's time for the expert to state her opinions about the important
issues in the case. How do you do this? The Federal Rules of Evidence allows flexibility, since FRE 702 permits an "opinion or otherwise." The traditional approach is to ask for just that: the opinion. Many jurisdictions
require that the opinion be expressed to a "reasonable degree of medical
or scientific certainty," otherwise the opinion is considered speculation
and objectionable.

Example:

> *Q.* Dr. Johnson, I'm now going to ask you your opinion about cer-
> tain things. First, do you have an opinion, to a reasonable degree
> of medical certainty, whether Mary Wilson's back injury was
> caused by the collision on June 1, 1999?
> *A.* Yes.
> *Q.* What is your opinion?
> *A.* My opinion is that Mary Wilson's back injury, the herniation of
> the disk at the L3-L4 level, the lumbar section of her spine, was
> caused entirely by the collision on that day.

The shortcoming of this approach is that it makes you repeat the phrase
"reasonable degree of medical or scientific certainty" each time you ask
for an opinion. Another way is to deal with it once.

Example:

> Q. Dr. Johnson, the law requires that you give your opinion to a rea-
> sonable degree of medical certainty. If you can't answer to a rea-
> sonable of medical certainty, please let us know, all right?
> A. Yes.
> Q. Doctor, in your opinion, was Mary Wilson's back injury caused by
> the collision on June 1, 1999?
> A. Yes.

This is effective, but there may be more effective ways. Remember that the jury likes expressions of certainty, whether it's from eyewitnesses or experts. Since the rules permit an "opinion or otherwise," you can ask it other ways.

Example:

> Q. Dr. Johnson, what did you conclude about the cause of Mary
> Wilson's back injury?
> A. I concluded that her back injury was caused by the collision on
> June 1, 1999.

Sometimes an expert can testify to something as a fact, not as an opinion. This again has the advantage of sounding certain and not merely an opinion over which reasonable experts may differ.

Example:

> Q. Dr. Johnson, will the scars on Mary Wilson's face ever go away?
> A. No. Scar tissue is permanent. It may change its appearance
> slightly over time, but it will never go away. The scars she has
> today will be with her for the rest of her life.
> Q. Is there any doubt about that?
> A. No.

b. *Hypothetical questions*

Finally, don't forget the hypothetical question. Before the Federal Rules of Evidence were enacted, the hypothetical question was the required method for getting opinions from nontreating or consulting experts. This was because such experts had no first-hand knowledge of the facts necessary to support their opinions. To get around this problem, experts were asked to "assume" certain facts were true, and then were asked their opinions about the assumed facts. Since the hypothetical question needed a proper foundation, there had to be evidence admitted to support each assumed material fact. If there was none, the hypothetical question was improper and the expert, having no first-hand knowledge of the relevant facts, could not testify to his opinions. Needless to say, lawyers often fought over whether all material facts were properly included in the hypothetical question, and over other technical aspects of this rule.

The hypothetical question requirements were justifiably criticized as being cumbersome and unnecessary. The enactment of the Federal Rules of Evidence, particularly Rules 703 and 705, have practically eliminated the hypothetical question in federal courts and state courts that have adopted the rules. Despite these changes, a few state jurisdictions still require them, and some lawyers still like to use them even though they are no longer required. That's because a hypothetical question allows you to summarize the evidence and elicit an opinion on a critical trial issue, such as causation or permanence of injuries. For this reason, hypothetical questions are still sometimes used at the end of a party's case in chief.

Example:

Q. Dr. Adams, I'm going to ask you to assume certain facts as true. I will then ask your opinions based on those facts. Assume:
1. A man is 30 years old, 5 feet 10 inches tall, weighs 175 pounds.
2. Before June 1, 1999, he was in perfect health. He worked as a school teacher. He enjoyed hiking and camping with his wife and daughters, playing basketball, and working around the house.
3. On June 1, 1999, while crossing the street, he was struck on his left side above the knee by a pickup truck and knocked down on the pavement.
4. He was immediately unable to move his left leg, and experienced shooting pains up and down his leg.
5. He was taken to the hospital, examined, and X rayed. The diagnosis was a transverse fracture of the left femur nine centimeters above the knee.
6. The fracture was set and casted. The cast was kept on for 22 weeks. The cast was then removed, and therapy began and continued for several months.
7. Three weeks ago the leg was examined again. At that time the leg was still substantially smaller than the other, the man experiences pain whenever he tries to walk, and an examination disclosed that arthritis had developed at the fracture site.
8. He can't engage in sports, can't work around the house, and can't do physical activities involving the use of his leg because of the pain.

Dr. Black, based on these facts, do you have an opinion, to a reasonable degree of medical certainty, whether there is a causal connection between the injury to the leg and the development of arthritis?
A. Yes.
Q. What is your opinion?

You can also ask the expert's opinion about any other issues, such as permanence of injury, and ability to resume former employment. A simple, clear hypothetical, reviewed with the expert, which parallels the earlier presentation of the facts, can be an effective persuasion tool at trial.

6.   Bases for opinions

a.   Sources for opinion

In most situations, particularly when the witness is a nontreating or consulting expert, you will want to bring out the sources of the information the expert relied upon. This will demonstrate that the expert, even if not dealing directly with the problem at the time, nevertheless obtained all the important information so that her opinion is reliable. A common example would be a nontreating orthopedist or psychiatrist.

Example:

Q. Dr. Andrews, before we get to the reasons why you concluded that Mr. Jones is a danger to himself and others, let's review the sources of information you had available to assist you. What information did you have?

A. Several things. I had Mr. Jones' complete medical records, from childhood to the present date. I also had his psychiatric records, including his hospitalization in the state mental hospital in 1994. I had the psychological tests that were administered by the hospital at that time. Finally, of course, I examined Mr. Jones after being directed to do so by the court.

Q. Was the information you received adequate to evaluate Mr. Jones' mental condition and determine if he should be civilly committed because he represents a danger to himself and others?

A. Yes.

Q. Was there any additional information you would have wanted to assist you in evaluating Mr. Jones?

A. No, it was a complete workup. The file contained everything a psychiatrist hopes to have available.

Experts frequently get, and rely on, second opinions from their colleagues. This should be brought out when it occurs, since it strengthens the opinion when the views of other experts have been considered.

Example:

Q. Dr. Gibson, is it customary for psychiatrists like yourself to consult with other psychiatrists before reaching a professional opinion?

A. Yes, it's very common in psychiatry.

Q. Did you consult with other experts in this case?

A. Yes, I consulted with Dr. Monet and Dr. Jacobs, who are experts in treating paranoid schizophrenia.

Q. Did your consultations with them help you in evaluating the patient in this case?

A. Yes, they were very helpful.

Experts can also base their opinions on learned treatises, since FRE 803(18) states that if "relied upon by the expert witness in direct examination," statements contained in learned treatises may be read into evidence, but may not be received as exhibits." This is a powerful tool and is particularly useful to support the opinion of the expert who is young and inexperienced.

Example:

Q. Dr. Wilson, what else did you rely on in reaching your opinions?
A. I relied extensively on Saunder's Treatise on Orthopedics, which is a recognized treatise, perhaps the most authoritative treatise, in the field.
Q. What statements from Saunder's Treatise on Orthopedics did you rely on?
A. The chapter on trauma, particularly the section on traumatic arthritis.
Q. Do you have that treatise with you?
A. Yes, I do.
Q. Dr. Wilson, please read the statements from Saunder's treatise on Orthopedics that you relied upon in reaching your opinions.
A. The part I relied upon is in Chapter 8, on page 447. It says there: "Trauma as the cause of joint arthritis should never be overlooked. The medical literature is replete with case histories of painful joint arthritis activated by traumatic injuries."

In some jurisdictions the lawyers are permitted to put a blowup of the section of the treatise relied upon in front of the jury as it is being read. However, the exhibit is not, under Rule 803(18), actually admitted as an exhibit.

FRE 703, effective in 2000, complicates matters, because it provides that "facts or data that are otherwise inadmissible shall not be disclosed to the jury by the proponent of the opinion or inference unless the court determines that their probative value in assisting the jury to evaluate the expert's opinion substantially outweighs their prejudicial effect." You can expect the opposing lawyer to object whenever the expert is asked to testify in detail about the sources underlying the expert's opinion.

Example:

Q. Dr. Andrews, one of the bases for your opinion that Mr. Jones is a danger to himself and others is your interview with Mr. Jones?
A. That's right. I did a two-hour interview and evaluation.
Q. You interviewed Mr. Jones' spouse and children?
A. Yes.
Q. Tell us what Mr. Jones and the family members told you during those interviews.
Counsel: Objection, your honor.

What is the judge likely to do in these circumstances? First, the judge will want these issues raised before trial. As the proponent of the expert, you want the direct examination to go smoothly, so you should raise any anticipated objections to the expert's testimony in a pretrial motion. Second, the judge under FRE 703 has a great deal of discretion. If the judge feels that the direct examiner is trying to "back door hearsay" under the guise of asking the expert for the bases of the expert's opinions, the judge may sustain the objection.

b. *Sources for opinion meet* Daubert *standards*

If the basis of the expert's testimony includes scientific tests and methods, the opposing party will usually ask for a pretrial "Daubert hearing" to determine the admissibility of the testimony and the underlying tests. At the hearing, the following kinds of questions should be asked:

(Tests)
Q. What tests were done, and why?
Q. What other available tests were not done, and why not?
Q. What standards were used for the tests?
Q. How many times did you do the tests?
Q. Can the tests be replicated, and have they been?
Q. Did the tests fit the facts of this case?
Q. Did the tests exclude other possible causes?
Q. Was the testing done as part of general scientific research, or was the testing done for purposes of this litigation?
Q. Who paid for the tests?
Q. Did the expert reach his conclusions first, then gather support for it?

(Error rate)
Q. What was the error rate of the tests, and how was it calculated?
Q. Did the error rates meet the level of 95 percent certainty, so that the tests are "statistically significant?"
Q. Are there standards for the technique used?
Q. Who developed those standards and why?
Q. Were those standards complied with in this case?
Q. If not, why not?

(Peer review)
Q. Have the theories and studies been published?
Q. When and where were they published?
Q. Were they peer reviewed, and, if so, by whom?
Q. Who paid for the publication?
Q. If not published, why not?
Q. Did you participate in writing the publication?
Q. Did the publication come out before you were hired as an expert in this case?

(General acceptance)
Q. What is the relevant scientific community?
Q. Has the technique or theory been generally accepted by that scientific community?
Q. How do you know?
Q. Is the technique or theory used in the scientific world, or is it used only in the courtroom?

If the expert fails on some of these points, his testimony will be highly suspect. If the expert didn't do all the tests that should have been done, didn't check for error rates, the tests have not been peer reviewed, the tests were done for purposes of litigation rather than general scientific advancement, the testing was paid for by an interested party, or the conclusions were reached before support for the conclusions were found, it is unlikely that the trial judge, relying on *Daubert* and *Joiner*, will allow the expert to testify at trial.

If the expert's testimony survives the *Daubert* analysis, the essence of these questions and answers should be repeated before the jury at trial, since the jury will need a basis on which to assess the expert's credibility and the test's validity.

c. Basis for opinion

The last step is to ask the expert the basis for each opinion. The conventional way is to ask it immediately after the opinion has been brought out.

Example:

Q. Professor Johnson, do you have an opinion whether or not the design of this toaster oven is unreasonably dangerous?
A. Yes I do.
Q. What is your opinion?
A. My opinion is that the oven's design is unreasonably dangerous.
Q. Professor, what are the reasons for your opinion?

Once again, however, keep in mind that the jury likes certainty. Constantly using the word *opinion* reminds the jury that the testimony is only that — an opinion — and people can have differences of opinions. If the expert can testify more positively, have him do so.

Example:

Q. Professor Johnson, after you examined and studied this toaster oven, were you able to come to any conclusions?
A. Oh, yes.
Q. What were they?
A. First, I concluded that this toaster oven is unreasonably dangerous.
Q. Why?

The expert might, in appropriate circumstances, be even stronger.

Example:

> Q. Professor Johnson, is this toaster oven unreasonably dangerous?
> A. It certainly is.
> Q. Why is it unreasonably dangerous?

d. Exhibits and visual aids

How should the expert explain the reasons behind his opinions and conclusions? Put the expert in the teacher mode. Use exhibits and visual aids that illustrate the testimony. Get the expert out of the witness chair and in front of the jury.

Example:

> Q. Dr. Sullivan, you brought a model of the elbow joint with you today, correct?
> A. Yes.
> Q. Does this model, Plaintiff's Exhibit #8, already in evidence, accurately show the bones, muscles, ligaments and other structures in the elbow joint?
> A. It does.
> Q. Will it help you in explaining the reasons for your opinions?
> A. Definitely.
> Q. Dr. Sullivan, using the model, explain why Mr. Gable's elbow joint will never have a normal range of motion.
> A. Certainly. First, . . .

The expert can then give a short lecture, directly to the jury, using the model to illustrate his points.

Example:

> Q. Professor Johnson, I'm placing the toaster oven on the table in front of the jury, and a diagram, a cross section of the oven, next to the table. These are Plaintiff's Exhibits #4 and #9, already in evidence. With the court's permission, may Professor Johnson step down from the witness chair and continue his testimony before the jury?
> Court: He may. (Witness stands by the exhibits.)
> Q. Professor Johnson, why is the toaster oven unreasonably dangerous?
> A. Several reasons. First, look over here where the electrical cord enters the metal housing. . . .

Whenever possible, have the exhibits the expert will refer to during his testimony already admitted in evidence. Don't use the expert for mundane tasks like establishing the foundations for exhibits that can be admitted in other ways. For example, make sure the hospital records are in evidence before the treating physician testifies. (This can be done during discovery through a Request to Admit Facts, before trial through a Pretrial

Memorandum and rulings on the admissibility of exhibits, or at trial through another witness.) That way the expert can freely refer to the records, and read from them, without giving the opposing side an opportunity to object on the basis that the witness is reading from something not in evidence. However, the expert should probably qualify exhibits that will be used as visual aids during his testimony, such as anatomical charts and models, since he is the most credible witness and can easily establish the necessary foundation.

e. Explanations

How long should the explanation take? Should the explanation come out in one answer, or should it be periodically interrupted by questions? That depends on how complex the topic is and how good the communication skills of your expert are. However, keep in mind the concept of "sound bites." Television news thrives on 10- to 15-second sound bites, and persons regularly interviewed on TV know that these kind of sound bites are best because they give the listeners information in digestible bites. When your expert is a capable communicator, consider giving him a free rein. If the expert is more ponderous and tends to carry on, you will need to structure the testimony to create periodic breaks. If your adversary makes objections based on "the question calls for a narrative," and the judge sustains the objections (although most do not), make the questions more focused.

Example:

> Q. Professor Johnson, why is it unreasonably dangerous? . . .
> Q. What's the next reason? . . .
> Q. Any other reasons?

Put yourself in the jury's shoes. If the jury could ask questions now, what would it want to know, and how would it ask it? Simply put those questions to the expert.

Example:

> Q. Professor, what's so dangerous about having the electrical cord next to the heating element? . . .
> Q. Why is a properly made o-ring critical for the valve to work right?

Get the expert to use simple visual images and analogies, since these sink in and are remembered.

Example:

> A. The rubber around the power cord insulates it. If it's put too close to a heat source, the rubber will dry out, develop cracks,

and start flaking off the wire. This creates a dangerous electrical shock hazard. That's exactly what happened here.

A. The o-ring does the same thing as the rubber washer in the end of your garden hose. The washer forms a tight seal so that water won't leak out. The o-ring is supposed to do the same thing in the valve. In this case, however, the o-ring was manufactured with a groove cut in it, which allowed the acid to leak out of the valve and drip on the floor.

Finally, get the expert to avoid technical terms whenever possible. For example, a doctor can easily testify without using the phrase "distal part of the leg." It is accurate enough if she says "lower part of the leg," and the jury will immediately understand the testimony. If the expert does need to use a technical term, have the expert immediately explain what that means without talking down to the jury. Don't say: "Dr., I'm afraid some of the jurors may not understand what distal means." Don't say: "Dr., I don't know what distal means." The first sounds patronizing, the second sounds dishonest. Just ask the expert what the term means. The explanation should be in clear, simple English.

Example:

Q. What did you find?
A. The X rays showed a comminuted fracture of the femur.
Q. Doctor, what's a comminuted fracture?
A. It's a fracture in which the bone has been forced out of position far enough that it has punctured the skin.

When a technical term is at the heart of the case, and the expert needs to use it, it might be more effective to have the expert explain the term using a diagram, model, or illustration to make it visual and real.

Example:

Q. Doctor, what did you find?
A. I found a herniated disk at the L3-L4 level.
Q. What is a herniated disk?
A. A disk is herniated when the material inside the disk, which has the consistency of Jello, seeps out through a crack in the outer layer of the disk and enters the surrounding tissue.
Q. Could you show us what it looks like, using Plaintiff's Exhibit #4 in evidence?
A. Sure. This illustration is a drawing of two vertebrae and the disk between them. The disk is colored pink. Over here (pointing) you can see where some of the material in the disk has pushed out of the disk and has entered the hole in the vertebra where the spinal cord goes. The material that has pushed out of the disk is called the herniation.
Q. Where is the L3-L4 level?

A. That's the disk between the third and fourth lumbar vertebra. That's right in the small of your lower back, where it curves in.

We are now ready to put these various ideas and techniques together.

§8.5. Examples of direct examinations

The following direct examinations illustrate the variety of ways experts can be presented effectively as witnesses during trial.

1. Treating physician in personal injury case

In the following example, an orthopedist testifies to her treatment of the plaintiff following an automobile accident in a personal injury case.

Example:

Q. Dr. Klein, please introduce yourself to the jury.
A. My name is Michelle Klein. I'm a doctor specializing in orthopedics. I have a private practice in town.

(Introduction)

This introduction tells the jury immediately the role the witness plays in the case.

Q. Dr. Klein, you treated Mr. Gable at the Mercy Hospital emergency room on June 6, 1999?
A. Yes.
Q. And you supervised his recovery and therapy afterwards?
A. That's right.
Q. Dr. Klein, are you prepared today to tell us about Mr. Gable's elbow and what the future holds for him?
A. Yes.
Q. Dr. Klein, let's start by learning a little about you. You went to Stanford University?
A. Yes.
Q. And medical school at Yale?
A. That's right.
Q. When did you graduate from Yale Medical School?
A. In 1976.
Q. Where did you do your residency?
A. At Massachusetts General Hospital in Boston.
Q. Tell us about the residency training.
A. My residency was in orthopedics, which is the area of medicine that deals with

(Qualifications)

Note how the questions alternate between leading and nonleading. This is proper, since these facts are not in dispute, and it makes the expert appear modest and unassuming.

injuries and diseases of the bones, muscles, and joints. It's a four-year program. What you do is treat patients with orthopedic problems under the supervision of orthopedic specialists, and become experienced in diagnosing and treating the conditions that patients have. I completed the residency in 1985.

Q. Dr. Klein, you're licensed to practice medicine in this state?

A. Yes, since 1981.

Q. I believe you're also board-certified as a specialist in orthopedics, right?

A. Yes.

Q. Aren't all orthopedists board-certified?

A. No.

Q. How does a doctor become board-certified in orthopedics?

A. Each medical specialty is controlled by a board. In orthopedics it's the American Board of Orthopedics. You are eligible to take the exam, which is a two-day exam, after completing your residency. I took the exam, passed it, and became board-certified in 1986.

Q. Is being board-certified the highest level of certification recognized in your field?

A. Yes.

Q. Dr. Klein, you also teach, correct?

A. Yes, I'm a clinical assistant professor at the state university medical school.

Q. What do you teach?

A. I teach in the orthopedics residency program, helping doctors become specialists in orthopedics.

Q. How long have you been teaching there?

A. It's been eight years.

Q. Are you on the staff of any hospitals?

A. Yes, I have staff privileges, which means that I can treat patients, at University Hospital and St. Mary's Hospital.

Q. Dr. Klein, let's turn now to your actual experience treating patients. You have your own practice in orthopedics, right?

A. Yes.

Q. Tell us about your practice.

A. I've had my own office since 1981 here in town. My practice is full time, and is limited to patients with orthopedic problems.

Board-certification is probably the most impressive "paper credential."

Teaching is also an impressive credential.

Most jurors will be more impressed with hands-on experience than with paper credentials.

Q. Have you ever treated patients with joint problems?

A. Of course.

Q. Have you treated patients with joint dislocations?

A. Yes. I probably see a dislocation every other day in my office.

Q. Dr. Klein, in this case Mr. Gable suffered a dislocation of his right elbow. Have you ever treated patients with that particular problem before?

A. Many times. Elbow dislocations are quite common. You see them often in athletes and children.

Q. Since 1986, about how many patients have you treated for elbow dislocations?

Bringing out the numbers is important.

A. I can only estimate. I see that about once a week, so I've treated several hundred elbow dislocations over the years.

Q. Dr. Klein, let's turn now to June 6, 1999, when you treated Mr. Gable at the Mercy Hospital emergency room. How did you come to treat him there?

(Diagnosis)

A. I was the orthopedist on call that day. I was called when Mr. Klein was brought by ambulance to the emergency room.

Q. Tell us what happened in the emergency room.

A. I met Mr. Klein in the ER a few minutes after he arrived. He was on a stretcher in one of the examining rooms. He was in pain, but he was coherent and I found out from him what happened.

Q. What was that?

A. He said he was in an automobile collision. He had braced himself before the crash, and the force of the crash threw him forward. He thought his arm was broken.

The patient's statement is properly admissible as a statement made for diagnosis and treatment under FRE 803(4).

Q. What did you do?

A. Two basic things. I gave him a physical examination. He seemed to have no injuries other than an elbow dislocation in his right elbow. It was rather obvious, because of the bone displacement, that his elbow was out of alignment. I then had X rays taken of his right arm with a portable X-ray unit. The X rays showed that no bones in the arm were broken, but that Mr. Gable had a posterior dislocation of the elbow joint.

Describe the key terms using simple English.

Q. What's a posterior dislocation?

A. That's when the bones of the lower arm, the ulna and radius, are pushed back and behind the bone of the upper arm, the humerus. This often happens when people fall and instinctively put their arm out to brake the fall. The elbow can't take that kind of stress, and dislocates at the joint.

Q. Dr. Klein, I'm showing you a model of an elbow joint, marked Plaintiff's Exhibit #6 in evidence. Using the model, could you explain what happens to the elbow joint in a dislocation?

An exhibit is always important so that the jury can visualize the diagnosis.

[Model of Elbow Joint]

PLAINTIFF'S EXHIBIT #6

A. Yes. In a posterior dislocation, the lower arm is pushed back, behind the upper arm, like this (demonstrating). The joint is normally held together by several ligaments, which are colored blue on this model. The ligaments are like nylon straps. They are flexible, but only for the normal range of motion of the joint. A dislocation stretches and sometimes tears the ligaments, since the bones in a dislocation are separated beyond the normal range of motion of the joint (demonstrating). There may also be other damage, most commonly bleeding into the joint and soft tissue damage.

Q. How did you treat Mr. Gable?

A. The standard treatment for this type of injury. He was taken up to surgery and given a general anesthetic. I then set this arm while he was unconscious, took another series of X rays to make sure the bones were

A computer animation would also be effective here.

Note how the doctor uses ordinary English to describe her demonstration. This is much better than using technical medical terms.

in proper alignment at the elbow, and then put a cast on the arm, which held the arm in a right angle.

Q. How did you set the arm?

A. It's a standard procedure. When the patient is unconscious, the muscles relax. With the help of the surgical staff, you steadily pull and turn the lower arm until it is back to its proper location. Most of the time, you can pop the lower arm back in place without surgery. That in fact happened with Mr. Gable.

Simple English is again used to describe a medical procedure.

Q. Did Mr. Gable get any medication following your setting the elbow?

A. Yes, he was prescribed a pain killer and an anti-inflammatory drug to keep down the swelling. Again, that's standard treatment.

Q. How long did Mr. Gable remain at the hospital?

A. He was discharged a few hours later. Like all surgical patients, he spent some time in the recovery room to make sure his vital signs were normal. After he woke up, I talked to him, gave him the prescriptions for the medications, and made arrangements to see him in my office in four weeks. Later that day his wife took him home.

Q. Dr. Klein, let's turn next to the time you removed Mr. Gable's cast and therapy began. When did that happen?

(Therapy)

A. One month later. I saw Mr. Gable in my office. I sawed off the cast using a vibrating saw and examined the arm. It was in the condition you would expect.

Q. What condition was that?

A. The arm was smaller, because the muscles shrink when not used. The range of motion was approximately 10 degrees to either side of a right angle, like this (demonstrating).

Make it visual whenever possible.

Q. Why couldn't the arm move more?

A. In an injury like this, the ligaments are damaged. Putting the arm in a cast gives the ligaments time to begin healing. Unfortunately, the ligaments also quickly lose their ability to stretch, limiting the range of motion.

Q. So you were expecting it?

A. Yes, it always happens in injuries like this.

Q. Dr. Klein, tell us about the therapy program you put Mr. Gable on.

A. It was the standard therapy. To regain the normal range of motion, the patient soaks his elbow in hot water for 10-15 minutes, then slowly stretches the arm back and forth. This stretches the ligaments. This needs to be done three or four times a day. If all goes well, most patients regain full range of motion in a few weeks time.

Q. Is this painful?

A. Sure. It's painful for everyone, and the amount of pain is related to the amount of damage to the ligaments and soft tissue.

Q. Did the therapy work for Mr. Gable?

A. Yes.

Q. How do you know?

A. Because the range of motion got much better. The next time I saw him, about four weeks after removing the cast, he had regained most of the normal range of motion.

Q. How much had he regained?

A. He could flex his arm like this (demonstrating) all the way up. He could extend his arm like this (demonstrating) most of the way, but was still missing the last 20-30 degrees of full extension (demonstrating).

Again, make it visual.

Q. Did you discuss this with him?

A. Yes, I told him to keep doing the therapy to try to get full extension.

Q. Did he ever regain full extension of the right arm?

A. No. He kept doing the therapy for several more weeks, but never regained the last 20-30 degrees of extension.

Q. Doctor, why was that?

A. Not all patients with elbow dislocations regain full range of motion, no matter how hard they work at the therapy. The reason is that the ligaments, after being stretched and torn in a dislocation, lose some of their elasticity. They just never stretch as well again. In addition, the torn ligaments develop scar tissue when they heal. Scar tissue does not stretch, so again the ligaments lose some of their elasticity. This keeps the elbow joint from regaining full range of motion.

(Explanation)

A "why" question puts the expert in the teacher mode.

Q. Have you had other patients with an injury like Mr. Gable who have also not regained full range of motion afterwards?

A. Yes. I'd say about 15 percent never regain it completely, based on my experience. That number is also consistent with the medical literature on the subject.

Q. Dr. Klein, is Mr. Gable's limited range of motion in his right elbow a permanent condition?

A. Yes. Given the length of therapy, and the time since the injury, in all likelihood that's the way his arm is going to be for the rest of his life.

Q. Let's turn finally to what all this means to Mr. Gable. You know he worked as an automobile mechanic, right?

A. Yes, he told me about his job.

Q. Will Mr. Gable ever be able to work again as an automobile mechanic?

A. No, I don't think so.

Q. Why not?

A. Two basic reasons. First, he does not have full range of motion in the elbow joint. His job as a mechanic requires that he have full range of motion in both arms. Second, and just as important, his right elbow joint is not as strong as it once was. The ligaments have been damaged, and have lost strength. Again, his job requires full strength in both arms. In short, his elbow is simply not up to taking the kind of repetitive strain that is put on the arm in mechanic work.

Q. Dr. Klein, isn't there something you, or other orthopedic specialists, can do to get Mr. Gable's right elbow back to normal?

A. Unfortunately, no. Doctors can't perform miracles. I'm afraid Mr. Gable's elbow is as good now as its ever going to get. This is the way it's going to be for the rest of his life.

(Prognosis)
Note that the doctor is not asked her "opinion"; FRE 702 permits other forms.

Effect of condition on patient's job, and the reasons for it, are critical.

This last question highlights the permanence of the condition.

2.   Pathologist in homicide case

In the following example, a medical examiner testifies to the cause of death and other issues in a homicide case.

Example:

Q. Dr. Stein, please tell what you do?

A. I'm the chief medical examiner in this county. I'm a pathologist, which is that branch of medicine that studies the causes of diseases, injuries, and deaths.

Q. How long have you held the position of chief medical examiner?

A. Five years.

Q. Dr. Stein, what are your duties as the chief medical examiner?

A. My job is to determine the cause of death of every person in the county who dies outside of a hospital, or dies under suspicious circumstances. I try to determine if the death was a homicide, suicide, accident, or from natural causes. Either I or one of the other pathologists in my office does the autopsy and lab tests to determine the cause of death.

Q. Did you do the autopsy on a Vernon James to determine the cause of death?

A. I did.

Q. When?

A. On June 2, 1999, the day after he was brought to the morgue.

Q. Were you able to determine the cause of death of Vernon James?

A. Yes.

Q. What was it?

A. He died from a gunshot wound to the head, which lacerated his brain, causing massive hemorrhage and death.

Q. Dr. Stein, before we get into the details of your autopsy, let's learn a little more about you. Tell us where you received your education.

A. I went to the state university, received my bachelor degree in chemistry in 1985, and received my medical degree in 1989. After that I did a three-year residency in pathology at the university hospital.

Q. Are you board-certified?

A. Yes.

Q. What does board-certified mean?

A. It means you have met the requirements of the specialty board, which in pathology is the American Board of Pathology.

(Introduction)

This introduction begins with an impressive point — that the expert is chief medical examiner.

(Opinion)

Here the expert's "opinion" is brought out early. The expert's credentials are then explored in greater detail.

(Qualifications)

Board-certification is highlighted.

Q. What are those requirements?

A. You need to have completed a residency in pathology, and have passed the exam, which is a two-day written exam.

Q. When did you become board-certified?

A. In 1993.

Q. Dr. Stein, do you teach?

A. Yes, I lecture at the police academy on pathology, and I am a clinical professor of pathology at the state university medical school.

Q. Have you ever testified before as a specialist in pathology?

A. Yes. As the chief medical examiner, I do most of the autopsies in suspected homicides, so I'm usually called to testify if those cases go to trial. I've been called as a witness about 50 times so far.

If the expert has previously been accepted as an expert in court, this is important. If the numbers are impressive, bring them out.

Q. Who calls you as a witness?

A. It's usually the prosecution, although I've been called by the defense a few times.

Q. Are you paid for your court appearances?

A. No. I'm a salaried employee of the county. Testifying is part of my job.

Q. Dr. Stein, let's talk now about your experience as a pathologist. Have you done autopsies to determine the cause of death?

A. Yes.

Q. How many times?

A. Well, that's my job. I probably do one autopsy a day, so in the five years that I've been the chief medical examiner I've done about 1,500 autopsies.

Impressive numbers again.

Q. Of those, how many involved deaths from gunshots?

A. I'd estimate about 200. Gunshot deaths are unfortunately quite common.

Q. Dr. Stein, tell us what is involved in an autopsy.

A. An autopsy is done to determine the cause of death. The first step is to examine the exterior of the body and note anything unusual. The second step is to examine the internal body organs, again looking for any abnormalities that may account for death. The last step is to take certain body parts, such as blood, urine, stomach contents, and send them to the lab for analysis, such as to determine the presence of alcohol, drugs, or other substances. As I'm doing the autopsy, I dictate my findings into a tape recorder, and I use the recording to prepare my written report of my findings.

Q. How long does an autopsy take?

A. It all depends. In a simple case, where the cause of death is obvious, it may be one or two hours. If the cause of death is not obvious, it may take much longer.

Q. Is that the procedure you took in your autopsy of Vernon James?

A. Yes.

Q. Dr. Stein, explain to us how you were able to determine that he died from a gunshot wound to the head.

A. Certainly. In a gunshot case it's often, but not always, apparent. In this case my examination of the exterior of the body revealed nothing unusual, except for two injuries to the head. An examination of the body cavity revealed nothing unusual. All the organs — heart, stomach, liver, and so on — were normal. My examination of the head revealed what appeared to be a bullet entry wound just above the right ear. There was also what appeared to be a bullet exit wound in the head about three inches above the left ear.

Q. How can you tell if it's a bullet wound?

A. You can't always tell for sure. But when you see what looks like an entry wound, and then also see what looks like an exit wound, that's usually strong evidence of a gunshot wound.

Q. How can you tell if it's an entry or an exit wound?

A. You can usually tell by the appearance of the wound. An entry wound from a bullet is usually quite small. This is because the skin is elastic and stretches as the bullet enters. The exit wound, by contrast, is usually larger, and can be much larger, depending on the type of bullet.

Q. What further examination did you do?

A. I peeled back the skin at the wound locations. I could see a round entry wound in the skull above the right ear. The injury above the left ear was much more extensive. The skull had been fractured extensively, and pieces of bone were missing.

> The expert is put in the teacher mode.

> Bring out the explanations in simple English.

Q. What did this tell you?

A. It confirmed my initial impression of an entry and exit wound.

Q. What else did you do?

A. I examined the brain. To do this you use a saw to remove part of the skull, which then allows you to examine the brain.

Q. What did you find?

A. There was massive trauma, which means damage, to the brain itself. There was massive hemorrhaging, which means blood loss, throughout the brain. I was then able to find bone fragments near the entry point, which means that the force of the bullet pushed small bits of the skull into the brain. At the exit point, there were several pieces of bone missing, which meant that the force of the bullet at the exit pushed bone pieces out of the head. By examining the brain itself, I could follow the path of the bullet from the entry point to the exit point, because the bullet causes significant visible damage to the brain as it passes through. Finally, I found no bullet or bullet fragments inside the skull.

The doctor immediately explains medical terms.

Q. From your examination, what did you conclude?

A. That Vernon James died from a bullet wound that entered his head above the right ear, left his head three inches above the left ear, and that the cause of death was trauma to the brain and massive hemorrhaging of the brain, caused by the bullet.

(Opinion)

Note that the expert is *not* asked his "opinion"; asking for the expert's conclusion is stronger, and is proper under FRE 702.

Q. Doctor Stein, I'd like to ask you about several other things. First, could you determine the path of the bullet from your autopsy?

A. Yes.

Q. What was it?

A. The bullet went in a straight line from the entry to the exit wounds.

Note how much else the expert can establish in addition to the cause of death.

Q. How can you tell that?

A. Except for the skull, the inside of the head is all soft tissue. A bullet would not change its path inside the skull because it was passing through the brain.

Q. Have you prepared an anatomical exhibit to illustrate your findings?

A. Yes.

Q. This diagram, State's Exhibit #8, does it fairly and accurately show the direction and path of the bullet?

A. Yes, it does.

As always, visual aids are important.

```
┌─────────────────────────────────────────┐
│                                           │
│                                           │
│                                           │
│        [Anatomical Diagram of Head]       │
│                                           │
│                                           │
│               STATE'S EXHIBIT #8          │
└─────────────────────────────────────────┘
```

Q. Your Honor, we offer Exhibit #8 and ask permission to show it to the jury.

Court: Any objection?

Opposing counsel: No, your Honor.

Court: Very well. It's admitted. Show it to the jury.

Q. Second, were you able to determine the distance the firearm was from the head when the bullet was fired?

A. Yes, I determined that the firearm was more than two feet away.

Q. How can you do this?

A. Every firearm uses gunpowder to shoot bullets. The expansion of the exploding gunpowder is what pushes the bullet out the barrel. Once the bullet is out, the gunpowder is forced out of the barrel as well. If the end of the barrel is less than two feet away, bits of burning gunpowder residue will be blown into the skin of the head. The closer the barrel, the greater the amount of gunpowder residue around the entry wound. If the barrel is more than two or three feet away, you will not find gunpowder burns on the skin. In this case the skin around the entry wound had no gunpowder embedded in it, so I concluded the gun barrel was more than two feet away, and probably more than three feet away, from the entry wound.

Another useful point, as it negates the possibility of a suicide or self-inflicted injury.

Q. Can you tell how much further away it was?

A. No, there's no medical way to determine this.

Q. Could this gunshot wound have been self-inflicted, as in an accidental shooting or a suicide?

A. No.

Q. Why not?

A. A self-inflicted gunshot wound would have to have had the barrel more than two feet from the head to account for the absence of any gunpowder residue. It's impossible for a man of average size, like Mr. James was, to shoot himself in the head and have the barrel of the firearm be more than two feet away. Anyway, the great majority of suicides are committed with the gun barrel held against, or very close to, the body.

Q. Dr. Stein, could you determine from your autopsy the caliber of the bullet that killed Mr. James?

Again, this information may be important, and anticipates a possible cross-examination point.

A. Not exactly. The diameter of the circular entry wound in the skull was approximately 9 millimeters. This means that the bullet could not have been larger than that.

Q. What does that tell you?

A. The bullet could not have been larger than a .38 caliber or 9 millimeter. It could have been smaller, since a bullet that is wobbling will make a larger entry wound than the diameter of the bullet.

Q. Finally, Dr. Stein, could you determine from your autopsy the kind or shape of the bullet that killed Mr. James?

A. To some extent. There are two basic types of bullets on the market. One is a solid pointed bullet, the other is a hollow point bullet. Pointed bullets will enter and exit the skull without significantly changing shape, so they cause less internal damage and make a smaller exit wound. Hollow point bullets have a hollow or flattened tip, which is designed to flatten or fragment when it hits something. These bullets cause much greater damage to soft tissue like the brain, and are less likely to pass entirely through a body the size of the human head. So I was able to conclude that the bullet that killed Mr. James was in all probability a solid pointed bullet.

3.   Economist in wrongful death case

In the following wrongful death case, an economist testifies about the economic loss to the plaintiff caused by the death of the plaintiff's husband.

Example:

Q. Mr. Howard, please introduce yourself.   **(Introduction)**

A. I'm William Howard. I'm an economist and I teach at the state university.

Q. You're a professor of economics there?

A. Yes.

Q. Professor Howard, did I ask you to do a study of the deceased, James Adams, to determine the economic loss to his wife, Shirley Adams, caused by his early death?

A. Yes, you did.

Q. Did you complete your study?

A. Yes.

Q. And you were compensated for the time you used to do the study?

A. Yes, I charged my usual rate, which is $150 per hour for the time necessary to determine the economic loss.

Q. How much have you charged for your study to date?

A. It's been 30 hours so far, which comes to $4,500.

Q. Are you prepared today to tell us the economic loss, in dollars, to Mrs. Adams, caused by the death of her husband?

A. Yes.

Q. Professor Howard, before we get to that loss, and what you did to determine it, let's learn about what you've done to become an expert in computing economic losses. You're an economist, right?   **(Qualifications)**

A. Yes.

Q. What does an economist do?

A. An economist is a person who studies the conditions and laws that control the production, distribution, and consumption of wealth.

Q. How did you become an economist?

A. I received my undergraduate degree in economics from the University of North Carolina in 1980, and my Ph.D. in eco-

The relationship between expert and lawyer is immediately and candidly established, including fees.

nomics from the University of Illinois in 1984.

Q. Tell us about your work experiences.

A. Since 1985 I've been a professor at the University of Georgia. I'm in the economics department, where I teach and do research.

Q. You're a full professor?

A. Yes, I was promoted to full professor in 1993.

Q. Professor Howard, what in your education and experience was most helpful in doing your study of the economic loss to Mrs. Adams for the death of her husband?

A. Probably two things. My teaching has focused on the cost of labor in the American economy, and the effects of inflation and taxes on real wages in the economy. My research and publications also focus on these areas.

This is a good question to ask, because it focuses on the pertinent parts of the expert's background.

Q. You've written articles and books that deal with the cost of labor and the effects of inflation and taxes on labor costs?

A. Yes.

Q. How many?

A. Well, I have one book, *Labor and Wages*, and I've had about 20 articles published which deal with labor costs in our economy in the post-World War II era.

Publications are important if they are actually relevant to what the expert did in *this* case.

Q. Professor Howard, have you ever been asked to study economic losses in personal injury and wrongful death cases?

A. Yes, probably about 25 times over the past ten years.

Q. Did you ever testify as an expert witness in court in any of those cases?

A. Yes, in about ten of them.

Experience as a court-room expert will be impressive.

Q. Were any of those cases a wrongful death case like this one?

A. About half involved situations where a person had been killed and I was asked to determine the economic loss to the surviving spouse or children.

Q. Professor Howard, let's turn now to what you were asked to do and how you did it. You determined the economic loss to Mrs. Adams caused by the death of her husband, correct?

Another transition question.

A. Yes.

Q. Exactly what does economic loss mean?

A. It means I determined all the economic benefits that Mrs. Adams would have received from her husband had he lived a normal lifetime, and determined what the present dollar value of those benefits is.

Q. How did you do that?

A. I had to do several basic studies. First, I had to determine what Mr. Adams' income during his expected working lifetime would have been if he had lived a normal period of time. Second, I had to determine what his fringe benefits were and determine the value of those benefits. Third, I had to learn what his personal consumption patterns were and determine the value of it. Fourth, I had to learn what his contribution to household work was and determine its value. Fifth, I had to determine the effect of inflation and taxes on these things. And finally, I had to determine what the present value, in dollars, was for all these things put together.

Q. These steps are outlined on this exhibit, Plaintiff's Exhibit #7, correct?

A. Yes.

Define key terms the expert needs to use.

A visual aid is essential to understanding what the expert did here. Put the exhibit near the witness so the jury can see both easily. This exhibit is not offered in evidence, but a later summary chart will be.

Study of Economic Loss to Shirley Adams

1. James Adams' lifetime income

2. James Adams' lifetime fringe benefits

3. James Adams' personal consumption

4. James Adams' contribution to household work

5. Effect of inflation and taxes

6. Present value of economic loss

PLAINTIFF'S EXHIBIT #7

Q. Let's examine what you did step by step. The first step was to determine Mr. Adams' lost income over his estimated work life, correct?

A. Yes.

Q. How did you do that?

A. I had Mr. Adams' employment records, statistics on the accounting industry from the Bureau of Labor Statistics, and my own experience in the industry. Mr. Adams was a 30-year-old accountant when he died. He had been working at his firm, Arthur Anderson, for eight years, so I had a work history on which to base my calculations. He began at $30,000 and earned $46,000 at his death, so he had been averaging raises of 6 percent per year, and had been regularly promoted by his company. In the accounting industry, accountants generally work until age 65. I used these figures, as well as my knowledge of wage trends in the accounting industry, to project what Mr. Adams' income would have been for the 35 years between his death and his expected retirement age. Since he was in good health, I felt that the expected retirement age in the industry would apply to him. I also assumed that he would have continued to receive salary increases in the future at the same rate that he had in the past eight years. These figures were also supported by the Bureau of Labor Statistics wage trends for the accounting industry.

The expert is put in the teacher mode, explaining what he did and why he did it.

Q. Were you able to determine how much money Mr. Adams would have earned as an accountant between age 30, when he died, and age 65, when he would have normally retired?

A. Yes.

Q. What is the total amount?

A. I determined that had he lived, Mr. Adams would have earned $3,800,000 between age 30 and age 65.

Q. Let's turn to the second item, fringe benefits. How did you determine what these were?

A. Mr. Adams' fringe benefits, such as health and life insurance, pension, retirement and plans, averaged 22 percent of his salary

You could have the expert put the key numbers on the diagram. Here, however, the later summary chart will list them.

during the eight years he worked at Arthur Anderson. That figure is consistent with the industry average, and is also consistent with Bureau of Labor Statistics data. Since I had already determined what his lost income would be, I took 22 percent of that figure to determine the value of the lost fringe benefits.

Q.   What did the value of the lost fringe benefits over those 35 years come to?

A.   The lost benefits totalled $836,000.

Q.   Let's turn to the third item, personal consumption. What does that mean?

A.   Personal consumption is that part of our income that we spend on ourselves. For example, we spend money on housing, clothes, food, entertainment, vacations, and similar personal things. Personal consumption for our purposes must be taken out of the economic loss computation, since what a deceased person would have spent on himself while alive would not be available to the survivor. Hence, I needed to determine what Mr. Adams's personal consumption habits were, as a percentage of his net income.

The expert explains another key term.

Q.   How did you do that?

A.   I checked two sources. First, I examined Mr. Adams' checking account history, since his paycheck and expenditures were all done through that account. Second, I looked at labor statistics that show average personal expenditures for various income groups, age groups, and family size.

Q.   What did these sources tell you?

A.   They were very consistent. The labor statistics are that for a person of Mr. Adams' income, age, and family situation, 75 percent of his net income would be personal expenditures. His actual spending history, as shown in his checking account, was very close, so I used a 75 percent figure of net income to determine personal consumption for the future 35 years.

Q.   Let's turn to the next item, the value of lost household work. You included that in your study, correct?

A.   Yes.

Q.   What is lost household work and how do you determine it?

A. Mr. Adams did work around the home, such as yard work and house painting, that has economic value. Mrs. Adams lost that when her husband died, so lost household work is an economic loss to her.

Q. How did you determine the value of Mr. Adams' lost household work?

A. I did two things. First, I determined how much work Mr. Adams regularly did around the house. This information came primarily from Mrs. Adams' deposition, where she described what her husband routinely did. Second, I used labor statistics, for this area, to determine the market cost of hiring someone to do the work that Mr. Adams used to do. In this way I determined the fair market value of Mr. Adams' household work on an annual basis.

Q. What was the value of his lost household work?

A. I determined it to be six hours a week, at $6.00 per hour, or $1,872 per year, for this present year.

Q. Professor Howard, did you take into consideration the effects of inflation and taxes in your calculations?

A. Yes.

Q. Let's discuss inflation first. Why did you take inflation into account?

A. Any calculation of future income and expenses must take inflation into account, because inflation has been a fact of life in this country for several decades, and we will continue to have inflation in the future. Inflation is simply a recognition that both incomes and cost of purchases go up over time. For example, if a loaf of bread this year costs $1.00, and next year costs $1.05, this represents an inflation rate of 5 percent for one year.

Q. How did you determine what rate of inflation you would apply to future income and expenses?

A. I looked at the inflation rates over the past 40 years. They have varied from as little as 2 percent a year, to as high as 13 percent per year. If you eliminate the extremes, the inflation rate has generally been between 2 percent and 4 percent, and the average

Jurisdictions may vary on the admissibility of inflation and taxes on economic loss calculations, so research is necessary here.

over the past 40 years has been 3.3 percent. Therefore, I used the inflation rate of 3.3 percent per year and applied it to determine future income and expenditures.

Q. Why did you take future taxes into account?

A. My task was to determine the economic loss to Mrs. Adams. Mr. Adams' income, like all of us, is taxed by the federal, state, and local governments. Since Mr. Adams only would have gotten after tax dollars in the future, the loss to Mrs. Adams of her husband's lost future income must also be reduced by the taxes that would have been paid had he actually been alive and earned it.

Q. How did you determine the tax rate to apply to Mr. Adams' lost future income?

A. Much the same as with inflation rates. No one knows for sure what the future will bring, and that includes the tax rate. I did the next best thing, and looked at the tax rates over the past 40 years to determine what they would likely be in the future.

Q. What tax rate did you determine was appropriate?

A. I determined that the average total tax rate for federal, state, and local taxes, for someone in Mr. Adams' income bracket, averaged 26 percent over the past 40 years, so I used that percentage to determine the effect of future taxes on Mr. Adams' income, had he lived.

Q. Professor Adams, let's talk about the last item, present value. What does the term *present value* mean?

A. My job was to determine what the future economic loss to Mrs. Adams is, and then determine what the present value of that loss is. Finding out the present value of money to be received in the future recognizes the fact that money received now is more valuable than the same amount received in the future, because we can earn interest on that money if we receive it now. Economists call this the time value of money. For example, if I am entitled to get $105 one year from now, and a safe investment rate is 5 percent, that $105 one year from now is worth the same as $100 now,

Reduction of future lost income to present value is an important but difficult concept. The expert needs to explain it in nontechnical terms.

since I can put it in the bank and earn 5 percent interest for the next year. Because of this, I had to calculate all the economic losses Mrs. Adams will experience in the future because her husband died, and then determine what amount of money, if put in a safe investment today, would generate enough interest and principal to cover those economic losses over the next 35 years.

Q. How did you decide what rate of return to use to determine present value?

A. Much the same way as I determined the inflation rate and tax rate, by looking into how things have been in the past and using it as a guide to what will probably happen in the future. I looked at the rate of return safe investments, such as treasury bills and certificates of deposits, have earned over the past 25 years.

Q. What did you determine as the appropriate rate of return to calculate present value?

A. I determined that a rate of 5 percent would be the most appropriate rate. This is what economists call the discount rate, which is the rate used to reduce future loss to its present value in today's dollars.

Q. Professor Howard, let's put all this information together. You prepared a diagram to show how you did your calculations in this case, correct?

A summary chart allows the expert to highlight and repeat his work in a visual way. This exhibit should be introduced in evidence, since it is your key exhibit on damages.

A. Yes.

Q. I'm showing you Plaintiff's Exhibit #6. Does this diagram accurately show the calculations you did to determine the present value of all future economic loss to Mrs. Adams caused by her husband's death?

A. Yes, it does.

Q. Your Honor, we offer Exhibit #6 in evidence.

Court: Any objections, counsel?

Opposing counsel: No, Your Honor.

Court: Very well, Plaintiff's Exhibit #6 is in evidence. Continue.

Q. Your Honor, may Professor Howard continue his testimony by the diagram?

Court: He may.

Q. Professor Howard, please step over to the diagram, and stand so all the jurors can see your diagram. (Witness does so.)

Place the exhibit before the jury. The expert can then become a teacher again.

Summary of Economic Loss to Shirley Adams

1. Lost future income $2,812,000

2. Lost future fringe benefits $836,000

3. Personal consumption   (minus) $2,109,000

4. Lost household work $112,000

5. Total losses in future $1,651,000

6. Present value of future losses $495,000

PLAINTIFF'S EXHIBIT #6

Q. The first item is lost future income. Explain to us how you reached that amount.

A. Sure. As I mentioned, I calculated what Mr. Adams' income over the next 35 years would have been. That came to $3,800,000. That figure takes into consideration inflation, since it's inflation that drives up wages. However, that figure does not take into consideration taxes, which I had determined to be 26 percent. Therefore, I had to reduce the $3,800,000 sum by 26 percent to determine the after-tax income that Mr. Adams would have received had he lived. This resulted in the amount of $2,812,000 (pointing).

Q. How did you calculate the second item?

A. The second item is lost future fringe benefits. I had calculated them to be 22 percent of gross wages, which results in lost future fringe benefits of $836,000, the figure here (pointing).

Q. The third item?

A. That's personal consumption. I had calculated that Mr. Adams would have personally consumed 75 percent of his after-tax income had he lived. This amounts to 75 percent of $2,812,000, or the sum of $2,109,000. That figure must be subtracted from the totals to reach an accurate figure for the actual economic loss to Mrs. Adams.

Q. The fourth item?

A. That's household work. I had calculated that the value of Mr. Adams' contribution to work around the house was $1,872 per year at present. I then had to apply my inflation rate of 3.3 percent over the next 35 years to determine the value of the lost household work over Mr. Adams' normal work lifetime. This figure came to $112,000 (pointing).

Q. The fifth item, total losses in future, how did you reach that?

A. That's simply the result of adding lost future income, lost future fringe benefits, and lost future household work, and subtracting personal consumption, which produces the figure of $1,651,000.

Q. Finally, Professor Howard, how did you determine the figure for the present value of the total future losses?

A. The question is: How much money do we need to invest now, at a safe interest rate, to make sure that Mrs. Adams receives the total of $1,651,000 over the next 35 years, after which the account will be totally expended? I used the investment rate of 5 percent to reduce, or discount, that figure to its present value, and reached the sum of $495,000. In other words, the sum of $495,000, invested today at 5 percent, will allow Mrs. Adams to draw from that account the total amount of $1,651,000 over the next 35 years.

Q. Professor Howard, will that sum, $495,000, adequately compensate Mrs. Adams for the economic losses she suffered as a result of the death of her husband, James Adams?

A nice ending, reminding the jury what the calculations cover, and what they don't.

A. For her economic losses, yes.

4. Engineer in products liability case

In the following case, an engineer, employed by the defendant manufacturer, testifies about the design of a motorcycle helmet in a products liability case. The plaintiff was injured when he fell off his motorcycle on his face, bending his head down and breaking his neck. Plaintiff's expert has already testified that the helmet was unreasonably dangerous because the brim was too long and made of a rigid material, and that this design caused the plaintiff's injury. The witness is testifying in the defense case.

Example:

Q. Good morning, Mr. Smith. You're the engineer who designed the Best Helmet that this case is all about?

A. That's right.

Q. What's your job at Best Helmets?

A. I'm the chief engineer in the design and safety division.

Q. Mr. Smith, we're going to talk about the design of the helmet and the factors you took into consideration in designing it in a few minutes. First, let's begin by learning a little about you. Where did you study to become an engineer?

A. I received my B.S. degree from M.I.T., the Massachusetts Institute of Technology, in 1980, and my M.S. in structural and mechanical engineering from Cal Tech in 1987.

Q. Are you a licensed engineer?

A. Yes, I've been licensed in this state since 1987.

Q. Tell us about the jobs you held before beginning work for Best Helmets.

A. I worked for Underwriters Laboratory for three years. That's the lab that tests consumer products for safety considerations. I then worked for three years for Bell Helmets, a large manufacturer of helmets, before moving to Best Helmets. I've been with Best since 1993.

Q. What kind of work did you do for Underwriters Lab?

A. I tested various consumer products, like appliances and sports equipment, for safety aspects. If the product passed the safety tests, the product would get the UL seal of approval that you commonly see on products.

Q. How many products did you test for safety at Underwriters Laboratory?

A. Between 200 and 300.

Q. What did you do for Bell Helmets?

A. I was in the testing division. We tested new helmet designs for safety aspects before they were put on the market.

Q. What kinds of helmets did you test?

A. All kinds. Helmets for motorcycles, bikes, football, baseball, and other recreation.

(Introduction)

This first question lets the jury immediately know the expert's role in the case.

(Qualifications)

Practical experience is important here, particularly experience doing work similar to what is involved in the case — product safety testing.

Q. How many did you test for safety?   Impressive numbers.
A. Around 100.
Q. Let's talk about your work at Best Helmets. You're the chief engineer in the design and safety division, right?
A. That's right.
Q. What does your work involve?
A. My division, which consists of me, about five other engineers, and a support staff, designs new helmets for the automotive, motorcycle, and bicycle markets. After designing them we test them for safety.
Q. How many different helmets does Best sell?
A. Right now about a dozen different models.
Q. How many motorcycle helmet models?
A. We have two motorcycle helmet models.
Q. Were you involved in the designing and testing of those helmets?
A. Yes.
Q. Mr. Smith, let's talk about the Best Helmet, the Model 202, that's involved here. How long has that helmet been on the market?
A. That helmet was first marketed four years ago. We spent about two years in the design and testing phase before that.
Q. How do you go about designing a helmet like the Model 202?
A. There are several steps. It begins after the   These steps show how
    marketing division has determined that   careful the manufac-
    there is an adequate market for a new hel-   turer was in designing
    met. My division then does the preliminary   and testing the helmet
    design work, which today is done largely by   for safety.
    computer modeling. After the design work
    we determine what materials will be used
    to manufacture it. We then build proto-
    types, that is, several actual helmets, which
    we test ourselves, and also submit to inde-
    pendent labs for additional testing. Only if
    the helmet passes these steps does it go
    into actual production.
Q. Are there any independent standards for   Meeting safety stan-
    safety that you follow?   dards is a key point.
A. In the motorcycle helmet area there are
    three sources for safety standards: the
    Federal Motor Vehicle Safety Standard 218,
    the American National Standards Institute
    290.1, and the Snell Memorial Foundation
    Standard. These are all standards for the
    helmet's impact resistance and ability to

absorb energy from an impact. We follow all three.

Q. Do the standards have anything to do with testing?

A. Yes. We test each helmet to make sure it exceeds the safety standard. Then we send each helmet to an independent lab to verify our results.

Q. These procedures you just mentioned — were they followed in the development of the Model 202?

A. Yes sir. Every one of them.

Q. Mr. Smith, what things do you have to consider during this development process?

A. Several things. The first one, of course, is safety. Everyone wants to make a helmet that is as safe as possible, but no helmet can protect the rider completely. What we do is design the helmet to reduce the possibility of serious injury to the rider's head.

Q. You said head. Isn't a helmet supposed to protect the rider's neck as well?

A. Not really. A helmet's function is to protect the head by reducing the likelihood of injuries such as skull fractures, concussions, and facial disfigurement in the event the rider falls. The design of the helmet, and the materials used in its manufacture, can substantially reduce the likelihood and severity of such injuries. No helmet can significantly protect the rider's neck, because the neck is flexible, and a helmet cannot keep the head from being twisted or bent.

Q. What other things do you consider?

A. The other two are appearance and cost. The helmet has to look attractive, or else no one will buy it. The helmet has to be cost effective, or no one will buy it either.

Q. Let's talk a moment about cost. Why should cost be a consideration, when safety is the principal concern?

A. If we design a helmet that costs $900, no one will buy it, no matter how great the safety features are. All the motorcycle helmets on the market are priced under $200, and most are in the $100 to $150 range. Therefore, every manufacturer of helmets, including us, tries to design the safest helmet possible within

This is a critical point.

This anticipates a likely point on cross-examination.

these cost requirements, which are imposed on us by the buyers.

Q. Let's talk now specifically about the Best Model 202. Tell us about the design.

A. The Best Model 202 is an open face design. Helmets today come in two basic models. The full face is completely enclosed, except for the oval opening for the eyes, which is covered by a removable piece of clear plastic. The open face is just that: open in the front.

Q. Does the full face give more protection to the face?

A. Yes.

Q. Why do you and other companies sell open face models if they give less protection to the face?

Another key point, again anticipating the cross-examination.

A. Some riders refuse to wear a full face model. They don't like how it feels, and it's hotter. In humid areas they can fog up. Some would not use a helmet at all if the only choice was a full face model. Wearing an open face model is vastly superior to not wearing a helmet at all, so every manufacturer in the market today offers both models.

Q. Mr. Smith, you brought a Model 202 to court with you, right?

A. Yes.

Q. I'm showing you Defendant's Exhibit #5, in evidence. That's the Model 202, right?

Visual aids are always a good idea.

A. That's right.

[Best Helmet Model No. 202]

DEFENDANT'S EXHIBIT #5

Q. That's identical to the helmet that the plaintiff wore?

A. Yes.

Q.   Describe for us the key features.

A.   Well, as I said, this is an open face helmet, as you can see. The outside is made of a single piece of molded fiberglass. The inside of the helmet has a suspension system made of nylon webbing and foam, which again is a standard design. It has a chin strap, like all helmets. Finally, it has a brim, three inches long, above the open face area (demonstrating).

The examination now focuses on the brim, that part of the helmet the lawsuit is based on.

Q.   Who decided on the shape and length of the brim?

A.   My design and safety division did.

Q.   From a safety point of view, what factors did you take into consideration in the design of the brim?

A.   The main purpose of the brim in open face helmets is to help protect the face in the event of a fall. If a rider falls on his face, serious disfiguring injuries can happen to the face, particularly to the eyes and nose. The brim also shades the eyes from the sun, but that's not its main function.

Q.   Why did you design it three inches long?

A.   The brim needs to be long enough to provide adequate protection to the rider's eyes and face in the event of a fall. On the other hand, it should not be so long that it acts as a lever on the head in the event of a fall on the face. We designed the brim so that it would be just long enough to provide significant protection to the face, yet not create a significant danger of the brim becoming a lever in a fall. Our tests showed that a brim three inches long accomplished this best.

Q.   Why did you design the brim out of rigid material?

A.   Again, that was a result of the same considerations. Only a rigid brim provides adequate protection to the eyes and face in the event of a fall on the face. We considered a flexible or removable brim, but rejected that design as inadequate after testing it.

This testimony directly rejects the plaintiff's claim.

Q.   Mr. Smith, based on your training as an engineer, your years in motorcycle design and testing field, and your years designing and testing the Best Helmet Model 202, have you come to an opinion on whether the design of this helmet is reasonably safe?

(Opinion)

Here the expert's opinion is asked in the traditional way.

A. Yes. In my opinion, based on what I know of the field generally and this helmet in particular, it's a reasonably safe design.

Q. Mr. Smith, you know that the plaintiff hired a Professor Johnson to evaluate your helmet?

A. Yes.

Q. You know he has different opinions?

A. Yes, I read his report and his deposition.

Q. Do you agree with his opinions?

A. No, I certainly don't.

Q. Let's find out why. Professor Johnson says two things. First, he says that the brim was too long. Do you agree with his opinion?

A. No.

Q. Why not?

A. A brim shorter than three inches would not adequately protect the rider's eyes and face. That's the type of injury that we need to protect against most, because it is both serious and common. There are studies on how frequently motorcycle riders receive different types of injuries when they fall. Those studies are well known in this industry, and every manufacturer, including Best, uses the information when designing the safety features of a helmet. The fact of the matter is that eye and face injuries are many times more common than neck injuries. The reality is also that a helmet primarily protects the head, and can't protect the neck. Putting these facts together, what we did is design the brim primarily to protect the eyes and face, and our brim does that very well.

Q. Do you know any company today that makes the brim less than three inches long?

A. No one does that.

Q. Professor Johnson also says that the brim should have been built out of a flexible material. Do you agree with his opinion?

A. No.

Q. Why not?

A. We tested various flexible brims when we were designing this helmet and rejected them. The problem with a flexible brim is that it doesn't provide adequate protection to the eyes and face, the most common

The witness confronts the plaintiff's expert head-on.

serious injury. We found from our tests that when the helmet is pushed face first into the ground, with the weight of the rider on it, the brim is bent down, exposing the face to serious scraping or even worse injuries. That was unacceptable. We'd never design an open face helmet with a flexible brim.

Q.   Mr. Smith, is there such a thing as a completely safe helmet?

A nice ending question and answer.

A.   No. Helmets are no different than cars. You can't design a car that can completely protect drivers against every possible injury. Motorcycle riders can always hurt themselves if they fall, and no helmet can prevent all injuries. What we can do is understand what helmets can and can't do, understand what the most common and most serious injuries are, and design a helmet that works best to reduce the most serious and most common injuries. That's what we did with the Best helmet.

5.   Accountant in commercial case

In the following case, an accountant testifies to the losses the plaintiff incurred when his business, a tavern, was closed following a fire. The case is a contract action brought against the plaintiff's insurance company.

Example:

(**Introduction**)

Q.   Ms. Johnson, please introduce yourself to our jurors.

A.   I'm Sharon Johnson. I'm an accountant, and I work for the accounting firm of PricewaterhouseCoopers in this city.

Q.   Ms. Johnson, you were retained by the plaintiff, Smith's Tavern, to do an accounting study, right?

The expert's role in the lawsuit is quickly established.

A.   Yes. Actually, my firm was, and I was selected to do the actual work.

Q.   What were you asked to do?

A.   About six months ago I was asked to determine the total amount of the loss to the business resulting from the fire.

Q.   Did you do that?

A.   Yes.

Q.   Were you able to calculate a dollar figure for that loss?

A. Yes.

Q. Ms. Johnson, before we get to that figure and how you calculated it, let's first learn a little about you. You're an accountant, right?

(Qualifications)

A. Yes.

Q. What does an accountant do?

A. An accountant is a person who has been trained in the principles and procedures of accounting. Accounting is a system of recording business and financial transactions in books, analyzing them for accuracy, and reporting the results to businesses and government agencies.

Q. How did you become an accountant?

A. I went to the state university and majored in accounting, and got my degree in 1985.

Q. Are you a certified public accountant?

A. Yes.

Q. What does it mean to be a C.P.A.?

A. A certified public accountant is an accountant who has taken and passed a national examination that tests your knowledge of accounting principles and procedures. The examination tests on accounting theory, practice, auditing, and commercial law. I passed the exam and was certified in 1981. It also means I am licensed by the State Board of Accountancy.

C.P.A. is an important credential.

Q. Tell us about your work experience since you became a C.P.A.

A. I started out with the Internal Revenue Service, doing audits of tax returns. Three years later I joined Pricewaterhouse-Coopers, which is a large, national accounting firm. I've done a variety of work for them, such as auditing the books and records of companies, preparing tax returns, reviewing financial reports to stockholders and government agencies. For the past five years I've been in the litigation support division.

Q. What does that division do?

A. We provide accounting expertise for parties involved in lawsuits. We might be doing anything from analyzing records in a criminal tax fraud case to determining and verifying business losses in a bankruptcy case.

Q. Have you ever been asked to determine the

economic loss to a business caused by a disaster such as a fire or flood?

A. Oh yes, I do that regularly.

Q. How many times have you done that?

A. I've done economic loss analyses about 150 times since I've been in the litigation support division.

Q. Have you ever testified in court as an expert in the field of accounting?

A. Yes, about 15 times.

Q. Have you ever testified in court as an expert on economic loss evaluation?

A. Yes, almost all the 15 times have been in that area.

Q. Your Honor, we tender Ms. Johnson as an expert in accounting and economic loss evaluation.

Court: Any objection?

Opposing lawyer: No, your Honor.

Court: Proceed.

Q. Ms. Johnson, you and your firm are being paid for your work in this case, correct?

A. Yes, under our standard agreement we bill for our time spent on the case at the rate of $100 per hour.

Q. How much time has it taken you to determine the loss to Smith's Tavern?

A. Approximately 30 hours to date. That includes preparing my report and testifying at my deposition.

Q. Let's turn now to what you were asked to do and how you did it. You were asked to determine the total loss to Smith's Tavern caused by the fire on June 1, 1999, correct?

A. That's right.

Q. How did you decide what a loss would be for the purposes of your study?

A. I was given a copy of the insurance policy on Smith's Tavern, which leased the building from the owner. It was a standard lease policy, covering the loss of any contents owned by the lessee, the tavern. In addition, it had a rider, that is, additional coverage, for business interruption, covering all economic losses to the business caused by the business interruption.

Q. Tell us what categories were included in your computation of the loss.

A. There were four basic areas: lost profits,

Bring out impressive numbers regarding directly relevant experience.

In some jurisdictions a witness must be tendered as an expert before the direct examination can continue.

The expert's fees are candidly brought out.

Another transition question.

The methodology is described and broken down into components.

lost inventory, lost furnishings and equipment, and interest on a bank loan.

Q. Why didn't you include lost wages to the employees?

A. The policy covered losses to the business itself, not its employees.

Q. What sources did you use to compute the loss in each of those four areas?

A. Fortunately, the books and records of Smith's Tavern were not kept there, so all were available. Specifically, I had the ledger books showing all income and expenses, checking account records, inventory records and invoices for the period between June 1, 1996, when the business started, and June 1, 1999, when the fire started. I also had copies of the deposition testimony of Mr. Smith, the owner of the tavern, and the fire marshall who inspected the building after the fire.

Q. Are these the kind of sources experts like you regularly use and rely upon in calculating economic losses to businesses?

A. Yes.

Q. Were these books and records adequate for you to make these calculations?

A. Yes. Smith's Tavern kept good records. They were more than adequate to make an accurate calculation of the total loss.

Q. Were your calculations done according to accepted accounting methods and procedures?

A. Yes, I used basic accounting methods for this job.

Q. You've prepared diagrams for each of these four categories, right?

A. Yes, I've summarized my calculations for each category on a separate diagram. I also made a summary chart showing the total loss.

Q. Ms. Johnson, let's turn to the first category, lost profits.

A. Okay.

Q. What is meant by the term *lost profits*?

A. Profits are what is left after you subtract expenses from income for a certain period of time. Income is simply the total sales of food and liquor. Expenses include the cost of food and liquor, employee wages, rent,

Since the expert's opinion is reliable only if the information used was complete and reliable, the sources must be developed.

Under FRE 703, the sources need not be in evidence for the expert to use them as the basis for the opinions, if they are of the type regularly relied on by such experts.

Here the expert has a visual aid for each step of her calculations.

utilities, insurance, advertising, and similar things.

Q.   Was Smith's Tavern profitable in 1999 before the fire?

A.   Oh yes. It was a very profitable business.

Q.   Using the first chart, Plaintiff's Exhibit #10, which I'm setting up on an easel so everyone can see it, please explain how you calculated the lost profits.

Lost Profits	
Lost profits 6/1/99–9/1/99	$37,000
Lost profits 9/1/99–11/1/99	$15,000
Total lost profits:	$52,000
PLAINTIFF'S EXHIBIT #10	

A.   Sure. Smith's Tavern has been in business since June 1, 1996, three years before the fire. It had an established record. The business was closed because of the fire between June 1, 1999, and September 1, 1999. First, I needed to determine what the lost profits were for that three-month period. I looked at the books and calculated the profits for the same three-month period in the previous year, 1998, which was $29,000. I then calculated the profits for the three months just before the fire, which was $35,000. Since Smith's Tavern has been increasing its business steadily since it opened, I took that increase into account. That increase was about $2,000 for each successive three months. That's how I reached this figure (pointing), $37,000, for the lost profits for the three months the business was closed.

Q.   Your diagram also shows another figure for lost profits. Explain what that figure is for and how you reached it.

A.   Sure. When Smith's Tavern reopened on September 1, 1999, it took two months for

The expert becomes a teacher.

If the expert is comfortable on her feet, have her leave the witness stand and continue her testimony standing by the exhibits.

business volume to return back to its level before the fire. I looked at the average monthly profits for the six months just before the fire, which was $10,500. Two months is $21,000. Instead, the business made just $6,000 profit during those first two months. Hence, it lost the sum of $15,000 in the two months after reopening, which it would have made if there had been no fire. That's a conservative figure, because it doesn't take into consideration the fact that business was steadily increasing.

Q. So the total for lost profits is?

A. This figure (pointing), $52,000, being the total of $37,000, for lost profits while closed, and $15,000, for lost profits after reopening.

Q. Ms. Johnson, let's turn to the second category, inventory losses. That's represented by this diagram, Plaintiff's Exhibit #11?

A. Yes.

Lost Inventory	
Inventory on 5/24/99	$20,000
Deliveries 5/24/99–6/1/99	$2,000
Sales 5/24/99–6/1/99	$3,000
Total inventory on 6/1/99:	$19,000
PLAINTIFF'S EXHIBIT #11	

Q. How did you calculate inventory losses?

A. Inventory is the liquor and food in the tavern that was destroyed by the fire. I started by looking at the inventory records, which showed the last inventory was taken one week before the fire, and showed $20,000 of liquor and food on the premises. That's this figure (pointing). I then added deliveries of liquor and food during that last week, which was $2,000 (pointing). Finally, I subtracted the cost of liquor and food sold that last week, which I estimated from the sales receipts, which came to $3,000. This produced a figure for inventory at the time of the fire, $19,000 (pointing).

Q. How did you estimate the cost of liquor and food from the sales receipts?

A. In the restaurant and tavern business the cost of food and liquor averages approximately one third of the menu price. Sales of food and liquor that week were $9,000, so the cost of the food and liquor used that week must have been approximately $3,000.

Q. The third category is lost furnishings and equipment. Again using the next diagram, Plaintiff's Exhibit #12, how did you calculate those losses?

Lost Furnishings & Equipment	
Purchase price 6/1/96	$189,000
Depreciation 6/1/96–6/1/99	$81,000
Fair market value of furnishings and equipment on 6/1/99	$108,000
PLAINTIFF'S EXHIBIT #12	

A. Smith's Tavern owned all the furnishings and equipment that were destroyed in the fire. I totalled all the invoices, and checked them against the canceled checks, for all these items that were bought new when the business was started up in 1996. The furnishings included tables, chairs, decorations, things like that. The equipment was primarily kitchen and bar equipment, such as stoves, freezers, refrigerators, dishwashers, and appliances. The total for the purchase price of all the furnishings and equipment was $189,000. That's up here on the diagram (pointing). However, the furnishings and equipment were three years old when they were destroyed by the fire, so I had to determine how much they were worth at the time of the fire.

Q. How did you do that?

A. I depreciated the furnishings and equipment to determine their fair market value at the time of the fire.

Q. What does the term *depreciate* mean?

An important term is explained.

A. Depreciation means that certain kinds of property, like cars, appliances, computers, and furniture, wear out and lose value over time. Some things depreciate faster than others.

Q. How did you decide how to depreciate the furnishings and equipment at Smith's Tavern?

A. There are accepted depreciation schedules and methods. For instance, furnishings and equipment are considered to have a seven-year life. That is, after seven years they are considered worn out and have little value. So in this case they had lost three of their seven years of value. I used what accountants call the straight line method of depreciation, which is just computing what three-sevenths of the original price was, and subtracting it from that price. That's shown by the figures on the diagram. The furnishings and equipment had lost $81,000 of their original value in three years. So the actual value of the furnishings and equipment at the time of the fire was $108,000 (pointing).

Q. Is that value the fair market value of the furnishings and equipment on June 1, 1999?

A. Yes. I used straight line depreciation because it will be a reasonably accurate reflection of actual fair market value at any point in time in the seven-year life of these furnishings and equipment.

Q. Let's turn to the last category, interest on a bank loan. Tell us about that category, again using the diagram, Plaintiff's Exhibit #13, to illustrate what you did.

```
┌─────────────────────────────────────────┐
│        Interest on Bank Loan             │
│                                          │
│ Principal borrowed on 8/1/99   $155,000  │
│                                          │
│ Interest rate: 10 percent per year       │
│           ($42.47 per day)               │
│                                          │
│ Interest paid 8/1/99 to date:   $21,000  │
│                                          │
│         PLAINTIFF'S EXHIBIT #13           │
└─────────────────────────────────────────┘
```

A. Smith's Tavern took out a loan on August 1, 1999, with the First National Bank. That loan was in the amount of $155,000 and was used to buy inventory, furnishings, and equipment to start up the business again when the building that was being leased for the tavern was repaired after the fire. That loan was necessary because the insurance company had not paid out on the policy by August 1, when the building became available. The interest on the loan is at 10 percent. Hence, the total amount of interest paid on the loan from August 1, 1999, to today's date is $23,000. Each additional day's interest after today is $42.47. Those figures are all here on the diagram (pointing).

Q. Ms. Smith, let's put all four of the loss categories together. You've prepared a final diagram that does that, correct?

A. Yes, that's Plaintiff's Exhibit #14.

The summary chart. Make sure it is large and attractive, since it highlights your damages case and is the exhibit you want the jury to focus on during deliberations.

```
┌─────────────────────────────────────────┐
│          Summary of Losses               │
│                                          │
│ Lost profits                    $52,000  │
│                                          │
│ Lost inventory                  $19,000  │
│                                          │
│ Lost furnishings & equipment   $108,000  │
│                                          │
│ Interest on loan to date        $23,000  │
│                                          │
│ Total losses to Smith's Tavern: $202,000 │
│                                          │
│         PLAINTIFF'S EXHIBIT #14           │
└─────────────────────────────────────────┘
```

Q. What does the diagram represent?
A. This last diagram simply shows the addition of the four categories. Lost profits are $52,000 (pointing). Lost inventory is $19,000 (pointing). Lost furnishings and equipment totalled $108,000 (pointing). Finally, the interest on the bank loan to date is $23,000. Add them up, and you get a total of $202,000.
Q. And that figure represents?
A. The total losses, to today's date, that Smith's Tavern suffered as a result of the fire on June 1, 1999.

6. Safety expert in slip and fall case

Not all experts are of the M.D. and Ph.D. variety. Under the federal rules, persons who have developed expertise through training and experience can also testify as experts in trials. In the following example, the manager of a fast-food restaurant testifies about safety procedures that should be followed when mopping floors during restaurant hours. The case is a negligence action brought after the plaintiff slipped and fell on the wet floor of the defendant's fast-food restaurant.

Example:

Q. Mr. Johnson, you're the manager of the Burger King restaurant here in town?   **(Introduction)**
A. That's right.
Q. How long have you been the manager?
A. Seven years.
Q. Where did you work before that?
A. I was a shift manager at a McDonald's for 3 years, and at a Denny's as a management trainee and assistant manager for 2 years. Before that I was in college, and I worked as a waiter and bus boy for several restaurants.
Q. Tell us about your college education.
A. I graduated from the state university with a B.A. degree, and majored in business administration.
Q. Mr. Johnson, since graduating from college, how many years have you worked in the restaurant industry?   **(Qualifications)**
A. All of them — 12 years now.
Q. During those years, have you learned safety procedures for mopping floors during restaurant hours?   Here the witness' expertise is from training and experience, not formal education.

A. Yes.

Q. Where did you learn them?

A. Everywhere I worked. I learned procedures for mopping floors in college when I worked as a bus boy, and at Denny's when I went through the management trainee program.

Q. Did that program involve safety training?

A. Sure — all kinds, including floor cleaning.

Q. How about at McDonald's and Burger King?

A. The same thing. They taught all their employees safety procedures, including cleaning floors.

Q. As a manager at Burger King, do you teach those safety procedures to your employees?

A. Always. That's the first thing we teach a new employee, and we always make sure they follow the procedures we teach them.

Q. Let's talk about the safety procedures for mopping floors during restaurant hours. What are the procedures for?

The focus moves to floor mopping.

A. Floors in busy restaurants like fast-food restaurants get dirty, so they need to be mopped regularly, at least every three or four hours. This means the floors need to be mopped while customers are on the premises. Therefore, you need safety procedures so that the floor mopping is done without putting any of the customers in danger.

Q. What's the danger to the customers?

A. The obvious one. A wet floor can be slippery. If customers slip they can seriously injure themselves.

Q. Mr. Johnson, tell us the safety procedures you've learned and follow, based on your 12 years in the restaurant industry.

A. Sure. The safety procedures involve two basic ideas. First, use only a damp, not wet mop. This makes sure that there are no puddles on the floor at any time, and gets the floor dry again in the least amount of time. Second, put large "Caution — Wet Floor" signs on the floor between the area being mopped and each entrance to the restaurant, and leave them there until the floor is completely dry again.

Q. Why caution signs at each entrance?

A. You need to warn each person entering the restaurant that the floor may be wet and to use caution. You need to warn them *before* they walk on the wet area. The only way to do that is to put a caution sign at every entrance.

Q. Is that the procedure at Burger King?

A. Yes.

Q. At McDonald's?

A. Yes.

Q. And at Denny's?

A. Yes.

Q. And at the other places you've worked?

A. Yes.

Q. Have you ever heard of a floor mopping procedure used that is different from the one you just described for us?

A. No.

Q. Mr. Johnson, in this case the evidence has shown that the defendant's restaurant had only one caution sign in the middle of the area being mopped when Mrs. Adams fell. Based on your knowledge of floor mopping safety procedures in the restaurant industry, was that a safe procedure?   **(Opinion)**

A. No.

Q. Why not?

A. With only one sign, a customer coming into   **(Basis for opinion)**
the restaurant from any of its entrances might not see the caution sign before reaching the wet floor. The proper safety procedure is to have a caution sign for each entrance, and put the sign between each entrance and the wet area. That just wasn't done here.

§8.6. *Cross-examination*

An expert witness is like any other witness — she can be cross-examined effectively if you use a sound approach and do the required preparation. The purpose is always the same: an effective cross-examination should be safe, yet should give the jury enough ammunition to question or reject the expert's opinions and reasons, and should create impressions about the expert that will carry into the jury room during deliberations.

1. Preparation

Cross-examining experts takes additional preparation. After all, the expert is usually an experienced witness and usually knows more about the subject than you will ever know. You are playing on the expert's field, with the expert's ball. Consequently, cross-examining such a witness requires more on your part. There are several things you should do when you receive notice of your opponent's testifying experts.

First, use your own expert to help you understand, and then attack, the expert's probable testimony. Your own expert should be your best teacher on the subject and your guide in what to expect from the expert you will cross-examine.

Second, read the literature in the field. Your expert can give you the basic references. Reading these treatises and other scholarly works will make you familiar with the subject; they are also sources of potential impeachment under FRE 803(18).

Third, obtain a copy of everything the expert has ever published. The expert's résumé, which you should have through discovery, is the place to start. The expert's deposition is another place to check. However, don't trust the résumé or deposition to be complete, since experts may omit publications they are now dissatisfied with, and Rule 26(a)(2) of the Federal Rules of Civil Procedure requires disclosure of publications only for the past ten years. Do an author check in the appropriate data bases in a local university's library to get a full list of the expert's publications. These publications may become impeachment at trial.

Fourth, learn where the expert has previously testified as an expert and obtain a copy of that testimony whenever possible. Under Rule 26(a)(2), the expert must disclose in writing all cases in which the expert has testified by deposition or at trial within the past four years. To check the disclosure for accuracy, and for older testimony, check with specialized groups. For example, the Association of Trial Lawyers of America (ATLA) and the Defense Research Institute (DRI), plaintiff's and defendant's personal injury associations, often compile data bases of experts for their members. This previous testimony may become impeachment at trial. Talk to the lawyers who have cross-examined the expert in the past.

Fifth, review the expert's résumé to pinpoint any weaknesses in the expert's education, training, and experience, and to determine if the expert's true area of expertise is other than the specific one involved in this case.

Finally, review the expert's written report, now required under Rule 26(a)(2) of the Federal Rules of Civil Procedure and Rule 16 of the Federal Rules of Criminal Procedure, and the expert's deposition transcript. These will tell you what her probable testimony at trial will be.

2.   Cross-examination approach

Effective cross-examination of an expert is no different than of any other witness: you must have a sound analytical approach to the witness so that you can determine whether to cross-examine and, if so, how to organize and execute the cross-examination to carry out realistically attainable goals. This approach, discussed in detail in Chapter VI, involves the following basic considerations.

a. Should you cross-examine? Not every witness needs to be cross-examined. If the expert has not hurt you, or if you have no effective points to make, or your own experts have been more persuasive, consider not cross-examining. The decision to cross-examine is discussed in §7.2.

b. How should the cross-examination be organized? All cross-examinations have two possible basic purposes: eliciting favorable testimony, and conducting a destructive cross. Eliciting favorable testimony ordinarily comes before a destructive cross. If the expert has substantially helped you by agreeing to helpful facts, consider not attempting a destructive cross at all, although you have destructive ammunition. How a cross-examination should be organized is discussed in §7.3.

c. Effective cross-examinations have a structure that starts strong, ends strong, and keeps it simple. They maintain control over the witness by asking simple, leading questions and stop when the point is made. These are discussed in §7.4.

d. What favorable information can you elicit? Did the witness say things on direct that you can have her repeat on cross? Can the witness admit facts not yet mentioned that support your case? What must the witness admit that helps you? What should the witness admit that helps? These are discussed in §§7.3-7.5.

e. What discrediting or destructive cross-examination can you do? Are the witness's perception, memory, or communication skills vulnerable? Can the witness be impeached? Can you expose the witness's bias, interest, or motive? Has she made prior inconsistent statements? Can the witness be impeached by a treatise? These are discussed in §§7.6 and 7.7.

3. Specific cross-examination techniques

A good approach to any cross-examination is to ask yourself: what will I say about this witness in closing arguments? Planning the cross-examination is then a matter of determining what facts you can realistically make the witness admit during cross-examination that support your planned closing argument. The following topics are the most frequently explored areas on cross-examination of experts.

a. Qualifications

Most cases that are tried will have opposing experts with different opinions and conclusions. The jury will invariably compare the opposing experts and make decisions on which expert to believe and why. Comparing the qualifications of the experts is one way the jury decides which expert to believe.

Expert qualifications involve two things: education and training, and actual hands-on experience relevant to the case on trial. A common cross-examination is to show less than the highest degree or certification in the field.

Example:

> Q. Ms. Johnson, you're a psychologist?
> A. Yes.
> Q. You have a master's degree in psychology?
> A. Yes.
> Q. But a master's degree is not the highest degree in your field, is it?
> A. No.
> Q. The highest level of accomplishment is the Ph.D. degree, right?
> A. Yes.
> Q. That's commonly called a doctorate degree, right?
> A. Yes.
> Q. That takes at least two or three years of additional study, doesn't it?
> A. It depends, but often takes that long.
> Q. Persons who hold a doctorate degree are allowed to be called doctor, right?
> A. Yes.
> Q. But you haven't achieved the doctorate level, have you?
> A. Well, I'm working toward it.
> Q. Ms. Johnson, you haven't reached it yet, have you?
> A. No.

Example:

> Q. Dr. Smith, you're a resident at Mercy Hospital?
> A. That's right.
> Q. You're in the fourth year of the residency program in orthopedics?
> A. Yes.
> Q. When you complete the program you'll be an expert in orthopedics, correct?
> A. Well, I like to think I already have expertise in my field.
> Q. Well, you're still training under recognized orthopedics experts in the residency program, aren't you?
> A. Yes.
> Q. Those experts, they're board-certified in orthopedics, correct?
> A. Yes.
> Q. That means they've taken and passed the examination given by the American Board of Orthopedics, correct?
> A. Yes.
> Q. You haven't taken that examination yet?
> A. Well, I'll be eligible to take it when I finish my residency.
> Q. You haven't taken that examination yet?
> A. Not yet.

Juries are usually impressed by hands-on experience, since that's how most of them become competent at their jobs. If the expert has impressive academic credentials, but doesn't have nearly the hands-on experience your expert has, cross-examination can often effectively point this out.

Example:

Q. Professor Henderson, you're a professor in the engineering college at the state university?
A. Yes.
Q. And you've been at the university, teaching and writing, since you received your doctorate degree?
A. That's right.
Q. Professor, this case involves the design of the front wheel suspension of a passenger car. Have you ever designed a front wheel suspension?
A. No.
Q. Have you ever designed any part for a car?
A. No.
Q. Have you ever worked in the automobile industry?
A. No.
Q. Have you ever been employed as a design engineer in any industry?
A. No.
Q. Have you ever designed any product that was actually put into production?
A. No.

Frequently an expert will have substantial expertise, but it won't be in the specific area involved in the lawsuit. An effective technique is to build up the expert's specialized area of interest, then point out that it doesn't apply to the specific area involved in the lawsuit.

Example:

Q. Dr. Andrews, you're a psychiatrist?
A. Yes.
Q. You work at the Madden Mental Center?
A. Yes.
Q. Most of the patients there are referred by the court system, right?
A. Not all, but most are.
Q. Those patients are mostly defendants in criminal cases, right?
A. Again, not all, but most are.
Q. And the court asks your center to determine if those defendants are legally insane, right?
A. That's a common request.
Q. In fact, most of your practice is concerned with determining whether those defendants are legally insane, right?
A. Yes.
Q. And the most common mental condition you deal with is schizophrenia, right?
A. Well, that's not the only one, but it is certainly a very common one.
Q. Dr. Andrews, you've specialized in the area of diagnosing and treating schizophrenia, right?

A.   Yes.

Q.   In fact, you've become a recognized expert in that area, haven't you?

A.   Well, I like to think I have, but you really should ask my colleagues.

Q.   And you've written extensively on schizophrenia?

A.   I've written some.

Q.   Over 20 published articles?

A.   Yes.

Q.   Dr. Andrews, the question today is whether Mrs. Thompson should be civilly committed because she is a danger to herself or others, right?

A.   That's right.

Q.   This is not a criminal case, is it?

A.   No.

Q.   No one asked you to determine if Mrs. Thompson is insane, did they?

A.   No.

Q.   And Mrs. Thompson does not suffer from schizophrenia, does she?

A.   No.

In some jurisdictions the cross-examiner is permitted to "voir dire the witness" on her qualifications. This means that if the cross-examiner wishes to challenge the expert's qualifications to testify as an expert witness, he can do a cross-examination, limited to the expert's qualifications, before the expert can continue the direct examination. Unless you have a solid reason to believe that you can keep the witness from being qualified as an expert, which is difficult under the federal and most state rules, this type of cross-examination is better saved for the regular cross-examination. This is because a voir dire on qualifications is usually followed by the court stating that "the witness may continue her testimony," which is tantamount to telling the jury that the judge believes the witness is qualified and that the judge didn't think much of your attempt to disqualify her.

b.   Bias and interest

A biased witness is a witness whose testimony is slanted for one side and against the other. A cross-examination that can demonstrate bias is a powerful tool because it taints the expert's entire testimony. The most common kind of bias is the expert who typically testifies exclusively or predominantly for plaintiffs or defendants. This information is easy to get because under Rule 26(a)(2) of the Federal Rules of Civil Procedure the expert must disclose in a required written report each time during the past four years that he testified by deposition or at trial.

Example:

Q.   Dr. Williams, you were asked to be a witness in this case by the defense?

A. Well, the defense asked me to consult on the case.

Q. Part of your job was to be a witness for the defense if the case went to trial, right?

A. I agreed to be a witness if necessary.

Q. And that was for the defense, right?

A. If the defense wanted to call me, yes.

Q. Dr. Williams, you weren't planning to be called as a witness by the plaintiff, were you?

A. No.

Q. In fact, you make it a habit of testifying as a defense witness, don't you?

A. I'm available as a witness to whoever wishes to retain me.

Q. Over the past four years, how many times have you testified by deposition or at trial?

A. I think its been about 12 times.

Q. Well, your written report says its been exactly 12 times, right?

A. Yes.

Q. And of those 12 times, you also know how many of those times you were called by the defense, don't you?

A. Yes.

Q. How many times?

A. Each time.

Q. Twelve out of 12 times you were called by the defense, right?

A. Yes.

Another way to demonstrate bias is to use the expert's previous publications. If the expert's article has an obvious slant, or appeared in a publication that represents a particular point of view, this can effectively be established.

Example:

Q. Dr. Baker, you say that the defendant, Mr. Williams, doesn't have any serious psychiatric conditions?

A. That's right.

Q. In fact, you claim that Mr. Williams is a malingerer, right?

A. Yes.

Q. And a malingerer is a person who either fakes or exaggerates symptoms?

A. That's basically right.

Q. Dr. Baker, you wrote an article called "The Malingerer and How to Expose Him," right?

A. Yes.

Q. In that article you said, on page 27, quote: "A doctor can, by careful questioning, get *most* patients to make statements that will support an evaluation of malingering." Did I read from your article accurately?

A. Yes.

Q. Your article appeared in a magazine called DRI?

A. Yes.

Q. DRI stands for Defense Research Institute?

A. Yes.

Q. That's the magazine for defense lawyers in the personal injury field, isn't it?

A. I think so.

Another frequently used technique is to show that the expert has a financial interest in being a witness and is willing to be a hired gun for anyone.

Q. Mr. Sullivan, you've retired from your old employer, the Ajax Construction Company?

A. Yes.

Q. Now you work solely as a construction engineer for your own consulting business?

A. Yes.

Q. You advertise your services?

A. Well, I have professional announcements in certain journals.

Q. And those announcements state that your services as an engineer are available?

A. Yes.

Q. To anyone who will pay your fee, right?

A. Yes.

Q. You advertise in ATLA?

A. Yes.

Q. That's the magazine for plaintiff's lawyers, right?

A. Yes.

Q. You advertise in DRI?

A. Yes.

Q. That the magazine for defense lawyers, right?

A. Yes.

Q. And you advertise in the Journal of the American Bar Association, right?

A. Yes.

Q. And that one goes out to all the lawyers?

A. It has a large circulation.

Another technique, but one that should be used sparingly, is to show how much money the expert makes being a witness. This approach, however, can just as easily be used against your expert as well. Therefore, make sure that your expert compares favorably on these points.

Example:

Q. Professor Silverman, you're a full-time professor at the state university?

A. Yes.

Q. You teach?

A. Yes.

Q. Do research?
A. Yes.
Q. And publish articles?
A. Yes.
Q. The university expects you to do those things?
A. Yes.
Q. The university considers yours to be a full-time job, right?
A. Yes.
Q. But you also hold yourself out as a consultant?
A. Yes.
Q. You earn extra money doing that?
A. Yes.
Q. Professor Silverman, what's your hourly rate?
A. In this case it's $200 per hour.
Q. Is that your usual rate?
A. Yes.
Q. And how many hours have you put into this case?
A. About 50 hours.
Q. So you've earned how much on this case?
A. Approximately $10,000.
Q. How many other cases are you presently consulting on?
A. I think it's about six or seven others.

c. *Data relied on*

The opinions and conclusions of experts are valid only if the data on which those opinions and conclusions are based are themselves accurate. It is not uncommon for the expert to have based her opinions solely or principally on data and information received from the client, and yet have made no effort to verify that data or information. If you can show that the data and information are inaccurate or incomplete, the expert's opinions and conclusions must fall as well. In short, you can take the "power" away from the expert by attacking the reliability of the data the expert relied on.

Example:

Q. Dr. Crane, you never saw the defendant before this crime was committed, did you?
A. No.
Q. Never treated him for any psychiatric condition?
A. No.
Q. You were brought in after he was arrested?
A. Yes.
Q. And after he was charged with murder?
A. Yes.
Q. And after he had been held in jail?
A. Yes.
Q. The basis for your psychiatric evaluation is the interviews you had with the defendant, right?
A. That and the police reports.

Q. The police reports contained statements from other witnesses, right?

A. Yes.

Q. Did you ever interview those witnesses to see if they had additional information about the defendant's state of mind at the time this crime was committed?

A. No, I relied on the police reports.

Q. The police reports also contained statements from the defendant, right?

A. Yes.

Q. But you interviewed the defendant to get additional information about his state of mind at the time of the crime, right?

A. Yes.

Q. And he gave you additional information about himself?

A. Yes.

Q. Dr. Crane, did you ever talk to the police or witnesses to check that the information the defendant was giving you was accurate?

A. No, I based my evaluation principally on my interviews and evaluation of the patient.

Q. Did you ever talk to his family, friends, or schools to verify the information he gave you?

A. No.

Q. And when you did these interviews he knew that you were hired to evaluate a possible insanity defense, right?

A. He knew I was there to clinically evaluate him.

Q. So if the defendant gave you false or exaggerated information, your opinions may be affected, right?

A. Well, it's possible, but a trained clinician can usually tell if the patient is lying.

Q. And if a patient is a good liar, you sometimes can't.

A. It's possible.

Q. Dr. Crane, the field of psychiatry has lots of case histories where patients have successfully misled their psychiatrists, isn't that true?

A. There are known instances of that happening.

Example:

Q. Professor Strong, you say this drug is reasonably safe, right?

A. Yes, that's my conclusion.

Q. The basis for your conclusion is the result of tests conducted by the manufacturer?

A. Yes.

Q. That's the same manufacturer that's the defendant in this case?

A. Yes.

Q. That's the same manufacturer who stood to profit if this drug was put on the market?

A. Well, I assume they hoped it would be profitable.

Q. Professor Strong, did you ever conduct your own tests to determine if this drug is reasonably safe to the public?

A. No.

> *Q.* Did you ever ask that this drug be tested by an independent laboratory?
>
> *A.* No.
>
> *Q.* So the data on which you base your opinion all came from the defendant, right?
>
> *A.* Well, from the company and the people who did the actual tests.
>
> *Q.* Those people who did the tests, they were all employees of the defendant, weren't they?
>
> *A.* Yes.
>
> *Q.* If those tests were improperly designed, that would affect your opinion, wouldn't it?
>
> *A.* It might.
>
> *Q.* If those tests were improperly conducted, that would affect your opinion, wouldn't it?
>
> *A.* It might.
>
> *Q.* If those tests were improperly analyzed, that would affect your opinion, wouldn't it?
>
> *A.* It might.
>
> *Q.* Your opinion is only as good as the tests on which your opinion is based, right?
>
> *A.* That's true.

Remember that the expert opinions are only as good as the data that the expert had access to. Hence, any time you can establish that the expert "didn't know" an important fact, or "didn't do" something important, his credibility is affected. This approach works well if the reason the expert didn't know or do something is that the lawyer retaining the expert didn't give the expert that fact, or didn't ask the expert to do that something. The expert will be more likely to blame the lawyer for shortcomings than himself.

This approach can sometimes be used to show that the expert relied solely on reports and exhibits provided by the lawyer conducting the direct examination, and never received or considered material from the other lawyers.

d. Assumptions

Experts make assumptions. If you can expose the assumption, the opinion becomes suspect. You can then ask the expert if her opinions would change if the assumptions were different. If the expert agrees, you can later argue that the other side's expert supports your side, since your side's assumptions are true. If the expert disagrees, you can later argue that the expert is biased and will never change her opinion regardless of the facts.

Example:

> *Q.* Dr. Wexler, your opinion is that the defendant had a psychotic episode at the time he killed his wife?
>
> *A.* Yes.

Q. You concluded that he was in what you called a dissociative state at the time of the killing?

A. Yes.

Q. You based this clinical opinion in large part on your interviews and examination of the defendant, right?

A. That was certainly an important part of it.

Q. When you interviewed the defendant, he claimed that he didn't remember the actual killing, right?

A. Yes.

Q. And you interviewed him how long after the killing?

A. It was about a month later.

Q. Your clinical opinion is based in part on the defendant's claim that he couldn't remember the killing?

A. Well, many things formed my evaluation of this patient.

Q. And the defendant's claim that he couldn't remember the killing was one of those things, right?

A. Yes.

Q. Doctor, a patient in a dissociative state shouldn't remember an event that happened while he was in that state, should he?

A. You wouldn't expect it.

Q. So this defendant's claim that he didn't remember the killing was a significant fact to you, wasn't it?

A. Yes.

Q. Doctor, if the true fact was that the defendant remembered the killing after he did it, would that change your opinion that he was in a dissociative state when he did the killing?

A. It might.

Q. Doctor, if the true fact was that the defendant told someone shortly after the killing that he had just killed his wife, that would change your opinion, right?

A. It might.

Sometimes you can get an expert to agree that the known facts are consistent with another explanation. In this situation you effectively convert the expert to your position in the case.

Example:

Q. Officer Woods, you took Mr. Johnson's breath sample at 11:00 P.M., right?

A. Yes.

Q. That's when you arrested him at his house?

A. Yes.

Q. The accident he was involved in happened at 10:00 P.M.?

A. That's my understanding.

Q. You say he was intoxicated at 11:00 P.M. in his home?

A. The test showed he was well over the legal intoxication level.

Q. At 11:00 P.M., right?

A. Right.

Q. You weren't with Mr. Johnson between 10:00 and 11:00 P.M., were you?

A. No.

Q. You don't know if he drank alcohol during that time, do you?

A. No.

Q. Officer Woods, if Mr. Johnson were alcohol free at 10:00 P.M., and had drunk alcohol after the accident, he could have produced the test results you got, right?

A. It's possible, but he would have had to drink a lot.

Q. But you can't say whether he did or he didn't, can you?

A. No.

e. Prior inconsistent statements

A fertile ground for expert cross-examination is impeachment with the expert's prior inconsistent statements. Through discovery you can learn what the expert has published and in which previous cases, if any, the expert has testified either by deposition or at trial. You can then get those publications and sometimes the expert's previous testimony transcripts. Through discovery you can also get the expert's written report in this case and depose the expert before trial. The result is that you can usually get solid information on both what the expert will say at trial and what the expert has said in the past. The past statements can then be used to impeach if the expert's trial testimony differs.

Impeachment with a prior inconsistent statement should use the same technique as for any witness. (See §7.7.) The technique is in three steps: commit, credit, and confront — then stop. Commit the witness to the direct examination testimony you want to attack. Credit, or build up, the reliability of the prior statement. Confront the witness by reading the statement, then stop.

The better technique is to read the impeaching section, then ask the witness if you read it accurately. Don't make the witness read the impeaching section. You will do a better job of reading, putting the proper emphasis on the key words.

Example:

Q. Dr. Schmidt, you say that Mr. Gable should be able to regain full range of motion in his elbow joint?

A. That's right.

Q. The fact that Mr. Gable has only limited range of motion is explained, you say, by his unwillingness to complete the therapy?

A. I believe that's the principal reason.

Q. You say that his elbow injury was not severe enough to account for the limited range of motion he now has?

A. That's right.

Q. Dr. Schmidt, you wrote an article in the Journal of Orthopedics, right?

A. Yes.

Q. Your article is called "Dislocations and Treatment"?

A. Yes.

Q. Your article appeared in the January, 1995 edition of the Journal of Orthopedics?

A. Yes.

Q. The Journal of Orthopedics, that's a reliable authority in the field, isn't it?

A. Yes.

Q. In fact, you subscribe to it?

A. Yes.

Q. You sometimes rely on it yourself?

A. Sometimes.

Q. That's because you know the journal checks its articles for accuracy before publishing them, right?

A. I think so.

Q. Doctor, you know they checked your article before accepting it for publication, didn't they?

A. Yes.

Q. Dr. Schmidt, I'm going to read a section from your article —page 47, counsel. Please follow along with me to make sure I read it right. Your article says: "The medical literature is replete with instances where relatively minor injuries to joints have resulted in painful and permanent loss of motion." Doctor, did I read from your article accurately?

A. Yes.

Consider using a blow-up of the impeaching section in court, which will make the impeachment visual and dramatic. Many courts will permit this, even though the impeaching section is not admissible as substantive evidence under FRE 801(d)(1)(A).

f. *Treatises*

The expert can also be impeached by treatises. FRE 803(18) requires that the treatise or periodical be established as a reliable authority, either during the cross-examination, through your own witness, or through judicial notice. The impeaching portion can then be read, although the treatise itself is not admitted as an exhibit. Using a treatise to impeach is a powerful technique since a treatise represents the collective wisdom of the particular field.

The technique is much like impeaching with a prior inconsistent statement: commit, credit, confront — then stop. Commit the witness to the direct examination testimony you want to attack. Credit, or build up, the reliability of the treatise. Confront the witness by reading the impeaching portion of the treatise, then stop. Use the treatise itself during the impeachment, since it will look impressive. You might have photocopies of the impeaching page to give the judge and opposing lawyer so they can follow along, and another copy for the clerk to include in the record, since the treatise itself is not usually admitted as an exhibit. In some jurisdictions you are allowed to use a blow-up of the impeaching section in court.

Where necessary, have the witness explain technical terms in the impeaching treatise before you read from it. This will prevent the witness from defining the terms after hearing the impeaching section, when the expert might twist the meaning of the terms to lessen the impact of the impeachment.

Example:

> Q. Dr. Alberts, several factors can affect the reliability of eyewitness testimony, right?
> A. Yes.
> Q. These include the length of time the eyewitness had to see the robber?
> A. Yes.
> Q. The anxiety level of the eyewitness?
> A. Yes.
> Q. The lighting and distance between the eyewitness and robber?
> A. Yes.
> Q. And the length of time between the robbery and the lineup?
> A. Yes.
> Q. Dr. Alberts, the race of the eyewitness and robber has an effect on reliability, doesn't it?
> A. It may.
> Q. In this case the eyewitness was Caucasian, and the robber was African-American. You know that, don't you?
> A. Yes, I was aware of that.
> Q. That's commonly called a cross-racial identification, isn't it?
> A. Yes.
> Q. If the eyewitness and subject are of different races, that is, a cross-racial identification, that can affect the reliability of the identification, right?
> A. It may have some effect.
> Q. In fact, Dr. Alberts, it has a significant effect, doesn't it?
> A. It has some effect, but I wouldn't characterize it as significant.
> Q. Dr. Alberts, you know the book written by Dr. Helen Lipton called "Eyewitness Identification"?
> A. I do.
> Q. In fact, Dr. Lipton is one of the most prominent persons in the field of eyewitness testimony?
> A. Yes.
> Q. And her book, "Eyewitness Identification," that's a reliable authority in your field?
> A. Yes.
> Q. In fact, you probably have a copy of her book, don't you?
> A. I do.
> Q. Dr. Alberts, I'm going to read from Dr. Lipton's book called "Eyewitness Identification." You follow along to make sure I read

it right. On page 136 it says, quote: "Research has repeatedly shown that cross-racial identifications are approximately three times less accurate than identifications made between members of the same race." Did I read that right?

A.   Yes.

The "did I read it right" question is the safer final question if the witness has been difficult to control. Another approach is to ask the expert "do you agree with the treatise?" Regardless of the answer, the witness is impeached. This final question may be more effective if the witness has fairly answered your previous questions. On redirect, the obvious rehabilitation questions — "Why do you disagree with the treatise?" or "Why did you use a procedure other than the one recommended by the treatise?" — will have less impact.

g.   Experts disagree

Frequently you will have little ammunition to reduce the effectiveness of the expert's testimony. In those situations the best you can realistically-achieve is to level the playing field. Show that the experts on both sides are essentially equal and, in effect, cancel themselves out. This puts the task of deciding who's right in the hands of the jury, where it really belongs any-way. In this way you empower the jury to decide the case without needing to directly decide which expert's testimony to accept and which one's to reject. This is always a useful approach whenever the other side's experts are either more impressive or more numerous.

Example:

Q.   Dr. Johnson, you doctors don't always agree on everything, do you?

A.   No.

Q.   Sometimes one doctor will have one opinion, and another doctor will have a different opinion?

A.   Yes.

Q.   You've seen that happen?

A.   Yes.

Q.   That's happened in your practice as well?

A.   Sometimes.

Q   In this case you know that Dr. Smith's opinion is different from yours?

A.   Yes, I'm aware of that.

Q.   Your opinion is that Ms. Williams' injuries prevent her from returning to work as a typist?

A.   That's right.

Q.   Dr. Smith feels that Ms. Williams, following surgery and therapy, should be able to return to work?

A.   That's her opinion.

Q.   Dr. Johnson, you know Dr. Smith, don't you?

A.   Yes.

Q. She's a colleague of yours?
A. Yes.
Q. She's a good doctor, isn't she?
A. I think so.
Q. You respect her as a colleague, don't you?
A. Yes.
Q. And you respect her professional opinions?
A. Yes.
Q. This is one of those cases where two experts disagree?
A. It is.
Q. Dr. Johnson, when two experts disagree, it's up to the jury to decide what to believe, isn't it?
A. Yes.
Q. That's why we have the jury system, isn't it?
A. Yes.
Q. And you don't have any problem with our system — the jury decides — do you?
A. No.

If your approach is to level the playing field for the experts, you can sometimes use the opposing expert to build up your own expert. This is a useful approach if your expert is younger and less experienced.

Q. Dr. Jones, you weren't the treating doctor, were you?
A. No.
Q. Dr. Adams was the treating doctor?
A. That's right.
Q. Dr. Adams treated Mr. Elliot's leg at the hospital?
A. Yes.
Q. And treated him after his discharge?
A. Yes.
Q. Dr. Jones, you became involved after that?
A. Yes.
Q. And that was at the request of the defense?
A. Yes.
Q. To evaluate Mr. Elliot's leg, you reviewed the hospital records?
A. Yes.
Q. And Dr. Adams' records?
A. Yes.
Q. Let's talk for a moment about what Dr. Adams did at the hospital and later on. Dr. Adams did a good job of setting Mr. Elliot's leg?
A. Yes.
Q. That was good medicine?
A. Yes.
Q. What Dr. Adams did, that's what you would have done if you had been the treating doctor?
A. I can't say I would have used exactly the same procedures as Dr. Adams, but she certainly did competent work.
Q. The therapy that Dr. Adams prescribed, that's a standard therapy program for the kind of injury Mr. Elliot had?

> A. Yes.
> Q. You would have prescribed the same kind of therapy if you had been the treating doctor?
> A. Yes.
> Q. Again, what Dr. Adams did, that's good medicine, isn't it?
> A. Yes.
> Q. You don't have any criticism of the medicine Dr. Adams practiced on Mr. Elliot, do you?
> A. No.

Effective cross-examinations of experts principally create general impressions about the experts in the mind of the jury, because frontal attacks on competent, prepared experts almost always fail, and obviously so. Instead, successful cross-examinations create the impressions that control which of the competing experts the jury accepts on key issues. One expert appears friendlier, more down-to-earth. Another appears defensive. Yet another one looks like a hired gun. And yet another appears argumentative. Whatever it is, the impressions experts make frequently control which side's experts the jury will ultimately embrace.

§8.7. Examples of cross-examination

Now put all these concepts together. Remember that the jury will not remember the details of your cross-examination, but they will keep impressions of the witness that were formed during your cross-examination. Keep the basic organization and structure of cross-examinations in mind. Start strong and end strong. Keep it simple. Use leading questions when it is important to do so. Remember that the cross-examination's purpose is to have the witness admit facts that will support the themes of your case that you will emphasize in your closing argument. Above all, don't argue with the expert or try to show how much you know about the subject. This usually turns off the jury and makes it side with the expert.

The following example of a cross-examination is of the same doctor whose direct examination is at the beginning of §8.5.

Example:

> Q. Dr. Klein, good morning.
> A. Good morning.
> Q. "Patient, heal thyself." You've heard that phrase?
> A. Of course.
> Q. That's a phrase all doctors learn in medical school?
> A. Yes.
> Q. Every patient has to take responsibility for his own recovery, doesn't he?
> A. Well, a patient needs to be motivated to get better.
> Q. Doctors can't make a patient get better by themselves, can they?

A.   No, it usually requires a patient's cooperation.

Q.   A well-motivated patient is often essential for a full recovery, isn't it?

A.   That's often true.

Q.   It's particularly true where the patient has to do therapy to achieve a full recovery?

A.   I think that's accurate.

Q.   Dr. Klein, let's talk about medicine. Mr. Gable was prescribed Tylenol No. 3 with codeine at the hospital?

A.   Yes.

Q.   He stopped taking it a few days later?

A.   Yes, he said he didn't like the way it made him feel.

Q.   Dr. Klein, the field of medicine has thousands of medications, doesn't it?

A.   Yes.

Q.   And probably dozens of pain killers?

A.   Yes.

Q.   In fact, doctors have a book called the Physician's Desk Reference which describes all those medications?

A.   Yes.

Q.   You have that book in your office?

A.   Yes.

Q.   If Mr. Gable had asked you for another pain killer, you could have prescribed one?

A.   Yes.

Q.   And if he didn't like how that one made him feel, you could have tried yet another one?

A.   Yes.

Q.   Until you found one that didn't have side effects that Mr. Gable didn't like?

A.   Probably.

Q.   But Mr. Gable never asked you to prescribe another pain killer for him, did he?

A.   No.

Q.   So he did the therapy without pain medication?

A.   Well, he told me he was taking over-the-counter medication.

Q.   But no prescription pain medication?

A.   No.

Q.   At any time?

A.   No.

Q.   Dr. Klein, let's talk about the therapy you prescribed for Mr. Gable. The therapy is designed to return full range of motion for the joint, right?

A.   Right.

Q.   That therapy consisted of soaking the elbow in hot water, letting the heat penetrate the joint, then stretching the arm back and forth.

A.   That's right.

Q.   Three or four times a day?

A.   Yes.

Q.   Until full range of motion returns.

A.   That's what we hope for.

Q.   Most patients with an injury like Mr. Gable's do regain full range of motion?

A.   Most, but not all.

Q.   In fact, 80 to 90 percent of patients regain full range of motion?

A.   That's what the medical literature shows.

Q.   Those patients who regain full range of motion — they do the therapy, don't they?

A.   Yes.

Q.   If they didn't do it, they couldn't expect to recover fully, could they?

A.   No.

Q.   Therapy is sometimes painful, isn't it?

A.   Yes.

Q.   The patient has to be able to handle the pain before he can do the therapy fully, right?

A.   Well, the pain cannot be so severe that it keeps the patient from doing the required therapy.

Q.   And doctor, the pain can be helped by pain killing medication?

A.   Yes, although no medication will completely block the pain.

Q.   But pain killers can help?

A.   Yes.

Q.   After a while Mr. Gable stopped doing the therapy?

A.   Yes.

Q.   He said it stopped getting better?

A.   Yes.

Q.   He said it hurt?

A.   Yes.

Q.   And during this entire time he never asked you for a single pain killer to help him do the therapy, did he?

A.   No.

Q.   Dr. Klein, you know that the other doctor, Dr. Bradsky, has a different opinion?

A.   Yes.

Q.   He says that, with proper pain medication and supervised therapy, Mr. Gable should be able to regain full range of motion in his arm.

A.   Yes, I've seen his report.

Q.   You know Dr. Bradsky, don't you?

A.   Yes.

Q.   You consider him a good doctor?

A.   Yes.

Q.   And you respect his opinion?

A.   I do, although I disagree with him here.

Q.   Of course. But Dr. Klein, medicine is the kind of field where two experts can disagree over something, isn't it?

A.   Yes.

Q.   And in that situation, it's up to the jury to decide?

A. I guess so.

Q. And you don't have any quarrel with that — letting the jury decide?

A. No.

The following example of a cross-examination is of the same economist whose direct examination is in §8.5.

Example:

Q. Professor Howard, economists make assumptions, don't they?

A. Well, in a sense.

Q. Let's talk about some of the assumptions you made in this case. You assumed that Mr. Adams would work as an accountant at Arthur Anderson until age 65, right?

A. I assumed he would work as an economist in the private sector, yes.

Q. You assumed that?

A. Yes.

Q. But you can't guarantee that he would have done that, can you?

A. No, not 100 percent.

Q. You assumed that Mr. Adams would have worked continuously until age 65, right?

A. Yes.

Q. You didn't take into account the possibility that he could be laid off or fired?

A. No, I thought he had a good track record at Arthur Anderson.

Q. Professor Howard, you can't guarantee that he would never be laid off or fired over 35 years, can you?

A. No.

Q. You can't guarantee that Arthur Anderson will exist as an accounting firm over the next 35 years, can you?

A. No.

Q. You also assumed that Mr. Adams would live another 45 years, right?

A. Yes, that's what his actuarial life expectancy is.

Q. But you can't guarantee that, can you?

A. No.

Q. You assumed that his spending habits, what you call his personal consumption rate, would remain the same over the next 35 years?

A. Yes.

Q. Professor Howard, you know that many people, as they get older, spend less and less on themselves, right?

A. That's sometimes true.

Q. That's well documented in the professional literature, isn't it?

A. The literature notes such a trend in some individuals.

Q. But you assumed Mr. Adams' personal consumption would never change over his lifetime?

A. That's what I assumed in this case, yes.

Q. You made some assumptions about inflation too, didn't you?

A. Yes.

Q. You assumed that inflation would average 3.3 percent over the next 35 years?

A. That's right.

Q. Of course, you don't know that for a fact, do you?

A. No, its my best projection of the likely inflation rate.

Q. You did that by looking at the past 40 years?

A. Yes.

Q. And you think that the future 35 years will be like the past 40 years?

A. Well, that's my best projection of what's likely to happen.

Q. Again, you can't guarantee that, can you?

A. Of course not.

Q. Taxes, Professor, you made the same kind of assumptions there, didn't you?

A. I did the same type of projection, yes.

Q. You assumed taxes would be the same in the future as they have averaged over the past 40 years?

A. Yes.

Q. You assumed that a safe investment rate for the next 35 years would be 5 percent, right?

A. Yes.

Q. Again, you can't guarantee these either, can you?

A. Guarantee, no.

Q. Professor Howard, you can't predict the future, can you?

A. Economists can make what we feel are reliable projections into the future.

Q. But you can't predict it with certainty?

A. No.

Q. You can't guarantee that your projections will actually happen, can you?

A. I expect them to be accurate, but I can't guarantee them.

Q. Because no one can predict the future, can they?

A. No.

§8.8. *Redirect examination*

The most effective redirect examination takes place during direct examination, by anticipating and covering the points the cross-examination is likely to make. This will make a redirect examination unnecessary. Anticipating and refuting on direct is usually more effective than refuting on redirect.

In real life, of course, you can't always anticipate everything, and it's the same with cross-examination. Hence, redirect examination is often necessary. The basics of redirect examination are the same for any witness. (See §5.14.) The witness can clarify things. The witness can answer "why" questions, such as explaining the reasons for an inconsistent statement.

The witness can put things in context. These are particularly important with experts, who can often be given a freer rein on redirect examination.

As always, prepare for the possibility of redirect examination with the witness. Let the witness know that you may need to redirect, depending on what the cross-examination does. Above all, the redirect must sound positive, not apologetic. Show the jury that the only reason there is any redirect at all is because the cross-examination distorted matters, or took them out of context, and an explanation is necessary for the jury to accurately understand the situation.

Example:

    Q. Dr. Johnson, on cross-examination the other lawyer read part of a treatise on obstetrics. You remember that?

    A. Of course.

    Q. The sentence that was read said: "If the infant is not breathing, a 3.5 millimeter endotracheal tube is recommended, in conjunction with bag ventilation, to ensure that the infant receives a proper supply of air." You remember that?

    A. Yes.

    Q. Dr. Johnson, do you agree with what the treatise says?

    A. As a general rule, yes.

    Q. But you didn't follow it in this case?

    A. No.

    Q. Why not?

    A. The treatise is dealing with the normal situation of a full-term infant. In that situation what the treatise says is good medical advice. In this case we were dealing with an infant that was premature by several weeks. Trying to put an endotracheal tube in such a premature infant is extremely dangerous. I would never do that in this situation, and I don't know of any obstetrician who would either.

Example:

    Q. Dr. Smith, your emergency room report says, as was pointed out by the other side, "Impression: fracture of the left tibia, distal third." Is that correct?

    A. Yes.

    Q. But the patient in fact had a comminuted fracture of the left fibula, right?

    A. Yes.

    Q. How did that happen?

    A. An impression on the emergency room report is just that: the doctor's impression from examining the patient. You don't begin treating the patient until you make a final diagnosis. That diagnosis is not made until X rays are taken and, if appropriate, lab tests are done. In this case, the X rays showed that the fracture was in the fibula, not the tibia. I then treated the patient in accordance with my final diagnosis.

IX

CLOSING ARGUMENTS

§9.1.   Introduction

Closing arguments are the chronological and psychological culmination of a jury trial. They are the last opportunity to communicate directly with the jury. For that reason, it is imperative that the arguments logically and forcefully present your side's theory of the case, themes and labels, position on the contested issues, and the reasons your party should get a favorable verdict.

As with all other phases of the trial, the arguments must be organized and planned in advance of trial. They should be constructed to parallel both your opening statement and your case in chief. This parallel construction can be achieved only where each phase of the trial is planned in advance as an integral part of the overall trial strategy. Preparing for closings after the evidence is in should then be limited to reviewing the specific evidence you will mention in your argument that supports your points, and deciding how, if you are the party with the burden of proof, you will divide the available material between your closing and rebuttal arguments.

This chapter will discuss organizing and delivering effective closing arguments and present illustrative closing arguments in representative civil and criminal cases.

§9.2.   Jury instructions and instructions conference

Before the closing arguments can begin, you must know the instructions the judge will give to the jurors because you should use those instructions during your closing argument. While the practice in most jurisdictions is for the judge to instruct the jury on the law immediately following the lawyers' closing arguments, some courts instruct the jury immediately before the closing arguments. In federal courts, Rule 51, Federal Rules of Civil Procedure, and Rule 30, Federal Rules of Criminal Procedure, govern the instruction process, but do so only in general terms. Hence, you must know when to draft requested instructions and submit them to the judge and other lawyers, how to draft instructions and verdict forms, and how to argue and preserve the record at the instructions conference.

1.   When to draft jury instructions and submit them to the judge

Jury instructions should be filed with the judge, and served on other parties, as part of the pretrial memorandum or before trial. In civil cases most jurisdictions require the parties to submit their requested jury instructions, and state any objections to the other side's instructions, as part of the pretrial memorandum. During the final pretrial conference the judge will rule on objections to the requested instructions. Many judges have standing orders in civil cases on how requested jury instructions should be prepared and submitted.

In criminal cases, and sometimes civil cases, judges usually want the requested jury instructions at, or a few days before, the beginning of the trial. In these cases the judge will usually rule on which instructions will be given at the instructions conference, which is most commonly held just before closing arguments. Even if the judge only wants the instructions at the beginning of the trial, prepare them well in advance. Doing this is critically important, and doing it properly takes time. On the eve of trial you should be preparing your key witnesses and polishing your planned opening statement, cross-examinations, and closing argument, not drafting jury instructions.

2.   How to draft jury instructions

There are several categories of instructions: general instructions, burdens of proof, elements and definitions of claims and defenses, measure of damages, and verdict forms. Your job is to draft each of them in a way that correctly states the law applicable to the case.

Many jurisdictions have approved "pattern" or "uniform" instructions for frequently tried cases, such as common criminal charges, and automobile negligence and contract cases. In these jurisdictions, preparing jury instructions is relatively easy. You simply select the appropriate instructions and reproduce them. Some jurisdictions have their pattern instructions available on computer so that printing the appropriate instructions is even easier.

The instructions are usually numbered, marked to reflect which side requested them, and cited to the sources of the instructions (except for an unmarked, or "clean set," for the judge). For example, plaintiff's first instruction might be marked "Plaintiff's Instruction #1; Pattern Jury Instruction #14." The judge then gets one set of marked and unmarked instructions from each party. Each party gets a marked set of the requested instructions from every other party. (The unmarked instructions are the actual instructions that will be given to the jury at the end of the trial, in those jurisdictions where the instructions are both read and given to the jury.)

If your jurisdiction has no applicable pattern jury instructions, you must draft them. The authority for the instructions is usually a statute, case law, or a pattern instruction adapted from another jurisdiction. Most judges again want an unmarked set as well as a marked set of instructions from each party. The marked instructions should again be numbered, show which side requested the instruction, and show the source of the instruction. For example, defendant's first instruction might be marked "Defendant's Instruction No. 1; Based on Arizona Revised Statutes Ch. 4, Sec. 13."

In recent years social science research has extensively studied the comprehensibility of jury instructions and has concluded that, because of their excessive use of legal terminology and complex grammar, many instructions either are not understood or are misunderstood by many jurors. The basic findings of this research are:

  a.   Use common words, not legalese, whenever possible.
  b.   Use simple sentences; avoid subordinate clauses.
  c.   Avoid double negatives.
  d.   Use the active voice.
  e.   Avoid abstract instructions; tailor instructions to case.
  f.   Avoid unnecessary instructions.

Hence, many jurisdictions have approved simpler pattern jury instructions in recent years. If in your jurisdiction lawyers still draft instructions, following these basic rules will improve jury understanding of the applicable law.

3.   How to draft verdict forms

There are two basic types of verdict forms, the general verdict and the special verdict (sometimes called a "special interrogatory"). Most jurisdictions use general verdicts. A general verdict simply asks the jury to announce which side won. The jurors sign the verdict form, which reflects their decision.

Examples:

(Choose one)
"We the jury find in favor of the plaintiff and against the defendant. We find plaintiff was damaged in the amount of $_____."
    or
"We the jury find in favor of the defendant and against the plaintiff."

(Choose one)
"We the jury find the defendant guilty of the crime of murder."
    or
"We the jury find the defendant not guilty of the crime of murder."

If there are multiple parties, the verdict forms must be modified accordingly.

The special verdict, which is sometimes used in civil cases, asks the jury to answer certain questions. In federal court special verdicts are discretionary with the judge. Several states also make special verdicts discretionary, and a few require them. Special verdicts usually require the jury to answer questions based on the elements of the claims and defenses in the case.

Example:

1. Did plaintiff prove that defendant was negligent?
    Yes____ No____
2. If your answer to question #1 was "yes," answer this question:
    Did plaintiff prove that defendant's negligence caused the accident?
    Yes____ No____
3. If your answer to question #2 was "yes," answer this question:
    What amount of money did plaintiff prove is necessary to compensate the plaintiff for her injuries?
    $_____

If given the choice, which type of verdict should you seek? The side expecting to win, and the side with a stronger emotional case, will usually prefer a general verdict. If, however, there are future plaintiffs, all of whom have separate cases against the same defendant, the first plaintiff will probably want (and the defendant should resist) special verdicts directed to defendant's conduct so that issue preclusion, formerly called collateral estoppel, may apply to the later cases. In a products liability case, for example, plaintiff may want a special verdict to ask "Is the defendant's product unreasonably dangerous?" If the jury answers "yes," later plaintiffs can argue that the defendant is precluded from relitigating this issue in a later trial.

Special verdicts are frequently favored by the defense, since defenses are often technical, and the defense usually looks for inconsistency in the verdicts. In addition, in multiple-party cases where the exposure of a particular party is relatively low, that party may want special verdicts directed to its role in the case.

4. How to argue and preserve the record at the instructions conference

The instructions conference, held to "settle instructions," decides on the wording of the instructions and whether they will be submitted to the jury. Instructions conferences are frequently held in the judge's chambers.

The judge will usually go over the requested instructions, first plaintiff's, then defendant's, one by one, and rule on any objections. While this is going on, make sure that a record is being made! The better practice is to have the court reporter present during the conference. In some jurisdictions, however, the court reporter is sometimes excused during the conference, and afterwards the judge and lawyers summarize what happened on the record. If the latter occurs, make sure that the court reporter takes down all your objections and reasons.

If claimed error occurs during the instructions conference, it is your duty to make sure that the trial record adequately shows that error. First, make sure your objections to instructions are specific. Most jurisdictions require that you state specific reasons why your instruction should be given and why your opponent's should not be. Second, make sure that the judge rules on all your proposed instructions. Most jurisdictions do not allow you to claim error based on the judge's failure to consider your instructions unless the record is clear that you submitted them, expressly asked the judge to rule on them, and obtained a ruling. Third, make sure that your instructions, which the judge denied, are submitted to the court clerk for inclusion in the trial record. (If your instructions were filed with the clerk before trial, they will be part of the trial record.) Most jurisdictions require that the denied instructions be physically preserved in the trial record for appeal.

Finally, learn your jurisdiction's waiver rules. Some require only that the record clearly show your objections at the instructions conference in order to raise error on appeal. Others require that you renew your objections before and after the instructions are read to the jury. Many require that you raise any claimed error in a motion for a new trial.

§9.3. Closing arguments from the jury's perspective

The instructions conference has just been completed, and the jurors have been brought back to the courtroom. The following ritual usually occurs next:

Judge: Are both sides ready?
Plaintiff's lawyer: Ready, your Honor.
Defendant's lawyer: Ready, your Honor.
Judge: Members of the jury, we are now going to hear the closing arguments of the lawyers. The closing arguments are the lawyers' opportunity to argue to you why you should return a verdict in their favor. The rules are as follows. Plaintiff argues first, then defendant. After the defendant is done, plaintiff gets to make a short rebuttal argument. In other words, because plaintiff has the burden of proof, plaintiff gets to argue first and last. Plaintiff, please proceed.

What are the jurors thinking and feeling at this point? First, they are tired. Sitting, listening, and watching a trial is tiring, physically and emotionally. Second, the jurors are informed. They have watched and listened and know the evidence that the two sides have presented. Third, they are opinionated. Despite the judge's instructions to keep an open mind, the jurors have naturally developed opinions and attitudes about the lawyers, parties, evidence, and who should probably win. Fourth, they know the time for them to decide is near, and they are anxious and worried about deciding the case correctly. Experienced lawyers understand what the jurors are thinking and feeling and use this knowledge to organize and deliver their closing arguments. They understand that a good closing argument not only persuades the undecided and uncertain jurors, but also provides ammunition to the favorable jurors so that they become stronger advocates on their behalf during the deliberations.

What does all this say about closing arguments? Effective closing arguments, from the jury's perspective, have several basic characteristics.

1. The first minute

The first minute or two of your closing argument should communicate three things to the jurors: your theme, why the jury should find in your favor, and your enthusiasm about your case.

Think back to the themes you first raised in your opening statement. (See §3.2.) Your themes — "cheating," "promises," "police brutality," "revenge," "greed," "pain," "responsibility," and so on — were the anchors around which you constructed your case. These need to be incorporated into your closing argument.

First impressions are lasting impressions. This was true in your opening statement and during your direct and cross-examinations of the witnesses; it will remain true during closing arguments. Hence, your first minute must grab the jurors in a way that will compel them to continue listening. Consider beginning on a strong note.

Example (plaintiff in personal injury):

One second. That's all it would have taken. One second, and none of us would be here. One second, but that defendant couldn't even spare that.

Example (defendant in personal injury):

Taking responsibility for your own actions. We said at the beginning that this was a case about someone refusing to take responsibility for his own actions, and now we know why, don't we?

Example (prosecution in criminal case):

Folks, that defendant killed, and he killed for one reason: revenge. The evidence has made that perfectly clear.

Example (defendant in criminal case):

Once again, an innocent man has been framed, and there's nothing funny about it. And it's got to stop now.

The traditional approach was to begin gradually, thanking the jury for its service to our system of justice and their attention to the case, and build from there. While some lawyers still adhere to this approach, it is rapidly declining, principally because lawyers now understand that the first minute of the closing argument is a critical time in which you should make important points and the jury decides whether you have anything interesting and useful to say. Use the opportunity.

2.   Argue!

Argument is not a summation. No one — certainly not the jury — wants to hear a flat recitation of what the witnesses said during the trial. The jurors heard and saw the evidence, and they neither want nor need to have it recited line by line.

Instead, a good argument *argues!* An argument takes your themes, your theory of the case, the supporting evidence, and the law and molds them into a persuasive whole. It is logic and emotion brought together. An effective argument makes the jurors want to do what you want and to feel good about it afterwards. The specific ingredients of effective closing arguments are discussed in the next section.

3.   Efficiency

Jurors have limited attention spans. At the end of the trial their attention span is, if anything, shorter because they are tired, have heard the evidence, and are opinionated. Hence, your closing argument must be efficient. Keep in mind that most persons can maintain a high level of attention for only 15 to 20 minutes. Therefore, your argument cannot overload the jury. Instead, it should focus on the themes, the key evidence, and the law, and it should strip away the peripheral information. Key ideas should be repeated, since repetition is so important for retention.

For the lawyer the message should be clear. Most closing arguments take about 20 to 40 minutes. Using more time is counterproductive: Jurors will be overwhelmed by details and will respond by shutting you out. Instead, it is more effective to use fewer, but key, details, stick with your most important points, and do this before the jury wants to tune you out.

§9.1.   Strategic considerations

Experienced trial lawyers know that effective closing arguments invariably have certain characteristics and techniques that largely account for the argument's effectiveness. These are discussed below.

1.   Use your themes and labels

Think back to your opening statement. You selected your themes and labels and wove them into your opening statement. The same thing should be done in your closing argument as well.

Example:

As the plaintiff in a personal injury case in which plaintiff's damages are primarily pain and suffering, your theme might be: *"The only companion Louise Burch has today is her pain."*

Example:

As the defendant in a criminal case, your theme might be: *"The real victim in this case is Bobby Smith. Bobby is the victim of an unreliable identification and a victim of a shoddy police investigation."*

Try to make your closing argument memorable. Jurors, like anyone else, remember things stated in a distinctive way. If the jurors adopt your theme, they become advocates for you during jury deliberations.

Example:

As the plaintiff in a personal injury case in which a major concern is comparative negligence, your theme might be: *"Mary Jones was where she had a right to be, doing what she had a right to do."*

Example:

As the defendant in a criminal case in which the principal issue is the defendant's state of mind, your theme might be: *The prosecution brought you lots of facts, but they didn't bring you the truth.*

Think back to your labels. Your "labels" were the terms you used to describe the parties, events, and other important things during the trial. Labels were important because they conveyed attitudes and messages. People were called "the plaintiff," "Ms. Johnson," or "Liz," depending on the message you wanted to send to the jury. A vehicle was called a "car" or a "fancy sports car," again depending on the messages you wanted to send. You need to keep the labels consistent, all the way through your closing argument.

2.   Argue your theory of the case

Previous chapters have repeatedly emphasized that you must develop a theory of the case in advance of trial and stick with it throughout the trial. Your closing arguments should present your theory of the case explicitly to the jury, and demonstrate why your theory most logically incorporates and explains both the contested and undisputed facts admitted at trial.

3.   Argue the facts and avoid personal opinions

We no longer live in an age where dazzling oratory consistently wins trials. Jurors are too well informed and perceptive to be easily spellbound. They usually follow the court's instructions and decide the case on the evidence. This means that today's jurors are persuaded by facts. The closing arguments that have staying power, that jurors remember during deliberations, are those that argue the facts.

Arguing facts involves more than a simple recitation of the testimony. It involves analysis. Juries decide cases on the basis of impressions — what they think the truth is — based on the way the parties have presented the evidence. Effective trial lawyers selectively pick and emphasize those parts of, and inferences from, the evidence that, when presented as an integrated whole, create an impression that convinces the jury that their side should win.

Refer to specific witnesses and their testimony when arguing the facts. A "fact" becomes a fact only when a jury accepts it as true. Hence, you must tell the jury why something is a true fact by reminding them what witness or witnesses said it, how it was said, and why it makes sense.

Example:

> *Keep in mind that the defendant was going 40 mph in a 30-mph zone. How do we know this? Well, both Mrs. Phillips and Mr. Jackson told us so. Remember where they were standing? Both were standing right on the corner and saw the defendant's car go by. They were in a perfect position to see how fast he was going. That's why we know he was going 40 mph.*

It is improper for a lawyer to directly state his personal beliefs and opinions about the credibility of witnesses or the quality of the evidence presented during the trial. Statements like "I think that" or "I believe that" are objectionable. These phrases are both improper and unpersuasive and are best eliminated entirely from your trial vocabulary.

4.   Use exhibits and visual aids

Successful courtroom techniques maximize the use of exhibits and other demonstrative aids. Chapter VI reviewed how to use exhibits in your case in chief. Do not forget these techniques now. Closing arguments should use at the appropriate places those exhibits admitted in evidence that corroborate and highlight the main points of your argument.

Exhibits do more than augment the closing arguments. They also provide refreshing breaks. Psychological studies have shown that the average person is able to devote his uninterrupted attention to one topic for only a few minutes. Accordingly, any argument that drones on for 5 or 10 minutes on any one point, regardless of how effective its content is, will lose the jury. Exhibits, in addition to their obvious value as a tool of persuasion, can provide that refreshing change of pace that recaptures the jury's attention.

Think broadly. Consider using not only the exhibits already formally admitted in evidence, but also visual aids such as flow charts, chronologies, check lists for key facts and arguments, and check lists for the elements of claims, damages, and defenses. By the end of the trial, jurors are looking for new and fresh ways of receiving evidence and arguments. While such visual aids will not go to the jury room during deliberations (since they are not formally "evidence"), they can have enormous influence during the closing arguments.

In closing arguments, however, exhibits are the same double-edged sword they are during witness examinations: They both attract and distract. Accordingly, keep the exhibits you intend to use during closings out of sight until you need them, and after showing them to the jury put them out of sight. Doing this will make the exhibits supplement your argument, rather than distract and detract from it.

Example:

Folks, the key document in the case, the one that tells us what the verdict has to be, is Defendant's Exhibit #7. That's the letter the plaintiff wrote before this dispute started, and before he had a reason to twist the facts. Let's take another look at it. [Lawyer puts exhibit on easel.] The key paragraph is right here [pointing], where he wrote: "I see no reason why this project cannot be completed by or before June 1, 2000." So there's the proof, right before your eyes.

5. Use instructions

Closing arguments that selectively utilize instructions have a greater impact on the jury. By suggesting that the court's instructions of law as well as the facts support your side, a doubly effective argument can be fashioned. If, for example, you are arguing that a witness should not be believed because he was impeached, tell the jury that the court will instruct them that a prior inconsistent statement can properly be considered in determining a witness' credibility. Argue your facts, then argue that the law permits or even approves your interpretation of those facts. The key to utilizing this technique is to follow your factual argument immediately with the corresponding instruction so that the association is firmly fixed in the jury's mind.

How the jury is actually instructed and how the lawyers can use the instructions vary widely. Some judges only read the instructions; others both read and give them to the jury. Some judges require that lawyers quote verbatim from any instructions they use, while other judges disapprove of direct quotes and require that instructions be paraphrased. Learn what your judge's practices are.

Instructions frequently woven into the closing arguments include those covering the elements of claims and defenses, measure of damages, burdens of proof, credibility of witnesses, and definitions of critical legal terms.

Example:

As the defendant in a criminal case, you might argue: *"The prosecution wants you to believe the testimony of their star witness, who's a snitch who cut a deal with those prosecutors to save his own skin. Trouble is, you can't trust that kind of person. And its not just me saying that. Take a look at the instruction his Honor will give you. [Lawyer puts blowup of jury instruction on easel.] It says right here 'You should consider the testimony of a witness testifying in exchange for immunity with more caution than the testimony of other witnesses, since he may have had reason to make up stories or exaggerate what others did because he wanted to strike a good bargain with the government about his own case.' Doesn't that fit this case perfectly?"*

Sometimes you will want to build up the usefulness or significance of an instruction, so that the jury will pay particular attention to it.

Example:

Folks, in this situation the law does a wonderful thing. The law says . . .

Example:

So you're probably asking: what should we do? Once again, we look to the law for guidance.

6.   Use rhetorical questions

Since in most jurisdictions the jury cannot ask questions during the trial, having unanswered questions can be a very frustrating experience. Experienced lawyers recognize this and try to anticipate those questions the jurors would probably ask if they could.

Example:

As plaintiff in a personal injury case, you might argue: "*You're probably saying to yourself: Mr. Jones, that's a lot of money you're asking for. Why should we award him $300,000? You're right, of course. That is a substantial sum of money. But in this case Jane Smith's injuries have been devastating.*" Then argue that the amount requested is the bare minimum necessary to adequately compensate the plaintiff for his injuries.

Rhetorical questions can also be used effectively to challenge your opponent with difficult or unanswerable questions. If he fails to answer these questions, the jury will undoubtedly remember it.

Example:

As the prosecutor in a criminal case, you might argue: "*In this case, the evidence showed that the defendant just happened to be one block from where the robbery occurred moments earlier, just happened to have a nickel-plated revolver on him, just happened to have $47 in his pocket, and just happened to be wearing a red velour shirt. If he's so innocent, I'm sure his lawyer will have a great explanation for how all these things just happened at the same time when he argues to you.*"

Example:

As plaintiff in a personal injury case, you might argue: *"Why didn't the defendant just keep his foot on the brake until the light changed? It was only two more seconds. Why didn't he wait just two seconds? That's the question they never want asked, and it's the question they can't answer."*

Example:

As defendant in a criminal case, you might argue: *"Where are the fingerprints? If Bobby was really the burglar, really ransacked that house, as they claim, wouldn't you expect to find his fingerprints all over the place? Or at least on something? Where are the fingerprints?"*

7.   Use analogies and stories

Analogies and stories, if short and pertinent, can be effective in defining and crystalizing an idea in the jury's mind. They must be short, because the time for arguing is limited, and pertinent, because a story told for its own sake, without making a point, is counterproductive. Analogies tie the evidence to the jurors' own experiences in life.

Example:

In a criminal case where the prosecution has had to call an unsavory witness, you might make the following argument: *"If you find a maggot in your food, you throw it all away. The prosecution here wants you to ignore the maggot and eat the rest of the plate anyway."*

Example:

If your case involves largely circumstantial evidence, you might make the following argument: *"Imagine you're at home just before going to bed. It's clear outside. The next morning you wake up, look outside, and see that the lawn is covered with snow. You didn't actually see the snow fall, but there's no doubt that it snowed that night."*

In both cases you can use the analogy or story to make a point and then continue by showing the jury why it has significance in this case.

8.   Argue strengths

Argue your strengths, not just your opponent's weaknesses. Successful arguments are those that have a positive approach and concentrate on the evidence produced at trial that affirmatively demonstrates your party should prevail. Jurors soon realize that arguing extensively your opponent's weaknesses occurs only when you have little good to say about your own case. Negative arguments often create negative impressions. This is particularly important for the prosecution in a criminal case because of the prosecution's high burden of proof.

9.   Deal candidly with weaknesses

While your closing argument should positively argue your strengths, this does not mean that you should entirely avoid weaknesses. Every trial will have some weaknesses. If it did not, the case would have been settled before trial.

Confronting weaknesses has two advantages. First, your weaknesses are your opponent's strengths. By addressing them first, you can in part deflate his later argument so that the jury does not hear those points for the first time from your opponent, the way he wants them argued. Take the wind out of his sails by raising his points first, and they will sound hollow and tired when he argues them. Second, the jury will respect your honesty and candor when openly and candidly discussing those weaknesses. Since your credibility as an advocate is critically important, this consideration should not be downplayed. Remember that jurors, like everyone else, are influenced by whom they like. Make sure that's you and your party.

Example:

Folks, I have a problem here. I've been talking about Bobby's testimony, and why it makes sense to believe what he told us. But some of you might say: "If what he says now is true, then why did he tell the police that he wasn't even there?" That's a good question, and to answer it we need to get into the head of a sixteen-year-old kid and learn why he would deny knowing anything when the police first talked to him.

Closing argument is the time to solve problems, not ignore them. This is time to deal openly with the jury's concerns about the case, and discuss them candidly.

10.   Force your opponent to argue his weaknesses

For the same reasons that you want to concentrate on your strengths, force your opponent to argue his weaknesses. A common method is to ask rhetorical questions during your argument that challenge your opponent to explain his weaknesses.

Example:

If, as the defense has been claiming all along, the collision happened the way the defendant said it did, why isn't there any corroboration? Wouldn't you expect that of all the people who witnessed the collision, they could find one person who

would back them up? I'm sure Mr. Smith, when he argues, will answer this ques-
tion that we've all been asking and wondering about.

When it is your opponent's turn to argue, he may take the bait and attempt to answer the question, thereby arguing a weakness and creating a
negative impression. A few well-selected questions can often produce this
desired effect. However, be careful — make sure your opponent doesn't
have an obvious, effective response.

11.   How do you deliver your closing argument?

How should you deliver your closing argument? The simple answer is: in
whatever way persuades the jurors to decide in your favor. What things are
the jurors looking for?
     First, the jurors are looking for conviction. They are looking to see
which lawyer *really believes* his side should win, as contrasted with the lawyer
who is merely making a closing argument because it's expected. Therefore, your most important concern is to present your closing argument in
a way that demonstrates your total conviction in your case and your un-
wavering commitment to your side. The delivery style that accomplishes
this is as varied as trial lawyers are numerous. Some are emotional and pas-
sionate, others quietly compelling. However you do it, one thing is clear:
The jury must feel that you firmly believe in your case.
     Aside from projecting conviction, there are several things you need to
consider that will improve the persuasiveness of any argument. First, unless restricted to a lectern, closing arguments are usually made directly in
front of the jury box, approximately halfway from either end. You should
stand close enough to maintain eye contact with each of the jurors, yet not
so close that they feel uncomfortable. You should ordinarily stay several
feet from the first row of jurors, so that those wearing bifocal glasses have
no difficulty seeing you, moving closer only when necessary to show exhibits to them. Many courtrooms have lecterns, and some judges require
you to make your arguments from the lectern. If you wish, or are required,
to use it, make sure that the judge will allow you to move it to the location
you want. However, don't use the lectern unless required, because it places
a barrier between you and the jury.

Example:

     In the schematic diagram shown on the next page, you would nor-
mally make your closing arguments near the area marked "X."

Presenting an effective closing argument involves both a physical and verbal style. They must be harmoniously combined to continuously project
the belief that your side, based on the evidence, is entitled to win.
     Your physical, or nonverbal, style must support your verbal presenta-
tion. First, maintain periodic eye contact with each juror, but neither single out any one juror nor ignore others. This is most effectively done by
directing an idea, in one or two sentences, to a specific juror, then direct-

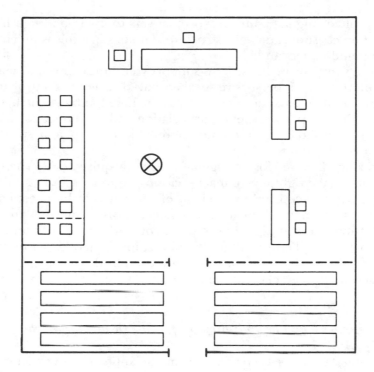

ing your next point to another juror. Maintain eye contact with the juror you are talking to. Doing this will make each juror feel that you are individually talking to him.

Second, control your body movement so it reinforces your speech. Stand straight, with your feet planted firmly, and lean forward slightly. This stance is positive and authoritative. Avoid wandering around constantly, since this merely serves as a distraction. However, changing your position from time to time can effectively signal that you have completed one topic and are moving to another.

Third, use gestures that reinforce your points. Such gestures are those that draw jurors' attention to your face, since this is where the words are coming from. Accordingly, the gestures must be from the upper body, which include facial expressions, head and shoulder movement, and hand gestures that are above waist level. Avoid tapping feet, moving legs, slouching, playing with objects in your pockets, or using your hands while they are down at your sides, since these are all lower-body movements that distract jurors from concentrating on your speech.

Your verbal style must also be appropriate for persuasive speech. A closing argument is not an opening statement, which is basically informational speech. A closing argument must be forceful. A safe approach is to view a closing argument as a discussion with the jury, in the same manner you would present your views on an important issue to a gathering of neighbors at someone's house.

Use plain, forceful, and active language, avoiding either slang or formal, stilted language. Jurors expect lawyers to use good English. Keep your sentences short and your structure simple, since this is much easier to follow and understand.

Also, vary your verbal style to support your arguments and maintain juror interest. Good, persuasive speakers have learned to control and use the variables that make up speech. These include loudness, pitch, speech rate and rhythm, pauses, silence, articulation and pronunciation. Each of these can and should be used and modulated to keep your speech patterns forceful and interesting.

Making effective closing arguments is an acquired skill. There is no such thing as the right way to make a closing argument. Every trial lawyer through experience learns what kind of presentation he is comfortable with, that seems natural for his personality and style, and that appears to work for him. Accordingly, do not try to copy or imitate another lawyer's style. That style will only work for him. Learning from others is important, but always adapt what you learn to your own individual style. Only the delivery style that you feel comfortable with will be effective with a jury.

§9.5.   *Contents and organization of effective closing arguments*

In opening statements, lawyers use a common approach — engaging, forceful storytelling — to introduce the jury to the case. In closing arguments, however, lawyers use numerous approaches, styles, and techniques to convince the jury to return a favorable verdict. The ways are limited only by lawyers' imaginations, and good trial lawyers are imaginative and creative.

Nevertheless, effective closing arguments almost invariably contain several components that are modified to meet the needs of a particular case. Except for the introduction and conclusion, trial lawyers commonly vary the order in which these components will be used during the closing argument. These include the following:

1.   introduction
2.   issues
3.   what really happened and proof
4.   basis of liability/nonliability or guilt/innocence
5.   damages (in civil cases)
6.   instructions
7.   refuting the other side
8.   conclusion

1.   Introduction

Most trial lawyers today avoid the traditional introductory comments — thanking the jurors for their attention, or acknowledging how their lives have been disrupted by serving as jurors — and get immediately to the argument. This is because the modern approach recognizes the reality of the jurors' minds at this stage of trial: Jurors are tired, have heard the evidence, and are opinionated. Jurors want to hear what you want, and why your are entitled to what you want. They want to hear it clearly, efficiently, and in a way that captures and holds their attention. Hence, effective introductions today get immediately to the point, putting an important theme or fact immediately before the jurors. The traditional beginning — "May it please the court, counsel, members of the jury" — is still used in some places, but has been abandoned in others.

Example (plaintiff — civil):

    May it please the court, counsel, members of the jury. On June 15, 2000, Joan Carter's young life ended when that defendant, drunk and speeding, ran a red light, crashed into her car, and crushed the life out of her body. Her husband, and her children, are here today asking that you do her, and her family, justice.

Example (defendant — civil):

    This is a case about failing to take responsibility, and about a person — the plaintiff — who wants to be rewarded for failing to follow his doctor's orders.

Example (plaintiff — criminal):

    Being attacked in your own home is everyone's worst nightmare. Fortunately, it's only a nightmare for most of us. For Bob Martin, old, sick, and alone, it was a nightmare that became a reality during the evening of June 1, 2000.

Example (defendant — criminal):

    This case is about a tragedy. That's because when the police fail to do their job, when they fail to do a thorough investigation, when they take shortcuts, the wrong person can stand accused of a crime he didn't commit. That's a tragedy, and it's a tragedy that started for Bobby Abrams at 8:00 that August night.

    These kinds of introductions grab the jurors' attention, telling them that what you are about to say will be exciting and worth hearing. They say: Stay tuned, there's more coming. Accordingly, the quick, forceful introduction is becoming the standard way in which effective trial lawyers begin their closing arguments.

2. Issues

Somewhere, usually just before or just after dealing with the facts, you should state the issue in the case. You should state it in a way that the answer should be obvious, and then answer it anyway.

Example (plaintiff — civil):

    Folks, there's only one issue in this case. It's simply this: Was that defendant negligent when he drove his car and crashed into Mr. Smith's car? The answer is obvious: That defendant was negligent, that defendant was the only one who was negligent, and that defendant's negligence was the only cause of Mr. Smith's injuries.

Example (defendant — civil):

Plaintiff claims the only issue is whether the state was negligent in designing the curve in the road. That's not really the issue here. The real issue, the only real question you need to decide is: Did that plaintiff cause his own injuries? The evidence shows that the plaintiff was negligent because he was simply driving too fast, and that he injured himself through his own fault.

Example (plaintiff — criminal):

What's this case all about? It's simple: did that defendant intentionally, and without provocation from anyone, shoot and kill Bobby Jackson? The answer: of course! That defendant did precisely that, and that's why he's guilty of murder.

Example (defendant — criminal):

The prosecution would like you to believe that the only issue is whether Frank shot and killed Jackson. But that's not the issue here. There's not even a dispute over whether that happened. The real issue is: Did the prosecution disprove, beyond a reasonable doubt, that Frank was not entitled to defend himself against Jackson's assault? They haven't been able to disprove this, because it's simply true. It's perfectly clear here that Frank shot and killed Jackson because Jackson was about to attack him with a knife. That's not a crime. That's justified self-defense.

After stating the issue, you can then easily continue into your discussion of the facts in the case.

3.   What really happened and proof

Most trials are ultimately a contest to determine whose version of a disputed event or transaction is more likely true. Which side's version of reality will the jury accept as true? Inexperienced trial lawyers frequently make two interrelated mistakes: They spend too much time reviewing undisputed facts, and too little time arguing why the jury should accept *their* version of the key disputed facts. Hence, you need to focus on the key things: What are the key factual disputes in the case? How can I get the jury to accept my version? Once you have focused on the critical facts, you need to *argue* that you have more, or more credible, evidence so that the jury must resolve the dispute in your favor.

The key disputes in a trial usually involve one or more of three kinds of controlling issues. First, the issue may focus on the elements of required proof or the burden of proof. The question then becomes, what has been proven? Second, the issue may focus on inferences to be drawn from the evidence. The question then becomes, what do the facts mean? Third, the issue may focus on witness credibility. The question then becomes, who do you believe? In each situation, winning the jury over to your version of the disputed facts is central to a persuasive closing argument.

Marshaling the facts that support your side is not merely repeating what the witnesses have testified about. That's largely a waste of time. The jury wants to know what the evidence *means*, and how it fits together to form a clear picture. Think broadly about the kinds of proof you can marshal to win the war over the disputed facts. These should include the following:

1. client's testimony
2. other corroborating witnesses
3. exhibits
4. admissions from opponent's witnesses
5. common sense and human nature
6. probabilities and improbabilities
7. pleadings and discovery

The following are illustrations about how you can argue various things that may be in dispute. A common approach is to begin by telling the jury what really happened, from *your* perspective, and then move immediately to all the sources that make your version of what happened more plausible than your opponent's.

Example (plaintiff):

What happened on December 13, 2000, as John Smith was driving south on Clark Street? He could see the intersection of Main Street ahead. . . .

Example (defendant):

December 13, 2000, started out as an ordinary day for Bob Jones. After a normal day at the office, he was going home to have dinner with his family. Up ahead was the intersection with Clark Street, which he had driven through numerous times. He could see . . .

Both sides, in other words, want to create their picture of a disputed event that is more believable, and therefore more likely true, than the other side's. Both sides then need to bring out the facts that support their version.

Example (prosecution):

That tavern was well lighted. There were lights over the bar, lights over the front entrance, lights in the street that shined through the plate glass windows in front, and lights from the jukebox, neon signs, and candles on the tables. There was plenty of light for the patrons to see, observe, and identify the robbers.

Example (defense):

That bar wasn't well lighted. It was pretty much like any neighborhood bar.

Successful bars create moods, mostly through dim lighting. This bar was no exception. It had only a few dim lights spread around the room. This is hardly the kind of lighting you would want to have when correctly identifying the robbers is critical.

When referring to witness testimony, identify that witness to the jury and build up that witness' credibility.

Example:

You remember Ms. Williams, the sales clerk. She was standing right on the southwest corner of Main and Clark, just outside her store, and saw the whole thing happen.

Example:

Remember Dr. Good? He was the distinguished doctor with the silver hair. What are his qualifications? He's a board-certified specialist in orthopedics, the chief orthopedist at Rush Hospital. He's treated hundreds of fractures just like the one involved here.

Example:

Mr. Roberts has no ax to grind here. He doesn't know any of the persons involved in the crash. He just happened to be there and told us what actually happened.

Re-create for the jury the actual testimony of your key witnesses, bit by bit.

Example:

Remember when I asked Ms. Andrews . . . ? Remember her answer? She said . . . What was the last question I asked her? . . . Her answer to that question was . . .

Example:

What Mr. Roper said was so important that I got the transcript of what he told us during the trial. He said:

Q.   *What color was the light?*
A.   *It was red.*
Q.   *Are you sure?*
A.   *Yes. I was looking at it when the car went through the red light.*

Argue that your witnesses are the most reliable ones the jurors heard.

Example:

Isn't that the way it must have really happened? Who was in a better position to see what really happened? Who was the only witness who was looking at the in-

tersection before the cars actually collided? Who was the only person who saw the entire collision from beginning to end?

Exhibits should always be used to corroborate important points. Take the exhibit out when you want to use it, make the point, and then put it away when done.

Example:

What else proves it happened this way? Take another look at the diagram we brought you, Plaintiff's Exhibit #4. As you can see, the light is a three-second yellow light. According to all the witnesses, Mr. Black's car was only 30 to 40 feet from the crosswalk when the light turned, and he was only going 25 mph. It's obvious that the light was yellow when he drove into the intersection, and he had every right to be there.

Example:

Take a look at the insurance policy itself. It's in evidence — Defendant's Exhibit #1 — and you will be able to take it to the jury room later. Look particularly at page 4 of the policy. Right here it says that . . .

Admissions during trial from your opponent's witnesses can be particularly persuasive sources of proof. After all, if the opponent admitted something that helps you (and hurts the opponent), it's very likely to be true.

Example:

Throughout this trial we've been saying that the defendant was in a hurry, and that his carelessness caused this collision. The best evidence we have comes from the defendant's own mouth. Remember when I asked him: "Didn't you have a meeting in your office scheduled for 9:00 A.M.?" "Wasn't it an important meeting?" "You didn't want to be late for the meeting, right?" Remember when he admitted all those things? Well, that crash happened at 9:00 A.M., two miles from his office. Was he in a hurry? Of course! The defendant's own testimony proved it.

Common sense, human nature, probabilities, and improbabilities can all be persuasive sources of "evidence."

Example:

Does it make sense that a 68-year-old woman would get on a bus that way? Wouldn't she be extremely careful every time she got on a bus and climbed the steps? Isn't that particularly true for a woman who has arthritis?

Example:

The plaintiff wants you to believe that Mr. Johnson would risk the lives of himself, his wife, and his children, by making a left turn in front of oncoming traffic, just to save a few seconds. Does that make any sense?

Finally, look to the pleadings and discovery for admissions that make important points. Answers to the complaint, admissions in depositions, interrogatory answers, and responses to requests to admit facts are all potent sources of proof.

Example:

Remember when the plaintiff said he saw the child running across the street, and he tried to brake, but couldn't stop in time? However, the truth came out during the plaintiff's deposition, when I asked him: "Did you see the child before you hit him?" And his answer was: "No, he came out of nowhere." Isn't that the more likely truth, the only truth that explains why the defendant didn't stop his car for that little boy?

The artistry of good closing arguments is to weave all these kinds of supporting "facts" together into a coherent argument, that reinforces your key points, and makes the jury accept *your* version of what really happened.

4.   Basis of liability/nonliability or guilt/innocence

Immediately following their argument on what happened and why the facts compel the conclusion that it happened the way you claim, many lawyers will sum up the liability argument.

Example (plaintiff):

So what did the defendant do that was negligent here? He failed to keep a proper lookout for others. He failed to yield the right of way. He failed to drive with a speed that was safe for the weather that night. All this was negligence, and it also violated the rules of the road.

Example (defendant):

Members of the jury, the plaintiff did not look to see whether other cars were coming. He did not come to a complete stop at the intersection, but rolled ahead, assuming that the light would change sooner than it did. It's obvious that the plaintiff was negligent and that his own negligence was the real cause of this accident.

5.   Damages (in civil cases)

Plaintiffs in civil cases usually argue liability first, then damages. The idea is that you first convince the jury that the defendant is liable, then move to the damages that plaintiff is entitled to recover. This ends your closing argument on an emotional high point, reviewing the injuries and damages the plaintiff suffered and now has to live with.

In contract cases the damages that a plaintiff is entitled to are often apparent. Compensable losses, caused by the other party's breach, usually will be spelled out in the damages instruction, and evidence of those damages usually will come from concrete sources such as bills, checks, and other documents. Arguing damages then involves mentioning the permissible damages and showing the proof of those damages.

In tort cases, however, the intangible nature of damages such as pain and suffering make it more difficult to name a dollar amount for such damages. Most plaintiff's lawyers will first usually describe the impact the event has had on the plaintiff's life and then discuss the dollar amounts to which the plaintiff is entitled.

Example:

> *Before this collision Bob Smith was a healthy man. He was a successful businessman, moving up within the company. He enjoyed outdoor sports, camping, hiking, working around the house, the kinds of things most of us enjoy. What happened to Bob after the collision?*
>
> *(Symptoms) The car crashed into Bob's right side and he was knocked to the pavement. He felt a stabbing pain in his right leg. He couldn't move, and just lay there. Finally, someone called for an ambulance. . . .*
>
> *(Diagnosis) Dr. Good arrived at the hospital a short time after Bob got there. He examined Bob in the emergency room and ordered X rays. Those X rays showed that . . .*
>
> *(Treatment) Bob was in that hospital for 12 days. His cast was not removed for five months. During that time, he couldn't use his leg or exercise in any way. He couldn't work. All he could do was wait. Finally, when the cast came off, the doctors started Bob on the therapy program. Every day, four times a day, Bob would . . .*
>
> *(Prognosis) What is Bob Smith's condition today? He used to enjoy outdoor sports, camping, and hiking. Today he can't. He used to be able to do gardening and chores around the house. Today he can't do that either.*
>
> *(Damages) Members of the jury, the law says that if someone is injured because someone else was negligent and caused the injuries, that person is entitled to be compensated. There are several things we need to consider.*

In personal injury cases the following are usually considered permissible damages. Keep in mind, however, that jurisdictions vary both on the terminology used and whether each item is a separate element of damages. The safe approach is to use a large courtroom chart that lists the proper damages elements according to the damages instruction the judge will later give the jury. The damages elements may include the following:

a. medical expenses
b. future medical expenses
c. lost income
d. future lost income
e. nature and extent of injuries
f. physical disability and disfigurement
g. pain and suffering
h. future pain and suffering

Many plaintiff's lawyers tell the jurors what amount they are asking and then justify it by discussing each of the permissible elements. Jurors may resent your withholding the final figure by discussing the elements first, particularly when the amount is large.

Compute each element of damages precisely. The standard approach is to use a large chart, which lists the permissible elements of damages, and put dollar figures next to each element as you discuss them. This tells the jury that you have been careful and thoughtful.

Show how the damages you are asking for will help the plaintiff. Jurors will usually be more receptive to awarding large verdicts if they see how the money will help the plaintiff deal with her future.

Example:

For future medical expenses, we ask that you give Mrs. Jones $70,000. Why that amount? You heard how she will need a wheelchair for the rest of her life. Her life expectancy is 30 years. A wheelchair today costs, as we learned, more than $700 and lasts only about five years. That means she will need more than $4,200 just to have a decent wheelchair for the rest of her life. But that's only the beginning. She will need weekly physical therapy. That's going to cost at least $30 for each session, or $1,500 each year. These figures don't even include inflation, and we know that things cost more with each passing year. That's why her medical expenses for the future will add up to at least $70,000.

Most lawyers usually begin by discussing the out-of-pocket damages such as medical expenses and lost income; next, they move on to future losses such as future medical expenses and future lost income; then they end with the intangible elements such as disability, disfigurement, and pain and suffering. The thinking is that the last elements are the emotional high point of the damages and should be argued last.

Example:

Finally, folks, we need to talk about the kind of life Fred Woods has today, and will have for the rest of his life. In a land of normal people, what does it mean to be able to stand, walk, and lead a normal life like anyone else? What does a life feel like when it is restricted to a wheelchair? We suggest the sum of $300,000 is the least we should do to compensate Fred for what he has lost, and will never regain over the next 30 years of his life. If that figure is too low, it is your right and duty to change it. If the defense says it's too high, let the defense tell you why only $10,000 per year is too high. Whatever you do, however, keep one thing in mind. This is the one day, the only day, in Fred Woods' life where he can come before you and get justice for what happened to him.

Many jurisdictions ban making what is usually called a "per diem argument." This prevents plaintiff's lawyer from arguing that the jury should give the plaintiff a given amount, say $20 per day, for the rest of plaintiff's expected life. (More creative lawyers asked a set amount for each hour, minute, or even second of the plaintiff's life!) The effect of the argument, when the amount requested is multiplied by the plaintiff's actuarial life expectancy, is that the plaintiff is usually seeking an extraordinary amount. Most jurisdictions, however, permit asking for a certain amount and justifying it by showing that it is only a small amount for each year the plaintiff will probably live. For instance, plaintiff's lawyer may argue that for pain and suffering the plaintiff should receive $50,000, which is only $5,000 annually for the 10 years plaintiff is expected to live. The advantage of such an argument is that it shows the jury a rational reason for the damage request.

What should the defendant do? Defendants, of course, don't like to talk about damages at all, because discussing them may leave the impression that by doing so they are conceding liability. On the other hand, defendants are afraid that if they don't discuss damages, and the jury finds for the plaintiff on liability, it will simply accept the plaintiff's suggested damages and return a verdict in that amount. There is no simple answer. It depends on the amount of money at risk, and the relative strengths of the liability and damages evidence. In cases where both liability and damages are in issue, defendant needs to decide whether to discuss damages at all, and, if so, when. There are three common approaches.

First, the defense might decide to argue only liability, with the thinking that the liability argument will be stronger if damages are not even mentioned. This is good if the jury accepts the damages argument. If it doesn't, the risk is that the jury, having heard only the plaintiff's damages request, will give the plaintiff everything requested. This approach can be effective in contract cases where the damages amount is fairly certain.

Second, the defense might decide to argue liability first, then damages. This works well if the liability argument is weak and the real point is to hold down damages; the main part of the argument thus will focus on showing how exaggerated and unreasonable the plaintiff's request is. This approach is frequently used in tort cases where damages is the principal issue.

Third, the defense might decide to argue damages first, then liability. This works well if you want to discuss damages but want to end up on a high note, your liability argument. The key is to start by denying liability, then shift to the damages issue without sounding defensive. This is a common approach where both liability and damages are seriously in dispute.

Example:

It's clear from the evidence that plaintiff caused his own injuries, so he's not entitled to recover anything from us. Even so, plaintiff's lawyer talked about damages for so long, we need to look at his claims to see if they hold up, see if they're reasonable.

Example:

We're simply not responsible for what happened. But if you disagree, we need to talk about what they've asked for, and see if that's reasonable.

After discussing how the plaintiff's damages claims have been exaggerated and are not supported by the evidence, you can then credibly return to the liability issue.

Example:

Folks, what they're asking for, $300,000, is totally unreasonable. However, as we discussed before, that's not even the real issue here. The real issue, the only issue, is: Was the plaintiff himself negligent? And the only answer to that question must be: Yes, he was.

When the defendant is discussing the damages, should the defense only attack the plaintiff's damages numbers, or should the defense also suggest alternative numbers? Again, defendants hate to make this decision. Some defense lawyers like to suggest an alternative figure, especially if plaintiff's request looks like serious overreaching.

Example:

Just because you ask for it doesn't make it reasonable. If plaintiff's requested amount — $300,000 — is unreasonable, and it is, what would be reasonable? We suggest that if plaintiff were entitled to anything, the amount of $50,000 would be more than adequate to compensate him for his medical bills, lost work, and any other losses. That amount, and no more, is reasonable, and it's fair.

Of course, if the defendant suggests an alternative amount, there is a substantial likelihood that the jury will, when it discusses damages, treat the plaintiff's and defendant's suggested amounts as the maximum and minimum possibilities and reach a verdict somewhere in between these extremes. For that reason, some defense lawyers prefer only to attack the plaintiff's damages request, without suggesting a specific dollar amount.

Example:

Plaintiff has asked you for $1,000,000. What that means is that he will receive around $50,000 for every year of his life, without ever touching the $1,000,000. That $50,000 each year is more than he ever earned in any year of his life! And that's simply not reasonable.

Finally, defendant needs to decide how to deal with the issue of comparative negligence. One approach is simply to argue that the plaintiff was totally at fault. The problem is that if the jury rejects the argument, it may then accept the plaintiff's argument that the defendant was totally at fault. If there is substantial evidence of negligence by both parties, the defense may want to concede that both were negligent, and ask the jury to apportion fault accordingly.

Example:

You may decide that Mr. Williams was at fault here. If you do, we accept your decision. But keep in mind that the plaintiff was also at fault here. It wouldn't be fair, and it wouldn't be right under the facts, to put all the blame on Mr. Williams and none on the plaintiff. The plaintiff, after all, was obviously negligent too. So if that is your decision, the only fair thing to do is find each of them 50 percent responsible.

This kind of argument will almost guarantee that the jury will find the defendant at fault. If, however, you can get the jury to accept the idea that the plaintiff deserves part of the blame, you will have effectively reduced the damages the defendant will have to pay. In addition, the jury may respect your candor in acknowledging that the defendant bears some responsibility for what happened, and will be more willing to accept the other things you will argue, such as exaggerated damages.

Most states today follow some form of comparative negligence in tort cases. In those, many allow liability to be apportioned among all responsible persons, even if a person is not a named party in the trial. In other words, the jury may need to apportion liability among not just the plaintiff and defendant, but also any settled parties and any persons that were never sued (sometimes call "nonparties at fault"). For example, if plaintiff sues two defendants, one of them settles before trial, and an unknown driver was also involved in the collision but left the scene before his identity could be determined, the jury may need to apportion liability among all four persons (plaintiff, defendant, settled defendant, and nonparty at fault), the total liability adding up to 100 percent. In these situations, plaintiff will try to put as much liability as possible on the defendant; the defendant will try to put most of the liability on the settled defendant, the nonparty at fault, or the plaintiff. These situations can become complicated, and you need to know how the liability allocation issue will be presented to the jury before deciding how you will argue it.

6.   Instructions

The key instructions the court will give the jury should be incorporated into your closing argument. Instructions usually given to the jury include:

a.   burden of proof
b.   elements of claims, damages, and defenses
c.   definitions of important legal terms
d.   credibility of witnesses
e.   using common sense and experiences in life
f.   sympathy should not be considered

Effective closing arguments tie specific instructions to specific points in the argument. For example, in criminal cases defense lawyers almost always use the burden of proof instruction when arguing that the prosecution has failed to prove its case beyond a reasonable doubt. In both civil and criminal cases plaintiffs commonly refer to the elements instruction for the claims to demonstrate that they have in fact proved what the law requires them to prove.

Jurisdictions differ on how you can use instructions during closing arguments. Most allow you to read verbatim from the instruction and even show the instruction to the jury, like any other exhibit in evidence, during the argument. A few jurisdictions do not permit you to read verbatim but do allow you to refer to specific instructions and paraphrase them.

The key to effective use of instructions is to use the instruction in conjunction with the point you are making.

Example:

Can you believe what Mr. Watkins said? He's a good friend of the defendant. On top of that, he's a convicted felon. We can't afford to trust him. And it's not just my saying so. Judge Hawkins, when she instructs you on the law, will tell you that the testimony of a person who has been convicted of a crime should be taken with particular caution.

Example:

Judge Hawkins will instruct you that you should consider any bias and interest of a witness when you judge the credibility of that witness. Why is that instruction so important here? The plaintiff's case depends almost entirely on the testimony of John Roberts, the plaintiff's friend and business partner. Doesn't it make sense that Roberts would, and did, shade his testimony to help the plaintiff? After all, if he helps the plaintiff he helps himself.

Example:

The court will tell you that if you find that we were not negligent, then you are not to consider damages because there will be no reason to do so. That instruction ties right into what this case is all about. The plaintiff has not shown that we did anything wrong. Therefore, you will not need to discuss their claimed damages at all.

Example:

The key word in this case is "know." Did Bobby know there were illegal drugs in the truck when he drove it across the border? Her Honor will tell you that the prosecutors must prove, beyond a reasonable doubt, that Bobby knew the drugs were there. Did they? Of course not. There's been absolutely no evidence proving this.

7. Refuting the other side

Almost all jurisdictions give plaintiff (the party with the burden of proof) the right to make both a closing argument and a rebuttal argument. Plaintiff in those jurisdictions has a choice to make: Should he anticipate the defendant's closing argument, or save any refutation for his own rebuttal argument?

Many lawyers mention the defendant's likely claims in the closing argument. The logic is that the jury will not hear the defendant's arguments for the first time from the defense. By anticipating the defense's arguments, you can raise and refute them before the defense has a chance to argue.

Psychological research has shown that persons are more resistant to counterarguments if they have been given reasons to resist them beforehand.

Example:

What has the defense been claiming here? They want you to believe that Mrs. Smith was in such a hurry that she made a left turn in front of oncoming traffic. They also want you to believe that she made that left turn without even checking for oncoming traffic. But those claims don't hold water. That's because . . .

The defendant, of course, arguing second and not having a rebuttal argument, must spend more time on the plaintiff's claims and refute them during the defense's closing argument.

Example:

What does the plaintiff claim happened? They would have you believe that Mr. Jones drove into the intersection after the light had turned red. Well, let's go back to the corner of Main and Clark Streets and see whether that holds up.

Many defendants expressly discuss the fact that they only get to talk once, and that the plaintiff has a second chance — rebuttal — to talk.

Example:

Folks, this is my last time to talk with you. I don't get a second chance, the way the plaintiff [prosecution] does. So when the plaintiff [prosecution] argues again, keep in mind that I won't have a chance to respond to what they say. I'm going to count on you to see if their argument holds up. I'm going to rely on you to ask: But where's the evidence of that? Where's the proof?

Some defendants also like to challenge the plaintiff with difficult questions just before concluding the defense argument. The idea is that plaintiff, when starting the rebuttal argument, will be tempted to respond to the defense immediately, and in doing so will sound weak and uncertain.

Example:

Members of the jury, the prosecution has been claiming since the beginning of the trial that this is a case of murder. But murder requires proof, beyond a reasonable doubt, that Bobby intended to kill or do great bodily harm. But what's the evidence been? Its uncontradicted that Bobby was scared to death of Jimmy. Jimmy was much bigger, and had threatened him in the past. The last thing in the world Bobby needed, and wanted, was to get into a fight with Jimmy. So if Bobby was scared to death of Jimmy, and desperately wanted to avoid him, how could Bobby have intended to kill? That's the question the prosecution has never answered, and that's the question they don't want you to think about. See if they answer it, or even try to answer it, when they get up a second time.

8.   Conclusion

The end of your closing argument should smoothly and efficiently conclude your argument. It should appeal to the jury's sense of fairness and justice. It should remind the jury of a key theme or other important point. Most effective conclusions today end crisply and dramatically so that the last phrases linger tellingly in the air.

Example (plaintiff — civil):

　　Above all, remember this. This is Bob Smith's only day in court. This is the only time he can come before a jury and receive proper compensation for the injuries the defendant caused. This is the only time he can receive justice. We are confident you will give him that.

Example (defendant — civil):

　　Folks, my company, the Ajax Insurance Company, doesn't pay cheaters. Never has, and never will. The plaintiff tried to cheat us by making a fraudulent claim on a fire insurance policy. That's wrong, and that's cheating. Don't let him get away with it here.

Example (plaintiff — criminal):

　　When that defendant took his gun and shot an unarmed man, a man who was doing absolutely nothing wrong, he intentionally snuffed out the life of another human being. Members of the jury, that's what the crime of murder is all about.

Example (defendant — criminal):

　　What does all this add up to? The prosecution has failed miserably here. They failed to prove Frank was there. They failed to prove that he had anything to do with that robbery. Because of that, let Frank go. Let him go back to his job, his family, and his life.

§9.6.   *Rebuttal*

Plaintiff, who ordinarily has the burden of proof, in most jurisdictions has the right to argue first and last; that is, plaintiff has the right to make a closing argument and, after the defense has argued, a rebuttal argument. How should plaintiff best utilize this advantage? Two questions are involved. First, how should plaintiff apportion his ammunition between the closing and rebuttal? Second, how should time be apportioned between the two?
　　Plaintiff should fully cover all the key points in the closing argument and resist the temptation to save all the best arguments for rebuttal. "Sandbagging" has dangers. First, it will make the plaintiff's closing argument weaker, something to be avoided at all costs. Second, defendant, sensing that the plaintiff has sandbagged, can waive his closing argument,

preventing plaintiff from arguing in rebuttal. Third, defendant ca[]
a narrow closing argument involving one or two issues, again preve[]
plaintiff from arguing the unmentioned issues in rebuttal. (For examp[]
defendant might argue only liability, preventing plaintiff from arguing
damages in rebuttal.) Knowing how strictly the court will sustain scope of
rebuttal objections is obviously important. Finally, keep in mind that the
jury is tired and will tune you out and become hostile if the rebuttal argument drags on or simply repeats old arguments.

Apportioning the time between the opening and rebuttal arguments
is usually left up to plaintiff. (Some judges, however, limit the time the parties may argue so plaintiff must plan and reserve enough time for the
planned rebuttal.) Most plaintiffs will use two or three times as much time
on the closing argument as on rebuttal. This will allow for a full closing argument yet reserve enough time for an adequate rebuttal. For example, a
plaintiff might use 20 to 30 minutes for closing and 5 to 10 minutes for rebuttal.

The rebuttal argument, like all parts of the trial, must be planned in
advance. Here, coordination between the closing and rebuttal arguments
is important. Decide what arguments, stories, analogies, or other routines
each will use. Make sure neither argument steps on the other's toes so that
the rebuttal will be fresh for the jury. Put yourself in the defense's shoes.
What points would you probably argue if you were representing the defendant? What are your best responses to those likely arguments?

Just as there is no single "right way" to organize and deliver a closing
argument, experienced trial lawyers vary greatly in the way they organize
and deliver rebuttal arguments. Nonetheless, many structure their rebuttal along the following lines:

a.   introduction
b.   your strongest points
c.   defendant's contentions and your refutation
d.   conclusion

Notice the emphasis on *your* strong points. Many trial lawyers make a
serious mistake during rebuttal: They merely respond to questions raised
during the defense's closing argument. This usually makes the rebuttal argument sound defensive, negative, and passive, which is exactly what the
defense wants to accomplish. A clever defense lawyer during his argument
will throw out a series of questions and challenge the other side to answer
them during the rebuttal. Resist the temptation. Use your rebuttal to hit
your best points in a fresh way. Periodically weave in selected defense contentions you have anticipated when your refutation is strong. Above all,
keep the rebuttal active and positive.

§9.7.   *Examples of closing arguments*

The following closing arguments are from the same cases as the opening
statements examples in Chapter IV.

'er): *People v. Sylvester Strong*

r Strong, has been charged with murdering
'5, 2000. The prosecution claims that the shoot-
prior incident. The defense claims the shoot-
se.)

ₚₗosecution

...y it please the court, counsel, members of the jury.

At the beginning of the case, during the opening statements, we said that this was a case of murder. What has that evidence we brought you proved?

We now know that the defendant, Sylvester Strong, shot and killed the victim, Shelley Williams, on the 2300 block of Bloomingdale Avenue on April 25, 2000. We know that the victim was completely unarmed when he was shot, and we know that he was shot two times in the back, the second shot coming when he was lying face down on the sidewalk, helpless and unprotected. In short, we have shown, and the defense concedes, that Sylvester Strong killed Shelley Williams; and the only remaining question is whether that killing is a murder as well!

How did Shelley Williams come to die so tragically? Shelley, his mother, Rosie Garrett, and various other family members and friends were in two cars, returning from the north side of Chicago. As the cars turned from Winnebago on to Bloomingdale, the first car, driven by Shelley, stopped. He saw the defendant, Sylvester Strong, riding down Bloomingdale on a bicycle. Shelley got out of his car and walked over to where the defendant had stopped and started talking to him. Shelley stopped and talked to the defendant because he had heard that the defendant had sworn at his mother at a party the previous day. Shelley motioned to his mother, who had parked at the corner, to get out and come over. This she did. Shelley then asked her: "Is this the boy that cussed you out?" She answered, "Yes, it is." Shelley told him to apologize directly to his mother.

(Introduction)

The traditional introduction here is done simply.

The simple theme: murder.

(Issue)

The issue is stated as positively as possible.

(What happened)

Notice that the narrative of the occurrence closely parallels the prosecution's opening statement. This always reinforces the impression that you have delivered on the representations you made during the opening statement.

Suddenly, George Howard, the defendant's brother-in-law, ran up to them, with a handgun. He fired two shots in the air. The defendant then grabbed the gun from Howard, saying: "Give me the gun — you're not trying to shoot him." The defendant then pointed the gun at Shelley, who said: "I don't want to fight," while waving his arms. Shelley backed up, and the defendant fired the first shot, hitting him in the arm. Shelley turned to run, and the defendant fired the second shot, hitting him in the back. Shelley fell, face down, on the sidewalk, next to a fire hydrant by the corner of Bloomingdale and Winnebago. That's when the defendant walked over and fired the third shot into the back of a helpless and unarmed victim.

Note also that the narrative is done in an active, "you are there" style.

The defendant then ran westbound on Bloomingdale. Rosie yelled for someone to stop him. Clarence Williams, the victim's brother, jumped into the victim's car and drove down Bloomingdale to cut the defendant off and keep him from escaping. Clarence jumped out of the car, and kicked the defendant in the head to keep him from running away.

Other people, including the defendant's wife, who was armed with a baseball bat, came to the scene. Rosie took the bat away from her, then started beating the defendant with it. We don't deny that one bit. She kept on hitting the defendant, who had just shot her son to death, until the police arrived.

Not contesting that the defendant was beaten is probably the better approach, since it prevents the defense from making a big issue out of it.

Shelley Williams was taken to a nearby hospital, but it was too late. The three gunshots had done their job. Shelley Williams was dead by the time he reached the hospital. The autopsy later showed that the fatal shot entered Shelley's lower back, traveled in an upward direction, piercing the lungs so that they filled up with blood, and pierced his heart as well.

That, in a nutshell, is what our evidence has proved here. That evidence has proved, beyond a reasonable doubt, that on April 25, 2000, the defendant, Sylvester Strong, intentionally shot and killed the victim, Shelley Williams, with a

(Basis of guilt)

This summary closely parallels the elements of murder.

handgun, and that there was absolutely no justification for the shooting. That is why this evidence has proved that the defendant is guilty of murder.

The elements of murder could be put on a large chart and used here.

How do we know it really happened this way? Remember when Rosie Garrett testified? What did she tell us? She told us she'd been following her son's car to Bloomingdale Avenue, when she saw her son Shelley stop his car, get out and walk over to the defendant, who'd been riding down the street on a bicycle. She saw them talking, then Shelley motioned for her to join them. When Shelley asked her if this was the man who had previously insulted her and cussed her, she said, "Yes." Shelley then demanded that the defendant apologize directly to her. What else did Rosie Garrett tell us? Suddenly George Howard appeared and fired a gun two times into the air. The defendant then grabbed the gun from him, yelling: "You're not trying to shoot him — give me the gun!" Rosie Garrett then stood there as the defendant, methodically and deliberately, fired three shots into her son, killing him on the spot. What did Rosie do next? Realizing that the gun was now empty, she grabbed a baseball bat from Sylvester's wife and, seeing the defendant trying to escape, did what any reasonable person would have done under the same circumstances. She ran to where the defendant was and started hitting him with the bat to keep him from getting away, until the police arrived a couple of minutes later.

(Corroboration)

The corroboration takes the essential parts of the important witnesses and repeats the testimony. This should be done by referring directly to the heart of the witness' testimony.

Admitted diagrams and photographs could be used here to illustrate the witnesses' testimony.

Who else told us it happened this way? Clarence Williams, the victim's brother, who graduated from high school, enlisted and served in the Army in Vietnam, and, since his return, has been working as a master mechanic for General Motors, also testified. Everything he saw and heard corroborated Rosie Garrett. Of course, since he remained by his car, he couldn't hear all of the conversation between Shelley, his mother, and the defendant. However, he could see that Shelley did nothing to provoke the defendant, and could see that neither Shelley nor his mother was armed in any way. What he told us he saw next was that George Howard came

Using rhetorical questions is often an effective way of introducing a new topic.

up, fired a handgun into the air, the defendant grabbed it and emptied the gun into his brother's back. Seeing the defendant running away, he jumped into the car, chased the defendant, and cut him off a short distance away. He then kicked the defendant to keep him from getting away until the police came. Folks, everything Clarence Williams told us about that day supports, is consistent with, and corroborates, Rosie Garrett's testimony.

Who else testified? Remember Willie Williams? He was only an acquaintance of the victim, not a family member, who happened to be with them that afternoon. He doesn't have any axe to grind here. He's not biased in favor of any side here. He simply told us what he saw that day to the best of his memory. What did he see? Since he had run a short distance away when the first shots rang out, he was a little further away than the others, but he did turn to see the defendant pull the trigger of the gun three times, shooting the victim three times, the last time when he was lying helpless on the sidewalk.

What about the other witnesses? All of them — the police officers who arrived at the scene, the ballistics expert who confirmed that this handgun matched the bullets removed from the victim's body, and the pathologist who performed the autopsy and learned that the fatal shot pierced the victim's lungs and heart — as well as the exhibits admitted in evidence, all of these are consistent with the eyewitness.

Corroboration by exhibits, physical evidence, and expert testimony should always be mentioned.

Use the admitted exhibits during the argument to maintain juror interest.

Now, you're probably going to ask yourself, why did this shooting happen? What motive was there? It's clear that the defendant shot and killed Shelley Williams because he got angry when forced to apologize to Rosie Garrett and, as so often happens, a gun was nearby. Please keep in mind, however, that we are not required to prove a motive for the shooting. The Court will instruct you on this point later. All we are required to prove, and we have proved, is that the defendant shot and killed Shelley Williams, he intended to do it, and was not justified in doing it.

A weakness in the case is that there is no apparent motive in the case sufficient to cause a murder. The best the prosecution can do is to suggest one, then remind the jury that the law does not make motive a required element of murder.

What would the defense have you believe? The defendant claims that on the day before, April 24, there was a party where he and Rosie Garrett had words. He, however, would have you believe that Rosie Garrett, not he, was using all the foul and insulting language. He claims that after the police arrived and broke up the argument, Rosie and some others said they would come back tomorrow and finish it. What does he say about the 25th? The defendant would have you believe that he was merely riding his bicycle down the street when he was confronted by Shelley, who immediately started swearing at him. He claims that George Howard came by, and suddenly everyone was getting out of the two cars with baseball bats and two-by-fours. They surrounded him, and for no apparent reason, started beating him. He claims he was already bloodied and couldn't really see because of all the blood in his face, when he heard the gunshots and somehow got the handgun from George Howard. He then claims that he fired blindly, solely to get this armed mob off him.

They also called Ada May, the defendant's mother-in-law. Her recollection, to no one's surprise, was exactly consistent with the defendant's when it came to the argument the day before. As far as the 25th is concerned, she really couldn't remember any details, although she was sure, again to no one's surprise, that she saw Rosie Garrett beating the defendant with a baseball bat.

We have, then, a classic case of testimony that, as far as what happened on April 25 is concerned, is contradictory, and it's your duty to decide where the truth lies. In other words, you've got to decide which witnesses are telling the truth. When you decide on the credibility of the witnesses, the court will tell you that you should consider their demeanor while testifying, gauge it against other testimony, measure it against your common sense and experiences in life, and see if the witnesses have any bias, interest, or motive that could affect their testimony.

The witnesses we called were all hardworking, decent people who told you what happened. Their

(Other side and refutation)

Note that the other side's contentions are stated to make clear that you don't believe they are true. Using the "he claims that" types of predicates clearly establishes that.

A little sarcasm in appropriate circumstances can be effective.

Credibility of witnesses, where you have two diametrically opposed versions of the facts, must be argued. It's always effective to refer to the credibility instruction the court will give.

Common sense should always be argued, since

testimony was consistent on every important fact. They all said that the victim was completely unarmed when he was shot. They were not contradicted in any way during the cross-examinations. Finally, doesn't what they say make sense? Doesn't it square with your experiences in life? The *only way* the victim could have been shot the way he was — once in the arm, and twice in the back — is if it happened the way our witnesses say it did. It is totally impossible for the defendant, shooting "blindly" as he would have you believe, to just happen to shoot *only* the victim, and just happen to shoot him twice in the back. Not only does the physical and medical evidence contradict the defense, but the only witness who testified directly to this version of the events was the defendant himself. When you consider the credibility of his testimony, keep in mind that, if ever a man had a motive to distort the truth and fabricate a story, it's got to be the defendant in a criminal case charged with murder.

this is probably the single most important basis for the jury's decision on who is telling the truth.

Where the defendant testifies, his obvious bias should be pointed out.

Finally, there's one witness the defense simply can't get around, and that's Arthur Anderson. Mr. Anderson, you'll remember, is a friend of the *defendant*. If his testimony was going to be slanted toward anyone, it would be toward the defendant. Yet, what did he testify to? He told us he was on the street and saw the defendant with some other people, then saw George Howard run by with a gun and fire it. What did he see next? He saw the defendant grab the gun and say: "Give me the gun — you're not trying to hit him," then aim the gun at Shelley Williams and pull the trigger. He saw Shelley backing up, waving his arms and turning, and the gun went off a second time. He then saw the defendant walk over to where Shelley had fallen and put the third shot in his back. Immediately afterwards he saw the defendant run past him, and noticed that *at that time* there was absolutely no blood on his head, face, or clothes.

Showing that a witness who would be expected to testify favorably to the defense actually supported the prosecution's version of the facts is usually very persuasive. When this happens, the element of support in the testimony must be driven home.

So there you have it. When the defendant's own friend comes into court and, under oath, tells you what he saw, and his testimony totally contradicts the defense, you know for certain which side has been telling the truth here.

The court will instruct you that, under our law, a person commits the crime of murder when he: first, performs an act or acts which cause the death of another; second, intended to kill or do great bodily harm to another; and third, was not justified in killing the other person under the circumstances.

(Instructions)

The prosecution should usually tell the jury what the elements of the offense are, and argue that he's met each of the requirements. An elements chart would be useful here.

We have demonstrated, with convincing, credible, and consistent witnesses, that the defendant, Sylvester Strong, killed the victim, Shelley Williams, that he did so intentionally, and that by no stretch of the imagination was this a legitimate self-defense situation. These witnesses have demonstrated each of these propositions beyond a reasonable doubt. Accordingly, we ask that you return the only verdict that this evidence supports and fairness demands, a verdict finding the defendant, Sylvester Strong, guilty of the crime of murder. Thank you.

(Conclusion)

Closing argument — defense

Your Honor, Mr. Sklarsky, ladies and gentlemen of the jury, good morning.

(Introduction)

At the beginning of this case, when his Honor, Judge Cousins, was questioning you, he asked you whether you would follow the law, whether you would be fair, and whether you would hold the prosecutors to their burden of proving Sylvester Strong guilty beyond a reasonable doubt. There was a lot of talk about that and each of you indicated and promised that you would hold the prosecutors to their burden. Judge Cousins also asked you whether you would presume Sylvester innocent throughout this entire trial and through your deliberations and presume him so unless the State was able to prove him guilty beyond a reasonable doubt. All of you indicated that you presumed him innocent. Additionally, ladies and gentlemen, you were asked to use your common sense and experiences in life in evaluating the testimony of the witnesses. Based upon your responses: "Yes, I can follow the law," "Yes, I will hold the prose-

The defense's introductory remarks are often longer than the prosecution's. The defense often stresses that each juror promised to follow the law when the jurors were selected, and calls upon them to adhere to their promises.

cutors to their burden of proof beyond a reasonable doubt," "Yes, I will presume the defendant innocent unless he is proven guilty beyond
a reasonable doubt," you were selected as jurors in this case. We are calling upon you now,
ladies and gentlemen, to abide by those
promises that you made.

Let's now look at the evidence and see why the
prosecutors failed to prove Sylvester Strong
guilty beyond a reasonable doubt. As we told
you at the beginning, this is a case of self-
defense. We do not contest the fact that Shelley
Williams was shot and killed, an unfortunate
thing that has happened, and nothing that I
can say, nothing that anyone in this courtroom
can do can change this. That fact, however, is
not the issue in this case. The issue here is: Was
Sylvester Strong justified in defending himself
under the circumstances that existed on that
day? Our answer, ladies and gentlemen, is that
the evidence indeed shows that the State failed
to prove Sylvester Strong guilty beyond a reasonable doubt, because they did *not* prove, beyond a reasonable doubt, that when he shot
Shelley Williams he did *not* reasonably believe
that it was a necessity to defend himself against
death or great bodily harm.

Now why do I say this? Ladies and gentlemen,
basically it comes down to whose account of the
incident you believe. Do you believe the version
provided by Rosie Garrett, Willie Williams,
Clarence Williams, or Arthur Anderson on that
stand, or do you believe the defendant and Ada
May Howard? We have diametrically opposed
versions in this case as to what happened.

The four occurrence witnesses — we call them
occurrence witnesses because they are supposed to have been on the scene and observed
the occurrence — were Rosie Garrett, Willie
Williams, Clarence Williams, and Arthur
Anderson. They would each have you believe
that before April 25, the date of the shooting,
there had been absolutely no threats, no threat-
ening gestures made by members of the
Williams family directed to members of
Sylvester's family.

The theme: self-
defense.

(Issue)

The defense should
put the issue in terms
of the prosecutor's
burden of proof, since
this is the easiest statement of the issue to
answer.

The answer should
emphatically and im-
mediately follow the
statement of the issue.

**(Other side and refu-
tation)**

Since the prosecution
has the burden of
proof, the argument
addresses the prosecu-
tion's witnesses *before*
arguing the defense
version of what hap-
pened.

Rosie Garrett, the first occurrence witness, testified that on April 25, at the corner of Bloomingdale and Winnebago, she observed her son Shelley talking with Sylvester Strong. She claimed that the only thing that happened before the shooting was that Shelley asked her if Sylvester was the person who cursed her. She said Shelley got out of the car and told Sylvester, "I want you to apologize." So Sylvester apologized. Shelley then said, "No, don't apologize to me, apologize to my mother." As Sylvester was turning to apologize to his mother, according to Rosie Garrett's testimony, that is when George Howard came running down the street and shot in the air. She then claims that Sylvester ran over to George Howard, grabbed the gun, saying, "You are not trying to hit him," and started shooting. Rosie Garrett claims that just before the shooting there was no fighting, no cursing, no argument, everything was peaceful, low tones of voice, not yelling; just a quiet, peaceful conversation.

Clarence Williams also got on the stand. He said the same thing, nothing happening, no argument — in fact, he couldn't hear what was being said because the tape deck in the car was playing. He also claims that, for no apparent reason, George Howard ran down the street firing the gun. He claims that Sylvester then, again for no apparent reason, grabbed the gun and started shooting. And he claims that only after the shooting stopped did anybody on the street lay a hand on Sylvester Strong, and that was when Clarence caught him down here by the end of the street with the car and kicked him in the face.

Now, if you believe the version of what occurred on the day of April 25 given by Rosie Garrett, given by Willie Williams, given by Clarence Williams, given by Arthur Anderson, you would have to believe the following: That when George Howard ran down the street and fired the shots, he was firing them because he was berserk, because there was absolutely no reason at all to fire.

Their witnesses would have you believe there was only peaceful conversation, no fighting, no

Arguing that the prosecution's witnesses are incredible because their testimony is illogical and does not provide a common-sense explanation of the subsequent shooting is an effective approach.

hitting; not a darn thing happening to Sylvester when, for no apparent reason George Howard went berserk, and then Sylvester went berserk as well. We then got two berserk individuals in the street, just shooting up everybody for no reason at all. This simply defies common sense, and everybody in this courtroom knows it.

Let's look at some of the other things. You remember when we went through the addresses of all of the individuals? Did you notice how they all *just happen* to be from outside of this neighborhood? Doesn't it seem just a little suspicious that all these friends of Shelley Williams decided to be on Bloomingdale at the same time? Incidentally, they *just happened* to catch Sylvester out there in the street around the time Ada May said Shelley Williams would come over there to finish the mess that occurred the night before. Don't these coincidences alone create a reasonable doubt in your mind about whether their witnesses are telling the truth?

Take a look at the photographs of this street. The officer said that the distance between where the shots were fired, and where he saw Sylvester being beaten, was only around 100 feet. Other testimony showed there was nothing wrong with his legs and feet. The testimony also was that Clarence got into the car, drove down the street, and cut Sylvester off. If that's all true, then why couldn't he get more than a hundred feet away? There had to be something wrong with him or he would have gotten much further. Doesn't this prove that Sylvester was attacked *before* the shots were fired? Isn't the fact that he managed to get only one hundred feet explained *only* by the fact that he was already injured, and couldn't run very well?

Just as the prosecution used the available physical evidence, presenting the same evidence to contradict the prosecution is always a good tactic.

The issue in this case is *why* Sylvester Strong shot that gun. That is the *only* issue; and the *only* one that can tell us the reason for the shooting — why he shot — is this man, Sylvester Strong. He is the only one that can tell us what was going through his mind. The issue, stated in legal terms, is whether he reasonably believed, under the circumstances that existed at the time of the shooting, he would sustain great

Since the prosecution had more occurrence witnesses, pointing out that only the defendant can testify directly on the issue of intent is an effective argument.

bodily harm or death to himself if he didn't defend himself. Shelley Williams can't testify to
that, Clarence Williams can't testify to that, and
Arthur Anderson can't testify to that. Only
Sylvester can, and we heard him tell us what he
felt when he fired those shots. That's why this is
a case of self-defense.

How many shots did he fire? He testified that
he just kept on shooting. *Why did you shoot?*
Because they were trying to kill me. When did you
shoot? When they were coming at me, trying to get me.
The only person who could testify as to his intent is Sylvester himself.

I have only a few moments left, so we must go
on. The prosecutor talked a lot about the entrance of the bullets, and said that two of the
bullets entered Shelley Williams' back. He
wants us to believe that Sylvester Strong should
be convicted simply because two shots entered
Williams' back. Well, it's not as simple as that.

Just for a moment, put anyone else in that same
situation. A mob has surrounded you. They are
armed with bats and two-by-fours. You instinctively fire your gun. Do you stop to see whether
the first shot hits anyone? Do you stop to see if
anyone is turning while you shoot? *Of course not!*
You would fire that gun as fast and as often as
you could. Isn't that exactly what a reasonable
person would have done under these circumstances? Well, that is exactly what happened,
and only what happened, here. The question is
whether, when the first shot was fired, Sylvester
Strong reasonably believed that he was justified
in defending himself. If so, it does not make
any difference where that first shot or, for that
matter, any other shots actually struck.

(What happened)

Having refuted the
prosecution witnesses,
the argument now
gives the defense ver-
sion of what hap-
pened.

Judge Cousins will instruct you that a person is
justified in using deadly force when that person
reasonably believes that such force is necessary
to prevent imminent death or great bodily
harm to himself. Isn't that what really happened here? Isn't that what Sylvester Strong
must have been thinking when he fired that
gun? Under these circumstances, surrounded
by an angry mob, isn't what Sylvester Strong did

(Instructions)

The defense will natu-
rally stress the self-
defense instructions,
particularly the bur-
den of proof's being
on the prosecution.

exactly what any other reasonable person would have done if faced with the same situation? *Of course it is!* Because what he did was reasonable, Sylvester is simply not guilty of any crime. It's self-defense.

Judge Cousins will also instruct you that the prosecution has the burden of proof in this case, and that this burden of proof never shifts to the defendant. Although we presented evidence in this case, we are not required to prove anything. *We* do not have to prove that Sylvester Strong was justified in defending himself as he did. It is the *prosecution* that is required to *disprove* this proposition, and they have to *disprove* it beyond a reasonable doubt.

Who among you can't say that you have a reasonable doubt whether Sylvester reasonably defended himself here? Of course you have doubts! You have got to have doubts about that. If nothing else, the evidence you heard here is filled with doubt.

This case will be over soon. I have tried my best to show you what really happened on Bloomingdale Avenue during the afternoon of April 25, 2000. I have tried my best, but my job is done. This case now rests in your hands. When this case is over, you, I, and probably some others, will from time to time think back and reflect on this case. It may be in the morning during a spare moment. This case may suddenly come back to you at night when you are trying to fall asleep. Wherever you think of this case, you are probably going to ask one thing: Did I do Sylvester Strong justice? If you have doubts about this case, have them now. For him there is no tomorrow, no second chance. Ask yourself those hard questions now, because for him tomorrow is too late. If during your deliberations you keep that in mind, we are sure that you will return a verdict of not guilty.

I only have this one chance to talk with you. When I am finished, the prosecutor will have a second chance to get up and make what is known as a rebuttal argument. I don't have a chance to talk to you after him and rebut any-

(Conclusion)
There is nothing wrong in having an emotional conclusion to your argument, if it is appropriate to the case and is done in good taste.

Challenging the prosecutor to answer a difficult issue can be an effective approach. However, make sure

thing he might tell you. I am confident, however, that since you heard the evidence, you will be able to come up with an answer for anything he might tell you. When he gets up, ladies and gentlemen, have him explain to you how it was so unreasonable for Sylvester to defend himself under these circumstances. Have him explain to you why, when surrounded by an armed, angry mob, Sylvester was not entitled to protect himself and save his own life. Have him tell you what would have been more reasonable here. If you have a doubt as to what the right thing to do would have been, then you can't say that what Sylvester did was not reasonable.

the prosecutor does not have an obvious good answer he can use.

Ladies and gentlemen, we say again that this is a case of self-defense. The prosecution has not proved beyond a reasonable doubt that when Sylvester fired that first shot, he did not reasonably believe it was necessary to do so to defend himself. The prosecution has utterly failed to prove that issue beyond a reasonable doubt. Because of their failure, we ask you to return the only verdict this evidence demands. Let him go free. Let him return to his job, his family, and his friends. Find him not guilty.

Rebuttal argument — prosecution

Members of the jury.

(Introduction)

About what happened on Bloomingdale Avenue during the afternoon of April 25, 2000, there can be no doubt. We presented four credible, consistent eyewitnesses, all of whom told you the same thing. I'm not going to review their testimony again. Suffice it to say that all of them told us Shelley Williams was merely insisting that the defendant apologize to his mother for swearing at her; George Howard arrived and fired two shots in the air; the defendant grabbed the gun, saying, "Give me the gun — you're not trying to shoot him"; he aimed the gun and fired the first shot, hitting Shelley in the arm; as Shelley turned and ran, the defendant shot him in the back; Shelley fell face down, and took the third shot in his back, too. That, in a nutshell, is what four decent persons told us, under oath, happened.

(Your strongest points)

The rebuttal cannot be negative in tone.

Accordingly, get right into your strongest ammunition and hit hard.

Mr. Hill makes much of the fact that there were inconsistencies in their testimony. Of course there were! There always are minor inconsistencies. That's because every witness to an event sees it from his own vantage point, remembers it with different degrees of recall, and testifies about it, using his own verbal style and expressions. You ought to be suspicious of testimony that is perfectly identical because it usually means that the testimony is rehearsed. That obviously didn't occur here, because each eyewitness simply told you what he saw, in his own unique way.

(Other side's contentions)

Note that the defense's arguments are woven into the middle of the rebuttal. This keeps your refutation from creating a negative atmosphere.

What Mr. Hill *didn't* talk about is more revealing. He spent almost no time talking about the testimony of the four witnesses to this crime that we presented. Instead, he spent most of his argument talking about the defendant. Why do you suppose he decided to do that? Could it be that he wants you to forget that four persons saw the defendant shoot an unarmed, defenseless man three times, twice in the back? Could it be that by constantly talking about the defendant he's trying to appeal to your emotions and get you to ignore the evidence?

(Refutation and other strong points)

In the same vein, use your refutation to again raise the strongest parts of your proof.

Mr. Hill also chose not to talk about the significant corroboration of these witnesses. Remember Dr. Ibram, the pathologist, who told us about the autopsy he performed on the body of Shelley Williams? He told us that he found three bullet wounds in the body. One was in the arm, and two were in the back. Aren't his findings completely consistent with and corroborative of the eyewitnesses, all of whom told us they saw Shelley Williams raise his hands to protect himself when the first shot was fired, saw him turn and run when the second shot was fired, and saw him fall, after which the defendant deliberately put the third shot into his back?

Since shooting a man in the back is such a repulsive fact, cutting against the defendant, you can hardly mention it too much!

There's something about physical evidence that's impossible to ignore. It never lies, never forgets, and never disappears. It simply always is there, to prove which side is telling the truth. In this case, what does the physical evidence, the location of the bullet wounds, show? It conclusively proves that the way the four eyewitnesses told us this crime happened is true.

What about the defense they presented here? There's an old saying: "The defense doesn't have to prove anything, but if they decide to call witnesses, they'd better make sense and wash with the other evidence." That, needless to say, is hardly what happened here. The defendant's testimony made no sense, and it was flatly contradicted by the four eyewitnesses.

The defendant claims he was surrounded by an angry, armed mob that beat him with baseball bats and two-by-fours simply because he didn't apologize to Rosie Garrett. Does that make any sense? Your common sense and experience in how life works tells you it didn't happen that way. The defendant claims that he somehow managed to grab George Howard's gun and fired it blindly to get the mob off him. If that's so, isn't it simply amazing how all three bullets ended up in only one person, and two of the shots ended up in his back? Now that's truly amazing! Finally, the defendant tells you that he was bleeding profusely from the face and head, fell down repeatedly, and staggered the one hundred feet to where he was when the police arrived. If that's so, wouldn't you expect to see blood spots and blood smudges all along the path he took down Bloomingdale? Of course you would — if his story is in fact true. But what did Officer Genowski tell us? When he arrived at the scene, he saw the defendant on the ground, and there was blood at that spot. He then walked over to where Shelley Williams was lying, and saw blood there as well. He then checked the sidewalk and street between those two places, and did not see any blood anywhere else. That's absolutely positive proof that the defendant's story is not true. Again, it's the physical evidence that conclusively proves who's telling the truth here.

What this case comes down to, then, is whom you decide to believe. Are you going to believe Rosie Garrett, Clarence Williams, Willie Williams, Arthur Anderson, and the physical evidence as presented through Dr. Ibram and Officer Genowski? Or are you going to believe the defendant's story? There's no middle ground in this case.

There's nothing wrong with employing sarcasm and showing disbelief in appropriate situations.

Note that the prosecutor, through the use of sarcasm, leaves little doubt that he thinks the defendant is lying, but he never says it directly. Instead, he lets the jurors reach this conclusion on their own. This is the better approach.

(Conclusion)

Since you have four eyewitnesses to the defense's one, this should be repeatedly stressed.

Mr. Hill in his closing argument asked the prosecutor to tell you what would have been the reasonable thing to do. The reasonable thing for the defendant to do would have been simply to say, "I'm sorry," apologize to Rosie Garrett, and walk away. That's what a reasonable person would have done. But not the defendant. That's not the way he does things, and that's why he's in this courtroom today.

We proved that the defendant shot and killed Shelley Williams, that he fired that gun intending to kill or cause bodily harm to Shelley Williams, that the defendant was in no way justified in doing what he did; and we proved it beyond a reasonable doubt. In short, what the defendant did on the afternoon of April 25, 2000, is what the crime of murder is all about. Thank you.

Since the defense made the argument, you're entitled to respond to it directly, under the "invited reply" doctrine.

2.   Civil case (products liability): *Hi-Temp, Inc. v. Lindberg Furnace Company*

(Hi-Temp, a company that treats metal products in furnaces, purchased an industrial vacuum furnace in September 1999 from the defendant manufacturer. On December 31, 2000, the furnace exploded. Hi-Temp had the furnace repaired. Hi-Temp claims that a design defect in the furnace, particularly in a valve, was the cause of the explosion. Lindberg maintains that the furnace was safely designed and manufactured.)

Closing argument — plaintiff

Members of the jury, this is a case about product safety. When a company makes a product, it has a duty to design it, and make it, safe. That defendant, the Lindberg Furnace Company, designed and built the valve on this vacuum furnace that was unreasonably dangerous. It was defectively designed. Why is that so?

(Introduction)

The theme — product safety — is stated immediately.

We heard Don Lyons, the general vice-president of engineering for Hi-Temp, testify that in early 1999, Hi-Temp had entered into negotiations with Lindberg for purchase of a vacuum furnace. Mr. Lyons told us that during these negotiations, Hi-Temp told Lindberg they needed a furnace that could go at least as high as 2,150 degrees and would operate around the clock, seven days a week.

(Review of testimony)

The opening argument uses the witness-by-witness method of reviewing the evidence. This technique is useful if your witnesses were credible and convincing and

Based on these requirements, Lindberg designed and manufactured a furnace which they said had an Inconel shield good to 2,300 degrees, which they sold to Hi-Temp without any reservation whatsoever for $103,000. The furnace was put into service in September 1999.

We heard Dan Waller, the maintenance foreman from Hi-Temp, testify that for the next 15 months, until December 31, 2000, he was the person primarily responsible for maintaining that furnace. His duties included cleaning the Poppet valve, cleaning O-rings, replacing worn parts, and maintaining and cleaning all water lines of calcium and lime deposits. Whenever he had to, he would contact Gerald Scott of Lindberg and consult with him.

We also heard from Mr. Vern Molitar, the plant foreman. He testified that he was working the evening of December 31, 2000. That night the furnace had steel-plated turbine parts being processed for a customer.

Mr. Molitar told us that when he came to the plant, he was told that there was no vacuum in the furnace, that there was atmospheric pressure in the furnace, and it was supposed to be pumping down to a vacuum.

Mr. Molitar checked the entire unit. He examined the gauge settings and they were proper. He examined the pumps and they appeared proper. He examined the oil levels and they were proper. He examined the charts and he told us that when he examined the charts, he noted that on the previous cycle, the load in the furnace had achieved a temperature of 1,970 degrees and it also achieved vacuum. After Mr. Molitar's examination of this entire unit on the night of December 31, 2000, what he said was an explosion occurred.

He described this explosion as a tremendous shock wave, which felt like wind pushing at him. It was accompanied by a huge boom, something like an artillery gun. He saw black sooty smoke coming out of the unit. He did not see any flame, flash, spark, or fire, but as soon as

you want to remind the jury of this. Its drawback is that where many witnesses are involved, the technique can become boring to the jury.

It's always a good idea to briefly remind the jury who the witness was before summarizing his testimony.

(What happened)

Throughout the argument, plaintiff refers to the "explosion." "Explosion" is a much stronger term than "event," "incident" or "occurrence." Choosing your labels can have a significant impact on the jury's perception of what really happened.

the explosion was over and he looked into the unit, he saw that the load inside the chamber was pushed to one side.

After the explosion, other employees from Hi-Temp had a chance to examine the wreckage. We heard from several of them. All noticed that the load in the chamber had been pushed aside and that the pump and related parts had been damaged.

Immediately after the explosion, Hi-Temp hired Jim Davis to determine the cause of the explosion. Mr. Davis has a master's degree in mechanical engineering. He is a licensed professional engineer in several states. He is the president of an engineering firm and he has extensive experience in the laws of thermodynamics. For 11 years he has designed control systems for vacuum furnaces.

Since Davis is plaintiff's only expert, and the outcome of the case depends in large part on the jury's accepting his explanations, his testimony must be covered in detail.

His background credentials should also be reviewed in some detail, since they will have a significant impact on his credibility.

During Mr. Davis' initial visit to the plant, he examined the entire furnace wreckage. He examined the diagrams. He examined the charts and spoke to the witnesses. Based upon that initial visit, Mr. Davis was not able to come to a conclusion as to what occurred. The reason was that this pump had been crated along with the foreline valve and sent to Massachusetts, and he did not have an opportunity to inspect the pump. He reported on his first inspection that he could not come to a conclusion.

Mr. Davis then went to Massachusetts, where this pump had been sent, and he inspected it. He found the drift eliminator, the small metal guides on the foreline valve, had been bent around the foreline valve and rammed into the skirt of the adjacent pump.

Since the jury has heard the testimony and seen the exhibits, they will already be familiar with the technical terms used. Nevertheless, the summary should still be as simple as possible, using few technical terms. Here plaintiff has managed to reduce a difficult technical case to three basic parts — pump, foreline valve, and drift eliminator.

Based upon his inspection of the wrecked furnace, the pump, the foreline valve, and the drift eliminator, Mr. Davis concluded that this explosion was the result of a design defect in the furnace. That design defect made the furnace unreasonably dangerous.

(Basis of liability)

The theme is repeated.

Specifically, Mr. Davis said the defect in the furnace was that there was no locking device on the foreline valve when it was in the manual mode. This foreline valve could open when you had atmospheric pressure on top of it and a vacuum beneath it.

Mr. Davis said that a proper design of this furnace would have had a locking device so that in no case could the foreline valve accidentally open when the vacuum furnace was in operation.

Take another look at the diagram of the furnace. Mr. Davis' conclusions were based upon the following physical findings:

First, this drift eliminator was found bent around the valve and rammed into the skirt of the pump. Second, there were signs of a destructive push this way, in *toward* the chamber. Third, there was damage *inside* the chamber and a shifted load. Finally, the pump was in a shifted position.

Here the attorney is using a diagram of the furnace and referring to the important parts, which are labeled. The diagram, of course, was previously admitted as an exhibit.

Based upon these physical findings, it was Mr. Davis' conclusion that this damage that resulted could only be accounted for by a force that came from *above* the foreline valve. That's the only way to account for the destruction which rammed the drift eliminator around the valve, into the pump, and created the damage inside the furnace.

It is always important to explain *why* the expert's opinions and conclusions are reasonable and are supported by the facts.

He concluded the damage could *not* have originated from inside the furnace because if it had, all the damage would have been in an *outward* direction, yet there was none. All the forces went inward. Furthermore, the *only* force that could have caused the damage was a high-pressure force coming from the pressurized side of the foreline valve into the vacuum chamber.

(Anticipating defenses)

In the same vein, you should argue that the other side's position is illogical or not supported by the facts.

He explained that when you have atmosphere on one side of the foreline valve and a vacuum on the other side, if that foreline valve opens, the air pressure charges into the vacuum at something like twice the speed of sound. This speed easily accounts for the resulting damages in the vacuum chamber and is entirely consistent with what Mr. Molitar described as a shock wave pushing at him.

It is always effective to show that favorable witnesses corroborate each other.

Mr. Davis told us that a simple and feasible design system could have prevented what had occurred. All that would have been required was an automatic locking device on the foreline valve in the manual mode to prevent it from opening at a time when there was atmospheric pressure on one side and a vacuum on the other. In short, this valve had been designed and built so that it was unreasonably dangerous. It was a defective design, that defective design caused this explosion, and that's why this defendant is responsible.

What about the damages this explosion caused? Mr. Lyons, the plant manager, told you that immediately after the occurrence, he contacted the pump manufacturer in Massachusetts, who told him to ship the pump to them. Once the pump was shipped to Massachusetts, Hi-Temp learned that the pump was not repairable.

Mr. Lyons also ordered replacement parts for the furnace. We saw the invoices. There were 17 separate orders from Lindberg, totaling $30,575.01. There were 23 separate orders from other suppliers, totaling $8,231.83. These are parts that were necessary to put the equipment back into serviceable operation.

Mr. Lyons told us that it took a total of ten weeks, from January 1 to March 10, 2001, to determine the damage, make the orders, receive the shipments of the supplies necessary to put the unit back together, and install them.

Mr. Baker, the certified public accountant, determined what the lost gross earnings for Hi-Temp were during those ten weeks. Mr. Baker examined all the books and records and, using what he termed the general trend method, he calculated the loss to be $34,265.

He also determined that the labor cost to Hi-Temp for paying company employees to do the 560 hours of repair work came to $3,773.

When you total all the damages that have been before you, you get a number in excess of $55,000, the amount we are asking. You have a

(Damages)

Notice how the elements of damages are reviewed in detail, down to the precise amounts involved. It is dangerous to be sloppy in your damages argument. The jury may well interpret sloppiness or generalizations as an attempt to inflate the damages.

This is also a good time to put each element of damages on a poster board, so that the elements can be emphasized and a total reached before the jury.

business interruption loss in excess of $34,000. You have a labor charge of $3,700. You have the parts ordered from Lindberg for $30,500, and you have the parts ordered from other suppliers for $8,200. That totals to $76,400.

So why are we asking only for $55,000, instead of the $76,400? That's because some of the replacement items that were ordered by Hi-Temp admittedly were more costly than the items that were in there prior to the explosion.

The molybdenum shield for the furnace, and some of the other parts were more expensive than the parts they replaced. In addition, the damaged parts had been used for 15 months, and were no longer new. It would not be fair to treat the damaged parts as new. Therefore, we are reducing the damages from $76,400 to the sum of $55,000 to fully adjust for these changes.

(Anticipating defenses)

This is an effective argument to refute what will certainly be argued by the defense. It shows the jury how fair and reasonable plaintiff's damages request is.

(Conclusion)

The $55,000 amount is what fairly and exactly reflects the damages as a result of that explosion of December 31, 2000, an explosion that happened because that furnace, designed and manufactured by the defendant, was defective and unreasonably dangerous. When you have reviewed the evidence, ladies and gentlemen, it clearly supports a verdict of $55,000 in favor of Hi-Temp and against the defendant.

Closing argument — defendant

May it please the Court, Mr. Kaplan, ladies and gentlemen of the jury.

Notice how the defendant has chosen not to do the standard "thanking the jury" routine.

(Issue)

The issue in this case is quite simple. They claim that the vacuum furnace is designed with a foreline valve that's unreasonably dangerous and that this claimed condition caused $55,000 worth of damage. That's the whole dispute.

Now, I am going to talk for a moment about damages. Plaintiff spent time on this issue, and there are some things we need to discuss.

(Damages)

The defendant will often argue damages

Are we really talking about damage as a result of an occurrence, or are we talking about routine maintenance and upgrading? We know that the pump oils and gaskets have to be changed yearly. When were they changed last? We know that there was thermal insulation on the furnace when it was originally sold, and now they submit bills for graphite felt at a much higher price with a much higher service life.

We know there was an Inconel lining inside the furnace, and we know they ordered a new one. They started getting quotes in May of 2000, and ordered a replacement lining in September on a "rush basis." That was three months before this so-called explosion. Again, they're moving up to a longer service life and a more expensive material for a higher temperature rating. Ken Taylor told us that the only thing wrong with the pump was that a bent baffle had to be straightened out. This would take only about $100 worth of labor and materials, yet they want us to buy them a whole new pump at a cost of $6,400. Are they really repairing damages, or are they doing routine maintenance and upgrading of the furnace? How much life was left in the old materials? Obviously it couldn't have been much, since they were already replacing them.

Now, we heard Ken Taylor, the expert from Lindberg, testify that he could have repaired the furnace in two weeks. However, Lindberg was not asked to repair the furnace. Lindberg was not asked to quote a price on repairing the furnace. Lindberg was not asked to tell them how soon they could repair the furnace. Was Hi-Temp aggressively pursuing the repair of that furnace? Did they order any repair materials on a rush basis? The answer is obviously no. They dragged it out for ten weeks, a job that could be done in two.

Ten weeks of business interruption they are claiming for $34,000. If it really is business interruption, and the furnace can be repaired in two weeks, and the furnace is needed that badly, two weeks would amount to $7,300.

We're not talking about damage as a result of

before liability, since you cannot credibly argue the liability issue if you end up arguing damages.

an occurrence, but mostly about routine maintenance and upgrading of the furnace.

Now, the court will instruct you that the plaintiff in this case, Hi-Temp, had a duty to minimize its damages. They had a duty to aggressively pursue the repair of the furnace if it would save them money, and to the extent they failed to do that, they should not collect for the excess over what an aggressive pursuit of a repair would be.

Weaving the appropriate instructions into the argument is always an effective technique, since it puts a judicial stamp of approval on the argument.

Now, let's talk about why Lindberg is not liable to Hi-Temp in this case. You're going to say: "Mr. Quade, you've got a tough job. Your company made the furnace and you can't explain how it happened." Let me suggest why we can't tell you what happened, and why that's not our obligation.

(Basis of nonliability)

The rhetorical question is a good way to squarely confront a difficult problem.

Who loaded the furnace? Did the person that loaded the furnace testify? No. What was in the furnace besides the turbine blades? Did anybody come in and tell what they saw in that furnace when they loaded it? No. Who programmed the furnace? What program was it set for? We don't know.

The rhetorical question is also a useful device to raise questions your opponent should have answered but didn't.

What were the control switch settings? We don't know that either. And why is it a secret? I suggest that the reason we don't know what happened is that these persons never came forward, yet they are all employees of Hi-Temp.

Now, there is another missing piece of information that would be very important to all of us in determining what happened. Abel Navaret was the operator of the furnace, and had no other duties. Navaret still works for Hi-Temp. Where was he? What does he know about this? Why didn't they bring him in?

The court is going to instruct you that if a witness is under a party's control and not equally available to the other parties, and he doesn't come in to testify and no reasonable excuse is made for his not testifying, it is presumed that his testimony will be adverse to their side of the case. Their plant is only perhaps 20 miles from here. That's where Navaret is. They chose not to bring him in and they know what the law is.

Here again the relevant instruction is discussed and used to reinforce the argument.

The court is also going to instruct you on what the plaintiff has to prove in this case. The plaintiff has to prove five things, two of which we take no issue with. We intentionally made the furnace without an interlock on the foreline valve, and that condition existed when we turned over the furnace to Hi-Temp. There's no dispute about that.

The plaintiff will have to prove *all five* things, and the plaintiff can't prove the other three. First, does the design of the furnace without a locking device on the foreline valve constitute an unreasonably dangerous condition? The answer is no. That's one element of the remaining three that they haven't proved.

We heard three experts, Carl Seelandt, Ken Taylor, and Cris Dobrowalski testify that it does not constitute an unreasonably dangerous condition. It's a necessary design for servicing. You can't run the furnace, conduct an ordinary leak check, or do routine maintenance without it.

On that point, let's review what Mr. Dobrowalski said. He was our outside expert. He has no ax to grind, yet he corroborated our own people. He says the foreline valve mechanism is very reputable and safe. He was ashamed to say he doesn't do so well at his company in the design of their products.

You need the manual operation of the furnace to disconnect the pump. You need the manual mode so that an operator can use his brains and do the testing, checking, and maintenance such a furnace requires. Does this sound unreasonably dangerous? Of course not! Mr. Dobrowalski's conclusion was that the design of the foreline valve without an interlock in the manual mode does not constitute an unreasonably dangerous condition. So here we are, years later, and normally the industry progresses and you learn new things on the way, but we haven't invented anything better than the design that was used on this furnace.

So much for the proposition that the condition was an unreasonably dangerous one. The

(Instructions)

The defendant can use the elements instruction to his advantage, particularly if there are several essential elements and the defense is based on more than one, since the plaintiff should lose on the liability issue if it fails to prove each element by a preponderance of the evidence. A diagram of the five elements should be used here.

Showing that the "outside" expert corroborates the employee experts necessarily enhances the credibility of them all.

evidence shows that the plaintiff has not met its burden on that issue.

The second proposition that the plaintiff has not met its burden on is proximate cause. The condition which it claims renders the furnace unreasonably dangerous must be the condition that causes the damage in the furnace.

We have had three experts who have made their life's work vacuum engineering testify they don't know what caused the damage. As I said before, if you don't have any of the facts about what's in the furnace, how it's loaded, what the control settings are on, and who operated the furnace, you just can't determine it. But we also know that the condition in the product which they claim is unreasonably dangerous, didn't cause it. Simply opening the foreline valve, according to Carl Seelandt, Chris Dobrowalski, and Ken Taylor, could not have created the kind of damage that occurred. Three experts said this could not be the cause of the damage. The plaintiff has simply failed to prove that the damage was actually caused by any unreasonably dangerous condition in that furnace.

The third proposition that the plaintiff has failed to meet its burden on is damages, and I have already talked about that.

Now, a few words about Mr. Davis, the plaintiff's witness and only person who condemns the design. The case involves a vacuum furnace. Has Mr. Davis ever built one? No. Ever designed one? No. Has he ever run one? No. Has he ever leak-checked one? No. Has he ever read any of the literature on it? No. Has he ever run any experiments on it? No. Has he run any kind of tests? No.

Is this the kind of expertise you want to rely on to determine whether this furnace system is unreasonably dangerous? Of course not. You have to determine the credibility of the witnesses and the weight to be given to their testimony, and you should consider Mr. Davis' qualifications in deciding whether his testimony can be

Since the defense has three experts to the plaintiff's one, this advantage should be repeatedly stressed.

(Their side and refutation)

The safest way to attack an expert is to challenge his professional expertise, since this is not an attack on the expert himself, which always runs the risk of offending the jury.

accepted. When you look at his background, and particularly when you compare it to the expertise and experience of the three experts we presented, you can only reach one conclusion: Mr. Davis' opinion simply cannot be accepted.

In short, the evidence here has failed to show that the furnace and foreline valve were unreasonably dangerous, or that it caused the damage here. Lindberg purposely designed the valve to allow the operator to select between manual and automatic modes. The operator must be somebody who knows what he is doing when he operates a sophisticated machine. Lindberg gave its sophisticated industrial customers credit for having brains. Don't hold it against them.

Rebuttal argument — plaintiff

Ladies and gentlemen, I hate to get into arguments over witness' qualifications, but since Mr. Quade raised this issue I'm going to respond to it. He told you Mr. Davis was not qualified. Why? Simply because he hasn't spent his life in the vacuum furnace industry. They'd conveniently like you to forget that Mr. Davis is a mechanical engineer who has worked 11 years for a company that designs the control systems for vacuum furnaces.

If you want to argue about qualifications of experts, however, let's look at the witnesses that the defense called. First of all, they bring in Mr. Seelandt, who was an employee of Lindberg at the time of the occurrence. That's hardly the kind of neutral, unbiased expert you'd want to rely on. When was he first contacted and given sufficient facts upon which to testify? A few weeks ago!

How about Mr. Dobrowalski, the man who came here from Boston? Well, Mr. Dobrowalski is not a licensed professional engineer, as is Mr. Davis. Mr. Dobrowalski has only a bachelor's degree in electric engineering. The problem with Mr. Dobrowalski is this: He was also contacted only weeks ago by the defendant, and he told

This type of ending can have a much greater impact than the standard "request for a favorable verdict" ending.

Notice how little time is spent defending the qualifications of plaintiff's expert before the argument shifts to attacking the bias of defendant's experts. This converts a defensive response into an aggressive, affirmative argument.

There's nothing wrong with using a little sarcasm in appropriate situations.

you that even at that time he was not provided sufficient facts upon which to base his opinion. Doesn't that bother you a little bit?

Finally, they called Mr. Taylor, who they claim was so neutral and objective. Did he ever see the furnace? No. Did he ever examine the wreckage? No. Did he ever talk to any of the witnesses? No. But whom does he work for? Kinney Vacuum Company. And what do they manufacture? Vacuum pumps. And who buys their vacuum pumps? The defendant, of course. Doesn't that bother you a little bit?

Notice that this is a fairly strong attack on these defense experts, yet it does not go overboard. The plaintiff never *directly* argues that these experts were bought and paid for; instead, the jury is allowed to reach this conclusion on its own.

(Damages)

Let's go back to damages for a moment. Mr. Quade claims that the damages were not quite as bad as what we showed you. Obviously when you repair a unit with new parts, it is more valuable than it was before the occurrence. That's why we said that although the repair costs were $75,000, we are asking only for $55,000.

The weakest part of the defense argument was on the ten weeks repair time. Consequently, this is the point the plaintiff jumps on and argues the most.

Mr. Quade claims we could have put the thing back together in two weeks. Two weeks? What did the evidence show? On January 5, Hi-Temp ordered a series of parts from Lindberg. Half the parts didn't get from Lindberg to Hi-Temp until January 30. The other parts didn't arrive until February 16 and 18. They knew that the unit was down. If anybody could have accelerated the delivery, you would have thought it would have been the defendant, Lindberg. It took them seven weeks just to get the parts to Hi-Temp, and yet they claim they could have put the unit back together in two weeks. Their claim is simply preposterous.

Next, Mr. Quade complains that there are certain witnesses to the explosion that we haven't seen. However, Mr. Molitar testified he was on duty at the time. He examined all of the instruments, all of the pumps, all of the oil levels prior to the explosion. He knew what was in the furnace at the time. Rather than challenge what Mr. Molitar told us, Mr. Quade instead says: "Where is Abel Navaret? Why haven't we heard from him?"

However, remember what Mr. Taylor told us? Lindberg performed an investigation immediately after this thing. They had men in there immediately and, based upon what they learned in their investigation, if they for one moment thought Abel Navaret could help their case, they could have subpoenaed him into court. They have the same right to subpoena witnesses as I do. He's still up in Northlake. They knew that. Mr. Navaret could have been subpoenaed and been examined by Mr. Quade — if he for a moment thought Mr. Navaret would have helped the defense.

This is the standard reply to the "missing witness" argument.

Ladies and gentlemen, Mr. Quade's argument cuts both ways. You heard Mr. Taylor testify that Lindberg had many people investigate this loss. Where are they? Why does Lindberg rely on experts that they contacted a few weeks before trial rather than their own people that initially investigated this occurrence? If you want to interpret a witness' absence against the party who didn't bring them, then take a hard look at them.

Turning an argument around and using it against the other side is always effective (and something to consider before making an argument that can later be used against you).

Finally, it's important in this case to remember that Lindberg has not given you one plausible explanation of a force which could cause the extensive damage you saw, not one theory in all their investigations.

Instead, what do they tell you? They tell you Mr. Davis' theory isn't plausible. What did Mr. Seelandt say? He said it couldn't happen the way Mr. Davis explained it. He claimed that air rushing into the vacuum chamber couldn't produce such damage. Yet the damage was obviously there; and Mr. Seelandt, their own expert, couldn't explain it.

What did Mr. Dobrowalski tell you? He's simply a carbon copy of Mr. Seelandt. He's also quick to tell you that Mr. Davis is wrong, yet he can't explain it either.

What about having a locking safety system on the foreline valve of the furnace? That would have prevented the explosion from happening. That obviously could have and should have been included in its design and manufacture. The only reason you have been given for not having interlock protection is that then you would not be able to detect leaks. That's been the only reason that Lindberg has given.

Yet their own expert, Mr. Seelandt, admitted on cross-examination that you would *not* have to open the foreline valve to check for leaks in the system. He admitted that even if the foreline valve had a locking device, that would not prevent you from testing for leaks. Their own expert refutes their main argument.

Ladies and gentlemen, the evidence in this case has shown that in 1999, Hi-Temp purchased a furnace from Lindberg for $103,000. After this explosion, Hi-Temp spent $34,000 to repair it, and incurred other losses. Lindberg has denied responsibility for this occurrence for years. They have had Mr. Davis' report on the explosion at least since last year. Doesn't it seem strange they would deny responsibility all this time but wait until a few weeks before trial to contact two of their experts?

Lindberg's defense, at best, is that although they designed and manufactured the furnace, they can't explain how what wasn't supposed to happen, in fact, did happen. It's their furnace, they designed it, they made it, yet they can't explain it.

Of all the experts you have heard, Mr. Davis was by far the most persuasive. Mr. Davis is the only expert witness in this case who took the trouble to go to the plant, see the unit, inspect the wreckage, talk to the witnesses, examine the charts, and go to Massachusetts to examine the pump.

Based on that extensive study of the facts, Mr. Davis concluded that the explosion was caused when the foreline valve opened, allowing atmospheric pressure to rush into the vacuum chamber of the furnace. The foreline valve did not have a locking safety system which would have prevented the valve from improperly opening. This failure made the furnace unrea-

Notice how many times plaintiff has argued that the defendant's experts are "recent arrivals." This is probably plaintiff's best point to rebut the fact that the defense has three experts to plaintiff's one.

Immediately afterwards, plaintiff builds up, and contrasts, its sole expert, so that the jury's last thought is on that expert.

sonably dangerous, and this failure was the defect which was the direct cause of the explosion.

Accordingly, we ask that you return the only verdict this evidence warrants, a verdict in the amount of $55,000 in favor of Hi-Temp and against the defendant.

X

OBJECTIONS

§10.1. Introduction

In some ways making proper, timely objections is the most difficult skill for the inexperienced trial lawyer to master. This is difficult for two reasons. First, evidence is usually taught in law schools at a theoretical level, which, while important, has little to do with the contexts in which evidentiary and procedural problems routinely arise during trials. Trial lawyers learn to associate "buzz words" with appropriate objections until the association is automatic. A buzz word is simply a word or phrase that an experienced trial lawyer is conditioned to know is objectionable. For instance, when a lawyer starts a question with "Isn't it conceivable that . . . ," a trial lawyer will instantly react because the question necessarily calls for a speculative answer. Second, timeliness is essential when making objections, since making a late objection is often worse than not objecting at all.

The difficulty in mastering objections is that recognizing the buzz words and reacting to them in timely fashion can only be developed thoroughly through trial experience. They are difficult if not impossible to master in a textbook environment. (However, interactive video programs, which contain trial scenarios and require you to make correct and timely evidentiary objections, are excellent learning tools.)

Despite these problems, objections in a trial context can and should be studied to develop a methodology that, when joined with some actual experience, will result in ultimate mastery of this essential trial skill. This chapter will discuss when to make objections, how to make them, how to make offers of proof, and the types of evidentiary objections commonly encountered at trial.

§10.2. Making objections before trial

Whenever possible, it is usually advantageous for both the judge and lawyers to raise anticipated evidentiary issues before trial. The judge will appreciate it since it makes the trial run more smoothly (which jurors also appreciate) and it gives him time to make a careful, reasoned decision on the issues without the pressures of trial. Lawyers like it because it allows them to prepare their cases in light of the judge's rulings on those issues and, if on the losing side of the ruling, allows the opposing lawyer to make a good record for appellate purposes. It also reduces the possibility that the jury will hear inadmissible matters (and need to be instructed to disregard them, which is largely ineffective).

Evidentiary issues can be raised before trial in several ways: a pretrial motion to preclude evidence, a hearing on objections raised in a pretrial memorandum, and in motions in limine.

1. Pretrial motions to preclude evidence

A written pretrial motion to preclude testimony, usually filed well before trial, asks the court to bar evidence the other side will seek to have admitted at trial. The pretrial motion is the best way to get important issues, which will affect the way you plan for trial, decided well in advance. For example, if in a criminal case the defense knows that the prosecution will try to introduce evidence of other bad acts the defendant has committed, under FRE 404(b) a pretrial motion to preclude this evidence should be made. Regardless of the judge's ruling, the defense can then plan accordingly. If in a civil case the defendant knows the plaintiff plans to introduce evidence of subsequent design changes or the existence of insurance, the defendant should make a pretrial motion to preclude this evidence. Once again, regardless of the judge's ruling, the defendant can plan accordingly.

2. Pretrial memorandum and conference

In civil cases many judges require the parties to file with the court, well in advance of the trial date, a pretrial memorandum, sometimes called a "pretrial statement." The pretrial memorandum usually lists the planned witnesses, exhibits, and jury instructions for each party, and any objections to them by the opposing party. If there are objections to exhibits, the judge will usually hold a pretrial conference and rule on as many of the objections as possible before trial. Certain evidentiary objections, principally relevance and hearsay, can usually be ruled on before trial. Others, primarily foundation objections, cannot be, since the judge will usually need to hear foundation testimony from a witness before ruling on such an objection. Objections to the wording of requested jury instructions can often be resolved the same way.

3. Motions in limine

A motion in limine is simply a motion made before trial starts, during a recess, or just before a witness testifies. While the better practice is to raise anticipated evidentiary problems in a written pretrial motion, in the real world of trials this is not always possible. Lawyers sometimes learn a fact, or realize that the other lawyer intends to introduce certain evidence, just before the trial starts or even during the trial.

A motion in limine simply asks the court to rule on an evidentiary matter so that it need not be decided in the middle of a witness' testimony.

Example:

> *Lawyer:* Your Honor, before the jury comes out, we have an evidentiary matter we would like to take up before Mr. Williams begins his testimony.
>
> *Judge:* Very well, what is it?
>
> *Lawyer:* We just learned that Mr. Williams has a misdemeanor conviction for assault three years ago. That is not a prior conviction that should be usable under Rule 609 to impeach his credibility. We ask that the plaintiff be precluded from mentioning this conviction during the cross-examination.
>
> *Judge:* Counsel, any argument?
>
> *Opposing lawyer:* No, your Honor. We know of the conviction but were not planning to use it during our cross-examination.
>
> *Judge:* In that case, the prior conviction is precluded, and will not be mentioned during the trial.

The jury can then be brought into the courtroom and the trial continues.

§10.3. When to make objections during trial

Every trial involves numerous situations in which objections can be made. When to make objections, however, involves more than simply having proper situations in which to make them. It also involves almost instantaneous decisions on whether to make the objections at all. The following should always be considered.

1. Jurors dislike objections

Jurors see lawyers who make constant objections as lawyers who are trying to keep the real truth from them. Since your credibility as a lawyer has a critical influence on the outcome of the trial, minimize your interference while evidence is being introduced before the jury. The more objections you make, the more your credibility suffers. Anticipate evidentiary problems. Raise them before trial whenever possible. During the trial, try to make your objections out of the jury's presence, during recesses, motions in limine, and side-bar conferences. On the other hand, don't be afraid to make objections. Jurors have all seen enough television to know and expect that some objections will be made.

2.   Will the answer hurt your case?

Unless you are reasonably sure that the answer to a question will hurt your case, it is usually better not to object. If you make the objection and the court sustains it, the jury will naturally wonder what the answer would have been, had the witness only been allowed to answer. What the jury thinks the answer would have been is often worse than the actual answer. Ask yourself: will the ruling really make a difference? Save your objections for what you are reasonably certain will be damaging.

On the other hand, you must keep the judge in mind. Repeatedly failing to make a proper objection (because the answer won't hurt your case) can result later on in the judge overruling a proper objection (where the answer will hurt your case), since you have through your conduct conditioned the judge to assume that what was repeatedly asked earlier was proper. Object enough to let the judge know that you know when to make proper objections.

3.   Does your objection have a solid legal basis?

If you do make an objection, be reasonably sure you will be sustained. Have statutory and case authority ready to support the major objections you anticipate making during the trial. Making an objection and having it overruled is often worse than not making it at all, since the objection merely draws the jurors' attention to the question and eventual answer.

4.   Protect the record

Evidentiary objections must be made with two purposes in mind. First, to keep the jury from hearing improper evidence; second, to preserve any error on appeal.

You must make and protect your record. Errors in admitting evidence at trial are usually waived on appeal unless a proper, timely, specific objection was made during the trial.

5.   Can you use an objection as a tactical device?

Making an objection necessarily has the effect of breaking the flow and pace of the opponent's examination or argument. While it is unethical to make an unfounded objection solely to disrupt your opponent (or coach your witness), it is proper to make an objection whenever there is a legitimate evidentiary basis for it, even if the inevitable effect is to disrupt your opponent's presentation.

§10.4.   *How to make objections during trial*

FRE 103 governs rulings on evidence. The main considerations are the following:

1. Timeliness

Evidentiary objections must be timely. If a question is improper, an objection must be made before an answer to the question is given. Ordinarily, you should object to a question only when it is completed. If, however, the question itself is directly prejudicial as well as improper, you must object promptly when this first becomes apparent.

If an answer is improper, an objection must be made as soon as that fact becomes apparent. Although it is entirely proper (and necessary in order to protect the record) to object to a completed answer and, if sustained, ask that the answer be struck and the jury instructed to disregard it, this is obviously an unsatisfactory solution. You can't "unring the bell," nor will the jury be able to, although the instruction to disregard alerts jurors to the improper evidence so that they should not discuss it during deliberations.

Tell the court that you are making an objection. All too often lawyers begin to state the reasons for the objections without ever announcing that they are objecting.

Example:

> Counsel: Your Honor, it seems to me that what counsel is trying to do here is to delve into the . . .
>
> Court: Are you making a speech or do you have an objection in mind?

Tell the court you are making an objection before stating anything else.

Examples:

> *Objection, your Honor. . . .*
>
> *Your Honor, we object. . . .*

Most courts require that objections be made while standing. Be sure you know what the practice in your court is. Even if not required, standing up while making an objection is a good idea since it gets the attention of the judge, opponent, and the witness.

Most courts also require that only one lawyer for any party can make and, if necessary, argue an objection. Many courts also require that only the lawyer conducting the direct or cross-examination of a witness can make objections during the testimony of that witness. This keeps things simple, and prevents other lawyers representing a party from making additional objections.

2. Legal basis

Objections should state the legal basis for the objection. This should be done succinctly, without excessive argument.

Examples:

> *The question calls for a hearsay answer.*
>
> *The answer is unresponsive.*
>
> *The exhibit violates the original documents rule.*

If you wish to argue the matter, or your opponent attempts to make a long-winded, argumentative speech before the jury, ask for a side-bar conference. In that way the arguments on the objections can, as they should, be made without the jury hearing them.

Insist on a ruling. The objecting party is entitled to obtain a ruling on every objection made. Failure to obtain a ruling usually results in waiving any error on appeal.

Example:

> *Your Honor, may we have a ruling on our objection?*

Sometimes opposing counsel will withdraw the question being objected to before the court rules on the objection. When this is done, make sure that the next question is not essentially the same as the last. If it is, renew the objection.

Where, to preserve the record, you must have an answer struck and the jury instructed to disregard it, do so promptly and in a way that lets the jury know why it is being instructed.

Example:

> *Counsel:* Objection, your Honor, to the hearsay answer.
> *Court:* Objection sustained.
> *Counsel:* Your Honor, may we have the answer stricken and the jury instructed to disregard the improper answer?
> *Court:* Very well. The answer is stricken, the jury is instructed to disregard the answer.

Make sure that your objections, as well as any arguments for the objection, are directed to the judge. Don't argue directly with the opposing lawyer or try to interrupt him. The judge may let both sides argue on the objection at a side-bar conference, the usual procedure being to let the objector argue first and then have the other side respond before ruling on the objection. Be professional, make a legal argument, and make it to the judge. Show the judge why the evidence should be admitted or excluded, based on a specific evidentiary rule, and why that result is fair.

Finally, if an objection is sustained against you, think about how you can overcome the objection. Was the objection based on a significant rule of evidence, such as hearsay or privilege, or was it based on an improper form of questioning? If the former, you should always see if you can get the same, or nearly the same, evidence properly admitted. If the latter, simply rephrasing the question will usually get around the objection.

Inexperienced lawyers are usually intimidated by objections, and frequently abandon an important point or line of questioning when an objection is sustained. As the direct examiner, you should always ask: If the point is important, how can I overcome the objection and get the evidence properly admitted?

3. Procedure

The safest procedure is to make the objection, then hesitate a moment before stating a legal basis for the objection. If the basis for the objection is obvious, the court will ordinarily sustain the objection without requiring you to state the legal basis. This is the best of all possible worlds, because the court's ruling is proper if there is *any* proper basis for the ruling. By momentarily hesitating, you give the court a chance to sustain your objection without having to state a basis for it. Under FRE 103, stating a specific ground for your objection is necessary only if it is not apparent from the context of the question or answer. If you state a specific ground for an objection, but it's not a proper one, the court can overrule your objection, even if there is another proper legal basis for objecting.

Always be prepared, of course, to state the specific legal basis for any objection you make. If the court overruled your objection, you preserve error only if you state a proper legal basis.

Learn what your judge's practices are. Some judges always want you to state the basis for any objection and will ask you for the legal basis for your objection if you haven't stated it. Others will only ask for a basis when the reason is not apparent from the question or answer.

Finally, always remember that in many situations more than one legal ground may exist for excluding testimony or exhibits. For instance, a witness' testimony could violate the hearsay and privilege rules. A record, even where a proper business-records foundation was established, could still violate hearsay rules. A photograph could both lack a proper foundation and be unduly prejudicial. Accordingly, don't hang your hat on just one reason for excluding evidence. Where the evidence is damaging, develop alternative grounds why the evidence should be excluded.

If the trial judge ruled on an evidentiary objection before trial, must the objection be renewed during trial when the evidence is offered to preserve error on appeal? The federal courts are divided, some always requiring that an objection be renewed during trial and others holding that this was not always required. (State jurisdictions are divided on this issue as well.)

In 2000, FRE 103(a)(2) was amended by adding the following language: "Once the court makes a definitive ruling on the record admitting or excluding evidence, either at or before trial, a party need not renew an objection or offer of proof to preserve a claim of error for appeal." The key question is whether the trial court's ruling is "definitive." If, at the time of the ruling, the judge states that it is conditional or provisional, or that the matter may be reconsidered later, you must object again when the evidence is offered during trial. If you are not sure whether the ruling is definitive, renew your objection during trial.

§10.5.   Offers of proof

When your opponent's objection has succeeded in excluding important evidence, you must make an offer of proof. The offer is necessary for two reasons. First, it may convince the trial judge to reverse his ruling. Second, the offer will create a record so that the reviewing court will know what the excluded evidence was and be able to determine if the exclusion was improper, and, if so, whether the improper exclusion constituted reversible error. An offer of proof is required under FRE 103 whenever it is not apparent from the context what the excluded evidence is.

There are two principal ways to make an offer of proof. Under the first method the lawyer simply tells the court what the proposed testimony would be, either in a narrative or question-and-answer format. This must be done out of the jury's presence. Tell the court you would like to make an offer of proof and ask for a side-bar conference, or, if your offer of proof will be lengthy, ask that the jury be excused for a few minutes.

Example:

> *Counsel:*   Your Honor, if we were allowed to pursue this line of questioning, the witness would testify that one week after the robbery, the defendant tried to sell her a watch which we can prove was taken during the robbery.

Example:

> *Counsel:*   Your Honor, if allowed to answer the question objected to, the witness would testify as follows:
> *Q.*   What did he tell you at that time?
> *A.*   He said: "I think I'm going home. I've got to pay the plumbing contractor for the work he did."

The second method involves using the witness himself. Again out of the jury's presence, continue the examination of the witness, using the same questions to which objections had been sustained. In this way the reviewing court will have a verbatim transcript of the testimony the trial court excluded. Under FRE 103(b) the trial court can require an offer of proof in question-and-answer form.

The first method has the advantage of efficiency, the second, the advantage of completeness. Although the second is preferable because it creates a clear record, it is time-consuming and impractical. Repeatedly asking that the jury be excused so you can make an offer of proof will incur both the court's and jury's disapproval. Save this for the critical parts of your case.

The offer should conform to the usual rules of evidence, since there is no error when the trial court excludes evidence that, as disclosed by the offer of proof, is objectionable for any reason, even if the objections could be cured. The opposing counsel can make any appropriate objections during the offer of proof.

Where the evidence successfully objected to is an exhibit, it must be made part of the record so the appellate court can review it, if its exclusion is raised as error on appeal. During the trial the clerk will usually collect all exhibits. Make sure she receives all the exhibits you have offered in evidence.

§10.6.   *Evidentiary objections*

Any law student who has taken a course in evidence can define the basic evidentiary objections. Trial lawyers, however, do not react to evidence in terms of those definitions. By the time they could determine whether a given question or answer falls within an evidentiary definition, the objection would hardly be timely. Trial lawyers shorten this thought process by learning and reacting to "buzz words," those forms that objectionable questions and answers commonly take in an actual trial.

The following evidentiary objections are commonly encountered at trial. Note that the objections can be classified into two broad categories, objections directed to form and those directed to substantive evidence. Objections to form can usually be cured by rephrasing the question or answer. On the other hand, objections to substantive evidence, if sustained, will actually result in excluding evidence.

Example (form):

> Q.   Mr. Jones, is it possible that the driver of the other car didn't come to a complete stop at the stop sign?
> *Counsel:*   Objection, your Honor. Counsel is asking the witness to speculate.
> *Court:*   Sustained.
> Q.   Mr. Jones, did you see the other car as it approached the sign?
> A.   Yes.
> Q.   Describe what the car did.
> A.   It came to the corner, slowed down to around 10 mph, then kept going through the intersection without ever stopping.

In this example, the examining lawyer overcame the objection simply by rephrasing his questions in proper form to elicit the desired information. The objection only forced the examining lawyer to ask better phrased questions and ultimately obtain a better answer than he would probably have gotten to his original question. For this reason, it is often better not to object to questions that are improper in form only.

Example (substance):

> Q.   Mr. Jones, tell the jury what you heard the bystander, Shirley Smith, say about how this accident happened.
> *Counsel:*   Objection, hearsay.
> *Court:*   Sustained.

In this example, the objection has succeeded in excluding from evidence any statements by Shirley Smith. If there are no applicable exceptions to the hearsay rule, the statement simply cannot get into evidence, unless the proponent calls Shirley Smith as a witness to describe what she personally saw. If the proponent believes that a hearsay exception such as present sense impression or excited utterance applies, he should ask for permission to make an offer of proof out of the jury's presence.

The following objections are commonly encountered at trial during the presentation of evidence through witnesses and exhibits:

Objections to questions
a. calls for irrelevant answer
b. calls for immaterial answer
c. witness is incompetent
d. violates the best evidence rule
e. calls for a privileged communication
f. calls for a conclusion
g. calls for an opinion (by an incompetent witness)
h. calls for a narrative answer
i. calls for a hearsay answer
j. leading
k. repetitive (asked and answered)
l. beyond the scope (of the direct, cross, or redirect)
m. assumes facts not in evidence
n. confusing/misleading/ambiguous/vague/unintelligible
o. speculative
p. compound question
q. argumentative
r. improper characterization
s. misstates evidence/misquotes the witness
t. cumulative
u. improper impeachment

Objections to answers
a. irrelevant
b. immaterial
c. privileged
d. conclusion
e. opinion
f. hearsay
g. narrative
h. improper characterization
i. violates parol evidence rule
j. unresponsive/volunteered

Objections to exhibits
a. irrelevant
b. immaterial
c. no foundation
d. no authentication
e. violates original documents (best evidence) rule
f. contains hearsay/double hearsay
g. prejudice outweighs its probative value
h. contains inadmissible matter (mentions insurance, prior convictions, etc.)

1. Relevance (FRE 401 et seq.)

a. Definition

Relevant evidence under FRE 401 is evidence that has "any tendency to make the existence of any fact that is of consequence to the determination of the action more probable than it would be without the evidence." This definition incorporates both traditional relevance and materiality concepts. Relevance issues are directed to the sound discretion of the court.

In dealing with relevancy issues, it is useful to break the topic into sequential stages.

(1) Is it generally relevant (FRE 401-402)?
(2) Do FRE 403 considerations prevent admission?

Under FRE 403, relevant evidence may be excluded if its probative value is "substantially outweighed" by considerations such as unfair prejudice, confusion, delay, or waste of time. This balancing test is intentionally tipped in favor of admissibility.

If evidence is generally admissible under the FRE 401-403 balancing test, special relevance rules may nevertheless exclude the offered evidence.

(3) Do character trait rules apply (FRE 404, 405)?
(4) Do other acts rules apply (FRE 404(b))?
(5) Do habit rules apply (FRE 406)?
(6) Do policy exclusion rules apply (FRE 407–415)?
(7) Do privileges rules apply (FRE 501)?

Basic relevance objections are important and can usually be anticipated in advance of trial. Hence, the safest procedure is to raise likely issues through pretrial motions and motions in limine.

b. Objection

Your Honor, we object. The question calls for an irrelevant answer.

Objection, your Honor. The witness' answer is going into irrelevant matter.

Objection. The exhibit is irrelevant.

c. Examples

Relevancy objections during trial usually arise where circumstantial evidence is offered, because the probative value of the proffered evidence may not be readily apparent. These circumstantial evidence issues usually are based on one of the special relevancy rules such as other acts or habit evidence.

Since relevancy issues can be complex and may involve substantial areas of additional testimony, as the opponent you should usually insist on an offer of proof. Do not be satisfied by a conclusory assertion from opposing counsel that the proffered evidence is relevant or will be "connected up." Do not tolerate a long-winded narrative by opposing counsel before the jury, explaining why the proffered testimony is relevant. Ask for a side bar and request a full offer of proof. At the conclusion of the offer of proof, make any relevancy or other objections that are appropriate.

Consider the following example of permissible other acts evidence. In a burglary case, the prosecutor can prove that the defendant obtained a copy of the building's floor plan several weeks before the burglary. This is circumstantial evidence of a plan or opportunity, and is admissible under FRE 404(b) as a permissible use of other acts evidence.

2. Materiality

a. Definition

Evidence is material if it has some logical bearing on an issue in the case. What is at issue is determined by the elements of the claims and defenses raised by the pleadings.

The Federal Rules of Evidence have abandoned the term "materiality," which is now incorporated in the broad definition of relevancy contained in FRE 401. However, many state jurisdictions still differentiate between relevancy and materiality.

b. Objection

Objection, your Honor. This evidence is immaterial.

c. Examples

In the standard automobile case, the plaintiff must prove negligence, causation, and damages. Hence, proffered evidence that the defendant was insured is immaterial to the issues in the case.

In a worker's compensation case, since contributory negligence is not a defense, proof that the worker was negligent is immaterial.

3. Incompetent (FRE 601-606)

a. Definition

Incompetency refers to witnesses. A witness is incompetent if he suffers from a statutory disqualification that prevents him from testifying. The federal competency rules are in FRE 601-606. The only requirements are that a witness take an oath to testify truthfully and that he have personal knowledge about the matter he is testifying on. However, FRE 601 defers to state competency rules in federal civil diversity cases. Hence, you must also know the applicable state competency rules. Many states still have competency rules such as age requirements and Dead Man's Acts.

b.   Objection

*I object, your Honor. The witness is attempting to testify to a business trans-
action in violation of the Dead Man's Act.*

c.   Examples

Witness competency issues can usually be anticipated in advance, since
discovery rules in civil cases, and in some criminal cases, require disclosure
of witness lists. Today, however, incompetency disqualifications are uncommon and are usually limited to young age, infirm mind, and Dead Man's
Acts. Dead Man's Act issues can be complex and should always be researched thoroughly whenever the lawsuit involves the estate of a deceased.

4.   Privileged communication (FRE 501)

a.   Definition

Communications made in confidence between parties having certain
relationships are, upon objection, barred from disclosure. FRE 501 leaves
unchanged the prior law on privilege. The privileges are based on the policy that it is preferable to foster open, frank communications between persons having certain relationships by protecting these communications
from disclosure at trial. The most common privileges are attorney-client,
physician-patient, and husband-wife.

FRE 501 defers to state privilege rules in federal civil diversity cases.
Hence, you must know the state privilege rules as well. The state rules are
frequently different from the federal ones, particularly in the marital and
physician-patient privileges area, and the jurisdictions vary considerably
regarding what relationships are protected by privilege rules.

b.   Objection

*I object. The question calls for a privileged communication between attorney
and client. I claim the privilege for my client.*

c.   Examples

Problems in the privilege areas commonly center on who the holder
of the privilege is, whether the matter discussed is subject to a privilege,
whether the communication was made under confidential circumstances,
whether a waiver of the privilege has occurred, and whether the privilege
has been terminated.

Privilege issues can frequently be anticipated. These issues are usually
complex and must be thoroughly researched in advance of trial. If you anticipate a privilege problem, the best procedure is to raise it with a pretrial
motion, as part of a pretrial conference hearing, or in a motion in limine
so that the issues can be resolved before trial if possible. If the problem
suddenly arises during trial, the best practice is to object and ask for a side-
bar conference so that you can adequately argue the objection.

Consider the following example of an exchange where a privileged issue has been raised by the opposing counsel:

> *Q.*   Mr. Smith, what did you tell your lawyer about what happened at the intersection?
> *Counsel:*   Objection, your Honor. That is a privileged communication. May I be heard at side bar?

5.   Original documents (best evidence) rule (FRE 1001 et seq.)

a.   Definition

The original documents rule, often called the best evidence rule, applies principally to writings. The federal rule, contained in FRE 1001-1004, makes substantial changes from previous law.

The federal rule applies to any writing, recording, or photograph if it is "closely related to a controlling issue." If it applies, the general rule is that a "duplicate," such as a carbon copy or photocopy, is generally admissible to the same extent as the "original." However, if there is a genuine dispute over the writing's authenticity, such as a claim that the signature is forged or the contents have been altered, the original must be produced. Finally, in these situations the production of the original is excused if it is unavailable because, in good faith, it was lost or destroyed, it cannot be obtained by legal process, or the opponent has the original and refuses to produce it after being served with a notice to produce. The contents of the writing can then be proved by "other evidence," which includes duplicates as well as any other proof, such as oral testimony.

Keep in mind that some states still follow the traditional original documents rule, which usually requires production of the original.

b.   Objection

Objection, your Honor. This evidence is not the best evidence of the contract. Your Honor, we object to this exhibit on grounds of the best evidence rule.

c.   Examples

Best evidence objections arise less frequently because the federal rule generally permits the admission of duplicates. However, if the original is still required, three things must usually be proved. First, the nonproduction of the original must be accounted for before other evidence of its contents is admissible. Second, a duplicate must be shown to be accurate before it can be admitted (see §6.3(16)). Third, there must be proof that the original was in fact signed by the parties, if the writing is a legal document, such as a contract or promissory note.

Perhaps the most common example involves contracts. Consider the following:

Smith executes a contract with Jones. The original, bearing both Smith's and Jones' signatures, is placed in a file drawer in Smith's office. Copies of the contract are made and kept by both Smith and Jones. Two years later, Smith sues Jones for breach of contract. Jones denies having signed the contract, triggering the application of the rule and the requirement that the original be produced at trial. However, Smith cannot find the original of the contract. It's no longer in the file drawer. Smith and his office staff look everywhere for the original, without success. Just before trial they search again, without success. Under these circumstances, a copy of the contract, if properly authenticated, will be admissible at trial.

6.   Parol evidence rule

a.   Definition

The parol evidence rule bars from admission in evidence extrinsic oral evidence that modifies or contradicts a contractual instrument, freely entered into by competent parties, complete and clear on its face. Its purpose is to prevent a written agreement from being attacked and contradicted by oral testimony.

b.   Objection

Objection, your Honor. The question calls for an answer that violates the parol evidence rule.

c.   Examples

Violations of the parol evidence rule most frequently occur in contract cases when testimony relating to the execution of the contract is elicited. While it is proper (and necessary) to present evidence showing that the contract was signed by the parties, it is usually improper to elicit testimony between the parties as to what they intended the contract to do or what the terms of the contract mean to them.

Most problems involving the parol evidence rule concern the exceptions and whether they apply in a given situation. Exceptions include mistakes, incompleteness, ambiguities, and other uncertainties on the contract. Since the application of an exception will allow into evidence an entire additional line of inquiry, a prompt objection and insistence on an offer of proof is essential. Parol evidence objections can raise complex issues and should always be researched and raised in advance of trial, through pretrial motions or motions in limine, whenever possible.

7.   No foundation

a.   Definition

All exhibits must have the necessary foundations established before they can properly be admitted in evidence. The objection should be made when the exhibit is offered in evidence. It is always preferable for the proponent of the exhibit to offer it when the witness is still on the stand. If an objection is sustained, the witness is still there to supply any missing foundation elements.

b.   Objection

Objection, your Honor. There is no proper foundation for the exhibit.

We object. There has been no showing that the photograph accurately portrays the intersection as it existed on the date of the accident.

c.   Examples

A difficult decision involving exhibits is whether to object on foundation grounds. If the foundation problem can be solved easily, an objection may only force the other party to establish the missing element, at the same time enhancing the credibility and impact of the exhibit. Sometimes the better approach in these situations is not to object at all and to then mention the missing element in closing arguments (e.g., "Of course it's a picture of the intersection, but is it worth anything? No one ever said that's the way the intersection looked on the date of the accident.").

Where you definitely want to keep the exhibit from being admitted and there is a substantial likelihood that a proper foundation cannot be established, a timely objection is essential.

This objection is also frequently made in two other areas. First, it is made to lay and expert opinion testimony, since there must be a proper factual basis on which the opinion is based. Second, it is made if the proper foundations for in person and telephonic conversations have not been established.

8.   No authentication (FRE 901 et seq.)

a.   Definition

Writings and conversations must be authenticated to be admissible at trial. Signed writings such as contracts and notes must be shown to have been executed by a party or agent. This is true even if the signed writing can be qualified as a business record, since the business records exception solves only the hearsay problems, not the authentication requirement. (E.g., Smith signs a promissory note of the XYZ Company. The original is retained in the company's files. In a lawsuit on the unpaid note, the note can be qualified as a business record. However, the signature of Smith on the note must be proved before the note can be admissible against Smith.) Where conversations are involved, the identity of the parties to the conversation must be demonstrated.

b.   Objection

We object. This exhibit has not been authenticated.

Objection, your Honor. There has been no proof of who executed this document.

We object. There's no evidence that the witness knew who the person on the other end of the telephone was.

c. Examples

The same considerations involving foundation objections apply equally to authentication objections.

9. Hearsay (FRE 801 et seq.)

a. Definition

Hearsay is a statement, other than one made by the declarant while testifying at the trial or hearing, offered in evidence to prove the truth of the matter asserted. The statement may be oral, written, or nonverbal conduct intended as an assertion. The federal rule essentially follows the classic definition of hearsay. However, it treats certain categories of statements as nonhearsay.

b. Objection

Objection, your Honor, the question calls for a hearsay answer.

Objection, hearsay.

c. Examples

The most obvious and recurring hearsay problems arise when a question calls for, or a witness testifies to, out-of-court statements made by another person, and a nonhearsay use of the statement does not exist.

Q. What did Mr. Doe tell you about the accident?
Q. What did he say to you at that time?

These questions are objectionable if no exceptions to the hearsay rule, such as admission by parties or excited utterances, exist.

Hearsay problems can be more subtle, as when the form of the question does not obviously call for hearsay, yet the answer necessarily incorporates hearsay information.

Q. What did you learn from them?
Q. What did your investigation disclose?
Q. Did Dr. Johnson agree with you?
Q. What did your committee conclude?
Q. Was he a witness to the crash?

Answers to these questions will probably include facts obtained from other persons and, if in issue, will be hearsay and inadmissible unless an exception or a nonhearsay rationale exists.

In a related vein, questions sometimes use a "state of mind" formulation in an attempt to circumvent the hearsay rule.

Q. Were you aware that . . .
Q. Did you come to know that . . .
Q. Was it your understanding that . . .

Unless the witness's state of mind is an issue in the case, these questions will contain hearsay information that is not properly admissible.

Witnesses' answers often spontaneously fall into hearsay when the witness goes beyond the intended bounds of the question.

Q. Who was present at the meeting?
A. The eight people I mentioned previously.
Q. Did all of them talk during the meeting?
A. Yes. Mr. Jones, for instance, kept saying that . . .
Counsel: Objection, your Honor, hearsay.

"Double hearsay" is a common hearsay objection governed by FRE 805, and is raised principally when business records are introduced as exhibits. Keep in mind that the business records foundation eliminates only one level of hearsay (i.e., FRE 803(6) makes it unnecessary to call the maker of the business record as a witness). Qualifying a document as a business record does not mean that everything on the record is automatically admissible. Only that part of a business record made by, and containing first-hand information of, employees of the business are part of the record. Whenever the record contains information obtained from nonemployees, a second level of hearsay exists, and that information from nonemployees is not admissible unless a separate hearsay exception applies.

Consider, for example, a hospital emergency room report. It states "patient's blood pressure: 160/95" and "patient's temperature: 102." It also contains the patient's words: "patient says he was involved in car accident and thinks leg is broken." The patient's blood pressure and temperature were obviously taken by a nurse, and are properly part of the business record. The patient's words are a second level of hearsay, or double hearsay, because the patient is not an employee of the hospital (and has no "business duty" to report or record information accurately). However, the patient's statement falls within another hearsay exception, FRE 803(4), statements made for the purpose of diagnosis and treatment, and is therefore admissible. If no separate hearsay exception applied, the patient's words would have to be deleted before the rest of the emergency room report would be properly admissible as a business record.

Hearsay objections are very common at trial and can be made in a variety of ways. Two frequently heard objections, however, should *not* be made. One is that the evidence is "self-serving." This objection is poorly stated, since all evidence tends to serve its proponent. The real objection is that evidence is hearsay and no exception applies. The other objection is that "the statement was made out of the presence of the defendant" in a criminal case. This objection has no basis, since the presence or absence of a defendant, or any other party, has nothing to do with its hearsay analysis. Don't make this objection! It is probably derived from an inaccurate and misplaced extension of the admission-by-silence concept.

10. Leading (FRE 611)

a. *Definition*

A leading question suggests the desired answer to the witness. This is generally improper during direct examination. Qualifiers such as "if anything" and "did you or did you not" do not make a question proper where the rest of the question is leading. Under certain circumstances, such as preliminary questions, matters not in dispute, child witnesses, questioning hostile or adverse witnesses, and foundations for exhibits, the leading form is proper, since FRE 611(c) provides that leading questions on direct examination are proper if "necessary to develop the witness's testimony." Leading questions are also considered proper when proving a negative, since there is usually no other practical way to obtain such information. (E.g., "Were you present in the boardroom of your company on June 1, 2000 when Mr. Taft signed the contract marked Pl. Ex. #8?" "No.")

b. *Objection*

I object, your Honor. The question is leading.

Objection, your Honor. Counsel is leading the witness.

c. *Examples*

Q. You were scared, weren't you? (A nonleading form is: How did you feel?)

Q. Immediately after the robbery, did the victim scream? (A nonleading form is: Did the victim do anything after the robbery?)

Q. Did he or did he not look both ways before stepping off the curb into the intersection? (A nonleading form is: Did he do anything before stepping off the curb?)

Note that either question can be asked and a responsive answer obtained in a nonleading way. Since the questioner can cure the objection, it is sometimes better not to object unless this happens repeatedly, since the leading questions on direct usually detract from the impact of the answer.

11. Narrative (FRE 611)

a. *Definition*

A long narrative answer is objectionable because it allows a witness to inject inadmissible evidence into the trial without giving opposing counsel a reasonable opportunity to make a timely objection. By requiring the direct examiner to ask a series of specific questions to which the witness can give reasonably succinct answers, opposing counsel will have a reasonable opportunity to object. FRE 611(a) gives the court broad discretion to control the mode of interrogating witnesses.

b.   Objection

Objection, your Honor, the question calls for a narrative answer.

Objection, your Honor, the witness is giving a narrative answer.

c.   Examples

Q.   Tell the jury everything that happened that day.
Q.   Please describe in your own words how this collision occurred.
Q.   Tell us what you know about the plaintiff.

Each of these questions potentially calls for a long narrative answer. A timely objection will force the proponent to ask specific questions that will break the narrative into manageable segments.

Sometimes witnesses will "take off" on an otherwise proper question and go way beyond what the answer reasonably calls for. One or two objections that are sustained will usually train the witness not to give narrative answers.

On the other hand, narrative objections should not automatically be made whenever an appropriate situation arises. Often narrative answers are an ineffective way of presenting a direct examination. If the witness' answers ramble or appear disorganized, making a narrative objection will only help the direct examiner regain control over his witness.

12.   Conclusions (FRE 701)

a.   Definition

A conclusion is a deduction drawn from a fact or series of facts. In general, witnesses should testify only to facts. Conclusions, based on those facts, are for the jury to draw as it sees fit. FRE 701 has expanded the permissible extent of lay witness conclusions by permitting the witness to testify to inferences from facts actually perceived by the witness under certain circumstances.

b.   Objection

Objection, your Honor. The question calls for a conclusion.

We object. The witness is attempting to give his conclusion.

c.   Examples (questions)

Q.   Was he driving the car recklessly?

Q. You got there as fast as possible, didn't you?
Q. Didn't the defendant intend to kill the victim?

d.   *Examples (answers)*

Q. Describe what he looked like.
A. He was drunk as a skunk.

Q. What's the next thing he did?
A. He just quit trying, that's what.

Q. Describe the work the repairman did.
A. He didn't do any of the repairs competently.

13.   Opinions (FRE 701 et seq.)

a.   *Definition*

Expert opinions are generally proper only in those areas in which specialized knowledge will assist the trier of fact and the witness has been properly qualified as an expert (FRE 702). Lay witnesses can give opinions and inferences only where the opinion is based on the witness' perception of an event and is helpful to the jury in understanding the facts (FRE 701). Common examples are speed, time, distance, and sobriety.

b.   *Objection*

Objection, your Honor. The question calls for an improper opinion.

Objection. The witness has not been qualified as an expert.

We object. This matter is not a proper subject for expert opinion.

c.   *Examples*

The most common problems in this area involve issues of whether the subject matter is a proper one for opinion testimony, particularly when a lay witness is on the stand.

Q. (To lay witness) Was the design of the automatic clutch pedal of this forklift truck unreasonably dangerous?

Unless the lay witness has demonstrated some special knowledge in this area, such as a forklift truck operator would have, asking his opinion on a technical subject is objectionable. Answers that are objectionable as conclusions often run afoul of the opinion rule as well.

Although FRE 704 permits opinions on "ultimate issues," this does not permit all opinions, since the opinion must be helpful to the jury in understanding the evidence or resolving issues. An opinion on an "ultimate issue" is proper only if it helps the jury.

Consider the following testimony in a civil commitment proceeding:

Q. What was your psychiatric diagnosis?
A. (Psychiatrist) The defendant is a paranoid schizophrenic.
Q. Is he a danger to himself or others?
A. Yes.

Here the clinical diagnosis cannot be used by the jury to determine if the defendant was legally incompetent, so asking for an opinion on the ultimate legal issue is proper. (However, note the restrictions in FRE 704(b) governing mental state issues in criminal cases.)

Consider the following testimony in a personal injury case:

Q. What did you conclude from your investigation?
A. (Accident-reconstruction expert) The defendant crossed the center lane just before the impact.
Q. Was the defendant negligent?
Counsel: Objection, your Honor.
Court: Sustained.

Here the expert's opinion on negligence is improper, since the jury can use his investigation results to reach a legal conclusion, and the expert's opinion on negligence does not help the jury understand the facts or resolve issues.

14.   Repetitive (asked and answered) (FRE 611)

a. *Definition*

Questions and answers previously elicited and made by the same party should not be constantly repeated. The reasons are twofold: First, having the same questions and answers repeated wastes time. Second, it places undue emphasis on those questions and answers repeated. This rule applies equally to direct and cross-examinations. While the federal rules have no specific rule against repetitive questions and answers, FRE 611(a) gives the court discretion in controlling examinations of witnesses to "avoid needless consumption of time." (The cross-examiner, of course, may ask the same questions previously asked during the direct examination.)

b. *Objection*

Your Honor, we object. The question is repetitive.

Objection, your Honor. That question has already been asked and answered.

c. *Examples*

The most common problems arise when a lawyer attempts to repeat the substance of the previous question (that elicited a particularly favorable answer), but phrases it in a slightly different way. The significant determination is not whether the new question is identical to a previous question, but whether the new question reasonably calls for the same answer that has previously been given. If it does, and the lawyer constantly is using this method to repeat and emphasize what he considers important testimony, make the objection.

15. Assuming facts not in evidence

a. Definition

This objection often occurs during examinations, particularly cross-examinations, when the introductory part of the question assumes a fact that is not in evidence and the existence of which is in dispute.

b. Objection

Your Honor, we object. The question assumes a fact not in evidence.

Objection, your Honor. There's no evidence that . . .

c. Examples

With lay witnesses, the objection most commonly arises on cross-examination where the question includes as a fact something that has not been shown to exist.

> *Q.* You were more than 50 feet from the skid marks, weren't you?
> *Q.* After you ran from the scene, you never looked back, did you?

If there has been no evidence of any skid marks, or that the witness ran from the scene, these questions are improper.

16. Misstates evidence/misquotes witnesses

a. Definition

A question that misstates and distorts evidence or misquotes a witness is improper, whether this is done during the examination of witnesses or during closing arguments.

b. Objection

Objection, your Honor. Counsel is misstating the evidence.

Objection, your Honor. There's no evidence that . . .

c. Examples

Misstatements and misquotes usually occur in two types of situations. First, a lawyer in a question refers to evidence produced earlier during the trial, but does so inaccurately. Second, some lawyers habitually repeat a witness' last answer as part of the next question, but again, do so inaccurately.

> *Q.* You hit the man, didn't you?
> *A.* Yes.
> *Q.* After attacking him, what happened?

Where inaccurate repetition occurs, a prompt objection is essential.

17.   Confusing/misleading/ambiguous/vague/unintelligible

a.   Definition

A question must be posed in a reasonably clear and specific manner so that the witness can reasonably know what information the examiner is eliciting.

b.   Objection

Objection, your Honor. The question is confusing and ambiguous.
Objection. The question is too vague.

c.   Examples

Confusing, ambiguous, and vague questions usually arise where the evidence has involved many occurrences, witnesses, and conversations. The examiner will ask a question about an event or conversation without stating, or it being apparent, which one the question is directed to.

> *Q.* Who was present at *that* meeting?
> *Q.* What did *he* say during the March 13 meeting?

In both examples the question is unclear if there was more than one meeting or many persons present. Object, and force the examiner to state which meeting or which person he is referring to.

18.   Speculative

a.   Definition

Any question that asks the witness to speculate or guess is improper. This is because cases should be decided on facts, and guesswork from a witness on what might be the facts or what possibly could have happened is irrelevant. On the other hand, witnesses are permitted to give estimates and approximations, most commonly of distance, time, speed, and age. In addition, greater latitude is given during the examination of expert witnesses, and questions that are essentially speculative in nature will often be permitted.

b.   Objection

Your Honor, we object. The question is speculative.

Objection. Counsel is asking the witness to guess.

c.   Examples

Q.   Isn't it possible that . . .
Q.   It's conceivable that . . . , isn't it?
Q.   If the car had been farther away you would have been able to avoid hitting him, wouldn't you?

19.   Compound

a.   Definition

A compound question is one that brings up two separate facts within a single question. It is objectionable because any simple answer to the question will be unclear.

b.   Objection

Objection, Your Honor, to the compound question.

We object, your Honor, to the double question.

c.   Examples

Q.   Did you go to Smith's Tavern on the 13th and to Frank's Tavern two days later?
Q.   Did you go to Smith's store on the 13th and, if so, did you buy anything?

If only one of the two facts in each question is true, neither a "yes" nor a "no" response will be accurate. The real danger of the compound question is that the witness will give a simple, innocent answer that is only partially correct. Opposing counsel will then attempt to use the well-intentioned but inaccurate answer during closing arguments. The objectionable question can, of course, be easily divided into two or more separate questions.

20.   Argumentative

a.   Definition

Any question that is essentially an argument to the jury is improper. Such a question elicits no new information. It simply states a conclusion and asks the witness to agree with it. These "questions" should be saved for closing arguments.

b.   Objection

Objection, your Honor. The question is argumentative.

We object. Counsel is arguing with the witness.

c.   Examples

Q.   Since you were 80 feet away, it was raining and dark, and the whole robbery took only a few seconds, you couldn't have had a good opportunity to see the robber's face, could you?

This objection is sometimes made during opening statements, where the statement goes beyond stating the facts and improperly characterizes the facts. For example, stating that "the defendant is a violent, vicious brute" in an opening statement is improper; in closing arguments it may be proper, if the characterization is a fair inference from the admitted evidence. Keep in mind that judges vary widely on what they consider improper arguments in opening statements.

21.   Improper characterization

a.   Definition

A close relative of the argumentative and conclusory question, improper characterizations in both questions and answers are really argumentative and conclusory. Since characterization is something that the jury, not the lawyer or witness, should infer, if appropriate, the question is improper.

b.   Objection

Your Honor, we object to counsel's characterization.

Objection, your Honor. The witness' characterization is improper.

c.   Examples

Q.   He was attacking you like a frenzied dog, wasn't he?
Q.   How much money did you lend to this financial wizard?
A.   He was acting like a spoiled brat who had his favorite toy taken away.

22.   Unresponsive/volunteered

a.   Definition

An answer that does not directly respond to a question is objectionable as unresponsive. Where the answer goes beyond what is necessary to answer the question, that surplusage of the answer is objectionable. In many jurisdictions only the party calling the witness can make the objection. This is because if the answer is otherwise properly admissible, there is no point in striking the answer as unresponsive. If the answer is objectionable for another reason, the objector need only object on the proper evidentiary grounds. However, today some jurisdictions allow either party to object on the basis that an answer was unresponsive or volunteered.

b. Objection

Objection, your Honor. The answer is not responsive to my question. I ask that the answer be stricken.

I object to the volunteered portion of the answer and ask that everything after . . . be stricken.

c. Examples

Most problems occur when a witness is so eager to tell his story that he uses each question as a springboard for a long narrative answer. Adequate pretrial preparation of witnesses should prevent this problem before it occurs. When it does occur, however, you should promptly reestablish your control over the witness.

Q. Mr. Smith, please listen to my question and answer only that question.

Keep in mind that unresponsive answers can damage both sides. When you are the direct examiner, such answers ruin your pace and logical presentation of your evidence. For the cross-examiner, the danger always exists that the witness will say something prejudicial that is inadmissible.

23. Prejudice outweighs probativeness (FRE 403)

a. Definition

This objection is principally directed to exhibits, although it can also apply to testimony. Merely because an exhibit has probative value does not guarantee that the exhibit will be admissible. Exhibits, although probative, may be extremely prejudicial. Where the prejudicial impact is substantial, and its probative value slight, the court can exercise its discretion and exclude the exhibit.

b. Objection

Objection, your Honor. The exhibit's prejudicial impact substantially exceeds its probative value.

Objection. This exhibit is not admissible under Rule 403.

When making the objection in the jury's presence, it is better simply to refer to Rule 403, since stating that the evidence is prejudicial will stimulate the jury's curiosity.

c. Examples

This objection is most commonly made against photographs, usually in color, of the deceased in homicide cases. It is also sometimes raised where personal injury plaintiffs are asked to display their injuries to the jury.

Often the exhibit has been, or can be, duplicated by other less inflammatory evidence. In those situations the exhibit can be challenged not only as being prejudicial, but cumulative as well.

Whenever such a situation arises, a prompt objection or a motion in limine is essential. An inflammatory exhibit, once before the jury, can hardly be retracted. The objection should be anticipated and made out of the jury's hearing whenever possible.

24. Cumulative (FRE 611)

a. Definition

The court has discretion to control repetitive evidence introduced during trials. When one witness after another parades into court reinforcing the previous witness while adding nothing new, or a series of exhibits all demonstrate the same things, the witnesses and exhibits are unnecessarily cumulative and are therefore objectionable.

b. Objection

Objection, your Honor. This photograph is entirely cumulative.

We object to this evidence. It's already been covered by four other witnesses.

c. Examples

Cumulative witnesses are commonly incurred where reputation evidence is involved. A party may choreograph a parade of witnesses, all attesting to the good reputation of a particular person. The time to object is when the jury or judge appears to become restless or bored.

Cumulative exhibits are most commonly photographs. Where each additional photograph adds nothing of consequence to exhibits already in evidence, an objection may be appropriate.

25. Beyond the scope (FRE 611)

a. Definition

Under FRE 611(b), cross-examinations should be "limited to the subject matter of the direct examination and matters affecting the credibility of the witness." Redirect examinations, in turn, should be limited to matters raised during the cross-examination. This controls the efficient and orderly presentation of evidence in each party's case in chief. Where the cross or redirect examination attempts to pursue matters not covered by the preceding examination, an objection is proper.

This objection may also be raised during rebuttal testimony and re-buttal closing arguments. Rebuttal testimony is proper only when it con-tradicts substantial evidence previously presented by your opponent. In the same vein, the plaintiff's rebuttal argument is proper only when it re-sponds to matters raised during the defendant's closing argument.

b.   Objection

Objection. This is beyond the scope of the direct.

We object, your Honor. This matter wasn't mentioned during the direct exam-ination.

We object to this argument, your Honor. We never discussed damages in our closing argument, so plaintiff can't discuss it in rebuttal.

c.   Examples

Scope objections are most commonly encountered during witness ex-aminations when the cross-examiner attempts to elicit facts from the wit-ness in areas not previously covered during the direct examination. Where the witness can give favorable testimony in new areas to the cross-exam-iner, he must usually call the witness as his own, in his case in chief, and elicit the testimony at that time. Note, however, that under FRE 611(b) the court in its discretion may permit the cross-examiner to inquire into new matters during the direct examination, provided that the inquiry is done in a nonleading way. Whether the court will permit you to do this will de-pend largely on how substantial the new matters are and how lengthy the additional examination will be. (Most state jurisdictions follow the federal scope-of-cross rules. A few, however, follow the English, or "wide open" rule, which permits cross-examination on any relevant matter, regardless of whether it was previously mentioned on direct.)

On redirect examination the problem usually arises when the exam-iner realizes he has forgotten to ask a certain line of questions or establish the foundation for an exhibit, and attempts to do so after the cross-exam-ination. If this happens, ask the court to permit you to reopen the direct examination for this limited purpose.

Scope objections to rebuttal testimony or rebuttal closing arguments are proper in similar situations. When the rebuttal testimony attempts to present entirely new evidence, or a rebuttal closing argument ventures substantially beyond the matters covered by the defendant's argument, an objection should be sustained.

26.   Improper impeachment (FRE 613)

a.   Definition

Impeachment rules are technical and have several requirements. The cross-examiner must have a good faith basis for raising the impeaching matter; the matter must in fact be impeaching; it must be raised on cross;

and the witness must be given a reasonable opportunity to admit, deny, or explain the impeaching matter. If the witness denies or equivocates, the matter must be proved up with extrinsic evidence if it is noncollateral. (See §7.7 for a detailed discussion of the various impeachment methods and requirements.)

Under FRE 613(a), a witness can be cross-examined with a prior inconsistent written statement without the cross-examiner first showing it to the witness. Under FRE 607, any party can impeach any witness, including its own.

b.   Objection

We object, your Honor. This is improper impeachment.

c.   Examples

Problems with impeaching with a prior inconsistent statement are usually found in four areas. First, the cross-examiner may not read verbatim the impeaching statement when he asks the witness to admit it. Where a report, written statement, or transcript is involved, it must be read verbatim. Paraphrasing or summarizing is improper. Second, the impeaching statement cannot be taken out of context to distort its meaning. Under FRE 106, you can require your opponent to read the entire relevant portion of the impeaching statement. Third, the cross-examiner may attempt to introduce in evidence at a later time an impeaching statement without ever having given the witness an opportunity to admit or deny the statement during the cross-examination. Fourth, the cross-examiner may fail to prove up the impeachment where required.

In each case, the remedy is the same: Object promptly to prevent the improper impeachment from getting before the jury. If the cross-examiner failed to prove up where required, you must move to strike and ask that the jury disregard it to preserve error.

§10.7.   Other objections

In addition to objections made during the presentation of evidence, other objections can be made during the course of the trial. This section will review the more common objections that can be made during jury selection, opening statements, and closing arguments.

1.   Jury selection

Objections commonly made during the jury selection process include the following.

a.   Mentioning insurance

Under FRE 411 and parallel state evidentiary rules, it is usually improper to mention to the jury that any person involved in the case was or was not covered by liability insurance. This necessarily follows since the existence of insurance is irrelevant to the issue of negligence, while its disclosure is inevitably prejudicial.

However, lawyers conducting the voir dire examination of the jurors in personal injury and other tort cases, particularly plaintiff's attorneys, are vitally interested in knowing whether any of the prospective jurors have ever worked for insurance companies or related enterprises. Accordingly, many jurisdictions permit the lawyers during the voir dire examination to inquire on this subject indirectly. Asking, "Have you ever worked for the claims department of any company," or similar questions is often permitted, since such a question does not directly suggest that a party to the suit was insured. You must, of course, determine in advance whether and how explicitly your judge will permit this topic to be raised.

b. Discussing law

It is usually improper for counsel to discuss in detail the law applicable to the case, or to ask jurors whether they agree or disagree with the law. Advising the jury of the applicable law is a judicial function. The only appropriate consideration is whether the juror will commit himself to follow the law as the judge gives it, and this is usually something the judge covers herself. However, some judges will permit discussing the applicable law in general terms. Determine what your judge's attitude is in advance of trial.

c. Discussing facts

In many jurisdictions it is improper to tell the jury the details of the case it will hear. Attorneys often attempt to determine what jurors' reactions to the evidence will be by revealing portions of it during the voir dire, then challenging those jurors who had negative reactions to it. That this is commonly done accounts in large part for the recent trend of having the voir dire conducted by the court, with the lawyers' participation limited to asking questions solely about jurors' backgrounds.

2. Opening statements

Objections commonly made during the opening statements include the following.

a. Arguing the law or the instructions

Opening statements permit the lawyers to tell the jury what they anticipate the evidence at trial will be. Accordingly, it is usually objectionable to review or discuss in detail the law or instructions applicable to the case. Courts, however, differ widely on how strictly they require counsel to adhere to this rule.

b. Argumentative

The opening statements should tell the jury the anticipated facts that will be presented during the trial. Accordingly, it is improper to make the opening statement argumentative, such as arguing the credibility of witnesses and other evidence the jury will hear, or arguing inferences and deductions from that evidence. These are appropriate only during closing arguments. Again, judges differ widely in how strictly this rule is enforced.

c. Mentioning inadmissible evidence

It is always improper to bring before the jury, during opening statements or at any time, evidence that is inadmissible. Common forms of inadmissible evidence are:

1. evidence that has been suppressed by pretrial motions or motions in limine
2. privileged matters, such as attorney-client or husband-wife conversations, inadmissible under FRE 501
3. evidence of settlement negotiations in civil cases and plea negotiations in criminal cases, inadmissible at any time under FRE 408 and 410
4. subsequent repairs, made after an event, inadmissible to prove negligence in connection with that event under FRE 407
5. evidence of payment of, or promise to pay, medical and related expenses resulting from injury, inadmissible to prove liability under FRE 409

d. Mentioning unprovable evidence

It is improper to mention evidence that, although true, is incapable of being proved at trial. Where a witness has died or cannot be found for trial, it is improper to state what that witness' testimony would be. Where exhibits have been lost or destroyed, it is improper to tell the jury what such exhibits contain. The test here is good faith. A lawyer can include in his opening statements only evidence that he in good faith believes is both available and admissible at trial.

e. Giving personal opinions

It is improper to tell the jury your personal opinion on any evidentiary matter. Such personal opinions are not proper because they directly inject the credibility of the trial lawyer into the trial. Accordingly, phrases such as *I think* or *I believe* are best left out of your trial vocabulary.

f. Discussing the other side's evidence

It is improper to tell the jury during opening statements what you expect the other side to present as evidence during the trial, since the other side is not obligated to present evidence and can elect to present whatever it chooses. This is a problem usually limited to criminal cases, where it is highly prejudicial for the prosecutor to suggest what the defense will prove, since the defendant is never required to prove anything.

3. Closing arguments

Objections commonly made during closing arguments include the following.

a. *Misstating evidence*

It is improper to misstate evidence or misquote testimony admitted during the trial. However, it is proper to argue reasonable inferences and deductions from such evidence. Trial judges are usually reluctant to sustain such objections absent a clear violation, since what the evidence actually admitted at trial was involves memory and recollection, which can and do often differ. Accordingly, judges often overrule such objections, but remind the jurors that they heard the evidence and should rely on their recollections in determining whether counsel's statements of the evidence are accurate. This objection is best saved for obvious gross misrepresentations and misstatements.

b. *Misstating law and quoting instructions*

It is improper in some jurisdictions to read the court's instructions verbatim to the jury during closing arguments. However, it is usually permissible in those jurisdictions to refer to the instructions the court will actually give and paraphrase their contents to the jury. When this is done, the paraphrasing or other reference to the instructions must be fair and accurate.

Most jurisdictions take the approach that any instructions used during arguments can be read verbatim or paraphrased accurately. You must learn what the practice is in your jurisdiction.

c. *Using an impermissible per diem damages argument*

In some jurisdictions it is improper when arguing damages in personal injury cases to ask for a specific dollar amount on any element of damages on a per diem basis and then multiply that figure by the actual life expectancy of the injured party. This usually leads to astronomical figures (e.g., asking for $25 per day for pain and suffering will yield $365,000 over a 40-year life expectancy). Many jurisdictions permit the damages argument to ask for only one lump-sum figure for each proper element of damages. A few jurisdictions bar suggesting a specific dollar amount for pain and suffering damages. As always, make sure you know what the permissible methods of arguing damages are in your jurisdiction.

d.   Giving personal opinions

It is improper for counsel to inject his personal opinions, beliefs, and attitudes into the case at any time. Therefore, such comments as *I think* and *I believe*, unless clearly and directly linked to the evidence, are improper. Since these phrases often draw objections when used, they are best excised from your trial vocabulary.

e.   Appealing to jury's bias, prejudice, and pecuniary interest

Our jury trial system requires the jury to reach a verdict without resorting to bias or prejudice. That verdict should be based solely on the evidence admitted during the trial and the court's instructions on the applicable law. Accordingly, suggesting to the jury that they may be personally affected by a given verdict is improper, even if done indirectly. For example, it is improper to suggest that the jury's taxes will go up, or their property values will go down, if they decide against a governmental party.

f.   Personal attacks on parties and counsel

It is always improper to engage in personal attacks on opposing counsel or the other parties in the trial. This should never be done, for both legal and persuasive reasons. Nothing can diminish your credibility before the jury faster than resorting to this type of argument. Never let things get personal, either at this or any other stage of the trial. Commenting on a party's race, religion, national origin, political affiliations, or other personal characteristics is in most instances highly improper.

g.   Prejudicial arguments

A large number of arguments are improper because they are prejudicial comments having little or nothing to do with the evidence. Each substantive area of trial work has developed substantial case law on improper arguments. For instance, in personal injury cases it is improper to argue the wealth or poverty of the parties, the effect of income taxes on a money judgment (in most jurisdictions), or the effect of a judgment on insurance rates and other indirect costs of living. It is improper to ask the jury to put itself in the shoes of any of the parties, since this is really a direct appeal to the juror's emotions and hence violates what is commonly called the "golden rule" (e.g., in a paraplegic case, you cannot argue, "If someone came to you and said, 'I'll give you $1,000,000, but you'll have to spend the rest of your life lying on your back,' would you take it?"). In criminal cases it is improper to argue that the defendant will commit more crimes if released, that the jury has a moral obligation to protect society from the defendant, or that the defendant may attempt to retaliate personally against the jury hearing the case.

From a tactical point of view, your approach to making objections during these phases of the trial is essentially identical to the evidentiary phases. Always remember that jurors dislike objections that appear to keep interesting information from them. Where you can anticipate problems, you should raise them out of the jury's hearing whenever possible. Maximize your use of pretrial motions, motions in limine, and side-bar conferences. Where you cannot resolve problems in advance, use your objections sparingly. Consistent with protecting your client's interests and making a good record, save your objections for important situations, when you are reasonably certain that the court will sustain your objections. Utilizing such an approach usually develops a favorable impression on the jury, an impression that can pay dividends when the jury is deliberating on the verdict.

XI

TRIAL PREPARATION AND STRATEGY

§11.1.   Introduction

The "secret" to effective trial preparation is no secret at all. It's preparation, preparation, and more preparation! It's 90 percent perspiration, 10 percent inspiration. It's preparing sooner, not later. Hence, the trial lawyer who starts preparing for trial early, does it systematically and thoroughly, and incorporates an understanding of psychology into that preparation is more likely to achieve a successful result at trial.

§11.2.   Trial preparation timetable

When should you take the numerous steps that are necessary to be fully prepared to try a case to a jury? The easy answer is earlier rather than later. Time pressures intensify as a trial date approaches, and emergencies are an inevitable part of trial work.

How early is early? In busy trial practices, such as state prosecutors and public defenders, trial lawyers usually have a few days at best to prepare for trial. In major cases, trial lawyers may need months to prepare for trial. The following chronology of events should be a useful guide for most cases.

4–8 weeks before trial

Review pleadings
File amended pleadings if necessary (and still permitted)
Review discovery
Amend and supplement discovery if necessary (and permitted)
File motions to exclude evidence
Obtain rulings on pending motions if possible
Serve trial subpoenas (if not already done)
Learn how the judge conducts the trial
Learn how the courtroom is set up

3–4 weeks before trial

Organize trial notebook
Prepare jury instructions
Prepare exhibits folders
Prepare witness folders
Order courtroom exhibits and visual aids (large charts, photo enlargements)
Order courtroom equipment (projectors, screens, TV monitors)
Obtain rulings on motions if possible
Check on service of trial subpoenas

2–3 weeks before trial

Brainstorm: refine theory of the case, themes, labels
Brainstorm: focus on the people, storytelling, key disputes
Prepare proposed jury selection strategy
Prepare jury voir dire questions
Prepare opening statement
Prepare closing argument
Prepare direct examinations
Prepare cross-examinations
Check on availability of your witnesses
Schedule witnesses for trial preparation

1–2 weeks before trial

Discuss possible stipulations with opponent
Prepare client for testimony and courtroom presence
Prepare witnesses for testifying at trial
Check on availability of your witnesses
Check with court on trial date

week before trial

Keep in touch with your witnesses
Advise witnesses when they will probably be needed
Keep preparing client
Keep preparing witnesses

Refine order of witnesses
Refine exhibits list
Refine planned cross-examinations
Rehearse your opening statement and closing argument
Check with court on trial date, starting time, and schedule

Should you blindly follow this chronology? Of course not. Every case has its own pulse. The underlying purpose of the chronology, however, is sound: Do as much as you can early to minimize the emergencies and unexpected demands on your time that inevitably arise as the trial date approaches. This allows you to focus your time in the final days on key tasks, such as delivering an effective opening statement, having well-prepared witnesses ready to testify, and refining your planned cross-examinations. The more time you have to think, rehearse, and refine, because other tasks are completed, the better your trial performance will be.

§11.3.   Organization of litigation files and trial notebook

Ours is an age of records, and the field of law is no exception. Everything is routinely recorded and duplicated. Even a simple case can, and invariably will, generate extensive paperwork. Consequently, litigation files must be organized, divided, and indexed to provide immediate and accurate access to their contents at any time. Trial notebooks must be organized to provide an outline and quick reference for the actual trial. The lawyer who is organized will appear prepared, confident, and professional to the jury, judge, client, and opponent.

1.   Litigation files

There is no magic in organizing litigation files. Most law firms have systems for the types of cases the firms routinely handle. The important point is that your system must be logical, clearly indexed, and bound whenever possible. It should be in place when litigation starts, not just when a trial seems likely.

Litigation files are usually divided into several categories. The files should have tabbed dividers for each category. In larger cases, categories may be further divided. For example, discovery could be further divided into initial disclosures, interrogatories, documents requests, depositions, and requests to admit facts. Correspondence could be divided into correspondence with client, lawyers, and others. Whenever possible, the divider contents should be bound in chronological order.

The following file organization and categories are commonly used:

1. *Court documents*
    a.   pleadings
    b.   discovery
    c.   motions
    d.   orders
    e.   subpoenas

    2. *Attorney's records*
        a. chronological litigation history
        b. retainer contract, bills, costs
        c. correspondence
        d. legal research
        e. miscellaneous
    3. *Evidence*

Documents and records that may become exhibits at trial should be placed in clear plastic document protectors whenever practical. (This prevents them from being marked up during the litigation process.) While the exhibits will depend on the specific case, the following are commonly involved.
        a. bills, invoices, statements, receipts
        b. correspondence between parties
        c. business records and public records
        d. photographs, diagrams, maps, charts

(These exhibits will later be placed into a separate exhibits folder.) Other exhibits, such as physical objects and large diagrams and models, should be protected and safeguarded in a secure location.

2. Trial notebook

Organizing materials for trial differs from organizing litigation files. Litigation files are designed to be all-inclusive. Trial materials, by contrast, include only those materials that will actually be used during the trial; they need to be organized in a way that parallels how they will be used at trial. The standard way trial lawyers organize their trial materials today is through a trial notebook. (Some trial lawyers are beginning to use portable computers in the courtroom to store materials such as pleadings, discovery, depositions, and business records for easier access and quicker retrieval. Litigation and courtroom software is being constantly refined and improved so that substantial parts of a trial notebook can be effectively computerized.)

A trial notebook is simply a three-ring notebook containing appropriately tabbed sections that parallel the trial process. The notebook itself should be a three-ring notebook, $1\frac{1}{2}$ to 2 inches thick, which will hold standard letter-sized ($8\frac{1}{2}'' \times 11''$) paper. A notebook with a locking mechanism for the rings, a label slot on the binding, and a pocket inside the front cover for "do lists" is the most useful style. If your case is too large to fit into one notebook, simply use two or more notebooks and divide the materials accordingly. For example, you might have your facts, pleadings, discovery, and motions in one notebook (or portable computer), the remaining sections in another.

The three-ring notebook should have a series of color-coded tabbed dividers, made of stiff paper, plastic covered, with reinforced holes and tabs.

How the trial notebook is divided and organized is up to the individual trial lawyer, and various systems exist. Commercial trial notebooks and forms are available, although their designs are generally inflexible. The important point is that you can and should organize your trial notebook to be useful for *you*.

A common organizational system is the following:

1. facts
2. pleadings
3. discovery
4. motions
5. charts
6. jury
7. openings
8. plaintiff
9. defendant
10. closings
11. instructions
12. law

Two untabbed dividers, at the front and back of the trial notebook, will keep sheets from tearing out of the notebook.

These trial notebook sections should contain the following:

1. *Facts*
   a. summary sheet containing the parties, lawyers, addresses, and telephone numbers, and a summary of the pleadings, if useful
   b. reports such as police reports, investigator's reports, and other fact summaries
   c. chronology of events, if useful
2. *Pleadings*
   a. amended pleadings, in order
   b. pretrial order, if it amends pleadings
   c. copy of applicable statutes, if statutory claims
3. *Discovery*
   a. initial disclosures
   b. interrogatories and answers
   c. requests to produce documents and responses
   d. deposition summaries
   e. requests to admit facts and responses
4. *Motions*
   a. motions, responses, and orders, in order
   b. pretrial memorandum and order
   c. anticipated trial motions
5. *Charts*
   a. trial chart (elements of claims, defenses, and proof)
   b. witness list (your witnesses, addresses, telephone numbers)
   c. exhibit list (for each party)

6. *Jury*
   a. jury chart form and challenges record
   b. juror profile outline
   c. requested voir dire questions to submit to judge
   d. checklist of your voir dire questions
   e. copy of applicable jury selection statutes and rules
7. *Openings*
   a. outline of your planned opening statement
   b. blank pages for notes on opponent's opening statement
8. *Plaintiff*
   a. if plaintiff, an outline of each direct examination
   b. if defendant, an outline of each anticipated cross
9. *Defendant*
   a. if plaintiff, an outline of each anticipated cross
   b. if defendant, an outline of each direct examination
10. *Closings*
    a. blank pages to note ideas during trial for closings
    b. outline of your planned closing argument
    c. blank pages for notes on opponent's closing argument
    d. outline of your planned rebuttal argument, if plaintiff
11. *Instructions*
    a. your proposed jury instructions
    b. opponent's proposed jury instructions
12. *Law*
    a. rules of evidence — federal and state
    b. your trial memorandum
    c. opponent's trial memorandum
    d. copy of key statutes
    e. copy of key cases

The trial notebook will then organize and contain everything you need to conduct the entire trial, except for the following:

1. Exhibits

Exhibits should be placed in a separate file folder, inside plastic document protectors if necessary, and premarked as exhibits whenever permitted by local rules. You should also have additional copies of these exhibits for your own reference, and for the judge, jury, opponent, and witness. A useful system is to have the original and several copies of each exhibit in a separate file divider.

2. Witness folders

There should be a separate file divider for each witness expected to testify at trial. Each divider should contain a copy of each statement the witness has made, such as deposition transcripts, reports, and statements to police and investigators. It should also contain a copy of each exhibit the witness will use or qualify for admission during the examination. These folders are essential both during the preparation of witnesses before trial and during trial to refresh recollection on direct or impeach during cross-examination. The witness file dividers should be kept in a separate file folder.

3. Transcripts

Transcripts of depositions, hearings, and other proceedings should be in a separate file folder.

4. Jury instructions

If jury instructions have not been submitted to the judge before trial, the originals and required copies should be kept in a separate file folder.

5. Notepads

You should have letter-sized notepads, three-hole punched with a stiff back for note-taking during the trial. Such notes can then easily be placed in the appropriate sections of the trial notebook.

The trial notebook, exhibits, witness folders, transcripts, jury instructions, and notepads can be kept secure in a catalog case, which every trial lawyer should have.

Finally, learn how your trial judge conducts a trial, and examine the courtroom in which the case will be tried. Every judge has personal preferences on how a trial should be run, and these can influence your presentation. Courtroom layouts, sound systems, lighting, and equipment vary significantly, and these can have an important influence on how witnesses testify and what exhibits you can use persuasively during the trial.

§11.4. Elements of claims and defenses

Trials involve two basic concepts. First, evidence at trial must be legally sufficient. It must meet the burden of proof on each element of each claim or defense raised in the pleadings. This concept is legal and is directed to the judge. Second, evidence at trial must be persuasive. It must be understood, absorbed, remembered, and accepted by the trier of fact. This concept is psychological and is directed to the jury.

The easy way to prepare for the legal sufficiency of your case (and the legal insufficiency of your opponent's case) is to organize a trial chart. A trial chart is simply a visual way of outlining your trial evidence. Using the jury instructions, which itemize the elements of the claims and defenses involved in your case, the trial chart should list each required element for each claim and defense. The trial chart should then show the source of proof for each element, whether by witnesses, exhibits, pleadings, admissions in discovery, or other source.

Example (plaintiff):

Trial Chart

Elements of claim:	*Proof:*
(Count I — Contract)	
1. Contract terms	1. Contract (Pl. Ex. #1)
2. Contract executed	2. a. Answer to complaint
	b. Def. admission in deposition
	c. Def. interrogatory answer
3. Pl. performed	3. a. Pl. testimony
	b. Pl. letter to def. (P#2)
	c. Pl. records (P#5)
4. Def. breached	4. a. Pl. testimony
	b. Def. records (P#3)
	c. Contractor who completed job
5. Pl. damages	5. a. Pl. testimony
	b. Contractor who completed job
	c. Pl. checks (P#8)
	d. Contractor's records (P#9)

The trial chart should be continued for each element of your required proof and your opponent's anticipated proof.

When completed, the chart is an effective method for identifying areas where your (and your opponent's) proof is strong and where it is weak. It will identify the areas where you should strengthen the proof if possible, where your opponent's attack is likely to come, and where the critical issues at trial will be. Finally, the chart is useful during trial when making and opposing motions for directed verdicts.

When your legal analysis, through your trial chart, is completed, preparation can then focus on the psychological aspects of the upcoming trial.

§11.5. *Psychological principles of jury persuasion*

Reflect back on the psychological principles discussed in Chapter II. How do jurors make individual decisions? Jurors are mostly affective thinkers who use deductive reasoning to make decisions. They care more about the people than the legal issues. They use their attitudes and beliefs to filter information and decide what to believe. They reach decisions quickly, based on relatively little information. After reaching decisions they believe are fair, they selectively accept, reject, or distort new information so that it "fits" their already reached decisions. Jury selection is primarily concerned with learning jurors' likely attitudes about issues important to the case, and determining which jurors will be receptive, which ones resistant, to each side's party, theory of the case, themes, and labels.

How do jurors reach group decisions? When jurors begin deliberating, group dynamics become important. Whether a juror is a persuader, participant, or nonparticipant largely determines how much influence that juror will have with the other jurors in reaching a group decision — the verdict. Jury selection is also concerned with determining how "strong" each juror is likely to be during deliberations, so that peremptory challenges can be used against persuaders likely to be hostile to that side.

What influences these jurors? Credible witnesses, who testify clearly, simply, and dynamically, are important. So are visual aids and exhibits, because seeing has more impact than hearing. Jurors like stories that focus on the people, not the legal issues. Vivid, visceral, and visual evidence makes a difference. Efficiency in presenting information is important, since jurors have limited attention spans, and limited interest in learning new things. Using themes, labels, and repetition, and ordering the information advantageously, has much to do with whether the jury accepts and remembers it.

These psychological principles can be distilled into six key concepts that should influence trial preparation and the trial itself. They are:

1.   Prepare from the jury's point of view
2.   Develop a theory of the case
3.   Select themes and labels
4.   Emphasize the people
5.   Use storytelling techniques
6.   Focus on the key disputed facts and issues

Let's apply these concepts to trial preparation, beginning with the theory of the case.

§11.6.   Theory of the case

What is a "theory of the case"? Your theory of the case is simply a logical, persuasive story of "what really happened." It must be consistent with the credible evidence and with the jury's perception of how life works. Your theory of the case must combine your undisputed evidence and your version of the disputed evidence that you will present in storytelling form at trial.

When do you develop your theory of the case? Your version of what really happened is a process that begins when your case starts and steadily develops as the discovery in the case progresses. When discovery is completed, you should have a good grasp of the undisputed evidence, where the evidence is in dispute, and what the key factual disputes are. By this time, and *before* you begin other trial preparation, you must decide on what your theory of the case will be, because your trial preparation needs to focus on proving your theory and discrediting your opponent's theory.

How do you go about developing a theory of the case? This requires several steps. First, review the elements of each claim (or defense) in the case and prepare the jury instructions if you have not already submitted them to the court. Second, analyze how you intend to prove (or disprove) each of those elements through admissible testimony and exhibits. Third, analyze the contradictory facts that your opponent has available to determine the key issues that will be disputed at trial, and what witnesses and exhibits your opponent will probably use to prove his side of those issues at trial. These steps should already have been completed by preparing your trial chart. Fourth, research all possible evidentiary issues that may arise to all of the likely proof so that you can realistically determine what will be admissible at trial. Finally, review all the admissible evidence you and your opponent have on the key disputed issues to identify each side's strengths and weaknesses. This is where the critical contests during the trial will be. You must then plan how you can bolster any weaknesses you have and how you can persuasively attack your opponent's weaknesses.

Trials are in large part a contest to see which party's version of disputed events the jury will accept as true and which party's version of "what really happened" is more plausible. This ongoing process of developing logical, consistent positions on disputed facts and integrating them harmoniously with the undisputed facts to create a persuasive story of what really happened is what trial lawyers call developing a theory of the case.

Consider the following:

Example:

In an automobile negligence case, the plaintiff pedestrian was struck by defendant's car at an intersection. Some evidence will place the plaintiff within the crosswalk with the walk light green. Other testimony will place the plaintiff outside the crosswalk, jaywalking across the intersection.

As plaintiff, your theory could be one of the following:

a. Plaintiff was in the crosswalk and had the right of way (ordinary negligence).
b. Plaintiff may have been outside the crosswalk but was injured because the defendant could have stopped his car but didn't (last clear chance).
c. Both plaintiff and defendant may have been negligent, but defendant bears most of the fault (comparative negligence).

Example:

In a murder case, the prosecution's evidence will show that after a violent argument the victim was shot by a man some witnesses will identify as the defendant.

As defendant, your theory could be one of the following:

a. Defendant did not do the shooting (identification).
b. Defendant did the shooting, but was justified in defending himself (self-defense).
c. Defendant did the shooting, but the circumstances do not make the shooting a murder (manslaughter or lesser charge).

As you can see, your position on the facts, both disputed and undisputed, must be developed well in advance of trial. Each disputed fact must be analyzed and a position taken on it that is consistent with your theory of the case. Only then can you move on to the next stages of your trial preparation.

Most trials, where the issues are close, are usually decided on a few pivotal points. It may be an admissibility issue on a critical exhibit or a key witness' testimony. It may be the impression a crucial witness makes on the jury. It may involve how effective your cross-examination of a key witness is. Whatever the issues, thorough trial preparation must include determining what those issues will be at trial. In short, you must find out what the crucial issues will be, how you want to articulate those issues to the jury, and how to prepare for the critical issues more thoroughly and convincingly than your opponent so that the jury will resolve these issues in your favor. All these considerations must come together in deciding on your theory of the case.

§11.7.   Themes and labels

Jurors cannot absorb all the information that a trial produces, so they use subconscious strategies to deal with sensory overload. One strategy, supported by psychological research, is to identify key points or themes that help jurors process information more quickly. A theme is simply a memorable word or phrase that summarizes your position on a critical issue. A trial lawyer must identify the critical issues involved in the case, develop themes for them, and state them in memorable ways so that the jurors will use *your* themes in processing the contested facts and resolving the disputed issues.

Themes should be emotionally compelling. They should incorporate the jurors' sense of fairness and universal truths. They should be simple and have immediate meaning. They should focus on people, not issues. In short, themes must translate legalese into simple, compelling, human propositions that are consistent with the attitudes jurors already hold about people, events, and life in general.

Consider, for example, a breach of contract case. If plaintiff's case is based on proof that defendant defrauded her, the theme might be "this is a case about trust" or "two people made promises to each other, and now one doesn't want to live up to his word."

Consider a personal injury case. If plaintiff's case is based on proof that defendant ran a red light, the liability theme might be "people who take chances hurt others" or "this is a case about breaking the rules of the road." The damages theme might be "Mary Smith's only companion is her pain."

Consider a wrongful death case. If plaintiff wishes to emphasize damages, the theme for the plaintiff spouse might be "this is a case about loneliness" or "as we grow older, the thing we fear most is being alone."

In every case you can, and should, develop themes for the key issues on liability and damages. These will, if they are carefully chosen and expressed, become focal points for the jurors' thinking. If the jurors use *your* themes as a reference point during deliberations, you have a much better chance of getting a favorable verdict.

Both sides, of course, need to consider the themes the other side is likely to use and plan accordingly. You need themes that not only summarize your side, but are also effective antidotes to your opponent's likely themes.

The same careful planning should also go into your selection of labels. What are "labels"? Labels are simply the ways you will refer to the people and events during the trial. Labels convey meanings and values to the jury, since how we characterize things influences how others perceive them.

Consider how language can affect perception. Calling two cars hitting each other a "collision," "crash," "impact," or "smash" conveys a different impression than calling it an "accident" or "two cars hit each other." Asking a witness "how slowly was the car moving" conveys a different image than asking "how fast was the sports car traveling." Referring to a witness as "Bobby" conveys a different stature than "Mr. Williams." Referring to a party as "the defendant" sends different signals to the jury than "Mr. Smith." "That corporation" says something different than "Grandma's Cookies."

The careful trial lawyer selects labels for parties, events, things, and action that send signals to the jury on how it should perceive those parties, events, things, and action. Once selected, those labels must be used consistently throughout each stage of the trial.

§11.8.   *Dramatize, humanize, visualize using people stories*

Jurors, like everyone else, are a product of their environment. Most people stop learning when they finish their formal schooling, and most of what they learn later comes through the medium of television. Therefore, they have been trained to expect drama, an emphasis on personalities, and sophisticated visual effects. They expect everything quickly, in simple, digestible sound bites. They expect interesting visual aids. And they want it all to be easy and enjoyable. Anything less and you've violated the "boring rule," and jurors will quickly change channels.

The lesson for trial lawyers is obvious. First, use storytelling techniques. Search for interesting, dramatic, different ways to present your case. Jurors expect a certain energy level from lawyers and witnesses. Try to re-create what happened through "word pictures" rather than merely tell the jury what happened. Put the jury in the picture so it can feel, not just see, what happened. Second, focus on the people, not just on the events. People do things for a reason. Jurors want to know not just what happened but also what motivated the people behind the events. Jurors want to know about the key players so they can decide whom to silently cheer for. Third, use visual aids as much as possible. Watch how news programs integrate visuals with narration. Notice how highway billboards attract attention and send simple messages quickly. These are the techniques that are effective with the public. Why not bring that knowledge into the courtroom? Carefully prepared exhibits can persuasively summarize your liability and damages cases, and the exhibits will keep persuading the jury during its deliberations. Finally, do it simply and quickly. Jurors expect information in five- to ten-minute segments (that TV training again). Focus on your themes and key facts and repeat them. A courtroom is no different than a classroom. People learn better when a few key ideas are repeated from time to time.

§11.9.   Focus on the key disputed facts and issues

Finally, focus on the key disputes in the case and gather the evidence that will convince the jury to accept your version of the disputed facts. If that evidence is witnesses, prepare the witnesses so that they are dynamic, confident, detailed, and vivid, particularly on the key disputes. If the evidence is exhibits, make sure they are more visually appealing than your opponent's. Wars are often won or lost because of a key battle. The same holds true for trials.

For example, the outcome of a personal injury case may depend on which side's version of an intersection collision the jury will accept. The outcome of a contract case may depend on which side's version of a critical meeting and the conversation held during that meeting the jury will accept. In both cases, you need to prepare the witnesses and exhibits so that they are more convincing — dynamic, confident, detailed, and vivid — on the key disputed facts than the other side.

You are now ready to use your organizational system and your understanding of the psychology of persuasion to actually plan and implement the various tasks that make up preparing for a jury trial.

§11.10.   Opening statements and closing arguments preparation

Work backward. Plan your closing argument first. Everything else then follows. This advice is given by many experienced trial lawyers, and there's a good reason for it: It works.

Why? Because the backward approach makes you think about the elements of the claims and defenses, your theory of the case, themes and labels, undisputed evidence, and key areas where the evidence is in dispute. It makes you think about integrating these concerns into a persuasive whole — your closing argument. It makes you think about what is important and what is merely interesting or peripheral. Your closing argument must do two basic things. It must win the war over the high ground — whose themes will be more appealing to the jury — and win the war over the disputed facts — whose version of the disputed events the jury will accept as true. In short, planning the closing argument first will tell you what to emphasize and what to cover lightly, or not at all, in the other stages of the trial. If it's not important enough to mention during closing arguments, it's probably not important enough to mention during the other stages either.

If you plan your closing first, you will then know what needs to be in your opening statement. Your opening should do several things. First, it should state your themes and theory of the case. This should be done quickly, in the first minute or two. The themes should then be repeated periodically during the opening statement, so that if the jury retains one idea, it should be your themes. Second, it should describe what happened in storytelling form. Decide on the visual aids and exhibits to use during the opening statement that will supplement your storytelling, and that are part of an overall visual strategy. Third, it should anticipate problems and weaknesses by weaving them into your storytelling. Finally, it must be delivered forcefully, with few or no notes at all. The opening statement must show that you have a winning case, and that you, through your conduct and attitude, believe in it.

How do you outline your opening once you've decided what will be in it? One thing you should *not* do (although many inexperienced trial lawyers do) is write out what you will say and use it verbatim during your opening statement. The reason becomes clear once you've seen it done this way. People write differently from how they speak, and a written opening doesn't sound right when delivered to a jury. If you must write out your opening (security blankets are sometimes a necessity), be sure to reduce it to an outline before you give it, and don't memorize what you've written.

An opening statement outline should be on one page whenever possible (and it's possible in almost every case). It should be in large print, noting the "buzz words" that will trigger recall if needed. Some lawyers also put down key dates, names, and events as a protection against a memory block in the middle of the opening statement. The outline can then be put on counsel table or a podium for reference if necessary. When you give the opening statement, however, it is absolutely essential that you get away from notes, look squarely at the jurors, and tell them about the case from your point of view.

Example (plaintiff in an intersection collision):

Opening statement

1. This is a case about: people in a hurry hurting others
    taking chances
    little injury can end a career
2. Bob Johnson's background — self-made man
    family man
3. Intersection — where Bob's life changed
4. How it happened — Bob's eyes
    witnesses
    crash, crushed, snapped, and so on
5. Aftermath — hospital — excruciating pain
    head injury, no pain killers
6. Aftermath — rehabilitation — Bob learned reality
    doctor — never return to normal
7. Today — Bob's situation — learning to cope
    Bob's family — lost what taken for granted
8. Request for verdict — do the right thing

How do you prepare your closing argument? As suggested earlier, organize your main points, based on your theory of the case, themes and labels, undisputed evidence, and your version of the disputed facts. These will tell you what you need to argue at the end of the case (as well as what to emphasize in your opening and witness examinations).

Reserve several blank pages at the front of the closing arguments section of your trial notebook. During the trial, as you hear key testimony from witnesses, statements by lawyers, and questions (if permitted) from jurors, see key exhibits, and have those periodic brainstorms, write them down on the blank pages. These add up during a trial. These specific references to witness testimony and other sources become the details that provide the support and substance of your arguments. Your final preparation for closing arguments, therefore, consists of selecting from these notes the points you want to add to the closing arguments you have already organized and noting them on your closing outline.

Your outline will be organized much like your opening statement. Since a persuasive argument must come from the heart and cannot be read, your outline should be that and nothing more — one or two pages of notes, in large print, containing the key points you want to argue, in the order you want to argue them, with the references to your themes, exhibits, and testimony. The only reading you should do will be reading from key exhibits or quoting from key testimony.

§11.11. Jury selection preparation

If you know your theory of the case and your themes and labels, have your closing argument outlined and your opening statement prepared, know what your client and key witnesses are like and what they will say, you can plan your jury selection strategy. This involves two basic tasks: developing a profile of favorable and unfavorable jurors, and outlining proposed voir dire topics and drafting requested voir dire questions for the judge.

What's a jury profile? This is simply a description of juror backgrounds that you believe are likely to favor, and disfavor, your side. How do you do this? In large cases, lawyers can afford the luxuries of hiring jury psychologists to survey the community to determine its attitudes about issues pertinent to the trial and hiring mock juries to test their theories and themes. In most cases, however, trials lawyers must rely on their experience, knowledge of the community, and perhaps intuition to do the same thing — determine if certain types of jurors, based on their backgrounds and experiences, are likely to be attitudinally disposed toward or against your side. Putting these demographics and experiences on a profile makes them easier to apply during the jury selection process when you exercise your peremptory challenges.

Example:

Plaintiff has sued a trucking company for personal injuries arising from a collision between her car and defendant's truck. Plaintiff is a homemaker with two small children. Defendant is a large national corporation.

Juror Profile — defendant

Unfavorable:	*Favorable:*
Homemakers	Professionals
Young women	Middle-aged jurors
Blue collar	Managerial-level employees
Low income	Middle/white-collar incomes
Previous plaintiffs	Insurance industry employees

In some civil cases, jurors who are favorable on liability may be unfavorable on damages. Consequently, you must refine your juror profile thinking to account for how strong you are on these two areas. For example, if plaintiff is strong on liability but marginal on damages, plaintiff's juror profile should emphasize the jurors that will be favorable and unfavorable on damages.

Once you have identified the backgrounds of likely unfavorable jurors (an admittedly inexact task), you will know what kinds of questions to ask during voir dire. If lawyers will do the voir dire questioning, you need only make a checklist of the topics you must cover during your questioning. If the judge will do all or some of the questioning, you will need to draft proposed voir dire questions and submit them to the judge. This is usually done by filing a request, using the formality of a motion, with the court before trial.

Example:

PLAINTIFF'S REQUESTED VOIR DIRE QUESTIONS

Plaintiff requests that the following questions be asked of the jury during the court's voir dire:

1. Have you ever been a plaintiff in a lawsuit?
2. Have you ever . . .? If so, . . .?
3.

Finally, your trial notebook should have a jury chart to record the basic background information about each juror obtained during the voir dire examination so that you can review it before deciding which jurors to challenge.

The type of diagram or chart depends on how jury selection will be conducted. If the strike system is used, all jurors in the venire will be questioned before any challenges are made. Under this system you can use a legal pad to record the basic information about each juror. (Some lawyers use a form to record the background information of each juror; this allows you to do less writing to record the information and spend more time watching the jurors. Better yet, have someone else write down the information so you can concentrate on the jurors.)

If a traditional system is used, jurors will usually be called into the jury box and only those jurors will be initially questioned. As challenges are exercised and jurors are excused, new jurors replace the excused jurors and are also questioned. Under this system it is necessary to develop a way to keep track of jurors in the box. Most lawyers use a jury box diagram to record juror names and backgrounds. When a challenge is exercised, the juror is crossed off and a new box created. (Square yellow Post-it notes work exceptionally well here.)

Example: (jury chart):

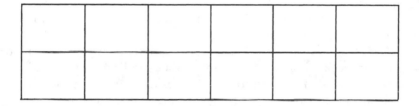

The diagram will cover most of a page. In each of the squares you then simply record in abbreviated form the basic background information obtained during the questioning, as demonstrated below.

> **John Doe** — 40 — carpenter — self-cmp. 10 yrs. — 3C in grade school — W part-time bookkeeper 15 yrs. — owns home Chicago, N. side — 2 yrs. army

§11.12.   *Witness selection and preparation*

1.   Witness selection

Your case in chief will be presented principally through the witnesses you call and the exhibits you introduce. With witnesses you must decide three basic things: whom you will call as witnesses, what you will have these witnesses say, and how you will organize all this in your trial notebook.

Whom you call as witnesses to prove your case is frequently not an issue. You simply must call the witnesses you know of to establish a prima facie case, and there is no room for choices. Most of the time, however, you will have choices. For example, of the several occurrence witnesses available, which ones will you call? Which witnesses will you call to introduce and explain business records to the jury? Which of the police officers who responded to the scene of the accident or crime should you call? In deciding whether to call certain available witnesses, remember the following considerations:

1. Do not overprove your case. Many lawyers call far too many witnesses, thereby boring the jury or, even worse, creating the impression that the lawyer doesn't have confidence in her own witnesses. In general, calling a primary witness and one or two corroboration witnesses on any key point is enough. It's usually best to make your case in chief simple, fast, and then quit while ahead.

2. Use strong witnesses. Stick with strong, likeable witnesses and avoid marginal or weak witnesses who can be damaged by cross-examination, unless such witnesses are essential to establishing a prima facie case.

3. Don't try to prove everything. You are required only to prove the elements of your claims and defenses or to refute the other side's. Avoid calling witnesses merely because they have something interesting to say. Stick to your game plan and prove only your claims and theory of the case. Every added witness gives your opponent an opportunity to hurt your case. Don't give him unnecessary opportunities.

4. Don't sandbag. Do not fail to call a strong witness because you plan to call that witness in rebuttal. First, it's a psychologically bad strategy to save a strong witness for late in the trial. Jurors listen to and are persuaded by witnesses while their minds are still open and undecided. By the rebuttal stage jurors have usually made their minds up about the case, and the strong witness will have little impact. Second, your opponent may surprise you by resting or by presenting evidence in an area not related to your witness' testimony, thereby preventing you from calling him in rebuttal. The court may also rule that since the witness could have been called in your case in chief, the witness is an improper rebuttal witness.

2. Witness preparation

Preparing witnesses for trial is not the same as preparing witnesses for depositions. This is not the time to learn what the case is all about or to obtain interesting information. You should know from discovery what the witnesses can contribute to your case. You also know, from your preparations so far, what you are legally required to prove, what your theory of the case is, and what your themes and labels will be for the trial.

Preparation for trial involves culling out of what each witness *can* say those things the witness *will* say that will prove your case, and preparing each witness to do this persuasively. Witness preparation involves both testimony selection and testimony preparation. Keep the following in mind:

1. Witnesses should be prepared for trial individually by the lawyer who will do the direct examination of that witness. Having an "associate" prepare witnesses rarely works well. Only when you have personally prepared a witness, know precisely what he will testify about, have a feel for the kind of witness he is, and understand how to ask questions that trigger the good responses can you effectively present that witness at trial. Remind the witness that it is perfectly proper to get together to prepare the witness for testifying at trial (and the jury will usually be told this in an instruction).

2. Review with the witness everything where the witness is "down on paper." This includes depositions, other sworn testimony, oral and written statements, interrogatory answers, and any reports the witness made. These are the sources for refreshing recollection on direct examination and impeachment on cross-examination. These should all be in the witness folder that you have already prepared. Have the witness read these, or read them to the witness, if necessary. Point out particularly important areas and any areas where the statements differ with each other. Determine if the witness' current memory differs from these statements. If so, and the witness insists that his present recollection, not the earlier statement, is accurate, explain how the opposing lawyer may impeach him with the statement and show how this is done.

3. Review with the witness all exhibits he will identify or authenticate. Explain how you will need to "lay the foundation" for exhibits and show how this is done.

4. Review the probable testimony of other witnesses to see if any inconsistencies exist between any of the witnesses. If so, see if there are any explanations for important inconsistencies that can be brought out through the witnesses at trial if opposing counsel makes an issue of them.

5. Prepare the direct examination of the witness and review it with the witness — repeatedly. Make sure the witness can actually testify to what you anticipate he can. Make sure he can lay the proper foundation for all necessary exhibits. Once the general outline of the direct examination is clear, go over the actual questions you intend to ask on direct. Above all, *practice the actual examination with the witness!* Do it in your office. Do it in an empty courtroom. Do it as though the jury were watching. Do it repeatedly until both you and the witness are comfortable with the examination (but stop if the examination begins to sound rehearsed). Is this time-consuming? Of course. But it's the only way to properly prepare a witness.

6. Prepare for the cross-examination of the witness. Review the areas that you anticipate the cross-examination will cover. Have another lawyer conduct practice cross-examinations using the same tone and attitude as the cross-examiner is likely to use at trial. Above all, *practice the actual cross-examination with the witness.* Talking about the cross-examination can only go so far. The witness needs the experience of actually being cross-examined in a realistic environment.

7. Prepare the witness for his courtroom appearance. Decide on what he should wear. Jurors expect neat, conservatively dressed witnesses, with clothes appropriate to the witness' background. For most witnesses this means a suit or jacket and tie. For witnesses who wear uniforms, work attire may be effective. Explain how the courtroom is arranged and where the judge, lawyers, court reporter, court clerk, bailiff, and spectators sit. Explain how the witness will enter the courtroom, where and how he will take the oath, where he will sit while giving his testimony, how he should sit and appear while there, and how he will leave the courtroom. If the witness is a party that will sit with you at counsel table, remind him that the jury will be watching and assessing him, even when he is not testifying. Instruct him not to whisper or interrupt you when court is in session. Instead, have him write on a notepad anything he wants to tell you when you are occupied with witness testimony or other critical matters.

8. Prepare the witness for the procedural and evidentiary rules that govern his testimony. Some lawyers have printed instructions they give each witness.

Example:

Instructions for Witnesses

a.   Listen carefully to each question. Answer only that question. Do not ramble on or volunteer information. Look at the jury when answering questions. Speak loudly and clearly so that the last juror can hear you easily. Do not look at the judge or at me for help if asked difficult questions.

b.   If you do not understand a question, say so and the lawyer will probably rephrase it. If you do not *know* an answer to a question, say so. If you do not *remember* an answer, say, "I don't recall" or "I don't remember." The lawyer may show you your previous statements to jog your memory. If you can only approximate dates, times and distances, give only your best approximations. If you cannot answer a question with "yes" or "no," either the lawyer will ask another question or you will be allowed to explain your answer. Give positive, clear, and direct answers to every question whenever possible.

c.   Use your own vocabulary. Use the words you normally use and feel comfortable with. Don't use someone else's vocabulary, "police talk," or other stilted, artificial speech.

d.   Be serious and polite at all times. Do not exaggerate or understate facts. Don't give cute or clever answers. Never argue with the lawyers or judge. The lawyer on cross-examination may attempt to confuse you, have you argue with him, or have you lose your temper. Resist these temptations. Never argue. Never lose your temper.

e.   You will be allowed to testify only to what you personally saw, heard, and did. You generally cannot testify to what others know, or to opinions, conclusions, and speculations.

f.   If an objection is made by either lawyer to any question or answer, stop. (The lawyers will usually stand up when they object.) Wait for the judge to rule. If she overrules the objection, answer the question. If she sustains the objection, simply wait for the next question. Never try to squeeze an answer in when an objection has been made.

g.   After the cross-examination, the direct examiner may ask more questions; this is called "redirect examination." The cross-examiner may also ask more questions; this is called "recross-examination." On direct and redirect examination leading questions are usually not permitted. On cross- and recross-examination leading questions are proper.

h.   Above all, *always tell the complete truth according to your best memory of the events and transactions involved.*

3.   Direct examination outline

How do you create an outline of your planned direct examination in your trial notebook? There are two common methods.

a.   *The Q & A method.* Under this approach, every question you intend to ask the witness (and a summary of the expected answer) is written out. This is the method frequently employed by inexperienced lawyers during their first few trials. Its advantage is that you can draft your questions in proper form in advance. The disadvantages are that, unless you are a great actor, your questions will invariably sound as though they are being read from a script — hardly the impression you want to convey. This approach also weds you to the script and hinders your flexibility in asking logical follow-up questions. If you do use this method for your first few trials, never show your questions and answers to your witness, since they may then be discoverable (the other side may argue that they were used by the witness to prepare for testifying, possibly making them discoverable at trial under FRE 612).

b.   *The witness summary method.* Under this approach, used by most experienced trial lawyers, you outline the key things the witness will testify about on direct. You then simply follow the outline, asking the questions that elicit the desired answers. The advantages are that your questions will sound fresh and spontaneous, and you retain flexibility to ask follow-up and clarifying questions. A convenient way to organize the direct under this approach is to note at the top of the outline the exhibits the witness will work with or qualify and the witness' prior statements (which will be in the witness' file folder). The rest of the page is then split into three columns: dates and times, witness testimony, and exhibits. This makes it visually simple to know where you are and what you should do next. As the examination progresses, you simply check off what has been done as it occurs.

Example (John Doe — direct examination):

Exhibits: 1. wallet (P#2)
             2. building photo (P#1)
             3. lineup photo (P#6)
Statements: 1. grand jury transcript of 6/20/00, pp. 1-8
                2. statement to police in report, p. 7

1. Background   name, age, address
                        how long there
                        work and school
                        residence — neighborhood
                        family

2. 5/20/00   where living
                        describe building
                        describe apt. layout
                        doors, locks, lights   *ID photo* — P#1

3. 2:00 A.M.   in apt.
                        TV, beer, lights

4. What happened   two men broke in door
                        describe men   *ID def.*
                        guns, describe
                        took wallet, describe
                        men searched apt.
                        took things, describe
                        threats, ran out

5. Aftermath   called police, arrived
                        spoke to them

6. Lineup   9:00 A.M. call
                        to station
                        talked to police
                        viewed lineup, ID def.   *ID photo* — P#6
                        shown wallet, ID it   *ID wallet* — P#2

All the direct examination outlines should be put in your trial notebook (under plaintiff or defendant, depending on whom you represent) in the order you plan to call them in your case in chief.

4. Witness list

Finally, you need to keep a list of witnesses in the charts section of your trial notebook. The witness list will show each witness' name, home address and telephone, work address and telephone, any other information useful for locating and scheduling him during the trial, and a one-sentence synopsis of the witness' role at trial. Some lawyers put the list in alphabetical order. Others put the list in the order in which the witnesses are expected to testify at trial. The witness list is critical for keeping in touch with the witnesses as the trial date approaches and during the trial.

Example (witness list — plaintiff):

Frank Miller

123 North, Chicago (works at home)
H (312) 888-1123   W (same)

accountant who prepared defendant's tax returns

Mrs. Sharon Jones

2300 N. Clark, Chicago (works 8-12)
H (312) 888-9876   W (312) 726-8231

bookkeeper at defendant's company

H ( )   W ( )

§11.13.   Exhibit selection and preparation

If you have prepared your witness examinations, you already know what exhibits you intend to use during trial. Now is your opportunity to think about exhibits one more time. You need a strategy that incorporates both "exhibits," that will be formally admitted in evidence, and "visual aids," that are not formally admitted in evidence but can supplement opening statements, closing arguments, and expert testimony. Ask yourself: What visual aids will help the jury understand my case better? What additional exhibits would be persuasive on the issues of liability and damages? If so, what witnesses do I need to qualify them for admission at trial? Although in many jurisdictions your exhibits are already limited to what has been disclosed in discovery and covered by the pretrial memoranda and order, this is not always so. Creative thinking now still produces good ideas.

When in doubt, choose more visual exhibits, not fewer. Plan how your exhibits can be creatively prepared. Bigger is better: Enlargements of photographs and documents are more effective than letter-sized originals. Color attracts more attention than black and white. Putting important documents and records on foam-core poster boards will draw more attention than sheets of paper. Think how you can make your exhibits more attractive than the other side's exhibits.

Plan what the necessary foundation for each exhibit is and who the best witness is to provide it. Plan when in the direct examination of that witness the exhibit should be first used and qualified for admission. If the exhibit can be marked or highlighted, plan how this can be done most effectively and train the witness to do this during the direct examination.

Finally, you need to keep a list of exhibits in the charts section of your trial notebook. The exhibits list will show, for each party, the exhibit number, exhibit description, and boxes to check showing the evidentiary status of the exhibit — if offered, admitted, refused, reserved, or withdrawn. The exhibits list is essential for you to keep track of the admissibility status of your, and your opponent's, exhibits during trial.

Example (exhibits list — plaintiff):

#	*Exhibits marked for identification*	*Offered*	*Admitted*	*Refused*	*Reserved*	*Withdrawn*
1	Construction contract	x	x			
2	Final payment check	x			x	
3a-g	Monthly progress reports (7)	x	x			

§11.14. *Order of proof*

The last step in preparing your case in chief is deciding the order in which you will present your evidence. Your proof will come from four possible sources: witnesses, exhibits, stipulations, and judicial notice. You have total control over the order in which you will present your evidence, and you are limited only by the availability of your witnesses. Hence, the principal question is: what order of proof will present my case most effectively?

There are several considerations you should keep in mind in deciding on the order of proof. These include the following:

a. Present your case in chronological order or some other logical progression, as viewed from the jury's perspective. Jurors follow testimony most easily when it is ordered chronologically, particularly when occurrence evidence is involved. Since jurors are familiar with chronological storytelling, use the same approach with your case unless there is a compelling reason to alter your approach. This is probably the most important consideration in determining your order of proof and will usually override competing and conflicting considerations.

b. Start with a strong, important witness to give the jury a good initial impression of your case.

c. Finish with a strong witness. Jurors generally remember what they hear and see first and last. These are the psychological principles of primacy and recency. Use them to your advantage.

d. Begin each morning and afternoon session with a strong and interesting witness whenever possible. Jurors are fresh and retain information better at the beginning of court sessions.

e. If you must call your opposing party or another adverse witness during your case in chief, it is usually safer to call him during the middle of your case. If the witness does more damage than he helps, he will not have started your case in chief on a bad note, and you can immediately follow him with favorable testimony. On the other hand, lawyers sometimes prefer to take a risk and begin their case in chief by calling the opposing party as an adverse witness. This can work well if the witness is unprepared or will make a bad impression on the jury.

f. Call important corroboration witnesses immediately after the primary witness has testified. This usually has the effect of driving home important points that the jury will then accept as true. On the other hand, jurors are easily bored. Avoid calling several corroboration witnesses to the same point. Overkill adds nothing, and boring the jury is costly. Sometimes a corroboration witness can be called later so that the jury does not repeatedly hear the same evidence.

g. Several witnesses are sometimes necessary to establish technical elements of proof. These can be boring witnesses. Unless doing so will interrupt the logical progression of your case, these witnesses can sometimes be interspersed with more interesting witnesses. In any event, these technical witnesses should be efficiently presented. Keep in mind, however, that technical witnesses may be necessary both to provide foundations for critical exhibits you want to introduce at a certain time and as predicate witnesses for other witnesses, unless the court will allow you to call witnesses out of turn on your representation that you will "connect it up." (For example, chain-of-custody witnesses are necessary predicate witnesses before an expert can testify to the results of laboratory tests on the evidence involved.)

h. Reading depositions, stipulations, and documentary evidence is inherently less interesting and usually boring. See how you can make this come alive. Choose a good witness for reading in deposition testimony. Enlarge key documents to make them more appealing. Intersperse this kind of evidence with more interesting proof, unless it will disrupt the orderly presentation of your case.

i. Get your exhibits in evidence and show them to the jury as soon as possible. Jurors understand and retain what they see much better than what they hear. Use photographs, diagrams, models, maps, and summary charts (particularly if enlarged), and recordings, movies, and in-court demonstrations whenever possible. Jurors remember dramatic visual presentations. Work particularly on having such exhibits summarize your liability and damages proof. If, for example, the jury will use your intersection diagram during deliberations as their reference exhibit when they discuss liability, this will be a powerful influence.

j. Alternate lay witnesses and expert witnesses to keep the jury's attention.

k. An expert often is a good final witness because he can effectively summarize the evidence in your case. This will capsulize your case just before you rest.

l. Finally, remember that your planned order of proof must remain flexible. Witnesses, particularly experts, have busy schedules and can be available only at certain times. Last-minute problems invariably arise, requiring you to adjust your expected order. Remember also that the above consid-erations can and often will compete with each other so that there is no one way in which your proof should be ordered. As usual, there is no simple solution to these conflicts. Each case must be analyzed, and the advantages and disadvantages of each order considered, to arrive at an order that appears reasonable, one that presents your case in a logical, progressive way that is easy for the jury to follow and understand.

The following examples give simple illustrations of one way in which the proof could be organized in common civil and criminal cases.

Example (plaintiff in pedestrian collision case):

1. plaintiff
2. eyewitness
3. police officer at scene
4. ambulance driver
5. doctor at emergency room
6. treating physician
7. former employer on damages
8. spouse on damages

Example (prosecution in murder case):

1. eyewitness to shooting
2. first police officer at scene
3. ambulance driver
4. doctor at emergency room
5. pathologist on cause of death
6. second eyewitness
7. arresting police officer
8. detective on defendant's admissions

§11.15. *Cross-examination preparation*

Your final trial preparation task is to prepare the cross-examination of your opponent's witnesses. This has been saved for last for a reason. Cross-examination preparation cannot be focused until you know exactly what your theory of the case is, what themes and labels you will use, and what the key factual disputes will be during the trial.

Effective cross-examinations require preparation. Discovery, in both civil and most criminal cases, makes it possible to determine what your opponent's witnesses will probably say at trial. Since you know what the direct testimony of these witnesses will be, you can and should prepare your cross-examinations in advance as well.

Preparation for cross-examinations should include the following:

a. Outline each witness' probable testimony on direct examination, including the exhibits she is likely to identify and qualify for admission.

b. Review all depositions, statements, and reports the witness made. For parties, review the amended pleadings and interrogatory answers as well.

c. Ask yourself the key question: What will I say about this witness during closing arguments? Your cross-examination should elicit only enough information to support your closing argument, and nothing more. Put another way, many, perhaps even most, cross-examinations fail because they are unrealistic and attempt too much.

d. Consider what the witness must admit that is favorable to your side. What exhibits of yours can she identify and qualify? What facts can she testify to that help you? Where has she made previous statements that "lock her in" on testimony that will help your side?

e. Consider what the witness is reasonably likely to admit that is favorable to your side. What testimony is she likely to give that sounds improbable? What testimony is in conflict with other witnesses? What testimony contradicts common sense and the jurors' experiences in life? What testimony conflicts with the exhibits?

f. Consider what impeachment you have of the witness' probable testimony. Will her testimony conflict with any of her previous statements and reports? Do her previous statements conflict with each other?

g. When you have reviewed the available materials and have collected possible cross-examination ideas into three basic categories — favorable testimony, likely admissions, and impeachment — you need to arrange your cross-examination into specific points. The fewer good points you have, the more likely the jury is to remember them. The jury will never remember ten specific things you cover on cross. Try to keep your major points to a handful, and make sure that they all contribute to your theory of the case, themes, and closing argument. Avoid unimportant points entirely, since they only dilute your strong points.

h. Arrange the points you have decided to cover on cross-examination in an intelligent order. Obtain favorable admissions before you attempt to impeach.

i. Start crisply on a strong point and end crisply on another strong point. Your best points should come first and last, because jurors remember best the things they hear first and last (the principles of primacy and recency).

Sounds like a lot of work? Of course it does. However, successful cross-examinations are almost entirely the product of hard work, thorough preparation and planning, and an understanding of what you can realistically accomplish. There's simply no other way to do it.

When you've completed the cross-examination preparation for each witness, you still need to organize your planned cross-examination and put it in your trial notebook. A common problem of inexperienced trial lawyers here is a lack of organization. During the direct examination they feverishly take notes, and this rarely does anything worthwhile. The better approach is to *take only those notes that will help your cross-examination.* (If necessary, have someone else take full notes of your opponent's direct examinations.) This is easily accomplished if you organize your cross notes so that you can integrate anything useful the witness says on direct into your notes.

A common system is to outline the planned cross-examination on one side of a sheet of paper, by specific topics. The other half of the sheet is blank; this is where you will note anything specific the witness says on direct that you can use on cross. This will limit your note-taking during the direct, giving you more time to watch the witness testify, which is usually more useful anyway. Some lawyers put a short synopsis of the witness' expected direct testimony, and a list of prior statements, at the top of the page. (The prior statements should be in that witness' folder.)

Example (John Smith — cross-examination):

Direct: Witness will probably testify he was walking down the street late at night, was accosted by a man he claims was the defendant, who claimed he had a gun, and was robbed of $35, and later identified def. in lineup.

Statements: statement to police (pp. 6-8 of reports)
grand jury transcript of 6/20/00

Cross-examination	Direct examination
1. late at night dark, no lights near	1.
2. happened suddenly, not expecting trouble	2.
3. worried about being hurt, looking for gun	3.
4. never saw gun (GJ transcript, p. 7) (statement, p. 8)	4.
5. description to police, general never noted scar on face	5.

Under this system, the only notes you will make during the direct examination are on any specific facts the witness makes that help you on the points you have planned to make on cross. These notes can be made on your cross outline next to the topic involved. In this way your direct examination notes are useful because they are immediately correlated to your planned cross-examination.

All the cross-examination outlines should be put in your trial notebook (under plaintiff or defendant, depending on whom you represent) in either alphabetical order or in the order you anticipate your opponent will call these witnesses at trial.

§11.16.   *Examples of trial strategy*

1.   The case — *Robert Johnson v. Mary Smith*

On June 1, 2000, at approximately 5:30 P.M. Robert Johnson's and Mary Smith's cars collided in the intersection of Main and Broadway. Johnson was driving southbound on Main Street toward the intersection with Broadway. Smith had been driving northbound on Main Street and had stopped in the intersection, waiting to make a left turn to go west on Broadway. Johnson was alone in his car, a six-year-old Jaguar sports car. Smith's husband was a passenger in her car, a one-year-old Buick sedan.

Johnson was on his way home from the shop where he worked as an automobile mechanic. Smith was driving her husband, who had been feeling nauseated most of the day, to their doctor's office.

According to Johnson, as he was driving southbound on Main, the light turned yellow when he was about three car lengths from the intersection. It was too late to stop, so he continued into the intersection on the yellow light. He was still traveling about 25 mph, the same speed as the other rush-hour traffic in front of and behind him. Just as he entered the intersection, a car (Smith's car) that had been stopped in the intersection, facing northbound and waiting to make a left turn, suddenly made the left turn in front of him while the light for Main was still yellow. Johnson slammed on his brakes, but it was too late. Johnson's car slammed into the right side of Smith's car.

According to Smith, she was stopped in the northbound lane of Main, waiting to make a left turn on Broadway. The oncoming stream of cars prevented her from making the turn. The light turned yellow, she waited until the light turned red for Main, and then made her left turn. As she was making her left turn, a car, coming southbound on Main, ran the red light and crashed into the right side of her car.

The force of the crash threw Johnson forward. He braced himself by instinctively locking his arms on the steering wheel, but the force of the collision broke his right upper arm and dislocated his right elbow. He also received a classic whiplash injury to his neck. Smith and her husband were shaken up by the collision but did not require medical attention. Both cars were extensively damaged.

Other than Johnson and Smith, the collision was witnessed by a pedestrian at the corner, Ben Jones, and Smith's husband, Robert Smith. Jones' testimony will be consistent with Johnson's. Robert Smith's testimony will be consistent with his wife's.

Police soon arrived. They noted that Johnson's car had about 10 feet of tire skid marks behind it. Main and Broadway Streets are both two-lane roads with parking on both sides of the streets. The single traffic light hanging over the center of the intersection has a three-second yellow light.

Johnson was taken by ambulance to a local hospital. His arm was examined, X-rayed, diagnosed as an elbow dislocation, and put in a cast. His neck was examined, X rays showed no fractures, and he was diagnosed as having a moderate whiplash injury. Johnson was discharged the next day.

During the month following his injuries Johnson stayed at home recuperating. His whiplash injury slowly got better, but he still was in substantial pain from the neck and arm injuries. He took prescription medication for the pain.

A month later Johnson's orthopedic specialist removed the cast. (Johnson had seen this specialist two years earlier for neck pain caused by a mild arthritis, which had responded to heat and medication treatment.)

The rehabilitation program began. It consisted of heat treatment and arm-stretching exercises to regain full pain-free motion and strength in the arm. Johnson stopped doing the exercises after several weeks, claiming that the pain, despite his medication, was too severe, and that it stopped improving his arm by the time he stopped. His doctor instructed him to resume therapy. Johnson did, but stopped after a few weeks for the same reasons. Today his elbow remains tender, especially when used extensively, and the range of motion has still not returned to normal.

Johnson was recently examined by a defense orthopedic specialist. That doctor's opinion is that Johnson should be able to regain full, pain-free use of the arm if Johnson would only continue with the therapy program.

Johnson is 35 years old, married with two children, and worked as an automotive mechanic. He tried to return to work since the collision, but the pain and loss of motion prevented him from doing the physical work required of a mechanic. His boss reluctantly fired him. Johnson has been living on unemployment benefits and savings, and his wife works to make ends meet. Johnson has lived in this town his entire life.

Smith is 60 years old, married with grown children. She and her husband are retired. They sold a small retail store they had owned and managed and moved to this town last year.

The case is scheduled for trial in a few weeks. Plaintiff's complaint alleges common law negligence and violation of statutory driving rules. The case will be tried under the state's comparative negligence law.

2.   Plaintiff's strategy

(Step into the mind of plaintiff's lawyer as he thinks through his approach to the upcoming trial.)

It's now three weeks from the trial date. I've done some of the basic trial preparations. I've reviewed the litigation file, filed all amendments and supplemental responses to discovery, had trial subpoenas issued, and set up my trial notebook. I've already prepared my trial chart, witness list, exhibit list, and proposed jury instructions. (Most of these were already submitted to the court in the joint pretrial memorandum.) I've organized witness folders for the expected witnesses and collected my exhibits in an exhibits folder.

It looks as if this one is really going to trial. My latest demand and the defense's last offer are still miles apart. They just don't see the issues, particularly damages, the way I do. It's time to get serious about putting this case together.

1.   Theory of the case

What's my theory of the case on liability? One thing to avoid is calling this a "who had the red light" case. The jury will probably think a 35-year-old mechanic is more likely to have run a red light then a 60-year-old woman. The better approach is to pick another theory that avoids "red light" issues.

How about calling this a "failure to yield" case? After all, my plaintiff was driving straight through an intersection, and the defendant, trying to make a left turn, turned directly in front of the plaintiff. The defendant had a legal duty to yield to oncoming traffic. Under this theory it doesn't really matter what color the traffic light was when the cars were both in the intersection. Plaintiff still had the right of way, and defendant still had the duty to yield until it was safe to make the left turn. It seems that this is also a better way to realistically impose 100 percent responsibility on the defendant.

Okay, that's it. As far as liability is concerned, I'm going to approach this case as a "failure to yield the right of way" case.

What's my theory of the case on damages? This is my major concern. What I need to avoid is a verdict in the $50,000 range. This would merely be compensation for plaintiff's medical expenses, a year's lost wages, and a little pain and suffering. I need to sell to the jury the fact that plaintiff's elbow condition is permanent, through no fault of his own, that it has reduced his lifetime earning capacity by approximately 50 percent, and that it seriously affects the quality of his life. I'd like to get a verdict in the $400,000 range. This is going to be very difficult.

My theory on damages needs to do three things. First, I'm going to avoid the whiplash injury as the basis for damages. It's a red herring. The arthritis in plaintiff's neck was a preexisting condition and is as likely a reason for his continuing pain as is the whiplash injury. I can't ask the jury to give serious money for this. The better tack is to buy credibility with the jury by taking this position.

Second, I need to sell the idea that a "seemingly minor injury can sometimes have devastating, career-ending consequences." If the jury accepts this idea, they will at least be willing to consider compensating plaintiff for his loss of earnings capacity. (Maybe some references to athletes who have had minor injuries, which were nevertheless career-ending, will work with sports-minded jurors.)

Third, I need to sell the idea that plaintiff truly tried to do the rehabilitation, but couldn't because of the pain, which was caused by the damage to the elbow structures. I need to sell the idea that people sometimes don't come back 100 percent from an injury of this kind. "He tried" is going to be an important part of this case. I need to sell the fact that plaintiff hates not being able to work and has every motivation in the world to recover completely.

2. Themes and labels

How do I create themes that will focus the jury's attention on my theory of the case? My themes must be easy to remember, be based on universal truths, and must explain why things happened as they did.

On the liability issue, my factual argument is going to be that the defendant, who was taking her nauseated husband to the doctor, was in a hurry and took a chance by guessing or assuming that the oncoming car would stop when the light turned yellow. I'm going to be careful not to suggest that she is a bad driver, only that the situation that day let her take a chance she might not otherwise have taken. A theme that captures this idea might be "people in a hurry take chances" or "people in a hurry can hurt others," or "it's dangerous to assume what other people will do."

On the damages issue, my themes are pretty clear. I'm going to argue that "common injuries can sometimes have devastating consequences" to explain how the elbow dislocation ended plaintiff's career as an auto mechanic or any other job that requires physical arm strength. I'm also going to argue that "not everyone bounces back 100 percent from an injury" to explain why the rehabilitation program did not restore the arm enough to return successfully to work.

What about labels for people, places, things, and events? I need to dignify the plaintiff; "Mr. Johnson" is appropriate. I need to watch attacking the defendant, who looks and sounds like everyone's model grandmother; "Mrs. Smith" sounds right. However, the Smiths owned a business before retiring. I'll want to mention that they "owned a business" whenever possible, to offset the jurors' possible fears that a plaintiff verdict may ruin the Smith's retirement years.

For the collision, I'll need to create "impact" word pictures. Words like "collision," "impact," "crash," "crunch," "smashed," and so on should draw the picture. For the injury to plaintiff, words like "thrown forward," "felt arm snap," and "arm dangled by his side" will picture what the injury was. For the rehabilitation period, words like "he tried to," "stretching the damaged ligaments," and "despite the pain" should create images of how painful the program was.

The key, then, is to work these themes into my opening statement and closing argument and work the labels into my entire presentation of the case.

3. Dramatize, humanize, visualize

I need to both "re-create" this collision for the jurors so that they can experience what the plaintiff experienced and show that the collision was sufficiently traumatic to account for his injuries and permanent effects on his life. I also need to make the plaintiff come alive as Robert Johnson, a human being and family man, one the jury can identify with, feel sorry for, and want to help. Only if I get the jurors in a frame of mind where they want to help will plaintiff get substantial damages. Graphic exhibits and "visual" testimony are going to be very important in this case.

4. Opening statement and closing argument

From my theory of the case and themes and labels, and the importance of dramatic, visual evidence, I already know the basics of my closing argument. I'll outline the basics now, and use notes I take during trial to provide the specifics that flesh out the argument. (In closing, I'll need to emphasize damages more than in my opening, since the last impression I want the jury to have is that the real question is what an adequate damages award is, not whether liability has been proved. I'll probably use a damages elements chart, based on the damages jury instruction, to thoroughly review them.)

These basic concepts — theories and themes and labels — must be carried into the opening statement as well. I could start out my opening statement with "this is a case where someone failed to yield the right of way to oncoming traffic, and it changed Mr. Johnson's life forever." Whatever it is, I want to get my theme on damages before the jury right away, and mention it several times during my opening.

However, I'll want to focus on liability in my opening. Even though my most difficult trial task is to sell my damages to the jury, I don't want to come across at the beginning of the trial as someone who's interested only in money. Instead, I'm going to concentrate on how the collision happened, and then describe what happened to the plaintiff's life and what the future holds for him, but avoid talking about dollars. I'll only ask for "substantial damages" or "compensation for what happened" to the plaintiff, but not mention dollar amounts. This will take the emphasis off money and instead focus on the plaintiff as a human being who now needs help.

Finally, I need to make what happened come alive. Standard chronological storytelling — through the *plaintiff's* eyes — to "re-create" how the collision happened, and what happened to the plaintiff afterward, should work well.

Will I want to use visual exhibits in the opening? While this is helpful in some cases, I'm going to avoid them here. A left-turn collision is easy to explain, so there's no necessity for using exhibits. Besides, I want to concentrate on the picture of the plaintiff as a human being, and exhibits won't do much for me there.

5. Jury selection

What kind of jury am I looking for? I obviously want a jury that will return a favorable verdict, but that's too general to be helpful. What are my strengths and weaknesses? I think I'm in pretty good shape on the liability issue — failure to yield. It's damages I'm worried about. Perhaps I need to focus on the jurors who will be inclined to award substantial damages in this kind of case. In short, it's time to develop a profile of favorable and unfavorable jurors.

On liability, favorable jurors are likely to be drivers, people who are familiar with the rules of the road and what it's like to drive in rush-hour conditions. I'm going to avoid jurors who have never driven, no longer drive, drive rarely, or are primarily rural drivers.

On damages, I want jurors who can understand mathematics and will follow my lost-future-income proof, particularly from my economic expert. I want jurors who are physically active, both in their jobs and in their leisure interests. I want jurors who are familiar with handling large sums of money who won't be turned off by the prospect of giving a substantial award of money. I'm going to avoid jurors who have desk jobs and are physically inactive. I'm also going to avoid jurors with medical backgrounds who have seen seriously injured persons and will not see the plaintiff's situation as serious. Finally, I'm going to avoid jurors who have had pain in their own lives, particularly older jurors who might see pain as an inevitable part of life.

What specific voir dire questions do I want asked? I need to know the jurors' socioeconomic levels, since I'm looking for jurors who will be willing to award perhaps $400,000 in damages if the facts warrant it. Therefore, I'll need to ask about residence, education, and jobs to identify jurors used to handling substantial sums of money. I also need to identify persons with sedentary lifestyles who would probably be unsympathetic to the plaintiff. Therefore, I'll need to learn about their interests, hobbies, and spare-time activities. I definitely need to discover if any jurors or their spouses or immediate family have medical backgrounds or employment, since jurors who have seen major physical handicaps will probably not see the plaintiff's condition as significant. Finally, I need to know if any jurors have been injured seriously or were plaintiffs in personal injury lawsuits, since I doubt such jurors will be sympathetic to the plaintiff.

6. Witnesses

I don't have much selectivity with witnesses. Possible witnesses include:

(liability)   plaintiff
                police officers at scene
                bystander/eyewitness

(damages)   emergency room doctor
                emergency room nurses
                ambulance attendants
                treating orthopedic specialist
                plaintiff's employer
                economic expert on lost future income
                occupational expert on future employment
                automobile repair witness on bills
                plaintiff's spouse
                plaintiff's children

Of these, I probably won't call the emergency room nurses, ambulance attendants, automobile repair witness (unless the defense won't stipulate to the admissibility of the records and their reasonableness), and plaintiff's children. I won't do anything dangerous, like call the defendant or her husband as adverse witnesses. I plan to keep my case clean and simple.

What do I need to focus on in my case in chief? Several things. First, I need to make the jurors like my plaintiff so that they will *want* to help him. I'll do this by showing he's an all-American guy who's held a good job for years and has a stable family life. I'll definitely *avoid* talking about money or financial damages during his direct examination. He'll talk only about his background, the collision, and particularly his motivation and attempts to rehabilitate his arm.

Second, I'll focus on the bystander/eyewitness to support the plaintiff's testimony on how the collision happened. The bystander is the only independent eyewitness, and he supports us.

Third, I'll use witnesses *other* than the plaintiff to prove damages. These will include the employer, spouse, occupational expert, and economist.

Finally, I'll need to prove that the plaintiff genuinely tried to regain full use of his arm, that he hates his life now, that his condition is probably permanent, and that it prevents him from ever working as a mechanic or other labor-intensive job. The hospital physician and the orthopedic specialist will be the key witnesses.

7. Exhibits

Several exhibits will be important in my case. On liability, I'll have photographs, enlarged to $30'' \times 40''$ or larger and mounted on foam-core poster boards, of the intersection. I'll probably use one aerial photo and two photos taken from the north and south showing the drivers' views of the intersection. I'll also want one looking north, taken *in* the intersection, to show the defendant's view (this should show how unlikely it is that defendant could watch the only overhead traffic light and oncoming traffic at the same time). I'll also need photos of the two damaged cars. Finally, and most important, I'll have a large, attractive intersection diagram on which witnesses will mark the key facts that summarize my liability case.

On damages, my main concern is proving permanence of injury. The X rays will be useful to visualize the displacement of the bones and explain the soft-tissue damage that must have occurred in the joint capsule. The doctors will need large color diagrams of the elbow joint and a working model of an elbow to explain where ligament damage and scarring probably occurred and why some patients never recover fully from this type of dislocation. The jury needs to see *inside* the plaintiff's arm to understand why his injury is a permanent, career-ending one. Finally, whatever visual aids the economist can provide to show plaintiff's lost future income, reduced to present case value, may be helpful (but I'll need to see them first).

8. Order of proof

In what order will I call these witnesses? My basic plan is to prove liability first, then damages. On liability, the logical choice is to call the plaintiff first, followed by the bystander, and the best police officer at the scene (the one who made the diagram of the intersection and prepared a report about the scene).

On damages, I have a choice. Should I present the medical evidence first or the economic-loss evidence first? The medical evidence should be first because I want to show the jury why the injury ended the plaintiff's ability to work as a mechanic before I start talking about money. This approach also will end my case in chief on damages, usually a sound order.

My order of proof will probably be as follows:

1. plaintiff
2. bystander/eyewitness
3. police officer at scene
4. emergency room physician
5. orthopedic specialist
6. plaintiff's spouse

7.   repair records witness (unless stipulated)
8.   plaintiff's employer
9.   occupational expert
10. economic expert

9.   Cross-examinations

Through the pretrial memorandum I know that the defense may call only three witnesses: the defendant, her husband (the passenger in her car), and an orthopedic specialist.

This alone tells me a great deal. First, it appears that the defense will attack my case on liability by challenging my version of what happened. I don't think the defense will win on liability, but since this is a comparative negligence jurisdiction, the defense may argue that plaintiff was also at fault and suggest that liability should be apportioned accordingly. Second, the defense will attack my claim of permanent injury through its orthopedic expert (who examined the plaintiff recently). Finally, it looks as if the defense will not contest, and perhaps even ignore, my economic proof on the theory that it's irrelevant because the injury is not permanent.

What will I need to do during my cross-examinations of these witnesses? My approach to the defendant and her husband will be similar. I need to bring out *facts* supporting my argument that defendant was in a hurry to get to the doctor and that her attention was on her husband. I also want to show that defendant could not watch the overhead traffic light and oncoming traffic at the same time. With the defendant's husband, I'll simply point out that he was feeling nauseated and couldn't have been paying much attention to the lights or traffic. I'll need to do this gently because the defendant and her husband seem to be nice people.

The cross of the orthopedic specialist will be important since his opinion is that plaintiff should even today be able to rehabilitate his arm fully if he tried. The most I can get out of him is probably two points, but they're important. First, he didn't treat the plaintiff and monitor his progress during the rehabilitation period. Second, not all patients with elbow dislocations recover completely, despite their best efforts. If I can get these points out, I'll quit, because I have enough for my closing argument.

Well, that's about it so far. Now I've got to start preparing my witnesses to implement my trial strategy. At the same time I've got to keep thinking my strategy through, again and again, refining and shaping it the way I want, and working with my witnesses repeatedly so that what I bring out during their examinations serves my strategy. Time for a fresh pot of coffee.

3.   Defendant's strategy

(Step into the mind of defendant's lawyer as she thinks through her approach to the upcoming trial.)

We offered $70,000 to settle this case (based principally on two years' lost wages, repair bills, and medical expenses); plaintiff rejected it. We're not going to raise our offer, and the insurance company says I should try it.

I will. I've got all the preliminary work done, my files are set up, and my trial notebook is organized. Time to start thinking through my trial strategy.

1.   Theory of the case

What's my theory on liability? It's unrealistic to expect an outright win on liability; getting a 50-50 split would be great, although the jury will probably put most of the liability on the defendant. I can't concede liability, however, and I need an approach that may put some of the blame on the plaintiff. If I can show that the plaintiff *may* have entered the intersection on the red light or without appropriate caution, the jury might split liability. After all, it was rush-hour traffic, and plaintiff was driving a Jaguar sports car. This image may help me.

What's my theory on damages? I'm much stronger here. Plaintiff wants to retire on this case, and I don't think the jury will let him do this. This is a case where a plaintiff suffers a common dislocation and won't do the therapy, or take the pain medication, necessary to rehabilitate the arm. Plaintiff wants to be able to sit around his house for the rest of his life and have the defendant pay for it. I can also show that plaintiff didn't follow doctors' orders. If plaintiff had done what the doctors told him, he would be back on the job and his damages would be minimal.

2.   Themes and labels

My themes are going to be important. I need something that will take the focus off the defendant and put it on the plaintiff, if the jury is going to apportion liability. My liability theme needs to suggest that plaintiff was careless.

The short ten-foot skid marks give me a start. They suggest that plaintiff never took his foot off the gas and applied the brakes until just before the impact. If plaintiff had simply braked even one second earlier, or had his foot ready to brake, this collision would never have happened. How about "plaintiff did not give Mr. and Mrs. Smith even one second of caution" or "one second of caution — that's what this case is all about." This then lets me argue that plaintiff bears responsibility for what happened.

On damages, my themes are obvious. "This is a case about a man who won't follow doctor's orders" and "the plaintiff won't try, and wants you to reward him for it." These themes strongly suggest that what the plaintiff is asking for is simply unfair.

Some labels I can use during the trial will create images that help me. Plaintiff was driving a "Jaguar" or a "fancy sports car." This will generate popular images of the typical speeding sports car driver. "Doctor's orders" is another label all jurors will instantly understand. In addition, plaintiff is just "lying around" and "not even trying," additional images that will help me on damages.

3.   Dramatize, humanize, visualize

I have one clear advantage. Mr. and Mrs. Smith come across as everyone's favorite grandparents. I'll need to personalize them, show the jury what kind of people they are, and make it difficult to return a large verdict against such nice people.

I also need to show that what happened could just as easily have seriously injured Mr. Smith and that he had good reason to be shaken up by the accident.

Most of all, I need to capture the jury's perspective of how this accident happened. I need to have the Smiths tell what *they* saw from *their* perspective. If I can get the jury to visualize what they saw — a sports car zooming through the intersection late — I have a good chance of putting a good portion of the liability on the plaintiff.

4. Opening statement and closing argument

From my theory of the case and themes and labels, I already have the basics of my closing argument. What do I need to accomplish during my opening statement? As defendant, I go second. I need to jar the jury's thinking away from the plaintiff's perspective. I need to get the jury mentally in the back seat of my car and watch the accident happen. To do that I need to tell a clear but attention-getting story of what the Smiths saw at Main and Broadway and how they were lucky not to be seriously injured.

I also need to suggest, but subtly, that plaintiff wants to retire on this case without any serious efforts on his part to rehabilitate his arm. I need to suggest overreaching and unfairness in what plaintiff is asking. However, I need to give the jury good reasons for reaching these conclusions. Therefore, I need to spell out how plaintiff failed to follow doctors' orders and do his therapy.

Do I need exhibits in my opening? Probably not; I can tell my case without them. If, however, plaintiff uses a large intersection diagram in his opening, I'll make sure that his exhibits are removed before I begin.

5. Jury selection

What am I looking for in the jury? I'd like jurors who will at least consider my liability case and can find both drivers contributed to the accident. However, my principal job is to keep damages down. I can live with a $50,000 verdict; it's a verdict in the $400,000 range (what I know the plaintiff is shooting for) that scares me to death! What kind of jurors could return such a verdict, and hence are jurors to avoid?

I want the "Buick set" — solid middle-class values, workers, middle-aged or older, property owners. I want jurors who have earned what they have through hard work. I'd love jurors with medical backgrounds, people who accept the idea that pain and physical discomfort are just part of everybody's life from time to time. I prefer desk workers who are physically inactive. Jurors to avoid, then, are the young, lower socioeconomic level, manual laborers, athletic, outdoor-oriented. These are probably the dangerous jurors who are capable of giving plaintiff what he wants. My voir dire questions, then, will simply focus on learning these backgrounds that fit my profile of dangerous jurors.

6. Witnesses

The three witnesses I have are no secret: the defendant, her husband, and my orthopedic expert. (I've decided not to call witnesses to contradict the plaintiff's occupational and economic experts. My attitude is that their opinions are based on false premises: that plaintiff's arm is permanently injured, so there's no reason to present contrary evidence. I'll handle these points in closing argument.)

My direct examinations of Mary Smith and her husband will focus on several points. First, I need to show they're nice people, have worked hard all their lives, and earned the right to retire. Second, I need to show that Mrs. Smith is a careful driver and that she was being *particularly* careful that day, since she had a nauseated husband in her car and she needed to drive smoothly. Finally, I need to show how the accident really happened, through *their* eyes, and how lucky they were to avoid serious injury.

My orthopedics expert is crucial. I need to accomplish two things. First, I need to have the doctor come across as a nice person, not some cold, unfeeling, arrogant doctor. Second, the doctor needs to show how the plaintiff could have, and should have, rehabilitated his arm. He needs to explain that there are two common reasons why rehabilitation fails: lack of motivation, and a medical problem with the arm. If the former, it's the patient's problem. If the latter, surgery can usually correct a physical reason for restricted range of motion in the joint. He needs to show that an otherwise healthy 35-year-old man should generally recover completely from such a dislocation, and in the plaintiff's case he found after examination of the arm that there is no apparent reason that rehabilitation, if actually carried through, would not succeed and get him back on his former job.

I need to prepare the doctor for cross-examination. I know that plaintiff's biggest point is that not everyone recovers completely from such an injury (and he will argue in closings that plaintiff is just one who can't recover completely and that this is not his fault). The doctor needs to point out that if there is an incomplete recovery, the reasons are either motivational or physical.

7. Exhibits

I need a good exhibit to offset plaintiff's intersection diagram. I'll use the same kind of diagram and put the key defense facts on it. If my exhibit looks as good as the plaintiff's diagram, it will support my closing argument that both parties bear responsibility for the accident.

On damages, I need to be sure my doctor has charts and models so he can use them to explain his testimony and keep the jury's attention at the end of my case.

8. Order of proof

This one's easy. I'll put the defendant and her husband on first, and end up with the doctor. He's my key witness on damages and should be my last witness.

9. Cross-examinations

My cross of the plaintiff will be important on liability as well as damages. If plaintiff's version goes unchallenged, the danger is that the jury will accept it and tune out before I get a chance to put my case on. Therefore, I need to get *my* theory of the case before the jury during the cross-examination.

On liability, plaintiff's cross will focus on one idea: When the light turned yellow, he didn't exhibit the kind of caution called for under the circumstances. I know (from the deposition) that when the light turned yellow, plaintiff never took his foot off the gas and held it near the brake; instead, he simply kept going. My argument will be that this is not the kind of caution a yellow light calls for. In addition, I need to suggest that his estimation that he was three car lengths from the intersection is just that: an estimation, and he's not really sure.

The bystander needs to be handled differently. I need to suggest on cross that he wasn't expecting an accident, wasn't paying close attention to the cars since he wasn't driving, and really only noticed what happened *after* it all happened.

The police officer represents an opportunity. I think the 10-foot skid marks he can testify about will help me. Perhaps I can get him to state that entering an intersection on a yellow light creates a potentially dangerous environment and that a prudent driver is always ready to brake quickly.

What about my cross-examinations of the occupational expert and economist? My closing argument will be that these witnesses are irrelevant because no permanent injury is involved. If I cross the occupational expert at all, it will be brief, perhaps suggesting that a 35-year-old could easily be retrained for other work, if that were necessary. My cross of the economist should also be short. Economists usually compute lost future income based on certain assumptions about future rates of inflation and prudent investment yields. The usual result of their calculations is that lost future income, when adjusted for inflation and reduced to present cash value, creates a sum which in the first year will generate more interest income than plaintiff ever earned in any year. (This usually sounds like an excessive amount to the jury.) I'll also need to stress that he assumed plaintiff's arm injury is permanent, and his entire calculations are based on that assumption. This should give me enough ammunition to argue that the economist's testimony rests on a false assumption, is excessive in any event, and should be ignored.

Plaintiff's spouse is one witness I'll go easy on, or perhaps avoid cross-examining entirely. There's nothing she's likely to say that will help my case. Better to get her off the stand quickly.

The two treating doctors are the last witnesses I need to plan. My direct examination of my orthopedic specialist will provide the points of my cross-examination of plaintiff's doctors. I'll try to get them to admit that a complete recovery after a common dislocation is expected; career-ending injuries are rare, and when they do occur there is usually a medical complication involved; patients unwilling to follow a prescribed therapy program often cause their own failure to recover completely; if pain is serious, a variety of medications can be tried to assist the therapy program; surgery can usually correct physical conditions that impede a full recovery. They must admit that plaintiff's X rays show no physical problem with the elbow joint.

What do I do next? I need to kick all these ideas around in my mind, refine them, and run them past someone with more trial experience. Then I'll start working with my witnesses. If all goes well at trial, the jury will put at least some of the liability on the plaintiff and will keep damages in the $50,000 range. I think that would be a successful trial result. Better set the alarm clock extra early tomorrow.

§11.17.   *Trial lawyer's self-evaluation guide*

When a trial is over, trial lawyers are only human. They bask in the warm glow of victory or sink into the despair of defeat. Once the trial is over, however, every trial lawyer should ultimately ask: What did I learn from this trial, what did I do well and not so well, and how can I get better?

Good trial lawyers get better because they learn from their experiences. They don't avoid critical self-analysis because "the jury was too stupid to understand my case" or other defensive attitudes. Good trial lawyers review their performances dispassionately and learn from their mistakes.

The following self-evaluation guide may help you review your trial performances in the future.

1.   **Strategy**

> Did I develop a persuasive theory of the case?
> Did I develop persuasive themes?
> Did I develop persuasive labels for people, places, events?
> Did I develop people stories?
> Did I identify the key disputed issues?
> Did I develop my important facts on the disputed issues?
> Did I pursue only what I could realistically accomplish?
> Did I anticipate my opponent's strategy?
> Did I anticipate problems and weaknesses?

2.   **Execution**

a.   *Openings*
> Did I present my theory of the case?
> Did I present my themes?
> Did I use my labels for people, places, events?
> Did I use storytelling to present facts and my case?
> Did I use persuasive exhibits?
> Did I realistically deal with my weaknesses?
> Did I accomplish my purposes efficiently?

b.   *Witnesses*
> Did my examinations serve my overall strategy?
> Did I use simple, factual, nonleading questions on direct?
> Did I elicit "word pictures" on direct?
> Did I present people stories on direct?
> Did I use simple, factual, leading questions on cross?
> Did I "save" my conclusions during cross for closings?
> Did I accomplish my purposes efficiently?

    c. *Exhibits*

       Did I make and use persuasive exhibits and visual aids?

       Did I use exhibits in openings, closings, and witness examinations?

       Did I provide legally sufficient and persuasive foundations?

       Did I effectively manage my own and my opponent's exhibits throughout the trial?

    d. *Closings*

       Did I argue my theory of the case?

       Did I consistently use my themes?

       Did I consistently use my labels for people, places, events?

       Did I develop the important facts and logical inferences to support my version of the key disputed issues?

       Did I use exhibits, instructions, analogies, and rhetorical questions?

       Did I use both logic and emotion?

       Did I accomplish my purposes efficiently?

3. Delivery

    a. *Verbal*

       Did I train my witnesses to create "word pictures"?

       Did I and my witnesses use "plain English"?

       Did I effectively modulate my voice to maintain the jury's interest and emphasize key points?

       Did I use pacing and pauses?

       Did I have any distracting verbal mannerisms?

    b. *Nonverbal*

       Did I avoid overusing notes during my opening and closing?

       Did I maintain eye contact with witnesses and jurors?

       Did I use reinforcing movement and gestures?

       Did I project appropriate attitudes?

       Did I have any distracting nonverbal mannerisms?

XII
BENCH TRIALS

§12.1. Introduction

"What you say about jury trials is all very interesting, but what if it's not a jury trial? How much of what we know about the psychology of persuasion in jury trials is applicable to bench trials?" A good question, and often asked. The question is important because "bench trials," also called "court trials" and "trials to the court," are common and probably getting more common.

There are two reasons why cases are not tried to a jury and instead become bench trials in which the judge is the trier of the facts. First, the case may involve claims to which there is no right to trial by jury. The claims may involve only equitable remedies, such as injunctions or specific performance. They may involve areas such as probate, domestic relations, juveniles, bankruptcy, or admiralty, in which state and federal law generally do not permit jury trials. The claims may be based on specific statutes, such as the Federal Tort Claims Act, that confer no such right. Second, the parties may either have made no timely demand for a jury trial or have waived their rights to a jury before the case proceeded to trial.

How often do bench trials occur? While complete national statistics are elusive, the following are good approximations. In criminal cases, about 10 to 15 percent of all trials are bench trials, although the percentages can vary significantly among state and federal jurisdictions. In civil cases, about 30 to 35 percent of all trials are bench trials. These percentages rise if the definition of a bench trial includes contested dispositive hearings, such as hearings on petitions for preliminary injunctions, and proceedings before quasi-judicial bodies, such as arbitrations and administrative hearings. Unless you are trying personal injury, employment (where plaintiffs usually demand a jury), or criminal cases (where defendants usually demand a jury), your next trial probably will be a bench trial.

The conclusion is clear: Bench trials are everyday occurrences in civil and criminal cases, in federal and state courts. Every competent trial lawyer needs to know how things are done differently in a bench trial.

§12.2.   The law of bench trials

The law of bench trials differs from that of jury trials in four basic respects: trial procedures may differ; evidentiary issues may be handled differently; findings of fact and conclusions of law may be required; and standards of review on appeal are different.

First, trial procedures may differ. FRE 611(a) gives the trial judge substantial power to control trial procedures, and some judges freely use that power. For example, a judge may decide to try the case in bits and pieces, hear witnesses out of turn, hear all the liability evidence first and the damages evidence second, restrict opening statements and closing arguments, hear the direct examinations of experts in statement form, and impose time limitations on each side's presentation of its case. Although a judge may impose these special procedures in jury trials, he is more likely to impose them in bench trials.

Trial procedure may differ in another way. In bench trials, the judge is likely to participate actively throughout the trial, from asking questions during opening statements and closing arguments, to questioning witnesses during their direct and cross-examinations, to telling lawyers about his concerns and interests as the trial proceeds.

Second, evidentiary issues may be handled differently. In jury trials, judges prefer to rule on evidentiary objections before trial (and out of the jury's presence) whenever possible. During bench trials, most judges hear and rule on evidentiary issues as they occur during the trial. Since judges have to hear the offered evidence to rule on the objections, usually little is gained by hearing the objections separately. Keep in mind too that although jurors may dislike frequent objections, judges are used to objections and may actually welcome them if they are directed at significant matters, are well founded, and simplify the case.

There is a clear preference for admissibility in bench trials. Judges frequently "let it in for what it's worth," knowing that this is generally a safe ruling. An appellate court is much more concerned with whether the trial judge failed to consider proper evidence than whether the judge heard improper evidence. The appellate court presumes that the trial judge is not improperly influenced by any erroneously admitted evidence.

Third, procedural rules frequently require the trial judge to make findings of fact and conclusions of law at the end of a bench trial. For example, in federal courts, FRCP 52(a) requires findings and conclusions in civil cases, while FRCrP 23(c) permits them in criminal cases. Some states follow the federal approach, while others permit the trial judge to make general findings that dispose of the case. The rules requiring specific findings of fact and conclusions of law are designed to engender care by trial judges and promote meaningful appellate review, since written findings and conclusions detail how the judge evaluated the evidence and reached her legal conclusions. The trial judge can request that the parties submit proposed findings and conclusions, but she should ultimately prepare her own. A memorandum opinion or an oral decision made on the record may be adequate under the federal rules, although these are not favored methods.

Finally, appellate standards make reversing a bench trial because of evidentiary error particularly difficult. Appellate courts presume the trial judge considered only evidence that was properly admitted for a proper purpose, presume the prejudicial impact of erroneously admitted evidence was slight, and presume the judge was not influenced by offered evidence that was properly excluded. If evidence was received over objection, and later the judge determines that the evidence was improperly admitted, appellate courts presume the trial judge was not improperly influenced by that evidence. Good trial judges know this and quickly learn how to keep objectionable matters out of their findings of fact and conclusions of law.

In addition, the trial judge's evidentiary rulings are reviewed by an "abuse of discretion" standard, and findings of fact are reviewed by a "clearly erroneous" standard. Only conclusions of law are reviewed by a "de novo" standard. Coupled with the harmless error rule in FRE 103, these standards are a formidable barrier to appellate reversal. There are only two areas where appellate reversals of bench trials frequently occur: where the record shows that the trial judge misunderstood the required elements of claims, damages, and defenses under the applicable substantive law, and where the record affirmatively shows that the trial judge relied on improperly admitted material evidence in reaching his decision.

These barriers to appellate reversal do not mean, however, that you should not make objections and procedural motions during a bench trial if you believe they have merit. Avoid making technical "form" objections that accomplish little other than to annoy the judge. However, you must make timely and well-founded objections on important substantive matters. If you do not object, the judge can consider the admitted evidence for any proper purpose. And evidentiary objections should always be forcefully argued so that you win them in the trial court.

Make sure the trial judge rules on your objections. Without a ruling, there is no possibility of appeal on that basis. When an objection to offered evidence is sustained, be sure to make a timely and sufficient offer of proof. This is necessary not only to preserve error for appeal, but also to let the judge know what the rejected evidence is so that she has an opportunity to change her ruling. All too often, lawyers think about offers of proof in jury trials but not during bench trials. This is a mistake.

§12.3.   Know your judge

How does your judge conduct bench trials? If you do not know, and he does not say, find out. During the final pretrial conference, ask the judge how he intends to try the case, if he wants to streamline the presentation of witnesses and exhibits, and whether he has any scheduling concerns that may cause the case to be tried in bits and pieces rather than in one block of time. If the judge expresses interest or concern about particular aspects of the case, take note and plan how to address matters during the trial. Ask the judge if he intends to rule on anticipated evidentiary issues before or during the trial. Some judges have standing orders on how they want trials conducted in their courtrooms.

Ask members of your firm and other lawyers about their experiences with the judge in your kind of case. Ask the judge's former law clerks and court personnel about their observations. Watch the judge during a bench trial or a contested motion hearing for clues on how she acts, thinks, and likes to receive information. Does the judge prefer to get information visually or aurally? If you cannot watch the judge, read a transcript of a bench trial or hearing to determine whether the judge prefers to listen or to receive information visually, for instance, through court papers, exhibits, and other visual aids. How actively does the judge question the lawyers during opening statements and closing arguments? How actively does the judge question the witnesses during direct and cross-examinations? This knowledge can influence how you present your case and how you and your witnesses can communicate with the judge most effectively.

What is your judge's practice background and judicial track record? People's life experiences influence their views. Judges are no different. They are not legal automatons who dispassionately dispense justice. Judges are human beings with attitudes about people, events, and life in general. Bench directories are a good source of information. *The American Bench* and *Almanac of the Federal Judiciary* are two directories that provide background information on state and federal judges. Many larger jurisdictions have directories that list the backgrounds and procedures of their judges.

How well does your judge know your kind of case? Remember that a judge may try between 20 and 50 cases each year. As the years go by, that judge develops both expertise and attitudes. A computer search of the judge's name should turn up his published articles, books, and trial court opinions, as well as reported appellate decisions of his cases. Those experiences strongly influence a judge's thinking, because he uses past case experiences to assess evidence.

How much does the judge already know about your case? Here, local trial procedure helps provide the answer. In the federal system, the judge will have lived with your case since it was filed, probably will have ruled on motions during that time, and probably will have held pretrial conferences with the lawyers. If the judge has heard and ruled on important motions, such as a motion for summary judgement or a motion to preclude expert testimony, the judge already will know almost all of the important facts of the case. In civil (but not in criminal) cases, the judge will have the final pretrial statement detailing the claims and defenses, uncontested and contested facts, witness lists and a summary of their expected testimony, and exhibits lists. In civil (but rarely in criminal) cases, the judge may want each party to submit a trial memorandum detailing anticipated evidentiary and procedural issues and the party's position on them. A trial memorandum always helps the judge prepare for the trial, but it is particularly important in a bench trial. Influencing the judge about anticipated issues is always more important than educating your opponent.

Procedures vary in state courts. In smaller jurisdictions, the court organization is usually like the federal system in that judges are assigned the case when it is first filed in the clerk's office; the case then stays with that judge for the duration of the process. In larger jurisdictions, however, many use a central assignment system in which some judges only rule on pretrial matters and other judges only try cases. When discovery is complete and the case is ready for trial, the presiding judge will assign the case to one of the trial judges for trial. That trial judge will never have seen the case file before and will know nothing about it. You need to educate that judge quickly and professionally. Court files may be incomplete or unorganized, so give him a bound, tabbed, and indexed set of pleadings, key motions, and orders. Give the judge (and opposing counsel) a trial memorandum detailing the claims, defenses, expected evidence, and anticipated evidentiary disputes. Ask the judge or his law clerk what else he needs to become familiar with the case.

What is the judge's history with the lawyers? The judge may not know about the case but may well know something about the lawyers from prior professional or personal contact and from courthouse gossip. Always remember that the legal profession has a long memory, and professionalism and reputation are important. The judge's impressions about the lawyers will largely be created during the first meeting with the judge after she has been assigned the case. Your conduct during that meeting (and all others) should always send the same message: I am competent, professional, well prepared, and eager to try this case. Trials involve a measure of trust, and lawyers who demonstrate they are trustworthy throughout the litigation process have a distinct advantage when the case is actually tried.

What is the judge's history with the testifying experts? Judges become familiar with the experts that plaintiffs and defendants regularly call as witnesses in commonly tried cases. Judges develop attitudes about them and learn who the good experts and the not-so-good experts are. (Trial lawyers do this; why wouldn't judges?) This history should influence who you retain as experts at the beginning of the case and which experts you choose to have testify at trial.

Finally, what is the judge's history with the parties? Some parties, such as local, state, and federal governments, and large corporations with a major local presence, are regularly involved in civil and criminal cases (and are often represented by the same lawyers). Judges become familiar with these parties and sometimes develop attitudes about them.

Once you know something about your judge, his experiences, and his likes and dislikes, you will be better able to present a case that the judge will find engaging and persuasive.

§12.4.   Bench trials versus jury trials

Why do trial judges conduct bench trials differently from jury trials? Three overriding judicial concerns are involved.

First, the most valuable commodity a trial judge has is time. Judges usually prefer settlements to trials and usually prefer bench trials to jury trials. If a case must be tried, judges want to try it as efficiently as possible, and a bench trial is an opportunity to save time. This means that the judge will want the lawyers to stipulate to as many facts and legal issues as possible. The judge will want to minimize evidentiary objections and limit them to important relevance and hearsay issues. The judge will focus quickly on the key disputed facts and issues, will want witnesses ready to testify about those key facts, and will actively discourage unnecessary repetition and proof on collateral matters. Remember that judges are professional observers and usually take extensive notes during a bench trial. Whatever they hear or see, they usually grasp quickly, and they will want you to move on to something else just as quickly.

Second, the judge's notion of what he wants to hear and see trumps the lawyers' notions of what he should hear and see. In jury trials, everything you do should be focused on the jury's point of view. In bench trials, everything should be focused on the judge's perspective. Trial judges are concerned about the elements of claims, damages, and defenses, and about how the disputed issues will be proved. Some judges will tell you how they view the issues in the trial, what they see as the key factual and legal disputes, and what they want to hear and see to resolve those disputes. During the trial, the judge will indicate through his questions to lawyers and witnesses where his concerns and interests lie. Heed the suggestions.

Third, in trying to achieve justice, judges often find ways to get around technical legal requirements to achieve what they believe is a just result. For example, in a civil case, the judge will know if an affirmative defense is a complete bar to any recovery by the plaintiff and may look for ways to avoid the affirmative defense. In a criminal case, the judge will know what the result of a finding of guilty on each count of the indictment will be under mandatory sentencing laws and may look for ways to avoid a lenient or harsh outcome. Judges (like jurors) will often be receptive to results that are compromises between an all-or-nothing outcome for the parties.

What does this mean for trial lawyers? Again, three overriding concerns are involved.

First, prepare thoroughly before trial so that you present your case clearly and efficiently to the judge. If you want the judge to treat your case seriously, you must treat it seriously, and that begins with preparation. Follow time limitations. Keep your witnesses informed of the trial schedule and have them available and ready to testify. When you make important substantive evidentiary objections, do it in a timely and forceful way that shows the judge you are well prepared on the facts and know the law of evidence.

Get to the heart of the disputes as quickly as possible, both in presenting your case and in cross-examining the other side's witnesses. Have your exhibits and visual aids organized intelligently and give your lists of witnesses and exhibits to the court clerk and opposing counsel. Focus on your best theory of the case and avoid alternative theories. Stick to the key facts, keep your presentation clear, and be ready to answer the judge's concerns and interests. Be flexible. A judge who is actively involved in the trial may want the lawyers to change direction and focus as the trial progresses. Communicating with the judge is an active process that involves verbal and nonverbal feedback. In short, watch the judge during a bench trial in much the same way as you watch jurors during a jury trial, and take heed of his messages.

Second, project a positive attitude. Judges are experienced, and they quickly sense who is ready and eager to be on trial and who would have preferred to delay or avoid the trial. The lawyer who projects the attitude that she's wanted this case to get to trial for a long time and expects to win it has an advantage. Show you care about your client and your case by treating all phases of the trial seriously. This includes acting seriously in the judge's presence and having your game face on during the trial. Lawyers learn to look nonchalant when something bad happens during a jury trial; the same attitude helps in a bench trial.

Projecting a positive attitude includes being candid and reasonable. Judges value candor. Be precise and accurate in stating facts and applicable statutory and case law. If your case has a weakness or a problem, address it quickly and openly. If the other side's evidentiary objection has merit, concede the point. Fight only the battles you have to and the ones you can win. If the judge is about to make a mistake, protect the judge (and the record) by tactfully pointing out and correcting the mistake. Lawyers who try to confuse, mislead, or deceive soon lose the respect and trust of the trial judge. When trust leaves, your influence vanishes. This always proves costly.

Judges in bench trials are trying to reach fair and reasonable decisions, and they value lawyers who want the same outcome. Overly aggressive lawyers who appear willing to win at any cost and who value winning big more than being fair and reasonable quickly lose influence. This also proves costly.

Third, keep in mind that an experienced judge is still a human being who reacts to evidence much like jurors do. Impressions, especially first impressions, are important. This means you need to develop a clear theory of the case. Select appropriate themes and labels and use them consistently during the trial. Keep your presentation interesting and moving forward. Focus on the people and show why your people are the good guys, the ones wearing the white hats. Use interesting storytelling techniques. Keep the human, emotional core of the case, discarding the theatrics and embellishments that might be appropriate in a jury trial. Keep your witness testimony focused and vivid. Use visual aids such as blowups, diagrams, charts, and summaries liberally. Judges spend all day listening to lawyers, witnesses, and court personnel talk, so they appreciate exhibits and visual aids that highlight and summarize key information. These visuals provide an important break from the usual routine.

In short, a bench trial should never be "just a bench trial" during which lawyers present evidence in a disorganized, unfocused, boring way, under the belief that it makes no difference because the judge "will sort it all out." A bench trial offers opportunities for strong advocacy by competent trial lawyers at each stage of the trial.

§12.5.   Stages of a bench trial

These judicial concerns are important, and they influence what trial lawyers do in each stage of a bench trial.

1.   Opening statements

An opening statement is an opportunity to persuade. Seize the opportunity whenever possible. What kind of opening statement should you make? How should it differ from an opening statement in a jury trial?

Judicial attitudes about opening statements range from "Please proceed with your opening statement" to "Counsel, I'm familiar with the facts and issues in the case and don't need any openings. Call your first witness." What accounts for the difference? Three factors are central: your jurisdiction's rules, your judge's attitude about opening statements in bench trials, and your judge's knowledge about the case from any previous contact with it.

Opening statements are largely discretionary. The federal system has no procedural or evidentiary rule governing them. State rules are largely silent as well. In states that do have a rule, it is usually general, permitting an opening statement that contains a concise and brief statement of the facts the lawyers intend to prove during the trial.

Some judges consider opening statements in bench trials a waste of time and bar them. At the other extreme, some judges want full opening statements. Most judges are probably somewhere in the middle. Find out your judge's preference. A good time to ask is during the final pretrial conference.

Some judges vary their procedures depending on their previous contact with the case. The trial judge who has had the case since it was filed will be familiar with the facts and issues. In such cases, judges often either bar opening statements or permit only brief ones. In state jurisdictions using the assignment system, the judge will know little about the case and is more likely to permit full opening statements.

If your judge's practice is to bar or severely restrict opening statements, the final pretrial statement becomes all the more important. If the parties file a joint pretrial statement and can agree on the statement of uncontested and contested facts, there is no problem. If the parties cannot agree, each side will draft its own version. Regardless of how the statement is created, make sure it clearly reflects your positions on the uncontested and contested facts and issues in the case.

If the judge does not want to hear opening statements, try to change the judge's mind by asking to make a "brief" opening statement that will focus on the key factual and legal issues. Many judges will relent if the lawyers ask to make short openings. If the judge relents, make sure you are brief and that your opening focuses her thinking. If you do not push the judge to let you make at least a short opening statement, the judge may well conclude that any opening statement you would have made would not have been important anyway. At worst, the judge may think you have a weak case.

If the judge permits an opening statement, what should it contain? How should it be delivered?

An opening statement in a bench trial should help the judge understand how you intend to prove your case. This necessarily involves both law and facts. The judge will be focusing on the elements of the claims, damages, and defenses and how the evidence correlates to those elements. After all, the judge probably will make written findings of fact and conclusions of law at the end of the trial. There is no problem talking about the law during a bench trial, so spell out the required elements of your case, point out which ones will be contested, and show how you intend to prove those contested elements. That's what the judge will focus on during the trial. A good opening statement provides the judge with an organization of the facts and how they relate to the legal issues, a chronology of events if appropriate, and a general understanding of what happened and who is involved. If visual aids will help the judge — and they almost always will — use them.

Do not assume the judge is an expert on the applicable law. While any judge knows the elements of a common negligence or contract claim and the usual burdens of proof in civil and criminal cases, he may not know the elements of less commonly tried civil claims, criminal charges, or affirmative defenses. He may not know the burdens of proof applicable to particular claims and defenses or the existence of certain presumptions. Now is the time to gently educate the judge on what needs to be proved. If the judge is up to speed on the law, he will let you know. A good procedure is to have a copy of the pattern jury instructions for the elements of every claim, defense, and permissible damages that would be given if the case were tried to a jury. If there are any disputes over what needs to be proved to make a *prima facie* case on a claim or defense, or over what the proper measure of damages is, give the judge a copy of the appropriate instruction.

Second, tell the judge about the key facts you will present that will prove what you legally need to prove. In a bench trial, the judge is not moved by overly emotional storytelling, blatant appeals to sympathy, or repetitions of your strongest points, but this does not mean that you should sterilize your facts either. Keep the jury trial basics — vivid people stories told in a chronological or other clear way — but avoid the histrionics that will turn a judge off. Keep the drama, but avoid the theatrics. Remember that judges form impressions quickly based on their previous case experiences. If your case is different from the usual case, make that clear. And always tell the judge what specific damages and other relief you are seeking at the conclusion of the trial. The judge cannot read your mind and should not have to.

Project a positive attitude when you give your opening statement, no matter how short. Judges quickly sense whether you believe in your case and whether you expect to win. An opening statement in a bench trial can incorporate more law, and although the factual narration may not have the drama and theatrics appropriate to a jury trial, it should never be dull. Address the judge directly, maintain eye contact, and use your voice and body language assertively. Your attitude sends important signals — about you, your client, and your case — at a time when the judge is sensitive to such signals.

If the judge asks questions during your opening statement, address them immediately, much as you would in an appellate oral argument. Nothing irritates a judge more than to have a lawyer ignore one of his questions. If you do not know the answer, admit that and tell the judge you will have an answer shortly. Too many lawyers think they should always know the answer, and, if they don't, they make one up on the spot. Tell the judge, "I don't know, your Honor, but I'll research it and file a brief on that point first thing in the morning."

Finally, evidentiary objections during opening statements are generally a waste of time in a bench trial. They accomplish little other than annoying the judge.

2. Direct examinations

The core of most cases is the direct examinations of your witnesses in your case-in-chief. In what order should you call them? How should you organize the individual direct examinations? How should you present the deposition testimony of absent witnesses? Should you call the opposing party as an adverse witness? These are key decisions in both jury and bench trials.

First, try to call witnesses in the same order you would in a jury trial: Start strong, end strong, and avoid weak witnesses whenever possible. In bench trials, starting strong is just as important since judges also form impressions quickly. Try to call a witness who can tell the whole story at the beginning of your case, particularly if the judge is trying the case with breaks. The reason is the same as in jury trials: Making an initial strong impression is key. Call the witnesses in the order that tells the story of your case most effectively. It usually is a mistake to call witnesses out of order on the theory that it makes no difference to the judge in a bench trial. It does.

Avoid calling unnecessary corroboration witnesses. Unless the case hinges on disputed versions of events, transactions, or conversations (in which case you will want to call additional witnesses to buttress your side's version), judges are seldom influenced by witnesses who only corroborate what the judge has already learned from other witnesses or exhibits. In fact, a judge may cut the testimony short once she sees the witness is contributing nothing new.

Be sure to make a timely request to exclude witnesses from the courtroom during the trial, something lawyers frequently forget in the more informal atmosphere of a bench trial. (Under FRE 615, the exclusion order does not apply to parties, their representatives, or other essential witnesses, and some judges permit expert witnesses to remain in the courtroom and listen to each other's testimony.)

Direct examinations must be focused, and this is particularly true in bench trials. The judge wants you to get to the core of the testimony quickly. Therefore, keep the background information short and get to the point. Remember that most of any witness's testimony will be undisputed, so a reasonable amount of leading to elicit undisputed but necessary testimony will be permitted. However, when you elicit core testimony, make sure the witness does the testifying.

You can streamline the direct examination by incorporating stipulations and pretrial statements. For example, if the witness is testifying about a particular business meeting, you might say: "Your Honor, Stipulation No. 6 covers when and where the meeting took place and who was present," and then immediately examine the witness about the conversations during that meeting. You might say: "Your Honor, in the Final Pretrial Statement the parties agreed that the defendant had authority to enter into binding contracts," and then go directly into the terms of the oral contract. The judge will appreciate efforts to cut through the preliminary and uncontested information quickly to get to the heart of the matter.

Efficiency and focus, however, should not come at the price of diluting the impact of the direct examination. Witnesses need to be prepared so that they testify forcefully and persuasively. Avoid the common mistake of thinking that since it is "just a bench trial" the judge wants only the facts and cannot be influenced by effective testimony. Judges appreciate well-prepared witnesses who communicate effectively as much as jurors do, and they hate lengthy, boring testimony as much as anyone else does. Keep the testimony vivid and visceral, leaving out only the theatrics. This is particularly true when the case hinges on the credibility of witnesses who testify to differing versions of disputed events or transactions. Think of ways to present the testimony creatively, remembering to incorporate exhibits and visual aids into the examinations whenever appropriate. Judges, like jurors, often would rather see it than just hear it.

Direct examinations in bench trials differ from jury trials in one important way. The judge may participate actively in the examinations. This can take two forms. Some judges will tell you where they want the direct examination to go. For example, the judge may say, "Counsel, I think I understand the background to this dispute now. I'm particularly interested in this witness' memory of the conversation between the presidents of the two companies." Some judges will tell you where they do not want the direct examination to go. For example, the judge may say, "I think I've heard enough about how the company generates and creates its records from other witnesses. Let's move on to something else." Heed the advice.

The other way judges participate is by directly questioning the witnesses. The questions may be to get additional information. For example, the judge may ask, "Ms. Williams, why didn't you write your memo about this meeting until three days later?" The questions may be to get clarifications, for example, "Mr. Johnson, I didn't follow you there. Exactly where were you when you had this conversation?" Some judges will ask questions during the examination, while others will try not to interrupt the examination and ask questions only at the end of the direct or cross-examination. Expect these interruptions, prepare your witnesses for them, and make sure that they answer the judge's questions immediately and candidly.

How should you present the deposition testimony of unavailable witnesses? Ask the judge. Most judges want the lawyers to mark up the deposition transcript to highlight what they believe is admissible and important. Some judges want the lawyers to make summaries of the relevant portions and to excerpt the actual questions and answers on key points. If the deposition was videotaped, most judges want to watch only the parts the lawyers designate as important. Whatever the method, you can be sure that the judge does not want you to read, with a "witness" on the stand, the questions and answers from the entire deposition transcript. Nor does the judge want to read extensive portions of any transcript. Make sure that the transcript or videotape is marked as an exhibit and is formally admitted in evidence.

Finally, should you call an adverse party as a witness in your case-in-chief? Lawyers, particularly for plaintiffs, often call the adverse party early in their case-in-chief, either hoping to catch the party unprepared or expecting that the party will make a bad impression and damage his own case. Calling the adverse party, of course, involves the risk that the strategy will fail. Is the risk different in a bench trial?

Remember that the judge is an experienced and sophisticated observer who understands the underlying strategic considerations. As such, your decision to call an adverse witness is less likely to surprise him and perhaps less likely to influence him. If you must call an adverse witness to establish a necessary element of a claim or defense, the judge will understand why you are calling that witness and assess the situation appropriately. On the other hand, if the only reason you are calling the adverse party is to badger him — all you have is showmanship, not substance — the judge will quickly understand that as well. Always ask yourself: What impact will this have on my judge?

3.   Cross-examinations

Should you cross-examine a particular witness? In jury trials, jurors expect cross-examination to follow every direct. Therefore, lawyers ordinarily conduct some cross-examination of almost every witness in a jury trial. Bench trials, however, are different. The judge understands cross-examination and neither expects nor wants you to cross-examine unless you have something important to bring out. Put another way, judges have little patience with long-winded, rambling, unfocused cross-examinations, especially on collateral points that will not change the outcome of the case. This is not a good idea in a jury trial and it is a terrible idea in a bench trial. When judges see these things happening, they usually will not hesitate to tell you. Do not let your cross-examinations reach that point.

Avoid trivial impeachment. In the heat of battle, lawyers sometimes feel that any inconsistency, no matter how minor, must be forcefully brought out. Remember, however, that judges understand impeachment, and they know what is meaningful and what is not. They know that witnesses, being human, rarely say exactly the same thing when repeatedly describing events and transactions. Minor differences, such as "the car was going about 25 mph," and "I think the car was going 25 to 30 mph," are not worth bringing out. The judge will quickly assess trivial impeachment for what it is: The lawyer has nothing significant to bring out during cross-examination of this witness.

Judges, being experienced, want you to do two things when you cross-examine: get to the point and avoid the theatrics.

First, get to the point. Judges usually get the point of the cross-examination much more quickly than the average juror. For example, if you wish to show that a witness is biased in favor of the opposing party, simply bring out the fact showing the basis for bias — "The plaintiff owes you $100,000, doesn't she?" — and leave it alone. The judge will immediately understand the point; nothing more is necessary.

Second, avoid the theatrics. Judges are relatively immune to the atmosphere lawyers generate during cross-examination, particularly when it comes to impeachment. Before a jury, impeachment should progress step by step — the commit, credit, and confront method — and be accompanied with an attitude that signals to the jury how it should view the impeachment. Judges, on the other hand, know the impeachment technique and the reason for it but differ in their reactions to it.

Some judges just want the bottom line — the actual impeachment — without the customary build-up. For example, if a witness testifies that he saw the crash, on cross examination you can simply ask him about making a prior inconsistent statement — "You told Officer Smith right after the crash that you only saw the cars after they had already collided, isn't that right?" — and leave it alone. The judge will immediately understand the point. Some judges like to see the impeaching document. If that is the case, have an extra copy available for the judge.

Other judges (often the ones who were experienced trial lawyers themselves) enjoy seeing good lawyers employ good impeachment technique. With such judges, the impeachment technique can approximate what you would do in front of a jury. How do you know what your judge likes and wants? Look and listen for the judge's verbal and nonverbal cues. If the judge looks resistant or put off, adjust appropriately.

In some situations, judges may have more patience than jurors. Although they want you to get to the point, judges may let you go on longer during cross-examination than jurors might, so long as you continue to establish important points. This is particularly so if the cross-examination involves financial, technical, or scientific information and the witness is an expert. Jurors quickly get bored or confused; judges are more likely to understand that you are scoring points.

4. Exhibits

Should you use exhibits and visual aids during bench trials? If so, how will the judge rule on admissibility issues? How should you select the exhibits and visual aids? And how should you present them during the trial?

Some lawyers mistakenly think that since the case is "just a bench trial," it is not worth the time and expense to make serious courtroom exhibits because the judge likely will not be influenced by them. Talk to judges and you hear a different message: "I spend almost all my time listening to people talk. Why wouldn't I appreciate visual aids in a bench trial?" The point is clear: Judges, just like jurors, appreciate effective courtroom exhibits, find them influential, and want you to use them during bench trials.

Second, how will the judge rule on admissibility issues? Judges dislike dealing with technical foundation issues during trial. It is time-consuming and rarely accomplishes anything. Hence, they usually pressure the parties to stipulate to the admissibility of, or at least the foundation for, each side's exhibits before trial. (This means you must decide, before trial, which of your and your opponent's exhibits you are willing to admit in evidence by stipulation.) If that does not work, many judges deal with foundations informally at trial, rather than requiring a technically precise foundation, and pay attention only to serious relevancy or hearsay objections. When it comes to admitting exhibits, the "I'll let it in for what it's worth" approach is common.

For trial lawyers the message is clear. In bench trials, judges do not want to be bothered with technical foundation issues. They want to focus on the big picture. Save your evidentiary objections for key exhibits and make only serious and well-founded relevancy and hearsay objections.

Third, how should you select exhibits and visual aids for a bench trial? The short answer is: exactly the way you would if it were a jury trial. Judges are human. They enjoy seeing exhibits and learn and remember better by seeing rather than by hearing. It is a big mistake to assume that judges will not be influenced by exhibits and visual aids. Courtroom exhibits send a positive message to the judge: This lawyer believes in his case and believes it is important, so he spent time and money to ensure that his exhibits make his case clear.

Consider using blowups of photographs, diagrams, records, documents, and other visual aids. Mount them on posterboard or make them part of a computer presentation (particularly if the courtroom has the necessary technology already in place). Make them colorful and attractive. Judges, like jurors, particularly appreciate charts, diagrams, and summaries that show chronologies of events, steps in processes, and compilations of technical or detailed information. You might use exhibits in conjunction with witness testimony, the same way you would in a jury trial. Consider using computer animations and simulations that visualize and explain your expert witness testimony.

Use FRE 1006 to condense the presentation of voluminous records. FRE 1006 permits making summaries of voluminous writings, recordings, and photographs that cannot be conveniently examined in court. Even though a summary is admissible without having the documents on which the summary is based first admitted in evidence, good practice dictates that the underlying documents be available in case the judge asks for them. If appropriate, cross-index the summary to the underlying documents. Judges love FRE 1006. It is a great rule to streamline the presentation of documentary evidence, and judges expect you to use it.

In bench trials involving more than a handful of documents, prepare a tabbed and indexed exhibits book or ring binder of your exhibits for the judge (and extra copies for opposing counsel and witnesses). Number the exhibits and tab them chronologically, by count, or in another logical way so that judge, lawyers, and witnesses can quickly find the appropriate exhibit. This kind of preparation again sends positive signals to the judge. Many judges have their own preferred ways of identifying, marking, and organizing documents for trials. Find out if your judge has preferences and, if she does, follow them.

If the judge does not want his own set of exhibits, have a courtesy copy of each exhibit available as it is being discussed by the witness. For example, if the witness is testifying while using a blowup of an intersection diagram, give the judge a letter-sized copy of the exhibit. Many judges like to annotate their copy of the exhibit with notes as the witness testifies.

Finally, do not just give the judge a pile of preadmitted exhibits, thinking that the judge can, or will want to, "figure out" what the exhibits show. Not all exhibits are self-explanatory. Complicated records, such as financial and accounting records, need explanations and interpretations from witnesses, often experts, who can make sense of them and point out their significance. In these situations, the witness is the guide that takes the judge through the exhibits, explaining what they show and how they tie in to the other exhibits.

5.   Experts

Expert witness testimony in bench trials often differs substantially from jury trials. The reason is FRE 611(a), which gives the trial judge power to control the "mode of interrogating witnesses." Many judges use that power here, and it affects three areas of expert testimony: the expert's qualifications, the way the expert's testimony is presented, and questioning by the judge.

First, the judge is likely to short-circuit the expert qualifications and other background information to save time. Many judges ask the parties to stipulate to the qualifications of all the experts as meeting the minimum standards of FRE 702. Since almost all experts meet those standards, most lawyers will stipulate. Many judges then ask for the expert's resume or CV (curriculum vitae) in lieu of actual testimony about the expert's education, training, and experience. The CV is commonly regarded as either a business record or otherwise reliable hearsay. The CV is marked as an exhibit and admitted. Since this happens so frequently, make sure you have a clean copy of the expert's CV available and that the CV details the expert's background appropriately, so that the judge can make an accurate credibility assessment. Remember that most experts write their CV to impress other experts in their field. For courtroom purposes, make sure their CV will impress the judge.

Second, judges vary their procedures in taking testimony from experts, particularly on direct examination. Many judges treat experts like any other witnesses, with the usual direct, cross, and redirect examinations conducted by the lawyers. However, some judges like to get the expert's direct examination in written statement form, sometimes called a "written direct." Only the cross and redirect examinations are done by actual questioning in court. (This is a common procedure in bankruptcy courts, where direct examinations are usually presented in affidavit form.) The idea is that having the direct examination in written form, rather than live testimony, saves time. Some judges ask for the expert's written report and use it in lieu of live testimony. If the judge wants some form of written direct, find out before trial and prepare the expert accordingly. If the judge wants to use the expert's report in lieu of live testimony, make sure the expert prepares her written report so that it clearly spells out her opinions and the reasoning she used to reach her opinions.

Third, judges often become actively involved in questioning the experts, both on direct and on cross. After all, if the judge is going to decide the case, the judge will want his questions answered. Welcome this as an opportunity. If the judge signals through his questions where his interests and concerns are, this is valuable information. Some judges ask questions whenever they want, while others try to wait until the direct or cross is completed before asking questions. Prepare your experts for this and make sure they immediately and directly answer the judge's questions.

Judges generally relax the technical requirements for expert testimony and permit latitude on both direct and cross to get to core issues quickly. For example, form objections such as leading or compound questions routinely are overruled, because judges want to get to the heart of the testimony quickly. Save your objections for important matters.

Trial judges are the last generalists. They have substantial knowledge in many areas but are experts in few. Do not assume that your judge is an expert on medicine, financial and accounting procedures, technology, or whatever else is involved in your case. Find out before trial. Make your expert the teacher and guide who explains what she did and why she did it. Do it without the expert sounding or acting condescending. Use visual aids to illustrate the expert's explanations. If the expert is being too basic or is moving too fast, the judge will probably let you know by telling you directly, through his questions to the expert, or through his nonverbal responses. Heed the signals and modify the expert's presentation accordingly.

On cross-examination, remember that experienced judges have seen all the routine cross-examinations that are done of common types of experts. For example, every civil trial judge has seen economists cross-examined on the discount rate they used to determine the present cash value of lost future income. In a bench trial, this kind of information can be covered very quickly on cross-examination.

Finally, keep in mind that trial judges become familiar with the experts who frequently appear in court. These include doctors, economists, engineers, and malpractice experts who are the daily fare in commonly tried cases. The trial judges soon know, from their own experience and from talking to other judges, who usually testifies for plaintiffs, who usually testifies for defendants, and who are the experts of last resort. Over time, trial judges may have formed attitudes about some of those experts, and their attitudes come into play when those experts testify. Learn about your expert's experiences with your judge early, preferably when you first consider retaining the expert.

6. Closing arguments

The closing argument is your last opportunity to persuade. In a bench trial, what kind of closing argument is effective, and how does it differ from a jury trial? How should you deliver it? What kind of involvement does the judge have?

For judges, the decision in most bench trials is primarily analytical, not emotional. This is not to say that emotion plays no part, because judges are hardly blind to the human consequences of their decisions. Rather, it means that as the judge is listening to the arguments, he is thinking of his decision, not just in general terms, but in terms of the elements of the claims, damages, and defenses raised in the pleadings. The judge is thinking: Has the plaintiff proved the elements of her claims and damages? Has the defendant proved the elements of any counterclaims and affirmative defenses? Have they been proved to the required level of proof? After that comes the emotional part: Is this a fair and just result, or does the case allow for compromise? In short, the judge is thinking: Can I rule for one side, and should I? Good lawyers understand this and make arguments that address both concerns.

First, show the judge that you have proved what you are required to prove (or disprove). A sound approach is to structure your argument around the elements instructions for the claims, damages, and defenses that would be given if you were arguing a jury trial. Some judges appreciate having a written outline of your argument with bullet points. (In fact, some judges may ask that the lawyers submit their closing arguments in written form.) Refer explicitly to the particular witness testimony and exhibits that prove (or disprove) these elements. The judge will have to do this later anyway. Use visual aids, particularly those that summarize key facts, chronology of events, and relationships of parties and witnesses. Be accurate. Avoid misstating or exaggerating facts. Most judges take detailed notes during bench trials; if they get the sense that your "proof" of any required element requires stretching the facts, you're in trouble — in the present case and in future cases as well.

Give the judge a precise computation of your suggested damages, including percentages of relative liability for each party, present cash value of lost future income, prejudgment interest to date, and other compensable damages. Show how each item of damages was calculated and the evidence on which it is based. Prepare visual aids that make your requested damages clear, much as you would in a jury trial. Do not expect the judge to make these technical computations on her own.

Second, show that this is the right and fair outcome. Remember that in a bench trial a judge can usually find a reason to make the case come out the way he thinks it should come out and justify that outcome in his findings and conclusions. Just like jurors in a jury trial, the judge wants to feel good about the result. Avoid making exaggerated claims or taking untenable positions that an experienced judge (and an appellate court) will find implausible. This is particularly so when asking for damages. Judges know what is reasonable and what jurors and other judges are likely to do given the facts at hand. The lawyer who appears to want a fair and reasonable result will have more influence with the judge.

This means that you need to be sensitive to the judge's instinctive inclination to find a compromise outcome that is still supported by the facts. Always ask yourself: If the judge were to reach a compromise outcome, what would it likely be, and can I live with that result? If so, argue why such an outcome is fair and is the least that should be done. If not, show why the outcome is unfair and why another outcome is the right one.

Third, address the concerns the judge has expressed during the trial through his comments and questions to witnesses and lawyers. Every judge sends signals during the course of a trial. Now is the perfect (and last) time to address these concerns and incorporate them into your argument.

How should you deliver a closing argument in a bench trial? First, make it substantially shorter than it would be before a jury. Judges often impose time limits. Even if they do not, they expect your argument to be short and to the point. Second, avoid the theatrics that may be appropriate in a jury trial. Overly emotional arguments and "war stories" that may be appropriate to make a point before a jury usually turn judges off. Stick to the law and the facts.

This does not mean that the closing arguments should be boring. Avoid the theatrics, yet show you are serious about the case, committed to your client, and have the winning facts. This is largely a matter of tone. Address the judge directly, maintain eye contact, and use your voice and body language assertively. Never give the judge a reason to think that you are just going through the motions or "making a record."

Finally, what does the judge do during the arguments? Again, judges differ. Some judges sit and listen quietly, take notes by hand or on a laptop computer, and never interrupt. When this happens, lawyers never know whether the judge is actually listening because she is undecided or whether she already has decided what to do and is just waiting for you to finish. Since you never know for sure what the judge is thinking, keep arguing! (An exception may be in criminal cases in which the defendant is going to trial only to preserve error to appeal the judge's dispositive pretrial ruling, usually on a motion to suppress evidence or a confession. In such cases, your closing should be short, since you know the judge will find your client guilty based substantially on the evidence or confession, and you will then appeal from the judgment.)

Most judges ask questions during the closing arguments in bench trials. The questions can be about the evidence, elements of claims, damages, and defenses, and applicable case law. When this happens, lawyers never know whether the judge has genuine questions because he is still undecided or whether the judge has already made up his mind and is merely making sure that his grasp of the facts and law is defensible. Since you never know for sure, answer the judge's questions immediately and directly. A closing argument in a bench trial can closely approximate an appellate oral argument, where the lawyer's prepared argument is frequently interrupted with questions from the bench. Answering the judge's questions is always more important than your planned argument. If you do not know the answer, be candid. Tell the judge that you do not know and offer to file a memorandum on the point quickly.

During the arguments, the judge may signal, or even flatly state, which way he is inclined to rule. Deal with that reality. Try to modify his thinking rather than clash directly with it, much the way you would handle a judge's tough questions in an appellate oral argument.

7. Findings of fact and conclusions of law

In a bench trial, the judge may be required to make findings of fact and conclusions of law. In federal courts, FRCP 52(a) requires them in civil cases, and FRCrP 23(c) permits them in criminal cases. Some states follow the federal approach, while others permit the trial judge to make general findings that dispose of the case.

How will the trial judge make his findings of fact and conclusions of law, if he is required to make them? The recurring advice applies here as well: Know your judge.

Some judges like to decide the case immediately after the closing arguments and rule from the bench. Some take a short recess, then come back on the bench to announce the decision. Other judges always take time before announcing a decision and often do it in conjunction with issuing the findings and conclusions.

Some judges prefer to make the findings of fact and conclusions of law on the record by dictating them in open court or reciting them in a memorandum order. This is common when the facts are uncomplicated and the issues simple. Other judges want the lawyers to draft proposed findings and conclusions and submit them to the court. Still other judges want transcripts of witness testimony to incorporate into the findings of fact. If judges want submissions from the lawyers or transcripts of testimony, it will be some time before they will be able to hand down their findings and conclusions.

If the judge wants the lawyers to draft proposed findings of fact and conclusions of law, a common procedure in state courts, use the opportunity. Spell out the elements of the claims, damages, and defenses. Recite the testimony of the witnesses and admitted exhibits. Show how the elements have been proved (or not proved) by the evidence. While the judge will probably draft the final findings and conclusions herself, your proposed findings and conclusions will serve as a blueprint, and the judge may incorporate parts of your proposed findings and conclusions into her final decision.

Under FRCP 58, it is the entry of judgment (not the issuing of the findings and conclusions) that terminates the case and starts the clock running for purposes of appeal. The date final judgment is entered is critical, since the time for filing a notice of appeal cannot be extended.

§12.6. Conclusion

In summary, what do you need to know to try bench trials effectively? First, understand how bench trial procedures differ from jury trials. Second, understand how your assigned judge conducts the bench trial in your case. Third, recognize that the judge is an experienced jury of one. He wants you to be efficient, wants you to present the evidence his way, and wants his decision to achieve justice. Finally, prepare as if the case is a jury trial, then modify it appropriately for a bench trial. Keep the drama and human interest, lose the melodrama and theatrics. In short, if you know how to try a case persuasively to a jury, you know how to try one persuasively to a judge as well.

FEDERAL RULES OF EVIDENCE

(as amended through December 1, 2000)

ARTICLE V.   PRIVILEGES

ARTICLE VI.   WITNESSES

ARTICLE VII.   OPINIONS AND EXPERT TESTIMONY

ARTICLE VIII.   HEARSAY

ARTICLE IX.   AUTHENTICATION AND IDENTIFICATION

RULES OF EVIDENCE FOR UNITED STATES
COURTS AND MAGISTRATES

ARTICLE I.   GENERAL PROVISIONS

Rule 101.   Scope

These rules govern proceedings in the courts of the United States and before United States bankruptcy judges and United States magistrate judges, to the extent and with the exceptions stated in rule 1101.

Rule 102.   Purpose and construction

These rules shall be construed to secure fairness in administration, elimination of unjustifiable expense and delay, and promotion of growth and development of the law of evidence to the end that the truth may be ascertained and proceedings justly determined.

Rule 103.   Rulings on evidence

(a) Effect of erroneous ruling.   Error may not be predicated upon a ruling which admits or excludes evidence unless a substantial right of the party is affected, and

(1) Objection.   In case the ruling is one admitting evidence, a timely objection or motion to strike appears of record, stating the specific ground of objection, if the specific ground was not apparent from the context; or

(2) Offer of proof.   In case the ruling is one excluding evidence, the substance of the evidence was made known to the court by offer or was apparent from the context within which questions were asked.

Once the court makes a definitive ruling on the record admitting or excluding evidence, either at or before trial, a party need not renew an objection or offer of proof to preserve a claim of error for appeal.

(b) Record of offer and ruling.   The court may add any other or further statement which shows the character of the evidence, the form in which it was offered, the objection made, and the ruling thereon. It may direct the making of an offer in question and answer form.

(c) Hearing of jury.   In jury cases, proceedings shall be conducted, to the extent practicable, so as to prevent inadmissible evidence from being suggested to the jury by any means, such as making statements or offers of proof or asking questions in the hearing of the jury.

(d) Plain error.   Nothing in this rule precludes taking notice of plain errors affecting substantial rights although they were not brought to the attention of the court.

Rule 104.   Preliminary questions

(a) Questions of admissibility generally.   Preliminary questions concerning the qualification of a person to be a witness, the existence of a privilege, or the admissibility of evidence shall be determined by the court, subject to the provisions of subdivision (b). In making its determination it is not bound by the rules of evidence except those with respect to privileges.

(b) Relevancy conditioned on fact.   When the relevancy of evidence depends upon the fulfillment of a condition of fact, the court shall admit it upon, or subject to, the introduction of evidence sufficient to support a finding of the fulfillment of the condition.

(c) Hearing of jury.   Hearings on the admissibility of confessions shall in all cases be conducted out of the hearing of the jury. Hearings on other preliminary matters shall be so conducted when the interests of justice require or when an accused is a witness and so requests.

(d) Testimony by accused.   The accused does not, by testifying upon a preliminary matter, become subject to cross-examination as to other issues in the case.

(e) Weight and credibility.   This rule does not limit the right of a party to introduce before the jury evidence relevant to weight or credibility.

Rule 105.   Limited admissibility

When evidence which is admissible as to one party or for one purpose but not admissible as to another party or for another purpose is admitted, the court, upon request, shall restrict the evidence to its proper scope and instruct the jury accordingly.

Rule 106.   Remainder of or related writings or recorded statements

When a writing or recorded statement or part thereof is introduced by a party, an adverse party may require the introduction at that time of any other part or any other writing or recorded statement which ought in fairness to be considered contemporaneously with it.

ARTICLE II.   JUDICIAL NOTICE

Rule 201.   Judicial notice of adjudicative facts

(a) Scope of rule.   This rule governs only judicial notice of adjudicative facts.

(b) Kinds of facts.   A judicially noticed fact must be one not subject to reasonable dispute in that it is either (1) generally known within the territorial jurisdiction of the trial court or (2) capable of accurate and ready determination by resort to sources whose accuracy cannot reasonably be questioned.

(c) When discretionary.   A court may take judicial notice, whether requested or not.

(d) When mandatory.   A court shall take judicial notice if requested by a party and supplied with the necessary information.

(e) Opportunity to be heard.   A party is entitled upon timely request to an opportunity to be heard as to the propriety of taking judicial notice and the tenor of the matter noticed. In the absence of prior notification, the request may be made after judicial notice has been taken.

(f) Time of taking notice.   Judicial notice may be taken at any stage of the proceeding.

(g) Instructing jury.   In a civil action or proceeding, the court shall instruct the jury to accept as conclusive any fact judicially noticed. In a criminal case, the court shall instruct the jury that it may, but is not required to, accept as conclusive any fact judicially noticed.

ARTICLE III.   PRESUMPTIONS IN CIVIL ACTIONS
AND PROCEEDINGS

Rule 301.   Presumptions in general civil actions
and proceedings

In all civil actions and proceedings, not otherwise provided for by Act of Congress or by these rules, a presumption imposes on the party against whom it is directed the burden of going forward with evidence to rebut or meet the presumption, but does not shift to such party the burden of proof in the sense of the risk of nonpersuasion, which remains throughout the trial upon the party on whom it was originally cast.

Rule 302.   Applicability of state law in civil actions
and proceedings

In civil actions and proceedings, the effect of a presumption respecting a fact which is an element of a claim or defense as to which State law supplies the rule of decision is determined in accordance with State law.

ARTICLE IV.   RELEVANCY AND ITS LIMITS

Rule 401.   Definition of "relevant evidence"

"Relevant evidence" means evidence having any tendency to make the existence of any fact that is of consequence to the determination of the action more probable or less probable than it would be without the evidence.

Rule 402.   Relevant evidence generally admissible;
irrelevant evidence inadmissible

All relevant evidence is admissible, except as otherwise provided by the Constitution of the United States, by Act of Congress, by these rules, or by other rules prescribed by the Supreme Court pursuant to statutory authority. Evidence which is not relevant is not admissible.

Rule 403.   Exclusion of relevant evidence on grounds
of prejudice, confusion, or waste of time

Although relevant, evidence may be excluded if its probative value is substantially outweighed by the danger of unfair prejudice, confusion of the issues, or misleading the jury, or by considerations of undue delay, waste of time, or needless presentation of cumulative evidence.

Rule 404.   Character evidence not admissible to prove conduct; exceptions; other crimes

(a) Character evidence generally.   Evidence of a person's character or a trait of character is not admissible for the purpose of proving action in conformity therewith on a particular occasion, except:

  (1) Character of accused.   Evidence of a pertinent trait of character offered by an accused, or by the prosecution to rebut the same, or if evidence of a trait of character of the alleged victim of the crime is offered by an accused and admitted under Rule 404(a)(2), evidence of the same trait of character of the accused offered by the prosecution;

  (2) Character of victim.   Evidence of a pertinent trait of character of the victim of the crime offered by an accused, or by the prosecution to rebut the same, or evidence of a character trait of peacefulness of the victim offered by the prosecution in a homicide case to rebut evidence that the victim was the first aggressor;

  (3) Character of witness.   Evidence of the character of a witness, as provided in rules 607, 608, and 609.

(b) Other crimes, wrongs, or acts.   Evidence of other crimes, wrongs, or acts is not admissible to prove the character of a person in order to show action in conformity therewith. It may, however, be admissible for other purposes, such as proof of motive, opportunity, intent, preparation, plan, knowledge, identity, or absence of mistake or accident, provided that upon request by the accused, the prosecution in a criminal case shall provide reasonable notice in advance of trial, or during trial if the court excuses pretrial notice on good cause shown, of the general nature of any such evidence it intends to introduce at trial.

Rule 405.   Methods of proving character

(a) Reputation or opinion.   In all cases in which evidence of character or a trait of character of a person is admissible, proof may be made by testimony as to reputation or by testimony in the form of an opinion. On cross-examination, inquiry is allowable into relevant specific instances of conduct

(b) Specific instances of conduct.   In cases in which character or a trait of character of a person is an essential element of a charge, claim, or defense, proof may also be made of specific instances of that person's conduct.

Rule 406.   Habit; routine practice

Evidence of the habit of a person or of the routine practice of an organization, whether corroborated or not and regardless of the presence of eyewitnesses, is relevant to prove that the conduct of the person or organization on a particular occasion was in conformity with the habit or routine practice.

Rule 407.   Subsequent remedial measures

When, after an injury or harm allegedly caused by an event, measures are taken that, if taken previously, would have made the injury or harm less likely to occur, evidence of the subsequent measures is not admissible to prove negligence, culpable conduct, a defect in a product, a defect in a product's design, or a need for a warning or instruction. This rule does not require the exclusion of evidence of subsequent measures when offered for another purpose, such as proving ownership, control, or feasibility of precautionary measures, if controverted, or impeachment.

Rule 408.   Compromise and offers to compromise

Evidence of (1) furnishing or offering or promising to furnish, or (2) accepting or offering or promising to accept, a valuable consideration in compromising or attempting to compromise a claim which was disputed as to either validity or amount, is not admissible to prove liability for or invalidity of the claim or its amount. Evidence of conduct or statements made in compromise negotiations is likewise not admissible. This rule does not require the exclusion of any evidence otherwise discoverable merely because it is presented in the course of compromise negotiations. This rule also does not require exclusion when the evidence is offered for another purpose, such as proving bias or prejudice of a witness, negativing a contention of undue delay, or proving an effort to obstruct a criminal investigation or prosecution.

Rule 409.   Payment of medical and similar expenses

Evidence of furnishing or offering or promising to pay medical, hospital, or similar expenses occasioned by an injury is not admissible to prove liability for the injury.

Rule 410.   Inadmissibility of pleas, offers of pleas, and related statements

Except as otherwise provided in this rule, evidence of a plea of guilty, later withdrawn, or a plea of nolo contendere, or of an offer to plead guilty or nolo contendere to the crime charged or any other crime, or of statements made in connection with, and relevant to, any of the foregoing pleas or offers, is not admissible in any civil or criminal proceeding against the person who made the plea or offer. However, evidence of a statement made in connection with, and relevant to, a plea of guilty, later withdrawn, a plea of nolo contendere, or an offer to plead guilty or nolo contendere to the crime charged or any other crime, is admissible in a criminal proceeding for perjury or false statement if the statement was made by the defendant under oath, on the record, and in the presence of counsel.

Rule 411.   Liability insurance

Evidence that a person was or was not insured against liability is not admissible upon the issue whether the person acted negligently or otherwise wrongfully. This rule does not require the exclusion of evidence of insurance against liability when offered for another purpose, such as proof of agency, ownership, or control, or bias or prejudice of a witness.

Rule 412.   Sex offense cases; relevance of alleged victim's past sexual behavior or alleged sexual predisposition

(a) **Evidence generally inadmissible.** The following evidence is not admissible in any civil or criminal proceeding involving alleged sexual misconduct except as provided in subdivisions (b) and (c):

(1) Evidence offered to prove that any alleged victim engaged in other sexual behavior.

(2) Evidence offered to prove any alleged victim's sexual predisposition.

(b) **Exceptions.**

(1) In a criminal case, the following evidence is admissible, if otherwise admissible under these rules:

(A) evidence of specific instances of sexual behavior by the alleged victim offered to prove that a person other than the accused was the source of semen, injury or other physical evidence;

(B) evidence of specific instances of sexual behavior by the alleged victim with respect to the person accused of the sexual misconduct offered by the accused to prove consent or by the prosecution; and

(C) evidence the exclusion of which would violate the constitutional rights of the defendant.

(2) In a civil case, evidence offered to prove the sexual behavior or sexual predisposition of any alleged victim is admissible if it is otherwise admissible under these rules and its probative value substantially outweighs the danger of harm to any victim and of unfair prejudice to any party. Evidence of an alleged victim's reputation is admissible only if it has been placed in controversy by the alleged victim.

(c) **Procedure to determine admissibility.**

(1) A party intending to offer evidence under subdivision (b) must:

(A) file a written motion at least 14 days before trial specifically describing the evidence and stating the purpose for which it is offered unless the court, for good cause, requires a different time for filing or permits filing during trial; and

(B) serve the motion on all parties and notify the alleged victim or, when appropriate, the alleged victim's guardian or representative.

(2) Before admitting evidence under this rule the court must conduct a hearing in camera and afford the victim and parties a right to attend and be heard. The motion, related papers, and the record of the hearing must be sealed and remain under seal unless the court orders otherwise.

Rule 413.   Evidence of similar crimes in sexual assault cases

(a) In a criminal case in which the defendant is accused of an offense of sexual assault, evidence of the defendant's commission of another offense or offenses of sexual assault is admissible, and may be considered for its bearing on any matter to which it is relevant.

(b) In a case in which the Government intends to offer evidence under this rule, the attorney for the Government shall disclose the evidence to the defendant, including statements of witnesses or a summary of the substance of any testimony that is expected to be offered, at least fifteen days before the scheduled date of trial or at such later time as the court may allow for good cause.

(c) This rule shall not be construed to limit the admission or consideration of evidence under any other rule.

(d) For purposes of this rule and Rule 415, "offense of sexual assault" means a crime under Federal law or the law of a State (as defined in section 513 of title 18, United States Code) that involved —

(1) any conduct proscribed by chapter 109A of title 18, United States Code;

(2) contact, without consent, between any part of the defendant's body or an object and the genitals or anus of another person;

(3) contact, without consent, between the genitals or anus of the defendant and any part of another person's body;

(4) deriving sexual pleasure or gratification from the infliction of death, bodily injury, or physical pain on another person; or

(5) an attempt or conspiracy to engage in conduct described in paragraphs (1)-(4).

Rule 414.   Evidence of similar crimes in child molestation cases

(a) In a criminal case in which the defendant is accused of an offense of child molestation, evidence of the defendant's commission of another offense or offenses of child molestation is admissible, and may be considered for its bearing on any matter to which it is relevant.

(b) In a case in which the Government intends to offer evidence under this rule, the attorney for the Government shall disclose the evidence to the defendant, including statements of witnesses or a summary of the substance of any testimony that is expected to be offered, at least fifteen days before the scheduled date of trial or at such later time as the court may allow for good cause.

(c) This rule shall not be construed to limit the admission or consideration of evidence under any other rule.

(d) For purposes of this rule and Rule 415, "child" means a person below the age of fourteen, and "offense of child molestation" means a crime under Federal law or the law of a State (as defined in section 513 of title 18, United States Code) that involved —

(1) any conduct proscribed by chapter 109A of title 18, United States Code, that was committed in relation to a child;

(2) any conduct proscribed by chapter 110 of title 18, United States Code;

(3) contact between any part of the defendant's body or an object and the genitals or anus of a child;

(4) contact between the genitals or anus of the defendant and any part of the body of a child;

(5) deriving sexual pleasure or gratification from the infliction of death, bodily injury, or physical pain on a child; or

(6) an attempt or conspiracy to engage in conduct described in paragraphs (1)–(5).

Rule 415. Evidence of similar acts in civil cases concerning sexual assault or child molestation

(a) In a civil case in which a claim for damages or other relief is predicated on a party's alleged commission of conduct constituting an offense of sexual assault or child molestation, evidence of that party's commission of another offense or offenses of sexual assault or child molestation is admissible and may be considered as provided in Rule 413 and Rule 414 of these rules.

(b) A party who intends to offer evidence under this Rule shall disclose the evidence to the party against whom it will be offered, including statements of witnesses or a summary of the substance of any testimony that is expected to be offered, at least fifteen days before the scheduled date of trial or at such later time as the court may allow for good cause.

(c) This rule shall not be construed to limit the admission or consideration of evidence under any other rule.

ARTICLE V.   PRIVILEGES

Rule 501.   General rule

Except as otherwise required by the Constitution of the United States or provided by Act of Congress or in rules prescribed by the Supreme Court pursuant to statutory authority, the privilege of a witness, person, government, State, or political subdivision thereof shall be governed by the principles of the common law as they may be interpreted by the courts of the United States in the light of reason and experience. However, in civil actions and proceedings, with respect to an element of a claim or defense as to which State law supplies the rule of decision, the privilege of a witness, person, government, State, or political subdivision thereof shall be determined in accordance with State law.

ARTICLE VI.   WITNESSES

Rule 601.   General rule of competency

Every person is competent to be a witness except as otherwise provided in these rules. However, in civil actions and proceedings, with respect to an element of a claim or defense as to which State law supplies the rule of decision, the competency of a witness shall be determined in accordance with State law.

Rule 602.   Lack of personal knowledge

A witness may not testify to a matter unless evidence is introduced sufficient to support a finding that the witness has personal knowledge of the matter. Evidence to prove personal knowledge may, but need not, consist of the witness' own testimony. This rule is subject to the provisions of rule 703, relating to opinion testimony by expert witnesses.

Rule 603.   Oath or affirmation

Before testifying, every witness shall be required to declare that the witness will testify truthfully, by oath or affirmation administered in a form calculated to awaken the witness' conscience and impress the witness' mind with the duty to do so.

Rule 604.   Interpreters

An interpreter is subject to the provisions of these rules relating to qualification as an expert and the administration of an oath or affirmation to make a true translation.

Rule 605.   Competency of judge as witness

The judge presiding at the trial may not testify in that trial as a witness. No objection need be made in order to preserve the point.

Rule 606.   Competency of juror as witness

(a) At the trial.   A member of the jury may not testify as a witness before that jury in the trial of the case in which the juror is sitting. If the juror is called so to testify, the opposing party shall be afforded an opportunity to object out of the presence of the jury.

(b) Inquiry into validity of verdict or indictment.   Upon an inquiry into the validity of a verdict or indictment, a juror may not testify as to any matter or statement occurring during the course of the jury's deliberations or to the effect of anything upon that or any other juror's mind or emotions as influencing the juror to assent to or dissent from the verdict or indictment or concerning the juror's mental processes in connection therewith, except that a juror may testify on the question whether extraneous prejudicial information was improperly brought to the jury's attention or whether any outside influence was improperly brought to bear upon any juror. Nor may a juror's affidavit or evidence of any statement by the juror concerning a matter about which the juror would be precluded from testifying be received for these purposes.

Rule 607.   Who may impeach

The credibility of a witness may be attacked by any party, including the party calling the witness.

Rule 608.   Evidence of character and conduct of witness

(a) Opinion and reputation evidence of character.   The credibility of a witness may be attacked or supported by evidence in the form of opinion or reputation, but subject to these limitations: (1) the evidence may refer only to character for truthfulness or untruthfulness, and (2) evidence of truthful character is admissible only after the character of the witness for truthfulness has been attacked by opinion or reputation evidence or otherwise.

(b) Specific instances of conduct.   Specific instances of the conduct of a witness, for the purpose of attacking or supporting the witness' credibility, other than conviction of crime as provided in rule 609, may not be proved by extrinsic evidence. They may, however, in the discretion of the court, if probative of truthfulness or untruthfulness, be inquired into on cross-examination of the witness (1) concerning the witness' character for truthfulness or untruthfulness, or (2) concerning the character for truthfulness or untruthfulness of another witness as to which character the witness being cross-examined has testified.

The giving of testimony, whether by an accused or by any other witness, does not operate as a waiver of the accused's or the witness' privilege against self-incrimination when examined with respect to matters which relate only to credibility.

Rule 609.   Impeachment by evidence of conviction
of crime

(a) **General rule.**   For the purpose of attacking the credibility of a witness,

(1) evidence that a witness other than the accused has been convicted of a crime shall be admitted, subject to Rule 403, if the crime was punishable by death or imprisonment in excess of one year under the law under which the witness was convicted, and evidence that an accused has been convicted of such a crime shall be admitted if the court determines that the probative value of admitting this evidence outweighs its prejudicial effect to the accused; and

(2) evidence that any witness has been convicted of a crime shall be admitted if it involved dishonesty or false statement, regardless of the punishment.

(b) **Time limit.**   Evidence of a conviction under this rule is not admissible if a period of more than ten years has elapsed since the date of the conviction or of the release of the witness from the confinement imposed for that conviction, whichever is the later date, unless the court determines, in the interests of justice, that the probative value of the conviction supported by specific facts and circumstances substantially outweighs its prejudicial effect. However, evidence of a conviction more than 10 years old as calculated herein, is not admissible unless the proponent gives to the adverse party sufficient advance written notice of intent to use such evidence to provide the adverse party with a fair opportunity to contest the use of such evidence.

(c) **Effect of pardon, annulment, or certificate of rehabilitation.** Evidence of a conviction is not admissible under this rule if (1) the conviction has been the subject of a pardon, annulment, certificate of rehabilitation, or other equivalent procedure based on a finding of the rehabilitation of the person convicted, and that person has not been convicted of a subsequent crime which was punishable by death or imprisonment in excess of one year, or (2) the conviction has been the subject of a pardon, annulment, or other equivalent procedure based on a finding of innocence.

(d) **Juvenile adjudications.**   Evidence of juvenile adjudications is generally not admissible under this rule. The court may, however, in a criminal case allow evidence of a juvenile adjudication of a witness other than the accused if conviction of the offense would be admissible to attack the credibility of an adult and the court is satisfied that admission in evidence is necessary for a fair determination of the issue of guilt or innocence.

(e) **Pendency of appeal.**   The pendency of an appeal therefrom does not render evidence of a conviction inadmissible. Evidence of the pendency of an appeal is admissible.

Rule 610.   Religious beliefs or opinions

Evidence of the beliefs or opinions of a witness on matters of religion is not admissible for the purpose of showing that by reason of their nature the witness' credibility is impaired or enhanced.

Rule 611.   Mode and order of interrogation and presentation

(a) Control by court.   The court shall exercise reasonable control over the mode and order of interrogating witnesses and presenting evidence so as to (1) make the interrogation and presentation effective for the ascertainment of the truth, (2) avoid needless consumption of time, and (3) protect witnesses from harassment or undue embarrassment.

(b) Scope of cross-examination.   Cross-examination should be limited to the subject matter of the direct examination and matters affecting the credibility of the witness. The court may, in the exercise of discretion, permit inquiry into additional matters as if on direct examination.

(c) Leading questions.   Leading questions should not be used on the direct examination of a witness except as may be necessary to develop the witness' testimony. Ordinarily leading questions should be permitted on cross-examination. When a party calls a hostile witness, an adverse party, or a witness identified with an adverse party, interrogation may be by leading questions.

Rule 612.   Writing used to refresh memory

Except as otherwise provided in criminal proceedings by section 3500 of title 18, United States Code, if a witness uses a writing to refresh memory for the purpose of testifying, either —

(1) while testifying, or

(2) before testifying, if the court in its discretion determines it is necessary in the interests of justice,

an adverse party is entitled to have the writing produced at the hearing, to inspect it, to cross-examine the witness thereon, and to introduce in evidence those portions which relate to the testimony of the witness. If it is claimed that the writing contains matters not related to the subject matter of the testimony the court shall examine the writing in camera, excise any portions not so related, and order delivery of the remainder to the party entitled thereto. Any portion withheld over objections shall be preserved and made available to the appellate court in the event of an appeal. If a writing is not produced or delivered pursuant to order under this rule, the court shall make any order justice requires, except that in criminal cases when the prosecution elects not to comply, the order shall be one striking the testimony or, if the court in its discretion determines that the interests of justice so require, declaring a mistrial.

Rule 613.   Prior statements of witnesses

(a) Examining witness concerning prior statement.   In examining a witness concerning a prior statement made by the witness, whether written or not, the statement need not be shown nor its contents disclosed to the witness at that time, but on request the same shall be shown or disclosed to opposing counsel.

(b) Extrinsic evidence of prior inconsistent statement of witness. Extrinsic evidence of a prior inconsistent statement by a witness is not admissible unless the witness is afforded an opportunity to explain or deny the same and the opposite party is afforded an opportunity to interrogate the witness thereon, or the interests of justice otherwise require. This provision does not apply to admissions of a party-opponent as defined in rule 801(d)(2).

Rule 614.　Calling and interrogation of witnesses by court

(a) Calling by court.　The court may, on its own motion or at the suggestion of a party, call witnesses, and all parties are entitled to cross-examine witnesses thus called.

(b) Interrogation by court.　The court may interrogate witnesses, whether called by itself or by a party.

(c) Objections.　Objections to the calling of witnesses by the court or to interrogation by it may be made at the time or at the next available opportunity when the jury is not present.

Rule 615.　Exclusion of witnesses

At the request of a party the court shall order witnesses excluded so that they cannot hear the testimony of other witnesses and it may make the order of its own motion. This rule does not authorize exclusion of (1) a party who is a natural person, or (2) an officer or employee of a party which is not a natural person designated as its representative by its attorney, or (3) a person whose presence is shown by a party to be essential to the presentation of the party's cause.

ARTICLE VII.　OPINIONS AND EXPERT TESTIMONY

Rule 701.　Opinion testimony by lay witnesses

If the witness is not testifying as an expert, the witness' testimony in the form of opinions or inferences is limited to those opinions or inferences which are (a) rationally based on the perception of the witness and (b) helpful to a clear understanding of the witness' testimony or the determination of a fact in issue, and (c) not based on scientific, technical, or other specialized knowledge within the scope of Rule 702.

Rule 702.　Testimony by experts

If scientific, technical, or other specialized knowledge will assist the trier of fact to understand the evidence or to determine a fact in issue, a witness qualified as an expert by knowledge, skill, experience, training, or

education, may testify thereto in the form of an opinion or otherwise, if
(1) the testimony is based upon sufficient facts or data, (2) the testimony
is the product of reliable principles and methods, and (3) the witness has
applied the principles and methods reliably to the facts of the case.

Rule 703.   Bases of opinion testimony by experts

The facts or data in the particular case upon which an expert bases
an opinion or inference may be those perceived by or made known to the
expert at or before the hearing. If of a type reasonably relied upon by experts in the particular field in forming opinions or inferences upon the
subject, the facts or data need not be admissible in evidence in order for
the opinion or inference to be admitted. Facts or data that are otherwise
inadmissible shall not be disclosed to the jury by the proponent of the
opinion or inference unless the court determines that their probative
value in assisting the jury to evaluate the expert's opinion substantially outweighs their prejudicial effect.

Rule 704.   Opinion on ultimate issue

(a) Except as provided in subdivision (b), testimony in the form of
an opinion or inference otherwise admissible is not objectionable because
it embraces an ultimate issue to be decided by the trier of fact.

(b) No expert witness testifying with respect to the mental state or
condition of a defendant in a criminal case may state an opinion or inference as to whether the defendant did or did not have the mental state or
condition constituting an element of the crime charged or of a defense
thereto. Such ultimate issues are matters for the trier of fact alone.

Rule 705.   Disclosure of facts or data underlying
expert opinion

The expert may testify in terms of opinion or inference and give reasons therefor without first testifying to the underlying facts or data, unless
the court requires otherwise. The expert may in any event be required to
disclose the underlying facts or data on cross-examination.

Rule 706.   Court appointed experts

(a) Appointment.   The court may on its own motion or on the motion of any party enter an order to show cause why expert witnesses should
not be appointed, and may request the parties to submit nominations.
The court may appoint any expert witnesses agreed upon by the parties,
and may appoint expert witnesses of its own selection. An expert witness
shall not be appointed by the court unless the witness consents to act. A

witness so appointed shall be informed of the witness' duties by the court in writing, a copy of which shall be filed with the clerk, or at a conference in which the parties shall have opportunity to participate. A witness so appointed shall advise the parties of the witness' findings, if any; the witness' deposition may be taken by any party; and the witness may be called to testify by the court or any party. The witness shall be subject to cross-examination by each party, including a party calling the witness.

(b) Compensation.   Expert witnesses so appointed are entitled to reasonable compensation in whatever sum the court may allow. The compensation thus fixed is payable from funds which may be provided by law in criminal cases and civil actions and proceedings involving just compensation under the fifth amendment. In other civil actions and proceedings the compensation shall be paid by the parties in such proportion and at such time as the court directs, and thereafter charged in like manner as other costs.

(c) Disclosure of appointment.   In the exercise of its discretion, the court may authorize disclosure to the jury of the fact that the court appointed the expert witness.

(d) Parties' experts of own selection.   Nothing in this rule limits the parties in calling expert witnesses of their own selection.

ARTICLE VIII.   HEARSAY

Rule 801.   Definitions

The following definitions apply under this article:

(a) Statement.   A "statement" is (1) an oral or written assertion or (2) nonverbal conduct of a person, if it is intended by the person as an assertion.

(b) Declarant.   A "declarant" is a person who makes a statement.

(c) Hearsay.   "Hearsay" is a statement, other than one made by the declarant while testifying at the trial or hearing, offered in evidence to prove the truth of the matter asserted.

(d) Statements which are not hearsay.   A statement is not hearsay if —

(1) Prior statement by witness.   The declarant testifies at the trial or hearing and is subject to cross-examination concerning the statement, and the statement is (A) inconsistent with the declarant's testimony, and was given under oath subject to the penalty of perjury at a trial, hearing, or other proceeding, or in a deposition, or (B) consistent with the declarant's testimony and is offered to rebut an express or implied charge against the declarant of recent fabrication or improper influence or motive, or (C) one of identification of a person after perceiving the person; or

(2) Admission by party-opponent.   The statement is offered against a party and is (A) the party's own statement, in either an individual or a representative capacity, or (B) a statement of which the party has manifested an adoption or belief in its truth, or (C) a statement by a person authorized by the party to make a statement concerning the subject, or (D) a statement by the party's agent or servant concerning a matter within the scope of the agency or employment, made during the existence of the relationship, or (E) a statement by a coconspirator of a party during the course and in furtherance of the conspiracy. The contents of the statement shall be considered but are not alone sufficient to establish the declarant's authority under subdivision (C), the agency or employment relationship and scope thereof under subdivision (D), or the existence of the conspiracy and the participation therein of the declarant and the party against whom the statement is offered under subdivision (E).

Rule 802.   Hearsay rule

Hearsay is not admissible except as provided by these rules or by other rules prescribed by the Supreme Court pursuant to statutory authority or by Act of Congress.

Rule 803.   Hearsay exceptions; availability of declarant immaterial

The following are not excluded by the hearsay rule, even though the declarant is available as a witness:

(1) **Present sense impression.**   A statement describing or explaining an event or condition made while the declarant was perceiving the event or condition, or immediately thereafter.

(2) **Excited utterance.**   A statement relating to a startling event or condition made while the declarant was under the stress of excitement caused by the event or condition.

(3) **Then existing mental, emotional, or physical condition.**   A statement of the declarant's then existing state of mind, emotion, sensation, or physical condition (such as intent, plan, motive, design, mental feeling, pain, and bodily health), but not including a statement of memory or belief to prove the fact remembered or believed unless it relates to the execution, revocation, identification, or terms of declarant's will.

(4) **Statements for purposes of medical diagnosis or treatment.** Statements made for purposes of medical diagnosis or treatment and describing medical history, or past or present symptoms, pain, or sensations, or the inception or general character of the cause or external source thereof insofar as reasonably pertinent to diagnosis or treatment.

(5) **Recorded recollection.**   A memorandum or record concerning a matter about which a witness once had knowledge but now has insufficient recollection to enable the witness to testify fully and accurately, shown to have been made or adopted by the witness when the matter was fresh in the witness' memory and to reflect that knowledge correctly. If admitted, the memorandum or record may be read into evidence but may not itself be received as an exhibit unless offered by an adverse party.

(6) Records of regularly conducted activity. A memorandum, report, record, or data compilation, in any form, of acts, events, conditions, opinions, or diagnoses, made at or near the time by, or from information transmitted by, a person with knowledge, if kept in the course of a regularly conducted business activity, and if it was the regular practice of that business activity to make the memorandum, report, record, or data compilation, all as shown by the testimony of the custodian or other qualified witness, or by certification that complies with Rule 902(11), Rule 902(12), or a statute permitting certification, unless the source of information or the method or circumstances of preparation indicate lack of trustworthiness. The term "business" as used in this paragraph includes business, institution, association, profession, occupation, and calling of every kind, whether or not conducted for profit.

(7) Absence of entry in records kept in accordance with the provisions of paragraph (6). Evidence that a matter is not included in the memoranda reports, records, or data compilations, in any form, kept in accordance with the provisions of paragraph (6), to prove the nonoccurrence or nonexistence of the matter, if the matter was of a kind of which a memorandum, report, record, or data compilation was regularly made and preserved, unless the sources of information or other circumstances indicate lack of trustworthiness.

(8) Public records and reports. Records, reports, statements, or data compilations, in any form, of public offices or agencies, setting forth (A) the activities of the office or agency, or (B) matters observed pursuant to duty imposed by law as to which matters there was a duty to report, excluding, however, in criminal cases matters observed by police officers and other law enforcement personnel, or (C) in civil actions and proceedings and against the Government in criminal cases, factual findings resulting from an investigation made pursuant to authority granted by law, unless the sources of information or other circumstances indicate lack of trustworthiness.

(9) Records of vital statistics. Records or data compilations, in any form, of births, fetal deaths, deaths, or marriages, if the report thereof was made to a public office pursuant to requirements of law.

(10) Absence of public record or entry. To prove the absence of a record, report, statement, or data compilation, in any form, or the nonoccurrence or nonexistence of a matter of which a record, report, statement, or data compilation, in any form, was regularly made and preserved by a public office or agency, evidence in the form of a certification in accordance with rule 902, or testimony, that diligent search failed to disclose the record, report, statement, or data compilation, or entry.

(11) Records of religious organizations. Statements of births, marriages, divorces, deaths, legitimacy, ancestry, relationship by blood or marriage, or other similar facts of personal or family history, contained in a regularly kept record of a religious organization.

(12) Marriage, baptismal, and similar certificates. Statements of fact contained in a certificate that the maker performed a marriage or other ceremony or administered a sacrament, made by a clergyman, public official, or other person authorized by the rules or practices of a religious organization or by law to perform the act certified, and purporting to have been issued at the time of the act or within a reasonable time thereafter.

(13) Family records. Statements of fact concerning personal or family history contained in family Bibles, genealogies, charts, engravings on rings, inscriptions on family portraits, engravings on urns, crypts, or tombstones, or the like.

(14) Records of documents affecting an interest in property. The record of a document purporting to establish or affect an interest in property, as proof of the content of the original recorded document and its execution and delivery by each person by whom it purports to have been executed, if the record is a record of a public office and an applicable statute authorizes the recording of documents of that kind in that office.

(15) Statements in documents affecting an interest in property. A statement contained in a document purporting to establish or affect an interest in property if the matter stated was relevant to the purpose of the document, unless dealings with the property since the document was made have been inconsistent with the truth of the statement or the purport of the document.

(16) Statements in ancient documents. Statements in a document in existence twenty years or more the authenticity of which is established.

(17) Market reports, commercial publications. Market quotations, tabulations, lists, directories, or other published compilations, generally used and relied upon by the public or by persons in particular occupations.

(18) Learned treatises. To the extent called to the attention of an expert witness upon cross-examination or relied upon by the expert witness in direct examination, statements contained in published treatises, periodicals, or pamphlets on a subject of history, medicine, or other science or art, established as a reliable authority by the testimony or admission of the witness or by other expert testimony or by judicial notice. If admitted, the statements may be read into evidence but may not be received as exhibits.

(19) Reputation concerning personal or family history. Reputation among members of a person's family by blood, adoption, or marriage, or among a person's associates, or in the community, concerning a person's birth, adoption, marriage, divorce, death, legitimacy, relationship by blood, adoption, or marriage, ancestry, or other similar fact of his personal or family history

(20) Reputation concerning boundaries or general history. Reputation in a community, arising before the controversy, as to boundaries of or customs affecting lands in the community, and reputation as to events of general history important to the community or State or nation in which located.

(21) Reputation as to character. Reputation of a person's character among associates or in the community.

(22) Judgment of previous conviction. Evidence of a final judgment, entered after a trial or upon a plea of guilty (but not upon a plea of nolo contendere), adjudging a person guilty of a crime punishable by death or imprisonment in excess of one year, to prove any fact essential to sustain the judgment, but not including, when offered by the Government in a criminal prosecution for purposes other than impeachment, judgments against persons other than the accused. The pendency of an appeal may be shown but does not affect admissibility.

(23) Judgment as to personal, family, or general history, or boundaries. Judgments as proof of matters of personal, family or general history, or boundaries, essential to the judgment, if the same would be provable by evidence of reputation.

Rule 804.   Hearsay exceptions; declarant unavailable

(a) Definition of unavailability. "Unavailability as a witness" includes situations in which the declarant —

(1) is exempted by ruling of the court on the ground of privilege from testifying concerning the subject matter of the declarant's statement or

(2) persists in refusing to testify concerning the subject matter of the declarant's statement despite an order of the court to do so; or

(3) testifies to a lack of memory of the subject matter of the declarant's statement; or

(4) is unable to be present or to testify at the hearing because of death or then existing physical or mental illness or infirmity; or

(5) is absent from the hearing and the proponent of a statement has been unable to procure the declarant's attendance (or in the case of a hearsay exception under subdivision (b)(2), (3), or (4), the declarant's attendance or testimony) by process or other reasonable means.

A declarant is not unavailable as a witness if exemption, refusal, claim of lack of memory, inability, or absence is due to the procurement or wrongdoing of the proponent of a statement for the purpose of preventing the witness from attending or testifying.

(b) Hearsay exceptions. The following are not excluded by the hearsay rule if the declarant is unavailable as a witness:

(1) Former testimony. Testimony given as a witness at another hearing of the same or a different proceeding, or in a deposition taken in compliance with law in the course of the same or another proceeding, if the party against whom the testimony is now offered, or, in a civil action or proceeding, a predecessor in interest, had an opportunity and similar motive to develop the testimony by direct, cross, or redirect examination.

(2) Statement under belief of impending death. In a prosecution for homicide or in a civil action or proceeding, a statement made by a declarant while believing that the declarant's death was imminent, concerning the cause or circumstances of what the declarant believed to be impending death.

(3) Statement against interest. A statement which was at the time of its making so far contrary to the declarant's pecuniary to proprietary interest, or so far tended to subject the declarant to civil or criminal liability, or to render invalid a claim by the declarant against another, that a reasonable person in the declarant's position would not have made the statement unless believing it to be true. A statement tending to expose the declarant to criminal liability and offered to exculpate the accused is not admissible unless corroborating circumstances clearly indicate the trustworthiness of the statement.

(4) Statement of personal or family history.   (A) A statement concerning the declarant's own birth, adoption, marriage, divorce, legitimacy, relationship by blood, adoption, or marriage, ancestry, or other similar fact of personal or family history, even though declarant had no means of acquiring personal knowledge of the matter stated; or (B) a statement concerning the foregoing matters, and death also, of another person, if the declarant was related to the other by blood, adoption, or marriage or was so intimately associated with the other's family as to be likely to have accurate information concerning the matter declared.

(5) Forfeiture by wrongdoing.   A statement offered against a party that has engaged or acquiesced in wrongdoing that was intended to, and did, procure the unavailability of the declarant as a witness.

Rule 805.   Hearsay within hearsay

Hearsay included within hearsay is not excluded under the hearsay rule if each part of the combined statements conforms with an exception to the hearsay rule provided in these rules.

Rule 806.   Attacking and supporting credibility of declarant

When a hearsay statement, or a statement defined in Rule 801(d)(2) (C), (D), or (E), has been admitted in evidence, the credibility of the declarant may be attacked, and if attacked may be supported, by any evidence which would be admissible for those purposes if declarant had testified as a witness. Evidence of a statement or conduct by the declarant at any time, inconsistent with the declarant's hearsay statement, is not subject to any requirement that the declarant may have been afforded an opportunity to deny or explain. If the party against whom a hearsay statement has been admitted calls the declarant as a witness, the party is entitled to examine the declarant on the statement as if under cross-examination.

Rule 807.   Residual exception

A statement not specifically covered by Rule 803 or 804, but having equivalent circumstantial guarantees of trustworthiness, is not excluded by the hearsay rule if the court determines that (A) the statement is offered as evidence of a material fact; (B) the statement is more probative on the point for which it is offered than any other evidence that the proponent can procure through reasonable efforts; and (C) the general purposes of these rules and the interests of justice will best be served by admission of the statement into evidence. However, a statement may not be admitted under this exception unless the proponent of it makes known to the adverse party sufficiently in advance of the trial or hearing to provide the adverse party with a fair opportunity to prepare to meet it, the proponent's intention to offer the statement and the particulars of it, including the name and address of the declarant.

ARTICLE IX.   AUTHENTICATION AND IDENTIFICATION

Rule 901.   Requirement of authentication
or identification

(a) **General provision.**   The requirement of authentication or identification as a condition precedent to admissibility is satisifed by evidence sufficient to support a finding that the matter in question is what its proponent claims.

(b) **Illustrations.**   By way of illustration only, and not by way of limitation, the following are examples of authentication or identification conforming with the requirements of this rule:

(1) **Testimony of witness with knowledge.**   Testimony that a matter is what it is claimed to be.

(2) **Nonexpert opinion on handwriting.**   Nonexpert opinion as to the genuineness of handwriting, based upon familiarity not acquired for purposes of the litigation.

(3) **Comparison by trier or expert witness.**   Comparison by the trier of fact or by expert witnesses with specimens which have been authenticated.

(4) **Distinctive characteristics and the like.**   Appearance, contents, substance, internal patterns, or other distinctive characteristics, taken in conjunction with circumstances.

(5) **Voice identification.**   Identification of a voice, whether heard firsthand or through mechanical or electronic transmission or recording, by opinion based upon hearing the voice at any time under circumstances connecting it with the alleged speaker.

(6) **Telephone conversations.**   Telephone conversations, by evidence that a call was made to the number assigned at the time by the telephone company to a particular person or business, if (A) in the case of a person, circumstances, including self-identification, show the person answering to be the one called, or (B) in the case of a business, the call was made to a place of business and the conversation related to business reasonably transacted over the telephone.

(7) **Public records or reports.**   Evidence that a writing authorized by law to be recorded or filed and in fact recorded or filed in a public office, or a purported public record, report, statement, or data compilation, in any form, is from the public office where items of this nature are kept.

(8) **Ancient documents or data compilation.**   Evidence that a document or data compilation, in any form, (A) is in such condition as to create no suspicion concerning its authenticity, (B) was in a place where it, if authentic, would likely be, and (C) has been in existence 20 years or more at the time it is offered.

(9) **Process or system.**   Evidence describing a process or system

used to produce a result and showing that the process or system produces an accurate result.

(10) **Methods provided by statute or rule.** Any method of authentication or identification provided by Act of Congress or by other rules prescribed by the Supreme Court pursuant to statutory authority.

Rule 902. Self-authentication

Extrinsic evidence of authenticity as a condition precedent to admissibility is not required with respect to the following:

(1) **Domestic public documents under seal.** A document bearing a seal purporting to be that of the United States, or of any State, district, Commonwealth, territory, or insular possession thereof, or the Panama Canal Zone, or the Trust Territory of the Pacific Islands, or of a political subdivision, department, officer, or agency thereof, and a signature purporting to be an attestation or execution.

(2) **Domestic public documents not under seal.** A document purporting to bear the signature in the official capacity of an officer or employee of any entity included in paragraph (1) hereof, having no seal, if a public officer having a seal and having official duties in the district or political subdivision of the officer or employee certifies under seal that the signer has the official capacity and that the signature is genuine.

(3) **Foreign public documents.** A document purporting to be executed or attested in an official capacity by a person authorized by the laws of a foreign country to make the execution or attestation, and accompanied by a final certification as to the genuineness of the signature and official position (A) of the executing or attesting person, or (B) of any foreign official whose certificate of genuineness of signature and official position relates to the execution or attestation or is in a chain of certificates of genuineness of signature and official position relating to the execution or attestation. A final certification may be made by a secretary of embassy or legation, consul general, consul, vice consul, or consular agent of the United States, or a diplomatic or consular official of the foreign country assigned or accredited to the United States. If reasonable opportunity has been given to all parties to investigate the authenticity and accuracy of official documents, the court may, for good cause shown, order that they be treated as presumptively authentic without final certification or permit them to be evidenced by an attested summary with or without final certification.

(4) **Certified copies of public records.** A copy of an official record or report or entry therein, or of a document authorized by law to be recorded or filed and actually recorded or filed in a public office, including data compilations in any form, certified as correct by the custodian or other person authorized to make the certification, by certificate complying with paragraph (1), (2), or (3) of this rule or complying with any Act of Congress or rule prescribed by the Supreme Court pursuant to statutory authority.

(5) **Official publications.**   Books, pamphlets, or other publications purporting to be issued by public authority.

(6) **Newspapers and periodicals.**   Printed materials purporting to be newspapers or periodicals.

(7) **Trade inscriptions and the like.**   Inscriptions, signs, tags, or labels purporting to have been affixed in the course of business and indicating ownership, control, or origin.

(8) **Acknowledged documents.**   Documents accompanied by a certificate of acknowledgment executed in the manner provided by law by a notary public or other officer authorized by law to take acknowledgments.

(9) **Commercial paper and related documents.**   Commercial paper, signatures thereon, and documents relating thereto to the extent provided by general commercial law.

(10) **Presumptions under Acts of Congress.**   Any signature, document, or other matter declared by Act of Congress to be presumptively or prima facie genuine or authentic.

(11) **Certified domestic records of regularly conducted activity.** The original or duplicate of a domestic record of regularly conducted activity that would be admissible under Rule 803(6) if accompanied by a written declaration of its custodian or other qualified person, in a manner complying with any Act of Congress or rule prescribed by the Supreme Court pursuant to statutory authority, certifying that the record —

(A) was made at or near the time of the occurrence of the matters set forth by, or from information transmitted by, a person with knowledge of those matters;

(B) was kept in the course of the regularly conducted activity; and

(C) was made by the regularly conducted activity as a regular practice.

A party intending to offer a record into evidence under this paragraph must provide written notice of that intention to all adverse parties, and must make the record and declaration available for inspection sufficiently in advance of their offer into evidence to provide an adverse party with a fair opportunity to challenge them.

(12) **Certified foreign records of regularly conducted activity.**   In a civil case, the original or duplicate of a foreign record of regularly conducted activity that would be admissible under Rule 803(6) if accompanied by a written declaration by its custodian or other qualified person certifying that the record —

(A) was made at or near the time of the occurrence of the matters set forth by, or from information transmitted by, a person with knowledge of those matters;

(B) was kept in the course of the regularly conducted activity; and

(C) was made by the regularly conducted activity as a regular practice.

The declaration must be signed in a manner that, if falsely made, would subject the maker to criminal penalty under the laws of the country where the declaration is signed. A party intending to offer a record into evidence under this paragraph must provide written notice of that intention to all adverse parties, and must make the record and declaration available for inspection sufficiently in advance of their offer into evidence to provide an adverse party with a fair opportunity to challenge them.

Rule 903.   Subscribing Witness' Testimony Unnecessary

The testimony of a subscribing witness is not necessary to authenticate a writing unless required by the laws of the jurisdiction whose laws govern the validity of the writing.

ARTICLE X.   CONTENTS OF WRITINGS, RECORDINGS, AND PHOTOGRAPHS

Rule 1001.   Definitions

For purposes of this article the following definitions are applicable:

(1) **Writings and recordings.**   "Writings" and "recordings" consist of letters, words, or numbers, or their equivalent, set down by handwriting, typewriting, printing, photostating, photographing, magnetic impulse, mechanical or electronic recording, or other form of data compilation.

(2) **Photographs.**   "Photographs" include still photographs, X-ray films, video tapes, and motion pictures.

(3) **Original.**   An "original" of a writing or recording is the writing or recording itself or any counterpart intended to have the same effect by a person executing or issuing it. An "original" of a photograph includes the negative or any print therefrom. If data are stored in a computer or similar device, any printout or other output readable by sight, shown to reflect the data accurately, is an "original".

(4) **Duplicate.**   A "duplicate" is a counterpart produced by the same impression as the original, or from the same matrix, or by means of photography, including enlargements and miniatures, or by mechanical or electronic re-recording, or by chemical reproduction, or by other equivalent techniques which accurately reproduce the original.

Rule 1002.   Requirement of original

To prove the content of a writing, recording, or photograph, the original writing, recording, or photograph is required, except as otherwise provided in these rules or by Act of Congress.

Rule 1003.   Admissibility of duplicates

A duplicate is admissible to the same extent as an original unless (1) a genuine question is raised as to the authenticity of the original or (2) in the circumstances it would be unfair to admit the duplicate in lieu of the original.

Rule 1004.   Admissibility of other evidence of contents

The original is not required, and other evidence of the contents of a writing, recording, or photograph is admissible if —

(1) Originals lost or destroyed.   All originals are lost or have been destroyed, unless the proponent lost or destroyed them in bad faith; or

(2) Original not obtainable.   No original can be obtained by any available judicial process or procedure; or

(3) Original in possession of opponent.   At a time when an original was under the control of the party against whom offered, that party was put on notice, by the pleadings or otherwise, that the contents would be a subject of proof at the hearing, and that party does not produce the original at the hearing; or

(4) Collateral matters.   The writing, recording, or photograph is not closely related to a controlling issue.

Rule 1005.   Public records

The contents of an official record, or of a document authorized to be recorded or filed and actually recorded or filed, including data compilations in any form, if otherwise admissible, may be proved by copy, certified as correct in accordance with rule 902 or testified to be correct by a witness who has compared it with the original. If a copy which complies with the foregoing cannot be obtained by the exercise of reasonable diligence, then other evidence of the contents may be given.

Rule 1006.   Summaries

The contents of voluminous writings, recordings, or photographs which cannot conveniently be examined in court may be presented in the form of a chart, summary, or calculation. The originals, or duplicates, shall be made available for examination or copying, or both, by other parties at a reasonable time and place. The court may order that they be produced in court.

Rule 1007.   Testimony or written admission of party

Contents of writings, recordings, or photographs may be proved by the testimony or deposition of the party against whom offered or by that party's written admission, without accounting for the nonproduction of the original.

Rule 1008.   Functions of court and jury

When the admissibility of other evidence of contents of writings, recordings, or photographs under these rules depends upon the fulfillment of a condition of fact, the question whether the condition has been fulfilled is ordinarily for the court to determine in accordance with the provisions of rule 104. However, when an issue is raised (a) whether the asserted writing ever existed, or (b) whether another writing, recording, or photograph produced at the trial is the original, or (c) whether other evidence of contents correctly reflects the contents, the issue is for the trier of fact to determine as in the case of other issues of fact.

ARTICLE XI.   MISCELLANEOUS RULES

Rule 1101.   Applicability of rules

(a) **Courts and magistrates.**   These rules apply to the United States district courts, the District Court of Guam, the District Court of the Virgin Islands, the District Court for the District of the Canal Zone, the United States courts of appeals, the United States Claims Court, and to United States magistrate judges, in the actions, cases, and proceedings and to the extent hereinafter set forth. The terms "judge" and "court" in these rules include United States bankruptcy judges and United States magistrate judges.

(b) **Proceedings generally.**   These rules apply generally to civil actions and proceedings, including admiralty and maritime cases, to criminal cases and proceedings, to contempt proceedings except those in which the court may act summarily, and to proceedings and cases under title 11, United States Code.

(c) **Rule of privilege.**   The rule with respect to privileges applies at all stages of all actions, cases, and proceedings.

(d) **Rules inapplicable.**   The rules (other than with respect to privilege) do not apply in the following situations:

(1) **Preliminary questions of fact.**   The determination of questions of fact preliminary to admissibility of evidence when the issue is to be determined by the court under rule 104.

(2) **Grand jury.**   Proceedings before grand juries.

(3) **Miscellaneous proceedings.**   Proceedings for extradition or rendition; preliminary examinations in criminal cases; sentencing, or granting or revoking probation; issuance of warrants for arrest, criminal summonses, and search warrants; and proceedings with respect to release on bail or otherwise.

(e) **Rules applicable in part.**   In the following proceedings these rules apply to the extent that matters of evidence are not provided for in the statutes which govern procedure therein or in other rules prescribed by the Supreme Court pursuant to statutory authority: the trial of minor and petty offenses by United States magistrate judges; review of agency actions when the facts are subject to trial de novo under section 706(2)(F) of title 5, United States Code; review of orders of the Secretary of Agriculture under section 2 of the Act entitled "An Act to authorize association of producers of agricultural products" approved February 18, 1922 (7 U.S.C. 292), and under sections 6 and 7(c) of the Perishable Agricultural Commodities Act, 1930 (7 U.S.C. 499f, 499g(c)); naturalization and revocation of naturalization under sections 310-318 of the Immigration and Nationality Act (8 U.S.C. 1421-1429); prize proceedings in admiralty under sections 7651-7681 of title 10, United States Code; review of orders of the Secretary of the Interior under section 2 of the Act entitled "An Act authorizing associations of producers of aquatic products" approved June 25, 1934 (15 U.S.C. 522); review of orders of petroleum control boards under section 5 of the Act entitled "An Act to regulate interstate and foreign commerce in petroleum and its products produced by prohibiting the shipment in such commerce of petroleum and its products produced in violation of State law, and for other purposes," approved February 22, 1935 (15 U.S.C. 715d); actions for fines, penalties, or forfeitures under part V of title IV of the Tariff Act of 1930 (19 U.S.C. 1581-1624), or under the Anti-Smuggling Act (19 U.S.C. 1701-1711); criminal libel for condemnation, exclusion of imports, or other proceedings under the Federal Food, Drug, and Cosmetic Act (21 U.S.C. 301-392); disputes between seamen under sections 4079, 4080, and 4081 of the Revised Statutes (22 U.S.C. 256-258); habeas corpus under sections 2241-2254 of title 28, United States Code; motions to vacate, set aside or correct sentence under section 2255 of title 28, United States Code; actions for penalties for refusal to transport destitute seamen under section 4578 of the Revised Statutes (46 U.S.C. 679); actions against the United States under the Act entitled "An Act authorizing suits against the United States in admiralty for damage caused by and salvage service rendered to public vessels belonging to the United States, and for other purposes," approved March 3, 1925 (46 U.S.C. 781-790), as implemented by section 7730 of title 10, United States Code.

Rule 1102.   Amendments

Amendments to the Federal Rules of Evidence may be made as provided in section 2072 of title 28 of the United States Code.

Rule 1103.   Title

These rules may be known and cited as the Federal Rules of Evidence.

INDEX